PROGRAMMING WITH

JavaScript

Algorithms and Applications for Desktop and Mobile Browsers

John David Dionisio
Loyola Marymount University

Ray Toal
Loyola Marymount University

JONES & BARTLETT
LEARNING

World Headquarters
Jones & Bartlett Learning
5 Wall Street
Burlington, MA 01803
978-443-5000
info@jblearning.com
www.jblearning.com

Jones & Bartlett Learning books and products are available through most bookstores and online booksellers. To contact Jones & Bartlett Learning directly, call 800-832-0034, fax 978-443-8000, or visit our website, www.jblearning.com.

Substantial discounts on bulk quantities of Jones & Bartlett Learning publications are available to corporations, professional associations, and other qualified organizations. For details and specific discount information, contact the special sales department at Jones & Bartlett Learning via the above contact information or send an email to specialsales@jblearning.com.

Production Credits
Publisher: Cathleen Sether
Senior Acquisitions Editor: Timothy Anderson
Managing Editor: Amy Bloom
Director of Production: Amy Rose
Marketing Manager: Lindsay White
V.P., Manufacturing and Inventory Control: Therese Connell
Associate Photo Researcher: Lauren Miller
Composition: Northeast Compositors, Inc.
Cover Design: Kristin E. Parker
Cover Image: Light: © yienkeat/ShutterStock, Inc.; Laptop: © Haywiremedia/ShutterStock, Inc.
   Photo display: © James Thew/ShutterStock, Inc.; SmartPhone: © lassedesignen/Fotolia.com
   App Icons: © abdulsatarid/ShutterStock, Inc.
Printing and Binding: Courier Kendallville
Cover Printing: Courier Kendallville

Library of Congress Cataloging-in-Publication Data
Dionisio, John David N., 1970-
  Programming with JavaScript : algorithms and applications for desktop and mobile browsers / John David Dionisio, Ray Toal.
     p. cm.
  Includes bibliographical references and index.
  ISBN-13: 978-0-7637-8060-9 (pbk.)
  ISBN-10: 0-7637-8060-X (pbk.)
  1. JavaScript (Computer program language) 2. Computer algorithms. 3.
Application software—Development. I. Toal, Ray. II. Title.
  QA76.73.J38D57 2013
  005.3—dc23
                    2011018738

6048

Printed in the United States of America
15 14 13 12 11   10 9 8 7 6 5 4 3 2 1

Dedication

Love and thanks as always to Mei Lyn, Aidan, Anton, and Aila for their support.

JDND

Contents

Preface

What comes to mind when you hear the terms *programming* and *computer science*? Game-playing, socially challenged geeks? Computers? Those are certainly the popular images. In reality, however, *anyone* can program,[1] and computer science is about much more than computers. You are just as likely to see people programming phones, robots, navigation systems, and factory machinery as you are desktop computers.

Programming with JavaScript: Algorithms and Applications for Desktop and Mobile Browsers is an introduction to some of the main ideas and principles of computer science, with some forays into the related disciplines of software engineering and information technology. It aims to convey these principles *by encouraging you to develop fundamental skills in programming*. Computer science deals with many things—computation, algorithms, software systems, data organization, knowledge representation, language, intelligence, and learning—but it is programming experience that enables you to gain a better understanding of these topics, and the tools to explore them in depth.

Objectives

This book aims to:

- Introduce the field of computing by showing that it is a natural science, encompassing computer science, software engineering, computer engineering, information systems, and information technology.

---

[1] "Anyone can" means that great programmers can, and do, come from any background, not that programming can be learned without effort [Bra07].

- Dispel common myths about what computing is and show that computing provides a foundation for careers in many different areas, including medicine, law, business, finance, entertainment, the arts, education, economics, biology, nanotechnology, and gaming.

- Teach a respect for programming aesthetics, standards, style conventions, and judicious commenting early in the text, with the goal of preventing common bad habits from ever forming.

- Convey the power of JavaScript (as compared to other languages) by covering difficult material that is traditionally not taught to beginners. Some of this advanced material is isolated into sections marked with an asterisk (*) or is included in the appendices.

- Show that programming is not just about getting programs to work correctly, but is also about constructing programs that are readable, easily modifiable, and that run efficiently.

- Provide relevant case studies in distributed computing, touch-based user interfaces on phones and tablets, and graphics for both the student looking forward to employment and the professional programmer looking to keep current in modern software technology.

Organization

We've structured this text so that you can read it cover to cover if you like. It tells a story about computing, programming, and especially JavaScript, outlined as follows:

- Introduction to the field of computing (*Chapter 1*)

- Theory and practice of (JavaScript) programming (*Chapters 2–8*)

    - Getting started with programming (*Chapter 2*)

    - Data (*Chapter 3*)

    - Programming in the small I: Statements (*Chapter 4*)

- Programming in the small II: Functions (*Chapter 5*)

- Programming in the small III: Events (*Chapter 6*)

- Programming in the large I: Software systems construction (*Chapter 7*)

- Programming in the large II: Distributed computing (*Chapter 8*)

■ Advanced topics (*Chapters 9–10*)

While you need not read the text exactly cover to cover, you may want to keep the chapter dependencies in mind, shown here:

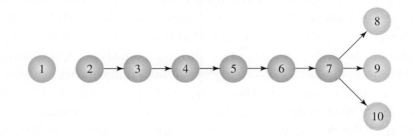

Note that Chapter 1 stands alone: it's optional. Readers who want to jump right in to programming can start with Chapter 2.

Audience

This text is designed as a primary resource for a first-year college course in computer science or software engineering. No previous programming experience is assumed. However, advanced students and professional programmers new to JavaScript should also find the text useful, as we do not shy away from technical areas of the language perceived as difficult or "advanced." In fact, we believe that professional programmers can benefit a great deal from the numerous review questions and exercises spread throughout the text, as well as our coverage of modern topics in the JavaScript world, including ECMAScript 5, HTML 5, Ajax, jQuery, Graphics, and Animation.

JavaScript

A note to instructors: We enthusiastically adopt JavaScript as the language with which to train new computer scientists. JavaScript has not traditionally found much traction in introductory university-level computer science courses; this is probably due to various misunderstandings about the language [Cro01]. We argue, however, that JavaScript is an *ideal* language for such courses.

First, thanks to the ubiquity of web browsers, every student already has access to a JavaScript interpreter; no download or installation is required. Second, the language finds middle ground in the debate between professors who claim that beginning students should focus not on programming but on abstract algorithms given in pseudocode, and those who argue that students require hands-on programming experience to make concepts stick. JavaScript features a surprisingly clear and simple syntax; students can start programming immediately without fretting about classes, "public static" methods, the mysterious void, consoles, packages, and so on. We realize many schools have tried the simple-language approach in CS1 with ML, Scheme, Ruby, or Python, but with the rise of the Web as a platform for running applications (both on desktop and mobile devices), none of these languages can boast nearly the same degree of popularity as JavaScript.

Finally, as functional programming, long thought of as being of interest only to academic computer scientists, becomes more important in the new world of multicore processors and Big Data, JavaScript as a teaching language makes a great deal of sense. Functional programming in JavaScript tends to be fairly accessible to beginning students, perhaps more so than languages known for having "too many parentheses" or a reliance on special constructs like blocks, continuations, or generators.

Additional Resources

Visit go.jblearning.com/Dionisio for answers to end-of-chapter exercises, source code, PowerPoint Lecture Outlines, errata, and additional bonus material outside the scope of this text.

Acknowledgments

We'd like to express our thanks to Loren Abrams, Turn Media; B. J. Johnson, Claremont Graduate University; Philip Dorin, Loyola Marymount University; Daniel Bogaard, Rochester Institute of Technology; Michael Hennessy, University of Oregon; and Laurence Toal, Wellesley College, for their careful readings of early drafts and many constructive comments. Thanks also to Kira Toal and Masao Kitamura for providing several images, and to Jasmine Dahilig, Tyler Nichols, and Andrew Fornery for their assistance in preparing ancillary materials. We are also grateful for the excellent support from the staff at Jones & Bartlett Learning, including Tim Anderson, Senior Acquisitions Editor; Amy Bloom, Managing Editor; and Amy Rose, Production Director, without whose professionalism and hard work this book would not have been possible. We'd also like to thank Caskey Dickson and Technocage, Inc., for hosting our cross-site scripting examples. Without them, there would be no sites to cross!

CHAPTER 1

The Field of Computing

CHAPTER CONTENTS

Introduction

Computing is the science of information processes. It addresses questions such as "What is information?" and "How can information be encoded, processed, stored, and transmitted?" Computing scientists study information processes in nature and perform experiments to better understand these processes. The experimental side of computing science consists of building and programming artificial computing devices.

This chapter takes a broad overview of the field of computing, looking at various disciplines within the field, careers that its practitioners may pursue, and several popular (and unfortunate) myths about the field. The material will hopefully give you a good feel for what computing is about and motivate you to continue to the next chapter, where you will begin programming in JavaScript.

1.1   Computing Is a Natural Science

Over the last 20 years or so, people have come to realize that computing is not limited to artificial computing machines. *Computational processes*, by which systems operate according to rules of some sort, have been observed in nature and in society [Den07]. Consider:

- Information about an organism is encoded in its DNA, and biological processes replicate, transcribe, and translate this information—a series of processes, or computations, known as *the central dogma of molecular biology* (see Figure 1.1).

- Chemical reactions proceed according to various rules. If you mix hydrogen and oxygen, nature runs the program $2H_2 + O_2 \rightarrow 2H_2O + E$.

- Social structures and communities evolve in ways that are impacted by environmental, governmental, and other forces.

- Financial markets can be viewed as computational systems reacting to buy and sell orders, fear and panic, and controlling government intervention.

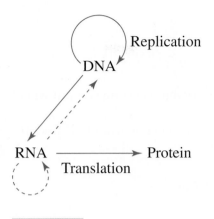

FIGURE 1.1
The central dogma of molecular biology [Cri70].

- Neural processes are computational. In a biological neural network, neurons receive input signals (from other neurons) and, based on these inputs, transmit output signals (to other neurons).

We study the information processes found in natural phenomena in order to better understand the world around us. We observe these processes and record our findings. We construct computing devices to help us model these findings. We perform experiments—that is, we write computer programs—with these models to answer "what if" questions. We apply our study of computing by building information systems for our businesses, organizations, governments, and personal use.

1.2 The Five Disciplines of Computing

Today many people recognize five major areas in the study of computing.

1.2.1 Computer Science

Computer science is the theory and practice of computation, algorithms, software systems, data organization, knowledge representation, language, intelligence, and learning. Computer scientists look for, and apply, answers to questions such as these:

- What can and cannot be computed?

- How fast can certain computations be carried out?

- How much information needs to be stored to carry out a certain computation?

- How can information be efficiently and securely encoded, stored, and retrieved?

- How do we design information processes (programs)?

- How do we know our programs are correct?

- How can computational theories help to explain intelligence and consciousness?

Computer science is concerned with the nature of computation and its application to other fields of study. Like philosophy and mathematics, and to some extent education, it treats knowledge itself as an object *of* study, rather than simply as a tool *with which* to study. Information processes are expressed using programming languages, which are defined using ideas from the field of linguistics. Computational methods are used to study biological, social, and economic systems. The branch of computer science known as *artificial intelligence* includes elements from psychology: for problem-solving computers to deliver answers you can trust, they should be able to explain their reasoning process in a way to which humans can relate.

1.2.2   Software Engineering

Software engineering involves the design, organization, and construction of (often large-scale and mission-critical) software systems, with a focus on product efficiency, reliability, robustness, testing, maintenance, and cost-effectiveness (see Table 1.1). Software engineers analyze business requirements and design software systems to meet those requirements. They focus on both putting together small fragments of code and wiring together subsystems to make large systems. Software engineers, also known as *developers*, work in collaborative, team-oriented environments.

A system that is ...	will ...
correct	do exactly what it has been specified to do.
reliable	not crash (that is, it will not stop running unexpectedly).
efficient	operate within reasonable time and space constraints.
understandable	allow its developers and users to figure out why it does what it does.
reusable	be built from components that can be used in other systems.
scalable	be able to be extended to handle larger and larger amounts of data, with only a reasonable amount of increased support cost.
maintainable	allow bugs (errors) to be easily isolated and fixed.
usable	do what its users want and expect.
economical	be produced on time and under budget, and cost a reasonable amount to run.

Table 1.1

Properties of Well-Engineered Software

1.2.3 Computer Engineering

Computer engineers design digital systems such as communications networks, computers, smart phones, digital audio and video players and recorders, monitoring and navigation systems for automobiles and aircraft, alarm systems, X-ray machines, and robotic instruments such as laser surgical tools. Many computer engineers are trained as electrical engineers, but specialize in electronics and digital systems and generally have more exposure to computer hardware and software.

1.2.4 Information Technology

The profession of information technology, or IT, includes people working on the construction, maintenance, and troubleshooting of an organization's computing infrastructure—computers, networks, email systems, websites, databases, telephony, and similar systems. In addition to programming, IT professionals often perform complex configuration, customization, and upgrading functions.

1.2.5   Information Systems

The field of information systems (IS) is concerned with the design of "computing solutions" for companies, nonprofit organizations, educational institutions, and governments to support their missions and improve their effectiveness. Unlike the other four disciplines, many institutions teach IS in business schools.

Much of the focus in IS is on the *use* of computing technology such as databases and communication tools. Programming still plays a role but has a different feel from the programming done by professionals in other disciplines. IS professionals are more likely to use *spreadsheets*, in which computations are expressed as formulas embedded within tables of data. Figure 1.2 shows a spreadsheet in which cell **E8** holds the value =SUM(B8:D8), which means that it should display the (computed) sum of values in cells **B8** through **D8**.

	mammoth.xls				
New Open Save Print Import	Copy Paste Format	Undo Redo	AutoSum Sort A–Z		
	Sheets	Charts	SmartArt Graphics	WordArt	
	A	B	C	D	E	F

	A	B	C	D	E
1	Mammoth Mountain, CA Snowfall (inches)				
2		Aug-Oct	Nov-Mar	Apr-Jul	Total
3	2004-05	85.6	423.1	61.4	570.1
4	2005-06	0.0	455.8	122.7	578.5
5	2006-07	4.0	186.5	31.5	222.0
6	2007-08	11.0	302.0	20.5	333.5
7	2008-09	10.0	416.5	43.5	470.0
8	2009-10	34.0	421.5	102.4	557.9
9	2010-11	10.0	595.5	63.0	668.5
10	Average	22.1	400.1	63.6	485.8
11					

Normal View   Ready

FIGURE 1.2

A spreadsheet.

1.3   Careers in Computing

Computing is now understood as a broad field of study; therefore, competence in one or more of the computing disciplines prepares you for careers in any of the following areas:

- **Biology**. The increasing importance of **genetics** and **computational biology** has given the field of biology more of a digital feel. Many life processes can be modeled as information processes. Computer scientists and biologists routinely collaborate in biological database research and in other endeavors.

- **Search, Data Mining, and Information Retrieval**. The value of information is such that many people are willing to pay good money for services that quickly extract desired information from massive amounts of (mostly irrelevant) data, given fuzzy search criteria. The efficient extraction of information from large data sets has long been a central problem in computer science.

- **Entertainment**. Computers have long played a role in **film** and **television**, and not just in **animation**. Production processes for most forms of entertainment, even live theater, use a great deal of hardware and software, making computing skills very valuable in the industry.

- **Digital Media Distribution**. Fewer and fewer people obtain movies and music by driving to a library or store. People with computing expertise work on problems related to reliable and secure delivery of media, efficient routing of streamed data through the increasingly congested Internet, and issues surrounding copyrights and royalties.

- **Gaming**. Gaming is a multibillion dollar industry, and many consumers' apparent willingness to spend continuously on new game products has attracted many programmers to careers in game development and production. Creating good game software is very difficult, requiring skills not only in computer graphics, modeling, and algorithms but also in math, physics, psychology, and creative writing.

- **Mobile Applications**. Many software applications that used to sit on a computer's hard drive are now run as web applications fetched on demand from a remote server. A similar shift to mobile applications is under way, many of which take advantage of a device's physical location (determined by a global positioning system (GPS)). New ways of interacting with mobile devices and applications will come from computing professionals.

- **Nanotechnology**. Nanotechnology involves the design and use of atomic-sized devices that work together (in huge numbers) to create effects that humans can see. These devices require sophisticated programming. Many articles have been written about the importance of uses of computer science in nanotechnology [MS03, Mac09].

- **Security, Defense, and Cyberwarfare**. The high value of an organization's (or nation's) information infrastructure means that workers with specialized knowledge and skills in security and cryptology will remain in demand for the foreseeable future. A computing background is important to develop these skills because encryption and decryption are computational processes.

- **Aerospace**. Modern aircraft, satellites, space stations, and robotic space explorers are carrying out their computational tasks every nanosecond. These are complex tasks, with billions of bytes of information being transferred, requiring time-sensitive, or *real-time*, processing. The design of these massively complex systems is a major aspect of the field of software engineering.

- **Business, Law, and Medicine**. Professional schools in these fields desire undergraduates from diverse backgrounds, particularly those with strong logical and analytical skills. **Medical imaging** and **business information systems** have long been closely allied with computer science, and the information infrastructures of **healthcare providers** and **insurers** now require a workforce with sophisticated computing skills. Issues surrounding patents and intellectual property require both legal and computing expertise to resolve.

A fairly comprehensive set of resources for those considering careers in computing can be found at the Association for Computing Machinery (ACM) Computing Careers site, `http://computingcareers.acm.org/`. The site provides not only posters and brochures but also information such as the top 10 reasons to major in computing, descriptions of the various computing fields, a FAQ section, and links to career sites. In addition, the United States Bureau of Labor Statistics publishes occupational outlooks for hundreds of different jobs in the country, including education and training requirements, earnings, and job prospects. Data for software engineers and computer scientists, for example, can be found at `http://www.bls.gov/oco/ocos303.htm` and `http://www.bls.gov/oco/ocos304.htm`, respectively.

1.4 Myths about Computing

The following myths have done a great deal to harm the image of computing as a field and kept much-needed talent away:

- **Myth**: "The only people who study computing are introverted, nerdy geeks."
  Fact: The stereotypical image of the programmer may have changed since the 1940s (see Figure 1.3), but computing, especially programming, has always

FIGURE 1.3
Programmers circa 1947.

been a highly *collaborative* field. Occasionally, a solo programmer can create a moderate-sized work of art, but the majority of today's software systems are of a size and complexity well beyond any single individual's ability to create and manage. Computing is a field with talented people who have varied interests. Unfortunately, negative popular media images seem to have more effect on young people who would otherwise excel in an information profession.

- **Myth**: "All computing jobs are being offshored." **Fact**: Besides the obvious exaggeration inherent in the word "all," a percentage of offshored jobs is due to local demand for workers exceeding supply, not just to cost. Not every job *can* be offshored: there is intangible value to having highly skilled information workers on site.

- **Myth**: "Computing is only about programming boring desktop and laptop computers." **Fact**: The number of microprocessors in *embedded devices* dwarfs the number in personal computers. Robots, smart weaponry, cars of the future, factory machinery, (smart) phones, and digital assistants are a few of the many programmable devices requiring computing skills to build and produce.

- **Myth**: "Computing ended with the dot-com bust." **Fact**: The dot-com bust of the early 2000s followed an unsustainable industry boom. The years since the bust have brought fantastic improvements in search, video sharing, social networking, news distribution, and mobile computing. Computers continue to get smaller, cheaper, and faster. Nearly every business has an online presence, and people expect online *services* from them as well, and expect these services to run well on their mobile devices.

- **Myth**: "There's no need to study computing—my art class or business class will teach me all I need to know to be a great programmer." **Fact**: Software systems are some of the most complex things humans have created. The knowledge and experiences gained from building these systems, particularly the countless failed systems and the reasons for these failures, have been captured in the literature and culture of computer science and software engineering, not business and art.

Chapter Summary

- Computing is a natural science, not just an artificial one. Information processes provide models for behavior within biological systems, matter and energy, and societal and economic systems.

- The five disciplines of computing are computer science, software engineering, computer engineering, information technology, and information systems.

- Computing professionals hold careers in a wide variety of fields, including but not limited to biotechnology, aerospace, entertainment, information retrieval, law, business, medicine, media, gaming, and cybersecurity.

- Many myths about the computing disciplines have kept many (often young) people away from the field.

Exercises

All of the exercises in this chapter ask you to do some research and perform activities that go beyond what you have read in the chapter.

1. Read Peter Denning's "Computing Is a Natural Science" [Den07], and write a one- to three-paragraph review of the article.

2. Do some reading on DNA transcription. Explain the terms "coding strand" and "mRNA synthesis." How do these terms relate to your best guess as to what a computer program is or does?

3. The five computing disciplines listed early in the chapter are taken from the ACM Computing Careers materials at `http://computingcareers.acm.org/?page_id=6`. This taxonomy of computing fields is very broad; those with interest in programming tend to focus on computer science and software engineering. Do some research and list around 20 subdisciplines of computer science and software engineering.

4. Computer science is a rather young field. Look up information on the computer science faculty of your school, your alma mater, or a college you hope to attend some day, and find out in which fields these people received bachelor degrees.

5. Make a list of any interdisciplinary courses offered in the computer science department at your favorite college.

6. See if you can find any reliable data to answer the following two (surprisingly vague) questions. Which is the most popular programming language in the world today? Which programming language is most commonly taught in freshman computer science courses?

7. If you know people with programming experience, do a survey and record, for each person, their three favorite programming languages. Then ask them about languages they despise. EXTRA CREDIT: If your interviewee becomes very animated and uses scathing language to denigrate a particular programming language, ask (as a follow-up question) whether that language's designer was truly incompetent or was perhaps just trying to design a language for some purpose other than what your interviewee might have tried to use the language for.

8. For each of the following programming languages, research one or two interesting facts: JavaScript, Ruby, Io, Lua, Self, Java, Python, C, ActionScript, Smalltalk, LISP, Ada, bash, SQL, and Go.

9. Try to recreate the spreadsheet from Figure 1.2. If you are new to spreadsheets, by all means ask a friend for help.

10. If you were able to recreate the spreadsheet in the previous exercise, insert rows for past (or future) ski seasons.

11. Research several encryption methods in use today, namely, Blowfish, AES, and RSA. How widely used is RSA? Why is it said that RSA is not known to be *provably secure*?

12. Read or skim one article on each of the following: computational biology, computational neuroscience, computational social science, and computational linguistics.

13. Browse the *ACM TechNews* at `http://technews.acm.org/`. Read not only a handful of articles from the current week but also peruse the archives (found at `http://technews.acm.org/archives.cfm`). Make a list of 10 to 20 interesting headlines that highlight the breadth of computing applications in the everyday world.

14. What are the arguments for and against the proposition that the human brain is a kind of computer?

15. Read a biography of Alan Turing. Give some reasons why he is known as the founder of the field we know today as computer science.

16. The answer to the question "Which was the first mechanical computer?" depends on a person's definition of a mechanical computing device, but there is general agreement on which was the first computer that was both *general purpose* and *electronic*. What was it called? What was it designed to do? Who were its first programmers?

17. Today we take for granted our ability to write programs that will run on many different computers. But this was not always the case: early machines were programmed, by human programmers, using numerically encoded instructions in the computer's own *machine language*. For a single program to run on different machines, it needs to be *compiled* (translated) into the machine language of the machine on which it will be run. One of the first compilers (possibly *the* first compiler) was written by Grace Murray Hopper. Read a biography of Admiral Hopper. What other contributions did she make to computer science?

18. Browse the course offerings at your favorite college's business school. Does the business school teach its own algebra and calculus classes, or are its students required to take those courses in the math department? Does the business school teach its own programming courses, or are its students required to take those courses in a computing (computer science or similar) department?

19. Which franchise has generated more revenue—the *Star Wars* movie franchise or the *Madden NFL* video game franchise? Which has generated more profit? Consider both raw sales numbers as well as revenue from derivative profits. As absolute figures may be hard to come by, be sure to qualify any estimates. Cite the sources used in your research.

20. Find a serious research article, or a news article backed by authoritative research, describing how negative portrayals of computing professionals in popular media have dissuaded people from entering the profession (or from entering university-level programs in computing). To what degree are the media portrayals accurate? To what degree are they inaccurate?

21. Give at least one myth about programming or computation from popular culture that was not included in this chapter.

CHAPTER 2

Programming

CHAPTER CONTENTS

Introduction

People write programs for a variety of tasks, such as to play music and videos, to organize personal data, and to find answers to questions that would take too long to work out with pencil and paper. Programming can reward you with feelings of accomplishment (from producing something useful) and power (from watching your commands being carried out by a device under your control).

In this chapter, we will explain what programming is and describe various ways in which you can write and run programs in the JavaScript programming language. We present several example programs—which we encourage you to try out as you read along—and discuss the building blocks from which programs are constructed. We close with a brief discussion on the kinds of things that must be kept in mind in order to craft excellent—not just working—programs. By the end of this chapter, you will be able to write and run some simple programs of your own design.

2.1   Learning to Program

Programming is the act of creating instructions for an *agent* to carry out. This very general definition includes the writing of musical scores (for musicians), recipes (for cooks), and architectural blueprints (for construction companies). Some people might insist that "programming" applies only to robots, computers, media players, consumer devices, guidance systems, factory machinery, and other mechanical agents. However, composers, recipe writers, and architects do have one essential thing in common with programmers: they have a vision in mind and must describe in detail how to make that vision a reality.

A *program*, or *script*, is an encoding of a process in some language. Thousands of *programming languages* exist today. These languages differ from human languages by having precisely defined syntax and semantics that keep them free of ambiguities such as those found in the sentence "He gave her cat food." The text of a program is called *code*, or *software*, while the physical agent that runs the software is called *hardware*.

Programming is a skill, and like all other skills, including martial arts, music, drafting, plumbing, carpentry, football, tennis, and so on, it requires time and practice; it takes years to master [Nor01]. Learning to program involves both building basic skills and understanding grand concepts. But learning is not done top-down (starting with the concepts) nor bottom-up (starting with building blocks too small to constitute real programs); rather, it is done middle-out. Like an apprentice, you begin by looking at and working with existing programs, from which the concepts eventually become apparent. So this chapter focuses on a series of examples that will give you a feel for what programs in JavaScript look like and how to run them. In subsequent chapters, we will get more technical.

Review and Practice

1. Define, in your own words, the terms *program* and *programming language.*

2. Give at least four distinct interpretations of the English sentence "He gave her cat food."

2.2 Getting Started

Programming can be done on thousands of kinds of devices and in thousands of programming languages. We will feature a programming language you almost certainly already have available—JavaScript. Nearly every modern home, school, or workplace computer, or smart phone or tablet, runs JavaScript "out of the box" because JavaScript programs run inside your web browser. No download, installation, or setup is necessary. JavaScript's integration with your browser enables draggable objects, scrollable maps, animated and real-time effects, three-dimensional (3D) rendering, and more, without browser plug-ins or extensions. JavaScript is not only an extremely powerful language [Cro08a], but also perhaps the most popular language in use today [Cro08b].

To write and run JavaScript programs, you will need:

■ A web browser

That's it! While technically this single requirement can come with a variety of qualifying statements (e.g., it has to be a "modern" web browser; JavaScript must be enabled; you must have a "modern" implementation of JavaScript), in this text we take the optimistic (and likely) stance that the web browser you use today is ready and willing to run JavaScript without any showstoppers. So fire up that browser and start with the simplest way to write and run JavaScript: your browser's own address box.

2.2.1   The Browser Address Box

Type the following into your web browser's address box (see Figure 2.2):

```
javascript:alert("Hello World!")
```

Hit the *Enter* or *Return* key, and your browser should respond with a window that says, surprisingly enough, "Hello World!"

Figure 2.1 illustrates how this program looks on a particular browser (Firefox) running under a particular operating system (Ubuntu); the program should look substantially the same on other platforms.

FIGURE 2.1

The "Hello World" script in action.

FIGURE 2.2

Entering JavaScript code in the browser's address box.

Review and Practice

1. "Go to" the address `javascript:alert(1 + 2 + 3 + 4)`.

2. "Go to" the address `javascript:alert("1" + "2" + "3" + "4")`.

2.2.2 Runner Pages

You may have realized there is little hope of writing the next mapping service, photo-sharing site, or social network in your browser's little address field. For more space in which to write scripts, you can employ a JavaScript "runner," such as the one hosted at `http://javascript.cs.lmu.edu/runner` (see Figure 2.3).

Type a script into the text area on this page, then click the [Run] button. For the trivial example from Section 2.2.1, enter:

```
alert("Hello World!");
```

This is identical to what you typed into the browser address box earlier *except* for the `javascript:` prefix. That prefix is not part of the language; it is a marker that tells the browser how the address text is to be interpreted.[1] So not surprisingly, clicking [Run] (try it now!) results in exactly the same behavior as before. This is because the browser is running exactly the same program; the only difference lies in *how* you entered this program into the web browser.

---

[1]Technically, the marker is called a *protocol*. You have undoubtedly seen other protocols, such as `http`.

FIGURE 2.3

A simple web page for running JavaScript programs.

To help you acclimate to this environment, we have provided a handful of small scripts for you to type in and run. We will not describe *how* they work just yet; the focus right now is on getting you used to *running* programs. Keep in mind that you will need to type things exactly as shown; if the program does not behave as described, review what you typed to make sure it matches the code in the text. Although we are leaving these scripts unexplained for now, you should look for connections between the scripts as written and their behavior when run. Take the time to experiment by making small changes and observing the behavior of your modified scripts.

- This program plays a small game of Mad Libs based on a popular 1940s show tune:

```
alert("I like " +
    prompt("Please enter a city:") + " in " +
    prompt("Please enter a month:") + ", how about you?");
```

■ This program simulates a single die roll. Each time you run it, you will get a random number from one to six:

```
alert("You rolled a " +
    (Math.floor(Math.random() * 6) + 1) + "!");
```

■ This script illustrates how JavaScript can manipulate text:

```
var message = prompt("Enter a sentence:");
alert("Shouted: " + message.toUpperCase());
alert("Toned down: " + message.toLowerCase());
```

■ The following script tells you how many days remain until midnight on the upcoming New Year's Day. Its correctness depends on whether you have set the time and date on your computing device properly.

```
var now = new Date();
var newYear = new Date(now.getFullYear() + 1, 0, 1);
var days = (newYear - now) / 86400000;
alert("From " + now + ", " + days + " days until the New Year!");
```

■ This script runs another script entered by the user. Which do you think is more intriguing—the fact that this is even possible in JavaScript or the fact that such a script can be this short?

```
eval(prompt("Type in a script:"));
```

What do you think happens when the script you type in at the prompt is the program itself?

■ Because the scripts you execute in the runner are running in a web browser, they have access to the web page elements. You can see an example in the following script, which changes the background color of the page to green:

```
document.body.style.backgroundColor="green";
```

To restore the original background color, reload the page.

To make our programming introduction a little more fun, we have enhanced our runner with John Resig's *jQuery* library, making a number of special effects available right away.[2] Enter and run these three scripts:

- This script makes the words "JavaScript Runner" on the page red and much larger, and makes the script area border very thick:

```
$("h1").css("color", "red").css("font-size", "4em");
$("textarea").css("border-width", "5px");
```

  To undo the effects, reload the page in your browser.

- This script moves the title text a thousand pixels to the right, slowly, over a three-second (3000-millisecond) duration:

```
$("h1").animate({"margin-left": "+=1000"}, 3000);
```

- Finally, enter and run this script to make the entire page "self-destruct" (fade away, actually) in five seconds:

```
$("body").fadeOut(5000);
```

  Reload the page to bring it back to life.

Review and Practice

1. If you have not already done so, enter and run each of the preceding scripts in the runner.

2. Enter and run the following erroneous one-line script:

```
alertt("Hello");
```

   Note the typo—the extra "t." How was the error reported?

---

[2]In Section 7.5 we will show you how to use jQuery in your own scripts so you can use them outside of the runner.

2.2.3   Interactive Shells

One of the most useful (and fun) ways to program is to use an *interactive shell*, a tool in which you can write a little bit of code and watch it run immediately. For example:

You type:	`5 + 3`
The machine responds:	`8`
You type:	`15 > 3`
The machine responds:	`true`
You type:	`Math.sqrt(100)`
The machine responds:	`10`
You type:	`"deliver".split("").reverse().join("")`
The machine responds:	`reviled`

Figure 2.4 shows a screenshot of a shell session using the JavaScript shell from `squarefree.com`. For practice with the shell, see if you can duplicate the preceding session now.

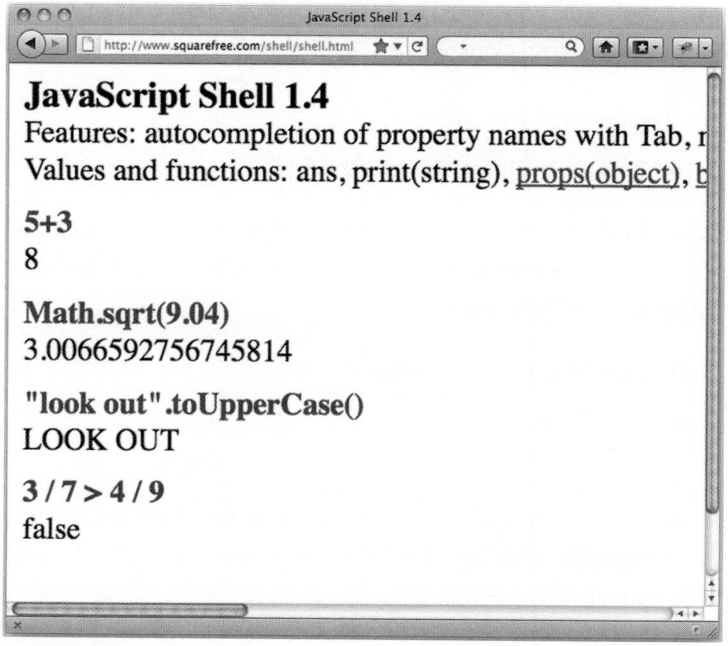

FIGURE 2.4

Using a JavaScript shell.

We won't describe all of the features of the shell in this book, as full documentation is online at `http://www.squarefree.com/shell/` and several hints appear on the shell page itself, but two of them are so useful we would be remiss not to mention them:

- Instead of retyping your previous input, use the up arrow key. This will load your previous input into the typing area—a feature you will appreciate every time you need to fix a typo.

- If your input requires multiple lines, use *Shift+Enter* (hold down the *Shift* key while pressing *Enter*) to begin the next line.

You will find the shell very useful while studying the example code snippets appearing in the text and will use it frequently as you both learn about JavaScript through self-directed experimentation and test ideas while developing your own scripts.

Other shells besides the one at `squarefree.com` exist; indeed, most modern web browsers have a built-in shell of their own. Look for a menu item (often in the Tools menu) with a name like JavaScript Console or Developer Tools.

Review and Practice

1. Evaluate `Math.exp(Math.PI) - Math.PI` in the shell.

2. Enter and run in the shell the random number script and the shouting script from Section 2.2.2. (You will need to use *Shift+Enter* for multiline scripts as stated in the shell instructions.)

3. Enter and run the following erroneous one-line script:

   ```
   alertt("Hello");
   ```

   Note the typo—the extra "t." You should see an error message displayed by the shell itself. Do you prefer this method of error reporting to that used by the test page from the previous section?

2.2.4 Files

The three approaches just discussed—the browser address box, the runner, and the shell—are fine for scripts that you write and use yourself, but what if your program is written for someone else? You can't expect others to type (or paste) your code into a runner or shell every time they want to run it. After all, you don't run your web browser, email program, instant messenger, word processor, or video player by first typing its code!

Instead, we distribute programs the same way we distribute documents, spreadsheets, photos, videos, and songs—in *files*. Because we aim to teach programming and not how to use a computer, we will assume you are able to create files with a text editor, find files on your computer, and drag files around your desktop—or at least have access to someone who can teach you how to do these things.

Let's adapt our die-rolling script from Section 2.2.2 to a file-based script. Since JavaScript programs run within a browser, our goal is to load a web page containing a die-rolling script into the browser and see the script run. Our first script used the `alert` operation to display the die roll in a message window; our new and improved version will write the die values directly on the browser's page. Create a file called *roll.html* with the following contents:

```
<!doctype html>
<html>
  <head>
    <meta charset="UTF-8"/>
    <title>A single die roll</title>
  </head>
  <body>
    <p>You rolled a <script>document.write(1 +
    Math.floor(6 * Math.random()))</script>.</p>
  </body>
</html>
```

Drag this file into your web browser, or invoke your browser's open file function (by selecting the menu option *File→Open*) and choose this file. You should see something like Figure 2.5. Since the script generates a new random number each time it is run, you can repeatedly reload (refresh) this page to perform additional rolls.

Let's look more closely at the file. Web pages are *documents* authored in the HTML *markup language*. We do not assume you know HTML already, but we will

FIGURE 2.5

The die-rolling script running in a browser.

introduce it very quickly.[3] The most visible features of HTML are *elements*—in our file, these are `html`, `head`, `meta`, `title`, `body`, `p` (for "paragraph"), and `script`. Elements are either delimited with *start tags* (such as `<html>`) and *end tags* (such as `</html>`) or represented with a single *empty tag* (such as `<meta/>`). Elements can optionally contain *attributes* (such as `charset = "UTF-8"`).

HTML is called a markup language because the tags "mark up" text in order to provide an underlying structure. The internal structure is that of a tree of *nodes*. The top, or *root*, node represents the document itself, while other nodes stand for the elements, the text, and other items, such as the document type, which we will explain in Chapter 6. Figure 2.6 shows the internal structure of the example document. You do not need the ability to draw such trees when you are learning HTML, but it is very helpful to understand that HTML documents are represented this way. When we write sophisticated scripts in Chapter 6, a deeper understanding of these trees will be crucial.

A document's `head` gives information about the document, such as the character set in which the file is written[4] and the title that appears on the browser's title bar, while the `body` contains the displayable content of the page. In our example, the body consists of a single paragraph (`p`) with three parts, the second of which is a `script` element containing JavaScript code. The script's `document.write` operation places a random number into the text of the enclosing document.

Embedding a script containing `document.write` directly inside an HTML document may be the simplest way to use JavaScript within a web page, but when

---

[3]If you find this introduction too cursory, we will be going more slowly and in-depth in Chapter 6. You can also go through the W3C's training materials at `http://www.w3.org/wiki/HTML/Training` or visit HTML Dog at `http://htmldog.com`.

[4]The `meta` element is optional, but it is good practice to include one. The reasons are somewhat technical, so we will defer an explanation of this element to Chapter 6.

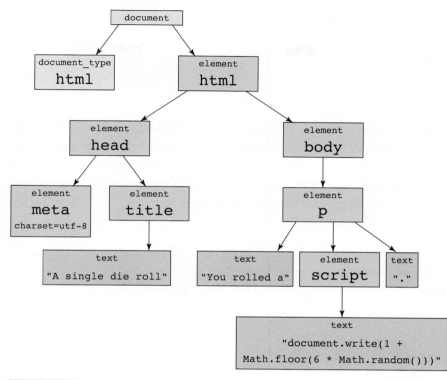

Document model for the first HTML page (*roll.html*).

pages become large, the mixing of HTML and JavaScript becomes hard to read. Therefore you will often see

- the document and script(s) residing in separate files and

- scripts handling input and output by manipulating the HTML elements.

Going this route, our new HTML file (call it *singleroll.html*) becomes:

```
<!doctype html>
<html>
  <head>
    <meta charset="UTF-8"/>
    <title>A single die roll</title>
  </head>
```

```
  <body>
    <p id="message"></p>
    <script src="singleroll.js"></script>
  </body>
</html>
```

Things are a little more complex in Figure 2.7; the HTML and JavaScript code work together a bit more indirectly than before. We have given our **p** element an **id** attribute that enables our script to find the element and insert text into the paragraph itself. Note that our script is no longer embedded in the document, but, according to the **src** attribute on the **script** element, now resides in a separate file, *singleroll.js*, which we will write as follows:

```
document.getElementById("message").innerHTML =
    "You rolled a " + (1 + Math.floor(6 * Math.random())) +
    ".";
```

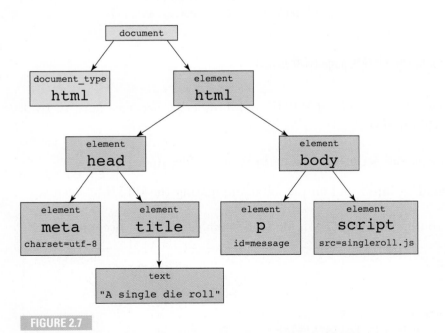

FIGURE 2.7

Document model for the second HTML page (*singleroll.html*).

The incantation `document.getElementById("message").innerHTML` refers to the part of the document inside the element that has the ID `message`. The symbol = tells JavaScript to copy the value on its right-hand side into the location on its left-hand side. The right-hand side is a text message announcing that a user rolled a particular value. It is pieced together from three fragments, the second of which is a mathematical expression for computing a random integer in the range $1 \ldots 6$. Whew!

Now let's look at a larger program, one that lives in a web page with text fields and buttons, communicating with its user in a nicer way than via `alert` and `prompt`. This script will introduce some advanced features of the language that we will not discuss in detail until later chapters, but a sneak peek at these features is important in understanding JavaScript's role in web programming.

This next program will contain a document with a form field for entering a temperature value and buttons for converting between Celsius and Fahrenheit. We start with a document file called *temperature.html* containing the following text:

```
<!doctype html>
<html>
  <head>
    <meta charset="UTF-8"/>
    <title>JavaScript Temperature Converter</title>
  </head>
  <body>
    <h1>Temperature Conversion</h1>
    <p>
      <input type="text" id="temperature" />
      <input type="button" id="f_to_c" value="F to C" />
      <input type="button" id="c_to_f" value="C to F" />
    </p>
    <p id="result"></p>
    <script src="temperature.js"></script>
  </body>
</html>
```

Figure 2.8 shows this page after a user has entered the value 40 and hit the `C to F` button.

FIGURE 2.8

A script running in a browser.

The body of this HTML document begins with an **h1** (<u>h</u>eading-level <u>1</u>) element. This normally renders large, bold text and is very common for page headings. Next comes a paragraph containing three items:

- An **input** box of type **text**, into which you can type or paste text. We have given this element the ID **temperature** so that our script will be able to access its value.

- An **input** element of type **button** labeled **F to C**. We have given this button the ID **f_to_c** so that our script can refer to it.

- An **input** element of type **button** labeled **C to F**. We have given this button the ID **c_to_f** so that our script can refer to it.

The last displayable item is a paragraph with the ID **result** into which the script will write the result of its temperature conversion computation. Finally, the **script** element's **src** attribute tells us the script is stored in an external file named *temperature.js*. Here is the script:

```
var report = function (celsius, fahrenheit) {
    document.getElementById("result").innerHTML =
        celsius + "\xb0C = " + fahrenheit + "\xb0F";
};
```

```
document.getElementById("f_to_c").onclick = function () {
    var f = document.getElementById("temperature").value;
    report((f - 32) / 1.8, f);
};

document.getElementById("c_to_f").onclick = function () {
    var c = document.getElementById("temperature").value;
    report(c, 1.8 * c + 32);
};
```

Our script contains:

- A *function* called `report`, which writes sentences such as 40°C = 104°F into the HTML document, where the actual Celsius and Fahrenheit values are supplied from outside the function. Functions will be described in Chapter 5. The character sequence `\xb0` produces the degree symbol (we will see why in Chapter 3).

- *Event handlers* for button clicks. When the `f_to_c` button is clicked, the script computes the equivalent Celsius temperature (using the formula $c = \frac{f-32}{1.8}$) and passes this computed value, along with the input Fahrenheit value, to the reporting function for display. A similar event handler, computing $f = 1.8c + 32$, is defined for the `c_to_f` button. Event handlers will be described in detail in Chapter 6.

You need not understand this script completely right now. We mentioned at the beginning of the chapter that our focus is, for now, *only* on providing you a few examples to become accustomed to the look and feel of JavaScript. The next few chapters will cover enough technical details to enable you to fully understand the script and write code of similar complexity.

Review and Practice

1. Locate, in Figure 2.5, the document's title.

2. Explain the differences between the following output strategies: (1) `alert`, (2) `document.write`, and (3) modifying the values of HTML elements.

2.3   Elements of Programs

Now that you have seen how to *run* programs, let's turn our attention to how to *create* them. After all, one of the goals of this book is to help you become a capable JavaScript programmer.

In order to create programs, we need to know about the elements from which they are constructed; thus, it is time to start introducing some technical vocabulary. Perhaps the three most important of these program elements are

- **expressions**, which compute values,

- **variables**, which store data for later use, and

- **statements**, which perform the actions of the script.

2.3.1   Expressions

An *expression* is a fragment of code containing values and operations, which we *evaluate* to produce a new value. JavaScript, like most programming languages, gives you a great many ways to form expressions. The following are some sample expressions and their evaluations. You can probably guess what many of these expressions mean, but a few may look pretty unusual:

```
2                               ⇒   2
2 + 8.1 * 5                     ⇒   42.5
(2 + 8.1) * 5                   ⇒   50.5
9 > 4                           ⇒   true
9 > 4 && 1 === 2                ⇒   false
"dog" + "house"                 ⇒   "doghouse"
"Hello".length                 ⇒   5
"Hello".replace("e", "u")      ⇒   "Hullo"
[2,3,5,7,11].join("+")         ⇒   "2+3+5+7+11"
(function (x) {return x * 5;}(8))  ⇒   40
```

Values include *numbers*, *text*, and *truth values* (**true** and **false**). Notice the quote marks surrounding text. Though it may sometimes be confusing to beginners, the distinction between numbers and text is extremely important! Text values in JavaScript are enclosed in quotes while numbers are not. Therefore 42 is the number forty-two, but "42" is a two-character sequence of text. Expressions may contain *operators*, such as + (addition), * (multiplication), === (equal to), and > (greater than). The meaning of an expression with multiple operators depends on the placement of parentheses and the *precedence* and *associativity* of the operators. Precedence tells you which operators need to be applied before others; for example:

- 5 + 2 * 4 means (5 + (2 * 4)) and not ((5 + 2) * 4) because multiplication has *higher precedence* than addition.

- 1 < 10 && 2 >= 5 means ((1 < 10) && (2 >= 5)) as opposed to, say, ((1 < (10 && 2)) >= 5) because the *relational operators* such as less than and greater than have higher precedence than the *logical operators* && (AND-ALSO) and || (OR-ELSE).

The precedence of some common JavaScript operators is listed in the following table, in decreasing order. Operators sharing a table row share precedence.

Precedence	Operators	Description
Highest	!	not
	* / %	times, divided by, modulo
	+ –	plus, minus
	< <= > >=	less than, less than or equal to, greater than, greater than or equal to
	=== !==	equal to, not equal to
	&&	and also
Lowest	||	or else

Associativity rules kick in to disambiguate expressions with operators that are on the same precedence level. For example:

- 5 – 2 – 4 means ((5 – 2) – 4) and not (5 – (2 – 4)) because subtraction *associates to the left*. Colloquially, left associativity means "do the **left**most subtraction first."

- 6 * 5 / 2 * 8 means (((6 * 5) / 2) * 8), again because of left associativity (* and / have the same precedence).

All JavaScript operators associate to the left except for a very small number that associate to the right. The complete set of all 52 JavaScript operators, with their precedence and associativity, appears in Appendix A in Table A.2. The table looks scary, but don't worry—you don't have to memorize it! Simply heed the following advice and you will avoid surprises:

> **When in doubt about precedence, use parentheses.**

The JavaScript shell (introduced back in Section 2.2.3) can be very useful for honing your skills with operators and expressions. One useful study technique is to say the meanings of expressions out loud as you type them into the shell, then look at the responses from the shell and make sure you understand *why* they were produced. To encourage you to get started, here are some suggested expressions to try, along with their English descriptions.

- 2 * 4 < 100 / Math.sqrt(11)

  Is 2 times 4 less than 100 divided by $\sqrt{11}$?

- 17 % 3

  The remainder of 17 divided by 3

- 22 * (16.5 + Math.PI)

  22 times the quantity 16.5 plus π

- "capybara".length === 2 || Math.pow(3,5) < Math.pow(5,3)

  Is the word "capybara" two characters long or, if not, is $3^5 < 5^3$?

Review and Practice

1. Rewrite the expression !x && y || z + 5 * 4 >= 3 == y && z in its fully parenthesized form.

2. Explain, in English, the meaning of x < y || x < z.

2.3.2   Variables

The values you compute when evaluating expressions may be needed multiple times in the course of a script, so JavaScript allows you to store them in *variables* for later use. We will introduce variables using the following script, which computes body mass index. Try it out in the runner or shell.

```
var KILOGRAMS_PER_POUND = 0.45359237;
var METERS_PER_INCH = 0.0254;
var pounds = prompt("Enter your weight in pounds");
var inches = prompt("Enter your height in inches");
var kilos = pounds * KILOGRAMS_PER_POUND;
var meters = inches * METERS_PER_INCH;
alert("Your body mass index is " + kilos / (meters * meters));
```

This script begins by *declaring*, or creating, the variable KILOGRAMS_PER_POUND and giving it the value 0.45359237. The variable METERS_PER_INCH is then created and given the initial value 0.0254. Next, a pop-up window asks the user for his or her weight in pounds and the input text is stored in the new variable pounds; this is followed with a similar capture of user input for the new variable inches. The script then looks up the values currently stored in the variables pounds and KILOGRAMS_PER_POUND, multiplies them, and stores the product in the new variable kilos. Next, the user's height in meters is computed and stored, and finally the body mass index is computed and alerted.

Since variables are (named) containers for values, it helps to visualize the running of a script by drawing variables as labeled boxes, as in Figure 2.9. This figure illustrates how the variables in our script get assigned during a run in which a user entered a weight of 155 pounds and a height of 72 inches. (Notice that the values for pounds and inches are obtained from a prompt, which always produces text, not numbers. As mentioned in the previous section, JavaScript text values must be given within quotes.)

We have followed good programming practice in naming variables: we have chosen names that reflect each variable's purpose in the script and used capitalization as a way to visually distinguish variables designed to hold fixed values (all capital letters) from those whose values depend on input, or are simply likely to

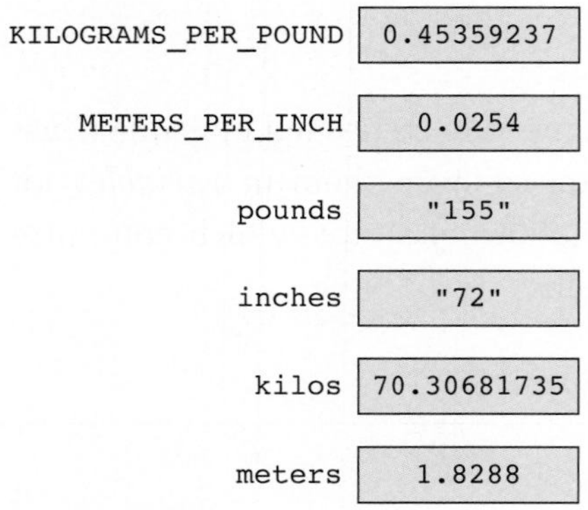

KILOGRAMS_PER_POUND	0.45359237
METERS_PER_INCH	0.0254
pounds	"155"
inches	"72"
kilos	70.30681735
meters	1.8288

FIGURE 2.9

Variables are containers for values.

change.[5] You don't have complete freedom in naming variables, however. There are two restrictions. Firstly, variable names must begin with a letter, the $ character, or the _ character, and contain only letters, digits, _'s, and $'s thereafter. Thus the following names are okay:

name	año	ORIGIN	last_known_value	lastKnownValue
$	$1	ButtonType	employee$name	$_$
x1	x2	comhábhar	_chromosome	__audioStream

while these are not (because they either begin with a number or contain a disallowed character):

    9times   give&take   root@whitehouse.gov   %Off   <=>

Secondly, you cannot use any of JavaScript's *reserved words*. These are words like `if`, `while`, and `var` that have special meanings in scripts.[6] We should also point out that `pounds`, `Pounds`, `POuNds`, and `POUNDS` are all different variables. The technical lingo for this fact is "JavaScript variables are case-sensitive"—the *case* of the letters (uppercase, lowercase) matters.

---

[5]The use of all capital letters for "constants" such as `METERS_PER_INCH` and lowercase for other variables is an example of a convention. The distinction is not required by the JavaScript language, but so many people follow this convention that failure to conform makes your code stand out in a negative way.

[6]The complete list of reserved words appears in Appendix A.

Our body mass index script provided an *initial value* to each of the variables it created. In practice, the initial value is not required; if omitted, the variable receives the special value `undefined`. In addition, although our script only wrote one value into each variable, it is possible to replace the value in a previously declared variable; this process is called *assignment*. The following script illustrates:

```
var minutes = 2;
var seconds = minutes * 60;
alert(seconds);
minutes = 5;
alert(seconds);
seconds = 10;
var hours;
alert(hours === undefined);
```

Some readers may find it helpful to trace the behavior of this script visually as we have done in Figure 2.10. We have shown "snapshots" of the variables at various points in the script. At first we have only `minutes`, then `seconds` comes into existence. The third snapshot shows that assignment places a new value into a variable *replacing the value that is already there*. The next snapshot shows another assignment, and the last one shows the effect of declaring a variable without an initial value: JavaScript gives it the special value `undefined`.

What happens if you *don't* declare a variable but try to use it anyway? Suppose in the following script the variable `next_song` was not defined:

```
alert(next_song);
```

This generates an error. The actual error notification you will receive depends on what you are using to run JavaScript; the JavaScript runner introduced in Section 2.2.2 simply pops up an error message (see Figure 2.11). If you are running a script associated with a web page, the browser itself will generally keep track of all the errors for you in a window of its own.[7]

---

[7] You can usually find this window by exploring your browser's menu.

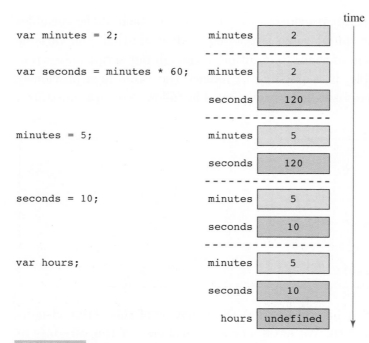

FIGURE 2.10

Variable declarations and assignments.

FIGURE 2.11

Use of an undeclared variable.

1. Rewrite the body mass index script so that it asks for and accepts input in kilograms and centimeters.

2. Is `first-guess` a legal variable name in JavaScript? Provide reasons for your answer.

3. What does the script `var size = 6; alert(Size);` do? (*Hint:* Pay attention to the case of the letters in the names.) Explain.

2.3.3 Statements

To build complete scripts, expressions and variables are wired together in *statements*. While expressions compute values, statements produce actions. A script is, in fact, a *sequence of statements*, each of which is *executed* when the script is run. JavaScript, like most programming languages, features statements for the following:

■ Declaring variables

■ Invoking predefined operations, such as `alert` and `prompt`

■ Replacing the value in a variable with a new value

■ Performing an operation only if some condition is true

■ Performing an operation repeatedly as long as some condition is true

So far, our example scripts have featured only statements of the first three types in the preceding list. We can take a quick peek at examples of the other two. Here is an example of a script that expresses happiness when you enter negative numbers and a bored politeness when you don't:

```
var n = prompt("Enter a number:");
if (n < 0) {
    alert("Cool, a negative number!");
} else {
    alert("Okay, thanks.");
}
```

And here is a script that displays how $1000 grows to $5000 if invested at a fixed 5% annual rate. You will need to run this script in our JavaScript runner (not the shell), as we are using jQuery and a special HTML `div` element tagged with the ID `footer` that we have put into the runner for scripts like this:

```
var total = 1000;
var year = 0;
while (total < 5000) {
    year = year + 1;
    total = total * 1.05;
    $("#footer").append("<div>After year " + year +
        " you have $" + total.toFixed(2) + "</div>");
}
```

This script begins by storing the value 1000 into the variable `total` and increases the value in this variable by successively multiplying by 1.05 (1000 → 1050 → 1102.50 → 1157.625 → . . .) until its value exceeds 5000. The variable `year` also advances, from 0 to 1 to 2 and so on. At each "step," we add an HTML `div` element to the footer (we strategically placed our footer `div` at the bottom of the runner page) to display the year and the total so far, formatted with JavaScript's `toFixed` operator to show exactly two places after the decimal point. See Figure 2.12.

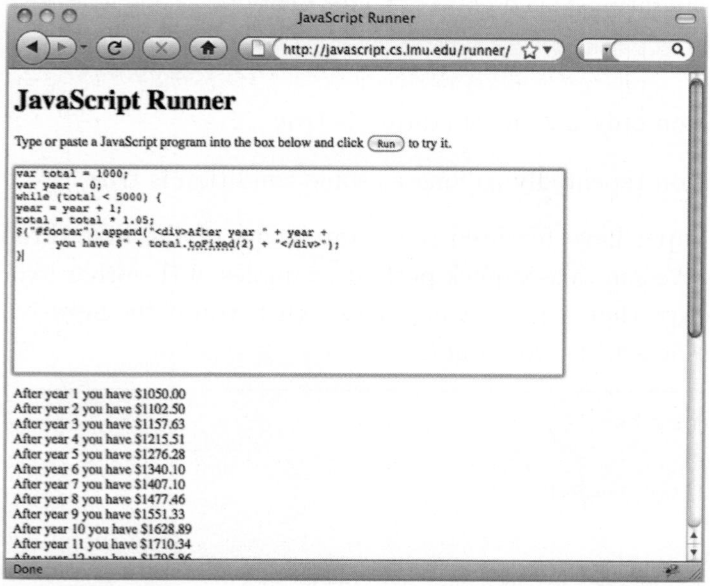

FIGURE 2.12
The compound interest script in the runner.

A full treatment of JavaScript statements will come later. In Chapter 4, we will greatly expand our repertoire of statements and cover the ones we have seen in much more depth. We hope, though, that for now, the little examples are starting to get you used to the "look and feel" of the language.

Review and Practice

1. Fill in the blanks: _____s are evaluated while statements are _____.

2. Modify and run the example script for determining how long it takes to quintuple your money for values of 2% and 35%.

2.4   The Practice of Programming

You are probably aware of the disastrous consequences of poor spelling, grammar, structure, or presentation in a resumé, report, sales brochure, advertisement, or college term paper. Speaking and writing skills are important factors in how people perceive and treat you. So it is with programming. Sloppy coding practices reflect poorly on the author, creating the perception that the coder is not capable or trustworthy enough to handle choice assignments or even an entry-level job.

The reasons for writing code carefully are not just aesthetic. For the same reason a building, ship, or appliance built with shoddy construction does not last (if it works at all), nontrivial software that is constructed without disciplined practice is hard to maintain and is much more likely to fail. Therefore thousands of books, articles, and websites have been devoted to the **art** of programming, the **science** of programming, software **craftsmanship**, and software **engineering**.

Because we have just scratched the surface of programming in this book, we are not ready to provide a complete set of guidelines defining quality code; we have much more JavaScript to cover before we can even say what many of these guidelines would even refer to! However, we can discuss a few features of readable scripts and mention tools that can perform some quality checks on your code. We will offer more programming tips for writing good (and sometimes elegant) code, and warnings against egregious practices resulting in bad (and sometimes evil) code, throughout the remainder of the text.

2.4.1   Comments

What are some desirable characteristics of software? Certainly correctness, reliability, robustness, and efficiency come to mind. But because most software systems are worked on by dozens if not hundreds of programmers and are frequently improved over time—often by people other than their original authors—it is crucial that the code also be readable, understandable, and maintainable.

The following script highlights a JavaScript feature you have not seen up to now—a feature that can, if used well, make your scripts more readable and understandable:

```
/*
 * This script prompts the user to enter four words: a noun, then
 * a verb, then an adjective, and finally an adverb.  It then alerts
 * a sentence using these four words.  The template for the sentence
 * is one that would make sense if the user entered "dog" for each
 * prompt.
 */

// Prompt for the four words
var noun = prompt("Enter a noun");
var verb = prompt("Enter a verb");
var adjective = prompt("Enter an adjective");
var adverb = prompt("Enter an adverb");

// Alert the composed sentence
alert("If you " + verb + " a " + noun + " during the " +
    adjective + " days of summer, you'll be " + adverb +
    " tired.");
```

The block between /* and */ at the beginning of the example, as well as the two lines starting with //, don't look like code; they appear to be plain English. That's because they *are* plain English; text placed between /* and */, as well as any text between two slashes (//) and the end of the line, are called *comments*. Comments allow human-speak to become part of a script, helping readers to understand the programmer's intent a little better. When JavaScript sees /*, it knows to skip over everything after that until it sees */. When JavaScript sees //, it ignores everything from there to the end of the line.

Virtually every programming language has a notation for comments. In HTML, comments begin with `<!--` and end with `-->`.[8]

```
<!-- The text of the comment goes here -->
```

The liberal inclusion of comments in code is highly encouraged in practice; no matter how great an expert one becomes in programming, it is often easier to read about something in natural language than in code. This is true whether you are reading code that you *didn't* write or are revisiting code that you wrote but haven't seen for some time.

Keep in mind, however, that writing *good* comments is a skill to be developed. First of all, comments should always be written to express ideas at a "higher level of abstraction" than the code itself. Comments explaining the *intent* of a script (or a portion of a script) are highly valued; comments that repeat the code, such as "`// Add three to x`," waste the reader's time. Secondly, make sure your comments are actually correct! Comments that disagree with the code can cause confusion and even mistakes, because other programmers will often read your comments to see how to combine your code with their own.

Review and Practice

1. Rewrite two or three scripts from this chapter with comments.

2. Why is it important to have comments that express the intent of the code, not exactly what the code does?

2.4.2   Coding Conventions

In many societies, individuality and free expression are highly valued, and a personal style running counter to the mainstream's mores is a matter of pride. Not so in programming.

Because programs have to be read, understood, and maintained by others, and often have to perform tasks for which failure can have terrible consequences, code should conform to accepted conventions. Scripts should be well structured,

---

[8]There are restrictions on the text inside an HTML comment: it cannot start with > nor -> nor contain two consecutive dashes (--) nor end with a dash. For details, see the official specification for HTML at `http://www.w3.org/TR/html5/syntax.html#comments`.

with consistent capitalization, punctuation, spacing, and formatting throughout. Inconsistencies in these areas are jarring to look at and are often a sign of programmer laziness or incompetence. Your scripts reflect your level of intelligence and professionalism, just as your speaking and writing do.

You can increase your chances of writing professional, quality code by following a style guide, such as the one at `http://javascript.crockford.com/code.html`. Of course, to read and get the most out of the entire guide, you need to know a lot of JavaScript; however, you *can*, and probably should, skim this guide at this early stage of your programming career to get a sense of what kinds of conventions good programmers try to adopt. Companies or organizations often produce extensive documents of coding conventions and best practices; one example is at `http://na.isobar.com/standards/`.

Many coding conventions are purely stylistic, such as "indent four spaces," "save your files with spaces, not tabs," "leave one blank line between functions," "put a single space on each side of an arithmetic operator," "fully capitalize variables whose value will never change," "never use a `with` statement," "declare all variables at the beginning of a function," and so on. Other rules are more substantive, such as "make sure your comments do not repeat what your code already says." We will encounter many such conventions, as well as coding dos and don'ts, throughout the book.

Review and Practice

1. Why is it so important to follow clear coding conventions?

2. What do the standards at `http://na.isobar.com/standards/` say about whitespace?

2.4.3   Code Quality Tools

Professional programmers routinely use tools to help them find instances of poor style and potential problems in their code. These tools are called *validators*, *verifiers*, or simply *code quality checkers*. Beginners can sometimes benefit from these tools but should keep in mind that effective use of such tools can only come after gaining a certain degree of programming competence.

One popular code quality tool is JSLint, which can be found at `http://www.jslint.com`. Enter or paste your script into the top box and hit the   JSLint

Options

☐ Stop on first error	☐ Tolerate debugger statements	☑ Allow one var statement per function
☑ Strict white space	☐ Tolerate eval	☑ Disallow undefined variables
☑ Assume a browser	☐ Tolerate sloppy line breaking	☑ Disallow dangling _ in identifiers
☐ Assume console, alert, ...	☐ Tolerate unfiltered for in	☑ Disallow == and !=
☐ Assume a Yahoo Widget	☐ Tolerate inefficient subscripting	☑ Disallow ++ and --
☐ Assume Windows	☐ Tolerate CSS workarounds	☑ Disallow bitwise operators
☐ Assume Rhino	☐ Tolerate HTML case	☑ Disallow insecure . and [^...] in /RegExp/
☐ Safe Subset	☐ Tolerate HTML event handlers	☑ Require Initial Caps for constructors
☐ ADsafe	☐ Tolerate HTML fragments	☑ Require parens around immediate invocations
	☐ Tolerate ES5 syntax	☐ Require "use strict";

The Good Parts	4	Strict white space indentation
		Maximum line length
Clear All Options	50	Maximum number of errors
	Predefined (, separated)	

```
/*jslint white: true, browser: true, onevar: true, undef: true, nomen: true, eqeqeq: true, plusplus:
true, bitwise: true, regexp: true, newcap: true, immed: true */
```

FIGURE 2.13

JSLint settings.

button. JSLint will report certain stylistic violations and potential problems in the pink text box. An options box lets you customize JSLint's behavior. For our purposes we suggest checking only Assume console, alert ... and Assume a browser. Because JSLint is continually being improved by its author, the actual option set may vary over time, but you should end up with something similar to Figure 2.13.

Using these settings, check the following slightly sloppy script:

```
// Here is a sloppy program that we will run JSLint on
var sum, i;
for(i = 1; i != 1000; j+= 1) {
    total += i;
}
alert(sum);
```

JSLint reports:

> Problem at line 3 character 4: Missing space between 'for' and '('.
> Problem at line 3 character 14: Expected '!==' and instead saw '!='.
> Problem at line 3 character 23: 'j' is not defined.
> Problem at line 3 character 24: Missing space between 'j' and '+='.
> Problem at line 4 character 5: 'total' is not defined.
> Implied global: j 3, total 4

Several of the error messages assume a somewhat advanced understanding of

JavaScript programming. If you ever cannot understand a JSLint suggestion, ask an experienced programmer or enter the error message into a web search engine. These learning moments will help you become acquainted with JavaScript a little faster. Be sure also to scan the tool's documentation at `http://www.jslint.com/lint.html`.

Code checking is an enormously useful and important part of software development; in many organizations, programmers are required to use automated checkers. Keep in mind, though, that satisfying a quality tool only means that your code conforms to certain standards, not that it functions correctly. You will want to write test suites or perhaps prove your scripts correct. Correctness proofs are (way) beyond the scope of this book, but we will cover testing in Section 7.7.

Review and Practice

1. Place the sloppy script from this section into JSLint and run the tool. Then correct the problems (within the tool itself), rerunning the checker until you have a script that is error-free.

2. Does the sloppy script from this section satisfy JSLint when all of the "Tolerate" boxes are checked?

2.5   The JavaScript Programming Language

Every programming language was designed for some purpose. For example, LISP was designed for artificial intelligence applications, Fortran for numeric processing, C for systems programming, ML for theorem proving, Smalltalk for graphical user interfaces, TeX for typesetting, Java (originally) for downloadable applets, and so on. JavaScript was designed to allow programmers to access and manipulate systems such as web browsers, image editors, word processors, and interactive documents. As web browsers exist on nearly every computer and smart phone today, and as JavaScript runs in nearly every browser, JavaScript has become one of the most popular programming languages in the world.

The term "JavaScript" is, perhaps surprisingly, simply a trademark referring to a dialect of an internationally standardized language called *ECMAScript* [ECM99, ECM09]. ECMAScript is the foundation of other languages, too, including Action-Script, which powers Adobe Flash. The scripting language found in the popular

Internet Explorer browser is officially named JScript, though everyone calls it JavaScript, too.

The JavaScript used in browsers today is almost certain to conform to ECMA-Script, third edition, or ES3 in geek-speak. In 2009, ECMAScript, fifth edition, or ES5, was standardized, and most major browsers have updated their JavaScript engines to support this new version (or a majority of features from it). ES5 is a superset of ES3; all ES3 programs are also ES5 programs, whereas ES5 adds many new features to ES3. In this book, we will clearly mark ES5 features when we use them, in case you are following along with a browser whose JavaScript engine is not quite ES5-ready.

You can find out which of the ECMAScript 5 features are supported by your browser by checking the compatibility table at `http://kangax.github.com/es5-compat-table/`.

Review and Practice

1. Which kinds of applications, besides web browsers, can host a JavaScript engine?

2. Which two editions (versions) of ECMAScript are the basis for modern JavaScript environments?

Chapter Summary

- Programming, or scripting, can be defined as the act of writing instructions for some agent to carry out.

- JavaScript programs (scripts) can be run as one-liners, in runners, in shells, or packaged in files and loaded into a web browser. Scripts can be given directly in HTML files but are more commonly packaged in separate files.

- Programs are put together from expressions (which compute values), variables (which store values for later use), and statements (which wire expressions together to produce actions).

- Variable names in JavaScript are strings of letters, numbers, dollar signs, and underscores; they do not start with a number. No variable can be a reserved word. Variable names are case-sensitive.

- Comments (if written well) increase a script's readability.

- Programs should not "just work"; they are a reflection of their author's professionalism and character and should be written in a consistent style.

- Code quality tools can be helpful in checking your code for poor style and potential problems. JSLint is a popular code quality tool for JavaScript.

- Virtually all JavaScript engines today conform to the third edition of the ECMAScript standard, while many newer engines conform to (much of) the fifth edition.

Exercises

1. Argue for or against the claim that writing a recipe for, say, Wu Hsiang Chi or Sambal Goreng Udang is actually programming.

2. While the terms *program* and *script* have virtually the same meaning in JavaScript, many software practitioners draw a great distinction between these terms. Research various definitions of these terms, as well as the terms *programming language* and *scripting language*. What makes a scripting language different from a programming language? Is the difference related to the idea that "scripts are for the actors while programs are for the audience"?

3. For each of the following English sentences, give as many interpretations as you can:

   (a) She poked the nanny with the umbrella.

   (b) I saw the astronomer on the hill with the telescope.

   (c) Time flies like an arrow.

   (d) Hershey bars protest.

4. Make a list of 10 ambiguous English sentences, similar to the examples in the previous exercise. If you have trouble coming up with 10, search the Web for some amusing ambiguous newspaper headlines; you'll have hundreds to choose from.

5. Give examples of programmable devices besides the ones listed in the beginning of this chapter.

6. Write a brief essay for or against the proposition that "the brain is hardware; the mind is software." Do a little research first to see what others have written about this topic.

7. Give a browser address (with the `javascript:` prefix) that will compute and alert the sum of the numbers 1, 4, 8, 16, and 25.

8. Give a browser address (with the `javascript:` prefix) that will compute and alert the number of years for 1 million minutes. Assume 60 minutes per hour, 24 hours per day, and 365.25 days per year.

9. In this chapter we saw that the `javascript:` prefix could be used in the address box to run JavaScript programs. Which other prefixes does your browser accept? (You can find the answer via a web search for "url protocols.")

10. Run this script in the JavaScript runner and describe what happens:

```
document.getElementById("scriptArea").style.backgroundColor=
    "yellow";
```

11. Run this script in the JavaScript runner and describe what happens:

```
document.getElementById("footer").innerHTML="blue";
```

12. Run this script in the JavaScript runner and describe what happens:

```
document.body.style.textAlign="right";
```

13. Run the following program a few times in a runner. What does the script do?

```
var number = Math.floor(Math.random() * 100) + 1;
for (var i = 1; i <= 10; i++) {
    var guess = prompt("Enter guess #" + i + " (1..100)");
```

```
    if (guess < number) {
        alert("Too small");
    } else if (guess > number) {
        alert("Too big");
    } else {
        alert("Got it");
        break;
    }
    if (i === 10) {
        alert("That's enough guessing");
    }
}
```

14. Evaluate each of the following in a shell:

    (a) `Math.atan(1) + Math.atan(2) + Math.atan(3)`

    (b) `Math.PI`

    (c) `1 < 5 < 10`

    (d) `-10 < -5 < -1`

    (e) `(function (x,y) {return 2 * x + y;}(3, 7))`

    You don't need to know what the expressions mean; the point of the exercise is to gain familiarity with the shell.

15. Modify the die-rolling application from Section 2.2.4 so that it rolls two dice instead of just one.

16. Modify the die-rolling application in the previous exercise so that it rolls two 20-sided dice.

17. Extend the following script:

```
alert("The " + prompt("Improper noun:")
    + " used to " + prompt("Adverb:")
    + " " + prompt("Verb:") + ".");
```

    to create longer, more interesting sentences. Run your script several times in the runner.

18. Draw a structure diagram (such as the one in Figure 2.7) for the temperature conversion HTML document discussed in Section 2.2.4.

19. Modify the temperature conversion document and script from this chapter so that it converts between Fahrenheit and the Kelvin scale.

20. Modify the temperature conversion document and script from this chapter so that it converts between kilograms and pounds.

21. Create an HTML page and associated script containing two text fields and one button. When the user clicks the button, the script writes the sum of the values in the two text fields onto the page. Use the temperature conversion document and script as a guide. Although we have covered very little web programming to this point, this exercise will force you to figure out the behavior of the existing temperature program in some detail as you try to adapt its elements to a new application.

22. Write each of the following expressions in their fully parenthesized equivalent form:

    (a) `2 * 5 - 7 / - 6 + 4`
    (b) `2 < 4 || true && false`
    (c) `1 < 2 < 3`
    (d) `! x || ! y && z`
    (e) `- - 4`

23. Express each of the expressions in the previous exercise in precise English.

24. Consider the body mass index script on page 35. If we remove the first four lines of this code and replace the uses of the (now-removed) variables with their initial values, we end up with a shorter version of the script:

```
var kilos = prompt("Enter your weight in pounds") * 0.45359237;
var meters = prompt("Enter your height in inches") * 0.0254;
alert("Your body mass index is " + kilos / (meters * meters));
```

Can we remove the variables `kilos` and `meters` in the same fashion? Why or why not?

25. Compare and contrast the shortened version of the body mass index script in the previous exercise with the original version from the chapter. Which version looks better to you? Why?

26. Run the following script in a freshly opened runner or shell:

```
alert(location);
```

Why do you think something was alerted, even though you did not define the variable `location`?

27. Write a script that asks (via prompt) for a user to enter a distance in miles, then alerts the equivalent distance in kilometers.

28. The universe has been estimated to be 156 billion light-years wide. Given that the speed of light is exactly 299,792,458 meters per second, write a script to determine the width of the universe in yottameters (Ym). A yottameter is 10^{24} meters.

29. Browse blogs or articles that address the question of whether software development is more of an engineering discipline or a craft. What are the arguments on both sides?

30. Check the following poorly formatted script with JSLint:

```
var x=0;var y=1;var sequence=[];
    while(y<1000){sequence.push(y);z=x+y;x=y;y= z;}
alert (sequence);
```

Use JSLint's suggestions to clean up the script.

31. Donald Knuth once wrote: "Let us change our traditional attitude to the construction of programs. Instead of imagining that our main task is to instruct a computer what to do, let us concentrate rather on explaining to human beings what we want a computer to do." Comment on this quote. Feel free to research what others have said on this topic.

32. Who designed JavaScript? What was it originally called? Why was its name changed to JavaScript? What year was JavaScript released?

33. JavaScript has been called the world's most misunderstood programming language. What are the reasons for this?

34. Why did the makers of the Internet Explorer browser call their scripting language JScript? Are there any differences between JScript and JavaScript? If so, do any matter in practice?

35. JavaScript runs in web browsers, Adobe Acrobat, and the productivity suite OpenOffice. What other environments does it run in?

36. Another JavaScript "runner" is hosted at `http://jsfiddle.net`. Enter and run several of the scripts from this chapter at `jsfiddle`.

37. Although this text focuses on JavaScript as a language for scripting web browsers, JavaScript is also used to write server-side code as well. Read about server-side JavaScript online and, if you are so inclined, install the `node.js` application (available at `http://nodejs.org`). Do not worry about writing anything in node for now; instead, experiment with node's shell. How is this shell similar to, and different from, the shell from `squarefree.com` discussed in this chapter?

CHAPTER 3

Data

CHAPTER CONTENTS

Introduction

Programs consist of both data and instructions for processing data. Many games, for example, feature players that are moved and drawn. Word processors hold lines of text, which are spellchecked, hyphenated, and positioned to flow around images, tables, footnotes, and other blocks of text. Search engines interpret queries, find matching content, and present results in a useful manner. Photo editors crop, sharpen, rotate, and scale images.

In this chapter, we will look at the different kinds of information that programs manipulate. We will see that data may come in primitive forms like numbers and text, as well as in structured forms that look as close to real-life objects as needed. By the end of this chapter, you will be able to express some nontrivial information structures that form the basis for arbitrarily complex scripts.

3.1   Data Types

In JavaScript, there are exactly six *types* of data:

1. *Booleans*, the two values `true` and `false`

2. Numbers, such as 81 and 4.21

3. Text, known in JavaScript as *strings* of characters

4. The special value `undefined`

5. The special value `null`

6. *Objects*

Data types are characterized not only by the values that belong to the type but also by the *operations* that are permitted on those values. For example, numbers can be multiplied, subtracted, and exponentiated, while strings can be trimmed, spliced, reversed, and capitalized. You will see all of JavaScript's data types, and a handful of operations, in the remainder of this chapter.

Unlike the previous chapter, which focused on acclimating you to running scripts without concern for detail, the material we cover here is intentionally quite technical at times. We have therefore included a fair number of example scripts. Each can be run in your favorite JavaScript environment, and we encourage you to run them exactly as presented here, as well as to experiment by making changes and running the resulting scripts.

3.2 Truth Values

The two values **true** and **false** show up again and again in programming. Here are a few examples you are likely to encounter:

```
var open = true;
var ready = false;
var gameOver = false;
var friendly = true;
var enabled = true;
```

They will also appear as the results of *comparisons*—expressions that compute whether one value is equal to (===), not equal to (!==), less than (<), less than or equal to (<=), greater than (>), or greater than or equal to (>=) another value.

```
alert(137 === 5);    // 137 equal to 5? No, alerts false.
alert(8 !== 3.0);    // 8 not equal to 3.0? Yes, alerts true.
alert(2 <= 2);       // 2 less than or equal to 2? Yes, alerts true.
var x = 16 > 8;      // Truth values can be stored in variables.
alert(x);            // Alerts true.
```

These values are called *Boolean values*.[1] We can apply several operators to these values, namely, **&&** (AND-ALSO), **||** (OR-ELSE), and **!** (NOT). If x and y are Boolean values:

- x && y is true if and only if x is true **and also** y is true.

- x || y is true if and only if x is true **or else** y is true.

- !x is true if and only if x is **not** true.

---

[1] In honor of George Boole, a 19th century mathematician and philosopher.

The reason that && and || are called AND-ALSO and OR-ELSE (as opposed to just AND and OR) will be given in Section 4.3.5.

Let's see the operators in action:

```
alert(4 < 5 && 15 === 6);    // Alerts false.
alert(1 === 2 || 15 > -5);   // Alerts true.
alert(!(3 <= 10));           // Alerts false.
```

You can "compute" with Boolean operators not unlike the way you would compute with numeric operators:

```
var x = 42;
var y = -1;
var bothPositive = x > 0 && y > 0;
var atLeastOneNegative = x < 0 || y < 0;
var exactlyOneNegative = x < 0 !== y < 0;
var atLeastOneNonPositive = !bothPositive;
```

Table 3.1 summarizes the workings of these three operators for all combinations of Boolean operands.

x	y	x && y	x || y	!x
true	true	true	true	false
true	false	false	true	false
false	true	false	true	true
false	false	false	false	true

Table 3.1

Boolean Operators

Review and Practice

1. Evaluate the expression `!(true && !false && true) || false`.

2. Evaluate the expression `false || true && false`.

3. Prove or disprove the following: if x and y hold Boolean values, then `!(x && y)` is always the same as `(!x || !y)`.

4. Write an expression that is true if and only if the value stored in variable x is between 0 and 10 (inclusive).

3.3 Numbers

The next data type we will visit is the number type. You write numbers in JavaScript pretty much as you would expect: `1729`, `3.141592`, and `299792458`. The letter `E` (or `e`) sandwiched between two numbers is read "times 10 to the power":

$$
\begin{aligned}
\texttt{3.6288E6} &\Rightarrow 3.6288 \times 10^6 \Rightarrow 3628800 \\
\texttt{5.390E-44} &\Rightarrow 5.390 \times 10^{-44} \\
\texttt{4.63e170} &\Rightarrow 4.63 \times 10^{170}
\end{aligned}
$$

3.3.1 Numeric Operations

Operators on numbers include + (addition), - (subtraction), * (multiplication), / (division), and % (modulo). The modulo operator computes the remainder after division:

```
alert(48 % 5);          // Alerts 3.
alert(31.5 % 2.125);    // Alerts 1.75.
```

Other operations include `Math.floor(x)`, which produces the largest *integer*[2] less than or equal to x; `Math.ceil(x)`, which produces the smallest integer greater than or equal to x; `Math.sqrt(x)`, which produces $\sqrt{x}$; `Math.pow(x,y)`, which

---

[2]The integers are $\ldots -3, -2, -1, 0, 1, 2, 3 \ldots$.

produces x^y (x to the power y); and `Math.random()`, which produces a random number between 0 (inclusive) and 1 (exclusive).

```
alert(Math.floor(2.8));     // Alerts 2.
alert(Math.floor(-2.8));    // Alerts -3.
alert(Math.ceil(2.8));      // Alerts 3.
alert(Math.ceil(-2.8));     // Alerts -2.
alert(Math.ceil(-5));       // Alerts -5.
alert(Math.sqrt(100));      // Alerts 10.
alert(Math.pow(2.5, 4));    // Alerts 39.0625.
alert(Math.random());       // Alerts something between 0 and 1.
```

The complete set of `Math` operations can be found in Appendix A on page 639.

JavaScript also contains several operators that work on the "internal representation" of integers, namely ~, &, |, ^, <<, >>, and >>>. These are rarely encountered in everyday scripts, so we will not discuss them here.

Review and Practice

1. Evaluate the following expressions: 1 / 8, 253E-2 * 10, 36 % 7 + 5, and 4 - 3 * 10 + 2.

2. What does `Math.floor(Math.random() *6) +1` produce? (Use a test page or shell, making sure to evaluate this expression several times.)

3. Evaluate the expression `Math.atan(1) + Math.atan(2) + Math.atan(3)`.

3.3.2   Size and Precision Limits

JavaScript numbers, like numbers in most programming languages, are not like the idealized numbers you encounter every day. For one thing, they need to fit in finitely sized, physical components inside a computing device. Thus, there is a largest finite number (JavaScript's is approximately 1.79×10^{308})[3] and a smallest finite number (approximately -1.79×10^{308}). Any computation producing a value larger than the largest finite number (or smaller than the smallest) yields the special value `Infinity` (or `-Infinity`).

---

[3] Or $2^{1024} - 2^{971}$ to be exact.

```
alert(2E200 * 73.987E150);    // Alerts Infinity.
alert(-1e309);                // Alerts -Infinity.
```

Not only are there limits to the *size* of numbers, but their *precision* is limited, too. Computations resulting in numbers that cannot be represented exactly will produce the nearest representable number. This may cause some surprises:

```
alert(12157692622039623539);      // Alerts 12157692622039624000.
alert(12157692622039623539 + 1);  // Alerts 12157692622039624000.
alert(1e200 === 1e200 + 1);       // Alerts true.
alert(4.18e-1000);                // Alerts 0.
alert(0.1 + 0.2);                 // Alerts 0.30000000000000004.
alert(0.3 === 0.1 + 0.2);         // Alerts false.
```

Many scripts never run into, or can easily tolerate, these approximations. However, sometimes the loss of precision means trouble (think of financial calculations). You should therefore have some sense of where approximations are likely to occur. The following points are particularly relevant:

- The representable numbers are packed most tightly around zero; in fact, more than half of them lie between -1 and 1. The farther you stray from 0, the more spread out they become.

- All integers between -9007199254740992 and 9007199254740992 inclusive are represented exactly. (You don't have to memorize those exact values; just remember that "counting" computations are safe within $\pm$ 9 quadrillion, more or less.) Beyond these limits, some, but not all, of the integers will be represented exactly.

- Computations involving (or yielding) very large numbers, very small numbers, or nonintegers will often produce nonexact results.

If you ever require the largest representable number, use the expression `Number.MAX_VALUE`. For the smallest, use `-Number.MAX_VALUE`. The expression `Number.MIN_VALUE` gives you the smallest representable number greater than zero, namely, 2^{-1074}.

Review and Practice

1. Evaluate the expression 152376357 * 349982379. Why is the final digit of the result not a 3?

2. Evaluate the two expressions (1E200 * 1E200) / 1E200 and 1E200 * (1E200 / 1E200), and explain why the answers are not the same.

3.3.3 NaN

The special value NaN, meaning *Not a Number*, appears when the result of an arithmetic computation is mathematically undefined:

```
alert(0 / 0);                    // Alerts NaN.
alert(Infinity * Infinity); // Alerts Infinity.
alert(Infinity - Infinity); // Alerts NaN.
alert(NaN + 16);                 // Alerts NaN.
alert(NaN === NaN);              // Alerts false.
```

The last of the preceding examples is surprising: NaN is not equal to anything, not even NaN! To test whether something is not a number, use isNaN:

```
alert(0 / 0 === NaN);       // Alerts false.
alert(isNaN(0 / 0));        // Alerts true.
alert(isNaN(2.718281828));  // Alerts false.
alert(isNaN(NaN));          // Alerts true.
alert(isNaN(Infinity));     // Alerts false.
```

We will see more details regarding NaN and isNaN in Section 3.8.

Review and Practice

1. Explain why Infinity + Infinity evaluates to ∞ but Infinity - Infinity evaluates to NaN. (*Hint*: Consider $(\infty + \infty) - \infty$ and $\infty + (\infty - \infty)$.)

2. Evaluate the expression -2 === Math.sqrt(-2 * -2).

3. Evaluate the expression isNaN(Math.sqrt(-1)).

3.3.4 Hexadecimal Numerals

Nonnegative integers in JavaScript can also be written in *hexadecimal notation*. Hexadecimal numerals count like so: 0, 1, 2, 3, 4, 5, 6, 7, 8, 9, A, B, C, D, E, F, 10, 11, ... , 19, 1A, 1B, ... , 1F, 20, ... , 9F, A0, ... , FF, 100, 101 ... , FFF, 1000, ... To write an integer in hexadecimal, prefix the numeral with 0x; for example:

```
alert(0x9);      // Alerts 9.
alert(0x9FA);    // Alerts 2554.
alert(-0xCafe);  // Alerts -51966.
alert(0xbad);    // Alerts 2989.
```

Note that you cannot use fractional parts nor scientific notation with hexadecimal.

Some versions of JavaScript treat integers beginning with a 0 as *octal numerals*. Octal numerals count like so: 0, 1, 2, 3, 4, 5, 6, 7, 10, 11, ... , 17, 20, ... , 27, 30, ... , 77, 100, 101, ... , 777, 1000, ... In these versions of JavaScript, you would see the following:

```
alert(07);       // Alerts 7.
alert(011);      // Alerts 9.
alert(-02773);   // Alerts -1531.
```

We recommend avoiding octal notation at all costs. We mention it only in case you accidentally type extra zeros at the beginning of a number and find your script producing strange results.

Review and Practice

1. Without using a shell, what is the numeric value of the JavaScript expression 0x10?

2. Determine if your JavaScript interpreter treats integers with leading zeros as octal.

3.4   Text

A *string* is a sequence of *characters*. In JavaScript, string values are written within double quotes (e.g., `"hello"`) or single quotes (e.g., `'hello'`), and *must fit on one line*.

3.4.1   Characters, Glyphs, and Character Sets

A character is a named symbol, such as:

PLUS SIGN
CYRILLIC SMALL LETTER TSE
BLACK CHESS KNIGHT
DEVANAGARI OM
MUSICAL SYMBOL FERMATA BELOW

Do not confuse a character with a *glyph*, which is a picture of a character. The glyph

$$K$$

could represent the character LATIN CAPITAL LETTER K, GREEK CAPITAL LETTER KAPPA, or CYRILLIC CAPITAL LETTER KA. Similarly, the glyph

$$\Sigma$$

could represent either the character GREEK CAPITAL LETTER SIGMA or SUMMATION SIGN. The glyph

$$\emptyset$$

could represent EMPTY SET, LATIN CAPITAL LETTER O WITH STROKE, or DIAMETER SIGN.

A *character set* is a particular set of characters, each having a unique number called its *codepoint*. JavaScript, like most modern languages, uses the Unicode character set. There is a tradition in Unicode to give the codepoint for each character in hexadecimal. Table 3.2 shows some codepoints for selected Unicode characters.

Codepoint	Character
F1	LATIN SMALL LETTER N WITH TILDE
3B8	GREEK SMALL LETTER THETA
95A	DEVANAGARI LETTER GHHA
F0A	TIBETAN MARK BKA- SHOG YIG MGO
11F4	HANGUL JONGSEONG KAPYEOUNPHIEUPH
13C9	CHEROKEE LETTER QUO
21B7	CLOCKWISE TOP SEMICIRCLE ARROW
265B	BLACK CHESS QUEEN
2678	RECYCLING SYMBOL FOR TYPE-6 PLASTICS
FE7C	ARABIC SHADDA ISOLATED FORM
1D122	MUSICAL SYMBOL F CLEF

Table 3.2

Codepoints for Selected Characters

For the complete codepoint mapping, see `http://www.unicode.org/charts`.

Why do codepoints matter? In JavaScript, you use codepoints to write strings with characters you might not be able to type on your keyboard. For example, the string "Привет" can be given as

```
"\u041f\u0440\u0438\u0432\u0435\u0442"
```

The two characters `\u` followed by four hexadecimal digits stand for the character whose codepoint is given by those digits. You can also use `\x` followed by *two* hexadecimal digits; therefore, you can write the string "Olé" two different ways:

```
"Ol\xc9"
"Ol\u00c9"
```

Some characters are not displayable at all, so the codepoint notation is required. Examples include LEFT-TO-RIGHT MARK (`\u200e`), RIGHT-TO-LEFT MARK (`\u200f`), and ZERO WIDTH NO BREAK SPACE (`\ufeff`). The first two of these characters appear in documents mixing text from languages read left to right (such as English and Spanish) with those read right to left (such as Hebrew and Arabic).

Escape	Description
\'	The single-quote character (used to get the single-quote character in a string surrounded by single quotes)
\"	The double-quote character (used to get the double-quote character in a string surrounded by double quotes)
\x*hh*	Where *hh* is a two-digit hexadecimal value, is the character whose codepoint is that value
\u*hhhh*	Where *hhhh* is a four-digit hexadecimal value, is the character whose codepoint is that value
\n, \t, \b, \f, \r, \v	The characters LINE FEED, CHARACTER TABULATION, BACKSPACE, FORM FEED, CARRIAGE RETURN, and LINE TABULATION
\\	The backslash character itself

Table 3.3

JavaScript Escape Sequences

The backslash character \ is used for more than just specifying characters by their codepoint; it combines with subsequent characters as shown in Table 3.3 to form what are called *escape sequences*.

The linefeed character, \n, causes the rest of the string to be written on the next line, and the tab character, \t, helps to align text in columns. The following one-line script alerts a string with tabs and newlines; Figure 3.1 shows the output.

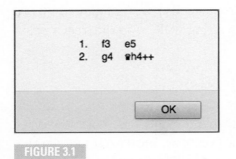

FIGURE 3.1

A string with tabs and newlines.

```
alert("1.\tf3\te5\n2.\tg4\t\u265bh4++");
```

The \u notation only works in JavaScript strings; to get characters in HTML documents, you use a different notation: surround the (hexadecimal) codepoint with &#x and a semicolon (";"). Examples:

Character	JavaScript	HTML
BLACK CHESS QUEEN	\u265b	&#x265b;
DIE FACE-1	\u2680	&#x2680;
DIE FACE-2	\u2681	&#x2681;
DIE FACE-6	\u2685	&#x2685;
TIBETAN LETTER DZHA	\u0f5c	&#x0f5c;

Let's create a slightly fancier die-rolling program to display die face characters directly in the HTML page. We will define a ⟨Roll⟩ button that when clicked generates a random integer in $\{0, 1, 2, 3, 4, 5\}$. Since the die face characters in Unicode have codepoints 2680 through 2685, the HTML is fairly easy to form. Here's a quick implementation:

```html
<!doctype html>
<html>
  <head>
    <meta charset="utf-8" />
    <title>Die Rolling</title>
    <style>div#die { font-size: 800% }</style>
  </head>
  <body>
    <div><input id="roller" type="button" value="Roll" /></div>
    <div id="die"></div>
    <script>
      document.getElementById("roller").onclick = function () {
          document.getElementById("die").innerHTML =
              "&#x268" + Math.floor(Math.random() * 6) + ";";
      }
    </script>
  </body>
</html>
```

A screenshot of the die-rolling script.

This script introduces the HTML `style` element, which we will cover in some detail in Chapter 6. For this document, we have introduced one style rule, which says, "For any `div` element whose `id` attribute is `die`, render text eight times larger than usual." Figure 3.2 shows a screenshot after rolling a 3. Your results may vary, however. Just because certain characters are defined in Unicode does not mean every browser is capable of displaying glyphs for them. Whether or not you (or your users!) can see particular characters depends on the *fonts* that are installed on the system.

Please note that our program was very small, so we can get away with embedding the script inside the HTML document. Remember to define scripts in separate files when your applications are longer (as discussed in Section 2.2.4). The same can be said for style rules. Because our page was very small, we placed style rules in the document head. In larger pages, style rules would appear in a separate file so that the document structure (HTML), its presentation (styles), and its behavior (JavaScript) are each in their own place. This *separation of concerns* is one of the many important concepts in software engineering.

Review and Practice

1. Look up, in a Unicode book or online reference, the codepoints for the following characters: COMMA, ORIYA DIGIT SEVEN, CANADIAN SYLLAB-ICS LWII, APPROACHES THE LIMIT, BRAILLE PATTERN DOTS-456, COFFIN, TETRAGRAM FOR RITUAL, and CJK STROKE HZG.

2. Write a one-line script to alert (the song title) "Такого как Путин."

3. Enter and run the die-rolling script from this chapter. Can your browser display the die face characters? If not, what is shown in their place?

3.4.2 String Operations

JavaScript provides dozens of string operations, such as finding the length (number of characters) in a string,[4] converting to upper- and lowercase, and replacing parts of the string.

```
alert("Hello, there".length);              // Alerts 12.
alert("Hello, there".toLowerCase());       // "hello, there".
alert("Hello, there".toUpperCase());       // "HELLO, THERE".
alert("Hello, there".replace("ello", "i")); // "Hi, there".
```

Sometimes you would like to know where in a string a certain character can be found or which character is at a given position. In JavaScript, the first character in a string is at *index* 0, the second at 1, the third at 2, and so on. The character at position p within string s is found with the expression s.`charAt`(p). Text within a string can be located with `indexOf` and `lastIndexOf`. The expression s.`substring`(x, y) produces a string consisting of all characters of string s from index x up to but **not including** the character at index y.

$$\text{"Some text".charAt(7)} \quad \Rightarrow \quad \text{"x"}$$
$$\text{"Some text".indexOf("me")} \quad \Rightarrow \quad 2$$
$$\text{"Some text".lastIndexOf("e")} \quad \Rightarrow \quad 6$$
$$\text{"Some text".substring(3, 7)} \quad \Rightarrow \quad \text{"e te"}$$

The + operator *concatenates* two strings:

$$\text{"dog" + "house"} \quad \Rightarrow \quad \text{"doghouse"}$$
$$\text{"2" + "2"} \quad \Rightarrow \quad \text{"22"}$$

Here is an example using `substring` and the concatenation operator to produce a phone number in a different format from the one given.

```
var phone = "(800) 555-1212";
var area = phone.substring(1, 4);
var prefix = phone.substring(6, 9);
var suffix = phone.substring(10, 14);
alert(area + "." + prefix + "." + suffix); // 800.555.1212
```

---

[4]We should be honest and say "more or less" here, because characters with codepoints greater than FFFF are counted twice. See Appendix C for details.

One extremely important aspect of JavaScript strings is that they are *immutable*. This means that you cannot change the characters within a string; nor can you change the string's length. For example, what do you think this code does?

```
var s = "Hello";
s.toUpperCase();
alert(s);
```

This alerts `Hello` because the second line simply performs a computation to uppercase a string but does nothing with the result! If the intent is to alert the uppercase version of the string, you can assign the uppercase string to a new variable or alert the `s.toUpperCase()` expression directly. Try it!

Review and Practice

1. What is `"abcdef".substring(3, 4)`?

2. Write a one-line script to alert the text "The backslash character (\) is cool."

3. Evaluate the expression `"dog".charAt(2).charAt(0)` and explain the result.

3.5   undefined and null

Usually in programming we are interested in capturing actual knowledge, such as how much something costs (a number), whether or not a player in a game is active (a Boolean), or the name of your supervisor (a string). But sometimes we want to capture the nonexistence of data or the uncertainty of data. Let's look at the supervisor example more closely. What might you say about your supervisor?

1. I have a supervisor and her name is Alice.

2. I definitely have no supervisor.

3. I may or may not have a supervisor; I really don't know.

4. I do know whether I have a supervisor, but I don't care to make this information public.

JavaScript gives you the special value `null` as a way to express the second scenario, and `undefined` for the third and fourth.

```
var supervisor = "Alice";    // The supervisor is Alice.
var chief = null;            // Absolutely, positively, NO chief.
var assistant = undefined;   // There might be an assistant.
```

Review and Practice

1. Explain in your own words the difference between `undefined` and `null`.

2. Why might it be a bad idea to use strings such as `"NONE"` and `"UNKNOWN"` instead of `null` and `undefined`, respectively?

3.6 Objects

3.6.1 Object Basics

In JavaScript, any value that is neither a Boolean, a number, a string, `null`, nor `undefined` is an *object*. Objects have *properties*, and properties have *values*. Property names can be strings (which you might have to place in quotes) or non-negative integers (0, 1, 2, . . .). Property values may be objects as well, enabling complex structures to be defined. An *object literal* is an expression defining a new object; several examples follow:

```
var dress = {
    size: 4,
    color: "green",
    brand: "DKNY",
    price: 834.95
};
```

```
var location = {
    latitude: 31.131013,
    longitude: 29.976977
};
```

```
var part = {
    "serial number": "367DRT2219873X-785-11P",
    description: "air intake manifold",
    "unit cost": 29.95
};
```

```
var p = {
    name: { first: "Seán", last: "O'Brien" },
    country: "Ireland",
    birth: { year: 1981, month: 2, day: 17 },
    kidNames: { 1: "Ciara", 2: "Bearach", 3: "Máiréad", 4: "Aisling" }
};
```

After defining an object, you may access its properties with either a dot or square brackets.

p.country	⇒	"Ireland"
p["country"]	⇒	"Ireland"
p.birth.year	⇒	1981
p.birth["year"]	⇒	1981
p["birth"].year	⇒	1981
p["birth"]["year"]	⇒	1981
p.kidNames[4]	⇒	"Aisling"
p["kidNames"][4]	⇒	"Aisling"

The dot-notation for properties is a bit more concise but cannot be used with integer properties (i.e., you can't say "a.1"), nor can it, in ES3,[5] be used if the property is a JavaScript reserved word (see page 628). In these cases, the bracket notation is required (e.g., a[10], a["var"]). Bracket notation is also required for property names containing spaces or certain other nonalphanumeric characters (e.g., part["serial number"]).

---

[5]Recall from Section 2.5 that ES3 is the old specification for JavaScript.

The properties of an object are not fixed; in fact, you can add and even delete properties, as in the following example:

```
var dog = {};              // An object with no properties.
dog.name = "Kärl";         // Now the object has one property.
dog.breed = "Rottweiler";  // Now the object has two properties.
delete dog.name;           // Now one property again.
```

When JavaScript is used for web applications, the elements that make up the web page are objects with their own properties. The following little web program demonstrates this; it makes a happy face jump around the browser by randomly placing it at a new random position every 2 seconds.

```
<!doctype html>
<html>
  <head>
    <meta charset="utf-8" />
    <title>Jumping Happy Face</title>
    <style>
      div#face {font-size: 500%; position: absolute;}
    </style>
  </head>
  <body>
    <div id="face">&#x263a;</div>
    <script>
      var style = document.getElementById("face").style;
      var move = function () {
        style.left = Math.floor(Math.random() * 500) + 'px';
        style.top = Math.floor(Math.random() * 400) + 'px';
      }
      setInterval(move, 2000);
    </script>
  </body>
</html>
```

The happy face itself is simply the character U+263A embedded in an HTML div with the ID "face." This element has a style property that is itself an object with properties that include position, left, and top. The script arranges, via setInterval, to run the move function[6] every 2000 milliseconds, or 2 seconds. The values of the style properties left and top are strings that can take various forms, one of which represents pixel offsets in the browser window and is denoted with values such as 288px. Our program assigns new style values each time the move function is run. JavaScript detects the style changes and refreshes the browser window. The program will run until you close the browser window or load another page.

Review and Practice

1. When must an object's properties be accessed with the square bracket notation as opposed to dot-notation?

2. What does the script

```
var pet = {name: "Oreo", type: "Rat"};
alert(pet[name]);
```

output? Why?

3.6.2   Understanding Object References

Objects differ from the other five types of values, collectively called *primitive values*, in two very important ways. Although quite technical, these two differences are so essential to understanding how to use objects correctly and efficiently that they must be memorized. The first is:

> **The *value* of an object expression is not the object itself but a *reference* to it.**

This can only be explained with pictures. Figure 3.3 shows how primitive values are stored directly inside variables (see variable a in the figure), while objects are not. Variables contain references to objects (see variable b).

Because object values are actually references, the assignment of an existing object value to a variable makes *a copy of the reference*, not of the object itself;

---

[6]Although functions will not be officially covered until Chapter 5, you should, we hope, be able to follow the general idea behind the code.

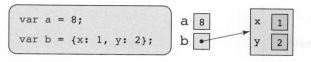

Object values are stored as references.

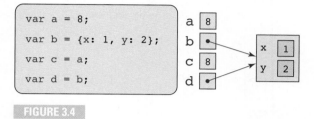

Assignment.

that is, *no new object is created*. If you think about it, assignment doesn't really work any differently for primitives than it does for objects; assignment between variables is always copying what is in one box into another box, regardless of whether that box holds a number or an arrow. Figure 3.4 illustrates the assignment of both primitives and object references, and should be studied carefully.

The second important way in which objects differ from the other types of values is:

Every evaluation of an object literal creates a brand-new object.

This fact is illustrated in Figure 3.5, where a script declares three variables and creates two objects. Although the two objects have exactly the same properties with the same values, there were two distinct object literals in the script, and therefore two distinct objects were created.

The fact that variables hold references and not objects requires us to think carefully about not only assignment but also equality testing. To evaluate the expression x === y, we ask "do x and y have the same value?" For variables referring to objects, we must ask whether each reference points to the *same object*. In Figure 3.5 we have a === b but a !== c. In the latter case we have two objects that look alike, but they are still two distinct objects.

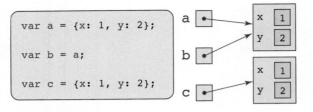

FIGURE 3.5

Three variables and two objects.

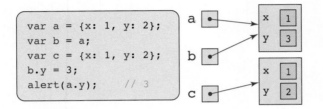

FIGURE 3.6

Updating a property of a shared object.

Because an object can be simultaneously referred to by more than one variable, either variable can be used to update the object's properties, and either can be used to see these updates. See Figure 3.6.

Review and Practice

1. Draw pictures that illustrate the variables **dress**, **location**, **part**, and p and their values given at the beginning of Section 3.6.1.

2. How does assignment of primitive values differ from that of reference values, if at all?

3. Evaluate the expression {x:1, y:2} === {x:1, y:2} and explain the result.

3.6.3   Object Prototypes

In Section 3.6.1 we created one dress, one location, one part, and one person object. What if you needed several of the same kind of object? You can define them straight up, of course, as in this collection of circles:

```
var c1 = {x: 4, y: 0, radius: 1, color: "green"};
var c2 = {x: 4, y: 0, radius: 15, color: "black"};
var c3 = {x: 0, y: 0, radius: 1, color: "black"};
```

But JavaScript lets you do something more elegant: you can create a prototypical circle on which other circles are based. Every JavaScript object has a hidden link to another object, called its *prototype*. When trying to read a nonexistent property in an object, JavaScript looks in the object's prototype. If the property is not in the prototype, it checks the prototype's prototype, and so on. The last object on this *prototype chain* should have the value `null` for its hidden link. If the property is not found anywhere on the chain, you will get an error.[7] Figure 3.7 shows a prototype circle, which is centered at $(0,0)$, with radius 1, and colored black; we have placed another circle at $(4,0)$ and colored it green. The hidden prototype link gives the new circle (`c1`) the same y-value and radius as the prototype. In fact, circle `c1` has four properties: `x` and `color` are called *own properties*, while `y` and `radius` are *inherited properties*.

You create an object from a prototype with `Object.create`. This is an ES5 operation, so old (ES3) JavaScript engines have to use another technique, which we cannot reveal until Chapter 5. Here is the ES5 code that creates the two objects in Figure 3.7:

```
var protoCircle = {x: 0, y: 0, radius: 1, color: "black"};
var c1 = Object.create(protoCircle);
c1.x = 4;
c1.color = "green";
// Note that c1.y === 0 and c1.radius === 1 (inherited properties)
```

Prototypes really shine when you derive many objects from them; in Figure 3.8 we have made two more circles. One of the two new circles has no properties of its own (pun intended); it happily inherits *all* the properties from the prototype.

---

[7]Technically, a `ReferenceError` will be thrown; these will be discussed in Section 4.5.2.

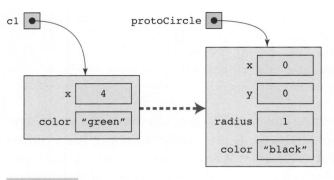

FIGURE 3.7

An object and its prototype.

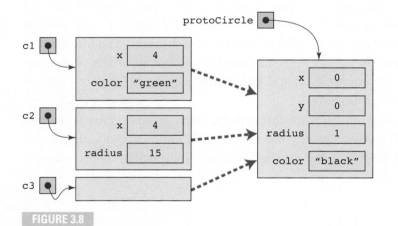

FIGURE 3.8

Multiple objects sharing a prototype.

Review and Practice

1. Define the terms *own property* and *inherited property* in your own words.

2. Write the code to create circles **c2** and **c3** in Figure 3.8.

3. In Figure 3.8, after running **protoCircle.radius = 5**, what would happen to the value of **c1.radius**? To **c2.radius**?

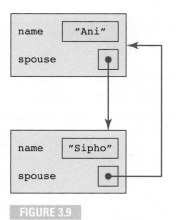

FIGURE 3.9

Objects that reference each other.

3.6.4   Self-Referential Objects

It is possible for an object to have a property whose value is a reference to itself, or for two objects to refer to each other, as in Figure 3.9. Notice that in such cases, it is not possible to describe all of the objects purely with object literals. (Try it!)

In such cases we can create partial objects with object literals and fill in the rest with assignment.

```
var mom = {name: "Ani"};
var dad = {name: "Sipho", spouse: mom};
mom.spouse = dad;
```

Review and Practice

1. Draw a picture of the objects resulting from the following declaration:

```
var p1 = {name: "Alice"};
var p2 = {name: "Bob", manager: p1};
p1.manager = p1;
```

2. What is the value of `p2.manager.manager.manager.name` in the previous question?

3.7   Arrays

An *array* is a special kind of object whose properties are consecutive nonnegative integers from 0 to some limit, together with a property called `length`. Arrays are special because you do not create them with regular object literals but instead with a special syntax:

```
var a = [];
var b = [8, false, [[null, 9]];
var days = ["p\u014d\u02bbakahi", "p\u014d\u02bbalua",
    "p\u014d\u02bbakolu", "p\u014d\u02bbah\u0101",
    "p\u014d\u02bbalima", "p\u014d\u02bbaono",
    "l\u0101pule"];
```

These arrays are illustrated in Figure 3.10.

This special syntax actually creates the properties 0, 1, 2, ... , and `length`. The `length` property is special, too: assigning to it may grow or shrink the array; newly added properties, if any, are set to `undefined`. An array may also be grown by assigning to a position beyond the end of the array.

```
var a = [9, 3, 2, 1, 3]; // a[0] is 9, a.length is 5, etc.
a[20] = 6;               // a[5] through a[19] now undefined.
alert(a.length);         // Alerts 21.
a.length = 50;           // a[21] through a[49] all undefined.
a.length = 3;            // a is now [9, 3, 2].
```

You can also create arrays by `split`-ting up a string across a given separator, extracting a `slice` from an existing array, or `concat`-enating two arrays. You can also `join` array elements together into a string while introducing a separator:

```
var s = "A red boat";
var a = s.split(" ");        // a is ["A", "red", "boat"].
var b = [9, 3, 2, 1, 3, 7];
var c = b.slice(2, 5);       // c is [2, 1, 3].
var d = c.concat(a);         // d is [2, 1, 3, "A", "red", "boat"].
alert(d.join("**"));         // Alerts 2**1**3**A**red**boat.
```

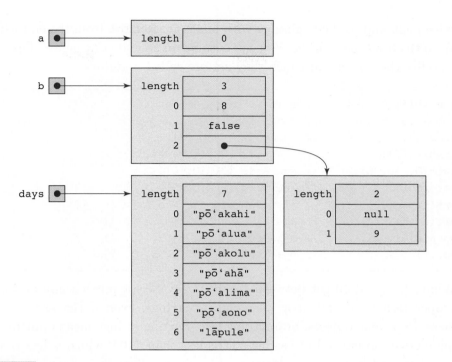

FIGURE 3.10

Arrays.

Note that the **slice** operation, when asked to create an array from the slice of b from positions 2 to 5, returned the array [b[2], b[3], b[4]]. This operation always includes the element at the starting position and excludes the one at the ending position; this is exactly the same behavior we saw with the **substring** operation back on page 69. That is, a.slice(x,y) creates a new array with elements a[x] through a[y-1], by design. There are two other forms of the **slice** operation:

```
var a = [9, 4, 1, 7, 8];
var b = a.slice(2);        // from index 2 to the end ([1, 7, 8)
var c = a.slice();         // all indices - makes a copy of a
```

The **split** operation does not change the string being split; nor do the **slice**, **concat**, and **join** operations change the arrays they operate upon. However, several operations *do* change the array objects themselves. You can add items to the end with **push** and to the beginning with **unshift**. Remove from the end with **pop** and from the front with **shift**. You can even **reverse** and **sort** arrays. Operations that modify the objects on which they act are called *mutators*.

```
var a = [];              // a is an array of length 0.
var b = [3, 5];          // b has length 2.
b.push(2);               // Now b is [3, 5, 2].
b.unshift(7);            // Now b is [7, 3, 5, 2].
a.push(3, 10, 5);        // Now a is [3, 10, 5].
a.reverse();             // Now a is [5, 10, 3].
alert(a.pop());          // Alerts 3 and changes a to [5, 10].
alert(a.shift());        // Alerts 5 and changes a to [10].
b.push(a[0], 1);         // b is now [7, 3, 5, 2, 10, 1].
b.sort();                // b is now [1, 10, 2, 3, 5, 7].
```

What? How did 10 get between 1 and 2? JavaScript put it there because the **sort** operation treats all array elements as strings, even if the array contains numbers, Booleans, objects, or anything else. Sorting strings means putting them in alphabetical order, and the string **"1"** is less than **"10"**, which is less than **"2"** (just like **"foot"** is less than **"football"**, which is less than **"goal"**). You *can* sort arrays using a numeric ordering as well; we will see how later in the text.

You can create arbitrarily complex structured data by placing arrays within object literals and creating arrays of object literals; for example:

```
var song = {
    title: "In My Head",
    track_number: 10,
    album: "Rock Steady",
    artist: "No Doubt",
    authors: ["Gwen Stefani", "Tony Kanal", "Tom Dumont"],
    duration: 205
};

var triangle = [{x: 0, y: 0}, {x: 3, y: -6}, {x: -4, y: -1.5}];
```

In practice, you will use regular objects to describe (individual) things, such as dresses, people, songs, and points, and you will use arrays to describe *lists* of things, such as songs on an album or the points of a polygon. Arrays are not the only way to form a collection of values; several exercises at the end of this chapter will introduce you to ways of wiring together objects to make different kinds of collections.

Review and Practice

1. Draw a picture of the variables `song` and `triangle` defined at the end of this section, as well as the objects they reference.

2. Draw a picture of the array referred to by the variable `a` after executing the following: `var a = [1, 2, 3, 4]; a.unshift(a.pop());`

3. Draw a picture of the array referred to by the variable `a` after executing the following: `var a = [1, 2, 3, 4]; a.push(a.shift());`

4. Describe the `split` and `join` operations in your own words.

3.8   Type Conversion

3.8.1   Weak Typing

Now that we have seen each of JavaScript's six data types, let's take a closer look at the operations on those types. We have seen a few operators so far, including:

Boolean **&&** *Boolean*	*number* **/** *number*
Boolean **||** *Boolean*	*number* **%** *number*
! *Boolean*	`Math.sqrt`(*number*)
− *number*	*string* **+** *string*
number **+** *number*	*string*`.toUpperCase`()
number **−** *number*	*string*`.indexOf`(*number*)
s*number* ***** *number*	*object* [*string*]

What happens if we give an operator one or more values of the "wrong" type? Let's experiment. Suppose a number is expected:

```
7 * false      ⇒  0
7 * true       ⇒  7
7 * "5"        ⇒  35
7 * " 5 "      ⇒  35
7 * " "        ⇒  0
7 * "dog"      ⇒  NaN
7 * null       ⇒  0
7 * undefined  ⇒  NaN
7 * {x: 1}     ⇒  NaN
```

Suppose a Boolean is expected:

```
! 5            ⇒  false
! 0            ⇒  true
! "dog"        ⇒  false
! ""           ⇒  true
! " "          ⇒  false
! null         ⇒  true
! undefined    ⇒  true
! {x: 1}       ⇒  false
```

And finally, suppose a string is expected:

```
"xyz" + false      ⇒  "xyzfalse"
"xyz" + true       ⇒  "xyztrue"
"xyz" + 7          ⇒  "xyz7"
"xyz" + null       ⇒  "xyznull"
"xyz" + undefined  ⇒  "xyzundefined"
"xyz" + {x: 1}     ⇒  xyz[object Object]
"xyz" + [1, 2, 3]  ⇒  xyz1,2,3
```

Here we see that JavaScript generally does not complain when operators are given values of the wrong type; instead, it tries to accommodate the programmer by performing *type conversions* to treat the wrongly typed value in a way that makes sense. It turns out that:

- When a number is expected: `false` is treated as 0, `true` as 1, strings as the number they look like, `null` as 0, and `undefined` as NaN. For strings, leading and trailing spaces are ignored, and a string that is empty or composed entirely of whitespace is treated as 0. A string that does not look like a number at all is treated as NaN. For an object x, JavaScript evaluates x.`valueOf()`.

- When a Boolean is expected: 0, the empty string (`""`), `null`, `undefined`, and NaN (as well as `false` itself) are treated as false, while all other values are treated as true. The former values are called *falsy* and the latter *truthy*.

- When a string is expected: JavaScript usually finds something reasonable, as you can see in the preceding examples. For an object x, JavaScript evaluates x.`toString()`.

We will provide a more detailed explanation of `valueOf` and `toString` on page 296. There is also a little detail we have to address about `&&` and `||`: they don't exactly expect Booleans. We will see why in Section 4.3.5.

Because of its penchant for implicit type conversions, JavaScript is called a *weakly typed* programming language. In a strongly typed programming language, expressions formed with values of the wrong type cause errors: scripts containing such ill-formed expressions will either not even be allowed to run, stop working altogether, or throw an exception[8] when the offending expression is evaluated.

Sometimes, these automatic conversions result in some surprises. One bit of odd behavior concerns `isNaN`, which you will recall is used to tell if something is not a number. You might expect Booleans, strings, and `null` to not be numbers, but experimentation shows us that `isNaN` doesn't work that way:

```
alert(isNaN(true));      // false, because true converts to 1
alert(isNaN(null));      // false, because null converts to 0
alert(isNaN("water"));   // true, and sensibly so
alert(isNaN("100"));     // false, because "100" converts to 100
```

---

[8]Exceptions will be covered in Section 4.5.2.

This means you should read **isNaN** as "cannot be converted into a number." A second surprise is the following confusion between numbers and strings that occurs very often when one is learning JavaScript:

```
var x = prompt("Enter a number");
var y = prompt("Enter another number");
alert(x + y);          // Concatenation, not arithmetic addition!
```

Entering 2 for each prompt will alert 22, because the result of evaluating a **prompt** is a string, and the + operator is (unfortunately) defined on strings as well as numbers.[9] Alerting **x - y** would have done numeric subtraction, however. The operator − is defined only on numbers, so JavaScript would have converted both string inputs. Multiplication and division are also "safe"; regardless, you must be always on your guard when it comes to numbers and strings.

3.8.2   Explicit Conversion

Because of the potential for string–number confusion, many JavaScript programmers prefer to make the conversion of strings to numbers more *explicit* in the code. This can be done in several ways:

$$
\begin{array}{lll}
\texttt{"3.14" - 0} & \Rightarrow & \texttt{3.14} \\
\texttt{"3.14" * 1} & \Rightarrow & \texttt{3.14} \\
\texttt{"3.14" / 1} & \Rightarrow & \texttt{3.14} \\
\texttt{+"3.14"} & \Rightarrow & \texttt{3.14} \quad \text{[Fastest]} \\
\texttt{Number("3.14")} & \Rightarrow & \texttt{3.14} \quad \text{[Clear but slow]} \\
\texttt{parseFloat("3.14")} & \Rightarrow & \texttt{3.14} \\
\end{array}
$$

The first three expressions work because −, *, and /, being numeric operators, will convert the string to a number before applying the (admittedly useless) operation. The fourth expression also uses a numeric operator, called *unary plus*. When

---

[9]This is considered by many to be a major design flaw in JavaScript. In fact, many other programming languages are very careful not to use + for strings; for example, PHP and Perl use the dot (.), ML uses the carat (^), and SQL uses the double pipe (||).

applied to a number, this operator does not really do anything, unlike its friend *unary minus*:

$$+4 \Rightarrow 4 \qquad \text{[Unary plus]}$$
$$-4 \Rightarrow -4 \qquad \text{[Unary minus]}$$

However, the fact that unary plus expects a number means that if given a string, JavaScript will convert that string to a number. The use of **+** for converting strings to numbers is rather cryptic, but the technique is convenient and not uncommon. Such handy programming forms are called *idioms*: they are not obvious to "outsiders" and must be learned (just like idioms in human languages).

Our earlier numeric addition script now becomes:

```
var x = +prompt("Enter a number");
var y = +prompt("Enter another number");
alert(x + y);          // Arithmetic addition (2+2=4)
```

You are encouraged to try this script and compare it with the previous attempt. What happens when you enter nonnumeric inputs?

What about the forms `Number(`*s*`)` and `parseFloat(`*s*`)` where *s* is a string? The former looks *clearer* (more readable) than the idiomatic form:

```
var x = Number(prompt("Enter a number"));
var y = Number(prompt("Enter another number"));
alert(x + y);          // Arithmetic addition (2+2=4)
```

However, many programmers shun `Number` because its use is *inefficient*: the JavaScript engine does too much work in running the code, slowing the script down and consuming more memory than necessary. It turns out that `Number` does not actually make a primitive number but rather an object with a number inside of it, which at least (thanks to weak typing) can be pulled out when the object is used when a number is expected. The JavaScript engine does more work for objects than for primitives; it has to find space for objects when they are created, and it needs to eventually get rid of them when they are no longer needed. There are times, however, when readability is more important than efficiency; we will discuss these issues further in Section 7.6.1.

We can explicitly convert strings to numbers with `parseFloat` and its cousin `parseInt`. These operations produce numbers from the beginning of a string, not necessarily the whole string, though leading and trailing spaces are ignored:

```
alert(parseFloat("23.9"));          // Alerts 23.9.
alert(parseFloat("5.663E2"));       // Alerts 566.3.
alert(parseFloat("   8.11  "));     // Alerts 8.11.
alert(parseFloat("52.3xyz"));       // Alerts 52.3.
alert(parseFloat("xyz52.3"));       // Alerts NaN.
alert(parseFloat("3 .5 .6"));       // Alerts 3.
```

The `parseInt` operation produces numbers without fractional parts; in fact, the `Int` in `parseInt` means, of course, "integer." Numbers with fractional parts allowed are known in computing circles as *floats*.[10]

```
alert(parseInt("23.9"));            // Alerts 23.
alert(parseInt("5.663E2"));         // Alerts 5.
alert(parseInt("5.663E7"));         // Alerts 5.
alert(parseInt("   8.11  "));       // Alerts 8.
alert(parseInt("52.3xyz"));         // Alerts 52.
alert(parseInt("xyz52.3"));         // Alerts NaN.
```

We can use `parseInt` to deal with numerals in any base from 2 to 36, which we will simply illustrate by example and then move on (for details on numeric bases, see Appendix B):

```
alert(parseInt("75EF2", 16));       // Alerts 483058.
alert(parseInt("50", 8));           // Alerts 40.
alert(parseInt("110101", 2));       // Alerts 53.
alert(parseInt("hello", 30));       // Alerts 14167554.
alert(parseInt("36", 2));           // Alerts NaN.
```

We will rarely, if ever, see `parseInt` and `parseFloat` in the remainder of this text.

---

[10]Why exactly are they called floats? The idea is that because the decimal point can appear anywhere within the number, it's as if it is allowed to "float around."

Review and Practice

1. Evaluate the following: `"5" + 5`, `5 + "5"`, `"5" * 5`, `5 * "5"`, `"5" * "5"`, `3 + null`, `"3" + null`, `"dog" + "house"`, and `"dog" - "house"`.

2. Based on your answer to the previous question, give the general rule regarding how JavaScript determines whether to treat `+` as numeric addition or string concatenation.

3.8.3 Loose Equality Operators

Since JavaScript, being weakly typed, tries to make values "match up" with each other typewise before applying operations such as `+`, `-`, `*`, `/`, `<`, and so on, it stands to reason that it might play the same type conversion game with equality operators. That is, if you would like to know whether x equals y, JavaScript's philosophy would be to try to find type conversions to make these values comparable. As it turns out, JavaScript gives you two ways to test equality: one with this implicit type conversion and one without.

The `===` operator compares two expressions and produces **true** if and only if the two expressions have the same value and have the same type,[11] while `!==`, as you know, produces the opposite truth value from `===`. These are known as the *strict equality operators*. JavaScript's other equality operators, `==` and `!=`, have been described as the "evil cousins" [Cro08a, p. 109] of the strict operators. The `==` operator does the type conversions before testing but goes overboard with its conversions and should probably be avoided.

The rules for `==` are well defined, even if hard to remember. They are given in full in the official JavaScript specification [ECM09, p. 80], but we can summarize the rules here. To evaluate x `==` y where x and y do not have the same types, JavaScript performs type conversions to attempt to make them comparable. In particular:

1. If one of x and y is a string and the other is a number, JavaScript will work with the numeric conversion of the string.

2. If one is a Boolean and the other is not, JavaScript will work with the numeric conversion of the Boolean.

---

[11] The one exception is that `NaN` is not equal to anything, not even `NaN`.

3. If one is an object and the other is a string or number, JavaScript will work with the conversion of the object into a string or number (we will see how this is done later in the text).

4. Finally, for some unknown reason, `undefined == null` and `null == undefined`.

Because of the complexity of these rules, we prefer the strict equality operators `===` and `!==`. Although the loose operators provide some "convenient coding shortcuts," such as automatically performing string to number conversions that we spent so much time discussing in the previous section, the fact remains that their behavior is quirky and hard to memorize.

> **Use `===` and `!==` instead of `==` and `!=`**

Review and Practice

1. Evaluate the following (using a shell), and provide an explanation for your results: `"7" == 7`, `"7" === 7`, `0 == " "`, `0 === " "`, `"0" == " "`, `"0" === " "`, `null == undefined`, `null === undefined`, `null == false`, `null === false`, `1 == true`, `4 == true`, `" " == false`.

3.9   The `typeof` Operator*

Occasionally you may find yourself with a value whose type you need to determine (it can happen). JavaScript's quirky `typeof` operator returns a string that describes the type of an expression. We say it is quirky because the value it returns sometimes makes sense and sometimes does not.

$$
\begin{array}{lcl}
\texttt{typeof 101.3} & \Rightarrow & \texttt{"number"} \\
\texttt{typeof false} & \Rightarrow & \texttt{"boolean"} \\
\texttt{typeof "dog"} & \Rightarrow & \texttt{"string"} \\
\texttt{typeof \{x:1, y:2\}} & \Rightarrow & \texttt{"object"} \\
\texttt{typeof undefined} & \Rightarrow & \texttt{"undefined"} \\
\texttt{typeof null} & \Rightarrow & \texttt{"object"} \\
\texttt{typeof [1, 2, 3]} & \Rightarrow & \texttt{"object"} \\
\texttt{typeof alert} & \Rightarrow & \texttt{"function"}
\end{array}
$$

There is no excuse for the type of `null` being `"object"`. It *does* make sense for arrays to have the type `"object"` because, after all, arrays are objects, but one wonders why functions, another kind of object (which we will see in Chapter 5), are treated specially by the `typeof` operator. It's just one of those things.

Review and Practice

1. Explain the output of the following:

```
var x = 2;
alert(typeof x + typeof "x");
```

2. Evaluate `typeof Infinity` and `typeof NaN` in a test page or shell.

Chapter Summary

- An expression is a fragment of code that is evaluated to produce a value.

- Every JavaScript value is either `undefined`, `null`, a number, a Boolean, a string, or an object.

- JavaScript numbers have size and precision limits, so many computations return approximate results.

- The expression `x === y` computes whether `x` and `y` are equal, while `x = y` assigns the value of `y` to `x`. The expression `x == y` is another kind of equality test but should generally be avoided because its behavior, while completely specified in the official language definition, is often unexpected.

- Objects in JavaScript contain a set of zero or more properties. An object's value is really a reference to the object, and it is not uncommon for two or more variables to contain references to the same object.

- An array is a special kind of object containing a collection of values, indexed from 0. Arrays also have a special `length` property. Updating the array may change the `length` property automatically, and updating the `length` property may cause the array to grow or shrink.

- JavaScript is a weakly typed language, meaning that most of the time when operators are given values of the wrong type, these values will be converted into values of the right type to allow the computation to proceed.

- The values 0, NaN, null, undefined, and the empty string ("") will be interpreted as false if used in a context where a Boolean value is expected. These values, together with false, are called *falsy*; all other values are *truthy*.

- There are many ways to make a string to number conversion explicit in JavaScript, including the unary plus idiom and the parseFloat and parseInt operations.

- JavaScript has 52 operators, though many of them are very rarely used.

Exercises

1. Read an article on George Boole. Then read an article on Claude Shannon. Discuss how the world might be different without their ideas.

2. Let $x = 10$, $y = 4$, $b =$ false. Evaluate the following expressions:

   (a) `x * y > 25 && !b || y % -3 !== 22`

   (b) `y * 4 === 2 || (b !== true)`

3. Show that when a and b are variables holding Boolean values, `!a && !b || a && b` always evaluates to the same result as `a === b`.

4. We saw in this chapter that `Math.sqrt(100)` evaluates to 10. The use of the dot makes it appear that `Math` is an object and `sqrt` is one of its properties. Is this true? Evaluate `Math["sqrt"](100)` in your favorite JavaScript environment and see if the result supports or refutes this hypothesis.

5. Use a shell to evaluate `~22`, `~105`, `~(-28)`, and a few other expressions involving `~` applied to whole numbers. Can you come up with a general rule for what this operator seems to do?

6. Execute the following script:

```
var celsius = prompt("Enter a temperature in \u00b0C");
var fahrenheit = 1.8 * celsius + 32;
alert(celsius + "\u00b0C = " + fahrenheit +  "\u00b0F");
```

   giving inputs of 0, 37, −40, and 100. Then execute with inputs such as dog, 2e600, 3ffc, and Infinity. For each execution, state whether your observed result made sense; if not, state why the result differed from your expectation.

7. Write a script similar to the one in the previous exercise that converts a user-supplied value in °F to °C. For now, do not worry about handling nonsensical input values; we will deal with such things in the next chapter.

8. Evaluate the following expressions: (a) 5 / 0, (b) 0 / 0, (c) Infinity + Infinity, (d) Infinity - Infinity, (e) Infinity * Infinity, (f) Infinity / Infinity, and (g) Math.sqrt(Infinity). Do these results make sense? Why or why not?

9. Write a one-line script that alerts a greeting message in Armenian, Arabic, Hebrew, Hindi, Chinese, or any other language that uses a non-Latin script.

10. Give a JavaScript string for the formula $\forall P.\ P0 \wedge (\forall k.\ Pk \Rightarrow P(k+1)) \Rightarrow \forall n.\ Pn$. Show how it is represented in HTML as well.

11. Modify the die-rolling web page from this chapter to roll five dice instead of just one.

12. Repackage the die-rolling web page from this chapter so that the HTML document and the script are in separate files.

13. Write an HTML document, with an embedded script, containing a single text field and buttons labeled floor, ceil, sqrt, sin, cos, tan, abs, and log. Clicking on any of the buttons should cause the corresponding mathematical operation to be applied to the value in the text field and to be displayed somewhere on the page. Because we have not covered a great deal of JavaScript yet, you can build this web page using the die-rolling page from this chapter as a guide and write a separate "onclick" function for each button. Later in the text, we will show how to write such applications much more efficiently.

14. Evaluate the following expressions:

    (a) `"one two three".split(" ");`

    (b) `"abracadabra".split("a");`

15. Write a JavaScript expression that produces **true** if a string *s* contains a comma and **false** otherwise.

16. Write a script that prompts for a string and alerts whether or not the entered string contains either a backslash character or a Telugu letter ddha (**U+0C22**).

17. Research the JavaScript **substring** operation. What happens if its first operand is larger than the length of the input string? What happens if the first operand is acceptable but the second operand is too large? What if one or the other operand is negative?

18. Let `p = { x: 1, y: [ 4, {z: 2} ] }`. What is `p.y[1]`?

19. What is the value of `({ x: 1, y: 2 }).y`? Would you ever write something like that?

20. What is the difference between `p["dog"]` and `p[dog]`? Write a script that illustrates this difference.

21. Explain the output of the following script in detail.

```
var employee = {
    name: "Kaela",
    department: "Technology"
};
alert(employee.salary === undefined);
```

Does this behavior make sense in light of the intended meaning of **null** and **undefined**?

22. In the program script on page 73, replace the `script` element with the following:

```
var style = document.getElementById("face").style;
setInterval(function () {
    style.left = Math.floor(Math.random() * 500) + 'px';
    style.top = Math.floor(Math.random() * 400) + 'px';
}, 2000);
```

Do you find this more or less readable? Why?

23. Draw a picture of the following object(s). Don't forget to show references as arrows.

```
{call: "mark", next: {call: "ready", next: {call: "set",
next: {call: "go", next: null}}}}
```

24. Draw a picture of the following object(s). Don't forget to show references as arrows. What do you think it means?

```
{op: "+", l: {op: "*", l: {op: "-", l: 3, r: 9}, r: 7},
r: {op: "/", l: 9, r: {op: "+", l: 8, r: 2}}}
```

25. Write a script that prompts for the abbreviation of a New England state and alerts the capital of that state. The first line should be:

```
var capitals = {ME: "Augusta", NH: "Concord", VT: "Montpelier",
    MA: "Boston", CT: "Hartford", RI: "Providence"};
```

For example, if your user inputs `NH`, your script should alert `Concord`.

26. Write variable declarations for the following:

   - An employee whose name is María, salary is 1000 USD, hire date is 2008-01-05, and who does *not* have a supervisor.
   - An array of the first 10 prime numbers.
   - The song "Johnny Tarr" by Gaelic Storm from the album *Tree*. Gather as much information about the track as you can.

27. Draw a picture of the following object:

```
[42, true, null, NaN, "nil", {}, undefined]
```

28. Recall this little script from the chapter:

```
var mom = {name: "Ani"};
var dad = {name: "Sipho", spouse: mom};
mom.spouse = dad;
```

What is the value of `mom.spouse.spouse.spouse.spouse`?

29. Here is an attempt to recreate the objects in the previous exercise:

```
var mom = {name: "Ani", spouse: {name: "Sipho", spouse: mom}};
```

Assuming that the variable `mom` was not previously defined, draw a picture of the resulting object. (*Hint*: You might want to use a shell or runner page for help.)

30. Draw a picture of the objects created by the following:

```
var players = {name: "Moe"};
players.next = {name: "Larry"};
players.next.next = {name: "Curly", next: players};
```

Can you write a cleaner set of statements that constructs the same object network?

31. Write a script that creates objects for people named Ani, Sipho, Tuulia, 'Aolani, Hiro, and Xue, such that:

- Tuulia is the mother of Sipho.
- Ani and Sipho are married.
- The children of Ani and Sipho are, in order, 'Aolani, Hiro, and Xue.

Define each of the objects with as many of the following properties as you can fill in: `name`, `mother`, `father`, `spouse`, and `children`. The `children` property should have an array value.

32. Draw a picture of the array referred to by the variable a after executing the following:

```
var a = [1, 2, 3, 4]; a.unshift(a.pop());
```

33. In mathematics, a *two-dimensional matrix* is an arrangement of values in rows and columns, such as:

$$\begin{pmatrix} 9 & 8 & 2 & -5 \\ \pi & 7 & 2.8 & 6 \\ -22 & 4 & 0 & 100 \end{pmatrix}$$

Matrices can be represented in JavaScript as arrays of arrays. Write a JavaScript array expression for the preceding matrix. Your array should have three elements, each of which is an array of four elements.

34. Let x stand for some completely arbitrary JavaScript expression. What can the expression !!x be used for?

35. Evaluate the following expressions and explain the results. (*Hint*: You may want to review Section 3.8 on type conversion for help.)

   (a) 5 < 10 < 20

   (b) -20 < -10 < -5

36. Write a script that prompts for a string of text and alerts the string made up of this value appended to itself twice. For example, if the user inputs "ho", your script should alert "hohoho". If the user inputs "888", your script should alert "888888888".

37. Explain the result of parseInt("250", 3).

38. Give the numeric value of each of the following expressions (write your answer in base-10): 791, 0x2e5, 2e5, 0791.

39. Write a script that prompts for a number in base-16 and alerts its value in base-10.

40. Determine the precedence of the `typeof` operator, relative to the addition, multiplication, and unary negation operators, by experimentation in the shell.

41. In mathematics, we are used to the fact that if $A = B$ and $B = C$ then $A = C$, a property known as the transitivity of equality. Because of implicit conversions, JavaScript's quirky `==` operator is not transitive. Demonstrate that transitivity does not hold. (*Hint*: Find a certain string A, a certain number B, and a certain string C for which A `==` B, B `==` C, but A `!=` C.) Is `===` transitive? Why or why not?

42. What JavaScript value should you assign to a variable x so that `typeof x === x` would be true?

CHAPTER 4

Statements

CHAPTER CONTENTS

Introduction

In the previous chapter, we saw how to write simple expressions, which are evaluated to produce values. But for scripts to be interesting, they need to do more than just evaluate expressions; they need to perform *actions*, which in JavaScript they do by executing *statements*. JavaScript has statements for declaring variables, evaluating expressions, and performing actions conditionally or repeatedly. There are also statements for disrupting the usual control flow, allowing you to construct fairly creative computations.

In this chapter, we will cover the most common JavaScript statements and study several scripts that illustrate them. Each of the scripts in this chapter is runnable on its own, so we encourage you to try them out as you read. By the end of this chapter, you will be able to write useful scripts for processing text, performing simple numerical computation, and managing simple data structures.

4.1   The Declaration Statement

We will begin our tour of JavaScript statements with a statement you've seen before—the *declaration statement*, also called the *variable statement*. This statement creates a new variable. You can provide an initial value in the declaration if you wish; if you do not explicitly give one, the variable will receive the value `undefined`.

```
var count = 0;
var dogs = ["Sparky", "Spot", "Spike"];
var response;
var malta = {latitude: 35.8, longitude: 14.6};
var finished = false;
var winner = null;
```

Here we have given explicit initial values to several variables—all of them, in fact, except for `response`. The variable `response` will therefore be created with an initial value of `undefined`.

You can introduce multiple variables in one statement, explicitly initializing some but not others.

```
var start = 0, finish = 72, input, output = [];
```

This statement initializes `input` to `undefined`.

Review and Practice

1. State the initial values given to the following four variables:

```
var x, y = 10;
var z = x, p = 10 * y + z;
```

2. Write a single variable declaration that declares two variables called `die1` and `die2` and initializes each of them to a (possibly different) random integer between 1 and 6, inclusive.

4.2 The Expression Statement

An *expression statement* evaluates an expression and ignores its value. This sounds silly, since it allows you to write useless scripts like the following:

```
2 + 2;              // Adds two and two, but ignores the result.
"Hello";            // Also legal but totally useless.
Math.sqrt(100);     // Does a computation, but ignores the result.
"a".toLowerCase();  // Computes a new string but ignores it.
```

But we can make useful statements out of expressions with *side effects*—actions that produce visible results, change the values stored in variables or object properties, or modify the structure of objects. The `delete` operator from page 73 produces side effects, as do alerts and assignments:

```
var x = 2;        // Declares x, initializing it to 2.
alert(x);         // Alerts 2.
alert(10 * x);    // Alerts 20.
```

```
var y;              // Declares y, without an explicit initial value.
alert(y);           // Alerts undefined.
y = x * 5;          // Assigns 10 to y, because x is still 2.
var z = y;          // Declares z, initializing it to 10.
y = "dog";          // Assigns "dog" to y, overwriting the old value 10.
alert(y + z);       // Alerts "dog10", because z is still 10.
```

Keep in mind that variable declarations and assignments simply place a value in a variable—nothing more, nothing less. They do not, for example, set up relationships between variables that must be maintained. In the preceding script, the declaration `var z = y;` did *not* make z and y the same variable, or require them to share the same value for the rest of their lives. It simply meant "create a new variable z whose initial value is y's current value." When we assigned a new value to y, the value of z did not change.

JavaScript has additional assignment operators besides =, including:

```
var x = 5;
x += 30;            // Same as x = x + 30, x now 35.
x -= 2;             // Same as x = x - 2, x now 33.
x *= -4;            // Same as x = x * -4, x now -132.
```

You can find the complete set of these combination assignment operators in Appendix A.

Let's now put together declaration and expression statements into a useful script.

```
/*
 * This is the first attempt at a script to find the number of
 * dollars and cents for a given number of pennies.
 */
var pennies = prompt("Enter a number of (U.S.) pennies");
var dollars = Math.floor(pennies / 100);
var cents = pennies % 100;
alert("That's " + dollars + " dollars and " + cents + " cents");
```

This script gives decent answers for 46588 ("465 dollars and 88 cents") and 46 ("0 dollars and 46 cents") and an acceptable, but grammatically awkward, answer for 109 ("1 dollars and 9 cents"). It even accepts fractions of pennies, with 897.5

yielding "8 dollars and 97.5 cents." However, for some inputs, our response is ugly at best and completely wrong at worst:

dog ⇒ NaN dollars and NaN cents
Infinity ⇒ Infinity dollars and NaN cents
−872 ⇒ −9 dollars and −72 cents
75q ⇒ NaN dollars and NaN cents
899.22 ⇒ 89 dollars and 99.22000000000003 cents
12345678901234567890 ⇒ 123456789012345660 dollars and 68 cents

What do these experiments tell us?

1. For nonnumeric inputs like `dog` and `75q`, the script correctly computes `NaN`, but the resulting English sentence looks ridiculous.

2. For negative inputs, we get the wrong answer! Were you surprised? After all, the script probably "looked right" to you. Apparently, looking right is not enough.

3. JavaScript's approximation of numeric results (we saw this back in Section 3.3) can haunt programmers even in the most innocent-looking code.

We would like our script to compute dollars and cents *only if* a user inputs a nice, nonnegative value that is neither too big nor a potential source of precision problems, and alert an error message otherwise. We'll see how in the next section.

Review and Practice

1. What is the value of x after executing `var x = 1; var y = x; y = 2;`?

2. Enter the following into the JavaScript shell and explain what you see:

```
alert(next_song);
next_song = "Incident on 57th Street";
alert(next_song);
```

3. Explain why negative inputs give unexpected answers in our dollars and cents script.

4.3   Conditional Execution

JavaScript provides a couple of statements and a few operators to allow us to write scripts that perform one set of actions under certain conditions and another set of actions under different conditions.

4.3.1   The if Statement

The `if` statement does at most one of a number of alternative executions, based on conditions you supply. The most general form of this statement has one `if` part, zero or more `else if` parts, and an optional `else` part. Each of the alternatives are statement sequences enclosed in curly braces. The conditions are evaluated in order, from top to bottom. As soon as one condition is true, its corresponding alternative is executed, thus finishing the entire `if` statement.

The following script illustrates an `if` statement with five alternatives:

```
var score = Math.round(Math.random() * 100);
if (score >= 90) {
    grade = "A";
} else if (score >= 80) {
    grade = "B";
} else if (score >= 70) {
    grade = "C";
} else if (score >= 60) {
    grade = "D";
} else {
    grade = "F";
}
alert(score + " is a " + grade);
```

Figure 4.1 illustrates the preceding statement in a UML (Unified Modeling Language) Activity Diagram. UML is a very popular language used to visualize software systems.[1] We will not be describing UML in detail in this book; instead,

---

[1]In fact, it is *the* lingua franca of modeling languages in software development today. While the UML itself is large, its most visible aspect is its 13 diagram types. In addition to activity diagrams, the UML features diagrams to describe the structure of types and objects, the state transitions of objects, the ways in which objects can interact, the organization and deployment of components, and several other aspects of object structure and behavior.

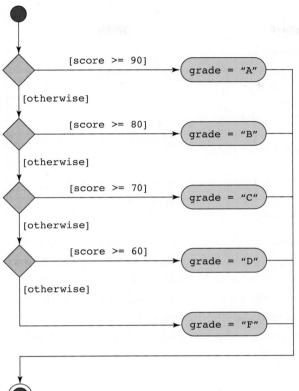

FIGURE 4.1

Activity diagram for an `if` statement.

see [Fow03] for an excellent introduction and guide. Fortunately, its notation is fairly accessible to a general audience; you can probably infer that the diagram expresses the fact that each condition is tested, one after the other, and that once a true condition is found, no more are tested.

The `if` statement can help us improve our dollars and cents script:

```
/*
 * This is the second attempt at a script to find the number of
 * dollars and cents for a given number of pennies.
 */
var pennies = prompt("Enter a number of cents");
if (isNaN(pennies)) {
```

```
    alert("That's not a number");
} else if (pennies < 0) {
    alert("That number is too small");
} else if (pennies >= 9E15) {
    alert("That number is too large");
} else if (pennies % 1 !== 0) {
    alert("I can only handle whole numbers");
} else {
    var dollars = Math.floor(pennies / 100);
    var cents = pennies % 100;
    alert("That's " + dollars + " dollars and " + cents + " cents");
}
```

This script accepts the user's input and then performs a series of *validation* checks. The first check ensures the input looks like a number (we saw `isNaN` back on page 62), the second ensures that it is nonnegative, and the third that it is not too large. This check is important because we want to deal only with exact integer amounts, and JavaScript has gaps in the integers it can represent above 9007199254740992. This is a rather messy number, and we don't care about its exact value anyway. We just want to pick *some* upper limit, so we will go with the simpler 9×10^{15}.

The final check rejects nonwhole values by taking the remainder of the value after dividing by 1. For whole numbers, this value should be 0; if it isn't, we alert yet another error message. Finally, if none of the error checks detects trouble, the JavaScript engine runs the computation of dollars and cents.

Review and Practice

1. Write an `if` statement that alerts a message if the variable `s` does not contain a string of length 16. (Note that this statement has no `else if` or `else` parts.)

2. Write an `if` statement that examines the value in the variable `x` and (1) adds it to the end of the array variable `values` if $x > 0$, (2) adds it to the front of `values` if $x < 0$, (3) increments the variable `zeroCount` if $x === 0$, or (4) does nothing otherwise.

4.3.2 The Conditional Expression

Sometimes you may prefer a *conditional expression* to an `if` statement: "*x* ? *y* : *z*" evaluates to *y* if *x* is truthy and *z* if falsy. For example, instead of

```
if (latitude >= 0) {
    hemisphere = "north";
} else {
    hemisphere = "south";
}
```

you can write

```
hemisphere = (latitude >= 0) ? "north" : "south";
```

Conditional expressions are sometimes used inside of expressions that build up strings, as in the following (here **present** is assumed to be a variable holding a Boolean value):

```
var notice = "She is" + (present ? "" : "n't") + " here.";
```

Review and Practice

1. Evaluate the expression `25 > -7 ? null : "next"`.

2. Rewrite the dollars and cents script, using the conditional expression to decide between using the word "dollar" and "dollars" and between "cent" and "cents."

3. Rewrite the conditional expression involving hemispheres to express the fact that the equator is in neither the northern nor southern hemisphere.

4.3.3 The `switch` Statement

Another kind of conditional statement, the **switch** statement, compares a value against a sequence of *cases* until it finds one that is equal to (`===`) the value and begins executing statements at that point. An optional **default** case will match any value at all.

```
switch (direction.toLowerCase()) {
    case "north": row -= 1; break;
    case "south": row += 1; break;
    case "east": column += 1; break;
    case "west": column -= 1; break;
    default: alert("Illegal direction");
}
```

A **break** statement will terminate the entire **switch** statement. It is considered good practice to finish each case with a **break**;[2] otherwise execution will "fall through" to the next case (without further comparisons to the remaining case expressions). For example, if we omitted **break**s in the preceding script, and the direction were **"east"**, what would happen? The value in **column** would be incremented, then decremented, and then an alert box would pop up informing you that **"east"** is not a legal direction.

Sometimes fall-through might be desired. Suppose that in a group of contest participants, everyone gets a certificate, but people who reach prize level 1 *also* get a backpack, and at prize level 2, people *also* get a ski vacation, and at level 3, they *also* get a car. This could be coded without **break** statements (see Figure 4.2):

```
/*
 * This script produces a set of prizes for a given prize level.
 * Contestants at one prize level get the prize for that level
 * plus all prizes at lower levels.  It uses an ugly form of the
 * switch statement where the cases are not walled off from
 * each other.
 */
var level = +prompt("Enter your prize level, 1-3");
var prizes = [];
switch (level) {
    case 3: prizes.push("car");
    case 2: prizes.push("ski vacation");
    case 1: prizes.push("backpack");
    default: prizes.push("certificate");
}
alert(prizes);
```

---

[2]Or a **return**, **throw**, or **continue** statement, which we will see later.

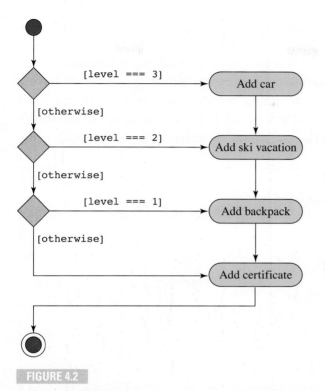

FIGURE 4.2

Activity diagram for a `switch` statement with fall-through.

Computations like this rarely occur in practice, so it is generally best to avoid cases that do not end in **break** (or another disruptive statement), lest they be confused with the more common pattern for switches. In fact, the JSLint code quality tool introduced back in Section 2.4.3 considers falling through to be an error! You can always find alternatives to fall-through switches; the end-of-chapter exercises will provide a couple problems for you to do just that.

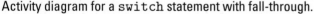

Review and Practice

1. Extend the direction example in this section to include northwest, southwest, southeast, and northeast cases.

2. Why does it not make sense to use a **switch** statement for the scores and grades example on page 104?

4.3.4   Avoiding Conditional Code with Lookups

Let's look at a situation that seems—at least to many beginning programmers—to call for an `if` statement, `?:` operator, or `switch` statement. Suppose we have a variable named `state` purportedly containing the name of a state in Deutschland (Germany), and we wish to assign to the variable `capital` the name of the state's capital, or the value `undefined` if the state name is unrecognized. We could write:

```javascript
// UGLY CODE - DO NOT DO THIS
if (state === "Baden-Württemberg") {
    capital = "Stuttgart";
} else if (state === "Bayern") {
    capital = "Munchen";
} else if (state === "Berlin") {
    capital = "Berlin";
} else if (state === "Brandenburg") {
    capital = "Potsdam";
} else if (state === "Bremen") {
    capital = "Bremen";
} else if (state === "Hamburg") {
    capital = "Hamburg";
} else if (state === "Hessen") {
    capital = "Wiesbaden";
} else if (state === "Mecklenburg-Vorpommern") {
    capital = "Schwerin";
} else if (state === "Niedersachsen") {
    capital = "Hannover";
} else if (state === "Nordrhein-Westfalen") {
    capital = "Düsseldorf";
} else if (state === "Rheinland-Pfalz") {
    capital = "Mainz";
} else if (state === "Saarland") {
    capital = "Saarbrücken";
} else if (state === "Sachsen") {
    capital = "Dresden";
} else if (state === "Sachsen-Anhalt") {
    capital = "Magdeburg";
} else if (state === "Schleswig-Holstein") {
    capital = "Kiel";
} else if (state === "Thüringen") {
```

```
    capital = "Erfurt"
} else {
    capital = undefined;
}
```

This code repeats a couple fragments for every state: `state ===` and `capital =`. The `switch` statement, which we will try next, removes the former, but forces us to add a `break` for every state—no real improvement:

```
// UGLY CODE - DO NOT DO THIS
switch (state) {
    case "Baden-Württemberg": capital = "Stuttgart"; break;
    case "Bayern": capital = "Munchen"; break;
    case "Berlin": capital = "Berlin"; break;
    case "Brandenburg": capital = "Potsdam"; break;
    case "Bremen": capital = "Bremen"; break;
    case "Hamburg": capital = "Hamburg"; break;
    case "Hessen": capital = "Wiesbaden"; break;
    case "Mecklenburg-Vorpommern": capital = "Schwerin"; break;
    case "Niedersachsen": capital = "Hannover"; break;
    case "Nordrhein-Westfalen": capital = "Düsseldorf"; break;
    case "Rheinland-Pfalz": capital = "Mainz"; break;
    case "Saarland": capital = "Saarbrücken"; break;
    case "Sachsen": capital = "Dresden"; break;
    case "Sachsen-Anhalt": capital = "Magdeburg"; break;
    case "Schleswig-Holstein": capital = "Kiel"; break;
    case "Thüringen": capital = "Erfurt"; break;
    default: capital = undefined;
}
```

The conditional expression, which we will use in our third try, removes the repetition in the assignment but not in the equality test:

```
// UGLY CODE - DO NOT DO THIS
capital =
      (state === "Baden-Württemberg") ? "Stuttgart"
    : (state === "Bayern") ? "Munchen"
    : (state === "Berlin") ? "Berlin",
    : (state === "Brandenburg") ? "Potsdam",
    : (state === "Bremen") ? "Bremen",
```

```
    : (state === "Hamburg") ? "Hamburg",
    : (state === "Hessen") ? "Wiesbaden",
    : (state === "Mecklenburg-Vorpommern") ? "Schwerin",
    : (state === "Niedersachsen") ? "Hannover",
    : (state === "Nordrhein-Westfalen") ? "Düsseldorf",
    : (state === "Rheinland-Pfalz") ? "Mainz",
    : (state === "Saarland") ? "Saarbrücken",
    : (state === "Sachsen") ? "Dresden",
    : (state === "Sachsen-Anhalt") ? "Magdeburg",
    : (state === "Schleswig-Holstein") ? "Kiel",
    : (state === "Thüringen") ? "Erfurt"
    : undefined;
```

At this point, we could philosophize that our inability to squeeze out all of the repetitive fragments of code must mean there is a better way to find capitals, and in fact there is. What are you left with when you take out all the code surrounding the tests and assignments? Just the states and the capitals! We don't need an elaborate computation to associate states with capitals; we can define the association in data, not code. All we need is a simple object:

```
var CAPITALS = {
    "Baden-Württemberg": "Stuttgart",
    "Bayern": "Munchen",
    "Berlin": "Berlin",
    "Brandenburg": "Potsdam",
    "Bremen": "Bremen",
    "Hamburg": "Hamburg",
    "Hessen": "Wiesbaden",
    "Mecklenburg-Vorpommern": "Schwerin",
    "Niedersachsen": "Hannover",
    "Nordrhein-Westfalen": "Düsseldorf",
    "Rheinland-Pfalz": "Mainz",
    "Saarland": "Saarbrücken",
    "Sachsen": "Dresden",
    "Sachsen-Anhalt": "Magdeburg",
    "Schleswig-Holstein": "Kiel",
    "Thüringen": "Erfurt"
};
```

We now simply write:

```
capital = CAPITALS[state];
```

to get the capital of the state whose name is contained in the variable **state**.[3] Think of this code as performing a *lookup* of the capital from a table of states and their capitals. When we use an object in this way, we speak of it as a *lookup table*, a *dictionary*, a *map*, an *associative array*, or a *hash*. A lookup table in general is said to map *keys* to *values*; here states are the keys and capitals are the values. Lookup code, when it is applicable, is better than conditional code for several reasons:

- There are no redundant code fragments, making the script shorter and easier to understand.

- The states and capitals appear right next to each other, making it easier to "see" the association.

- The code (the looking up) and the data (the lookup table) are naturally different things, and should not be tangled.

- The JavaScript engine can execute lookups considerably faster than conditional code.[4]

Here is another example. We will use a dictionary to associate numbers and letters on a phone keypad, as in Figure 4.3.

In order to convert a phone number with letters into numbers, we could use:

```
var LETTER_TO_NUMBER = { A: 2, B: 2, C: 2, D: 3, E: 3, F: 3, G: 4,
    H: 4, I: 4, J: 5, K: 5, L: 5, M: 6, N: 6, O: 6, P: 7, Q: 7,
    R: 7, S: 7, T: 8, U: 8, V: 8, W: 9, X: 9, Y: 9, Z: 9 };
```

---

[3]Or **undefined** if **state** does not contain the name of a state.

[4]The details are beyond the scope of this text, but the basic idea is that a JavaScript engine can usually "find" a key's value immediately just by looking at the form of the key. With conditional statements and expressions, each possible key has to be checked in order until the correct key is found.

A phone keypad.

So, for example, LETTER_TO_NUMBER["C"] === 2. Can we run the mapping in the other direction? A single number can map to multiple letters, so we will use strings:

```
var NUMBER_TO_LETTER = {
    2: "ABC", 3: "DEF", 4: "GHI", 5: "JKL",
    6: "MNO", 7: "PQRS", 8: "TUV", 9: "WXYZ"
};
```

Here we say, "Given a number n, the value of NUMBER_TO_LETTER[n] is a string containing all (and only those) letters associated with n on the keypad." We will make use of the first of these dictionaries in Section 4.4.2 when we introduce scripts for processing whole phone numbers.

Review and Practice

1. State, in your own words, when lookups can replace conditional code structures. (*Hint*: Could we have used a lookup strategy for the scores and grades example on page 104?)

2. Explain why the structures introduced in this section are called maps. Explain why they are called dictionaries.

3. Suppose you notice some code with the expression CAPITALS[Saarland]. What is (almost certainly) wrong with that?

4. Think up four or five examples of dictionaries in the "real world."

4.3.5   Short-Circuit Execution

Recall from Section 3.2 that if x and y are Booleans, the AND-ALSO and OR-ELSE operators have the following properties:

- x || y is true if and only if x or y is true (or both)

- x && y is true if and only if x and y are both true

Now if you are evaluating x || y and find that x is true, there is no need to evaluate y, since x || y will be true no matter what y is. Similarly, when evaluating x && y, discovering x to be false implies the entire && expression will be false—so there is no need to evaluate y. In fact, this is exactly how JavaScript evaluates these expressions: if enough is known by evaluating the first part, the evaluation of the second part is *short-circuited*, or skipped.

For example, the code fragment

```
if (t < 0 && t > 100) {
    /* do something here */
}
```

means exactly the same thing as

```
if (t < 0) {
    if (t > 100) {
        /* do something here */
    }
}
```

Now we see the reason for the names AND-ALSO and OR-ELSE. Saying "x and also y" suggests "**if** x is true, **then** (and only then) go see if y is also true." Similarly, saying "x or else y" suggests "**if** x is true, you're good; **else** you'll have to see whether y is true." The second part is evaluated conditionally.

The short-circuit operators have an interesting feature that we would be remiss to not point out: they don't actually *expect* Boolean operands! Notice:

```
alert(27 && 52);  // Alerts 52
alert(0 && 52);   // Alerts 0
alert(27 || 52);  // Alerts 27
alert(0 || 52);   // Alerts 52
```

In other words, JavaScript did not convert the numbers to Booleans. The official specification for the language says:

- To evaluate x && y, JavaScript first evaluates x. If x is falsy (false or convertible to false[5]), the entire expression produces the value of x (without ever evaluating y). Otherwise, the entire expression produces the value of y.

- To evaluate x || y, JavaScript first evaluates x. If x is truthy (true or convertible to true), the entire expression produces the value of x (without ever evaluating y). Otherwise, the entire expression produces the value of y.

This behavior makes it possible to write some clever-looking code. Suppose you have the variable `favoriteColor`, which you know to contain the name of your favorite color if you have one, or `undefined` if you don't. You can paint your car with your favorite color if you have one, *or else* black if you don't:

```
car.color = favoriteColor || "black";
```

This works because if `favoriteColor` contains a nonempty string, it is truthy and is therefore assigned to the color of `car`. If `favoriteColor` is `undefined` (which is falsy), the value of the || expression is by definition its second (right) operand, which is black.

There are some tricks we can play with the && operator too, but these are less common so we will leave them to the exercises at the end of this chapter.

Review and Practice

1. Evaluate the expression 3 && "xyz" || null.

2. Evaluate the expression 3 && "" || null.

3. True or false: For variables x and y, x && y is always the same as x ? y : x.

4. True or false: For variables x and y, x || y is always the same as x ? x : y.

---

[5]Recall from Chapter 3 that the values `undefined`, `null`, 0, "", and `NaN` are convertible to false.

4.4 Iteration

In the previous section we looked at ways to do different things under different circumstances. Now we will look at ways to do something over and over again.

4.4.1 The while and do-while Statements

JavaScript's **while** statement executes code repeatedly as long as a condition is true. The following example asks the user to enter a string of exactly five characters, and keeps on asking until the user follows the directions. While the user's input does not conform to the request, the script counts the number of attempts (and repeats the prompt). Only when an acceptable string is entered does the **while** statement finish.

```
var numberOfTries = 1;
while (prompt("Enter a 5-character string").length !== 5) {
    numberOfTries += 1;
}
if (numberOfTries > 1) {
    alert("Took you " + numberOfTries + " tries to get this right");
}
```

The general form of the **while** statement is

    while (*test*) { *stmts* }

First *test* is executed, and if it is truthy, *body* is executed and the whole statement repeats. This means the test happens before the body, and it may be that the body is never executed. The **do-while** statement, on the other hand, always executes the body at least once; its general form is:

    do { *stmts* } while (*test*) ;

We can rewrite the previous script to use the **do-while** statement:

```
var numberOfTries = 0;
do {
```

```
        var input = prompt("Enter a 5-character string");
        numberOfTries += 1;
} while (input.length !== 5);
if (numberOfTries > 1) {
        alert("Took you " + numberOfTries + " tries to get this right");
}
```

Figure 4.4 shows the activity diagram for our example script using the `do-while` statement. The iteration appears graphically as a cycle, or *loop*, through the reading, incrementing, and testing activities. Indeed, iteration statements are commonly known as loops, a term we will use frequently from now on.

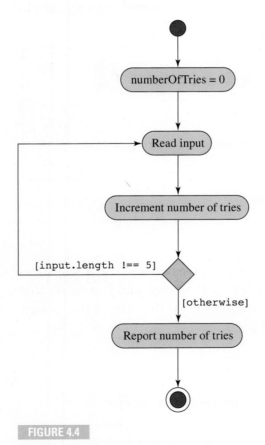

FIGURE 4.4

Activity diagram for a `do-while` statement.

4.4.2 The for Statement

The second kind of loop, the `for` statement, also loops as long as a condition is true, but is normally used to iterate through a fixed set of items, such as a range of numbers, the characters of a string, the indexes of an array, a chain of objects, and so forth. The general form of this statement is

for (*init* ; *test* ; *each*) { *stmts* }

The JavaScript engine runs the *init* code first, then as long as *test* is truthy, it runs the *body* followed by *each*. The *init* section normally, but not always, declares one or more variables. Here's our first example:

```
// Alerts that 4, 6, 8, 10, 12, 14, 16, 18, and 20 are even.
for (var number = 4; number <= 20; number += 2) {
    alert(number + " is even");
}
```

Here `number` is initialized to 4, and because this is less than or equal to 20, alerts `"4 is even"` and bumps `number` to 6. Now because 6 is less than or equal to 20, we next see `"6 is even"` and `number` becomes 8. The last value alerted is 20 because `number` will be subsequently bumped to 22 and the test condition will become `false`, ending the loop.

Our second example features a script that draws nested squares—the first with a side length of 10 pixels, the second with 20, the third with 30, and so on up to 300. This script is our first introduction to the HTML `canvas` element, part of the relatively new HTML5 standard and appearing on most, but not all, browsers. Run the following application, composed of an HTML file and a JavaScript file. Don't worry about the details of `canvas` yet—we will get to that in Chapter 9—but do pay attention to how the `for` statement generates squares of increasing sizes. You should see a picture like that in Figure 4.5.

```
<!doctype html>
<html>
  <head>
    <meta charset="UTF-8" />
    <title>Squares</title>
  </head>
```

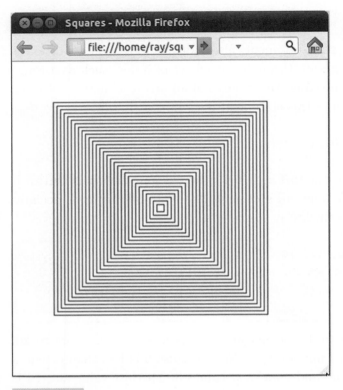

FIGURE 4.5

Screenshot of the square-drawing script.

```
<body>
  <canvas id="squares" width="400" height="400">
    Your browser does not support the canvas element, sorry.
  </canvas>
  <script src="squares.js"></script>
</body>
</html>
```

```
/*
 * This script draws nested squares whose sides have length 10, 20,
 * 30, 40, ..., 300, in the center of the canvas whose document id is
 * "squares".
 */
```

```
var canvas = document.getElementById("squares");
var ctx = canvas.getContext("2d");
var centerX = canvas.width / 2;
var centerY = canvas.height / 2;
for (var side = 10; side <= 300; side += 10) {
    ctx.strokeRect(centerX - side / 2, centerY - side / 2, side, side);
}
```

You will frequently use `for` statements when processing arrays. In the following example, we need to work with a list of words, namely, the strings `words[0]`, `words[1]`, `words[2]`, and so on. How do we "step through" this list? We create a variable—we will call it `i`—that increases by 1 for each iteration.[6]

```
// Alerts a string with the initial characters of each array item.
var words = ["as", "far", "as", "i", "know"];
var result = "";
for (var i = 0; i < words.length; i += 1) {
    result += words[i].charAt(0).toUpperCase();
}
alert(result);
```

Here is another example with arrays, illustrating a common pattern in which each array element is checked to see if it satisfies some condition:

```
// Alerts the number of zeros in an array.
var a = [7, 3, 0, 0, 9, -5, 2, 1, 0, 1, 7];
var numberOfZeros = 0;
for (var i = 0, n = a.length; i < n; i += 1) {
    if (a[i] === 0) {
        numberOfZeros += 1;
    }
}
alert(numberOfZeros);
```

---

[6]Why did we choose the variable `i` in our `for` statement? Answer: Tradition! Here `i` is playing the role of the index of the array elements, and "index" starts with "i." Programmers used `i` for this reason many decades ago and still do today.

Notice how this example also illustrates the declaration of *two* variables in the initialization section of the **for** loop. By initializing **n** to the length of the array, the loop's termination test becomes a little simpler.[7]

In addition to iterating through numeric ranges and array elements, **for** statements will often iterate through the individual characters in a string. Here is a script that asks the user to enter a phone number containing letters and responds with the numeric equivalent. We will step through each character in the user's input and do the following:

1. If the character is a digit, we will "pass it through" to the resulting string.

2. If the character is in $A \ldots Z$, we will look up the corresponding phone keypad digit and pass the digit through.

3. If the character is anything else, we will ignore it.

```
var LETTER_TO_NUMBER = { A: 2, B: 2, C: 2, D: 3, E: 3, F: 3, G: 4,
    H: 4, I: 4, J: 5, K: 5, L: 5, M: 6, N: 6, O: 6, P: 7, Q: 7,
    R: 7, S: 7, T: 8, U: 8, V: 8, W: 9, X: 9, Y: 9, Z: 9 };
var phoneText = prompt("Enter a phone number (letters permitted)");
var result = "";
for (var i = 0; i < phoneText.length; i += 1) {
    var c = phoneText.charAt(i);
    if (/\d/.test(c)) {
        result += c;
    } else if (c in LETTER_TO_NUMBER) {
        result += LETTER_TO_NUMBER[c];
    }
}
alert("The phone number is: " + result);
```

In this script, entering 1-800-GO-2-UTAH produces the response **The phone number is: 18004628824**, as digits are preserved, capital letters are translated, and the dashes are ignored.

---

[7]Because the initialization section is run only once and the termination test is run multiple times, simplifying the termination test may lead to faster code in some JavaScript engines. You don't need to be concerned with the details of why such "optimizations" work or don't work right now, but this pattern is not uncommon in the JavaScript world, so it is nice to be aware of.

Did you notice the two new features we slipped into this example?

- /\d/.test(c) evaluates to **true** if c is a string containing a digit (a character in 0...9).

- *x* in *object* evaluates to **true** if the given object has a property named *x*.

If we did not need to squeeze out the nonnumeric, nonletter characters, the script could be shortened. The **for** loop becomes simply:

```
for (var i = 0; i < phoneText.length; i += 1) {
    var c = phoneText.charAt(i);
    result += LETTER_TO_NUMBER[c] || c;
}
```

This says for each character in the original string, if there is a corresponding character in the **LETTER_TO_NUMBER** map, then use that mapped value; *otherwise use the original character itself.*

for loops are often seen iterating through another kind of sequence: linked structures of objects. The following code fragment sums all the scores in the object chain in Figure 4.6:

```
var total = 0;
for (var p = scores; p != null; p = p.next) {
    total += p.score;
}
alert(total);
```

Our last example of the **for** statement will illustrate *nested loops.* We will be producing the multiplication table shown in Figure 4.7.

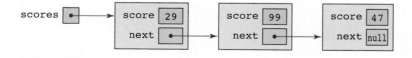

FIGURE 4.6

A chain of objects.

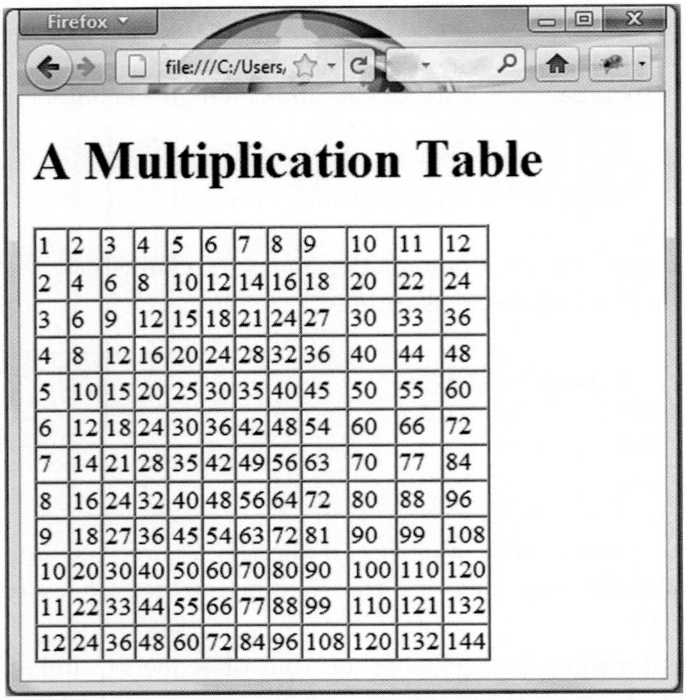

FIGURE 4.7

A JavaScript multiplication table.

We will place the title and the heading directly in the HTML and let the script generate the actual table with `document.write` operations. Our HTML file (*multiplicationtable.html*) is simply:

```html
<!doctype html>
<html>
  <head>
    <meta charset="UTF-8"/>
    <title>Multiplication Table</title>
  </head>
  <body>
    <h1>A Multiplication Table</h1>
    <script src="multiplicationtable.js"></script>
  </body>
</html>
```

Now let's develop the script that programmatically writes out the HTML for the table. The HTML elements we need to introduce are `<table>`, for the entire table; `<tr>`, meaning table row; and `<td>`, which stands for "table data," though you can think of it as a table cell. The table contains a list of rows, and each row contains a list of cells. The HTML we are shooting for is:[8]

```
<table border="1" cellspacing="0">
    <tr><td>1</td><td>2</td>...<td>12</td></tr>
    <tr><td>2</td><td>4</td>...<td>24</td></tr>
        .
        .
        .
    <tr><td>12</td><td>24</td>...<td>144</td></tr>
</table>
```

Our script writes the opening `<table>` tag, followed by the 12 table rows (via a `for` loop) each enclosed in `<tr>` elements, and finally the closing `</table>` tag. Each row requires a secondary loop to produce the table cells. As this loop is nested within another loop, it is called an *inner* loop.

```
var SIZE = 12;
document.write("<table border='1' cellspacing='0'>");
for (var i = 1; i <= SIZE; i += 1) {
    document.write("<tr>");
    for (var j = 1; j <= SIZE; j += 1) {
        document.write("<td>" + (i * j) + "</td>");
    }
    document.write("</tr>");
}
document.write("</table>");
```

Needless to say, you are encouraged to study and practice with this script.

---

[8]The meaning of the `border` and `cellspacing` attributes of the `table` element can be found in any HTML reference.

Review and Practice

1. Write a **for** statement that alerts 10, then alerts 9, and so on, until a final alert of 0.

2. Write a little script that computes the value of the product of the integers 1 through 20 (inclusive). Use a **for** statement.

3. What would happen if, in Figure 4.6, the value of the last object's **next** property were not **null** but rather a reference to the first object in the chain?

4. In the multiplication table script, the inner loop uses the variable **j** to iterate through the columns. What would the script have produced if the programmer had accidentally used the variable **i** for both the outer and inner loop indexes?

4.4.3   The for-in Statement

JavaScript includes a statement for iterating through the *property names* of an object. The language refers to this operation as an *enumeration* of property names. We will illustrate with an example:

```
var dog = {name: 'Lisichka', breed: 'G-SHEP', birthday: '2011-12-01'};
for (var p in dog) {
    alert(p);
}
```

This script will produce three alerts: one saying **name**, one saying **breed**, and one saying **birthday**. The order in which the properties appear is arbitrary. Let's try another object:

```
var colors = ['red', 'amber', 'green'];
for (var c in colors) {
    alert(c);
}
```

Think about what you expect this code to alert before you try it out. Remember that enumeration occurs on property *names*, not values.[9] The property names for the object referenced by the variable `colors` are 0, 1, 2, and `length`. However, when this code is run, you will only see 0, 1, and 2 alerted. Why don't we see `length`?

The reason has to do with the fact that each property of an object, in addition to having a value, has several *attributes*, among them:

Attribute	Meaning if true
`writable`	The value of the property can be changed.
`enumerable`	The property will appear during a `for-in` enumeration of properties.
`configurable`	The property may be deleted from its object and its attribute values may be changed.

It so happens that the `length` property on arrays has its `enumerable` attribute set to `false`. We know from earlier examples that its `writable` attribute is `true`. What about `configurable`? Bring up your favorite JavaScript environment and figure it out! How? You can create the `colors` array and then evaluate

```
delete colors.length;
```

and see what happens. If you have a JavaScript environment that supports the ECMAScript 5 standard (ES5),[10] you can try

```
Object.getOwnPropertyDescriptor(colors, "length").configurable
```

If you run any of the preceding examples through JSLint, you will notice that they will not pass unless the **Tolerate unfiltered for in** box is checked. The `for-in` statement actually iterates through all enumerable properties of an object, both own properties and inherited properties.[11] JSLint is simply reminding you that you might not want to go through every property on the prototype chain; for example, if you are interested only in the own properties of an object x, you can write:

---

[9] Were you thinking that this script would alert red, amber, and green? Don't feel bad: this is exactly what most languages except JavaScript actually do.

[10] Review Section 2.5 if you've forgotten about the different versions of JavaScript.

[11] Own and inherited properties were described on page 77.

```
for (var p in x) {
    if (x.hasOwnProperty(p)) {
        // do something . . .
    }
}
```

A final word on the topic of iteration statements:

> Use a `for` or `for-in` statement when iterating through a definite set of values: a range of numbers, the characters of a string, the indexes of an array, the properties of an object, and so forth. Use a `while` or `do-while` statement when the condition for exiting the loop isn't so obvious.

Review and Practice

1. Modify the little script with the dog to alert the following:

   ```
   The dog's name is Lisichka
   The dog's breed is G-SHEP
   The dog's birthday is 2011-12-01
   ```

   You must produce these alerts with a `for-in` statement and extract the property values with the *object*[*property*] notation.

2. Find out by testing, in a shell or runner page, whether or not an array's `length` property is `configurable`.

4.5   Disruption

Normally, statements are executed one at a time, in order. Conditional and iteration statements cause a small deviation from what is sometimes called *straight-line code,* but the deviation is inherent to the structure of the statement and trivial to spot. There are four statements, however, that aren't quite so structured; their effect on control flow is *disruptive*. These statements are

- **break**, which immediately abandons the execution of the currently executing **switch** or iteration statement;

- **continue**, which immediately abandons the rest of the current iteration within an iteration statement;

- **return**, which immediately abandons the currently executing function (functions will be covered in Chapter 5); and

- **throw**, which we will cover in Section 4.5.2.

4.5.1   break and continue

The **break** statement will immediately terminate an entire loop. This is especially useful when you are searching an array (or chain of objects) and would like to stop searching when you have found what you are looking for:

```
// Find the index position of the first even number in array.
for (var i = 0; i < array.length; i += 1) {
    if (array[i] % 2 === 0) {
        alert("Even number found at position " + i);
        break;
    }
}
```

The **continue** statement immediately starts the next iteration of a loop without finishing the current one. It is useful when some, but not all, of the iterations in your loop produce useful information. The **continue** statement says, "Whoops, there's nothing left to do in this iteration. I'll just go on to the next one." Here's an example:

```
// Computes the sum of all positive values in array.
var sum = 0;
for (var i = 0; i < array.length; i += 1) {
```

```
    if (array[i] <= 0) {
        continue;                // Skip nonpositives.
    }
    sum += array[i];             // Accumulate positives.
}
alert("Sum of positives is " + sum);
```

We are now ready to study a more complex script featuring the **break** statement—one that determines whether a user's input is *prime*. A prime number is an integer greater than 1 having no positive divisors other than 1 and itself. Prime numbers play an important role in modern cryptography; secure data transmission over the Internet today relies heavily on certain properties of prime numbers.

Our script will ask the user to input a number, but because users can input anything at all, we will have to check that the input is indeed a number. In fact, we will need to check more than that: we won't be able to do accurate tests for divisors on negative numbers, noninteger numbers, and numbers beyond JavaScript's contiguous range of integers, which you might remember goes up to some value just above 9 quadrillion (9×10^{15}) or so.

After these checks, we will look for integers that evenly divide the user's input. Which numbers should we test? If, for example, we want to know whether 107 is prime, we will need to ensure that it has no divisors other than 1 and 107, which means we need to check that none of $2, 3, 4, \dots, 106$ evenly divide 107. Even better, we need only test values up to $\sqrt{107}$ (see Exercise 24 at the end of the chapter). We can test these values in turn, but as soon as we find a divisor, we can stop looking (**break**!) and report that our value is not prime:

```
var SMALLEST = 2;
var BIGGEST = 9E15;
var n = prompt("Enter a number and I'll check if it is prime");
if (isNaN(n) || n < SMALLEST || n > BIGGEST || n % 1 !== 0) {
    alert("I can only test integers between " + SMALLEST +
        " and " + BIGGEST);
} else {
    var foundDivisor = false;
    for (var k = 2, last = Math.sqrt(n); k <= last; k += 1) {
        if (n % k === 0) {
```

```
                foundDivisor = true;
                break;
            }
        }
    alert(n + " is " + (foundDivisor  "not " : "") + "prime");
```

Our final example concerning **break** and **continue** examines the question, How do you break out of an "outer" loop? One way is to *label* the loop and mention this label in the **break** statement. Let's see how. Suppose we have an object recording the lottery picks for a group of people, such as:

```
var picks = {
    Alice: [4, 52, 9, 1, 30, 2],
    Boris: [14, 9, 3, 6, 22, 40],
    Chi: [51, 53, 48, 21, 17, 8],
    Dinh: [1, 2, 3, 4, 5, 6],
};
```

Further, suppose we want to know whether anyone has selected the number 53. We check each person's picks in turn, but as soon as we find a 53, we want to stop the entire search, not just the scan through the current person's picks.

```
var found = false;
Search: for (var person in picks) {
    var choices = picks[person];
    for (var i = 0; i < choices.length; i += 1) {
        if (choices[i] === 53) {
            found = true;
            break Search;
        }
    }
}
alert(found);
```

Interestingly, you are free to label any statement at all in your script, though it is probably rare to use labels for anything but outer loops—and even this case is fairly rare in practice.

Review and Practice

1. Rewrite the example with the `continue` statement in this section to use a `break` statement instead.

2. Rewrite the primality script to avoid the `break` statement. In other words, replace the `for` loop with a `while` loop that tests for either finding a suitable divisor or running out of divisors.

4.5.2   Exceptions

Sometimes, when a script is running, something goes wrong. Perhaps the problem is due to a coding error—perhaps you wrote code to compute $E = mc^3$ instead of $E = mc^2$, or wrote code to add when you meant to multiply. In these cases, the script keeps running, but it produces the wrong outputs. We say that such a script has a *bug* or is *buggy*. If you are lucky, you will look at the outputs and think "that can't be right" and review your script and correct the mistake.

But sometimes when running a script, the JavaScript engine comes across a statement that *cannot* be executed or an expression that *cannot* be evaluated. Now the script can't keep running. The engine will *throw an exception*. If you don't catch the exception—we will see how to do this momentarily—the script will immediately stop running. We call this a *crash*.

To understand this a little better, consider the following script:

```
alert("Welcome to my script");
var message = printer + 1;
alert("The script is now ending");
```

When the script is run, the first alert appears, but since the second statement requests the value of the undeclared variable `printer` (an error in JavaScript), the engine throws an exception. Because this exception is not caught, the entire script is aborted and the last alert is *never executed*. If you were to run this script in a just-opened JavaScript shell, you would receive a report of the uncaught exception, as shown in Figure 4.8.

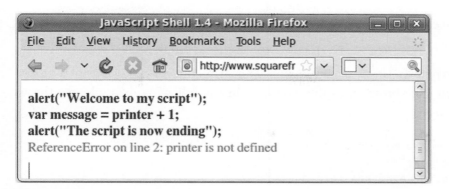

FIGURE 4.8

Exception notification in the JavaScript shell.

What other kinds of operations, besides using undeclared variables, are considered errors and result in JavaScript throwing exceptions? Figure 4.9 shows three cases:

- Setting an array's length to a negative number (a `RangeError`)

- Reading a property from the value `null` (a `TypeError`, because only objects have properties, and JavaScript cannot convert `null` into an object)

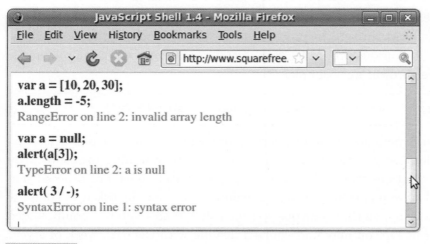

FIGURE 4.9

More exception notifications in the JavaScript shell.

- Executing or evaluating code that is not well-formed JavaScript (a `Syntax-Error`)

You can explicitly throw exceptions in your own code with JavaScript's `throw` statement. You can throw any value you like; in the following example, we throw a string:

```
alert("Welcome to my script");
throw "Ha ha ha";
alert("You will never see this message");
```

We mentioned that an uncaught exception causes a script to crash. To *catch* an exception, use a `try-catch` statement. The basic form of this statement is illustrated in another contrived example:

```
try {
    // This is a contrived example that just illustrates a point
    alert("Welcome to my script");
    throw "Ha ha ha";
    alert("You will never see this message");
} catch (e) {
    alert("Caught : " + e);
}
```

The `catch` clause initializes a variable (in this case, `e`, a rather common choice) to the value that was thrown. In practice, many JavaScript programmers like to throw objects with various properties that give information about the problem for which they were thrown; for example:

```
throw {reason: "class full", limit: 20, date: "2012-12-22"};
```

As you gain experience with JavaScript, you will find many cases where exceptions provide a very natural solution to certain programming problems. You should throw exceptions whenever you realize a computation cannot proceed sensibly with the data you currently have; for example, you may be asked to compute the balance due on a loan that someone specified should have interest compounded -5 times per year. Or you may find yourself dealing with the 64th week of a year or an encryption key that is the empty string. Sometimes you can recover from these exceptions by catching them.

Like most programming features, exceptions can be abused. Here is a script that asks the user to select one of three doors, numbered 1, 2, and 3, and win the prize hidden behind the chosen door.

```
// A script that might be better without exceptions
try {
    var PRIZES = ["a new car", "a broken stapler", "a refrigerator"];
    var door = prompt("Choose a door number  (1, 2, or 3)");
    var prize = PRIZES[door - 1];
    alert("You have won " + prize.toUpperCase() + "!!");
} catch (e) {
    alert("Sorry, no such door.");
}
```

Now if the user enters any value except 1, 2, or 3, the value of `prize` will be `undefined`, and the invocation of `toUpperCase` on `undefined` will throw an exception. The exception is caught and an error reported. This is by no means obvious from looking at the code; thus, we say the script exhibits convoluted logic. It relies on the fact that we were invoking `toUpperCase`, something unrelated to the "problem" of entering an invalid door number! We are better off checking the input immediately with a simple `if` statement.

Review and Practice

1. Does dividing by zero throw an exception in JavaScript?

2. If the prizes script were written without the `toUpperCase` invocation, would an exception ever be thrown? Why or why not?

3. Rewrite the example of the three prizes without using exceptions.

4.6 Coding Forms to Avoid

Because JavaScript is a powerful, industrial-strength programming language, it provides a great deal of flexibility in the way programmers can express computations. The language features several statements we have not covered, and many variations on the statements we did cover. It would not have been helpful to cram every statement and every statement variation into this chapter; after all, you did not learn the whole of your native language before beginning to speak it.

We have, however, presented enough useful information on statements for you to produce professional scripts. In fact, many things we left out were left out because they are features of JavaScript that are not only unnecessary but also, in our opinion, generally decrease the readability of code or increase the odds of introducing coding errors. Nevertheless, we will cover a few of these items now because you will see them used in other people's code and need to know what they mean.

4.6.1   Blockless Compound Statements

We presented the `if`, `while`, `do-while`, `for`, and `for-in` statements with the following general forms:

```
if (test) { stmts }
if (test) { stmts } else { stmts }
if (test) { stmts } else if (test) { stmts }
if (test) { stmts } else if (test) { stmts } else { stmts }
while (test) { stmts }
do { stmts } while (test) ;
for (init ; test ; each) { stmts }
for (var variable in object) { stmts }
```

The truth is, however, that where we have shown a sequence of statements enclosed in curly braces, JavaScript allows a single statement. It is perfectly legal to say

```
if (count === 0) break;
```

or

```
if (count === 0)
    break;
```

instead of the preferred

```
if (count === 0) {
    break;
}
```

The technical reason is that any sequence of statements enclosed in curly braces *is* itself a single statement, known as the *block statement*. You can therefore use a block statement anywhere a single statement is expected, but in practice, it looks foolish to use a block statement just for the heck of it. The following script is legal, though silly:

```
{{{{alert("Hello");}}}}
```

We strongly recommend that you follow modern coding conventions and use blocks *only* for **if** statements and iteration statements. We also strongly recommend that you *always* use blocks to build these statements, even if the short form saves typing. There are two primary reasons for this advice:

- It is visually jarring to look at code in which some statements use braces and some do not. It looks particularly bad when a single **if** statement has braces for some of its alternatives but not others. Lack of consistency gives the code an unbalanced, sloppy feel, requiring much more effort to figure out than necessary.

- The lack of braces makes code modification an error-prone undertaking. Here is a classic example. The following script alerts the squares of the numbers 0 through 9:

```
for (var i = 0; i < 10; i += 1)
    alert(i + " squared is " + (i * i));
```

The programmer decides to add a statement into the body of the loop to define a new variable to hold the computed square but forgets to add the braces:

```
for (var i = 0; i < 10; i += 1)
    var square = i * i;
    alert(i + " squared is " + square);
```

Because the `for` loop body is always the single statement following the parenthesized controlling expressions, this script declares the variable `square` and repeatedly assigns values to it, the last of which is 81. The alert comes after the `for` statement finishes. By this time, the value of `i` is 10, so the entire script produces the single alert "10 squared is 81." If you get into the habit of using braces without fail in your compound statements, you will never make this mistake.

> **Use block statements only within, and always within, `if` statements and iteration statements.**

4.6.2   Implicit Semicolon

The official JavaScript definition states that the following statements should end with a semicolon (;): the variable declaration statement, the expression statement (including assignments), the `do-while` statement, the `continue` statement, the `break` statement, the `return` statement (which we will see in the next chapter), and the `throw` statement. However, the language designers allowed programmers to leave off the statement-ending semicolons if they wish, relying on the JavaScript engine to figure out where one should have been. Unfortunately, this rule reduces your flexibility in splitting long statements across multiple lines of code. You can find the technical details regarding the handling of missing semicolons in [ECM09, Sec. 7.9], including advice on formatting statements to avoid getting burned with the automatic semicolon insertion policy.

4.6.3   Implicit Declarations

We have mentioned that the JavaScript engine throws an exception when you try to *use* a variable that has not yet been declared. If, however, you try to *assign to* an undeclared variable, JavaScript will automatically declare the variable for you.[12]

```
// Assume the variable next_song was never declared.
next_song = "Purple Haze";
```

---

[12]Technical note: The automatically declared variable is always a *global* variable. Global variables will be discussed in the next chapter.

This script does not throw an exception! Many people would probably say that it should; indeed, this implicit declaration is considered by many experts to be a language design flaw. An accidental misspelling of a variable name in an assignment results in the declaration of a new variable distinct from the variable you meant to assign to. The script keeps running until something happens "down the road," making the mistake hard to find. It would have been preferable if the engine threw the exception at the point of assignment, as the error would then be trivial to detect.[13]

You should never rely on this "feature" of JavaScript. JSLint wisely reports its use as an error.

4.6.4 Increment and Decrement Operators

Recall that to update the value of a variable, you use an assignment operator, such as = or +=, usually in an expression statement or `for` statement. You can also update variables with the ++ (increment) and -- (decrement) operators. These can be tricky! When placed in front of a variable, the operator updates the variable *before* the expression is evaluated. If the operator follows the variable, the variable is updated *after* the evaluation.

```
var x = 5;
x++;                // Now x is 6.
var y = x++;        // y gets 6, THEN x becomes 7.
var z = ++x;        // First x is bumped to 8, THEN z gets 8.
var w = ++y + z++;  // y gets 7 first, so w gets 15 and z gets 9 after.
```

The last line in this script is not pretty. Readers of this code have to think too hard to figure out what it does. The comment helps the reader's understanding but does not excuse the ugly code. Avoiding these operators removes the temptation to write cryptic and needlessly terse code [Cro08, p. 112].

4.6.5 The with Statement

Occasionally you will run across some code containing a `with` statement. While it may have seemed like a useful feature when the language was being designed, its

---

[13]Programming languages do exist that take this idea of "early error detection" one step further, and will simply refuse to even *run* programs that use undeclared variables.

inclusion is now thought by many to have been a mistake. We won't even describe the `with` statement in this book; instead, we refer you to [Cro08, p. 110] for a description of the statement and the reasons for avoiding it.

Review and Practice

1. Memorize the list of all statements that should be terminated with semi-colons.

2. Submit a script containing an implicit declaration to JSLint and note the error.

Chapter Summary

- A script is a sequence of statements, each of which produces some action. JavaScript statements include declarations, expression statements, conditionals, loops, and disruptive statements.

- We can store the results of evaluating expressions in variables and retrieve them at a later time. Variables should be declared before being used. If an initial value is not given in the declaration, the variable's initial value is `undefined`.

- Conditional code normally is written with the `if` statement, the `switch` statement, the `?:` operator, and the short-circuit operators. However, programmers can use dictionaries to replace some naïve uses of conditional code.

- The `while` statement features a test at the top of the loop; thus, its body may never be executed at all. The `do-while` statement has its test at the end and therefore always executes its loop at least once.

- The basic `for` statement is extremely flexible, allowing arbitrary initialization, test, and each-time code. The `for-in` statement iterates through those property names of an object whose `enumerable` attribute is `false`.

- The JavaScript engine throws an exception when it encounters a statement that it cannot execute or an expression that cannot be evaluated. You, the programmer, can throw exceptions explicitly with the `throw` statement. Exceptions are caught with `try-catch` statements.

- A block is a sequence of statements, enclosed in curly braces, that can be used as a single statement. It is considered good programming practice to always use blocks for the actions in an `if` statement and the bodies of iteration statements.

- JavaScript will insert semicolons that it thinks you might have left out. Programmers need to protect themselves by always explicitly using semicolons to terminate declaration, expression, `do-while`, `throw`, `return`, `break`, and `continue` statements.

Exercises

1. State the initial values of the variables `die1` and `die2` in the following script:

```
var die1, die2 = Math.floor(Math.random() * 6) + 1;
```

2. Suppose your friend tells you that an expression statement consisting only of a `prompt`, without assigning the result to a variable, is useless. Would you agree or disagree? Explain your answer using the following script (simulating a person who speaks but does not listen) for support:

```
prompt("Hi, how are you today?");
alert("Gee, that's great!")
```

3. Explain, in your own words, the difference between attempting to use a variable having the value `undefined` and using a variable that has not been defined.

4. What does the following script alert? Explain.

```
s = "Kunjalo!";
s.toUpperCase();
alert(s);
```

5. Suppose your little sister asks you why she couldn't find a "delete statement" in the official JavaScript definition, even though she writes statements like

```
delete player.winnings;
```

all the time. Knowing that she is the kind of kid who loves technical, precise explanations of linguistic features, what do you tell her? (*Note*: You have to say more than just "Delete is an operator, kiddo.")

6. What does the following expression represent?

```
Math.random() < 0.75 ? "Heads" : "Tails"
```

7. So far in this text, our approach to checking whether a number n is an integer is to evaluate the expression `n % 1 === 0`. Why does this work? An alternate approach is to evaluate the expression `Math.floor(n) === Math.ceil(n)`. Which approach do you prefer, and why? What do these expressions produce when $n = 9876543219876543.25$, and why? If this is not what you would have expected, what alternate ways can you think of to test for integers?

8. What is the expression `x < y ? x : y` good for?

9. Recall the following line from this chapter:

```
var notice = "She is" + (present ? "" : "n't") + " here.";
```

What would happen if we left off the parentheses? In other words, explain the meaning of the following:

```
var notice = "She is" + present ? "" : "n't" + " here.";
```

10. Rewrite the prize-level script to avoid **switch** statements without **breaks**. (*Hint*: There is a particularly nice solution to this problem involving the **slice** operation on arrays.)

11. Here is a poor, but functioning, **switch** statement containing the dreaded "fall-through." Rewrite this code fragment to avoid the **switch**:

```
var days = undefined;
switch (month) {
    case "Jan":
    case "Mar":
    case "May":
    case "Jul":
    case "Aug":
    case "Oct":
    case "Dec": days = 31; break;
    case "Apr":
    case "Jun":
    case "Sep":
    case "Nov": days = 30; break;
    case "Feb": days = leapYear ? 29 : 28; break;
}
```

(*Hint*: The month names in this code fragment show a commitment to a particular natural language; code like this should really be language-agnostic. Use numbers for months. Doing so should spark some ideas for getting rid of the `switch` completely.)

12. Modify the car-painting example so that the car is painted with your favorite color if you have one; otherwise it is painted with the color of your garage (if the color is known); otherwise it is painted red.

13. Write a script that prompts the user for a string containing numbers separated by spaces, then alerts the minimum value, the maximum value, and the sum. For example, if the input is 2 -9 3 4 1, then the script should alert `Minimum is -9, Maximum is 4, Sum is 1`. (*Hint*: Use the `split` operation on arrays to turn your input string into an array of values to compare.)

14. Write a script that repeatedly prompts a user to enter a word or phrase until the empty string is entered. After each (nonempty) word is entered, alert a random letter from the word.

15. Write a script that prompts the user for a string, then alerts whether or not the input string is a *palindrome*. A palindrome is a string that is spelled the same both forward and backward, such as `"I"`, `"bob"`, and `"racecar"`. Experiment with variations of the script that are insensitive to the case of

letters (allowing `"Abba"`) and that ignore nonletters (allowing `"Madam, I'm Adam"`).

16. Write a script that determines how many years it takes to reach an investment goal, as follows. Prompt the user for the initial amount of money, the annual interest rate (as a percentage), and the desired amount of money to end up with. Assume interest is compounded yearly. Use a `while` or `for` statement, adding to your current balance as you count the years. If you happen to know a formula that can obtain the result "in one step," incorporate this into a second script.

17. Write a script that prompts the user for an integer (in the range 1 to 10,000— you must check this) and reports the number of steps required in the *Collatz sequence* to reach the value 1. The Collatz sequence is a sequence of positive integers obeying the following:

    ■ If a number in the sequence, n, is even, then the next number in the sequence is $n/2$.

    ■ If a number in the sequence, n, is odd, then the next number in the sequence is $3n + 1$.

    For example, if your user inputs 10, then your script should produce the value 6 because the sequence

    $$10 \rightarrow 5 \rightarrow 16 \rightarrow 8 \rightarrow 4 \rightarrow 2 \rightarrow 1$$

    involves six steps. If the initial value is 1, then you should report zero steps.

18. Is it better to use a `while` or a `do-while` statement in the previous exercise? Why?

19. Recall the example script on page 121 that produced an acronym from an array of strings. Modify this script so that instead of creating an acronym from a fixed array, the user is first prompted to enter a string. Your new script should then `split` the input string, producing an array that is then processed by the acronym-generating code from this chapter.

20. Modify your script in the previous exercise so that instead of accepting data via `prompt`, the initial string is taken from an HTML input field. Use the temperature converter exercise from Chapter 2 as a guide.

21. In the example with the object chain on page 123, the chain was "terminated" with `null` rather than `undefined`. Why was this? In your answer, refer to the distinction between `null` and `undefined` from Chapter 3.

22. Explain, in your own words, the behavior of this script:

```
var i = 0;
while (i < 10) {
    continue;
    i += 1;
}
alert("All done");
```

23. Explain, in your own words, the behavior of this script:

```
for (var i = 0; i < 10; i += 1) {
    continue;
}
alert("All done");
```

24. Why, when testing whether a positive integer n is prime, is it necessary only to test divisors from 2 up to $\sqrt{n}$, instead of up to $n - 1$?

25. Suppose your friend says, "We can avoid the square root computation in the prime number script by making the termination condition of the loop `test * test <= n`." Is this an improvement? Why or why not?

26. One way to "speed up" the prime number-testing script is as follows:

   - If n is divisible by 2, you know immediately that n is composite.
   - Otherwise, test the divisors $3, 5, 7, 9, 11, \ldots, \sqrt{n}$.

   Why does this work? Rewrite the script to use this improved algorithm.

27. Research the JavaScript `with` statement. Look for articles (offline or online) that claim the statement is harmful. Summarize these arguments in a short paragraph of your own.

28. Modify the lottery example in this chapter to alert the name of the person who picked 53.

29. Try to evaluate an object literal expression in the JavaScript shell—for example, `{x: 0, y: 0}`. Now that you know about block statements and statement labels, explain the error message. How is it possible to evaluate an object literal in the shell? (*Hint*: Consider parentheses.)

30. In our discussion of blockless statements, we did not mention the `try-catch` statement. Why not? (You will likely need to consult a JavaScript reference to answer this question.)

31. One statement we did not cover in this chapter is the *empty* statement. Read about this statement in a JavaScript reference.

32. We did not cover in this chapter the `finally` clause of the `throw` statement. Read a full description of the `throw` statement in a JavaScript reference, and write a functional example script that uses the `finally` clause.

CHAPTER 5

Functions

CHAPTER CONTENTS

Introduction

A *function* is an object that carries out a specific computation, such as figuring sales tax, finding words in a document, or calculating the shortest route between two points on a map. A function is written once but can be used many times. All but the most trivial scripts contain functions.

This chapter shows how to define and use functions, and covers the technical details of function definition, parameter passing, scope, and function objects, while providing numerous examples. We will also introduce two of JavaScript's most useful and powerful features: the ability to pass functions as arguments to other functions and the ability to return functions from functions. By the end of this chapter, you will be able to define and use functions in your own scripts.

5.1　Black Boxes

Conceptually, a *function* receives inputs, performs a computation, and produces outputs. A function that computes the balance of an account after t years from a starting balance p and annual percentage rate r, with interest compounded n times per year, is illustrated in Figure 5.1.

To use this function, you send four values to the function and receive the computed balance in response. You need not know nor care that the function internally computes the formula $p \times (1 + \frac{r}{n})^{nt}$, nor what electromechanical processes inside the computer perform the arithmetic operations. You only care *what* the result of a function is, not *how* the result is computed. Because the "inner workings" of a function are invisible to its users, we think of functions as *black boxes*.

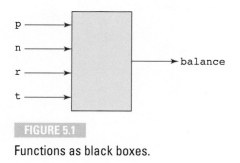

FIGURE 5.1

Functions as black boxes.

We see analogues of this idea in our everyday lives. We drive cars without an understanding of internal combustion or hydrogen fuel cells; we microwave food without an understanding of the underlying physics; we send instant messages, tweet, and make phone calls with no idea of how our text and voice are encoded and transmitted. We call this idea of seeing the big picture without worrying about details *abstraction*. Functions are abstractions of computations.

Review and Practice

1. Why are functions called black boxes?

2. Give an example of abstraction similar to the ones in this section.

5.2 Defining and Calling Functions

In JavaScript, a function value consists of a block of executable code, called its *body*, together with zero or more inputs, called *parameters*. Here is a function value that computes the cube of its sole parameter:

```
function (x) {return x * x * x;}
```

Functions are values just like numbers, truth values, strings, arrays, and conventional objects. You can, therefore, assign function values to variables:

```
var cube = function (x) {return x * x * x;};
```

To run, or *call*, a function, you *pass* it a parenthesized list of zero or more *arguments*. When called, the function first assigns to each parameter the value of the corresponding argument, then executes its body. A `return` statement, if any, passes the result of a computation back to the *caller*. The following script shows a function definition followed by three calls:

```
// Define the function - this does not run the body
var cube = function (x) {
    return x * x * x;
};

// Make three calls, running the body three times
```

```
alert(cube(-2));
alert(cube(10));
alert("There are " + (cube(3) - 1) + " cubes in a Rubik's Cube");
```

In the first call, we pass -2 to the function cube, which assigns -2 to x, computes -2 * -2 * -2, and returns this value (-8) to the point of call. This value is then itself passed in a call to the alert function, which you have seen before.

Functions can also have *names*. When a function has a name, you can call it without assigning it to a variable:

```
function cube(x) {
    return x * x * x;
};
alert(cube(-2));        // Alerts -8
```

This kind of definition, called a *function declaration* in JavaScript, is similar to, but not quite the same as, assigning the function to a variable with the same name. While many (perhaps most) programmers like the terseness of the function declaration, we prefer variable declarations. We have deferred our reasons until the end of this chapter, where they will make more sense; however, we feel the need to mention the existence of function declarations up front because they are so popular and you might wonder why we seem to be neglecting them.

Many functions have *no* parameters; for example:

```
var diceRoll = function () {
    return 1 + Math.floor(6 * Math.random());
};
```

To run this function, you must write diceRoll(), not diceRoll. The former expression *calls* the function; the latter simply *is* the function. This is important! Figure 5.2 illustrates the difference.

If a function completes its body without executing a return statement, it returns the value undefined. This is really just a technicality because functions

```
alert(diceRoll() + "\n"
    + diceRoll() + "\n"
    + diceRoll() + "\n"
    + diceRoll
);
```

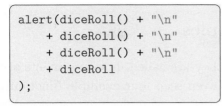

[JavaScript Application]

! 1
  6
  4
  function () {
      return 1 + Math.floor(6 * Math.random());
  }

OK

FIGURE 5.2

Function values versus function calls.

without **return** statements are generally called for their effect, not for any value they would produce:

```
var echo = function (message) {
    alert(message + ".");
    alert("I said: " + message + "!");
};
echo("Sanibonani");       // The natural way to call this function.
var x = echo("Hello");    // Assigns undefined to x, but not done in
                          // practice.
```

If you do not pass enough arguments to a function, the extra parameters will be initialized to **undefined**:

```
var show = function (x, y) {
    alert(x + " " + y);
};
show(1);                // Alerts "1 undefined".
```

Review and Practice

1. Write a script that defines a function that returns the average of two numbers, followed by a statement that alerts the result of calling this function with 3 and 5.

2. Write a function with no parameters that returns a two-element array containing two (possibly different) dice rolls.

5.3   Examples and More Examples

We now know how functions are written, how they are called, how arguments are passed, and how values are returned. We have even seen four example functions. To gain proficiency in writing functions, however, four examples are not enough.

5.3.1   Simple One-Line Functions

We will continue with a few simple "one-line" numeric functions. We will follow good programming practice by preceding each function with a comment that explains *what* the function does, not *how* it does what it does.

```
/*
 * Returns the area of a circle with radius r.
 */
var circleArea = function (r) {
    return Math.PI * r * r;
};
```

```
/*
 * Returns whether x evenly divides y.  For example
 * divides(5, 20) returns true, but divides(2, 17)
 * returns false.
 */
var divides = function (x, y) {
    return y % x === 0;
};
```

```
/*
 * Returns the price of an item after applying a discount.
 */
var discountedPrice = function (originalPrice, discountPercent) {
    return originalPrice - (originalPrice * discountPercent / 100.0);
};
```

You can, and will, use functions that you write to build up other functions:

```
/*
 * Returns whether a given year is a leap year, according to the
 * usual rules of the Gregorian calendar.  A year is a leap year
 * if it is (1) divisible by 4 but not 100, or else (2) is divisible
 * by 400.
 */
var isLeapYear = function (y) {
    return divides(4, y) && !divides(100, y) || divides(400, y);
};
```

Function calls are expressions, so it is very convenient to use a shell to try out sample calls. Enter the preceding functions and then verify the following evaluations:

circleArea(2.5)	⇒	19.634954084936208
circleArea(0)	⇒	0
divides(5, 70343450)	⇒	true
divides(7, 84934)	⇒	false
isLeapYear(1900)	⇒	false
isLeapYear(2000)	⇒	true
discountedPrice(999.95, 25)	⇒	749.9625000000001

These answers seem reasonable. If the final evaluation seems wrong to you, revisit the discussion in Section 3.3.2 on arithmetic computations in JavaScript often yielding approximate results.[1] However, let's now consider some rather unusual calls:

circleArea(null)	⇒	0
circleArea(false)	⇒	0
circleArea(true)	⇒	3.141592653589793
circleArea("dog")	⇒	NaN
divides("dog", 5)	⇒	false
divides("2", null)	⇒	true

---

[1]Real-world financial transactions, however, use sophisticated numeric algorithms to deal with rounding to the nearest cent and avoid the loss of money to round-off errors, but these algorithms will not be covered in this book.

As strange as they seem, these results are natural consequences of the type conversion rules we saw in Section 3.8. Recall that `true` gets interpreted as 1 and `"dog"` as NaN. We can work out the evaluations to see why the results came out as they did:

```
circleArea(true)  =  Math.PI * true * true
                  =  Math.PI * 1 * 1
                  =  Math.PI
                  =  3.141592653589793


divides("dog", 5)  =  5 % "dog" === 0
                   =  5 % NaN === 0
                   =  NaN === 0
                   =  false
```

Review and Practice

1. Write a function to compute the circumference of a circle with radius r.

2. Write a function to compute the surface area of a cylinder with radius r and height h.

5.3.2 Validating Arguments

Let's switch to the world of finance for the next example:

```
/*
 * Returns the balance after t years of an account
 * where the initial balance of p has been compounded n
 * times per year with an annual interest rate of r.
 */
var balanceAfter = function (p, n, r, t) {
    return p * Math.pow(1 + (r / n), n * t);
};
```

Let's test this for an initial balance of $1000, earning 5% compounded monthly, after 10 years, as well as for an initial balance of $1, doubling every year, after 20 years:

```
balanceAfter(1000, 12, 0.05, 10)   ⇒   1647.00949769028
balanceAfter(1, 1, 1, 20)          ⇒   1048576
```

So far so good. Now let's think about how the function behaves with unusual arguments. Does a negative rate make sense? Yes, it simulates paying interest instead of accumulating it. How about a negative number of years? Yes, it tells you the required starting balance that gets you to the given amount. But what if the number of compounding periods were negative?

```
balanceAfter(1000, -2, 0.05, 10)      ⇒   1659.234181850974
balanceAfter(1000, -0.06, 0.05, 10)   ⇒   2930.1560515835217
balanceAfter(1000, -0.05, 0.05, 10)   ⇒   Infinity
balanceAfter(1000, -0.02, 0.05, 10)   ⇒   NaN
```

What can it possibly *mean* to compound interest -0.06 times per year? Our function reports a final balance for negative compounding periods, but no bank would *ever* compound interest this way, as you can end up with outrageously large sums of money and, between -0.05 and 0, NaN dollars![2] We should fix our function; let's make it "say" that a negative value for compounding periods makes no sense (in our reality) by throwing an exception:

```
/*
 * Returns the balance after t years of an account
 * where the initial balance of p has been compounded n
 * times per year with an annual interest rate of r.  If n
 * is negative, the function throws a string saying so.
 */
var balanceAfter = function (p, n, r, t) {
    if (n < 0) {
        throw "Cannot compound a negative number of times";
    }
    return p * Math.pow(1 + (r / n), n * t);
};
```

---

[2]Mathematically, the result is a *complex number*, which JavaScript does not deal with directly. You can, however, define complex numbers on your own in JavaScript, though it does take some work.

Review and Practice

1. Evaluate the `balanceAfter` function for $p = 1000$, $n = 0$, $r = 0.05$, and $t = 10$. Even though the evaluation of the function at these arguments will cause a division by zero error, the answer still makes sense. Why do you think this is?

2. Rewrite the `balanceAfter` function to throw a `RangeError` object instead of a string.

5.3.3   Passing Object References as Arguments

Let's now move beyond functions on numbers and strings, and look at passing objects to functions:

```
/*
 * Returns the sum of all the elements in an array.
 */
var sum = function (a) {
    var result = 0;
    for (var i = 0; i < a.length; i += 1) {
        result += a[i];
    }
    return result;
};
```

Let's try it out:

$$\text{sum([])} \qquad\qquad \Rightarrow \quad 0$$
$$\text{sum([10, -3, 8])} \quad \Rightarrow \quad 15$$

Not too surprising. Our next example looks somewhat similar to, but *has a very different flavor* from, the previous example. Can you see what the main difference is?

```
/*
 * Uppercases all the strings in an array.
 */
var uppercaseAll = function (a) {
```

```
        for (var i = 0; i < a.length; i += 1) {
            a[i] = a[i].toUpperCase();
        }
};
```

The difference is that while the function `sum` returns a value, `uppercaseAll` does not include a `return` statement at all! Instead, it *changes the properties of the object passed to it*:

```
uppercaseAll([])                        ⇒  undefined
uppercaseAll(["abc", "", "ab"])         ⇒  undefined
var dogs = ["spike", "spot", "rex"]
uppercaseAll(dogs)                      ⇒  undefined
dogs                                    ⇒  ["SPIKE", "SPOT", "REX"]
```

Let's reinforce this important distinction by writing the nonmodifying version of uppercasing an array of strings. Instead of uppercasing the strings in the array argument, we will return a new array:

```
/*
 * Returns a new array that is equivalent to its input array
 * with its elements uppercased.
 */
var uppercaseStrings = function (a) {
    var result = [];
    for (var i = 0; i < a.length; i += 1) {
        result.push(a[i].toUpperCase());
    }
    return result;
};
```

Let's see this function in action:

```
uppercaseStrings([])                      ⇒  []
uppercaseStrings(["abc", "", "ab"])       ⇒  ["ABC", "", "AB"]
var dogs = ["spike", "spot", "rex"]
uppercaseStrings(dogs)                    ⇒  ["SPIKE", "SPOT", "REX"]
dogs                                      ⇒  ["spike", "spot", "rex"]
```

Notice that the argument, dogs, did not change. **Make sure you understand the difference between these last two functions.** The first one modifies properties of its argument; the second one leaves its argument alone and returns a new array.

Review and Practice

1. Give two functions for squaring every element in an array; that is, given [1, -4, 2], produce [1, 16, 4]. One function should return a new array; the other should change the argument itself.

5.3.4 Preconditions

Our next example raises an interesting question:

```
/*
 * Returns the largest element in an array.
 */
var max = function (a) {
    var largest = a[0];
    for (var i = 1; i < a.length; i += 1) {
        if (a[i] > largest) {
            largest = a[i];
        }
    }
    return largest;
};
```

Does it work?

$$max([7, 19, -22, 0]) \Rightarrow 19$$
$$max(["dog", "rat", "cat"]) \Rightarrow "rat"$$

So far so good. Our function relies on the > operator to compare successive values in the array, keeping track of the maximum value found so far (starting with the first element, a[0]). Now > knows how to compare numbers against numbers and strings against strings, but strangely, unless *both* values across > are strings, JavaScript will treat each value as a number and compare accordingly. Sometimes this is okay:

$$max([7, "19", -22, "0"]) \Rightarrow "19"$$

But when a value converts to NaN, things are not so nice. The expression x > y evaluates to false if either x or y is NaN. For example, 3 > NaN is false and NaN > 3 is also false! This means:

$$max([3, "dog"]) \Rightarrow 3$$
$$max(["dog", 3]) \Rightarrow "dog"$$

Shouldn't a self-respecting max function return the same value for two arrays that have exactly the same elements but in different orders? Perhaps, but consider that the values 3 and "dog" are really **incomparable**, so computing the maximum value of such an array is basically meaningless. Shouldn't we throw an exception in this case? Many languages do. Other languages refuse to even run programs that contain comparisons like this! JavaScript, however, happily runs such comparisons that give essentially meaningless results. You can try to detect these problems in your code if you wish, or you can provide a kind of "full disclosure" in the comment describing the function:

```
/*
 * Returns the largest element in an array.  If the array
 * contains values that are incomparable, the function returns
 * some unspecified, arbitrary value.
 */
```

Changing the comment does not change the way the function behaves one bit, but it does change the *contract* between the function and its users. With this comment, the function promises to deliver the maximum value as long as the caller passes only meaningful arguments; otherwise all bets are off. The constraints on the arguments demanded by the function are called *preconditions*. Preconditions are not checked by the function itself; failure to meet the preconditions simply leads to unspecified behavior. The term "precondition" is such a well-known and well-understood term in programming circles that we will adopt a convention for our comments that introduce preconditions:

```
/*
 * Returns the largest element in an array.  Precondition: All of the
 * elements in the array are mutually comparable.
 */
```

While thinking about nonsensical arguments, we should consider empty arrays. After all, "the largest element in an empty array" doesn't sound meaningful. Let's see how the function currently handles this case. First, the variable `largest` is initialized with `a[0]`, which is evaluated as `undefined` since there is no element at index 0 in the array. Then we go through a `for` loop zero times, which has no effect. Finally we return the value of `largest`, which is (still) `undefined`. So, as things stand, the maximum value in an empty array is `undefined`. If we are happy with this, we should state this in the function's comment. If not, we should begin the function with code to throw an exception if the array's length is zero. Your choice.

One final note about preconditions: like comments, you can overdo them. Saying that an argument isn't expected to be `NaN` may seem like being thorough, but most programmers would accept non-NaN-ness as an implicit precondition.

Review and Practice

1. Define the term *precondition* in your own words.

2. Which of the examples earlier in this chapter could have used preconditions in their introductory comments?

5.3.5   Separation of Concerns

We will now bring up an example that appears in nearly every introductory programming book—a prime number function. The function takes a value and returns whether it is prime. We gave a complete prime number script back on page 130, using `prompt` for input and `alert` for output. At that time, we were introducing full and complete scripts, without the complexity of such "advanced" JavaScript notions as functions! Now that we are much further along, we are going to *refactor* that script. Refactoring is the act of restructuring code to make it better, usually (but not necessarily) by breaking up a big messy block of code into smaller components. In this case we are going to **separate the user interaction from the main computation**. We will package the latter as a nice function:

```
/*
 * Returns whether n is prime. Precondition: n is an integer greater
 * than or equal to 2, and within JavaScript's main contiguous range of
 * representable integers.
```

```
*/
var isPrime = function (n) {
    for (var k = 2, last = Math.sqrt(n); k <= last; k += 1) {
        if (n % k === 0) {
            return false;
        }
    }
    return true;
};
```

Note very carefully: *The function simply returns whether its argument is prime; it does NOT alert a message saying so!* The rest of the script handles the prompting, the error checking, and the reporting of the result:

```
var SMALLEST = 2, BIGGEST = 9E15;
var n = prompt("Enter a number and I'll check if it's prime");
if (isNaN(n)) {
    alert("That wasn't a number");
} else if (n < SMALLEST) {
    alert("I can't test numbers that small");
} else if (n > BIGGEST) {
    alert("That number is too large for me to test");
} else if (n % 1 !== 0) {
    alert("I can only test integers");
} else {
    alert(n + " is " + (isPrime(n) ? "prime" : "composite"));
}
```

Our refactored code exhibits *separation of concerns*, a programming virtue yielding two primary benefits:

- Separating concerns makes complex systems understandable. Anyone needing to understand or diagnose a problem in a large system like a space shuttle or a financial services system must be able to identify subsystems with well-defined behaviors. A large system can never be understood by seeing it only as a collection of statements.

- By pulling out the prime number calculation into its own function, we have now created a *reusable* piece of code that we can drop in to any number of scripts that we write in the future. You have experienced the reusability of functions already: you have called `alert` and `Math.sqrt` without needing to have written their details on your own.

But how reusable is our prime number function? The script that called our sequence did a lot of error checking. If our function is really to be written once but called from hundreds or thousands of scripts, is it fair to expect these "callers" to all do the same error checking? Of course not. We can deal with the error checking in the function:

```
/*
 * Returns whether its argument is a prime number in the range 2..9e15.
 * Throws an exception if its argument is not an integer, or is out of
 * the range 2..9e15.
 */
var isPrime = function (n) {
    if (n % 1 !== 0 || n < 2 || n > 9E15) {
        throw "Number is not an integer or is out of range";
    }
    for (var k = 2, last = Math.sqrt(n); k <= last; k += 1) {
        if (n % k === 0) {
            return false;
        }
    }
    return true;
};
```

Note that *the function throws exceptions if it encounters problems; it does not alert errors!* This is crucial. In order for the function to be truly reusable, it should never take over user communication. Different users of your function may have different requirements for error reporting. Some will write them to a location on a web page while others may collect them in an array. Some will want to report errors in Zulu, Hawaiian, Irish, Urdu, or Hungarian, and it's not the function's job to anticipate every language.

> **When writing a function that computes values for its callers, throw exceptions to indicate errors.**

1. Why should functions generally not alert results or error messages?

2. Define the terms *refactoring* and *separation of concerns*.

5.3.6   The Fibonacci Sequence

Our last example for this section is a function that generates the *Fibonacci sequence*, a rather remarkable sequence whose properties show up in nature, music, and financial markets [PL07]. The sequence begins

$$0, 1, 1, 2, 3, 5, 8, 13, 21, 34, 55, 89, 144, \dots$$

Each value in the sequence (except the first two) is the sum of the previous two. Our function will build up an array `f`, starting at `[0,1]` and repeatedly adding the value of the last element (`f[f.length-1]`) to the value of the second-to-last element (`f[f.length-2]`). Because the function is to work on integers only, we will have to make sure our values do not exceed JavaScript's range of contiguous representable integers, which by now you are starting to recognize as $\approx 9 \times 10^{15}$. For now, we will cheat and just generate the first 75 numbers, knowing that these are safe. In the end-of-chapter exercises, you will explore getting as many values as you can.

```
/*
 * Returns an array containing the first 75 Fibonacci numbers.
 */
var fibonacciSequence = function () {

    // Start with the first two Fibonacci numbers
    var f = [0, 1];

    // Compute the 3rd through the 75th numbers
    for (var i = 3; i <= 75; i += 1) {
        f.push(f[f.length - 1] + f[f.length - 2]);
    }
    return f;
};
```

Try it out.

1. What is the highest Fibonacci number produced by the script in this section?

2. Rewrite the Fibonacci generator to accept an argument stating how many Fibonacci numbers to generate. Throw an exception if the argument passed is not an integer between 0 and 75, inclusive.

5.4   Scope

Functions allow you to bundle an arbitrarily complex computation into what appears to its callers a single, simple command. Consider the following function for computing the factorial[3] of a number:

```
/*
 * Returns the factorial of n.  Precondition: n is an integer between
 * 0 and 21, inclusive.  (Beyond 21, it returns an approximation.)
 */
var factorial = function (n) {
    var result = 1;
    for (var i = 1; i <= n; i += 1) {
        result *= i;
    }
    return result;
};
```

This function declares a parameter `n` and two variables of its own: `i` and `result`. Variables declared inside a function are called *local variables* and, like parameters, belong to the function and are completely distinct from any other variable of the same name elsewhere in the script. This is a very good thing. Consider:

```
var result = 100;
alert(factorial(5));    // Alerts 120.
alert(result);          // Still 100, of course
```

---

[3]The factorial of a number n is the product of all whole numbers from 1 to n. For example, the factorial of 5 is $1 \times 2 \times 3 \times 4 \times 5 = 120$.

We would not expect the global variable `result` to change just because we computed a factorial. Often, different parts of a script are written by different people. The author of the part of the script calling a function has no idea what variables might have been used inside the function. You would not be happy if you called the `alert` function and it changed some of your variables.

In JavaScript, variables declared inside a function, as well as the function's parameters, are said to have *function scope*, while those declared outside any function have *global scope* and are called *global variables*. Function-scoped variables are visible only within the function in which they are declared and are shielded from the outside world, as we have seen previously. The following smaller script makes the point more clearly:

```javascript
var message = "Pluto is only a dwarf planet";
var warn = function () {
    var message = "You're about to see something controversial";
    alert(message);
};
warn();         // Alerts "You're about to see something controversial"
alert(message); // Alerts "Pluto is only a dwarf planet"
```

Here we have two distinct variables that happen to have the same name. The scope of a global variable begins at the point of its declaration and extends to the end of the script, while the scope of a local variable is the body of the function in which it is declared. In this case, the local variable and global variable have the same name (`message`) and their scopes overlap. In the overlapping region, the innermost declaration takes precedence.

Although local variables are hidden from outside interference, global variables are visible from within functions, unless you specifically hide them:

```javascript
var warning = "Don't double-click the submit button";
var warn = function () {
    alert(warning);              // global variable is visible here
};
warn();         // Alerts "Don't double-click the submit button".
alert(warning); // Alerts "Don't double-click the submit button".
```

The fact that global variables are accessible within functions probably isn't surprising; in fact, we have made use of many global variables already: `alert`, prompt, isNaN, Math, and so on. Not being allowed to use them inside functions would be a huge impediment to getting anything done. However, it does mean we need to be careful of one potential problem:

```javascript
var message = "Time for a new game";
var play = function () {
    message = "Playing";  // OOOOOPS!!! Forgot "var"
    alert(message);
};
alert(message);    // Alerts "Time for a new game"
play();            // Alerts "Playing"
alert(message);    // Alerts "Playing". FAIL!!
play();            // Alerts "Playing".
```

The preceding script defined only one variable called message, and its value was updated by the function. Updating global variables within functions is nearly always considered very poor programming practice; the proper way for functions in a script to "communicate with each other" is through function arguments and return values, not through global variables. Programmers should strive to keep their use of global variables to a minimum; we will discuss the reasons behind this advice in Section 7.4.

> **Minimize the use of global variables. In particular, functions should "communicate" via parameters and return values instead of by updating global variables.**

The fact that the scope of local variables in JavaScript comprises the entire function body in which they are declared leads to another possible gotcha: while global variables don't exist until they are declared, local variables come into existence immediately when their function begins execution, *even if the variable is declared in the middle of the function body.* Consider the following code:

```javascript
var x = 1;
// At this point the global x exists, but the global y does not.
// Using y at this point would throw a ReferenceError.
var y = 2;
```

```
// At this point, the global y now exists.
var f = function () {
    alert(z);         // This is fine! Alerts undefined.
    var z = 3;
    alert(y + z);     // Alerts 5, of course.
};
f();
```

When a function is called, the JavaScript engine creates an object on the spot to hold the function's parameters and its local variables. The parameters are immediately initialized to copies of the arguments passed in the call, and all local variables are immediately initialized to **undefined**. This is why, in the previous example, using z before it was declared did not cause a **ReferenceError** to be thrown.

However, just because you *know* that local variables are usable before they are declared doesn't mean you *should* use them in their undefined state. In fact, purposely using variables before they are defined is sure to confuse almost anyone reading your code and would be considered very poor style. Many JavaScript style guides even go so far as to say that all local variables should be declared in the first statement of a function body; JSLint even has a setting to check for this.

Review and Practice

1. Define the term *scope*.

2. Name and describe the two kinds of scope in JavaScript.

3. What is alerted in the following script?

   ```
   var x = 1;
   var f = function (y) {alert(x + y);}
   f(2);
   ```

   What would the script alert if the parameter y were renamed to x?

4. Your friend has been asked to write a function called `nextSquare`, which returns 1 the first time it is called, then 4 the next time it is called, then 9, then 16, then 25, 36, 49, 64, etc.

```
var current = 0;
var nextSquare = function () {
    current += 1;
    return current * current;
};
```

Variable `current` is global. What can go wrong? What should you tell your friend? Can you propose a better way to implement `nextSquare`?

5.5   Functions as Objects

Recall that every value in JavaScript that is not `undefined`, `null`, a Boolean, a number, or a string is an object. Function values, therefore, are objects and, like all objects, can have properties. They can also (like all other values) be themselves properties of other objects. And if that is not interesting enough, we can use a special JavaScript operator to allow functions to manufacture a bunch of objects that all look and behave the same way—in effect, creating new data types. This section explores these and other interesting consequences of functions being objects.

5.5.1   Properties of Functions

Knowing that functions are objects, one question to ask is, What kind of properties would a function have? The short answer is that you can store whatever you like in a function object. Perhaps you would like to keep track of the number of times a function was called:

```
var average = function (x, y) {
    average.calls += 1;
    return (x + y) / 2;
}
average.calls = 0;

alert(average(4, 8));      // Alerts 6.
```

```
alert(average(10.5, 11));   // Alerts 10.75.
alert(average(0, 1));       // Alerts 0.5.
alert(average.calls);       // Alerts 3.
```

Other uses of properties for functions include counting the number of times certain results are generated (good for dice rolls or dealing cards), remembering the return value of a function for given arguments (which we will see in Section 10.3), and defining data relevant to a particular set of objects (introduced on page 278).

When a function object is created, JavaScript gives it two properties to start off. The first, `length`, is initialized with the number of parameters the function has:

```
var average = function (x, y) {
    return (x + y) / 2;
};
alert(average.length);      // Alerts 2 (one for x plus one for y).
```

We will defer coverage of the second predefined property, `prototype`, until Section 5.5.3.

Review and Practice

1. Modify the dice roll function from the beginning of this chapter so that it keeps track of the number of times it rolls each value. You can do this by assigning six properties to the function (one for each die face) or by using a single array property.

2. Do an experiment to see if it is possible to change the `length` property of a function.

5.5.2   Functions as Properties

Since functions are values, they can be, and often are, properties of objects. There are two main reasons for placing functions inside of objects. The first is to simply group a number of related functions together; for example:

```
var Geometry = {
    circleArea: function (radius) {
        return Math.PI * radius * radius;
    },
```

```
    circleCircumference: function (radius) {
        return 2 * Math.PI * radius;
    },
    sphereSurfaceArea: function (radius) {
        return 4 * Math.PI * radius * radius;
    },
    boxVolume: function (length, width, depth) {
        return length * width * depth;
    }
};
```

Grouping a number of functions into a single object helps us organize and understand large programs. Instead of trying to comprehend a system that has hundreds or thousands of functions, we humans do much better if the system features only a couple dozen software components. In a game program, for example, we would naturally create separate subsystems for players, landscapes, physics, messaging, equipment, graphics, and so on, each as a (possibly large) object.

The second reason for including functions as properties is to make programs *object oriented* rather than *process oriented*. For example, instead of thinking in terms of functions that *operate on* shapes, we can store functions as *properties of* shapes. Placing the functions inside the objects keeps the focus on the objects, making the functions play the role of *behaviors* of the objects:

```
var circle = {
    radius: 5,
    area: function () {return Math.PI * this.radius * this.radius;},
    circumference: function () {return 2 * Math.PI * this.radius;}
};
alert(circle.area());            // Alerts 78.53981633974483
circle.radius = 1.5;
alert(circle.circumference());   // Alerts 9.42477796076938
```

This example introduces the JavaScript *this* expression, a rather powerful expression that can have different meanings depending on its context. When the containing object is referenced in a call (such as `circle.area()` in the preceding example), `this` refers to the containing object.

Properties that are functions using the `this` expression are called *methods*. Thus we say our circle has an `area` method and a `circumference` method.

Review and Practice

1. What are the two main reasons for using function values for object properties?

2. What is the difference between process orientation and object orientation?

3. What does the following script alert? Why?

   ```
   var x = 2;
   var p = {x:1, y:1, z: function () {return x + this.x;}};
   alert(p.z());
   ```

4. What is a method, in your own words? Give an example.

5.5.3   Constructors

In the previous section we defined a single circle object. What if we needed many circles? We could write a function to produce them:

```
// BAD CODE - DO NOT DO THIS
var Circle = function (r) {
    return {
        radius: r,
        area: function () {
            return Math.PI * this.radius * this.radius;
        },
        circumference: function () {
                return 2 * Math.PI * this.radius;}
        };
};
var c1 = Circle(2);      // Creates a circle with radius 2.
var c2 = Circle(10);     // Creates a circle with radius 10.
alert(c2.area());        // Alerts 314.1592653589793
```

This looks okay on the surface, but this code has a serious flaw. Every time we create a circle, we create extra area and circumference methods, too. Figure 5.3 shows the result of creating the preceding two circles.

When we create multiple circles, we waste large amounts of memory storing redundant copies of area and circumference functions—a bad thing because memory is a finite resource. When your script runs out of memory, it crashes. Fortunately, JavaScript's prototypes, which we encountered back in Section 3.6.3, give us a solution:

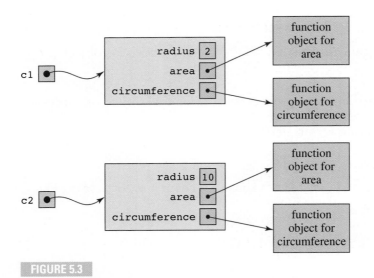

FIGURE 5.3

Improper creation of multiple copies of the same function.

```
/*
 * A prototypical circle, designed to be the prototype for all circles
 * created with the Circle function below.
 */
var protoCircle = {
    radius: 1,
    area: function () {return Math.PI * this.radius * this.radius;},
    circumference: function () {return 2 * Math.PI * this.radius;}
};

/*
 * Creates a circle with a given radius.
 */
var Circle = function (r) {
    var c = Object.create(protoCircle);
    c.radius = r;
    return c;
};
```

Each circle created by calling `Circle` gets its own `radius` property and a hidden link to a single, shared prototype containing the (sole!) `area` and `circumference` functions. That is well and good. One small flaw remains, though:

we used *two* global variables, `Circle` and `protoCircle`. It would be better to have only one, so let's make our prototypical circle be a property of the `Circle` function.[4] We now have a pattern for conveniently defining a set of objects of the same "type":

```
/*
 * A circle data type.  Synopsis:
 *
 * var c = Circle(5);
 * c.radius => 5
 * c.area() => 25pi
 * c.circumference() => 10pi
 */
var Circle = function (r) {
    var circle = Object.create(Circle.prototype);
    circle.radius = r;
    return circle;
};

Circle.prototype = {
    area: function () {return Math.PI * this.radius * this.radius;},
    circumference: function () {return 2 * Math.PI * this.radius;}
};
```

We can apply this pattern to produce a function for creating rectangles:

```
/*
 * A rectangle data type.  Synopsis:
 *
 * var r = Rectangle(5, 4);
 * r.width => 5
 * r.height => 4
 * r.area() => 20
 * r.perimeter() => 18
 */
var Rectangle = function (w, h) {
    var rectangle = Object.create(Rectangle.prototype);
    rectangle.width = w;
    rectangle.height = h;
```

---

[4]We could have made the function a property of the prototypical circle, too, or even created a new object of which both the creation function and the prototype are properties. You will explore these alternative approaches in the exercises at the end of the chapter.

```
        return rectangle;
};

Rectangle.prototype = {
    area: function () {return this.width * this.height;},
    perimeter: function () {return 2 * (this.width * this.height);}
};
```

Do you notice quite a bit of commonality (repetition) between our circle and rectangle examples? For each kind of object, (1) we create a prototype object, (2) we link the prototype to the objects we create with the construction function, and (3) we arrange for the function to explicitly return the object being created. Wouldn't it be nice if these three things were handled automatically somehow, to save us from repeating similar code for every kind of object? There is indeed a way.

First of all, you need not explicitly create prototype objects that you wish to share among a group of objects. Every function object in JavaScript automatically has a **prototype** property—they're free! As mentioned in Section 5.5.1, **prototype** is the second of the two predefined properties on functions; the first was **length**. Whenever a function is defined, its **prototype** property is initialized to a brand-new object. (This brand-new object has a property of its own, called **constructor**, but we won't be using it in this text.) Figure 5.4 shows a freshly created function for computing the average of two values.

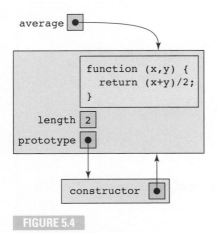

FIGURE 5.4

A JavaScript function object.

Secondly, when using a function to create objects, you don't have to explicitly link up the prototypes; nor do you have to return the newly created object, provided you use the magical operator **new**. When you prefix a function call with **new**, three things happen:

1. JavaScript creates a brand-new empty object and calls the function with the expression **this** referring to the new object.

2. The newly constructed object's prototype is set to the **prototype** property of the function.[5]

3. The new object is automatically returned from the function (unless you explicitly make the function return something else).

These rules look complicated, but an example should help make things clear. The following code features a circle-making function and shows how circle instances are created by calling the function with the **new** operator.

```
/*
 * A circle data type.   Synopsis:
 *
 * var c = new Circle(5);
 * c.radius => 5
 * c.area() => 25pi
 * c.circumference() => 10pi
 */
var Circle = function (r) {
    this.radius = r;
};

Circle.prototype.area = function () {
    return Math.PI * this.radius * this.radius;
};

Circle.prototype.circumference = function () {
    return 2 * Math.PI * this.radius;
};
```

---

[5]This can be confusing! The **prototype** property of a function object is not the prototype of the function; rather it is the prototype for all the objects *created by* the function.

```
var c1 = new Circle(2);    // Creates a circle with radius 2.
var c2 = new Circle(10);   // Creates a circle with radius 10.
alert(c2.area());          // Alerts 314.1592653589793.
```

The script begins with the creation of a function object, which we will refer to with the variable `Circle`. Like all functions, it is created with a second object serving as the value of its `prototype` property. We then add `area` and `circumference` functions to the prototype object. Next, we create a couple circle objects with the incantation `new Circle`. The operator `new` creates new objects whose prototype is `Circle.prototype`, giving us the situation in Figure 5.5.

A function such as `Circle` that is designed to be called with `new` is called a *constructor*. By convention, we name constructors with an initial capital letter, and we omit `return` statements, preferring to use JavaScript's automatic return of the newly constructed object. The reason for the capital letter convention will be given in the next section.

Aside: Because the operator `new` does so many things "behind the scenes," it takes some effort to understand. Constructor calls lacking a `return` statement are now returning objects instead of the usual `undefined`, and the newly created object's prototype is magically assigned to an object that we never explicitly created.

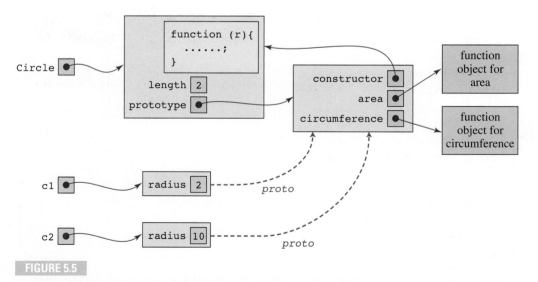

FIGURE 5.5

A constructor function and two created instances.

The indirectness of this approach is perhaps one reason why `Object.create` was added to the JavaScript language (as part of ECMAScript 5). Some JavaScript programmers suggest you exclusively use `Object.create` for new scripts, as it makes the link between objects and their prototypes more explicit. Explicit code is generally easier to read, easier to understand, and easier to work with. Another reason for sticking to `Object.create`, though, is philosophical: we can think simply in terms of objects (some of which are prototypical objects), rather than introducing additional notions of "types."[6]

We cannot dismiss constructors and the operator `new`, however. These have been around since the beginning of JavaScript, are used in thousands of existing scripts, and are the means by which many of the built-in objects of JavaScript are built, so you need to understand them. You will gain familiarity through practice; for now, review the basic steps:

To create and use a custom data type, such as for circles, using operator `new`:

1. **Write a constructor function that initializes properties unique to each circle via assignments such as `this.radius = r`.**

2. **Assign methods shared by all circles to `Circle.prototype`.**

3. **Create specific circles by invoking `new Circle()`. The prototype for each circle that is so created will automatically be `Circle.prototype`.**

Review and Practice

1. Explain how JavaScript's mechanism for prototypes simplifies the creation of new "types" of objects.

2. What is the significance of the `constructor` property in prototype objects? (*Hint*: What are the values of `c1.constructor` and `c2.constructor` in Figure 5.5?)

---

[6]This philosophical discussion is beyond the scope of this text. If you find it interesting, it is covered in many articles and texts on programming languages. Search for phrases such as "prototypal inheritance versus classical inheritance."

5.6   Context

In the previous section, we covered two of the four roles played by the expression `this`. We are now ready to give a complete discussion of this very useful and flexible expression. We say it is a flexible expression because its meaning depends on the *context* in which it is used.

Rule 1: When used at the top level of a script or within a global function, `this` refers to the global object—the object of which global variables are properties:

```
this.x = 2;            // Set the x property of the global object.
alert(x);              // Alerts 2.

var f = function (x) {
    this.y = x + 1;
};
f(2);                  // f is called as a global function.
alert(y);              // Alerts 3.
```

Rule 2: When used in a method body, `this` refers to the object through which the method was called. (We saw this earlier.)

```
var f = function (x) {
    this.y = x + 1;
};
var a = {y: 10, op: f};
var b = {y: 20, increment: f};

a.op(100);             // f is called through a.
alert(a.y);            // Alerts 101.
b.increment(43);       // f is called through b.
alert(b.y);            // Alerts 44.
```

Rule 3: When used in a function that was called with the `new` operator, `this` refers to the newly created object. (We saw this earlier as well.)

```
var Point = function (x, y) {
    this.x = x;
    this.y = y;
};
var p = new Point(4, -5);   // New point created.
var q = Point(3, 8);        // DANGER! DANGER! Sets global x and y!
```

That last line shows that we must be careful to always call constructors with **new** lest we clobber existing global variables and cause the script to run amok. To reduce the chance of these accidents, JavaScript programmers capitalize the names of constructors. Tools (such as our friend JSLint) can scan the code, looking for calls of functions with capitalized names not prefixed with **new**. If it finds any, the programmer can be scolded.

Rule 4: The function methods **apply** and **call** allow you to specifically define the object you want to use as the value of **this**.

```
var f = function (a, b, c) {this.x += a + b + c;};
var a = {x: 1, y: 2};
f.apply(a, [10, 20, 5]);   // Calls f(10, 20, 5), using 'a' as this.
f.call(a, 3, 4, 15);       // Calls f(3, 4, 15), using 'a' as this.
alert(a.x);                // Alerts 58.
```

```
var Point = function (x, y) {
    this.x = x;
    this.y = y;
};
var p = {z: 3};
Point.apply(p, [2, 9]);    // Now p is {x: 2, y: 9, z: 3}
Point.call(p, 10, 4);      // Now p is {x: 10, y: 4, z: 3}
```

These methods allow us to borrow (or hijack) existing methods and constructors and reuse them for objects other than those for which they were intended. The methods differ only slightly: **call** passes along its arguments, while **apply** bundles up the arguments in an array. We will see how they are used to implement a programming technique known as *classical inheritance* in Section 7.2.2.

Review and Practice

1. What are the four uses of `this`?

2. What is the difference between `apply` and `call`?

3. What does the following script alert (and why)?

```
var p = {x: 1, f: function (y) {this.x += y; return this.x;}};
var q = {x: 5};
alert(p.f(1));
alert(p.f.call(q, 3));
```

5.7   Higher-Order Functions

By now you have realized that functions save you from writing the same code over and over. If you had to, say, encrypt a large batch of credit card numbers, you certainly wouldn't duplicate the 50 or so lines of encryption code for each credit card. You would write a single encryption function with the credit card number as a parameter. Now your code follows the DRY (**D**on't **R**epeat **Y**ourself) principle—a good thing. When you repeat yourself, and you need to correct a mistake in your code, you would have to make the change in every repeated code fragment. This is not only time consuming but error prone—can you be sure you've made *all* of the required changes?

Sometimes, code repetition is more subtle. Consider these two functions:

```
var squareAll = function (a) {
    var result = [];
    for (var i = 0; i < a.length; i += 1) {
        result[i] = a[i] * a[i];
    }
    return result;
};
```

```
var capitalizeAll = function (a) {
    var result = [];
    for (var i = 0; i < a.length; i += 1) {
```

```
            result[i] = a[i].toUpperCase();
        }
    return result;
}
```

These two functions differ only in one small way. They both apply a function to each element in an array and collect the results; however, the first squares the elements while the latter capitalizes them. Can we code the common structure once and parameterize it by the small difference? JavaScript makes this very easy; the small difference is simply the function that gets applied to each array element!

```
/*
 * collect([a0, a1, a2, ...], f) returns the array
 * [f(a0), f(a1), f(a2), ...].  That is, it collects the
 * values obtained by applying f to all elements of a.
 */
var collect = function (a, f) {
    var result = [];
    for (var i = 0; i < a.length; i += 1) {
        result[i] = f(a[i]);
    }
    return result;
}
```

The actual function you perform on each array element (e.g., squaring or capitalizing) is now passed as an argument:

```
var square = function (x) {return x * x;};
var capitalize = function (x) {return x.toUpperCase();};

var squareAll = function (a) {return collect(a, square);};
var capitalizeAll = function (a) {return collect(a, capitalize);};
```

You can even get away without making variable declarations for the little **square** and **capitalize** functions:

```
var squareAll = function (a) {
    return collect(a, function (x) {return x * x;});
}
```

```
var capitalizeAll = function (a) {
    return collect(a, function (x) {return x.toUpperCase();});
}
```

Let's see our functions in action:

```
alert(squareAll([-2, 5, 0]));          // Alerts 4,25,0
alert(capitalizeAll(['hi', 'ho']));    // Alerts HI,HO
```

A function *f* that accepts another function *g* as an argument (and calls *g* within its body) is called a *higher-order function*. The function `collect` is a higher-order function. So is the built-in `sort` function. You may recall from Section 3.7 how `a.sort()` sorts array `a` alphabetically rather than numerically. You can, however, pass a *comparison function* to `sort` to make it sort differently. A comparison function is a two-argument function you write yourself to return a negative value when the first argument is less than the second, 0 if they are equal, and a positive value if the first is larger:

```
var a = [3, 6, 10, 1, 40, 25, 8, 73];
alert(a.sort());                                    // Alphabetically.
alert(a.sort(function (x, y) { return x - y; }));   // Numeric
                                                    // ascending.
alert(a.sort(function (x, y) { return y - x; }));   // Numeric
                                                    // descending.
```

Because you can tell the `sort` function to compare elements any way you please, you can write code to sort a set of objects in several different ways:

```
var team = [
    {id: 5, name: 'Paolo', age: 23, salary: 79850},
    {id: 9, name: 'Carla', age: 82, salary: 95226},
    {id: 1, name: 'Gretchen', age: 19, salary: 27500},
    {id: 7, name: 'Svetlana', age: 55, salary: 179200},
    {id: 2, name: 'Kemi', age: 69, salary: 99850},
];
```

```
// Sort by age ascending
alert(team.sort(function (p, q) { return p.age - q.age; }));

// Sort by salary descending
alert(team.sort(function (p, q) { return q.salary - p.salary; }));

// Sort by name ascending
alert(team.sort(function (p, q) {
    return p.name < q.name ? -1 : p.name > q.name ? 1 : 0
}));
```

We have just shown that functions *can* be passed to other functions, but we haven't really said *why* this matters, beyond the fact that it helps us to avoid duplicating some code—which is often a good enough reason. We will see in Chapter 6 that passing functions is common when setting up timers and communicating with user actions on a web page. It also happens to be one of the most dominant programming paradigms in artificial intelligence programming. And, as described in [Spo06], it aids the construction of massively large, distributed applications—something we will have more to say about in Section 10.4.

The term *higher-order function* applies not only to functions that accept functions as arguments but also to functions that return functions. These kinds of functions occur often in advanced JavaScript programming, but we can give a simple example now. Here are three simple functions:

```
var withParentheses = function (s) {return "(" + s + ")";};
var withBrackets = function (s) {return "[" + s + "]";};
var withBraces = function (s) {return "{" + s + "}";};
```

These functions are quite similar. How might we refactor them? Each of these functions can be manufactured (by another function) simply by telling the manufacturer which delimiters to use:

```
var delimitWith = function (prefix, suffix) {
    return function (s) {return prefix + s + suffix;}
};
var withParentheses = delimitWith("(", ")");
var withBrackets = delimitWith("[", "]");
var withBraces = delimitWith("{", "}");
```

The three functions `withParentheses`, `withBrackets`, and `withBraces` are called *closures*. Roughly speaking, a JavaScript closure is a function whose body uses variables from an en*clos*ing function. Closures play an integral role in some very sophisticated JavaScript structures, such as sequence generators and modules. We will study them further in Chapters 7 and 10.

Review and Practice

1. Define the term *higher-order function*.

2. Using the `collect` function from this section, write and test a function that negates each of the elements in an array.

3. Write a function that sorts an array of circle objects from page 175 by increasing the radius value.

4. Write a function with a single parameter x that returns a function that adds x to the new function's sole parameter.

5.8   Function Declarations versus Function Expressions*

One of JavaScript's great strengths—and to many computer scientists one of its most beautiful features—is that its functions are values "just like" Booleans, numbers, strings, arrays, and all objects. They can be assigned to variables, stored as properties of an object, passed as parameters, and returned from functions.[7] Hopefully you are not surprised at this! We mention it only because many other languages deny many of these capabilities to functions.

When we assign a function expression to a variable, as in

```
var circleArea = function (x) {
    return Math.PI * x * x;
};
```

---

[7]The technical term for values that can be used in all these ways is *first-class* value.

we make the "functions are just like other values" aspect of JavaScript apparent. But as mentioned at the beginning of the chapter, there is another way to create function objects:

```
function circleArea(x) {
    return Math.PI * x * x;
}
```

The latter form, officially known as a *function declaration*, works much the same as the former: it declares (somewhat magically) a variable called `circleArea` and initializes the variable with a function value. But these two forms of definition differ:

1. Function declarations cannot appear in certain places in your code.

2. The variable introduced by a function declaration obeys different scope rules than normal variables. (You can see exactly how in one of the exercises at the end of the chapter.)

In particular, function declarations can only appear globally in a script or at the "top level" of a function body. They are not permitted inside of a statement.[8] The code

```
if (true) {
    function successor() {return x + 1;}     // NOT ALLOWED
}
```

should be a syntax error according to the official ECMAScript specification [ECM09]. Alas, if only it were that easy! The specification notes on page 96:

> Several widely used implementations of ECMAScript are known to support the use of FunctionDeclaration as a Statement. However there are significant and irreconcilable variations among the implementations in the semantics applied to such FunctionDeclarations. Because of these

---

[8] Here are the gory details: A script is a sequence of statements and function declarations [ECM09, p. 100]. Ditto for function bodies. However, the block statement, used in structures like the `for`, `while`, and `try` statements, may contain statements only.

irreconcilable differences, the use of a FunctionDeclaration as a Statement results in code that is not reliably portable among implementations. It is recommended that ECMAScript implementations either
disallow this usage of FunctionDeclaration or issue a warning when
such a usage is encountered.

The moral here is never put a function declaration inside a statement, even if your
browser allows it.

Because of the restrictions on the placement of function declarations, the specialized scoping rules, and the fact that function declarations obscure the definition
of variables and make functions look different than other types of objects, we prefer to avoid them. Function expressions can *always* be used and, as we will see
later in this text, are all but required in most patterns of module creation, web
programming, and network programming. Although function declarations may be
convenient, they add nothing to the language's expressivity and are just "one more
thing to learn."

Whether or not you choose to use function declarations, their existence affects
the way we write certain expressions. Because function declarations begin with
the word `function`, the designers of JavaScript decided that no statement may
begin with this word, lest the reader be confused. This means if you want to *call*
a function expression directly (in which case we say the function is an *anonymous
function*), you must put parentheses around the call:

```
You type:    function (x) {return x + 5}(10)
Response:    SyntaxError on line 1: syntax error
You type:    (function (x) {return x + 5}(10))
Response:    15
```

But why would anyone define a function just to call it right away? The specific
example just shown is not useful at all, but this programming pattern is frequently
used to do some rather sophisticated things. We will encounter it for the first time
in Section 7.4.2.

Review and Practice

1. What are two reasons to avoid using function declarations in your scripts?

2. Experiment with anonymous function calls. Does JavaScript allow you to
   parenthesize both the entire call and just the function value in the call?
   Why or why not?

Chapter Summary

- A function value is a parameterized block of code that can be run (or "called") as often as you wish.

- When calling a function, we pass *arguments* to its *parameters*. Excess parameters are initialized to **undefined**. Functions can return results to the caller via a **return** statement. If a **return** statement is never executed, the function returns **undefined**.

- JavaScript functions are values and thus can be assigned to variables, stored in object properties, passed as arguments to other functions, and returned from functions.

- It is good programming practice to comment a function with *what* the function does, not *how* it does what it does.

- When writing functions that process objects, you must decide whether you want the function to change the properties of its object arguments or return new objects.

- JavaScript variables have either global scope or function (local) scope.

- JavaScript functions have two properties, **length** and **prototype**. The **prototype** object is used to store properties accessible to all objects created with the function, effectively allowing the definition of new types. You can add additional properties to functions.

- Functions that are properties of objects and that refer to other properties of the object via the **this** expression are called methods. Methods are a core concept in object-oriented programming.

- Higher-order functions—functions that take functions as parameters or return functions—simplify several programming tasks and can reduce the amount of common code in scripts.

- Functions can be defined with function declarations, by using function expressions directly, or by assigning function expressions to variables or object properties. Function declarations, while convenient, cannot be used in certain contexts, have less intuitive scoping rules, and obscure the fact that functions are values like any other.

Exercises

1. Write a function that returns the larger of its two arguments. For example, the call `larger(-2, 10)` should return 10.

2. Write a function that returns the average of its two arguments. For example, the call `average(-2, 10)` should return 4.

3. Write a function that returns the average of all of the items in an array. For example, `average([4, 5, 7, 2])` should return 4.5.

4. Explain the result of running this script, using the word "associativity" in your answer:

```
var cubeOf = function (x) {return x * x * x;};
alert("There are " + cubeOf(3) - 1 + " cubes in a Rubik's Cube");
```

5. Write a function that accepts two numbers and returns a random number between the two values.

6. Write a function that accepts three values and returns the median. The median of three values is the value that is greater than or equal to one of the other values and less than or equal to the remaining value.

7. Write a function that returns the number of zeros in a given array. For example, the call `numberOfZeros([4, 0, false, 5, 0])` should return 2.

8. Write a function that returns the number of occurrences of a given character in a string. For example, given the string `"Rat-a-tat-tat"` and the character `t`, your function should return 5.

9. The original version of the `balanceAfter` function in this chapter produced the value `NaN` at $p = 1000$, $r = 0.05$, $t = 10$, and $n = -0.02$. However, calculators on major search engines such as Google and Wolfram Alpha return a

perfectly good number. Search for the following terms on Google and record your answers:

(a) `1000*(1+(0.05/12))^(12*10)`

(b) `1000*(1+(0.05/1))^(1*10)`

(c) `1000*(1+(0.05/-2))^(-2*10)`

(d) `1000*(1+(0.05/-0.02))^(-0.02*10)`

In these searches, Google is telling you the ending balances for $1000 of principal after 10 years at 5% for compounding 12, 1, −2, and −0.02 times per year, respectively. Why can Google give you a better answer than `NaN` for $n = -0.02$?

10. Use the Wolfram Alpha decision engine (`http://www.wolframalpha.com/`) to determine why the original `balanceAfter` function from this chapter gives troublesome results for negative numbers of compounding periods. Ask Wolfram Alpha to graph the function $1000 * (1 + 0.05/n)^{10n}$ and explain what you are seeing for negative values of n.

11. What is produced by the `sum` function from this chapter when given an argument that is not an array? Is this worrisome? Discuss whether or not the function should be rewritten to check for a nonarray argument.

12. Explain, in your own words, the difference between the functions `uppercaseStrings` and `uppercaseAll` from this chapter. Which do you like better? Which of the two would seem to require "more work" for the JavaScript engine to evaluate? Which of the two seems to require "more work" for the programmer who needs to use the functions?

13. How would you go about rewriting the `max` function from this chapter to throw an exception when it discovers that two of its array elements are incomparable?

14. Search for and read a couple articles on refactoring. Explain the concept in your own words.

15. Test the `isPrime` function in a shell on the following arguments: `undefined`, `null`, `false`, `true`, `"4"`, `"2"`, `" 2 "`, and `[19]`.

16. The following is a modified but incorrect version of the Fibonacci generator
    we saw in this chapter. Run this script. Look at the last value generated.
    Why is it not the sum of the previous two values?

```
var fibonacciSequence = function () {
    var f = [0, 1];
    while (f[f.length - 1] < 9E15) {
        f.push(f[f.length - 1] + f[f.length - 2]);
    }
    return f;
};
```

Fix this script so it collects as many Fibonacci numbers as can be precisely
represented in JavaScript.

17. Explain, in detail, what is alerted by this script:

```
var x = 5;
var f = function () {alert(x); var x = 10; alert(x);};
f();
alert(x);
```

18. Explain, in detail, what happens when this script is run:

```
var shout = function () {
    var message = "HEY YOU";
    alert(message);
};
shout();
alert(message);
```

19. Explain, in detail, what happens when you run this script:

```
alert("Hello");
var alert = 2;
alert("World");
```

20. Here is one approach to defining a function, called `nextFib`, that behaves as follows: The first time it is called, it returns 1. The next time it is called, it returns 1. Then 2. Then 3. Then 5. Each time it is called, it returns the next Fibonacci number.

```
var a = 1; var b = 1;
var nextFib = function () {
    var old_a = a; a = b; b = old_a + b; return old_a;
};
```

What happens if between successive calls someone were to overwrite the values of global variables `a` or `b`?

21. Here is another version of the `nextFib` function from the previous exercise.

```
var nextFib = (function () {
    var a = 1;
    var b = 1;
    return function () {
        var old_a = a; a = b; b = old_a + b; return old_a;
    }
}());
```

Does this work? Does it solve the security hole illustrated in the previous exercise? Why or why not?

22. Given

```
var Point = function (x, y) {
    this.x = x;
    this.y = y;
};
Point.prototype.distanceToOrigin = function () {
    return Math.sqrt(this.x * this.x + this.y * this.y);
};
var p = new Point(-4, 3);
```

What are the values of the following?

(a) `p.x`

(b) `p.y`

    (c) `p.distanceToOrigin()`

    (d) `p.constructor`

23. Extend the `Point` object (and its prototype) in the previous exercise to a data type for three-dimensional points.

24. Rewrite the `Point` type from the previous exercise so that it uses `Object.create` instead of constructors, as follows. Create an object called `Point` with two properties. The first, called `prototype`, will be the prototype for all subsequently created points; it will hold the distance to origin method. The second, called `create`, returns a new point object—created with `Object.create`—whose prototype will be `Point.prototype`.

25. Write a JavaScript constructor function for points on the earth's surface. Each instance should have a latitude and a longitude. Validate the parameters to the constructor so that latitudes are in the range $-90\ldots90$ and longitudes are in the range $-180\ldots180$. In the prototype, supply the following methods:

    (a) `inArcticCircle`

    (b) `inAntarcticCircle`

    (c) `inTropics`

    (d) `antipode`

26. Implement the point type in the previous exercise using `Object.create` instead of constructors, as follows. Define an object called `Point`, which will be the prototypical point on the earth's surface; it should contain the four methods defined in the previous exercise. Add another method, called `create`, that will construct a new point—with `Object.create`—whose prototype is `Point` itself.

27. Write a constructor for movie objects. A movie has a title, an MPAA rating, a list of directors, a list of producers, a studio, and a release date.

28. If you have created a constructor function f, is f.`prototype` the prototype of f? If not, what is it the prototype of, if anything? Do you think that the name of this property was well chosen? If so, why? If not, why not?

29. Have a discussion, in comfortable chairs or in front of a whiteboard, comparing various mechanisms for creating new "types" of objects. Consider:

- The use of `Object.create` inside a creation function, using a prototype that is a property of the creation function

- The definition of a prototypical object containing a creation method that invokes `Object.create` to make itself the prototype of newly created instances

- The traditional approach with constructors and operator `new`

If you are a novice programmer, revisit this exercise after a year or so of study, and invite an experienced JavaScript programmer to your discussion.

30. JavaScript comes with a built-in object called `Date`, which is a constructor. Research this function and answer the following:

    (a) What does the expression `new Date()` produce?

    (b) What does the expression `new Date(2009, 0, 20)` produce?

    (c) If `d1` and `d2` refer to date objects, what does the expression `d1.valueOf() - d2.valueOf()` produce?

31. The JavaScript `typeof` operator, which we saw back in Section 3.9, produces the string `"object"` for `null` and for arrays. Write a function called `type` that behaves like the `typeof` operator except that it returns `"null"` for `null` and `"array"` for arrays. You will have to do some research to determine the best way to tell whether or not a value really is an array.

32. Write a function called `twice` that takes in a function f and a value x and returns $f(f(x))$.

33. Define a function called `toTheEighthPower` that takes in a value x and returns x^8. Use the `square` function defined in this chapter and the `twice` function you defined in the previous exercise.

34. Suppose your friend tried to implement the `squareAll` function from this chapter using the incorrect expression `collect(a, square())`. Explain why this is wrong.

35. Consider

```
alert(collect([-2, 5, 0], function (x) {return x * x;}));
```

Is this readable? Useful?

36. If you have a modern (ES5-compliant) JavaScript engine, then you will have some built-in higher-order functions that you can apply to your arrays. One of these is forEach. Try to determine the meaning of this function through experimentation. Run the following script and explain its output:

```
var a = ["red", "orange", "yellow", "green", "blue", "violet"];
for (var c in a) {
    alert(c);
}
for (var i = 0; i < a.length; i += 1) {
    alert(a[i]);
}
a.forEach(function (c) {alert(c);});
```

37. The following is an alternative implementation of the array sum function we saw on page 156. (*Note*: It will only work on modern ES5 browsers.)

```
/*
 * Returns the sum of all the elements in an array.
 */
var sum = function (a) {
    var result = 0;
    a.forEach(function (x) {
        result += x;
    });
    return result;
};
```

Do you like this better than the implementation in the chapter? Is it easier to read and understand? Regardless of your opinion, state the significance of the fact that this alternative solution does not use the indexing variable called i in the original version. Would a human, when summing up the values in an array, consciously make use of a variable like i?

38. Suppose you were asked by an employer, teacher, or friend to write a function that determines whether a given function would ever finish or would run forever. In other words, you are asked to fill this in:

```
// Returns true f(x) finishes; false if f(x) runs forever.
var finishes = function (f, x) {
    // Fill this in...
}
```

Before attempting to implement this function, consider:

```
var p = function (g) {
    if (finishes(g, g)) {
        while (true) { }
    }
};
```

So function p takes a function g and finishes whenever g(g) runs forever, and runs forever whenever g(g) finishes. What is the meaning, then, of the call p(p)? What does this suggest about the possibility of even writing the function finishes?

39. Run each of the following scripts and record their output. (Make sure each script is run "fresh" so you don't pick up any global variables that happen to be in existence from a previous run.)

```
f();
var f = function () {alert("Hello");};
```

```
f();
function f() {alert("Hello");};
```

What does this tell you about the differences in scoping between function expressions assigned to variables and function declarations?

40. Run each of the following scripts and record their output:

```
(function () {
f();
var f = function () {alert("Hello");};
}());
```

```
(function () {
f();
function f() {alert("Hello");};
}());
```

What does this tell you about the differences in scoping between function expressions assigned to variables and function declarations?

41. In this chapter, we have only discussed how named functions are used in function declarations. It is, however, possible to assign named functions to variables. In this exercise, you will perform some explorations on this behavior. For each of the following scripts, describe the output and create a hypothesis regarding what the official language rules might be:

```
var f = function g() {alert("Okay");};
f();
g();
```

```
var f = function g(n) {
    alert(n);
    if (n > 1) {
        g(n - 1);
    }
}
f(2);
g();
```

CHAPTER 6

Events

CHAPTER CONTENTS

Introduction

Thus far, most of the scripts in this book have communicated with their users via `prompt` when requesting input and `alert` when displaying output. By using `prompt`, the script itself dictates when it is ready to receive input. *Event-driven computing* is an alternative style of interaction that emerged with the development of graphical user interfaces that places the user in control: actions, whether typed characters, mouse movements, speech, gestures, or even the passage of time, fire *events*, which the script must handle at any time.

This chapter introduces the central concepts behind event-driven computing and shows how these concepts are implemented by JavaScript on interactive web pages. We will expand our coverage of HTML, detail JavaScript's support for events, and present a case study of a complete tic-tac-toe game playable in a web browser. By the end of this chapter, you will be able to write scripts that can work with a variety of user interface elements by responding to and processing events.

6.1   User Interaction

The use of `prompt` and `alert` for user interaction is an example of the classic "input-process-output" paradigm. A program stops what it is doing, waits for a user to submit data, processes the data, and finally presents results to its user.

Event-driven computing extends the idea of "input" to *events*—things that happen while a program is running, such as keystrokes, mouse movements, speech, gestures, or even the passage of time. The concepts of "process" and "output" extend to how these events are *handled*, from the time such events are detected to the point where their effects, if any, become perceivable. Most modern applications, whether running in a web browser or natively on a desktop or mobile device, use events.

6.1.1   A Programming Paradigm Shift

Every program begins execution at its first statement, executes one statement at a time, and terminates after executing its last statement. This is readily apparent for scripts that take input via `prompt` and finish by announcing a result with `alert`. But does this fact hold for interactive programs, such as the event-driven temperature conversion program from Section 2.2.4 (see Figure 2.8)? Reexamine the *temperature.js* code, reproduced here in its entirety, with the aforementioned "beginning-to-end" notion in mind:

```
var report = function (celsius, fahrenheit) {
    document.getElementById("result").innerHTML =
        celsius + "\xb0C = " + fahrenheit + "\xb0F";
};

document.getElementById("f_to_c").onclick = function () {
    var f = document.getElementById("temperature").value;
    report((f - 32) / 1.8, f);
};

document.getElementById("c_to_f").onclick = function () {
    var c = document.getElementById("temperature").value;
    report(c, 1.8 * c + 32);
};
```

This script does nothing more than define three functions: one for displaying the output within the browser and one each for performing a temperature conversion calculation, from Celsius to Fahrenheit and vice versa. *Nothing else actually happens.* The functions aren't ever explicitly called!

Indeed, upon loading the *temperature.html* file and executing the code in *temperature.js*, that is precisely what the user perceives as happening: nothing, yet. No temperature conversions are attempted until you click either the   F to C   or the   C to F   button. But the code that waits for something to happen and then looks for the proper code to execute in response to the event is *not* part of the script; that happens *magically*.

This represents the essential paradigm shift involved in event-driven computing: event-driven programs don't *really* finish when they reach their last statement. They are written as families of functions that are defined, not called, in the explicitly written code. A hidden entity (revealed in Section 7.6.4) takes care of calling these functions at the right moment.

The study of event-driven systems tends to focus on four mechanisms:

■ Because many events are associated with visible user interface elements such as buttons, text fields, and sliders, a key component of event-driven computing is a *mechanism for defining user interface elements.*

■ Because detected events frequently refer to or modify other user interface elements within a script, a *mechanism for programmatically accessing user interface elements* should also be available.

■ Because user interface elements *respond* to events—including but not restricted to mouse clicks, mouse movement, keypresses, speech and gesture detection, keyboard focus changes, the passage of time, and the arrival of network data—event-driven systems provide a *mechanism for assigning the code that will execute* when a particular event is fired.

■ Many events are accompanied by supplementary information. For example, mouse events involve mouse coordinates and one or more mouse buttons; keyboard events involve a particular key and possibly one or more modifier keys (Shift , Alt , Control , etc.). Thus, event-driven systems provide a *mechanism for reading information pertaining to an event.*

These mechanisms appear in one form or another for any event-driven system; it is a matter of learning what form they take, exactly, for a particular technology. In this text, we will look at how these elements are implemented within web browsers—the engines that we have been using to run JavaScript.

Review and Practice

1. State, in your own words, what is meant by the "paradigm shift" in terms of how event-driven scripts are coded as opposed to the scripts you have seen prior to this chapter.

2. What mechanisms are shared by all event-driven systems, regardless of the programming language or foundational technology?

6.1.2 Events by Example: The Temperature Converter Web Page

Let's revisit the *temperature.html* web page from Chapter 2:

```html
<!doctype html>
<html>
  <head>
    <meta charset="UTF-8"/>
    <title>JavaScript Temperature Converter</title>
  </head>
  <body>
    <h1>Temperature Conversion</h1>
    <p>
      <input type="text" id="temperature" />
      <input type="button" id="f_to_c" value="F to C" />
      <input type="button" id="c_to_f" value="C to F" />
    </p>
    <!-- Computation result will go here -->
    <p id="result"></p>
    <script src="temperature.js"></script>
  </body>
</html>
```

In the web browser/JavaScript milieu, the web page plays the role of the mechanism for defining user interface elements. The file, when opened in a web browser, initially looks like the screenshot in Figure 6.1.

FIGURE 6.1

temperature.html, freshly opened.

At this point, the browser is ready for any event you might trigger. The code in *temperature.js* does not define *every* event to which the program will respond; many default event handlers are already on standby. For example, clicking within the temperature text field triggers an event for which an explicit handler was not defined in our script. The default handler for this event sets the text field as having *focus*; that is, typed keys will be sent to this text field as opposed to, say, the browser's address box or search field. Focus is typically indicated through a special border highlight and the presence of a flashing insertion point within the text field.

The third-to-last line in *temperature.html* executes the JavaScript code contained in *temperature.js*. As mentioned in Section 6.1.1, this code is really all setup—it defines three functions that do not get called until later in the life of the program's execution.

The script in *temperature.js* illustrates the mechanism for programmatically accessing user interface elements as well as the mechanism for assigning the code that will execute for certain events—the *event handlers*. The expression `document` `.getElementById("f_to_c")` accesses the F to C button within the page. The assignment of a function value to the `onclick` property of this button *registers* that function as the event handler for `click` events on that button. When this button is clicked, the event is detected and the registered function is invoked.

The function first reads the current temperature (the `value` property of the text field that is accessed via `document.getElementById("temperature")`), then assigns it to the variable `f`. It then calculates the new values for Celsius and Fahrenheit and calls the `report` function with these values as arguments. `report` takes these values, forms a new string with them, and assigns that string to the `innerHTML` property of the `result` element within the web page. Modifying `innerHTML` changes what the user sees in the web browser window. Once this event is handled, the cycle starts anew for each click of either button and for any other events that may be detected by the web browser.

The temperature converter example does not require a mechanism for reading information pertaining to an event. Examples featuring event information will appear later in the chapter.

6.2   Defining User Interface Elements

In Section 2.5, we mentioned how JavaScript was designed to be embedded in host systems such as web browsers, image editors, word processors, and similar systems. JavaScript code runs in response to events that originate from the user interface elements of these systems. While JavaScript does not natively define these elements, it does provide (quite nicely) the ability to use functions as properties of objects that correspond exactly to these user interface elements.

For example, in a web environment, the elements are provided (as we saw in Section 2.2.4) via structured documents written in HTML. These documents are either delivered over the Internet by web servers or stored on your local computer as *.html* files, then *rendered* by web browsers into the visual representations with which we are familiar. Without JavaScript, these pages are *static*—once loaded, their content does not change. The only way to change the displayed content is to click on a link, restarting the connect-and-render cycle for a new web page. With JavaScript, the web page gains the ability to trigger *changes to itself*, thus becoming *dynamic* based on the user's interaction with the content on that page.

As JavaScript is most commonly used with web browsers, we focus on the interface elements used in web applications.

6.2.1   Web Pages Are Structured Documents

Recall from Section 2.2.4 that an HTML document is a structured collection of nodes. Each node has a *type* (one of document, document type, element, text, or eight others[1]), a *value*, and, if it is an element node, a set of *attributes*. Figure 6.2

---

[1] The other node types are comment, attribute, CDATA, entity, entity reference, processing instruction, notation, and document fragment.

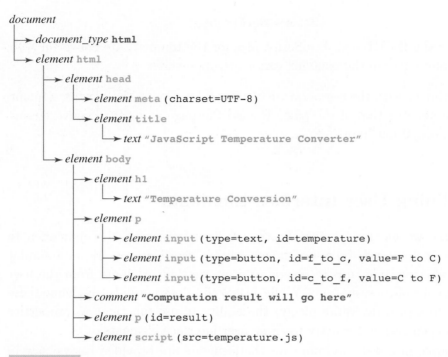

document
  → *document_type* **html**
  → *element* html
      → *element* head
          → *element* meta (charset=UTF-8)
          → *element* title
              → *text* "JavaScript Temperature Converter"
      → *element* body
          → *element* h1
              → *text* "Temperature Conversion"
          → *element* p
              → *element* input (type=text, id=temperature)
              → *element* input (type=button, id=f_to_c, value=F to C)
              → *element* input (type=button, id=c_to_f, value=C to F)
          → *comment* "Computation result will go here"
          → *element* p (id=result)
          → *element* script (src=temperature.js)

FIGURE 6.2

Internal structure of the temperature converter page.

gives the node structure for the temperature converter web page from page 201.[2]

HTML defines the set of available nodes and attributes, and the rules for constructing proper structures. The language has evolved through many versions; the current version is HTML5. You normally create HTML documents by writing sequences of characters, representing elements with *tags*: either start and end tags (e.g., `<body>` and `</body>`) or empty tags (e.g., `<meta/>`). There are two official ways to do this: the HTML syntax and the XHTML syntax. This text uses only the HTML syntax; the differences between the two are found in [W3C10a, Section 1.6].

While the complete set of rules defining the HTML syntax is quite extensive, the following should get you started:

1. Documents should begin with a document type declaration to tell the browser which flavor of HTML to expect (we have been using `<!doctype html>`, which signifies HTML5).

---

[2]We have simplified the tree just a tiny bit by removing all the little text nodes that contain nothing but spaces and newline characters that tend to live between elements.

2. The web page proper consists of a single `html` element, which consists of exactly two parts, in exactly this order: a `head` element followed by a `body` element.

3. The head contains information about the document, with child elements for the page title (`title`), links to other web resources (`link`), styling information (`style`), scripts (`script`), generic information (`meta`), and others. It is strongly recommended that you give, as the first subelement of `head`, a `meta` element that tells the browser in which character encoding your document is stored.[3]

4. The body contains the document's content and consists of a sequence of *block elements* such as paragraphs (`p`), headings (`h1`–`h6`), ordered lists (`ol`), unordered lists (`ul`), definition lists (`dl`), tables (`table`), data entry forms (`form`), preformatted text blocks (`pre`), block quotations (`blockquote`), scripts (`script`), generic document divisions (`div`), and more. The new HTML5 standard allows for specific document divisions, namely articles (`article`), heading groups (`hgroup`), headers (`header`), menus (`menu`), navigation sections (`nav`), asides (`aside`), and details (`details`).

5. Block elements contain text and other block elements. Runs of text can be marked up with *inline elements* to convey meaning to a reader. These include elements to denote emphasis (`em`), strong emphasis (`strong`), acronyms (`acronym`), abbreviations (`abbrev`), quotes (`q`), citations (`cite`), superscripts (`sup`), subscripts (`sub`), links to other documents (`a`, for "anchor"), generic inline spans (`span`), and more.

6. Several elements for multimedia content behave as inline elements: `img` (for images), `audio`, `video`, `object`, and `embed`. The `audio` and `video` elements are new in HTML5; `object` and `embed` are catch-all elements for browser plug-ins.

7. Some elements require subcomponents by design: ordered and unordered lists have list items (`li`); definition lists have terms (`dt`) and definitions (`dd`); tables may have a header (`thead`), body (`tbody`), and footer (`tfoot`), each of which has rows (`tr`) with cells that can be headings (`th`) or normal table data (`td`).

---

[3]We recommend writing `<meta charset="UTF-8"/>`. If you desire to know all of the details of character encodings in HTML, see `http://www.w3.org/International/questions/qa-html-encoding-declarations`.

8. Classic user interface elements include: buttons (`input type="button"` or `button`), text fields (`input type="text"`), drop-down boxes or lists (`select`), multiline text boxes (`textarea`), radio buttons (`input type="radio"`), checkboxes (`input type="checkbox"`), and more. HTML5 introduces `output`, `keygen`, `progress`, `meter`, and `command`, as well as additional `input` types such as `number`, `date`, and `email`.

9. A few elements can appear in either the head or the body, and a few elements can act as either block or inline elements.

There's more, of course; the ultimate authorities on all rules governing these elements are the complete *specifications* published by the Worldwide Web Consortium (W3C), such as for HTML5 [W3C10a] and for the older HTML 4.01 [W3C99] and XHTML 1.0 [W3C02]. These specifications are indeed quite long, but many useful summaries and examples appear on the Web.

In order to keep our focus on programming, and on event-driven programming in particular, our approach to HTML in this chapter is example-driven. Instead of a broad tour of HTML, we look only at the information needed to get to the good stuff, which is event handling using JavaScript. Anything beyond that becomes the realm of web page design—related, but not requisite, to the subject of this chapter.

Review and Practice

1. What is the difference between an element and a tag?

2. What is the difference between block and inline elements?

3. Draw a tree diagram for the temperature converter web page in Section 6.1.2.

6.2.2   Elements That Produce User Interface Controls

Since our treatment of HTML in this chapter is directed toward event-driven programming, we go right to the elements that play starring roles in building user interface elements into a web page.

The input Element

The input element defines web page components that look and work like many of the standard controls and widgets that can be found in current graphical user interfaces: buttons, text fields, and checkboxes, among others. The element's type attribute, specified as type="*type keyword*" within the element's start tag, determines the kind of user interface control that appears on the page. Some frequently used input types follow:

- type="button" produces a standard push button. The button's label (the text inside the control) is defined by adding a value attribute to the tag:

```
<input type="button" value="Roll Dice" />
```

The latest web standards also have a button element, which is equivalent to <input type="button"> but looks more intuitive (see Exercise 3 at the end of the chapter for more on button):

```
<button>Roll Dice</button>
```

- type="text" produces a standard text field, into which you can type whatever value you would like. For this type of input, the value attribute defines an initial value for the text field, if any:

```
<input type="text" value="Mumbai" />
```

The preceding tag produces the text field only; such fields are frequently accompanied by labels indicating the expected value, such as *First Name:* or *Phone Number:*. These labels can be included as plain text preceding the input tag. They can also be given an explicit connection using a label element:

```
<label for="firstNameField">First name:</label>
<input type="text" id="firstNameField" value="John" />
```

The label element behaves like any other text, with the exception that it is "bound" to the control that is identified in the for attribute. Thus, the control itself needs to be given an identifier using the `id` attribute. The web browser takes care of matching the IDs and ensuring that clicking on the label behaves like clicking on the associated control. You will see later on that giving *every* control an identifier using the `id` attribute is generally a good habit anyway (and frequently necessary), so this does not add much more work than you might initially expect.

■ `type="number"` produces a text field that restricts its input to numeric values. Some web browsers also provide a "spinner" control with this input type that lets users nudge the current value up or down. Additional attributes let you specify constraints on which numbers to accept, such as minimum and maximum values.

■ `type="password"` works like a text field but hides what the user types in order to shield passwords or sensitive data that need to be hidden from casual onlookers.

■ `type="checkbox"` produces a standard checkbox, typically rendered as a square control that can be checked or unchecked. An `input` tag with this type produces the control only; label text requires a `label` element, used in the same way as the `label` element for text fields. Thus, the complete checkbox markup looks like this:

```
<input type="checkbox" id="awakeCheck" />
<label for="awakeCheck">Are you awake?</label>
```

Label elements are more important for checkboxes and radio buttons than text fields, since users typically expect to be able to click on these controls' text in order to toggle the control.

■ `type="radio"` produces a standard radio button, typically rendered as a round control that is either activated or not. Like `type="checkbox"`, radio buttons need an associated `label` element for explanatory text.

Radio buttons differ from checkboxes in that they are meant to supply one of many mutually exclusive choices, such as for the answers to a multiple-choice question. Activating one radio button is supposed to deactivate all other radio buttons within the same family of choices.

To form this group affiliation, the `input` element should be given a `name` attribute. Radio buttons with the same `name` value will be considered to be part of the same group of options, and will therefore coordinate their values as the user clicks among them:

```
<p>Are you animal, vegetable, or mineral?</p>
<p><input type="radio" name="kind" id="animalRadio" />
  <label for="animalRadio">Animal</label></p>
<p><input type="radio" name="kind" id="vegetableRadio" />
  <label for="vegetableRadio">Vegetable</label></p>
<p><input type="radio" name="kind" id="mineralRadio" />
  <label for="mineralRadio">Mineral</label></p>
```

Additional keywords are accepted for `type`, but because our approach is "need to know," we will leave an exhaustive list to the many HTML references that are available.

The `select` Element

User interface controls that involve lists of choices can be included in a web page using the `select` element. The `select` element itself serves as a container for the overall list. Individual choices within the list are indicated using multiple `option` elements, one for each choice:[4]

```
<select>
  <option>Charles Babbage</option>
  <option>Ada Lovelace</option>
  <option>Alan Turing</option>
  <option>John von Neumann</option>
  <option>Kurt G&ouml;del</option>
</select>
```

The `select` element appears as a drop-down menu by default. If a `size="`*item count*`"` attribute is added, the element appears as a list whose height will accommodate the given number of items. The web browser provides a scroll bar if the number of `options` in the `select` element exceeds the given `size`.

---

[4]The `&ouml;` construct produces the ö symbol in web browsers. The last item in the list thus appears as "Kurt Gödel" when rendered.

Another important variant in the `select` element is the `multiple` attribute, which takes only the value `multiple` (easy enough to remember). If `multiple= "multiple"` is included in the `select` element's start tag, the resulting list will support multiple selection; that is, more than one `option` in the list can be selected at the same time.

The `textarea` Element

The last user interface element that we are presenting in this section is `textarea`, which is used for editing larger chunks of text, consisting of multiple lines. The `textarea` element accepts `rows` and `cols` attributes to determine its size on the web page. In addition, the `textarea` can be prefilled by including text between the element's start and end tags:

```
<textarea rows="5" cols="40">The last user interface element that we
are presenting in this section is textarea, which is used for editing
larger chunks of text, consisting of multiple lines.  The textarea
element accepts rows and cols attributes to determine its size on the
web page.</textarea>
```

Line breaks in the HTML source translate to the `textarea`, so you will need to keep default text on a single line if you want it to wrap "naturally" within the user interface control that appears on the web page.

Content and Container Elements

One last note on web page elements: Elements that produce user interface controls do not have the monopoly on events in HTML. Content and container elements can also detect and handle events, so we make brief mention of some of them here.

When rendered on a web page, these elements appear primarily as blocks or compositions of text and images—the stuff of web document content. However, they can still tell, for example, when a mouse moves over them or when they are clicked. This opens the possibility for some innovative and interesting means of interaction.

You have already seen a couple of these elements: p, for "paragraph," is a catch-all element for holding any text that can be construed as a traditional paragraph. Accordingly, the web browser default for displaying the text within a p element strongly resembles a paragraph: a block of word-wrapped text, with space above and below the text block. h1 to h6, for "heading," constitute the default outlining element for a web page—thus the numbering of distinct variants from 1 to 6. h1 constitutes the highest-level (broadest) sections of a document, with h2 to h6 marking further subsections.

The "container" elements div and span do not imply any particular type of content the way p and h1–h6 do. Instead, they serve to group other elements, giving the overall web document a containment scheme or structure. div, for "division," is used to enclose some cohesive portion of a web page. div elements are used for larger or broader content regions, and are thus rendered, by default, as self-standing blocks within their containing elements. span is also a general-purpose content element but is used more for "embedded" portions or "runs" within a larger piece of text. For example, specially formatted phrases within a paragraph, whether varying by font, color, or other characteristic, can be marked up with a span element. Thus, by default, a web browser keeps spans "inline" within their containing elements. div elements may contain span elements, but not the other way around.

Review and Practice

1. Write a *login.html* file that displays a standard login dialog, with prompts for username and password as well as Login and Cancel buttons.

2. What role does the label element play in defining web page user interfaces?

6.3 Programmatically Accessing User Interface Elements

As mentioned in Section 6.1.1, the next essential event-driven computing mechanism after defining user interface elements is the ability to access, or *script*, the user interface from a programming language. We have just seen how HTML provides the user interface definition mechanism for web applications. Next, we show how JavaScript uses a "bridge technology" called the *Document Object Model*, or DOM, to read, write, and otherwise manipulate this user interface.

6.3.1   The document Object

Let's cut immediately to some code and take a quick stab at proving to ourselves that document is indeed a host object, available anytime and anywhere to any JavaScript code that is running within a web browser. In the runner, execute the following:

```
alert(document);
```

At the very least, this should prove to you that document is indeed visible to JavaScript code with a minimum of fuss—just invoke it by name. Now let's take a peek at some of document's properties. Run this:

```
var i = 0;
for (var property in document) {
    alert(property);
    i = i + 1;
    if (i > 4) {
        break;
    }
}
```

You should see a sequence of five alert dialogs, each with a property name, such as bgColor, width, or getElementById. We cannot give you a definitive list here because different browsers may list document's properties in different orders (they may even include properties that other browsers don't have).[5]

The i counter limits the number of alert-ed property names to just five; without it, you would be hitting *Enter* or *Return* quite a few times. There is, however, a more convenient way to view all of document's property names. Try this:

```
for (var property in document) {
  document.write("<div>" + property + "</div>");
}
```

What happens now? You should see something resembling Figure 6.3. Note how your script has *changed the actual content of the web browser window*. This

---

[5]Need a refresher on for-in enumeration? It was covered in Section 4.4.3.

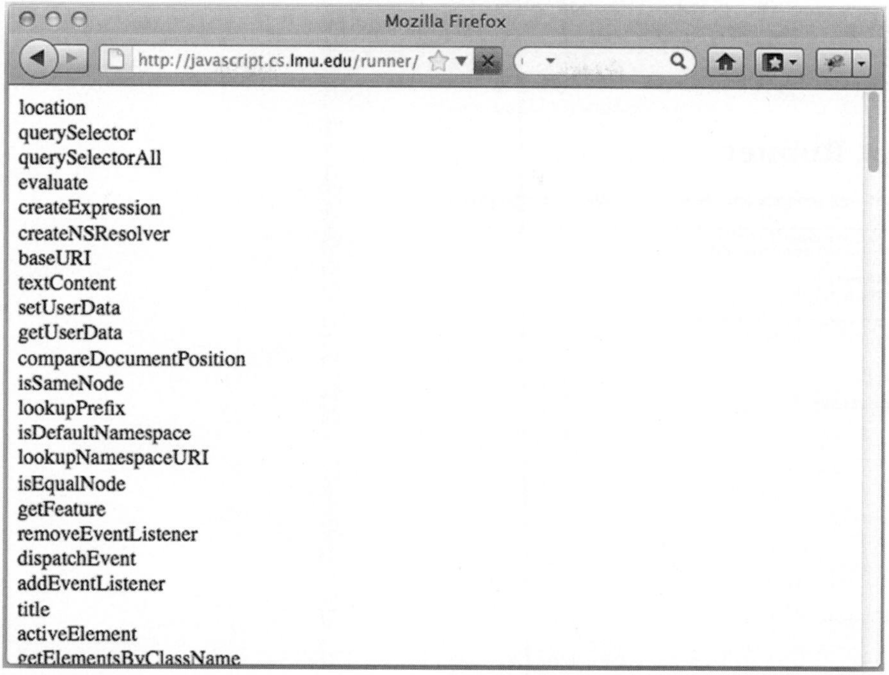

FIGURE 6.3

A web browser window, with its `document`'s property names written into it.

is one of the key properties of **document**—it is directly "wired" to a web page. The **write** function in **document** sends the given string right to that page; you are literally *writing* its content with this function. When **write** is invoked while a page is being processed—such as in *roll.html*—it behaves like a "typist" that is injecting HTML into the current page. However, when **write** is called *after* a page is loaded—such as via **javascript:** in the web browser's address field, through a JavaScript shell, or in our JavaScript runner page—a new, *blank* web page is created and the sent text is added to that.

It is not a stretch to imagine how a function can modify the web browser's content. It is a function after all, and can easily contain code that modifies what is displayed. What is unique about **document** is that functions are not the only mechanisms that produce changes to the web browser window—even certain *assignments* can accomplish the same thing.

To see this, we need to run some code within a page that has known content. Type the following into the JavaScript runner page:

FIGURE 6.4

The JavaScript runner page, with a script that has appended `document`'s property names to its content.

```
var footer = document.getElementById("footer");
footer.innerHTML = "<h3>document properties:</h3>";
var properties = [];
for (var property in document) {
    properties.push(property + " ");
}
footer.innerHTML += "<p>" + properties.join("<br/>") + "</p>";
```

In this program, `document.getElementById("footer")` returns some element of the runner page. But that's not the unusual thing: note how the mere *assignment* of a string to the `innerHTML` property of that object changes the web page—immediately and visibly (see Figure 6.4). This makes the interaction between JavaScript and its associated document feel very cohesive and natural: set a value, see the result.

6.3.2 Fun with DOM Properties

A quick examination of the HTML code that defines the runner page reveals the element whose `innerHTML` property became the recipient of `document`'s property names. Near the bottom of the markup is this line:

```
<p id="footer"></p>
```

This is a paragraph element whose `id` attribute was given the value `"footer"`. And, similarly to how the `document` host object represents the overall web page in JavaScript, the object returned by `document.getElementById("footer")` represents *this* particular p element in the language. Its `innerHTML` property represents the content between the element's start and end tags. The JavaScript runner page starts with nothing—the empty string—within this property. Assigning a string to `innerHTML` is just like typing that string between those tags.

Let's examine a few more properties before moving on. Type and run the following in the JavaScript runner page (`http://javascript.cs.lmu.edu/runner`):

```
document.getElementById("introduction").style.background = "red";
```

This code's effect should be pretty hard to miss. As before, we have a call to `getElementById`, this time with `"introduction"` as the argument. Again as before, we are touching a property of the object returned by that function—this time, a property named `style`. *Unlike* before, the `style` property is itself an object with additional properties. Here, we assign the value `"red"` to the `background` property of `style`.

Let's mess with `style` a little bit more. Try this:

```
var intro = document.getElementById("introduction");
intro.style.color = "blue";
intro.style.fontWeight = "bold";
intro.style.textDecoration = "underline";
intro.style.paddingTop = "100px";
```

As you might have guessed by now, the `style` property of a web element's JavaScript object representation is the one-stop place for anything that determines how the element is displayed: color, spacing, font, borders, visibility, positioning, and many more properties. In practice, though, you never assign style properties individually as shown here; instead, you would bundle up related styles and set them all at once. We will see how to do this in Section 7.6.1.

At this point, let's switch from assigning values to reading them. Specifically, let's look at the values that we can read from *user interface elements* like those presented in Section 6.2.2. The key here is that many of these values are *user-entered*, such as the state of a checkbox or the text in an input field. Try this script:

```
var scriptArea = document.getElementById("scriptArea");
var footer = document.getElementById("footer");
footer.innerHTML = "<pre>" + scriptArea.value + "</pre>";
```

When you run this script, you should find that the web page has been appended with something that looks almost exactly like the content of the runner page's text area. That's because it *is* the content of the runner page's text area; you have just asked JavaScript to access that text, then copy it to the bottom of the page (a.k.a., the "footer" **p** element that we used previously). Revisiting the HTML markup for the runner page, we see the following a few lines above the "footer" paragraph:

```
<p><textarea id="scriptArea" cols="80" rows="16"></textarea></p>
```

The expression `document.getElementById("scriptArea")` returns an object that represents the `textarea` element into which you type the code to run. Its `value` property returns the actual text—in this case, the very script that copies its code into the **p** "footer" element.

You may have noticed a subtle difference in what is assigned: to preserve the way the JavaScript code is entered, we "bookend" the code between `<pre>` and `</pre>` tags. These tags define a *pre*formatted web element: the text within this element is displayed exactly as typed—line breaks, spacing, and all—and frequently uses a different font. Go ahead—see what happens if you remove the `pre` tags. The code still works; the text is just displayed differently, because the `innerHTML` property, as its name implies, interprets its assigned value as HTML markup.

One last thing before we move on: when we say that the DOM exposes everything on a web page to JavaScript manipulation, we do mean *everything*. The following script demonstrates this flexibility. Even buttons, whose content is typically sacrosanct in most other environments (or else not easily changeable on the fly), are fair game in the DOM:

```
var runButton = document.getElementById("runButtonBottom");
runButton.value = "Please Execute This Script as Soon as Possible";
```

And not only can you manipulate components defined in your HTML documents, you can *create* new components as well:

```
var buttonPanel = document.getElementById("buttonPanel");
var newButton = document.createElement("input");
newButton.type = "button";
newButton.value = "I'm New!  But I Do Nothing...";
buttonPanel.appendChild(newButton);
```

Spend a few moments to infer the meanings of the **createElement** and **appendChild** methods, and try out the example in the runner page.

This completes our brief introduction to the more common user interface elements and their properties. You will eventually wish to become familiar with the full set of elements, and we have provided a complete list of elements and properties in Appendix A. For full details of each element's behavior, you will want to consult a print or online reference source, such as **https://developer .mozilla.org/en/DOM** and the authoritative standard defined by the W3C at **http://www.w3.org/DOM**. Web searches such as "HTML tutorial," "HTML reference," and "JavaScript DOM reference" also yield useful material.

6.3.3   A Place to "Play"

The design and construction of web documents and user interfaces is, on its own, a fairly expansive endeavor. It is important to gain experience through practice, and toward this end, we have prepared an HTML "playground" page with a number of user interface controls all set up and ready to be coded. The page can be found at **http://javascript.cs.lmu.edu/playground**, and a screenshot of its content is shown in Figure 6.5.

Before proceeding, we recommend that you drop by the page and look at how it is set up. Use your web browser's   View Source   or   Page Source   command (exact name and location depend on the browser) to examine the HTML that produces that page. Feel free to also copy that page into a local file so that you can edit and experiment with it.

6.3.4   Manipulating User Interface Controls

The HTML playground page provides us with enough user interface material to proceed with the next event-handling mechanism in JavaScript: reading from and writing to these user interface elements from JavaScript code.

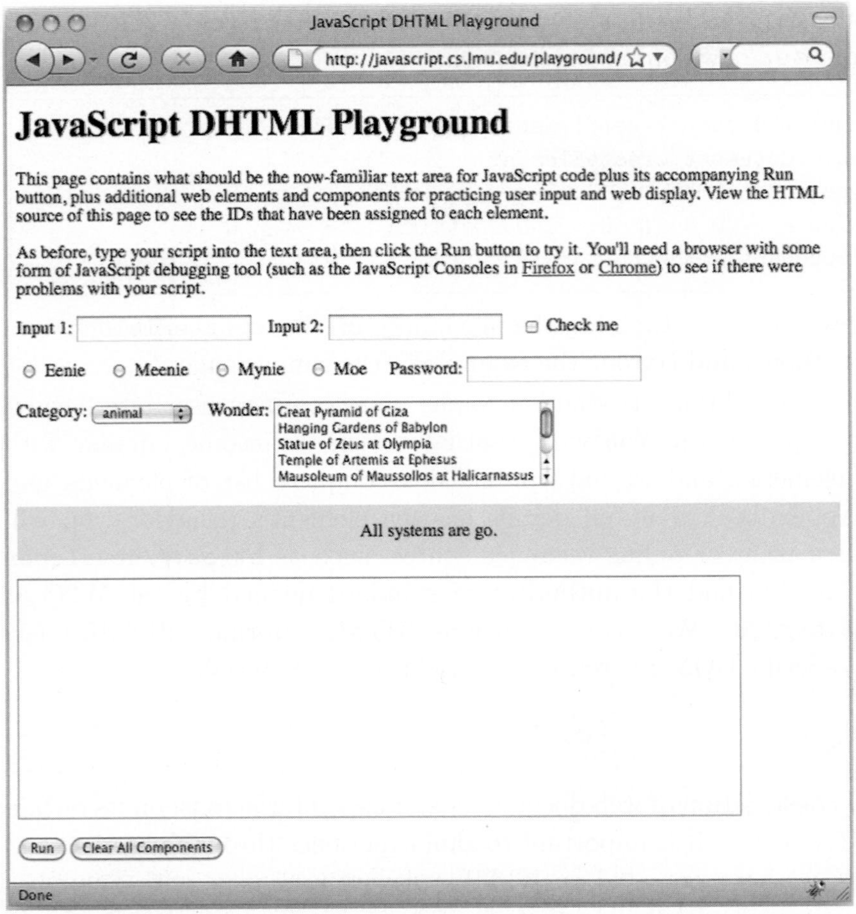

FIGURE 6.5

An HTML user interface "playground" page.

As seen previously, the key to manipulating web elements is to acquire the DOM object that directly represents this element; we can use the `getElementById` function for this.[6] All web page elements can accept an `id` attribute (e.g., `<p id="description">`); an element that has such an attribute can be retrieved as a JavaScript object "in a single bound" by `getElementById`. The main rule that you must follow is to make sure the value of an element's `id` property is *unique*. In other words, no two elements on the same web page may have the

---

[6]There are other ways, but this one will do for now.

same `id`. Otherwise, what can the DOM unambiguously return when you ask it to `getElementById`?

Take a moment to get to know the `id`'ed tags in the playground page, then type in the following script. Before hitting Run , enter numbers into the Input 1 and Input 2 text fields:

```
// Grab the elements that we need.
var input1 = document.getElementById("input1");
var input2 = document.getElementById("input2");
var status = document.getElementById("status");

// Read the required text and convert to numbers.
var number1 = +input1.value;
var number2 = +input2.value;

// Write the result.
status.innerHTML = number1 + " + " + number2 +
    " = " + (number1 + number2);
```

You have just written a simple adder![7] The script grabs the `input1` and `input2` text fields from the page, converts the text within those fields (their `value` property) into numbers via the unary plus operator (the fancy JavaScript idiom we saw back in Chapter 3), then adds the resulting numbers together. While addition itself may be trivial, the point of this script was to show you how assignment of IDs to HTML elements makes it extremely easy, with the help of `getElementById`, to access and modify the content of a web page—including content that can be changed by user input, such as the input fields.

Of course, the labeling and information on the playground page do not really scream "adder," so let's tweak its content accordingly with this script:

```
document.getElementById("header").innerHTML =
    "A Simple Dynamic HTML Adder";

document.getElementById("introduction").innerHTML =
    "This page adds two numbers.";
```

---

[7]Of course, the correctness of this adder is subject to the correctness of JavaScript arithmetic in general, as discussed in Chapter 3.

```
document.getElementById("instructions").innerHTML =
    "Type a number into each of the fields below, " +
    "paste the addition script into the text area, " +
    "then click the <i>Add</i> button.";

document.getElementById("input1Label").innerHTML = "Addend 1";
document.getElementById("input2Label").innerHTML = "Addend 2";
document.getElementById("status").innerHTML = "";
document.getElementById("runButton").value = "Add 'Em";

// Make everything else invisible.
var idsToHide = [ "check", "checkLabel", "row2", "row3" ];
for (var index = 0; index < idsToHide.length; index += 1) {
    document.getElementById(idsToHide[index]).style.display = "none";
}

// A final reminder that we need the separate adder script
// pasted in.
alert("Don't forget to paste/type in the adder script!");
```

Once this script is run, replace it with the pure addition script. Note how the changes "stick" for as long as you don't refresh the page. That's because the JavaScript objects that you have manipulated stay with the page until a new one is read into the browser's window. Web pages bookend JavaScript's life span; objects, variables, functions, and everything else are all discarded when a web page is closed, refreshed, or replaced, to be taken over by whatever DOM/scripts/variables are in the next page. It's the "circle of JavaScript life."

The following collection of one-liners shows how you are not restricted just to text values or the innerHTML property; feel free to run only the ones that interest you the most. Sometimes, a one-liner may affect more than one element. For example, selecting a radio button automatically deselects another, per the constraint provided by the name attribute. In addition, one of the lines has no immediate visible effect but affects the behavior of some lines after it. Can you identify which one?

```
document.getElementById("input1").disabled = true;
document.getElementById("check").disabled = true;
document.getElementById("check").checked = true;
document.getElementById("radio2").checked = true;
// The radio buttons are mutually exclusive.
```

```
document.getElementById("radio4").checked = true;
document.getElementById("password").value = "swordfish";
document.getElementById("password").readOnly = true;
document.getElementById("category").selectedIndex = 2;
document.getElementById("category").style.verticalAlign = "bottom";
document.getElementById("wonder").multiple = true;
document.getElementById("wonder").style.float = "right";
document.getElementById("wonder").options[1].selected = true;
document.getElementById("wonder").options[3].selected = true;
document.getElementById("status").style.border = "medium outset #0f0";
document.getElementById("status").style.textAlign = "right";
```

Note that none of the preceding scripts is event-driven. We have truly restricted the code to manipulation of the user interface with the same type of program that you have seen in previous chapters: start from the top, move through each statement in sequence. In doing so, we hope to drive home the point that the ability to manipulate a user interface with code is genuinely separate from the detection and handling of events. This is a good thing—more of that oft-mentioned separation of concerns virtue.

Before moving on, keep in mind that there truly is a vast variety of objects and properties within the DOM. One way to gain proficiency with these things is to find what is available (via books and online references) and experiment by manipulating these properties on some page with known content and IDs, such as our playground page or an HTML page of your own creation. Remember that it is safe to change, add, and delete things as much as you like, because everything you do goes quietly away once you close the window or visit another website.

6.3.5 Walking the DOM*

For readers interested in the details of JavaScript's relationship to the DOM, we will unwrap the **document** host object a bit more. As you have seen, **document** is the channel by which JavaScript code can modify or update the web page. This host object represents, exactly, the (document) node at the top of the document trees we have seen throughout the text, in Figures 2.6, 2.7, and 6.2. Indeed, all of the nodes in these trees are represented by JavaScript host objects; like all objects, they have properties. DOM objects, including **document** itself, have one or more of the following properties:

- **nodeType**: An integer in the range $1 \ldots 12$ describing the type of the node— e.g., 1 for an element, 3 for text, 8 for a comment, 9 for the document node itself (see Appendix A for the complete list).

- **nodeValue**: The "content" of a node, such as the text in a text node.

- **childNodes**: An arraylike object in which **childNodes[0]** references the first child of that object, **childNodes[1]** the second, and so on. Each child, in turn, may have a **childNodes** property of its own.

For DOM objects that are elements (**nodeType === 1**), there are two useful properties:

- **tagName**: The name of the element.

- **attributes**: An arraylike object containing attributes as "name–value pairs."

With this information, we can write a script to display the structure of a document. Writing a robust, general-purpose display script is hard, so as a first pass we will provide a script for you to drop in the familiar JavaScript runner page. It will write the node outline into the footer element.

```
/*
 * A script that displays the skeleton node structure of the
 * enclosing document in the element with id "footer".  This
 * is not an efficient script, and it leaves out some useful
 * information, such as attributes.  It is meant only to be a
 * first introduction to working with DOM nodes.
 */

var TYPES = ["", "element", "attribute", "text", "cdata",
    "entity_reference", "entity", "processing_instruction",
    "comment", "document", "document_type", "document_fragment",
    "notation"];

/*
 * Adds the subtree rooted at the given node into the given list
 * of nodes, indented four spaces per level.
 */
var showNode = function (list, node, indent) {
    var value = indent + TYPES[node.nodeType] + " ";
    if (node.nodeType === 1) {
        value += node.tagName;
    }
    list.push(value);
```

```
    for (var i = 0; i < node.childNodes.length; i += 1) {
        showNode(list, node.childNodes[i], indent + "    ");
    }
};

// Puts the outline into the footer element, formatted nicely
var list = [];
showNode(list, document, "");
document.getElementById("footer").innerHTML =
    "<pre>" + list.join("\n") + "</pre>";
```

Type or paste this code into the runner and execute the script. You will see an outline at the bottom of the page, the first few lines of which look like this:

```
document
    document_type
    element HTML
        element HEAD
            text
            text
            element META
            text
            element TITLE
                text
            text
            element SCRIPT
                text
            text
            comment
            text
            element SCRIPT
            text
        element BODY
            text
            element H1
                text

                .

                .

                .
```

This script begins by calling the `showNode` function on the `document` object, passing it an empty list and an empty string for "indenting." It "walks" the tree of nodes: at each node it adds information about the node (its type and its tag name if it has one) to a list, then processes each of its children, calling `showNode` on each child but with an indentation four spaces longer than the "current" indentation level. After all of the DOM nodes have been collected into the array, we join them with newline characters and wrap the whole list in a `pre` element (which we encountered a few pages back), so that the multiple space characters and newlines are respected. Finally, the `pre` element is placed at the bottom of the page, inside the `p` element with the "footer" id attribute.

Our little script can be improved. We have not shown attributes, nor the content of comment nodes nor of text nodes. Speaking of text nodes, why are there so many? Answer: Quite a few are blank. The text node under the `h1` element contains the text "JavaScript Runner" but the one between `body` and `h1` contains newlines and spaces! View the source of the runner page to see why.

Let's make these two improvements. To determine whether a value t consists entirely of whitespace (newlines, spaces, tabs, etc.), we will use the incantation `/^\s*$/.test`(t)—another one of the magical regular expressions that we will be getting to in Section 10.1. For attributes, we will write them on the same line as their containing element. Study the following enhanced script to see how the attributes are accessed:

```
/*
 * A script that displays the skeleton node structure of the
 * enclosing document, without text nodes containing only
 * whitespace, in the element with id "footer".  The script
 * needs work, though: it is not efficient and it may render
 * some attributes incorrectly.  Fixing it is an exercise for
 * the reader!
 */

var TYPES = ["", "element", "attribute", "text", "cdata",
    "entity_reference", "entity", "processing_instruction",
    "comment", "document", "document_type", "document_fragment",
    "notation"];

/*
 * Adds the subtree rooted at the given node into the given list
 * of nodes, indented four spaces per level.
 */
```

```javascript
var showNode = function (list, node, indent) {
    var value = indent + TYPES[node.nodeType] + " ";

    // Handle elements by showing tag names and attributes, if any
    if (node.nodeType === 1) {
        value += node.tagName;
        for (var i = 0; i < node.attributes.length; i += 1) {
            var a = node.attributes[i];
            value += " " + a.name + "=" + a.value;
        }
    }

    // If this is a text node containing all whitespace, bail
    if (node.nodeType === 3 && /^\s*$/.test(node.data)) {
        return;
    }

    // Add node to list and "descend" tree by processing children
    list.push(value);
    for (var i = 0; i < node.childNodes.length; i += 1) {
        showNode(list, node.childNodes[i], indent + "    ");
    }
};

// Puts the outline into the footer element, formatted nicely
var list = [];
showNode(list, document, "");
document.getElementById("footer").innerHTML =
    "<pre>" + list.join("\n") + "</pre>";
```

When executed from the JavaScript runner, we see:

```
document
    document_type
    element HTML
        element HEAD
            element META charset=UTF-8
            element TITLE
                text
            element SCRIPT type=text/javascript
                text
            comment
            element SCRIPT src=http://code.jquery.com/jquery-1.5.2.min....
```

```
element BODY
    element H1 id=header
        text
    element DIV id=scratch
        element P id=introduction
            text
            element INPUT type=button id=runButtonTop value=Run
            text
        element P
            element TEXTAREA rows=16 cols=80 name=scriptArea id...
        element DIV id=buttonPanel
            element INPUT type=button id=runButtonBottom value=Run
            element INPUT type=reset id=clearButton value=Clear
    element P id=footer
    element SCRIPT type=text/javascript
        text
    element SCRIPT type=text/javascript src=http://www.google-a...
    element SCRIPT type=text/javascript
        text
```

In addition to `childNodes` and `attributes`, you can also, given a node n, navigate the document with n.`parentNode`, n.`firstChild`, n.`lastChild`, n.`previousSibling`, and n.`nextSibling`. These methods, however, are generally more tedious to use than the venerable and efficient `document.getElementById`. You can also jump directly into the tree with `document.getElementsByTagName`. For example,

```
document.getElementsByTagName("p")
```

will return a collection of all of the p nodes in the document. There are also third-party JavaScript libraries that seek to make DOM access and manipulation easier and more powerful. We will learn about one such library, jQuery, in Section 7.5.

With practice, you won't have to run DOM walker scripts like the ones shown here to get a handle on a web page's structure. You will be able to infer it from the HTML source (particularly if it is well indented with good line breaks). Figure 6.6

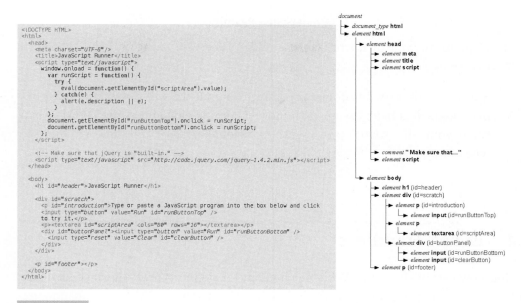

FIGURE 6.6

HTML and outline representations of the JavaScript runner page, with text and attributes (except id) elided for brevity.

displays the JavaScript runner page's overall DOM structure side by side with its source code. The correspondence is fairly easy to see.

As you deal with increasingly complex web pages, tools start to come in handy. Many web developer tools, such as the Firebug plug-in for Firefox and the built-in web inspector in WebKit-family browsers such as Apple's Safari and Google's Chrome, also include a *DOM inspector* tool as standard equipment. These inspectors are interactive versions of our DOM walker scripts, with features such as color coding, expanding or collapsing nodes as needed, and dynamic updates so that you see a web page's up-to-the-moment structure as JavaScript makes changes to it.

Complex pages with multiple levels also become prone to missed or mismatched tags, misspelled or incorrect attributes, and the like. For these syntactic issues, *validators* are indispensable. Validators read your HTML code and point out any errors or deviations from web standards. The W3C maintains a validation service at `http://validator.w3.org`, and some exercises at the end of the chapter will give you an opportunity to work with these tools.

Review and Practice

1. Explain, in your own words, the analogy that web pages and the DOM are like trees.

2. Speculate about what `document.getElementById` will do when the `id` being sought has been assigned to more than one element in the DOM. Then try it yourself—write up or create two elements with the same `id`, and see what happens.

6.4   Event Handlers

Having now established the Web's mechanism for defining user interface elements (HTML) and for programmatically accessing them (the DOM), we can now examine the mechanism for assigning the code that will execute when something happens on them. The code that runs in response to such happenings is called an *event handler*. JavaScript programs do not explicitly contain the code that waits for events to happen; instead, they simply register interest in certain events, leaving it to the system to detect when such events occur—thus the term *event-driven*.

Cutting to the chase, an event handler is simply a function. The simplest way to associate this function with a particular event is to assign it to a designated DOM property such as `onclick`, `onload`, `onkeydown`, or `onmousemove`, to name a few (the complete list of properties is in Appendix A). Once assigned, the function will be called when the corresponding event occurs. Many events refer to actions performed by a user—mouse activity triggers "mouse events," keyboard actions trigger "key events," etc. There are nonuser-triggered events too; you will read about particularly useful ones in Sections 6.6.4 and 8.4.

For convenience, most of this section presents code that is designed to run on our aforementioned playground page, found at `http://javascript.cs.lmu.edu/playground`. This gives us a known and consistent quantity in terms of predefined user interface elements. We will move beyond the canned playground page at the close of this chapter to develop a full-fledged, event-driven web page with content tailored to that application.

6.4.1 Anatomy of an Event Handler

The playground page does not, by default, handle any events in a custom way. Let's add a trivial event handler just to get things started:

```
// Alert something when the element with id "header" is clicked.
document.getElementById("header").onclick =
    function () { alert(this.innerHTML); };
```

When you run this script, nothing seems to happen. Something *has* happened, however: the playground page has now been told to handle `click` events on the page element whose ID is `header`. This element happens to be the large heading of the playground page. Click on it now and see what happens.

Simple, but perhaps not too useful. This example simply illustrates the core mechanism for designating event handlers—its "anatomy," so to speak.

Recall that every element in a web page is represented by some object within the DOM and is accessible via the `document` host object. Now, for such a user interface element:

■ Every event that can be reported by this element has a standard, short name, such as `click`, `mousedown`, `mouseup`, `focus`, and `blur`.

■ For each such event, the element has a property whose name is the event "nickname" preceded by the prefix `on`. For the preceding examples, these would be `onclick`, `onmousedown`, `onmouseup`, `onfocus`, and `onblur`, respectively.[8]

■ If a program is interested in a particular type of event for the element, it may do one of the following:

  – Assign a JavaScript function to the "`on` event" property of the element. This technique works on all browsers.

```
// Works in all browsers.
document.getElementById("header").onclick =
    function () { alert(this.innerHTML); };
```

---

[8]Note the naming convention: everything is in lowercase.

– Call the `addEventListener` function on the element, with the event's short name and the event handler as arguments. Be aware, though, that `addEventListener` is not supported on versions of the Internet Explorer browser prior to version 9.[9]

```
// Does not work on IE prior to version 9.
document.getElementById("header").addEventListener("click",
    function () { alert(this.innerHTML); }, false);
```

– Use a third-party JavaScript library such as jQuery to specify the event-handling behavior. We will officially introduce jQuery in the next chapter, but here's a sneak peek:

```
// Works on all browsers, but requires the jQuery library.
$("#header").click(function () { alert(this.innerHTML); });
```

For simplicity, we will use the first mechanism in the remainder of this chapter. In industrial-strength code, however, the third approach (a library) is most common: it provides the ability to assign more than one event handler of the same type to an element, it allows for customizing capture and bubble behavior (described later in this chapter), and it accommodates browser-specific implementations.

■ When the event happens, the assigned function is called. Within that function, the variable `this` is implicitly defined as the element in which the event took place.[10]

6.4.2   Event Handlers Are Functions Are Objects

The following example illustrates a control whose state influences whether or not another control is enabled. This behavior is frequently found in many web forms, as

---

[9]These earlier versions of Internet Explorer have a similar function called `attachEvent`. The two approaches differ in more than name only: they take different parameters, they have different capabilities regarding nested elements, and they treat the `this` expression differently.

[10]It is worth noting that this is not true of the nonstandard `attachEvent` function.

certain user choices may determine whether later choices may be applicable. Type
the following code into http://javascript.cs.lmu.edu/playground and run it:

```
/*
 * Enables or disables the category drop-down menu.
 */
var setCategoryEnabled = function (enabled) {
    // Recall that "!" in JavaScript means "not."
    document.getElementById("category").disabled = !enabled;
};

/*
 * Enables or disables the category drop-down menu based
 * on whether or not the "Check me" box is checked.
 */
var handleCheckClick = function () {
    setCategoryEnabled(this.checked);
};

// Sync up the drop-down and the checkbox.
setCategoryEnabled(document.getElementById("check").checked);

// Set the event handler.
document.getElementById("check").onclick = handleCheckClick;
```

After running this script, clicking on the checkbox, which corresponds to tog-
gling its checked property, will enable or disable the Category drop-down menu
accordingly, via its disabled property. Note that, in this case, we first assigned
the event handler function to the handleCheckClick variable. We then assigned
the "check" element's onclick property to that variable. Because functions in
JavaScript are objects in their own right, they can be assigned to variables, written
out on the fly, and passed around as arguments just like every other object—and
any of these activities may precede the function's eventual assignment to a web
element's event handler property. This grants you a lot of flexibility in terms of
how events are handled and managed through the life of a program.

The following example illustrates this flexibility. Before trying this out, reload the playground page to "reset" any event handlers that you might have assigned previously. Then, run this code:

```
/*
 * We prepare three possible event handlers in an array.
 */
var handlers = [
    function () {
        document.getElementById("input1").value = Date.now();
        setRandomHandler();
    },

    function () {
        alert("Hello events!");
        setRandomHandler();
    },

    function () {
        alert(prompt("Type something to capitalize:").toUpperCase());
        setRandomHandler();
    }
];

/*
 * Define a function that sets an event handler for the
 * "status" element at random.
 */
var setRandomHandler = function () {
    document.getElementById("status").onclick =
        handlers[Math.floor(Math.random() * 3)];
};

// Set the (initial) event handler.
setRandomHandler();
```

To see what it did, run it and click on the All systems are go. element multiple times. Note what happens each time: it's something different—and random! The current event handler, when called, does its work and then replaces itself with something different, simply by reassigning the "status" element's `onclick` property.

1. State whether you agree or disagree with this statement: "Event-driven programs cannot be read from beginning to end." Supply the reasons behind your answer.

2. Speculate about how one would *un*assign an event handler. Write up some test code to try it out, then look it up on the Web. How close was your initial guess to the actual mechanism?

6.5 Event Objects

The final core mechanism behind event-driven computing involves the delivery of information specifically pertaining to an event. In dynamic web programs, this mechanism takes the form of an *event object*, which holds supplementary information about the event that just took place. Different event objects have different properties. All event objects have a property called `type` holding the short name of the event. Mouse events have properties for their coordinates, relative both to the browser content (`clientX`, `clientY`) and to the overall screen (`screenX`, `screenY`). The `button` property indicates the mouse button that was involved in the event. The state of the keyboard, such as whether the *Shift* key was being held down at the time of the event (the `shiftKey` property), is also available. In addition to `shiftKey`, `altKey` indicates the state of the *Alt* key, and `ctrlKey` indicates the state of the *Control* or *Ctrl* key.

The actual property names and their interpretations differ greatly between the JavaScript implementations in the Internet Explorer browser and most other browsers. Details can be found in Appendix A. In addition, the way the events are delivered to your event handlers also differs! In Internet Explorer, the event object is stored in the global variable `event`. In other browsers, the event is passed as a parameter to your event handler. Let's see an example.

The following script sets up an event handler on the playground page's "wonders of the world" list. Take a moment to infer what it will do before actually trying it out:

```
document.getElementById("wonder").onclick = function (e) {
    if (!e) {
        e = event;
    }
```

```
    var status = document.getElementById("status"),
        selection = this.options[this.selectedIndex].text;

    status.innerHTML = e.shiftKey ? selection.toUpperCase() :
        e.altKey ? selection.toLowerCase() :
        selection;
};
```

The event handler copies the currently selected "wonder of the world" into the green status area. If we are running under Internet Explorer, no parameter is passed and e will be initially **undefined**; the first statement of the body takes care of setting e to the value of the global event object.

Cross-browser compatibility or incompatibility, especially for functionality as fundamental as event handling, is a significant real-world issue that can waste hours and hours of programmer time. The issue has improved gradually as standards have coalesced and web browsers have increasingly complied with those standards, but it has not (and may not) disappear completely. Third-party JavaScript libraries such as jQuery help to address this problem by "normalizing" these event-handling (and other browser) behaviors so that they look and act the same regardless of the browser. This normalization can be a significant time-saver and is arguably indispensable in production environments.

The remainder of the example is more or less uniform now that the major incompatibility across browsers has been addressed. The **select** element that holds this list has a **selectedIndex** property that indicates the index of the current selection. This index is then used to read the actual selection from the **select** element's **options** property, which is the array of all items in that list. In addition, *how* the selection gets copied is determined by whether or not the *Shift* or *Alt* keys are down. If the *Shift* key is down at the time of the mouse click, the selected item will be capitalized. If the *Alt* key is down, the lowercase version of the selected item appears.

Review and Practice

1. The "wonders of the world" event handler does not work correctly if it is assigned to **onchange** instead of **onclick**. Why?

2. What appears in the green status area if the *Shift* and *Alt* keys are *both* held down? Why?

6.6   Event Implementation Details

Additional mechanisms exist within event-driven systems beyond user interface definition, programmatic access, event handler setup, and event information delivery. While not as central to the overall paradigm as the preceding four, they still affect the implementation of an event-driven program. In this section, we cover the ancillary mechanisms that are particularly prominent within dynamic web programs.

6.6.1   Event Capturing and Bubbling

Enter and run the following script in the playground page:

```
document.getElementById("widgets").onclick = function () {
    alert("Widget area clicked!");
};
```

The moment you clicked on Run , were you surprised to see the alert saying that the widget area was clicked? A look at the HTML source provides an explanation: the entire bank of user interface controls is contained within a `div` element whose ID is "widgets." This is the element to which you have assigned the preceding `click` event handler. Thus, it stands to reason that clicking anywhere within this element triggers this event handler. Even clicking on distinct elements in their own right, such as the text fields, selection lists, buttons, etc., will trigger this event handler, as long as the clicked element is contained within the "widgets" `div` element.

So, observation 1: In web pages, an event handler is triggered as long as the event happened *within* the element to which the event handler function was assigned, whether or not another child or descendant element was also a direct recipient of that event.

Now, run this script without reloading the page, so that the prior event handler stays active (you may need to dismiss the "Widget area clicked!" alert one or more times):

```
document.getElementById("check").onclick = function () {
    alert("Checkbox clicked!");
};
```

With this event handler "installed," click directly on the checkbox component. Note how you see *both* alerts: the one saying "Checkbox clicked!" and the original one saying "Widget area clicked!" The checkbox alert appeared first, followed by the widget alert.

Observation 2: If an element contains another element, and both elements have an event handler assigned, then *both* event handlers are called if the event is triggered within the contained element. The event handler of the innermost element is called first.

This behavior is called *event bubbling*. To understand the origin of the term, refer to Figure 6.7, which illustrates the full web event life cycle: an initial *capturing* phase has the event "travel" through the outermost web element first (i.e., the document itself), then successively through any additional, contained elements that also intersect the event's location. Once the event reaches the lowermost element (or innermost, depending on how you think about the document's structure), it switches to the *bubbling* phase, and the event "bubbles" back up the element hierarchy.

Event handler registration via direct function assignment—i.e., the way we have been doing it so far—defaults to invocation during the bubbling phase. The

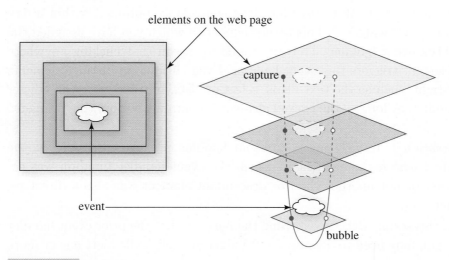

FIGURE 6.7

The event capturing and bubbling phases. Each circle represents a potential event handler invocation, if such a handler is assigned to that element for that phase (capturing or bubbling).

addEventListener approach to event registration mentioned earlier allows you to configure invocation to happen during either the capturing or bubbling phases (the details are beyond the scope of this text).

Bear with all of those widget area alerts one last time, and run this last script without reloading the page:

```
document.getElementById("templeOption").onclick = function () {
    alert("Temple clicked!");
};

document.getElementById("wonder").onclick = function () {
    alert("Wonder clicked!");
};

document.getElementsByTagName("body")[0].onclick = function () {
    alert("Body clicked!");
};
```

Congratulations if you correctly anticipated the resulting behavior: the event bubbles through multiple elements—arbitrarily many, in fact. The "innermost" element goes first, "bubbling" upward all the way to the overall document.

Not all events bubble. In particular, focus, blur, load, and unload do not. In addition, event objects have a stopPropagation function (called cancelBubble in Internet Explorer) that stops the bubbling process. To see this in action, insert a stopPropagation call in either the "templeOption" or "wonder" click handler, and click around again. Compare the resulting behavior to the behavior you saw previously.

At this point you are probably sick of all those alerts, so be sure to reload the playground page before moving on.

6.6.2   Default Actions

You might have observed, through all this discussion of events and event handling, that certain standard web browser behaviors seem like event handlers themselves. For example, clicking on a link to load a new web page can be viewed as a click handler on anchor (link) elements. Or, typing into a text field seems to be a keypress handler: "When a key is pressed, insert the corresponding character to the text field." The difference is that these behaviors are available automatically, or *by default.* And that is, in fact, what they are called—*default actions.* When event handlers are assigned to elements with default actions for those same events, the "custom" handlers are invoked first, with the default action taking place last. For example, if an anchor element has a `click` event handler, a mouse click triggers that handler, after which the web browser loads the URL specified by the anchor.

There are times, however, when you may wish to skip the default action. This can be done by calling the `preventDefault` function. This function resides with the event object that is passed to the event handler. Internet Explorer does not implement this method; instead you prevent default actions in Internet Explorer by setting the `returnValue` property in the event object to `false`.

As an example, the following script implements a behavior that can be found in many real-world forms: the restriction of keyboard input to just numeric symbols. The HTML5 `input type="number"` element "builds in" this functionality for the latest web browsers; however, it is still instructive to see how these kinds of constraints are implemented manually—after all, *someone* had to program them into the browser!

Two approaches are shown, one of which invokes the `preventDefault` function if available and assigns to `returnValue` if not:

```
/*
 * Eliminates all nondigits from the given string.
 */
var restrictToDigits = function (string) {
    return string.replace(/[^\d]/g, "");
};

/*
 * Checks if the given value is all digits.
 */
var isAllDigits = function (string) {
    return string.match(/^\d*$/);
};

/*
 * Rejects nondigit keypresses.
 */
var handleInputKeyPress = function (e) {
    if (!e) {
        e = event;
    }
```

```
        if (!isAllDigits(String.fromCharCode(e.charCode))) {
            // Make sure keypress doesn't cause a character to appear
            if (e.preventDefault) {
                e.preventDefault();
            } else {
                e.returnValue = false;
            }
        }
    }
};


/*
 * Rejects nondigits in this.value, and reselects the text field.
 */
var handleInputBlur = function () {
    if (!isAllDigits(this.value)) {
        alert("Sorry, only 0-9 are allowed here.");
        this.value = restrictToDigits(this.value);
        this.select();
    }
};


document.getElementById("input1").onkeypress = handleInputKeyPress;
document.getElementById("input2").onblur = handleInputBlur;
```

After running this script, try typing values into the page's   Input 1   and
Input 2   fields. If all went well,   Input 1   should now accept only digits 0 to
9, with all other characters rejected.[11]

For text input fields, the default action for keypresses inserts the character
represented by the pressed key into the field. In the case of our digit restricter, we
don't always want this to happen; we only want *digits* to get into the text field.
Thus, when our custom handler catches nondigits, `preventDefault()` treats them
like they never happened (from the point of view of the default keypress action for
Input 1   ).

---

[11] As written, keypresses such as shortcuts or accelerators may be rejected as well. We leave the
refinement of when `preventDefault` gets called as an exercise.

For comparison, Input 2 illustrates restriction to digits without using `preventDefault`. Input 2 will also accept only digits 0 to 9, but it checks for this only *after* you tab out of that field or click on another control. If the value in Input 2 contains anything other than 0 to 9, you will get an `alert` message to that effect when the field loses *focus* (i.e., it stops being the target of keypresses). A change in focus (i.e., becoming or ceasing to be the recipient of keypresses) is as much an event as a mouse click or a key hit. When an element receives focus (e.g., it is "tabbed into" or clicked on), the `focus` event takes place. When an element *loses* focus (e.g., it is "tabbed out of" or another element gets clicked), dynamic HTML engages in a little wordplay by invoking `blur` (i.e., the opposite of "focus" is "blur"—get it?).

6.6.3   Assigning Event Handlers

Thus far, we have been assigning event handlers in an ad hoc manner, primarily as scripts run after the fact from within the playground page and, way back in Section 6.1.1, from a script that is referenced near the end of the HTML page. It may not surprise you that the "after-the-fact" approach is used solely to help you learn about event handling; "in the wild," event handlers may be assigned from within the web page, as seen in the temperature converter example.

The `script` elements within a web page are read and executed in sequence, as they are encountered within the HTML source. When the script contains event handler assignment code (i.e., `element.event = function ( ... ) { ... };`), the main requirement is that the element being assigned already exists within the web page. That is why, in the temperature converter example, the `<script>` tag for *temperature.js* is located at the very end of the HTML source.

This approach can get unwieldy as a web page and its scripting code become more complicated: some scripts can modify the document as they run, and tags may be rearranged as the web page layout is edited. Thus, `script` elements that are scattered all over the page may become harder to track and debug. Wouldn't it be nice to have a standard, stable place for JavaScript references, while also not having to worry whether event handler assignment code is executed at a time when the affected element(s) already exists?

Enter the **load** event. This event is triggered by the *window* object, and signals when the web browser content has been completely read and the resulting document object model fully instantiated. The beauty of the **load** event is that you can assign its event handler early in the HTML source and be assured that the event handler itself is not invoked until the entire web page has been processed. This makes it an ideal event handler for assigning event handlers.

For example, *temperature.js* can be rewritten as follows:

```
var report = function (celsius, fahrenheit) {
    document.getElementById("result").innerHTML =
        celsius + "\xb0C = " + fahrenheit + "\xb0F";
};


window.onload = function () {
    document.getElementById("f_to_c").onclick = function () {
        var f = document.getElementById("temperature").value;
        report((f - 32) / 1.8, f);
    };

    document.getElementById("c_to_f").onclick = function () {
        var c = document.getElementById("temperature").value;
        report(c, 1.8 * c + 32);
    };
};
```

Written this way, the **script** element that runs *temperature.js* can be placed at a standard location, without worrying whether or not the **f_to_c** and **c_to_f** elements already exist at that point. The script can even be mentioned at the **head** element, with the actual event handler assignment taking place only after the entire document has been processed by the web browser.

There are other ways to assign events,[12] but we recommend **load** as a "good habit" approach for its stated benefits of guaranteeing that a web page is complete when the code is invoked and of allowing you to place almost all of your **<script>** tags in one place, such as the **head** element or right before the **body** element.[13]

---

[12]Including ways not explicitly discussed here, such as *intrinsic event attributes*.

[13]Ultimately, script loading and positioning turns out to be a much deeper issue than one might expect, especially with respect to performance. Online resources such as http://developer.yahoo.com/performance/rules.html and http://www.stevesouders.com serve to illuminate this further if you are interested.

6.6.4   Events Based on the Passage of Time

An event category that deserves special mention is based not on user activity on visible web page elements but on *the passage of time*. A JavaScript program can ask to be informed when a certain amount of real time has passed, either once or repeatedly. Since these events are not originated by user interface elements, handlers for them are set up in a slightly different manner. In the end, however, the overall mechanism remains the same.

Like any other event in JavaScript, these passage-of-time events are handled by functions. Unlike the other events, these functions are designated not by assignment to an element property but by the host functions `setTimeout` and `setInterval`.

Enter this script into `http://javascript.cs.lmu.edu/playground`, but don't click Run right away:

```
var timeoutStr = document.getElementById("input1").value;
var timeout = parseFloat(timeoutStr) * 1000;
document.getElementById("status").innerHTML = "Wait for it...";
setTimeout(function () {
        document.getElementById("status").innerHTML = "Liftoff!";
    }, timeout);
```

Before running the program, enter a number, in seconds, into the Input 1 text field. This is what should happen: the green status area should change to Wait for it ... and should stay that way for the number of seconds that you entered. Then, the message changes to Liftoff! .

You have just used the `setTimeout` function to *defer* the calling of a JavaScript function for a specific number of milliseconds (thus explaining the preponderance of 1000s in this section's examples). `setTimeout` returns immediately, allowing your code to do other things while the deferred function waits in the background until the designated amount of time has elapsed. In that time, your code may have done a whole bunch of other things, including additional computation and handling events. To see this in action, add an `alert` call right after the line with `setTimeout`, then run the script again. Note how the alert box appears immediately after you click Run , with Liftoff! appearing later (remember to type some number of seconds into Input 1 so that things don't happen too quickly).

Now try this program:

```
setInterval(function () {
        document.getElementById("status").innerHTML = new Date();
    }, 1000);
```

This time, you are using setInterval. Like setTimeout, setInterval defers the calling of a function for some number of milliseconds. Unlike setTimeout, setInterval *repeats* the function call between pauses (intervals) of the given amount of time. In the preceding example, the green status area of the runner page gets a by-the-second update of the current date and time. The function is called repeatedly for, well ... almost forever. Without writing additional code, you would need to reload a page, close the browser window, or visit a new site to end the repeated calls.

With additional code, you can exert better control over setTimeout and setInterval. When invoked, these functions actually return something—a value that serves as an *identifier* for the particular "deferred call" represented by the timeout or interval function. This identifier can subsequently be used in clearTimeout and clearInterval, respectively, to stop or cancel the pending function call(s). To use these functions, structure your code as shown:

```
// When starting a timeout or interval, save the returned ID.
var timeoutID = setTimeout(someFunction, someDuration);
var intervalID = setInterval(anotherFunction, anotherDuration);

/* ...any other code runs here... */

// Whenever a timeout or interval must be canceled, invoke:
clearTimeout(timeoutID);
clearInterval(intervalID);
```

Visit http://javascript.cs.lmu.edu/deferred for a concrete demonstration of this family of functions. The timer and interval functions play a prominent role in animation, so we will see plenty more of these functions in Chapter 9.

Review and Practice

1. What is the difference between event *capturing* and *bubbling*?

2. What are the advantages of putting all event handler assignment code within the `onload` event handler (except the `onload` assignment itself, of course)? Do you see any disadvantages?

6.6.5   Multitouch, Gesture, and Physical Events

As web browsers find themselves in increasingly diverse types of devices, the kinds of events to which they may potentially respond expand as well, depending on the input or sensor capabilities of that device. In this section, we cover a small sampling of these events. Note that most of the code examples here will only function as described when run in web browsers for devices that have the corresponding input methods, such as mobile/handheld and tablet computers.

At this writing, standards for these types of events remain in flux. The code provided in this section may need modifications as time passes, devices and their web browsers evolve, and standards coalesce. Relevant sources for the latest information on these events can be found with the W3C Web Events and Geolocation Working Groups [W3C11b, W3C11a] and in the developer documentation from vendors of devices capable of multitouch, gesture, and physical events [App11, Goo11].

Multitouch Events

Touch input resembles mouse input in that user actions—in this case a finger on a touch-sensitive display—occur as touches starting or ending (analogous to mouse button activity) and as movement across the display (analogous to mouse movement). But unlike mouse input, which can track a single two-dimensional point on a computer display, multitouch input can follow more than one such point concurrently. Further, mouse input separates movement from buttons; mouse movement can be detected whether or not a mouse button is held down. Touch input, however, has no such separation; movement cannot be detected unless fingers are touching the device.

These distinctions inform the way touch events are delivered and reported to a web browser:

- `touchstart` indicates the addition of a finger, or touch, to the list of known contacts on the device.

- **touchmove** indicates the motion of a previously known contact across the device.

- **touchend** indicates the removal or lifting of a finger or contact from the device.

Some devices also support a **touchcancel** event, which represents the end of a touch sequence outside of the deliberate lifting of a finger off the screen, such as movement out of the web browser's touchable content area.

As with all other event-handling approaches, the event handlers for these multitouch events receive an event object that holds information about the event, in this case a **TouchEvent** object. The main distinction between a **TouchEvent** and a **MouseEvent** is that touch events hold one or more *arrays* of **Touch** objects, one **Touch** for each finger that is currently on the screen. Mouse events, needing to track only one point of contact, hold all of this information immediately within the event object.

The touch arrays are standard JavaScript arrays: they all have the expected **length** property and have integer indexes starting at zero. If **event** represents the current touch event object, then **event.touches** is the array of all known touches on the web page, **event.targetTouches** is the array of all known touches on the actual element that is reporting the touch event, and **event.changedTouches** is the array of all touches that have changed since the last touch event was reported.

The web page at **http://javascript.cs.lmu.edu/text-touch** responds to touch events. It will appear to do nothing on computers that are not multitouch capable because its event handlers are attached exclusively to touch events. On a multitouch-capable device, however, the three paragraphs on the page will appear italicized when touched and will move their left margins left to right along with your finger. Best yet, you can do this to more than one paragraph concurrently, with multiple fingers on the screen as in Figure 6.8.

The JavaScript code can be found in *text-touch.js*. The overall program is a **window.onload** event handler, consisting of helper functions and event handler assignments. The bottom of the function assigns the event handlers, which are all functions defined in the lines prior:

```
// Assign the event handlers for all paragraph elements.
for (i = 0; i < paragraphs.length; i += 1) {
    paragraphs[i].ontouchstart = markParagraph;
    paragraphs[i].ontouchmove = shiftParagraph;
    paragraphs[i].ontouchend = unmarkParagraph;
```

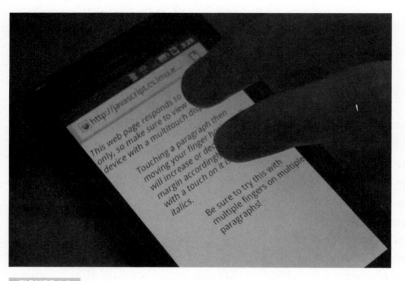

FIGURE 6.8

Using the touch event demonstration.

```
}

// Prevent possible default touch behaviors like scrolling and
// resizing.
document.body.ontouchmove = preventTouchDefault;
document.body.ongesturechange = preventTouchDefault;
```

Note the bottom two lines, which prevent default touch or gesture behavior such as scrolling or scaling. We want to disable these for this example so that manipulating the touchable paragraphs does not get disrupted by scrolls or scales.

Another useful touch-capable adjustment can be found in the `style` element of the web page's `head`:

```
user-select: none;
```

Setting this property keeps another set of default browser behaviors, pertaining to text selection and highlighting, from taking place while fingers are moving around the screen.

The actual event-handling code differs from other event handlers in its use of a `for` loop to process all of the changed touches in the current event. Note the `shiftParagraph` function, which adjusts the left margin of a touched paragraph according to the position of the touch:

```
shiftParagraph = function (event) {
    var i, touchCount, element;
    for (i = 0, touchCount = event.changedTouches.length;
            i < touchCount; i += 1) {
        element = getParagraphElement(event.changedTouches[i].target);
        element.style["margin-left"] = (event.changedTouches[i].pageX -
            element.startX) + "px";
    }
}
```

The `for` loop iterates through the `changedTouches` array within the provided `event` object and processes each touch. The `target` property of each touch object refers to the actual web page element that is currently being touched.

Gesture Events

Gesture input can be viewed as existing at a level above touch input: gestures are reported when particular sequences of touch events are detected. Gestures are analogous to mouse button clicks and double-clicks. Note how click events are actually specific sequences of the mouse button being pressed and then released. They motivate events of their own because they happen with sufficient frequency or are compellingly convenient, thus saving developers from having to write a lot of redundant code.

As a gesture event-capable web browser tracks sequences of touch events that can be interpreted as gestures in their own right, it can report the following events:

- **gesturestart** indicates the beginning of a multitouch gesture.

- **gesturechange** indicates a change in the current gesture, as driven by how the user's fingers are moving across the display.

- **gestureend** indicates the end of a multitouch gesture, typically due to a finger being lifted off the screen. Note that other fingers may still be in contact with the display, so that the lower-level touch events **touchmove**, **touchstart**, and **touchend** will still be reported even if the current gesture has already ended.

In current devices, supported gestures include *scaling*, typically enacted using two fingers moving closer together or farther apart by "pinching" the screen, and *rotation*, which is reported when two fingers are detected to be revolving around some axis that is perpendicular to the touch screen's plane. These gestures are reported in the `event.scale` and `event.rotation` properties of the event object that is passed into the gesture event handler. The `event.scale` property is a scalar from 0.0 to 1.0, while `event.rotation` is given in degrees.

A gesture event-handling sample page can be found at `http://javascript .cs.lmu.edu/text-gesture`. It will appear to do nothing on computers that are not multitouch capable because its event handlers are attached exclusively to gesture events. On a multitouch-capable device, however, the paragraphs on the page will appear italicized when a gesture begins within them (essentially two fingers on the paragraph). Their font size changes with a resizing "pinch" gesture, and their opacity changes when the fingers rotate. One caveat that you might note with this sample code is that scaling and rotation are handled concurrently within a single gesture, leading to possibly surprising behavior when a resize appears to come with an unintended rotation. Thus, in practice it is typically less confusing to process just scaling or just rotation when handling gestures.

The gesture sample code is actually somewhat more straightforward than the multitouch code because gestures are reported one at a time, as with most other web browser events. The `event.scale` and `event.rotation` properties are simply read as needed within the `changeParagraph` function (the designated `gesturechange` event handler) in order to make corresponding changes to the affected web page element:

```
changeParagraph = function (event) {
    var element = getParagraphElement(event.target), newOpacity;
    element.style["font-size"] = (element.startSize * event.scale) +
        element.sizeUnit;

    // Make 180 degrees of rotation correspond to 100% opacity.
    newOpacity = +element.startOpacity + (event.rotation / 180.0);
    newOpacity = (newOpacity < 0.0) ? 0.0 :
        ((newOpacity > 1.0) ? 1.0 : newOpacity);
    element.style.opacity = newOpacity;
}
```

Note that gesture events are currently even more preliminary than touch events, so the aforementioned events, objects, and properties, as well as any sample code, may only work on very specific devices or may require modifications over time.

Physical Events

Some web browser-capable devices have accelerometers and/or gyroscopes that allow the device to track its own physical movement and orientation, respectively. These actions remain perfectly inline with the event-driven computing paradigm, and standards that allow web browsers to detect such movement and rotation events are currently under development [W3C10b]. What follows is based on the content of this standards draft at the time this section is being written, along with existing web browser implementations of these standards.

Because these events are tied directly to physical motion, a basic understanding of three-dimensional coordinate systems and the laws of mechanics, including gravity, is necessary in order to use these events in intuitive and meaningful ways. Such concepts are beyond the scope of this section, however, so we leave that to further reading, and perhaps trial and error, on your part.

Physical device motion and orientation are reported as the following events, respectively:

- `devicemotion` indicates that a device has physically moved in space, with motion values reported in the corresponding `DeviceMotionEvent` that is passed into the event handler. Movement is reported in terms of *acceleration*, both with and without gravity (`accelerationIncludingGravity` and `acceleration` properties, respectively). The `interval` property indicates the time elapsed since the prior motion event (thus allowing programs to compute velocity and, to some extent, position based on the given acceleration vectors), while the `rotationRate` property reports a rate of change in the device's orientation during that interval. Both acceleration and rotation are given as three-dimensional vectors.

- `deviceorientation` permits reporting of *absolute* device orientation, as opposed to the relative value provided by the `rotationRate` property in `devicemotion` events. Orientation may be completely absolute or may be relative to some predetermined orientation; this will vary according to the sensors that are available on the device running the web browser.

Any `devicemotion` and `deviceorientation` event handlers must be attached to the top-level `window` host object. Associating these event handlers with any other web page element would be pretty meaningless because physical events affect the entire device anyway.

As with multitouch and gesture events, the following sample code comes with the same disclaimers on standards-in-progress and vendor-specific device support. The web page at `http://javascript.cs.lmu.edu/physical-events` demonstrates a raw "data dump" of any `devicemotion` and `deviceorientation` events that are reported by the web browser. Its event handlers consist solely of code that reads off the event object properties and copies them to the page, such as:

```
document.getElementById("acceleration-gravity-x")
    .innerHTML = event.accelerationIncludingGravity ?
        event.accelerationIncludingGravity.x : "not reported";
document.getElementById("acceleration-gravity-y")
    .innerHTML = event.accelerationIncludingGravity ?
        event.accelerationIncludingGravity.y : "not reported";
document.getElementById("acceleration-gravity-z")
    .innerHTML = event.accelerationIncludingGravity ?
        event.accelerationIncludingGravity.z : "not reported";
```

Depending on the device used for viewing this page, you will get anything from absolutely no data (meaning that the events are not even reported), to partial data (some "not reported"s, but some actual numbers), to a full, and constantly updated, set of values. If you do see any numbers, try moving and rotating your device in space, in all three dimensions, to see how they change. In addition, see what happens when you put down your device, so that it is supposedly "motionless." For computers with full accelerometer and gyroscope support in the web browser, what you see might surprise you.

After seeing `http://javascript.cs.lmu.edu/physical-events` on a supported device, you will probably agree that this is not the best way to get a feel for these physical event values. On the other hand, an intuitive presentation of these three-dimensional, fully spatial events requires techniques and tools that go beyond what we have seen so far; even Chapter 9 represents a mere introduction in this area.

Still, it would be nice to get a visual feel for these events and values. The `http://javascript.cs.lmu.edu/physical-colors` sample page makes an attempt at this while staying within the material that you have seen so far. Instead of regurgitating motion and orientation numbers, this page presents them as colors by reinterpreting the various x, y, z, alpha, beta, and gamma properties of the physical event objects as red, green, and/or blue values. If a particular physical event property is not supported or reported by a web browser, then that property's color swatch appears as a medium gray.

The conversion for acceleration, for instance, looks like this:

```
updateAccelerationColor = function (color, acceleration, scale) {
    color.r = acceleration ? ((acceleration.y > 0) ?
        possiblyClamp(acceleration.y * scale) : 0) : 127;
    color.g = color.r;
    color.b = acceleration ? ((acceleration.y < 0) ?
        possiblyClamp(-acceleration.y * scale) : 0) : 127;
};
```

Note, here, how the y coordinate of an acceleration value increases the red (r) and green (g) components of the color if it is positive, thus producing a shade of yellow, but increases the blue (b) component if it is negative.

It's better to see the program running than to read about it. Visit `http://java script.cs.lmu.edu/physical-colors` on a web browser that supports physical device events, and observe how the four color swatches on the page change as you move or turn the device. For devices that adhere to the directions specified in the standards-in-progress [W3C10b], the four color swatches (when supported) behave as follows, if you start by holding the device with its screen parallel to the ground and the top of the device pointing away from you:

- The *Acceleration* color swatch should turn yellow if you accelerate the device away from you, and blue if you accelerate the device toward you.

- The *With gravity* color swatch includes the downward acceleration due to gravity in its readings; for the most dramatic effect, orient the screen *perpendicular* to the ground first. In this orientation, the swatch should be blue when right side up, and yellow when upside down.

- The *Rotation rate* color swatch should turn green if the device is being turned clockwise in the same plane as the screen, then turn red if turned counterclockwise.

- The *Orientation* color swatch should turn green if the top of the device is facing north, and red if facing south, with intervening shades for all other directions.

All color swatches, except for *with Gravity* at certain angles and *Orientation*, should be black when the device is motionless because no significant velocity nor acceleration should be taking place during that time.

Review and Practice

1. Under what circumstances would you expect a web browser to support multitouch, gesture, and physical events?

2. How are multitouch events different from mouse events?

3. Why are gesture events characterized as being on a "higher level" than multitouch events?

6.7   Case Study: Tic-Tac-Toe

We conclude this chapter with a web page implementation of tic-tac-toe. You can access the example at `http://javascript.cs.lmu.edu/tictactoe/events`.

The idea behind this case study is to illustrate a functional, event-driven web application. The HTML for the page and its associated JavaScript are coordinated using event handlers to implement tic-tac-toe, with the two players taking turns on the same mouse.

6.7.1   Files and Connections

The application consists of two files: *tictactoe-events.html* and *tictactoe-events.js*. The game begins with the web browser loading the HTML file:

```
1  <!DOCTYPE HTML>
2  <html>
3    <head>
4      <meta charset="UTF-8"/>
5      <title>Tic-Tac-Toe: An Event-Driven Programming Case Study</title>
6      <script src="./tictactoe-events.js"></script>
7      <style type="text/css">
8        table { border: outset 1px rgb(128, 128, 128) }
9        td {
10         width: 50px; height: 50px;
```

```
11          vertical-align: middle;
12          border: inset 1px rgb(128, 128, 128)
13        }
14      tr { text-align: center }
15    </style>
16  </head>
17  <body>
18    <h1>Play Tic-Tac-Toe</h1>
19    <table>
20      <tr>
21        <td id="cell00"></td>
22        <td id="cell01"></td>
23        <td id="cell02"></td>
24      </tr>
25      <tr>
26        <td id="cell10"></td>
27        <td id="cell11"></td>
28        <td id="cell12"></td>
29      </tr>
30      <tr>
31        <td id="cell20"></td>
32        <td id="cell21"></td>
33        <td id="cell22"></td>
34      </tr>
35    </table>
36  </body>
37 </html>
```

The HTML document's `head` holds a `script` element that references *tictactoe-events.js*, which will play the game, and a `style` element that provides for some rudimentary formatting so that our tic-tac-toe grid looks decent.[14] The `body` consists of an `h1` title and, most importantly, a `table` element (lines 19 to 35) that defines the tic-tac-toe game board (see Figure 6.9). Note how `id` attributes are assigned such that the identifiers for the table cells follow a row-and-column sequence.

---

[14]We will have much to say about styling in subsequent chapters, including the fact that style information should really be in a separate file.

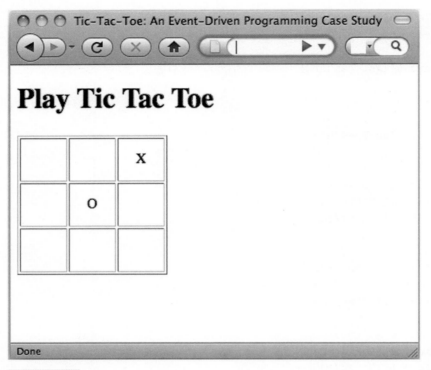

FIGURE 6.9

The rudimentary tic-tac-toe display.

6.7.2 Initialization

The structure of *tictactoe-events.js* follows the pattern that we have used previously: the JavaScript code consists of nothing more than variable declarations and assignments, the last of which assigns to the `window` object's `onload` property— the event handler that fires when the page is finished loading. It is important to do all of our DOM work after page load; otherwise the document objects we are trying to manipulate might not have been created.

```
1   /*
2    * An event-based tic-tac-toe game.
3    *
4    * This script starts with the variables and functions (state
5    * and behavior) that are needed by the game.  The last statement
6    * sets an onload event handler, which in turn sets up the event
```

```
 7  * handlers for the tic-tac-toe board.  The HTML source is
 8  * expected to set the board up for us.
 9  */
10
11  var squares = [];
12  var EMPTY = '\xA0'
13  var score;
14  var moves;
15  var turn = 'X';
16
17  /*
18   * To determine a win condition, each square is "tagged"
19   * from left to right, top to bottom, with successive
20   * powers of 2.  Each cell thus represents an individual
21   * bit in a 9-bit string, and a player's squares at any
22   * given time can be represented as a unique 9-bit value.
23   * A winner can thus be easily determined by checking
24   * whether the player's current 9 bits have covered any
25   * of the eight "three-in-a-row" combinations.
26   *
27   *      273                   84
28   *         \                 /
29   *           1 |   2 |   4  = 7
30   *         -----+-----+-----
31   *           8 |  16 |  32  = 56
32   *         -----+-----+-----
33   *          64 | 128 | 256  = 448
34   *         ===================
35   *          73   146   292
36   *
37   */
38  var wins = [7, 56, 448, 73, 146, 292, 273, 84];
39
40  var startNewGame = function () {
41      turn = 'X';
42      score = {'X': 0, 'O': 0};
43      moves = 0;
44      for (var i = 0; i < squares.length; i += 1) {
45          squares[i].firstChild.nodeValue = EMPTY;
46      }
47  };
```

```
48
49  var win = function (score) {
50      for (var i = 0; i < wins.length; i++) {
51          if ((wins[i] & score) === wins[i]) {
52              return true;
53          }
54      }
55      return false;
56  };
57
58  /*
59   * Sets the clicked-on square to the current player's mark,
60   * then checks for a win or cat's game.  Also changes the
61   * current player.
62   */
63  var set = function () {
64      if (this.firstChild.nodeValue !== EMPTY) {
65          return;
66      }
67      this.firstChild.nodeValue = turn;
68      moves += 1;
69      score[turn] += this.indicator;
70      if (win(score[turn])) {
71          alert(turn + " wins!");
72          startNewGame();
73      } else if (moves === 9) {
74          alert("Cat\u2019s game!");
75          startNewGame();
76      } else {
77          turn = turn === 'X' ? 'O' : 'X';
78      }
79  };
80
81  onload = function () {
82      // Note how we *really* rely on IDs being assigned properly.
83      var indicator = 1;
84      for (var i = 0; i < 3; i++) {
85          for (var j = 0; j < 3; j++) {
86              var cell = document.getElementById("cell" + i + j);
87              cell.indicator = indicator;
88              cell.onclick = set;
```

```
89            cell.appendChild(document.createTextNode(''));
90            squares.push(cell);
91            indicator += indicator;
92         }
93      }
94      startNewGame();
95 };
```

The initialization function iterates through every cell in the table and does the following:

- It gives each cell a unique identifier value. The identifier scheme is designed so that the program can easily tell when a player has gotten three in a row. (This is an example of "clever" coding being employed to save many, many lines of code at the expense of making the resulting code less transparent. Don't worry too much for now if you cannot follow all the details of the encoding scheme.)

- It assigns the `click` event handler to each cell. Since a click on each cell is handled in exactly the same way, the same function, assigned previously to the `set` variable, is assigned to every cell.

- It adds a *text node* object to each cell. This object contains the mark that is currently within each cell.

- It adds the cell to the `squares` array. Gathering the cells in this manner obviates the need to use `getElementById` later on; to process the cells later, we will simply iterate through the `squares` array.

Once the cells have been set up, we start a new game: we set the scores of each player to zero by initializing the `score` object, reset the `moves` count to zero, then set the text content of each tic-tac-toe cell to the nonbreaking space character (U+00A0).[15]

---

[15] In many browsers, having nothing but regular space characters in a table cell causes the table to look horrible. A reliable way to allow the cells to keep their intended width and height is to use the nonbreaking space.

6.7.3   Event Handling

Once the game has started, the program waits for mouse clicks by the players. Per the rules of tic-tac-toe, the first mouse click on a table cell is assumed to be from the X player, with O and X alternating from there.

The `set` function serves as the `click` event handler. The first thing it does is check whether the clicked cell's text value is no longer empty. If it isn't, then the cell has already been clicked on, and there is nothing else to be done.

If the cell is still empty, then its text is changed to the player whose turn it currently is (conveniently, the current turn is the same as the text to set). The move count is then incremented (which helps us determine when the board is full), and that player's score is increased by the value of the tic-tac-toe cell, effectively setting the "bit" that is represented by that cell. The `win` function then checks whether the current player has made a winning move.

If the player has won, then an `alert` declares this and a new game starts after the alert is dismissed. If there are no winners, the next thing checked is the move count: the moment nine moves have been made without a winner, the tic-tac-toe board must now be full, and we have a draw. If neither a winner nor the nine-move limit is found, then the game moves to the next turn, and the program waits for the next event.

6.7.4   The Business Logic

We close our case study with something that has both nothing and everything to do with event-driven computing: the so-called *business logic* of the tic-tac-toe game. The business logic of any system consists of the core data and computations within that system that are common regardless of the system's presentation or interaction with its end users. In that respect, it has "nothing" to do with event-driven computing because it is precisely that part of a program that does not depend directly upon the user interface. At the same time, the business logic of a system is what should remain stable or unchanging regardless of how presentation and interaction are implemented. Thus, business logic code must be written so that it is cleanly separated from presentation and interaction code. In that sense, now, business logic has "everything" to do with event-driven computing because not implementing it well (i.e., mixing it unnecessarily with event-handling code and its user interface elements) makes the program harder to maintain and to adapt.

For our version of tic-tac-toe, the business logic data consist of five variables: `turn`, `wins`, `squares`, `score`, and `moves`. Computations are performed in the functions `startNewGame` and `win`, and, partially, in `set`.

The `turn` variable stores the player who will make the next move, in terms of the player's mark of `X` or `O`. `wins` encodes the eight possible ways to mark three squares in a row: this is done by representing each of the nine squares as 1 bit in a 9-bit binary value. Both players start with a score of zero, or `000000000`. Marking the uppermost, leftmost square is equivalent to setting the rightmost bit to `1`, thus adding one to the score. Marking the middle square is equivalent to setting the fifth bit from the right to `1`, thus adding 16 to the score. Thus, a player who captures both squares gets a score of 17, or `000010001` in binary. Achieving three in a row involves being the first player to set the 3 bits that correspond to a row: `000000111` (7, the top row), `000111000` (56, the middle row), `111000000` (448, the bottom row), `001001001` (73, the left column), `010010010` (146, the center column), `100100100` (292, the right column), `100010001` (273, the top-left to bottom-right diagonal), and `001010100` (84, the bottom-left to top-right diagonal).

The `squares` array is the "bridge" to the user interface: it holds the table cell elements in the game board. The program builds this array so that it does not need to "walk" the DOM when starting a new game; it just iterates through the elements of this array to reset their symbols to the nonbreaking space. Finally, the `moves` variable is a simple counter that tracks the total number of turns taken by both players. Since there are only nine squares, there can be a maximum of nine moves. Reaching nine moves without a winner indicates the classic tic-tac-toe draw, or cat's game.

As for the functions, `startNewGame` takes care of setting the values of the aforementioned variables so that they represent a new game: squares are cleared, the scores and move count are reset, and the current turn is given to the `X` player. `win` determines whether a particular score represents a winning set of marks (i.e., three in a row). Finally, `set` connects the user interface to the business logic: a mouse click marks the clicked square appropriately, updates the current score, then checks for a winner.

Review and Practice

1. What symbol, if any, does the tic-tac-toe code use to represent a cell that has not yet been clicked by the user?

2. This case study uses a set of elements that you might not have seen before: `table`, `tr` (table row), and `td` (table data). If necessary, look up these elements on the Web (your guess on how they work and the purpose they serve probably won't be too far off). Based on this information, did the case study *have* to use these elements? Can you think of an alternative DOM setup for the tic-tac-toe game?

Chapter Summary

- Event-driven computing and programming represent a paradigm shift from the "do-this-then-this" execution approach of the programs that you have seen prior to this chapter.

- Event-driven systems consist of a mechanism for defining and accessing user interface elements, a mechanism for assigning code that *handles* events within these user interface elements, and a mechanism for delivering information about the event that took place.

- Some types of events are not initiated by the user, nor based on visible user interface elements. Web browsers, for example, can be set up to call a function based on the passage of time.

- Specific implementation issues regarding events in web browsers and JavaScript include the difference and relationship between event capturing and bubbling, the availability of default actions, and best practices regarding when and how event handler assignments should appear on a web page.

- It is advantageous to separate, as cleanly as possible, the data and internal computations within a program (its "business logic") from the way it is presented or formatted (its visual properties or layout) and the way it interacts with the user (its event handlers).

Exercises

1. Using the temperature converter code in Section 6.1.2 as a pattern, implement the following converter pages:

   - Feet to/from meters
   - Inches to/from centimeters
   - Pounds to/from kilograms
   - Degrees to/from radians (*Hint:* An approximation of π is available as `Math.PI`.)

2. Combine the five converters (temperature and the four converters in the previous exercise) into a single "unit converter" web page.

3. The temperature converter code in Section 6.1.2 (among other examples) uses `input` elements whose `type` is `button` for clickable buttons within the web page. These elements get their labels through their `value` attributes.

   An alternative element called `button` can also be used to create clickable buttons. Their temperature converter equivalents would look like this:

   ```
   <button id="f_to_c">F to C</button>
   <button id="c_to_f">F to C</button>
   ```

   (a) Modify the temperature converter code so that it uses buttons that are defined with these elements. Beyond the HTML tags, does anything else need to change?

   (b) Can you think of a functional difference between the two button-creating elements? (*Hint:* Take a close look at how each tag defines the different aspects of a button.) Do some Internet research to find the definitive answer.

4. The `confirm` function is a close relative of `alert`, displaying OK and Cancel buttons instead of a single OK button and returning `true` if the OK button was clicked and `false` otherwise.

Download a local copy of the JavaScript runner page and modify it so that, prior to running the script in the text area, a confirmation dialog appears to verify that the user really does want to run the code. Clicking OK should proceed with code execution, while clicking Cancel should not.

5. Implement a web page that performs tip calculations. At a minimum, you will need an `input` element each for the original cost and for the tip rate, and a `button` to trigger calculations. Use `input type="number"` to make input processing a little easier.

6. Enhance the tip calculation web page from the previous exercise by including a bank of radio buttons indicating "Poor Service," "Good Service," or "Excellent Service." Clicking on each radio button fills the tip rate `input` element with a different value, commensurate with the quality of service provided.

7. Enhance the web page from Exercise 5 so that it no longer needs the `button` element: have the web page update the calculated tip as the user types or changes the values of the `input` elements.

8. Implement a web page that displays an "advanced search" form for books. The web page should consist of checkboxes for "Search by Title," "Search by Author," and "Search by Subject," each with an accompanying text input field for the desired title, author, and subject search terms, respectively.

Include a Search button that, when clicked, displays the criteria and terms that the hypothetical search will use. These criteria and terms should, of course, match whatever the user has checked and entered. If the user did not check on "Search by Author," for example, then the author search criterion should not be included.

Be sure to associate `label` elements with the checkboxes.

9. Many user interface elements, including `input` and `select`, have a `disabled` attribute that, when set, renders that user interface element inactive or unresponsive to the user.

Use the `disabled` attribute to enhance the usability of the "advanced search" user interface from the previous exercise so that when a search criterion is unchecked, its corresponding text input field is disabled.

10. Implement a web page that presents an "account sign-up" form, with text input fields for a user's real name, email address, login name, and password. The web page should also provide a Submit button that would hypothetically send the account sign-up request to the (again hypothetical) server. This web page should exhibit the following behaviors:

   (a) Login name and password are required fields; that is, if they are blank, the Submit button should be disabled.

   (b) Password entry should actually consist of two `input type="password"` elements and should implement the typical "please retype your password" feature of typical account sign-up forms. As with the required fields, the Submit button should be disabled if the values in the password fields do not match.

11. This multipart exercise centers around exploring a web page's DOM structure.

   (a) Code a typical "document-style" web page, showing a few sections with headings, a number of paragraphs, some links (`a` elements), and some images (`img` elements). Sketch the DOM structure of that page by hand.

   (b) Add a Show Structure button to the bottom of your page that, when clicked, runs a version of the DOM walker script on page 224 and displays its output at the bottom of the web page. How closely does the DOM walker output correspond to your hand-drawn outline?

   (c) Activate or install web developer tools on your browser of choice: install Firebug if using Firefox, or choose the Developer Tools command under the Developer submenu of the top-level Tools or View menu in Google Chrome. For Apple Safari, you will need to check Show Develop menu in menu bar in the Advanced section of the preferences dialog window; you will then be able to choose Show Web Inspector from the Develop menu that appears. Web browsers and their user interfaces are ever-evolving, so if these instructions don't seem to match what you are seeing, don't fret—do a quick web search to find the latest instructions for your current browser.

Open your web page using your chosen developer tool and navigate through its structure. Again, take note of the interactive outline that is shown and compare it to what you did by hand and what the DOM walker script displayed.

(d) Finally, submit your HTML code to the W3C validator at `http://validator.w3.org`. You may use either the file upload or direct input option. Does your page validate? If it doesn't, fix your page according to the reported errors and revalidate until all warnings and errors are gone.

(e) What does the validator say when you remove the `doctype` tag from your web page?

The `style` properties that you have seen in this chapter primarily involved visuals such as colors and fonts. A number of other properties pertain to spacing and layout. Here are a few, with additional details available on the Web:

- `display` determines how an element is, well, *displayed* in relation to other elements. Common values for this property include `block`, `inline`, and `none` (meaning "don't display the element at all").

- `float` positions an element toward an upper corner of its containing element: `left` for the top-left corner and `right` for the top-right corner.

- Space around elements consists of three layers. From the inside out, these properties are `padding`, `border`, and `margin`. Starting in the middle, `border` is actually a compound property that defines not only space around an element but also visuals such as a line or a simulated 3D inset. The `padding` properties then define space between an element's text or children and the border, while the `margin` properties define space between an element's border and neighboring elements.

Feel free to experiment with these properties in the succeeding exercises to improve the appearance or readability of your web pages.

12. Choose a control, preferences, or system settings panel from an operating system of your choice and put together a facsimile of that panel using a web page. Make full use of user interface elements such as the full range of `input` variations, `select`, and `textarea`.

13. Create a web page that displays a simple email message composition layout:

- Include a "toolbar" with Send , Attach File , Save Draft , and Cancel buttons.

- Provide labeled `input` text fields for *To*, *Cc*, and *Subject*.

- Implement a main `textarea` for the message body.

Make sure the web page remains readable even if its browser window is resized.

14. Keyboard input raises a question: when a key is pressed, which part(s) of a web page should be notified of the event? Mouse and touch input, by their very nature, have natural targets: event notification centers on the location of the mouse or touch event. Keyboard events do not have as obvious a target.

The concept of *focus* addresses this issue: at any given time, one specific element, be it a text field, a drop-down menu, a button, or another element, is designated as the primary recipient of keyboard events (around which the event bubbling and capturing cycle takes place). This element is said to have the *focus* at that time. User activities such as mouse clicks or pressing the Tab key change the currently focused element.

The acquisition and loss of focus are events in their own right: `focus` and `blur`, respectively. Knowing the element that has keyboard focus has a number of uses, one of which is the facilitation of context-sensitive help.

Implement a hypothetical user profile page with context-sensitive help. The page should consist of multiple labeled text input fields. Next to each text field, supply a brief explanation of the field that is initially invisible (i.e., the `display` style property is set to `none`). Set up appropriate `focus` and `blur` event handlers such that the explanation elements only appear when their corresponding text field gets the keyboard focus.

15. An `input` element of `type="file"` allows a web page to choose a file on the user's computer, usually for uploading or sending. Look up the properties and usage of this `input` element, and write a script in the JavaScript runner page that appends such an element to that page. Set up the element so that, when a file is chosen, the page displays an `alert` that displays the chosen file's name.

16. Implement a "media playback" facsimile web page that displays buttons for jumping to the beginning or end of a track/chapter, rewinding, fast-forwarding, and playing back. Use images or styles to give the media controls a distinct and recognizable look. Implement `click` event handlers that display the function of their respective buttons. Finally, make the playback button a toggle: it should alternate between Play and Stop with each click.

17. A *master–detail display* is a common navigation or browsing view that is used in applications such as file or media browsers, blog sites, and many others. It consists of a list or sidebar that holds a menu of individual items. As items are clicked, the full content of those items is displayed in a (typically) larger content area. An example of such a display is shown in Figure 6.10.

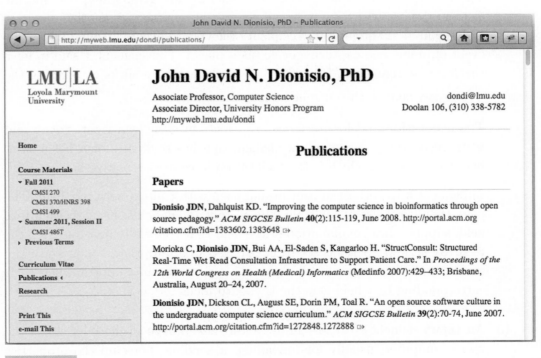

FIGURE 6.10

A master–detail display, with the *Publications* item as the current selection.

Implement, *on a single web page*, a master–detail display that lists at least five different web page elements (e.g., `input`, `div`, `body`) in its sidebar. When the user clicks on an element, the web page should display a brief description of that element.

(*Note:* This behavior can also be implemented with multiple web pages and links among them. Do not do it this way. Instead, handle `click` events on the sidebar elements by displaying their corresponding detail content in a main area.)

18. The HTML `iframe` element allows you to embed one web page's entire content within another one. The `iframe`'s `src` property holds its embedded page's URL.

    Using the `iframe` element, implement a rudimentary "browser in a browser" page. Place an `input` text field at the top of the page, alongside a Go button. Place an `iframe` below these controls. When the user types a URL into the text field and clicks on Go , the `iframe` should display the page at that URL.

    Don't worry that clicking on links within the `iframe` does not update your `input` text field; web pages are not actually allowed to do that for security reasons (more on this in Section 8.6.1).

19. Extend the "browser in a browser" from the previous exercise so that it maintains a URL history: every time the user enters a URL in the `input` text field, add that URL to a JavaScript array. Implement Previous and Next buttons, plus any necessary variables, so that the user can go backward or forward in the history and the `iframe` loads the corresponding web page accordingly.

    As before, don't worry about including clicked links in your history because your browser will not tell you about them.

20. Implement a "contact information" web page that solicits a user's name, address, email address, and phone number with a separate area code. Give the web page a Save button, and implement a `click` event handler that ensures that the supplied information satisfies the following rules:

    ■ The name may not be blank.
    ■ The zip code must consist of five digits.

■ The email address may not contain any spaces.

■ The area code must consist of three digits.

If all rules are satisfied, display an **alert** to that effect. Otherwise, tell the user what needs to be corrected.

21. Implement a "character counter" interface that displays a **textarea** element into which the user can type. As the user types text into the **textarea**, another element on the web page should list the number of characters typed so far.

22. Implement a "web checkout" interface that lists five hypothetical items for purchase. Each item should have a preset price, with an **input** element that allows the user to request a specific quantity for each item. Your web page should then:

   ■ Calculate and display the correct subtotal for the ordered items

   ■ Calculate and display the total shipping cost at a rate of $1.10 per individual item ordered

   ■ Calculate and display the total sales tax at a rate of 5%

   ■ Calculate and display the grand total for the order (subtotal + shipping + tax)

23. Implement a "seat selector" interface that starts by asking the user for a number of seats to reserve in a hypothetical theater or arena. The web page should display a floor plan for this venue using **input type="checkbox"** elements to represent a seat. The user enables or disables these checkboxes to indicate the seats to reserve, up to the number of seats that was originally requested (i.e., when the user has checked the requested number of seats, he or she must uncheck prior seats in order to change the "reservation").

24. Do a little taxonomy of species research on a favorite organism order (e.g., bats [*chiroptera*], armadillos [*cingulata*], owls [*strigiformes*]), then implement a three-level "drill-down" user interface that shows, successively, the following **select** elements:

   ■ A drop-down list of families within your chosen order

   ■ A drop-down list of genera within the chosen family

■ A drop-down list of species within the chosen genus

The user interface should start by showing only the first **select** element, without any family selected. As the user makes choices, the successive drop-down menus should reflect the possibilities determined by the previous drop-downs.

25. Create a web page with at least three levels of nested elements, such that its overall structure looks like this:

```
<div>
  <div>
    <div>
    </div>
  </div>
</div>
```

Give each element a **click** handler that identifies, through an **alert** dialog, the clicked-on element and whether or not the event is in the capturing or bubbling phase. Open the web page and, before clicking on various elements, predict the sequence of **alert** messages that you will see. Open the same page and click around using different web browsers as well, and determine which browsers have similar or different event behavior.

26. The key-by-key digit restricter example on page 238 (the **handleInputKey- Press** function) does not accommodate shortcut keys such as Control-C to copy or Control-V to paste (Command-C and Command-V , respectively, on Mac OS X browsers). On some browsers, this restriction even extends to basic editing keys such as arrows and backspace.

Modify the code so that these shortcut keys continue to perform their expected functions. (You may need to do a little research to figure this out. The basics are in the text, but the specifics are not.)

27. The key-by-key digit restricter example on page 238 has a loophole: it is possible to paste nonnumeric text into it (i.e., select nonnumeric text from anywhere, copy it to the clipboard, then paste it into the Input 1 text field

using a menu command or, if the previous exercise has been done, with the keyboard shortcut for Paste).

Close that loophole without resorting to the after-the-fact digit check that the example does for the Input 2 text field.

28. In Section 6.5, we noted that some web browsers report and deliver events to JavaScript programs in very different ways. In particular, Internet Explorer does not deliver the event object as a parameter to the event handler and instead defines a global **event** variable for that object, resulting in the repetition of blocks such as these in all event handlers:

```
if (!e) {
    e = event;
}
```

A common approach toward minimizing such repetition is to write "wrapper" functions that include these repeated blocks automatically. These functions take only the code that is *not* repeated as a function argument, then call that function alongside the code that does get repetitive.

Write your own **setClickHandler** wrapper function that takes care of the Internet Explorer event object difference transparently for **click** events. The function should take two parameters:

```
var setClickHandler = function (clickableElement, clickHandler)
{
    // Fill this in.
};
```

The **clickableElement** parameter should be the web page element to which you would like to assign a **click** event handler, and **clickHandler** should be a function that takes an **event** parameter. The **clickHandler** function may assume that its **event** argument is *guaranteed* to hold the event object, whether your program is running in Internet Explorer or another browser.

You can test whether your wrapper function works by running exactly the same code in multiple browsers. In all cases, the **click** event handler that you pass should always show that its **event** argument has been properly assigned.

29. Implement a "math drill" web page that displays an arithmetic question such as "9 × 5" or "5 + 3" and provides an `input` element for the user's answer. The web page should impose a time limit on providing the correct answer. If the user does not supply the right answer within the time limit, the page should inform the user that time has run out. When a correct answer is given or when time runs out, the page displays a new question. (*Tip:* Use the `Math.random` function to come up with the arithmetic questions. You will also need to use the `clearTimeout` or `clearInterval` functions when the correct answer is supplied before time runs out.)

30. Extend the "math drill" web page from the previous exercise so that it maintains a score showing the number of questions that the user got right versus the number of questions missed.

31. Extend the "math drill" web page from Exercise 29 so that it has a visible timer that counts down to zero. (*Hint:* You will need more than one passage-of-time event handler.)

32. Download and modify the tic-tac-toe case study so that it no longer automatically keeps track of whose turn it is. Instead, have a mouse click generate an X if no modifier keys are held down, and have it generate an O if the Alt key is held down. (*Hint:* As mentioned on page 200, this information is part of the event object that is passed to the event handler. Do some Internet research to determine exactly how this information is named and structured.)

33. Download and modify the tic-tac-toe case study so that it accepts keyboard input: let the number keys, as arranged on a keyboard's numeric keypad, represent the nine squares in the tic-tac-toe board (e.g., 1 represents the lower-left square, 9 represents the upper-right square).

    During a game, pressing one of these keys should be equivalent to the current player's clicking on the key's corresponding square. Keypresses for an already-occupied square should be ignored.

34. Download and modify the tic-tac-toe case study so that its cells respond to "rollovers" (i.e., `mouseover` and `mouseout` events): if the mouse moves over

a square that has not yet been marked, have the square appear green. If it moves over a square that is already occupied, have the square appear red.

(*Note:* Readers who have some advanced knowledge of web page authoring may be aware of approaches for this that do not involve JavaScript or event handling; note that the spirit of this exercise is to provide practice *specifically* with event handling, and not just to deliver the functionality by any available means.)

35. If you have access to a touch event-capable web browser, download and modify the tic-tac-toe case study so that it responds to touch events *instead of* mouse click events. (You will know that you have substituted things correctly if the page no longer works in a mouse-driven browser but still works on a touch-capable one.)

    To test your work, you may need to have a web server for hosting your modified tic-tac-toe case study because some devices that have touch-capable web browsers cannot open web pages as local files.

36. If you have access to a multitouch event-capable web browser, download and modify the tic-tac-toe case study so that it responds to touch events *and*, as in Exercise 32, no longer automatically keeps track of whose turn it is. Instead, let a one-finger touch generate an X and a *two-finger* touch generate an O. You may need to increase the size of the tic-tac-toe grid so that it accommodates two fingers more easily.

37. Compare the "touch-converted" tic-tac-toe implementations from the previous exercises to the original, mouse-driven versions on a touch-capable browser. Is there a discernible difference between how the touch-capable browser deals with touches that are "converted" to mouse clicks (in the case of the original tic-tac-toe implementation running under a touch-capable browser) versus "native" touch event handling (in the case of the touch-specific implementation from the previous exercise)? If so, speculate about the possible reasons for this difference in behavior.

CHAPTER 7

Software Construction

CHAPTER CONTENTS

Introduction

The preceding five chapters have covered the major elements of the JavaScript language and techniques for writing scripts to power simple interactive web pages. We are now ready to move from *programming-in-the-small* (the development of simple scripts) to *programming-in-the-large* (the development of systems with multiple, coordinating components). Just as you use different techniques to build a doghouse than you use to build a skyscraper, you employ different skills to construct large software systems than those used to write small scripts.

In this chapter, we will look at several issues relating to the design of large software systems. We will first extend the notion of *object-oriented programming* introduced in Chapter 5 and continue with a look at *modules*, JavaScript's set of built-in objects, and the popular jQuery library. We then introduce two topics with which all software developers must be familiar: performance analysis and unit testing. By the end of this chapter, you will be able to employ several advanced programming techniques for writing well-structured, efficient applications that involve multiple interacting components.

7.1   Software Engineering Activities

The task of producing a software system encompasses many activities. A business case must be made for the system; requirements must be gathered, defined, and organized; the system itself must be designed, planned, built, tested, integrated, deployed, and maintained. As we saw in Chapter 1, the field of *software engineering* studies how these activities are performed and coordinated to produce systems that are correct, reliable, robust, efficient, maintainable, understandable, usable, and economical.

Interestingly, JavaScript began life as a language for writing small scripts but has evolved to support very complex applications, including online word processors and spreadsheets, email clients, maps, and games. Programmers must approach the development of these systems in a disciplined, careful manner, using knowledge, tools, and results from the field of software engineering. Among other things, experienced programmers should

- be able to design, describe, implement, and connect software *components*,

- understand the performance implications of programming choices, that is, *why* one solution runs slower than, or requires more memory than, another,

■ know how to test components, and

■ know what solutions *already exist* for a given problem—whether built into JavaScript or available from someone else—so they do not "reinvent the wheel" while programming.

The remainder of this chapter covers several topics in the construction of non-trivial systems from components. The simplest component in JavaScript is the object, so we will begin by reviewing the role of objects in software development.

Review and Practice

1. What are some qualities of a software system that the field of software engineering tries to help you achieve?

2. What are some of the required skills a programmer should have?

7.2 Object-Oriented Design and Programming

Most of the scripts we have seen so far have been concerned with performing simple tasks. We have seen scripts that calculate body mass index, convert temperature values, determine if a number is prime, and format phone numbers. The *data* that these scripts processed were of secondary concern—the major focus was on the *algorithms* that carried out the tasks. We call such scripts *process-oriented*.

When software systems become large, we generally turn this focus around and assign primary importance to the data, treating the algorithms simply as *behaviors of objects*. This approach yields systems we call *object-oriented*.

7.2.1 Families of Objects

In previous chapters we saw how to create several objects with the same structure and behavior, such as multiple circle objects, multiple rectangle objects, and so on. The approach was to create these objects from the same prototype object, either by invoking `Object.create` or by defining constructors and using operator `new`. Because we only need one instance of each method, we placed the *methods* (behaviors) of the objects into the prototype.

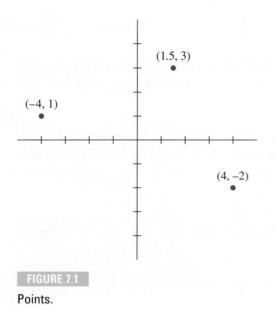

FIGURE 7.1

Points.

Let's review by means of an example. In computer graphics, we are often interested in manipulating points in a space. In a two-dimensional space, points have two *coordinates*, called x and y, written (x, y) (see Figure 7.1).

What behavior can we give to points? Here are three methods that can be useful. Given a point p, we would like to know

1. the distance from p to the origin $(0, 0)$,

2. the distance from p to another point q, and

3. the midpoint between p and another point q.

Our first pass at a point data type looks like this:

```
/*
 * A point data type.  Synopsis:
 *
 * var p = new Point(-3, 4);
 * var q = new Point(9, 9);
 * p.x => -3
 * p.y => 4
 * p.distanceToOrigin() => 5
 * p.distanceTo(q) => 13
```

```
 * p.midpointTo(q) => A point object at x=3, y=6.5
 */
var Point = function (x, y) {
    this.x = x || 0;
    this.y = y || 0;
};

Point.prototype.distanceToOrigin = function () {
    return Math.sqrt(this.x * this.x + this.y * this.y);
};

Point.prototype.distanceTo = function (q) {
    var deltaX = q.x - this.x;
    var deltaY = q.y - this.y;
    return Math.sqrt(deltaX * deltaX + deltaY * deltaY);
};

Point.prototype.midpointTo = function (q) {
    return new Point((this.x + q.x) / 2, (this.y + q.y) / 2);
};
```

We have introduced a new JavaScript idiom here—the use of || to allow us some flexibility in defining objects. Recall that when an argument is missing, its corresponding parameter is undefined. Because undefined is falsy, the expression undefined || x evaluates to x. We say, in this case, that arguments that are not passed in *default* to zero:

```
var p = new Point(5, 1); // Creates (5,1).
var q = new Point(3);    // Creates (3,0), as param y is undefined.
var r = new Point();     // Creates (0,0), as both params undefined.
```

Often we can add flexibility in other ways. Consider our midpointTo function, which we call like so:

```
var p = new Point(4, 9);
var q = new Point(-20, 0);
var r = p.midpointTo(q);
```

Some programmers might find this awkward and would prefer a midpoint function that takes both points as arguments. But where should this function go? (We hope you did not say "make it a global function.") The `Point` object itself is the perfect place:

```
Point.midpoint = function (p, q) {
    return new Point((p.x + q.x) / 2, (p.y + q.y) / 2);
};
```

Here is how this new function is called:

```
var p = new Point(4, 9);
var q = new Point(-20, 0);
var r = Point.midpoint(p, q);
alert("(" + r.x + "," + r.y + ")");   // Alerts (-8,4.5)
```

We can also use the main `Point` object to store other data related to points. For example, the point $(0,0)$ is known as the *origin*. Because it has a meaningful name, we would like to use it in our code. We can define the origin as a property of `Point` itself:

```
Point.ORIGIN = new Point(0, 0);
```

Do you see what is happening here? We have built up a rather interesting data type with *only a single global variable* (see Figure 7.2). When we begin to write much longer scripts, we will extend the technique even further. Perhaps we may write a large graphics library that, in addition to a `Point` type, might contain vectors, lines, and curves. Each of these constructors would themselves be properties of a single global variable named, perhaps, `graphics`.

Before moving on, recall from Section 5.5.3 that of the two mechanisms JavaScript provides to create object families, `Object.create` is no-nonsense and straightforward, while operator `new` does a lot of work behind the scenes and therefore takes time to master. You should be comfortable with both mechanisms. Perhaps you, like many others, will end up favoring `Object.create` for all your object construction needs. If so, you will have to deal with the fact that `Object.create`

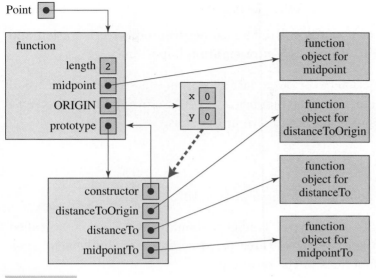

FIGURE 7.2

A data type for points with only a single global variable.

does not exist in many older browsers. In order to use this operation in these browsers, you will have to define it in terms of operator **new**. Here is one way:

```
/*
 * If Object.create does not exist in this JavaScript implementation,
 * define it!
 */
if (!Object.create) {
    Object.create = function (proto) {
        var F = function () {};
        F.prototype = proto;
        return new F();
    }
}
```

And one final note: The *standard library*—the built-in objects of JavaScript including arrays, strings, dates, errors, objects, and more—is built with the constructor and prototype mechanism. We will cover this library in more detail in the remainder of this chapter.

Review and Practice

1. Explain in your own words the difference between object orientation and process orientation. Why is object orientation important?

2. Add a `moveBy` function to the point data type from this section. The method takes two parameters, `dx` (the number of units to move in the x-direction) and `dy` (the number of units to move in y). Thus,

   ```
   new Point(1, 3).move(-5, 7)
   ```

   would cause the point to be located at $(-4, 10)$.

3. Create a `Triangle` data type. Triangles should have a property called `vertices`, which is an array of three (x, y) coordinates. Implement `area` and `perimeter` functions in the prototype.

7.2.2   Inheritance

We have defined "object-oriented" as "organized around objects instead of processes." There are some who argue, however, that for a programming *language* to be truly object-oriented (as opposed to simply "object-based"), it must also make it easy for the programmer to do two things:

- Define a hierarchy of types in which *subtypes* inherit the structure and behavior of their supertypes

- Isolate, or protect, portions of an object's state from interference by nonprivileged parts of a system

The former captures a certain relationship between objects, and the latter is about secure programming; both figure prominently in the construction of nontrivial systems. We will cover the first notion (hierarchy) in the remainder of this section and pick up the latter (information hiding) in the next.

The notion of a type hierarchy is illustrated in Figure 7.3. An arrow (with an open triangle arrowhead) from a type A to a type B means that A is a *subtype* of B, or "every A **is a** B." In the figure, we see that every human **is a** primate, every primate **is a** mammal, every mammal **is an** animal, every pelican **is a** bird, and so on.

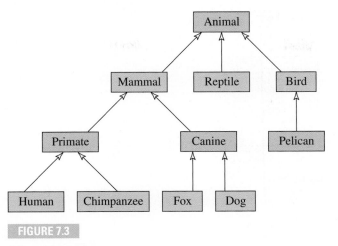

FIGURE 7.3

A type hierarchy.

To illustrate JavaScript's support for subtyping, let's create a type called `Circle` and a subtype called `ColoredCircle`. A colored circle **is a** circle that also has a color. To make things interesting, we will give colored circles a behavior of their own: a brightening function. We have three requirements:

1. Each colored circle shall have its *own* radius, center, and color properties.

2. All colored circles shall share a brighten method.

3. All circle operations, including those that already exist and those that may be added in the future, shall be accessible to colored circles.

Figure 7.4 illustrates the situation we wish to achieve. We want all colored circle instances to share a colored circle prototype and inherit all plain circle operations through the plain circle prototype. To give you a visual sense of this inheritance mechanism, we have also diagrammed a few circle instances and a few colored circle instances. Study the diagram to assure yourself that colored circles do have inherited area and circumference properties.

How can we create this setup in JavaScript code? We first build a circle type with a constructor and a prototype:

```
/*
 * A circle data type.  Synopsis:
```

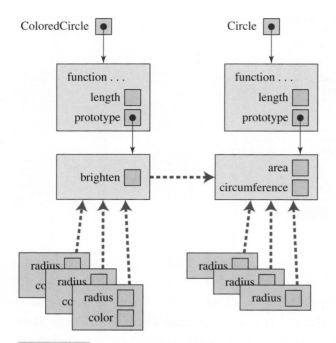

FIGURE 7.4

A type, a subtype, and several instances.

```
 *
 * var c = new Circle(5);
 * c.radius => 5
 * c.area() => 25pi
 * c.circumference() => 10pi
 */
var Circle = function (r) {
    this.radius = r;
};

Circle.prototype.area = function () {
    return Math.PI * this.radius * this.radius;
};

Circle.prototype.circumference = function () {
    return 2 * Math.PI * this.radius;
};
```

Then we build a constructor and prototype for `ColoredCircle`. Remember that in order for colored circles to inherit the behavior of basic circles (area and circumference computation), the colored circle prototype must be chained to the circle prototype.

```
/*
 * A colored circle data type, a subtype of Circle.  Synopsis:
 *
 * var c = new ColoredCircle(5, {red: 0.2, green: 0.8, blue: 0.33});
 * c.radius => 5
 * c.area() => 25pi
 * c.perimeter() => 10pi
 * c.brighten(1.1) changes color to {red: 0.22, green: 0.88,
 * blue: 0.363}
 */
var ColoredCircle = function (radius, color) {
    this.radius = radius;
    this.color = color;
};

ColoredCircle.prototype = Object.create(Circle.prototype);

ColoredCircle.prototype.brighten = function (amount) {
    this.color.red *= amount;
    this.color.green *= amount;
    this.color.blue *= amount;
};
```

If you prefer to build your types without the newer `Object.create` function, then instead of making the `Circle` and `ColoredCircle` objects constructors, you can make them the prototypes, each with creation methods, as in Figure 7.5. Here's the code:

```
/*
 * A circle data type.  Synopsis:
 *
 * var c = Circle.create(5);
 * c.radius => 5
 * c.area() => 25pi
 * c.circumference() => 10pi
 */
```

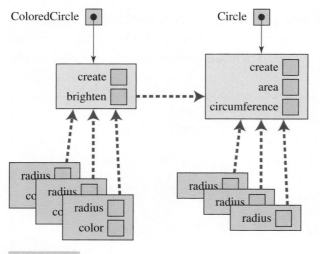

A type hierarchy with creation functions within prototypes.

```
var Circle = {};

Circle.create = function (radius) {
    var c = Object.create(this);
    c.radius = radius;
    return c;
};

Circle.area = function () {
    return Math.PI * this.radius * this.radius;
};

Circle.circumference = function () {
    return 2 * Math.PI * this.radius;
};
```

```
/*
 * A colored circle data type, a subtype of Circle.  Synopsis:
 *
 * var c = ColoredCircle.create(5, {red: 0.2, green: 0.8, blue: 0.33});
 * c.radius => 5
 * c.area() => 25pi
```

```
 * c.perimeter() => 10pi
 * c.brighten(1.1) changes color to {red: 0.22, green: 0.88,
 * blue: 0.363}
 */
var ColoredCircle = Object.create(Circle);

ColoredCircle.create = function (radius, color) {
    var c = Object.create(this);
    c.radius = radius;
    c.color = color;
    return c;
};

ColoredCircle.brighten = function (amount) {
    this.color.red *= amount;
    this.color.green *= amount;
    this.color.blue *= amount;
};
```

A more general and more powerful variation on this approach is explained in greater detail in [Lon10].

Review and Practice

1. Describe the notions of subtype and inheritance in your own words.

2. Explain the steps needed to create a subtype in JavaScript.

7.2.3 Information Hiding

Some people insist that in addition to the ability to define type hierarchies, true object-oriented programming must include a way to hide the internals of an object from all code except those methods specifically designed to act on the object. For example, you might have an account object holding a balance that is not allowed to be negative. You might try to prohibit illegal balances via methods:

```
/*
 * Creates an account object, with initial balance 0.
 */
var Account = function (id, owner) {
    this.id = id;
```

```
        this.owner = owner;
        this.balance = 0;
}


/*
 * Deposits or withdraws from an account, depending on whether the
 * amount is positive or negative, respectively.  If the transfer
 * would cause the balance to go negative, it is not applied and
 * an exception is thrown.
 */
Account.prototype.transfer = function (amount) {
    // A positive value is a deposit; a negative is a withdrawal.
    var tentativeBalance = this.balance + amount;
    if (tentativeBalance < 0) {
        throw "Transaction not accepted.";
    }
    this.balance = tentativeBalance;
}
```

As long as all updates to an account's balance field are made through the **transfer** method, the balance will not go negative. However, users of account objects are on the honor system here because nothing in the script prevents programmers from writing to the **balance** property directly:

```
var a = new Account("123", "Alice");
a.balance = -10000;
```

Is there a way to make it impossible to change a balance directly in JavaScript—to force all changes to go through method calls? There is! Remember that local variables (and parameters) of a function are invisible to outside code but are visible inside the function, including functions nested inside the function itself. We can make the balance a local variable inside the constructor:

```
var Account = function (id, owner) {
    this.id = id;
    this.owner = owner;
    var balance = 0;

    this.transfer = function (amount) {
        // A positive value is a deposit; a negative is a withdrawal.
```

```
        var tentativeBalance = balance + amount;
        if (tentativeBalance < 0) {
            throw "Transaction not accepted";
        }
        balance = tentativeBalance;
    }

    this.getBalance = function () {
        return balance;
    }
}
```

The `transfer` and `getBalance` methods have access to the variable `balance`—they're closures after all—but all code outside of `Account` does not. Try this in a shell:

```
var a = new Account("123", "Alice");
a.transfer(100);
alert(a.getBalance());    // Alerts 100
a.transfer(-20)
alert(a.getBalance());    // Alerts 80
a.transfer(-500);         // Throws "Transaction not accepted"
alert(a.getBalance());    // Alerts 80 (it didn't change)
alert(a.balance);         // Blank, because there's no such property
a.balance = 8;            // Uh-oh!! What is someone doing here?
alert(a.getBalance());    // Alerts 80, we're still safe.
alert(a.balance);         // Alerts 8. Hey! This is scary. Or is it?
```

What is the point of this example? Good question! There are several things to note. First, we *were* successful in designing a constructor that can create objects whose balances cannot be accessed directly: users *must* call `transfer` to change the balance, which is a good thing because the `transfer` method guards against overdrafts. Second, this level of protection only goes so far: we did not stop malicious users from adding a sneaky `balance` property to try to trick unsuspecting programmers into using it.[1] And third, we paid a price for this bit of information

---

[1]We will show how to do *that* in the next section.

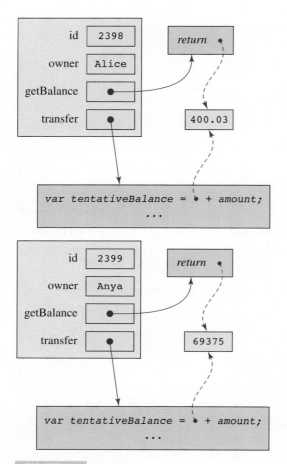

FIGURE 7.6

Simulating hidden properties.

hiding: instead of placing a single copy of each method in a prototype, *every account object you create will have its own transfer and getBalance functions.* This can get really expensive if you need many account objects. See Figure 7.6.

Hiding properties of an object is an example of *defensive programming.* Other examples include making a property of an object read-only, preventing the addition or deletion of properties to an object, and checking arguments passed to a function before using them. In the next section, we will look at some features introduced in ES5 that enable certain defensive programming techniques when working with objects.

1. What problem do local variables in a constructor solve? Why does the technique work?

2. The term *closure* was first introduced in Section 5.7. Review the definition there and explain why the transfer and balance functions in our account example are considered closures.

7.2.4   Property Descriptors*

If your JavaScript environment is based on ECMAScript 5, you can, among other things:

- Invoke `Object.preventExtensions(x)` to disallow the addition of new properties to object x, and `Object.isExtensible(x)` to see if you can add properties.

- Seal and freeze objects. `Object.seal(x)` prevents anyone from changing the structure of x in any way; `Object.freeze(x)` seals x and makes all of its properties read-only.

- Make individual properties read-only, nonenumerable, or nondeletable.

In an (ES5) object, every property has a *property descriptor*, which contains up to four *attributes* that specify how the property can be used. There are two kinds of descriptors. The first, the *named* property descriptor, has these four attributes:

Attribute	Meaning	Default Value
value	The value of the property.	`undefined`
writable	If `false`, attempts to write to this property won't succeed.	`false`
enumerable	If `true`, the property will appear in a `for-in` enumeration.	`false`
configurable	If `false`, attempts to delete the property or change any attribute other than `"value"` won't succeed.	`false`

The second, called an *accessor* property descriptor, has these four values (two of which are shared with the named property accessor):

Attribute	Meaning	Default Value
get	A function of zero arguments that returns a value. Can also perform additional actions.	`undefined`
set	A function of one argument used to "set" a value. Can also perform other actions, such as validation.	`undefined`
enumerable	If `true`, the property will appear in a `for-in` enumeration.	`false`
configurable	If `false`, attempts to delete the property or change any attribute other than `"value"` won't succeed.	`false`

You attach descriptors to properties via the ES5 functions `Object.create`, `Object.defineProperty`, and `Object.defineProperties`, and you can get the existing descriptors for (own) properties via `Object.getOwnPropertyDescriptor`. Examples:

```
var dog = Object.create(Object.prototype, {
    name: {value: "Spike", configurable: true, writable: true},
    breed: {writable: false, enumerable: true, value: "terrier"}
});
Object.defineProperty(dog, "birthday",
    {enumerable: true, value: "2003-05-19"}
);
alert(JSON.stringify(Object.getOwnPropertyDescriptor(dog, "breed")));
```

This code, thanks to the very convenient `JSON.stringify` function we will see in the next section, alerts

```
{"value":"terrier","writable":false,"enumerable":true,
 "configurable":false}
```

If you create an object with an object literal, all of its properties will get a descriptor with writable = true, enumerable = true, and configurable = true:

```
var rat = {name: "Cinnamon", species:"norvegicus"};
alert(JSON.stringify(Object.getOwnPropertyDescriptor(rat, "name")));
```

This code alerts

```
{"value":"Cinnamon","writable":true,"enumerable":true,
"configurable":true}
```

The named property descriptor provides a nice way to make a field *read-only* once it is set. (Check the property descriptor for `Math.PI` if you have a second.) The accessor property descriptor lets you perform checks (such as for overdrafts when attempting account withdrawals) before setting a property, or taking action (like logging access requests) when reading a property. The following (contrived) example shows the accessor property magic: you appear to be doing a simple assignment to the balance field, but because of its descriptor, a function kicks off that prevents a negative value from being accepted.

```
var account = (function () {
    var b = 0;
    return Object.create(Object.prototype, {
        balance: {
            get: function () {
                alert("Someone is requesting the balance");
                return b;
            },

            set: function (newValue) {
                if (newValue < 0) {
                    throw "Negative Balance";
                }
                b = newValue;
            },

            enumerable: true
        }
    });
}());
Object.preventExtensions(account);
```

Here's the object in action:

```
alert(account.balance);    // Calls get, (magically) alerts 0.
account.balance = 50;      // Calls set
alert(account.balance);    // Calls get, alerts 50.
account.balance = -20;     // Calls set, throws
alert(account.balance);    // Calls get, (still) alerts 50.
account.b = 500;           // Has no effect
alert(account.balance);    // Still alerts 50.
```

Review and Practice

1. Name the six attributes used in property descriptors. Which two can only go in a named descriptor? Which two can only go in an accessor descriptor? Which two can go in both?

2. What is the difference between `var a = {x: 1};` and `var a = Object.create(Object.prototype, {x: {value: 1}}); ?`

3. What does the following code alert, and why?

   `Math.PI = 3; alert(Math.PI);`

7.3   JavaScript Standard Objects

Objects serve as the building blocks of systems. Applications are built from many different *types* of objects. Healthcare applications have patients, physicians, facilities, medications, immunizations, appointments, and other objects. Human resources applications utilize employees, departments, and benefits. In entertainment, we see venues, engagements, performances, and artists.

JavaScript predefines for you a *built-in* set of primitives and objects useful across many different applications. These include the following values defined in the official ECMAScript specification:[2]

- **Primitives**: NaN, Infinity, undefined

- **Functions**: parseInt, parseFloat, isNaN, isFinite, encodeURI, encodeURIComponent, decodeURI, decodeURIComponent, eval

---

[2]The JSON object was introduced in ECMAScript 5; the rest all appear in ECMAScript 3.

- **Modules**: `Math`, `JSON`

- **Constructor functions**: `Object`, `Array`, `Function`, `Number`, `Boolean`, `String`, `Date`, `RegExp`, `Error`, `EvalError`, `RangeError`, `ReferenceError`, `TypeError`, `SyntaxError`, `URIError`

JavaScript programs are designed to run inside some *host environment*, like a cell phone, web browser, Adobe Acrobat, Adobe Photoshop, or Mac OS X's Dashboard, to name a few. Objects that you create in a JavaScript program, as well as the ECMAScript built-in objects just listed, are called *native* objects. In addition, JavaScript implementations include, as part of their standard library, dozens of additional *host objects* from their environment. You have already seen quite a few of these for web programming (`alert` and `prompt` probably come to mind).

In the remainder of this section, we will very briefly touch on a few of the more useful standard objects, while deferring reference material to Appendix A; for a complete (and necessarily long) description of the entire library, you will want to consult an online reference, such as `https://developer.mozilla.org/en/JavaScript/Reference`, the ECMAScript standard itself [ECM99, ECM09], or the W3C's DOM Reference (`http://www.w3.org/DOM/`).

7.3.1 Built-in Objects

The Built-in Primitives and Nonconstructor Functions

We covered the three built-in primitives `Infinity`, `NaN`, and `undefined` as well as the functions `parseInt`, `parseFloat`, and `isNaN` earlier. A description of the others follows:

- `isFinite(`n`)` produces `false` if n, when treated as a number, is `Infinity`, `-Infinity`, or `NaN`; otherwise it produces `true`.

- `encodeURI(`s`)` and `encodeURIComponent(`s`)` produce encodings of s according to the syntax of *Uniform Resource Identifiers*. These functions will be described in Chapter 8.

- `decodeURI(`s`)` and `decodeURIComponent(`s`)` produce the inverse operations performed by the corresponding encoding operations. These functions will be described in Chapter 8.

- eval(s) treats the string s as JavaScript code and evaluates it. Calling eval is slow because the string has to be compiled and interpreted.

Some examples:

```
alert(isFinite(-100));              // true
alert(isFinite(2E200 * 2E200));     // false
alert(isFinite("abcdef"));          // false, because converts to NaN
alert(isFinite(null));              // true, because converts to 0

var s = prompt("Enter a numeric formula");
if (/[^\d()+*/-]/.test(s)) {
    alert("I don't trust that input");
} else {
    alert(eval(s));
}
```

The eval function is controversial; some people even call it *evil*. Generally, a programming feature is called evil if it is easy to misuse and the consequences of its misuse are serious. The only reason to use eval in the first place is if you are importing code that is generated at run time.[3] But where would this code come from? If it comes from an untrusted source, a malicious agent could inject some code that wreaks havoc on your application.

As a rule of thumb, if you think you need to use eval, look for alternative ways to do what you want, as they likely exist. Creating and passing around closures take care of many of these cases, as does JSON.parse. If you do end up using eval, you must ensure that the code is safe—no infinite loops, no assignments, no calls, etc. In the preceding example code snippet, we made sure to call eval only if the string was made up exclusively of numbers, parentheses, and simple arithmetic operators. You might wish to start up a discussion with friends (or mentors) on whether this creates a sufficiently "safe" context to use an eval.

Math

The JavaScript Math object, which you saw briefly in Chapter 3, has a fair number of properties for mathematical constants (e, π, $\sqrt{2}$, $\ln 2$, and others) and functions.

---

[3]In other words, you would never write eval("x=3;") when just plain x = 3; would do!

You can find a description of every property of the `Math` object in Appendix A on page 639.

Object

The standard constructor function `Object` may be one of the most important objects in JavaScript, even though you never invoke it directly. It is called implicitly whenever you use an object literal:

```
var a = {};          // Same as var a = new Object();
var b = {x:1, y:2};  // Same as var b = new Object(); b.x=1; b.y=2;
```

Here's why this is so interesting. Because constructor functions define data types, the expression `var a = new Object()` says two things: `a` is an instance of `Object`, and `a`'s prototype is `Object.prototype`. So every object you create with an object literal gets all the behavior defined by `Object.prototype` (see Figure 7.7).

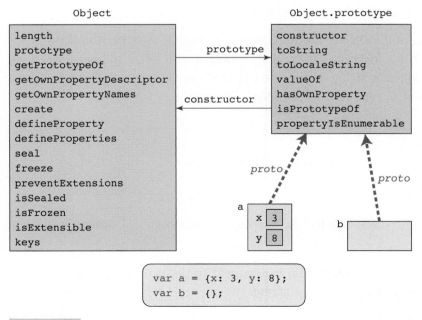

`Object` and `Object.prototype`.

What are these properties that every JavaScript object x gets?

- x.toString() produces a string representation of x. The implementation isn't super-useful, producing things like [object Object] and [object Math]; the reason for its existence will be revealed soon when we talk about overriding.

- x.toLocaleString() produces a string representation of x that is locale-specific; this method is intended to be overridden.

- x.valueOf() produces a primitive (generally a string or number) representation of x; this method is intended to be overridden.

- x.hasOwnProperty(p) produces true if p is an own property of x and false otherwise.

- x.isPrototypeOf(y) produces true if y is the prototype of x and false otherwise.

- x.propertyIsEnumerable(p) produces true if p is an own property of x and enumerable, and false otherwise.

The toString and valueOf methods are very special. Way back in Section 3.8 we laid out the rules for type conversion, pointing out what happens when an object x is used when a string is expected (x.toString() is called) and when a number is expected (x.valueOf() is called). Therefore:

```
var p = {x: 10, y: 5};
alert(p);              // Alerts [object Object].
alert(p - 5);          // Alerts NaN.
```

Why did we get these results? In the case of alert(p), JavaScript did the following:

1. Because alert expects a string, it arranged to perform a type conversion of the object referenced by p to a string.

2. It arranged to call p.toString().

3. It looked for a toString property of p but did not find one.

4. It looked in p's prototype (namely `Object.prototype`), where it did find `toString`.

5. It called `Object.prototype.toString`.

The important thing here is that `Object.prototype` *provides a default imple-mentation of* `toString`. You get it "for free," but you can *override* this behavior by supplying your own `toString`. We could write:

```
var p = {x: 10, y: 5};
p.toString = function () {
    return "(" + this.x + "," + this.y + ")";
};
alert(p);                 // Alerts (10,5).
```

Overriding plays a big part in object-oriented programming, as it allows certain objects to customize (in tech-speak: "specialize") the behaviors they inherit from other objects. These customizations often go at the level of types rather than individual objects (see Figure 7.8).

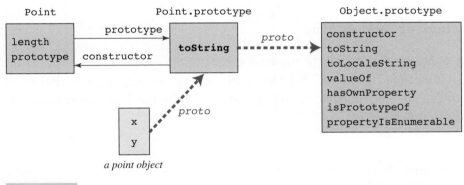

FIGURE 7.8

Overriding `toString`.

```
var Point = function (x, y) {
    this.x = x || 0;
    this.y = y || 0;
}
Point.prototype.toString = function () {
```

```
        return "(" + this.x + "," + this.y + ")";
};
alert(new Point(10, 5));          // Alerts (10,5).
```

The `Object` constructor also has properties of its own, all of which were introduced in ES5. We saw a few of these earlier in the book, albeit in an optional section. They all are described briefly in Appendix A on page 642, while a complete reference can be found, as always, in [ECM09].

Review and Practice

1. What is the significance of `Object.prototype`?

2. Describe overriding in your own words.

3. Write a script defining a data type for dogs, where dogs have a name and a breed, and whenever a dog is used where a string is expected, a string such as "Terrier Patch" or "Retriever Rover" is produced.

Boolean, Number, and String

JavaScript contains three slightly unusual constructors, sometimes called *wrappers*. These functions, `Boolean`, `Number`, and `String`, create objects that contain ("wrap") a single primitive, enabling you to use the method-call syntax (*object.method*) on primitives:

```
"hello".toUpperCase();   // same as new String("hello").toUpperCase()
var n = 2.7182818;
n.toFixed(4);            // same as new Number(n).toFixed(4);
```

Note that you do not need to call these constructors directly; they magically kick in whenever a primitive is used in a method call.

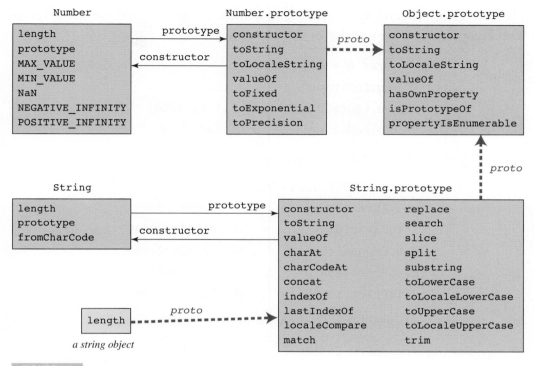

FIGURE 7.9

Number and String constructors.

What are the methods available to strings and numbers? (Let's neglect the useless `Boolean` constructor; it appears to have been added only for the sake of completeness.) Figure 7.9 shows us there are many. The complete set of `Number`, `String`, and `Boolean` methods is described in some detail in Appendix A; here, however, we show some of the more common methods in action. First, we have some numeric constants:

$$\text{Number.MAX\_VALUE} \approx 1.7977 \times 10^{308}$$
$$\text{Number.MIN\_VALUE} \approx 5 \times 10^{-324}$$

The `toString` property is overridden to show the number, and we get a bonus version for showing the number in different bases:

```
var n = 500
n.toString()    ⇒  "500"
n.toString(2)   ⇒  "111110100"
n.toString(16)  ⇒  "1f4"
```

You get three methods for formatting numbers as strings:

```
var x = 2984.83943992
x.toFixed(3)          ⇒   "2984.839"
x.toFixed(6)          ⇒   "2984.839440"
x.toExponential(5)    ⇒   "2.98484e+3"
x.toPrecision(3)      ⇒   "2.98e+3"
x.toPrecision(8)      ⇒   "2984.8394"
```

And, speaking of strings, here are some examples of string operations:

```
String.fromCharCode(1063)       ⇒  "Ч"
"Mississippi".charAt(1)         ⇒  "i"
"Mississippi".charCodeAt(1)     ⇒  105
"Mississippi".indexOf("ss")     ⇒  2
"Mississippi".lastIndexOf("ss") ⇒  5
"boo".concat("hoo", "hoo")      ⇒  "boohoohoo"
"Mississippi".slice(3, 7)       ⇒  "siss"
"Mississippi".split("ss")       ⇒  ["Mi","i","ippi"]
```

Array

Whenever you use an array literal, such as `[]` or `[10,20,30]`, the `Array` constructor is invoked. Your new array object gets properties for its data items and a special `length` property; it also gains over a dozen useful methods courtesy of `Array.prototype` (see Figure 7.10).

We covered arrays already in some detail in Section 3.7 and saw many examples. We will round out our coverage in Appendix A with a complete summary of every array method.

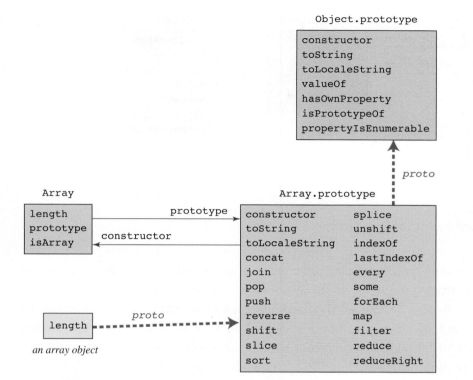

FIGURE 7.10

`Array` and `Array.prototype`.

Review and Practice

1. Give a short description of the JavaScript array methods `concat`, `join`, `push`, `pop`, `shift`, `unshift`, `reverse`, `slice`, and `splice`, and give an example of each. Refer to Appendix A as needed.

2. Experiment with the `Array` constructor. What does `new Array()` produce? How about `new Array(10)`? How about `new Array(4, 17, 26, false)`?

Function

You know quite well that functions are objects, but what kind of object? They are function objects, and they are created with the built-in constructor called `Function`. This constructor creates objects whose prototype value is, naturally,

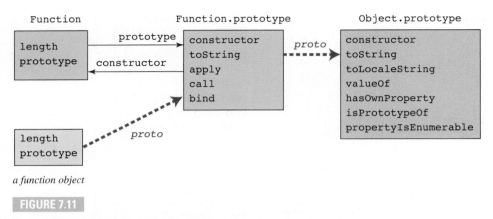

a function object

FIGURE 7.11

`Function` and `Function.prototype`.

`Function.prototype`. `Function.prototype` is a normal object whose prototype is `Object.prototype`, giving us the situation in Figure 7.11.

Back in Chapter 5 you saw the methods `apply` and `call`, which allow you to hijack the value of `this` in a function call. (You may want to review these now; see page 179.) ES5 added the method `bind`, which solves an interesting problem that often pops up in event handling. Remember the `setTimeout` method from Chapter 6? You pass it a function, and that function will be called after a certain number of milliseconds has elapsed. Try this in a shell or test page:

```
var greet = function () {alert("Hello, finally");}
setTimeout(greet, 5000);
```

You should see an alert pop up after 5 seconds. Now what if the function you want to pass to `setTimeout` is a method? The following does not work the way you might expect:

```
var Dog = function (name) {this.name = name;}
Dog.prototype.bark = function () {alert(this.name + " says WOOF");}
var star = new Dog("Bolt");
star.bark();
setTimeout(star.bark, 5000);
```

This code first alerts `"Bolt says WOOF"`, then 5 seconds after you dismiss that alert, a new pop-up appears saying `"says WOOF"`. Why is that? In the `setTimeout` case, we have already evaluated `star.bark` into a function object that includes a reference to `this` in its body. But this function is not called until later, and it is called in a context where `this` refers to the global object, not to Bolt. In fact, if you had created a global variable `name`, that string would appear in the second alert!

`bind` comes to the rescue here, by producing a function whose `this` value is guaranteed to be whatever value you pass to `bind`. You would invoke the delayed call with

```
setTimeout(Dog.prototype.bark.bind(star), 5000);
```

or even

```
setTimeout(star.bark.bind(star), 5000);
```

Binding context is pretty much part of the world of advanced JavaScript, so it's okay if you don't start using `bind` right away. Keep it in mind, however, when you find yourself passing methods to other functions and not seeing the results you expect.

Review and Practice

1. Explain the difference between `apply` and `call`.

2. Draw a picture similar to Figures 7.7, 7.10, and 7.11 that contains the functions `Object`, `Function`, `Array`, and `String`, their prototypes, and all prototype links.

Date

A JavaScript `Date` object represents an instant in time, encoded internally as a number of milliseconds since the *epoch*—midnight at the beginning of January 1, 1970 UTC, written 1970-01-01T00:00:00Z in ISO 8601 [ISO04] notation. Figure 7.12 illustrates how JavaScript dates are represented as points on a single time line, labeled in milliseconds. Three distinct date objects are shown on this line, and each date is rendered four different ways: ISO representations for both Zulu

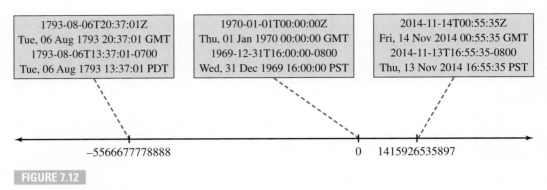

Dates are instants in time.

time[4] and the Los Angeles time zone, and two looser representations, one each for Zulu time and the Los Angeles time zone.

Date objects are instantiated with the **Date** constructor, which can be used in three ways:

- **new Date()**: The current instant of time, as understood by your computing device.

- **new Date(n)**: The instant of time n milliseconds past the epoch.

- **new Date($year, month, day, hour, minute, second, millisecond$)**: The given instant of time, in the current time zone that your computing device is set to. The year and month are required; a missing date defaults to 1 and other missing arguments default to 0. All values should be integers, with the month in the range 0 to 11 (January–December), the day in 1 to 31, the hour in 0 to 23, the minute and second in 0 to 59, and the millisecond in 0 to 999.

Date.prototype overrides **toString** and **toLocaleString** to provide human-readable date strings, and overrides **valueOf** to produce the "epoch time" (milliseconds since the epoch) of the date. For a full listing of the many methods available in **Date.prototype**, see an online reference. One caveat: Don't use **getYear** and **setYear**; use **getFullYear** and **setFullYear** instead. Rather than explaining each of the date methods, we will illustrate a few through a little script that tells you what day of the week you were born and how many days old you are:

---

[4]Zulu time, UTC (Coordinated Universal Time), UT1, and GMT (Greenwich Mean Time) are all essentially the same.

```
var y = +prompt("What year were you born in?");
var m = +prompt("What month were you born in (1-12)?") - 1;
var d = +prompt("What day of the month were you born on?");
var birthday = new Date(y, m, d);
var dayNames = "Sun|Mon|Tues|Wednes|Thurs|Fri|Satur".split("|");
alert("That was a " + dayNames[birthday.getDay()] + "day");
var today = new Date();
var differenceInMillis = today.getTime() - birthday.getTime();
var differenceInDays = Math.floor(differenceInMillis / 86400000);
alert("That was " + differenceInDays + " days ago");
```

In addition to the `getTime` method from `Date.prototype`, you can also generate "epoch time" values (milliseconds since the epoch) with `Date.UTC` and `Date.parse`. The former works like the seven-argument `Date` constructor we saw earlier, except it uses Universal time, not the machine's time zone:

```
var d = Date.UTC(2010, 9, 15, 20, 43, 8, 788);
alert(d);                       // 1287175388788
alert(new Date(d));             // Fri Oct 15 13:43:08 GMT-0700 (PST)
alert(new Date(d).toISOString()); // 2010-10-15T20:43:08.788Z
```

Note the use of the ES5-specific `toISOString` method.

`Date.parse` turns a date string into an epoch time, but the details regarding what kind of strings are allowed are somewhat complex. Modern ES5 implementations support ISO 8601 dates; older browsers do not. You will experiment in one of the end-of-chapter exercises.

Do be aware that date support in JavaScript is rather unsophisticated. It ignores leap seconds, only approximates daylight savings adjustments, and is limited to a proleptic Gregorian calendar with no cutoff date.[5] There is no direct support for alternate calendar systems, such as Julian, Buddhist, Coptic, or Ethiopic, and no direct support for computing periods of times, such as "4 years, 2 months, 3 weeks, and 2 days," rendered in ISO 8601 as `P4Y2M3W2D`.

---

[5] *Proleptic* means that the calendar rules are run indefinitely backward in time, even though no one was using the Gregorian calendar thousands of years ago. The cutoff date refers to the point in time that a country switched from the Julian to the Gregorian calendar. Details are beyond the scope of this text but can be found in Wikipedia's entry for Gregorian calendar.

Error Objects

Interestingly, 7 of the 15 built-in ECMAScript constructors define error types. Error objects are designed to be thrown. Although you can throw anything—strings, numbers, objects of your own creation, even `null`—you will often throw objects. For example:

```
if (month < 1 || month > 12) {
    throw new RangeError("Invalid month");
}
```

Each error constructor takes a single parameter—a message that becomes the value of the `message` property of the object. The seven built-in error "types" are:

Error Type	Thrown...
RangeError	when a value is too small or too large.
SyntaxError	when JavaScript source code is malformed.
TypeError	when a value does not have the expected type.
ReferenceError	when a reference to a variable cannot be resolved.
URIError	when a string cannot be encoded into a valid URI or URI component.
EvalError	(possibly) when an error other than a syntax error occurs in the execution of an eval call.
Error	whenever *you* like.

You will probably throw plain old `Error` most often in your own code. You may even wish to create your own error types that have meaning for your application—perhaps `SecurityError` if a user tries to do something without permission, or

`NavigationError` if someone asks for driving directions to an island with no ferry service.

Each of the error types has prototypes containing four properties: `constructor` (like all prototypes), `name` (containing the constructor name), `message` (with your custom description of the problem), and `toString`, which displays the name, a colon, and the message:[6]

```
var e = new TypeError("Array expected");
alert(e.name);          // Alerts TypeError.
alert(e.message);       // Alerts Array expected.
alert(e);               // Probably alerts TypeError: Array expected.
```

Review and Practice

1. In a JavaScript shell or runner, evaluate an expression that will throw a `ReferenceError`, one that will throw a `TypeError`, and one that will throw a `SyntaxError`.

2. Write a function that sums up the values in an array, throwing a `TypeError` if its argument is not an array.

JSON

The `JSON` object, introduced in ES5, contains two properties:

- `JSON.stringify(o)` produces the (textual) representation of object *o*.

- `JSON.parse(s)` produces the object described by string *s*.

JSON, the *JavaScript Object Notation*, will be described in detail in Section 8.2.3. For a taste of the notation, see Figure 7.13.

---

[6]That is what the ES5 standard says; in ES3 the JavaScript engine can display whatever it wants.

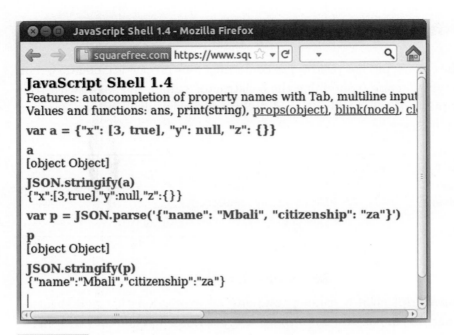

FIGURE 7.13

Using the JSON object.

You will find `JSON.stringify` incredibly useful during debugging.

Review and Practice

1. What does the acronym JSON stand for?

2. Although the `JSON` object was introduced in ES5, many pre-ES5 browsers support it. Find out if your browser does.

3. Why is `JSON.stringify(x)` better than just `x.toString()`?

7.3.2   Web Browser Host Objects

Host objects are those objects provided by the host environment. As web browsers are by far the most common host environment for JavaScript programs, we will briefly describe a few of the most widely used host objects.

alert and prompt

The alert and prompt functions that we have used quite often in this text are host objects because they involve resources that are managed by the web browser: pop-up or dialog windows, buttons, and text fields. Another sign of their being host objects is the way they are implemented in different browsers: the alert and prompt dialogs don't look the same across different browsers; the browser, not JavaScript, defines their look and feel.

document and Friends

Chapter 6 introduced you to the all-important document, and a few of its properties, including the ubiquitous getElementById. But the browser exposes a few other objects that you can script:

- window is the browser window that contains the currently running JavaScript code.

- navigator refers to the web browser application itself.

- screen refers to the user's display screen.

Using these objects is pretty much identical to using any other object—you can read or write them by accessing their properties, and you can make them do things by calling any properties that are functions. If the objects themselves are functions (such as alert and prompt), then you can call them from any context. The difference is that they are provided *by the web browser* and are not strictly a part of the JavaScript language.

The window object deserves some extra attention. In JavaScript, all global variables are actually properties of the one and only *global object*. In a browser environment, the global object contains a property called *window* whose value is a reference to the global object itself! This means the following script alerts true for each line:

```
alert(window.Number === Number);
alert(window.alert === alert);
window.alert(Object === window.Object);
window.alert(window.window === window);
alert(window.window.window.window.window === window);
```

DOM Objects

In the previous chapter, you saw how the components of a web page, such as buttons, text areas, paragraphs, divs, and so on, were exposed as objects that could be manipulated by scripts. There are many dozens of types of these DOM objects; we have listed these types and their properties and behaviors in Appendix A.

Review and Practice

1. What are the differences among native, built-in, and host objects?

2. If a JavaScript program works perfectly in one host environment but reports undefined objects when the same program is run in another environment, what possible cause would be your "prime suspect"?

3. The text so far has identified six web browser host objects. Name them.

4. Within web browser host environments, what makes `window` unique among host objects?

7.4   Modules

Most of the objects you encounter in programming belong to a type and are made with constructors—things like dates, strings, circles, rectangles, points, windows, errors, and buttons. Complex applications such as games and word processors might use several hundred types of objects. To keep things manageable, programmers divvy up their work into multiple scripts. Each script is a sequence of statements, many of which are variable declarations. Variable declarations at the top level of a script are global variables. If two different scripts defining global variables of their own with the same name are both included in the same page, we have a problem. Your page will think the two variables are really one. Because the consequence of this happening can be terrible (i.e., a script that runs fine on its own now crashes when some completely unrelated script just happens to be included in the same page), you will sometimes hear people say that an overreliance on global variables is evil.

7.4.1 Simple Modules

In JavaScript, we cannot do without global variables, but we can minimize their use. A *module* is an object that bundles up a number of related entities. You are familiar with a couple already; the `Math` and `JSON` built-in objects are essentially modules. The `Math` module bundles up what would ordinarily be 26 global variables into properties, as if it were defined as follows:

```
var Math = {
    E: ...;
    PI: ...,
    sin: function (x) {...},
    floor: function (x) {...},
    ...
};
```

Often the functions in a module will work together, and even share data. Usually this shared data should be made invisible to the rest of the system. Perhaps the simplest possible example of such a module is a sequence generator. A generator contains a function (usually called `next`) to return the next value in some sequence. The current value has to be hidden away somewhere so malicious code cannot disrupt the sequence. Suppose our sequence is generated with the transformation

$$x \rightarrow 4x - 3x^2$$

with starting value $x = 0.01$. For lack of a better term (at the moment), we will call our generator g. The first call of `g.next()` should return 0.01; the second call of `g.next()` should return $4(0.01) - 3(0.01)^2 = 0.0097$, and so on. Here is our first attempt:

```
/*
 * A very poor sequence generator.  It does not hide its state.
 */
var g = {
    x: 0.01,
    next: function () {
        var result = this.x;
```

```
        this.x = 4 * this.x - 3 * this.x * this.x;
        return result;
    }
};
```

What's wrong here? The variable x is exposed: we can disrupt the sequence by assigning to $g.x$. In order to hide this variable, we need to make it a local variable in some function. You've seen this trick before:

```
/*
 * A generator for the sequence x -> 4x - 3x^2 starting at 0.01.
 */
var g = function () {
    var x = 0.01;
    return {
        next: function () {
            var result = x;
            x = 4 * x - 3 * x * x;
            return result;
        }
    };
}();
```

Here we are assigning to g the result of *calling* a function with no arguments. What does that function call return? An object. What is in that object? A method called **next**, which delivers the items of the sequence. Can code that uses this module disrupt the sequence or dig into its current state? No. The method **next** is a closure, protecting the closed-over-variable x. We're good.

Now we will use the pattern of hiding state with a closure for a slightly more complex module. Our module will support a game in which players will line up. They may enter only at the end of the line and can take action only when they reach the front of the line. This line (or *queue*) can be implemented with a JavaScript array, but we should hide the array inside a module so none of the players can take cuts! We want this queue to be accessible *only* by adding players to the end and removing them from the front:

```
queue.add("Moe");
queue.add("Larry");
alert(queue.remove());  // Alerts "Moe"
```

```
queue.add("Shemp");
queue.add("Curly");
alert(queue.remove());   // Alerts "Larry"
alert(queue.remove());   // Alerts "Shemp"
```

To make this work, `queue` is defined as a function application expression, returning an object with two methods, each of which are closures using a shared, hidden array:

```
var queue = function () {
    var data = [];
    return {
        add: function (x) {data.push(x);},
        remove: function () {return data.shift();}
    };
}();
```

We hope you are starting to find this pattern natural. Entering and experimenting with the code in a runner or shell will help.

Review and Practice

1. What is the result of the 12th call of `g.next()`?

2. What happens in the queue module if you call `remove` too many times? Modify the module so that an exception is thrown in this case instead.

3. In the queue module, could we have used `unshift` for adding and `pop` for removing? Why or why not?

7.4.2   The Tic-Tac-Toe Game as a Module

The tic-tac-toe script from page 252 contains a large number of global variables, including `turn`, `score`, `squares`, `moves`, `win`, `set`, and others. If we were building a page containing several games including tic-tac-toe, there is a good chance that the scripts for other games would have used some of the same names. We would like to package up the game so that it introduces only one global variable with a unique name, or even *no* global variables.

We will show the no-global-variable approach here, starting with the HTML page. It will include scripts for various games and have placeholder `divs` for the games to be "dropped in."

```html
<!doctype html>
<html>
  <head>
    <meta charset="UTF-8"/>
    <title>Games Page</title>
    <script src="../scripts/chess-module.js"></script>
    <script src="../scripts/tictactoe-module.js"></script>
    <script src="../scripts/blackjack-module.js"></script>
  </head>
  <body>
    <h1>A Games Page</h1>

    <h2>A Chess Game</h2>
    <div id="chess"></div>

    <h2>A Tic Tac Toe Game</h2>
    <div id="tictactoe"></div>

    <h2>A Blackjack Game</h2>
    <div id="blackjack"></div>
  </body>
</html>
```

To make the tic-tac-toe script into a module, we will use the now-familiar technique of hiding that which is to be hidden in local variables. (You might be able to do that on your own.) But something else is different in this chapter—we didn't put any of the layout in the HTML at all. All we have is a `div` in which the script is supposed to create and run the entire game—structure, layout, and interaction. Such a self-contained, possibly complex, user interface component is often called a *widget*. Fortunately, scripts can build documents: use the `createElement` host function to construct new DOM elements and `appendChild` to attach them under an existing element.

Here's the complete script:

```
/*
 * A complete tic-tac-toe widget.  Just include this script in a
 * browser page and enjoy.  A tic-tac-toe game will be included
 * as a child element of the element with id "tictactoe".  If the
 * page has no such element, it will just be added at the end of
 * the body.
 */
(function () {

    var squares = [];
    var EMPTY = "\xA0";
    var score;
    var moves;
    var turn = "X";

    /*
     * To determine a win condition, each square is "tagged" from left
     * to right, top to bottom, with successive powers of 2.  Each cell
     * thus represents an individual bit in a 9-bit string, and a
     * player's squares at any given time can be represented as a
     * unique 9-bit value. A winner can thus be easily determined by
     * checking whether the player's current 9 bits have covered any
     * of the eight "three-in-a-row" combinations.
     *
     *      273                 84
     *        \                /
     *          1 |   2 |   4  = 7
     *        -----+-----+-----
     *          8 |  16 |  32  = 56
     *        -----+-----+-----
     *         64 | 128 | 256  = 448
     *        ==================
     *         73   146   292
     *
     */
    var wins = [7, 56, 448, 73, 146, 292, 273, 84];

    /*
     * Clears the score and move count, erases the board, and makes it
     * X's turn.
```

```
     */
    var startNewGame = function () {
        turn = "X";
        score = {"X": 0, "O": 0};
        moves = 0;
        for (var i = 0; i < squares.length; i += 1) {
            squares[i].firstChild.nodeValue = EMPTY;
        }
    };

    /*
     * Returns whether the given score is a winning score.
     */
    var win = function (score) {
        for (var i = 0; i < wins.length; i += 1) {
            if ((wins[i] & score) === wins[i]) {
                return true;
            }
        }
        return false;
    };

    /*
     * Sets the clicked-on square to the current player's mark,
     * then checks for a win or cat's game.  Also changes the
     * current player.
     */
    var set = function () {
        if (this.firstChild.nodeValue !== EMPTY) return;
        this.firstChild.nodeValue = turn;
        moves += 1;
        score[turn] += this.indicator;
        if (win(score[turn])) {
            alert(turn + " wins!");
            startNewGame();
        } else if (moves === 9) {
            alert("Cat\u2019s game!");
            startNewGame();
        } else {
            turn = turn === "X" ? "O" : "X";
        }
```

```
};

/*
 * Creates and attaches the DOM elements for the board as an
 * HTML table, assigns the indicators for each cell, and starts
 * a new game.
 */
var play = function () {
    var board = document.createElement("table");
    board.border = 1;
    var indicator = 1;
    for (var i = 0; i < 3; i += 1) {
        var row = document.createElement("tr");
        board.appendChild(row);
        for (var j = 0; j < 3; j += 1) {
            var cell = document.createElement("td");
            cell.width = cell.height = 50;
            cell.align = cell.valign = 'center';
            cell.indicator = indicator;
            cell.onclick = set;
            cell.appendChild(document.createTextNode(""));
            row.appendChild(cell);
            squares.push(cell);
            indicator += indicator;
        }
    }

    // Attach under tictactoe if present, otherwise to body.
    var parent = document.getElementById("tictactoe") || document.
        body;
    parent.appendChild(board);
    startNewGame();
};

/*
 * Add the play function to the (virtual) list of onload events.
 */
if (typeof window.onload === "function") {
    var oldOnLoad = window.onload;
    window.onload = function () {oldOnLoad(); play();}
} else {
```

```
                window.onload = play;
        }
}());
```

When the script is referenced in an HTML page, it is run. The script itself is just one function call. It calls a function whose body consists of 10 local variable declarations followed by one `if` statement.[7] The `if` statement makes an assignment to the global `onload` event handler. If there is no existing `onload` function, then the event handler is set to the `play` function. If one does exist, the handler will be assigned a new function that first calls the existing `onload` handler and then calls `play`. So the effect of the script is to start a game when the document finishes loading. We have written *unobtrusive JavaScript* in that our HTML page contains no references to the tic-tac-toe game other than the script that contains the game.

The game-playing code in the script is for the most part identical to the script from Chapter 6, with the obvious exception of the DOM-building code in the `play` method. We will leave you with the exercise of tracing out the activity of this method in building the DOM.

Review and Practice

1. Load the *games.html* page into a browser and play the tic-tac-toe game. Then change the `id` attribute of the tic-tac-toe `div` on the page to something else and reload the page. Verify that the tic-tac-toe board now appears at the bottom of the page.

2. Why is the tic-tac-toe module called a widget?

7.5   The jQuery JavaScript Library

Now that you are acquainted with techniques for building modules, you may be looking forward to writing some of your own. There are certainly few better ways to increase your programming aptitude than writing nontrivial, useful modules. But many times, you will want to take advantage of the thousands of modules other programmers have written for you.

---

[7]Note the parentheses around the function call—they have to be there! JavaScript treats any statement beginning with the word `function` as a function declaration (Section 5.8) and never a call of an anonymous function.

jQuery is one of the most widely used JavaScript libraries. Among other things, it greatly simplifies DOM programming and animations. Longtime JavaScript programmers will tell you of the many hours of their life wasted trying to get their scripts working on multiple browsers. jQuery takes care of these *cross-browser concerns* for you.[8]

Let's get started with jQuery. You can download the library from `http://jquery.com` and store the downloaded file in the same directory as your HTML and JavaScript files, or you may use a copy of the library stored on a public *content delivery network*, or CDN.[9] We will use the CDN at `http://code.jquery.com` in our examples; there are others, such as Microsoft's (see `http://www.asp.net/ajaxlibrary/cdn.ashx`), which are also free to use.

Our HTML document will reference both the jQuery library[10] and a script we are going to write momentarily:

```
<!doctype html>
<html>
  <head>
    <meta charset="UTF-8"/>
    <title>Some countries</title>
    <script src="http://code.jquery.com/jquery-1.6.4.min.js"></script>
    <script src="../scripts/simple-jquery-example.js"></script>
  </head>
  <body>
    <h1>Countries and their states (or provinces)</h1>
    <p>Click on a country to see some states or provinces</p>
    <ul>
      <li><span class="country">M&eacute;xico</span>
        <ul>
          <li>Chiapas</li>
          <li>Durango</li>
          <li>Hidalgo</li>
```

---

[8]jQuery is by no means the only library to simplify DOM programming and mitigate most cross-browser issues, nor was it the first. Other such libraries include MooTools, Dojo, and Prototype. jQuery supports Internet Explorer version 6 and up, all versions of Firefox, Opera 9 and later, and Safari 2 and later.

[9]A CDN consists of servers placed around the world that use techniques such as caching and serving data from the geographically closest server to end users, reducing overall Internet traffic.

[10]Generally, you should use the most recent version of jQuery available; at the time of this writing, this was 1.6.4.

```
        </ul>
      </li>
      <li><span class="country">Pakistan</span>
        <ul>
          <li>&#x67e;&#x646;&#x62c;&#x627;&#x628;</li>
          <li>&#x633;&#x646;&#x62f;&#x6be;</li>
          <li>&#x628;&#x644;&#x648;&#x686;&#x633;&#x62a;&#x627;&#x646;
            </li>
        </ul>
      </li>
      <li><span class="country">Brasil</span>
        <ul>
          <li>Par&aacute;</li>
          <li>Sergipe</li>
          <li>Maranh&atilde;o</li>
        </ul>
      </li>
    </ul>
  </body>
</html>
```

Now, here is our first example script. It illustrates simple animation and event handling:

```
/*
 * This is a first script using jQuery, illustrating the common
 * effect of showing "one child list at a time."
 */
$(document).ready(function () {

    // Hide all second-level lists with a roll-up effect
    $("ul ul").hide("slow");

    // Register listeners for clicking on top-level list items
    $(".country").click(function () {

        // First hide all second-level lists immediately
        $("ul ul").hide();
```

```
        // Then slowly expose the children of the clicked item
        $(this).next().show("slow");
    });
});
```

The jQuery library exports two global variables, `jquery` and `$`. Both refer to the same object, a function. The result of passing an expression to the function is a set of DOM objects to which you can apply dozens of interesting actions. The expression is called a selector; some examples include:[11]

- `$("img")`—the set of all `img` elements

- `$("#footer")`—the set of all elements with `id` attribute `"footer"`

- `$("div.contents")`—the set of all `div` elements with `class` attribute `"contents"`

- `$("div.contents ol")`—the set of all `ol` elements that are a descendant of a `div` element with class `"contents"`

- `$("div.contents > ol")`—the set of all `ol` elements that are a direct child of a `div` element with class `"contents"`

- `$("div:has(ol)")`—the set of all `div`s that have a nested `ol` element as a descendant

- `$("p:animated")`—the set of all `p` elements in the process of being animated

You can also pass a regular DOM element to the `$` function to create a set containing just that element. It is very common to see code with expressions such as `$(document)` and `$(this)`.

Once you have a set of DOM objects produced with `$`, you apply actions to the set. A small sampling of methods you can apply to a set follows:

- Effects: `animate`, `stop`, `slideUp`, `slideDown`, `fadeIn`, `fadeOut`, `fadeTo`, `show`, `hide`, `toggle`, etc.

---

[11]For the complete selector syntax (there are over 50 such forms in jQuery 1.6.4), consult the jQuery documentation at `http://api.jquery.com/category/selectors/`.

- DOM manipulations: `before`, `after`, `append`, `wrap`, `addClass`, `prepend`, `unwrap`, `remove`, etc.

- Event handler registration: `click`, `dblclick`, `mousedown`, `mouseup`, `mousemove`, `mouseenter`, `mouseleave`, `mouseover`, `scroll`, `keydown`, `keyup`, `keypress`, `hover`, `submit`, `focus`, `blur`, `ready`, `load`, `unload`

In our example script, the sole statement registers a function to run when the document is ready.[12] This function first uses the selector `"ul ul"` to hide, slowly, all the unordered lists that are inside of other unordered lists. We have highlighted the result of this selector in Figure 7.14, so you can see it does apply to the "second-level" lists.

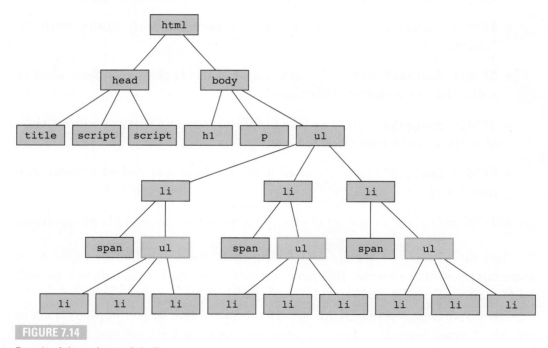

FIGURE 7.14

Result of the selector "ul ul".

Next, the script registers a function for clicks on country names. We have embedded the country names in `span` elements; registering the listener on the `li` elements would not have worked well (do you see why?). This click handler hides

---

[12]`$(document).ready($f$)` is strongly preferred to `window.onload = $f$`.

all the second-level lists, then slowly exposes (via **show**) all of the states of the country that was clicked. The target of the event was the span, and the list of states is a *sibling* of the span, selected by the jQuery method **next** (refer again to Figure 7.14 if you need help understanding this method).

Nearly every method in jQuery returns an element set. Sometimes, as with **next**, **prev**, **siblings**, **parent**, or **children**, you get a new element set. But often, you get the same element set. Either way, getting an element set makes possible a programming style called *method chaining*. Run this one-liner in the runner (**http://javascript.cs.lmu.edu/runner**):

```
$("#header").html("JS Runner").css("color","green").slideUp().slideDown
  ()
```

This selects the header element, then changes its inner HTML,[13] then changes its color to green, then slides it up (to hide it), then slides it down (to show it). The preceding code is equivalent to this inferior code fragment:

```
// This is an example of poor jQuery style.  Don't code like this.
var element = $("#header");
element.html("JS Runner");
element.css("color", "green");
element.slideUp();
element.slideDown();
```

There is more to jQuery than selectors and actions: the jQuery object has dozens of its own properties. Some are simple utilities:

- **$.isArray**($e$) returns **true** if e is a JavaScript array, and **false** otherwise.

- **$.contains**($e_1, e_2$) returns **true** if DOM element e_2 is a descendant of DOM element e_1, and **false** otherwise.

- **$.merge**($a, b$) merges the elements of array b into array a.

Others, such as **$.ajax**, **$.get**, and **$.post**, communicate with a web server; these will appear in the next chapter.

---

[13]Notice how jQuery's **html** method replaces the usual assignment to the **innerHTML** property.

In addition, jQuery ensures event objects, regardless of the browser being used, have a uniform interface. This saves programmers from dealing with the many differences between Internet Explorer and the rest of the modern browser family. Event objects are always passed to jQuery handlers, and event objects always contain the properties `target`, `currentTarget`, `timeStamp`, `preventDefault`, and `stopPropagation`, even when using Internet Explorer.

Besides solving, to a great extent, the "cross-browser problem" and simplifying DOM programming, jQuery has become an extremely popular library because it

- has a simple programming model: (1) find elements with selectors, then (2) apply actions to them;

- encourages programming with *unobtrusive JavaScript*;

- is relatively small and thus downloads quickly;

- is well documented; and

- has a large community of users, many of whom have contributed thousands of extensions known as plugins (see `http://plugins.jquery.com/`).

We cannot possibly cover the entire library in this text; the online documentation (`http://docs.jquery.com`) and entire books devoted to jQuery are readily available. We will be making use of jQuery throughout the rest of the text. And as we have mentioned before, the best way to learn is by doing, so don't skip the many end-of-chapter exercises that encourage you to explore this library.

Review and Practice

1. Explain the jQuery programming model.

2. Browse the index of jQuery functions on the page `http://api.jquery.com/`. How many functions are supported in the current version?

3. In the country and states example, why did we need `span` elements for the country names? What would have happened if we left out the `spans` and registered click listeners on `body > ul > li`?

7.6   Performance

In addition to creating code that is correct and maintainable, software designers and developers strive to create *efficient* code. Efficient scripts (1) do not take longer than necessary to run, (2) do not use up too much memory or other limited system resources, (3) do not take too long to load, and (4) respond quickly to user actions. We will cover each of these four kinds of efficiency in this section.

7.6.1   Run-Time Efficiency

A fast-running (efficient) script is usually better than an equivalent slow (inefficient) script. There is a wealth of information on writing efficient JavaScript code, including slideshows [Fuc09, Che10, Zak09b], video lectures [Zak09a], blog posts, articles, and a fair number of books. The science of improving your code to make it more efficient, known by the not-quite-accurate label of *code optimization*, is vast. We can't do justice to the entire topic, but we do have a little space to give you the big picture via a brief introduction—and a few examples, of course.

But first, a word of caution. Beware of speedups that make your code hard to read and hard to maintain [New99]. You should never trade readability for miniscule gains in performance—only tune for speed when it matters. For instance, suppose your script takes 5 minutes to run and you find a block of code that can be sped up by 0.5 milliseconds by replacing it with some clever, nearly unreadable (but functionally equivalent) code. If that block of code is executed only once (i.e., it's not in a loop), then you would only reduce your running time from 300 to 299.9995 seconds; the time you spent designing and writing the new code, and the headaches you will give to those reading it, is *not* worth the speedup. However, if the block of code appears in a loop that runs 100, 000 times, your running time is reduced from 300 to 250 seconds, which is quite significant![14]

The most basic (and self-evident) principle behind writing efficient code is this: perform computations in as few "steps" as is reasonable. Avoid both *useless*

---

[14]Donald Knuth made this point quite eloquently (and now famously) in a 1974 paper [Knu74]: "Programmers waste enormous amounts of time thinking about, or worrying about, the speed of noncritical parts of their programs, and these attempts at efficiency actually have a strong negative impact when debugging and maintenance are considered. We should forget about small efficiencies, say about 97% of the time: premature optimization is the root of all evil. Yet we should not pass up our opportunities in that critical 3%."

computations and *repeated* computations. For instance (talking about "useless" computation), you wouldn't look for a name in a phone book by scanning every name from the beginning. Often you can organize data to get what you need very quickly. We will see an example of this in Section 10.2.2.

The way to avoid needlessly repeating the same computation multiple times is to compute a value once, save the result in a local variable, and use the variable in place of subsequent computations. We saw this technique in prime number scripts from previous chapters. We did not write

```
for (var k = 2; k <= Math.sqrt(n); k += 1) {
    // body of for-loop
}
```

but rather

```
for (var k = 2, last = Math.sqrt(n); k <= last; k += 1) {
    // body of for-loop
}
```

in order to compute the square root only once. Square roots are expensive to compute, while looking up the value of a local variable is about the cheapest operation you can do. But it isn't just function calls (like `Math.sqrt`) and expressions involving operators that qualify as "expensive" enough to do only once; even examining the value of a nonlocal variable or an object property involves a bit of work:

- To access a nonlocal variable, the scope chain has to be searched. When executing code inside a nested function, global variables may take time to reach (see Figure 7.15).

- To access a property of an object, the JavaScript engine has to search the object to see if it has a property with the given name; failing that, it has to search the prototype chain.

These observations have led to several programming idioms such as:

```
// It is possible to do multiple assignments in the first section
// of a for-statement.  Each will be done only once.  This means
// the test to exit the loop can be done with a local variable.
for (var i = 0, n = a.length; i < n; i += 1)
```

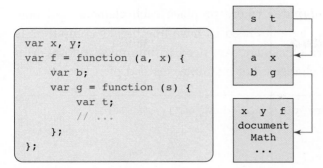

```
var x, y;
var f = function (a, x) {
    var b;
    var g = function (s) {
        var t;
        // ...
    };
};
```

FIGURE 7.15

Scope chain search.

```
// Reference the document locally to avoid always searching the
// scope chain.
var doc = document;
```

```
// Store this frequently accessed function locally.
var el = document.getElementById;
el("next").onclick = ...;
el("footer").value = ...;
```

Remember to only play these games if you are using the computation more than once, and only if it makes the code more readable. However, you may be able to relax the "more readable" requirement if the (unoptimized) code is running too slowly and the time savings are significant.

There's more, of course. Although JavaScript is technically a programming language that lives independently of the Web, it would be irresponsible not to mention the performance pitfalls involved in working with the DOM, as well as approaches to avoiding them. We could spend an entire chapter, or indeed another book, on this topic, but we will address just two issues here. (The exercises at the end of the chapter contain links to more comprehensive sources and give you a chance to practice with the techniques.)

First, many changes to the DOM, such as adding or removing elements, changing margins or alignment, resizing images, or moving elements, cause the browser to immediately *reflow* the page. This is an expensive operation in which the browser traverses the entire DOM and computes where to place each element and how much space to reserve for it. Text elements need to have line breaks computed as well. To make dynamic pages work efficiently, you need to minimize reflows. You do this by "batching" your DOM changes. For example, instead of

```
var intro = document.getElementById("introduction");
intro.style.color = "green";
intro.style.fontStyle = "italic";
intro.style.paddingBottom = "50px";
intro.style.fontSize = "300%";
```

you should write

```
var intro = document.getElementById("introduction");
intro.setAttribute("style",
    "color:green;font-style:italic;padding-bottom:50px;font-size:300%"
);
```

This sets all the styles at once, without reflowing between changes.[15] Another way to batch changes is to make them "off-document," then add the entire modified element structure at once. Review the DOM building code in the tic-tac-toe module in Section 7.4. We created many elements, ultimately wiring them up under a single **table** element. Only after all of the elements were connected did we finally add the table to the document.

If you cannot build up an off-document structure rooted at a single element (as we did with the **table** element), you can use a **DocumentFragment**. Let's go right to the example:

```
// BAD CODE: This is an inefficient way to add elements to a document.
var list = document.getElementById("days");
var days = "Sun,Mon,Tue,Wed,Thu,Fri,Sat".split(",");
for (var i = 0, n = days.length; i < n; i += 1) {
    var item = document.createElement("li");
    item.innerHTML = days[i];
    list.appendChild(item);
}
```

---

[15]Better yet, just attach a CSS class to the element. We will see how in Section 9.2.2.

Because the list element (with ID **days**) already exists in the document, each addition of a list item invokes a reflow. Instead, use a document fragment:

```
var list = document.getElementById("days");
var days = "Sun,Mon,Tue,Wed,Thu,Fri,Sat".split(",");
var fragment = document.createDocumentFragment();
for (var i = 0, n = days.length; i < n; i += 1) {
    var item = document.createElement("li");
    item.innerHTML = days[i];
    fragment.appendChild(item);
}
list.appendChild(fragment);
```

Adding the document fragment as a child of an element is just like adding all of the fragment's components as children, but without reflowing after each addition.

The second source of DOM inefficiency is the dreaded **HTMLCollection** object. Many DOM calls, like **getElementsByTagName**, only appear to produce arrays; instead they produce *live objects*—objects whose values change magically whenever the DOM changes. Look closely at the following script:

```
1  var doc = document;
2  var paragraphs = doc.getElementsByTagName("p");
3  alert(paragraphs.length);
4  doc.body.appendChild(doc.createElement("p"));
5  alert(paragraphs.length);
```

On line 2, we create a local variable called **paragraphs**, containing all of the **p** elements in the current page. Then we alert its length. On line 4, we create a new **p** element and add it to the page. On line 5, we see that our local variable's length has increased! The creation of a new element on line 4 clearly added to the page's DOM, but you might not have expected it to change our little collection that we apparently squirreled away into a local variable. But it does. The live object referenced by **paragraphs** is like a view into the DOM. Whenever you reference it, the JavaScript engine is likely running code to find all the elements in the collection again.

The moral here is that naïvely manipulating **HTMLCollection** objects in a loop can have huge performance consequences. We will explore some of these consequences in the end-of-chapter exercises.

1. Memorize the quote from Donald Knuth given in this section—the one that includes the phrase "premature optimization is the root of all evil." What does he mean by "premature"?

2. Consider the advice "only look for optimization opportunities inside of loops." Why would someone make such a statement?

3. Why is it generally less efficient to access global variables than local variables?

4. What are the two major sources of inefficiency in DOM programming mentioned in this section?

7.6.2   Space Efficiency

Memory, like disk storage, network bandwidth, and other kinds of space for holding and transmitting data, is a finite resource. Your JavaScript engine has a limited amount of memory to work with. When you create objects or call functions, the engine needs to obtain memory. When an object is no longer needed, or a function returns (without being captured by a closure), memory can be reclaimed so that it can be allocated again in the future.

If an object is referenced only by a variable that is local to a function, the variable goes out of scope when the function exits so the object's memory can be reclaimed. But if an object is captured by a global variable, you may sometimes wish to manually disassociate the object from the variable by assigning a different value to the variable. In Figure 7.16, we have assigned the value `null` to a variable that formerly contained an object reference.

Every object you create takes up storage space. When an object ceases to be referenced from any variable, it becomes *garbage*. The assignment to c in Figure 7.16 created garbage; we have highlighted this fact by drawing the detached object with a dashed line. The JavaScript engine eventually (and automatically) *reclaims* garbage, freeing up storage space for new objects that will be created later. Generating garbage is a good thing! If you "hold on" to objects you will never use again, you might eventually fill up all available memory and your script will stop working. A script that fails to detach objects that it will never use again

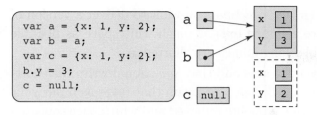

FIGURE 7.16

Assigning `null` to a variable.

is said to have a *memory leak*. If you have too many memory leaks, your script will eventually run out of memory and crash.

In addition, some scripts simply ask for too much memory. We have seen examples of poor memory utilization before in our lead-up to explaining function prototypes for sharing object behavior: every object literal or function expression creates a new object. We should therefore share large objects whenever possible.

Review and Practice

1. What happens in your favorite browser when your script runs out of memory? Write a script that fills up memory to find out.

2. What causes garbage to occur?

3. What is a memory leak? Why are memory leaks bad? How do you prevent them?

4. Local variables should "go away" when their containing function returns, thus freeing up the space they were using while their function was alive. But as we pointed out in this section, this only happens if the function is not "captured by a closure." What exactly does this mean? Illustrate your answer with diagrams.

7.6.3 Load-Time Efficiency

Suppose you have just created a lovely script—10,000 lines of beautifully formatted, readable code, with precise indentation, nice long variable names, crisp modules, and descriptive comments. To get the script to your users, all these long variable names and spaces and comments need to be transferred over the network to their devices. To shorten the *load time* you want to deliver a version of your script in which comments are stripped out, as much whitespace as possible is squeezed out, and, where possible, long names are shortened.

Hopefully you did not think even for a second that *you* should write the shortened code yourself! No, you employ a *minifier*, a program that takes as input your nice script and outputs a version with comments removed and whitespace squeezed out. Many people have written minifiers and have made them available for free. Try a web search for "JavaScript minifier."

In addition to minification, large scripts can be compressed using standard tools like `zip` or `gzip`. If the web server is set up to tell the client that the scripts are zipped, the browser should be able to uncompress the scripts after they are delivered. The details of setting up a server are beyond the scope of this text, however. Note that the time it takes for the browser to uncompress the script needs to outweigh the savings in network transfer time for this technique to have any benefit.

A relative of minification is *obfuscation*. An obfuscator will take in your script and produce an equivalent, difficult-to-read script. The obfuscated script may or may not be smaller than the original. The obfuscator's purpose is to make it difficult and time-consuming for end users to figure out the programmer's "trade secrets."

Here is an obfuscation of the temperature converter script we saw way back in Chapter 2, produced at `http://www.javascriptobfuscator.com/`. We have modified it so that it fits on the printed page; the actual obfuscation comprises just one line of code.

```
var _0x44a9=["\x69\x6E\x6E\x65\x72\x48\x54\x4D\x4C","\x72\x65
\x73\x75\x6C\x74","\x67\x65\x74\x45\x6C\x65\x6D\x65\x6E\x74\x
42\x79\x49\x64","\xB0\x43\x20\x3D\x20","\xB0\x46","\x6F\x6E\x
63\x6C\x69\x63\x6B","\x66\x5F\x74\x6F\x5F\x63","\x76\x61\x6C\
x75\x65","\x74\x65\x6D\x70\x65\x72\x61\x74\x75\x72\x65","\x63
\x5F\x74\x6F\x5F\x66"];var report=function (_0xf30ax2,_0xf30a
x3){document[_0x44a9[2]](_0x44a9[1])[_0x44a9[0]]=_0xf30ax2+_0
x44a9[3]+_0xf30ax3+_0x44a9[4];} ;document[_0x44a9[2]](_0x44a9
[6])[_0x44a9[5]]=function (){var _0xf30ax4=document[_0x44a9[2
```

```
]](_0x44a9[8])[_0x44a9[7]];report((_0xf30ax4-32)/1.8,_0xf30ax
4);} ;document[_0x44a9[2]](_0x44a9[9])[_0x44a9[5]]=function (
){var _0xf30ax5=document[_0x44a9[2]](_0x44a9[8])[_0x44a9[7]];
report(_0xf30ax5,1.8*_0xf30ax5+32);};
```

Not everyone uses obfuscators. Many (if not most) programmers take pride in their work and are thrilled when end users look at it. Others dislike obfuscators because the very idea of hiding the code is in opposition to the values of open source [Ope02], one of which is that users of software should have access to the source code they are running.

Review and Practice

1. Explain *minification* and *obfuscation* as they apply to JavaScript code. What is the purpose of each?

2. Run the tic-tac-toe script from this chapter through the minifier of your choice. What are the script sizes before and after minification?

7.6.4 User Interface Efficiency

One efficiency concern deserves to have a section all to itself: the responsiveness of the user interface. When a user presses a button, clicks on a link, or drags an object, feedback must be presented immediately. Users get frustrated when nothing seems to happen. How hard is it to ensure the system is responsive? After all, when an event occurs, the event handler runs right away, right? Well, not quite. It actually doesn't start running until the event handlers for all previous events have finished.

In Chapter 6, we said there was a "hidden caller" that invoked the event handlers.[16] This hidden caller is known as *the main event loop*. In JavaScript-like

---

[16]In the earliest event-driven systems, this caller *wasn't* hidden, and *did* have to be coded by the programmer. The fact that this code has now been sufficiently generalized and structured so that it is the same for all event-driven programs, with differences seen only in specific event handlers, is a testament to the ongoing evolution of user interface technologies.

syntax, it looks roughly like this:

```
while (!timeToQuit()) {
    var event = waitForNextEvent();
    if (hasHandler(event)) {
        invokeHandler(getHandlerFor(event));
    }
}
```

where:

- `timeToQuit` represents how the program determines whether it should end.

- `waitForNextEvent` is the 800-pound gorilla. It encapsulates the computation that detects when something takes place within the system, then captures the information pertaining to this event within some object assigned to an `event` variable. This can be quite involved, with hooks ranging all the way to a system's hardware and input/output devices.

- `hasHandler` represents the check for whether code has been registered to run for this event.

- `getHandlerFor` is a corollary of sorts to `hasHandler`; it represents the retrieval, in whatever form is defined by the system, for the code that comprises the event handler.

- `invokeHandler` represents the invocation mechanism used by a system for running the event handler's code. Frequently, the event handler is simply a function, so `invokeHandler` would be a standard function call.

These days, knowledge of the main event loop is considered supplementary; many programmers successfully write event-driven code without having an explicit awareness of the main event loop as a concrete concept. However, presenting the main event loop as shown here exposes a "gotcha" that many programmers encounter sooner rather than later.

The concern is this: while an event handler is being invoked, *no other events are being processed.* Events are queued up while the event handler executes. Only after a handler finishes can subsequent events be processed. If one handler performs a lengthy computation, the system will seem unresponsive or perhaps even frozen from the user's point of view. Whenever an application feels sluggish or jerky while the rest of the system seems to be running along fine, chances are that the currently executing event handler is running long and is therefore preventing the main event loop from processing subsequent events.

Here's a concrete illustration. Load the following page (with the associated script) into a browser, and press the Find It button to launch a calculation to find the millionth prime number. While the computation is taking place, try to type into the text area.

```html
<!doctype html>
<html>
  <head>
    <meta charset="utf-8" />
    <title>Let's find a prime number</title>
  </head>
  <body>
    <div>The millionth prime number is
      <span id="answer"><button id="go">Find it</button></span>
    </div>
    <p>While computing, try typing into this box:</p>
    <textarea rows="10" cols="50"></textarea>
    <script type="text/javascript" src="nthprime.js"></script>
  </body>
</html>
```

```javascript
/*
 * This script responds to clicking on the button with id "go"
 * by computing the millionth prime and writing it to the element
 * with id "answer".  TERRIBLE CODE: Clicking on the button will
 * hang the user interface until the computation finishes!
 */
document.getElementById("go").onclick = function () {
    Find: for (var n = 2, count = 0; count < 1000000; n += 1) {
        for (var k = 2, last = Math.sqrt(n); k <= last; k += 1) {
            if (n % k === 0) {
                continue Find;
```

```
            }
        }
        count += 1;
    }
    // Because the silly for loop goes too far...
    document.getElementById("answer").innerHTML = (n - 1);
}
```

You should find yourself unable to type, but after a minute or so the computation will finish, the result will be written on the page, and your interactivity will be restored. (If you don't notice a lock-up because your browser's JavaScript engine is blazingly fast, change the script to find the 5- or the 20- or the 100-millionth prime.)

There are two ways to keep a script responsive during a long-running computation. The first is to break the computation into chunks. In the following improved script, a helper function computes 10,000 primes, then schedules itself to run again after 50 milliseconds. During the breaks, other events can be handled. Reload the page with this new script and notice that typing in the text area is possible during the computation:

```
/*
 * This script responds to clicking on the button with id "go"
 * by computing the millionth prime and writing it to the element
 * with id "answer".  The computation works by computing 10,000
 * primes at a time, with 50-ms delays between chunks.  After each
 * chunk, we write progress information to the "answer" element.
 */
(function () {
    var n = 2, count = 0;
    var findMore = function () {
        Find: for (; true; n += 1) {
            for (var k = 2, last = Math.sqrt(n); k <= last; k += 1) {
                if (n % k === 0) {
                    continue Find;
                }
            }
            count += 1;
            if (count === 1000000) {
                document.getElementById("answer").innerHTML = n;
```

```
            return;
        } else if (count % 10000 === 0) {
            document.getElementById("answer").innerHTML =
                "(found " + count + " so far)";
            setTimeout(findMore, 50);
            n += 1;
            return;
        }
    }
    }
    document.getElementById("go").onclick = findMore;
}());
```

If you have a very recent browser, you can employ *web workers* to fix the long-running handler problem. A web worker is code that *runs on a different thread of control* than does the main event loop. You will research web workers and reimplement the millionth-prime finder page with them in one of the end-of-chapter exercises.

> **Ensure all event handlers run quickly. Break up long-running actions into chunks or use web workers to keep the script responsive.**

Review and Practice

1. What *does not happen* in the main event loop during the handling of a particular event?

2. Write a script that creates an event handler with an infinite loop and attaches it to a button. Click the button and report what happens.

7.7 Unit Testing

The last area of software construction we will cover in this chapter is one of the most important: testing. The cost of software failure can be high and can include loss of property or human life. It is irresponsible to release code that has not been tested.

What kinds of testing should be performed? Who is supposed to test, and when? How can we construct good tests? And why, really, must we test? Let's tackle the easy questions first. There are at least three considerations when testing:

- How much of the system are you testing?

    - *Unit testing* helps ensure that individual components, such as JavaScript objects, function as advertised.

    - *Integration testing* helps ensure that components can communicate with each other properly.

    - *System testing* helps ensure that a fully built system has no defects from a user's point of view.

- Which aspects of the system are you testing?

    - *Performance testing* checks to see if the system runs within specified temporal and spatial constraints.

    - *Regression testing* checks to see if the latest fixes and enhancements broke something that used to work.

    - *Stress testing* ensures that the system holds up under excessive load or when run in an environment without reasonable resources.

- Are you testing the code itself or its overall behavior?

    - *Black box testing* looks only at inputs and outputs and makes sure the outputs are as expected, ignoring the underlying implementation.

    - *White box testing* "exercises" an implementation with an eye toward getting good *code coverage*. Yes, access to source code is needed to do this.

A software development organization will have roles for personnel to perform *quality assurance* (QA) and *user acceptance testing* (UAT). These roles focus on black box, system, performance, regression, and stress testing. The programmers themselves are responsible for (white or black box) unit testing and integration tests. (In practice, integration tests tend to look like unit tests, so we will cover only unit tests here.)

Review and Practice

1. Why is unit testing important?

2. Why does UAT normally involve only black box as opposed to white box testing?

7.7.1   An Introductory Example

Your unit tests should aim at ensuring that all of your functions, objects, and modules work as expected. Let's start with a very simple example—a little statistics module:

```
/*
 * A small module containing statistics functions.
 */
var Stats = {

    /*
     * Returns the mean (average) of the elements in a. Precondition:
     * a is an array of finite numbers.
     */
    mean: function (a) {
        var sum = 0;
        for (var i = 0; i < a.length; i += 1) {
            sum += a[i];
        }
        return sum / a.length;
    },

    /*
     * Returns the median of the elements in a. Precondition: a is an
     * array of finite numbers.
     */
    median: function (a) {
        var b = a.sort(function (x, y) {return x - y;});
        var mid = Math.floor(b.length / 2);
        return b.length % 2 !== 0 ? b[mid] : (b[mid-1] + b[mid]) / 2;
    },
```

```
/*
 * Returns the range (difference between the max and min) of the
 * elements in a. Precondition: a is an array of finite numbers.
 */
range: function (a) {
    return Math.max.apply(Math, a) - Math.min.apply(Math, a);
}
};
```

What tests are required? One important rule is to be thorough. When testing functions, think of all possible kinds of inputs you might see—especially "edge" cases like empty arrays, zero, negative numbers, very tiny numbers, very large numbers, infinity, empty strings, objects with no properties, undefined, null, and so on. Look at places in the code where decisions are made and test each outcome; in our statistics example, we see that the median is computed a little differently for even-length and odd-length arrays. Look also for strong claims that can be made about the unit under test. In the statistics functions, the order of array elements is not supposed to matter, so our test cases should consist of a good mix of orderings.

Once you determine the scenarios you need to test, make a note of the operations and their expected results; for example:

Test Case	Expected
Stats.mean([2, 8, 11])	7
Stats.median([1, 17, 6, 0, 5])	5
Stats.range([2, 8, 11])	9
Stats.range([])	NaN
etc.	

Next, you need to write your tests. Read that last sentence again: you need to *write* tests. Testing is *programming*, not sitting at a keyboard running code to see if it works. A real-world system will have thousands of tests, all of them needing to be run often—hundreds of times a day. When a change is made to the code, the whole test suite needs to be rerun. Humans cannot be expected to manually type and run every test one at a time in front of a computer screen. You need code that runs the entire batch of test cases, checking whether the results are as expected and recording the number of successes and failures. The code that does the running and bookkeeping of the tests is called a *testing framework*. While you could write your own testing framework, it is best to use an existing one; this frees you to focus on your job—writing good tests.

Review and Practice

1. Why are edge cases (also known as boundary cases) important in testing? Do some research on the topic.

2. Extend the table of tests in this section.

3. Why do we need testing frameworks?

7.7.2 The QUnit Testing Framework

While you can choose among many free testing frameworks, we will focus on just one: QUnit. QUnit is well documented at `http://docs.jquery.com/QUnit/`. Like many JavaScript testing frameworks, you use an HTML page as the context for running and reporting:

```
<!doctype html>
<html>
  <head>
    <!-- INCLUDE THE QUNIT SCRIPT HERE -->
    <!-- INCLUDE YOUR SCRIPT HERE -->
    <!-- INCLUDE YOUR TESTS HERE --->
  </head>
  <body>
    <!-- INCLUDE DOM ELEMENTS FOR REPORTING HERE -->
  </body>
</html>
```

When this page is loaded (or reloaded), the tests will run and the reports will be generated inside the body. The only required DOM element is an ordered list element with ID `qunit-tests`:

```
<ol id="qunit-tests"></ol>
```

However, in practice, you will want to make your reporting much more comprehensive, and even pretty. QUnit can render a professional-looking report with the test suite name and a status bar (green if all tests pass, red if at least one failure), among other things. It is built to work with jQuery and comes with a nice style sheet.[17] Our full, jQuery-enhanced test page is as follows:

```html
<!doctype html>
<html>
  <head>
    <title>Stats Test</title>
    <link rel="stylesheet"
      href="http://code.jquery.com/qunit/git/qunit.css"
      type="text/css"
    />
    <script src="http://code.jquery.com/jquery-latest.min.js"></script>
    <script
      src="http://code.jquery.com/qunit/git/qunit.js"
      ></script>
    <script src="../scripts/statistics.js"></script>
    <script src="statistics-test.js"></script>
  </head>
  <body>
    <h1>Statistics Test Suite</h1>
    <h2 id="qunit-banner"></h2>
    <div id="qunit-testrunner-toolbar"></div>
    <h2 id="qunit-userAgent"></h2>
    <ol id="qunit-tests"></ol>
  </body>
</html>
```

Now for the tests themselves. Tests cannot run until the document is ready; since we are using jQuery, we can wrap our entire test suite in the usual `$(document).ready` call. A test suite contains *assertions*. An assertion is expressed by one of the following three functions:

- ok(*condition*, *message*)—passes if *condition* is truthy.

- equals(*actual*, *expected*, *message*)—passes if *actual* == *expected*. Note that this method uses the sloppy == instead of the recommended ===.

---

[17]We will talk about style sheets in Section 9.2.2.

- `same`(*actual*, *expected*, *message*)—is similar to `equals`, except that it uses `===` and, if there are arrays or objects, also performs comparisons on the components of these objects. For example:

`equals({x:1, y:2}, {x:1, y:2})`	⇒ `false`
`same({x:1, y:2}, {x:1, y:2})`	⇒ `true`
`equals(null, undefined)`	⇒ `true`
`same(null, undefined)`	⇒ `false`
`same({x:1,y:[true,"xyz"]}, {x:1,y:[true,"xyz"]})`	⇒ `true`

Assertions can include messages that will be written to the test report. The messages are optional, but if you don't have them, the output will be rather hard to follow. Here now is our test suite for the stats module:

```
/*
 * Unit tests for the statistics module.
 */
$(document).ready(function () {

    test("Mean Tests", function () {
        same(Stats.mean([1]), 1, "1 element mean");
        same(Stats.mean([1, 7]), 4, "2 element mean");
        same(Stats.mean([-2.5, 10, -7.5]), 0, "3 element mean");
        ok(isNaN(Stats.mean([])), "mean of [] is NaN");
    });

    test("Median Tests", function () {
        same(Stats.median([9, 6, 4, 100]), 7.5, "median of four");
        same(Stats.median([3]), 3, "median of one");
        same(Stats.median([10, 12]), 11, "median of two");
        same(Stats.median([6, 3, 4, 1, 2, 5, 7]), 4, "median of many");
        ok(isNaN(Stats.median([])), "median of [] is NaN");
    });

    test("Range Tests", function () {
        same(Stats.range([9]), 0, "range of 1 element");
        same(Stats.range([1, 7]), 6, "range of 2 elements");
        same(Stats.range([-5, 4, -10, 8, 15, -7]), 25, "range of many
            elements");
```

```
        ok(isNaN(Stats.range([])), "range of [] is NaN");
    });
});
```

Let's break down the output of this test, shown in Figure 7.17:

- The red bar means we had at least one failure.

- `Mean Tests (0,4,4)` means 0 failures, 4 passes, and 4 total tests in the "Mean Tests" group.

- `Median Tests (0,5,5)` means 0 failures, 5 passes, and 5 total tests in the "Median Tests" group.

- `Range Tests (1,3,4)` means 1 failure, 3 passes, and 4 total tests in the "Range Tests" group.

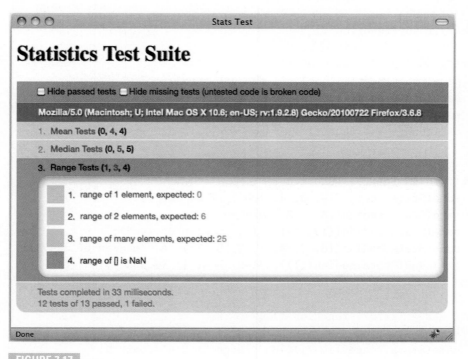

FIGURE 7.17

QUnit output for the statistics test.

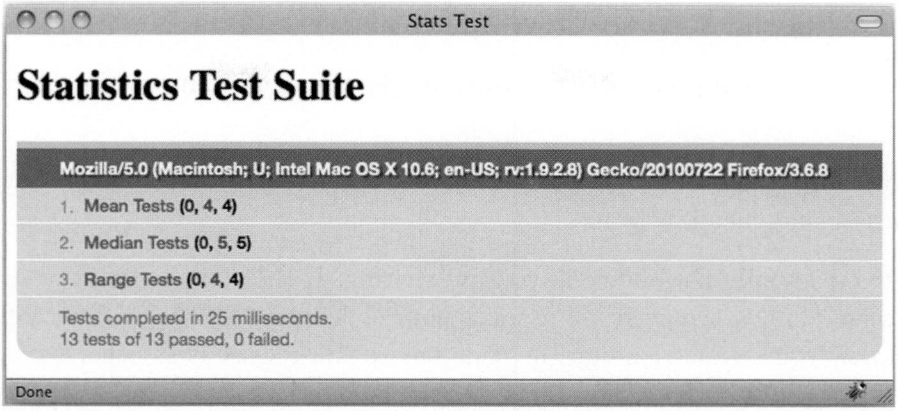

Figure depicting a browser window titled "Stats Test" showing:

Statistics Test Suite

Mozilla/5.0 (Macintosh; U; Intel Mac OS X 10.6; en-US; rv:1.9.2.8) Gecko/20100722 Firefox/3.6.8

1. Mean Tests **(0, 4, 4)**
2. Median Tests **(0, 5, 5)**
3. Range Tests **(0, 4, 4)**

Tests completed in 25 milliseconds.
13 tests of 13 passed, 0 failed.

FIGURE 7.18

QUnit output for the statistics test, after fixing the code.

The failed assertion was the one that expected the range of an empty array to be NaN. If you investigate the problem further, you will see that our implementation of `range` returns $-$Infinity, not NaN. This is easy to fix; after fixing the code, rerun the test (all you have to do is reload the browser page!) and you will see the green[18] of Figure 7.18.

There is quite a bit more to QUnit than we have shown here of course; consult the online documentation for details. Also see the companion website where we have included tests for many of the examples in the text.

Review and Practice

1. Build and run the statistics module, its test script, and its testing page from this section. Load the test page to run the tests and verify that all but one test pass.

2. Fix the `range` function and rerun the test.

3. Add 5 to 10 more test cases for the statistics module and run them. Become familiar with the process of editing your source code and tests and reloading the page to test immediately.

---

[18]Do a web search for "Keep the bar green to keep the code clean."

7.7.3   Testing in the Software Development Process

Unit testing is a common practice in the software development industry for many reasons:

- Testing helps you catch bugs early in the development process, when they are easiest and cheapest to fix.

- Unit tests actually use the code you are writing. If the calls made by your tests seem clunky, the eventual users of your code won't be happy. You will then know you should redesign the code before you release it to others.

- When you have a good set of tests in place, you can refactor with confidence!

It takes experience to write good tests and to know when to write them. Some programmers like to follow the philosophy of *Test-Driven Development* [Bec02], or TDD, where tests are written before the code itself. Regardless of the philosophy employed, getting into the habit of thorough testing pays many dividends—you will find yourself spending more time coding and less time debugging.

> **Review and Practice**
>
> 1. What are some of the benefits of unit testing?
>
> 2. What does it mean that having a test suite in place allows you to "refactor with confidence"?

Chapter Summary

- An object-oriented, as opposed to a process-oriented, view of the world is helpful when constructing large software systems.

- Objects can be built with constructors, or with `Object.create` and friends, introduced in ECMAScript 5.

- Many people see inheritance and information hiding as important aspects of object-oriented programming.

- A module is a grouping of related primitives and objects that serves as a unit in a larger script. Modules are often built in JavaScript using closures.

- jQuery is one of the most popular JavaScript libraries and does an excellent job of simplifying DOM programming.

- There are many aspects to performance, including run-time, load-time, memory, and user interface aspects.

- Unit testing is important when programming in any language. QUnit is a popular JavaScript testing framework.

Exercises

1. For the following types of objects, give a reasonable set of properties:

   - Country
   - Restaurant
   - Music album
   - Basketball team
   - Movie

2. Consider the following code:

```
var Circle = function (r) {
    this.radius = r;
};
Circle.prototype.area = function () {
    return Math.PI * this.radius * this.radius;
}
var c = new Circle(10);
```

   What is the value of `c.constructor`? List all the own properties of `c`. List all the enumerable properties of `c`.

3. Implement the `Circle` and `Rectangle` constructors and prototypes from this chapter. Also implement a constructor and prototype for a `Polygon` data type that has the same look and feel. (You may notice that the perimeter and area implementations for polygons are a bit more complex than for circles and rectangles.)

4. One of your colleagues has devised the following test to determine whether an expression refers to a circle object—that is, one created with the circle constructor in the previous exercise:

```
// Incorrect function for determining whether c is a circle.
var isCircle = function (c) {
    return c.constructor === Circle;
}
```

Give three reasons why this is a poor solution.

5. Based on your answer to the previous exercise, argue for the claim that the `constructor` field is completely useless.

6. Is the `constructor` field writable? Should it be?

7. We saw in Chapter 5 that creating a function creates two objects—one for the function itself and a new object assigned to its `prototype` property. What is the reason for this second object? Does it strike you as a wasteful implementation strategy, given that many functions will never be used as constructors? If so, why do you think this strategy was chosen?

8. In the colored circle example from this chapter, the constructor for `Colored-Circle` repeated code that also existed in the `Circle` constructor—namely, the assignment to the `radius` field. Design a mechanism by which this code can be shared (written once but used by both create methods).

9. Implement, with constructors and prototypes, two types, **Person** and **Employee**. Each person has a name, a birthdate, and a method to get the person's age. An employee **is a** person, who also has an employer, a hire date, and a salary. Be sure to properly allocate properties among objects and prototypes.

10. Implement the **Person** and **Employee** data types from the previous exercise using the technique of Figure 7.5.

11. Research the `instanceof` operator. Referring to Figure 7.4, explain why the expression `c1.instanceof Circle` has the value `true`.

12. Implement a type (with constructors and prototypes) designed to hold a sequence of objects with *only* two methods: one to add an object to the end

of the sequence and one to get the value of the kth element in the sequence. Be sure to hide the sequence implementation (*Hint*: probably an array) inside the object so that no code can add objects anywhere other than the end or can change or remove any of the objects.

13. Repeat the previous exercise using `Object.create`.

14. In Figure 7.6, we showed that the price of hiding properties within objects was that each object with the hidden property required its own copies of functions to access the private data. Is this a problem when the number of objects is small?

15. Write a script to determine which, if any, of the properties of `Object.prototype` are enumerable.

16. Can you assign to any of the global variables for built-in objects such as `isNaN`, `Infinity`, `undefined`, and so on? Experiment and report on your findings.

17. Do some research on JavaScript's `eval` function. Look at at least four sources, including the ECMAScript specification itself. Write a three-page paper or a decent-length blog post on the function. Why is it controversial? What kind of attacks can be carried out on a script with an `eval` function that does not check its input?

18. Write a function of two arguments, b and x, that computes $\log_b x$.

19. What is the prototype of `Object.prototype`? (Write a script to find out.)

20. Here is a small script:

```
Object.prototype = {};
var x = {};
alert(x);
```

Before running the script, what do you think it will do? Now run the script. Explain, in detail, what happened and why.

21. Implement a data type for people. Each person has a name, a birthdate, a mother, and a father. Since genealogy data are never complete, the father and

mother properties can be **null**. Override **toString** to produce the person's name. Also include a method to return a person's age.

22. Write a function that takes in a string and returns the reversal of the string. For example:

$$
\begin{array}{lcl}
\texttt{reversal("")} & \Rightarrow & \texttt{""} \\
\texttt{reversal("a")} & \Rightarrow & \texttt{"a"} \\
\texttt{reversal("string")} & \Rightarrow & \texttt{"gnirts"}
\end{array}
$$

23. Build a web interface to the string reversal function you wrote in the previous exercise. Your web page should have a single input box and a button labeled Reverse . Clicking the button should cause the text in the input box to be replaced with the reversal of its current contents.

24. Build a little JavaScript application that allows the user to type (or paste) into a text area and press a button to see a sorted list of all the words in the text area displayed just underneath the text area. For simplicity, treat "words" as sequences of one or more basic Latin letters—i.e., the "unaccented" letters A–Z and a–z. To extract these words from your text, you will use the incantation

```
s.split(/[^A-Za-z]+/)
```

where s is your text. This produces an array of words that you will sort and then render by writing into an element in your web document using the techniques from Chapter 6.

25. Write a script that produces an HTML table of 100 rows and 2 columns. The left column contains the values 0.1, 0.2, 0.3, ... , 10. The second column contains the square root of the number to its left, shown with exactly four digits after the decimal point. Use the document methods **createElement** and **appendChild** to produce the table, and the **Number** method **toFixed** to format the values in the second column.

26. For each of the methods in **Array.prototype**, state whether the method either (1) may possibly change or (2) cannot possibly change the array object on which it is called.

27. In the barking dog example on page 303 used to illustrate the `bind` method, could we have used `call` in place of `bind`? Why or why not? If so, try to come up with an example in which `call` and `bind` differ.

28. Read the Wikipedia article on ISO 8601 in its entirety. List three advantages that using this notation has over all other notations.

29. Obtain access to four different web browsers and determine whether they support ISO 8601 natively. For each browser, give the result of evaluating each of the following:

    (a) `Date.parse("December 5, 2000")`

    (b) `Date.parse("5-DEC-2000")`

    (c) `Date.parse("2000-12-05")`

    (d) `Date.parse("2000-12-05T17:22:05Z")`

    (e) `Date.parse("2000-12-05 17:22:05")`

    (f) `Date.parse("December 5, 2000 09:20 PM")`

30. What is the "epoch time" at the instant of your birth, within a million or so milliseconds? Demonstrate with a script.

31. Wikipedia states that Dante Alighieri died on September 14, 1321. This date probably uses the Julian calendar (which was commonly used in Italy at the time). Consider the date 500 years (to the day) from this date. What date would a resident of Italy at this new time say it was, assuming the person is using the Gregorian calendar? Why is the built-in `Date` object a poor approach to solving this problem?

32. Gain an understanding, through a little research (Wikipedia is fine), of the differences between UT1 and UTC. Can JavaScript be said to support either? Write a script to determine the number of seconds between midnight, Zulu time, on 2005-12-31 and midnight, Zulu time, on 2006-01-01. Did you get 86400 or 86401? Why?

33. The generator $x \to 4x - 3x^2$ we saw in this chapter is a variation of the *logistic map*—a generator that often comes up when discussing chaos theory. The actual logistic map is a family of sequences of the form $x \to x + rx(1 - x)$

for some value r. In our case, we used $r = 3$. We could parameterize our generator to take r, and, for good measure, the starting value as well:

```
/*
 * A generator for the famous logistic map.
 */
var logistic = function (r, start) {
    var x = start;
    return {
        next: function () {
            var result = x;
            x = x + r * x * (1 - x);
            return result;
        }
    };
};
```

Show how to use this function to construct the example generator function g from this chapter.

34. Implement the `queue` object from this chapter using `Object.create`.

35. We implemented our tic-tac-toe module with a function whose body contained many variable statements. Many JavaScript experts recommend that all function bodies contain only one variable statement in which all of the variables are declared. Rewrite the tic-tac-toe module using this guideline.

36. Implement a tic-tac-toe module with a 16-square board (4×4).

37. What are some libraries that are similar to jQuery? Make a list of capabilities, strengths, and weaknesses of each.

38. What is, in detail, the difference between using jQuery's document `ready` event and the host-supplied window `onload` event?

39. Modify the jQuery example in this chapter (countries and states) so that the "current" country's states slide up before the next chosen country's states slide down.

40. Rewrite the temperature conversion example from Chapter 2 using jQuery.

41. Rewrite the tic-tac-toe module from this chapter using jQuery.

42. Browse the jQuery plugins at `http://plugins.jquery.com` and write a script of your own design that uses one or more of the plugins.

43. Research three or four articles (or blog posts) that focus on the evils of "premature optimization." Write your own short summary of the issue. Provide examples from your research (and don't forget to cite your sources).

44. In [Zak09b], Nicholas Zakas found that in rewriting

```
var process = function (data) {
    if (data.count > 0) {
        for (var i = 0; i < data.count; i += 1) {
            processData(data.item[i]);
        }
    }
}
```

to

```
var process = function (data) {
    var count = data.count,
        item = data.item;
    if (count > 0) {
        for (var i = 0; i < count; i += 1) {
            processData(item[i]);
        }
    }
}
```

the rewritten code ran 33% faster on the Internet Explorer browser (in 2009). Run timing tests of your own for this code fragment, using several browsers.

45. Run this code in a runner or shell:

```
var p = document.getElementsByTagName("p");
for (var i = 0; i < p.length; i += 1) {
    document.body.appendChild(document.createElement("p"));
}
```

What happens? Why?

46. Consider this code:

```
var doc = document;
var spans = doc.getElementsByTagName("span");
for (var i = 0, n = spans.length; i < n; i += 1) {
    spans[i].innerHTML = "********";
}
```

What happens if this code is run on an HTML document with nested span elements? (Don't guess—experiment.)

47. One way to deal with the fact that HTMLCollection objects induce a recomputation of the collection on each access is to compute the collection once, then copy the elements into an array. Write a JavaScript function to perform a copy from an HTMLCollection to an array.

48. Read about the web page analyzer YSlow (http://developer.yahoo.com/yslow/). Install it in a local copy of Firefox and analyze our tic-tac-toe module. Try correcting the problems it identifies. Perform this exercise with two or three friends.

49. Compare jQuery 1.6.4 (http://code.jquery.com/jquery-1.6.4.js) with its minified version (http://code.jquery.com/jquery-1.6.4.min.js). Besides the removal of most whitespace and comments, what changes were made in producing the minified script?

50. In the script we used in this chapter to compute the millionth prime in chunks, we used an anonymous function to close over the variables n and count so that each periodic invocation of function findMore would be able to pick up where the last one left off. The anonymous function kept these two variables private as well, so no other scripts could accidentally modify them and cause havoc with the computation. Consider the following approach to this problem, which does not use the anonymous function:

```
document.getElementById("go").onclick = function () {
    var n = 2, count = 0;
    var findMore = function () {
```

```
        // ... Body of findMore is same as before...
    }
    findMore();
}
```

Critique this alternative approach. Is it better or worse than the one we gave earlier? Describe as many advantages and disadvantages as you can.

51. A fun way to approximate the value of π is to generate thousands or millions of random points in the square of width 2 centered at the origin, and to determine how many such points land within 1 unit of the origin. See Figure 7.19.

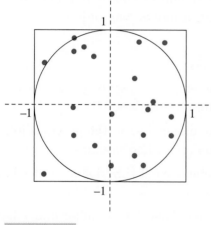

Randomly generating points for approximating π.

Because the area of the square is 4 units and the area of the inner circle is π units, one should, if enough random points are generated, have an estimate of $\frac{\pi}{4}$ by dividing the number of points within one unit of the origin by the total number of random points generated. Write a web page with a button labeled   Estimate Pi   that will trigger the generation of tens of thousands of random points from which you will generate your estimation. Write your script along the lines of the chunked prime finder: generate and test 1000 or so points at a time, with a 20- to 50-millisecond delay between chunks.

Write the running estimate into an element on the page so you can watch your estimate converge.

52. Read about web workers (specifications are, of course, on the Web), and write a script for the millionth-prime finder web page from this chapter. With a worker, you will not have to "chunk" your function, but you might want to disable the finder button while the worker is running.

53. Consider the problem of writing a "money bag" object. A money bag contains money of various denominations—for example, 13 U.S. dollars, 4 Angolan kwanzas, 17 Mexican pesos, 23 Japanese yen, 18 Yemeni rials. You can add money, remove money, and examine the contents of the bag. Attempts to remove more of a currency than exists should be considered an error. Write 15 interesting unit tests, in English, for a money bag object. We will start you off with a few:

   - Upon creation, the money bag is empty.
   - After adding 2 U.S. dollars to the empty money bag, the bag contains only 2 U.S. dollars—nothing more, nothing less.
   - After adding 4 Laotian kips to the money bag in the previous item, the bag contains exactly 2 U.S. dollars and 4 Laotian kips.
   - After adding 3 Laotian kips, we now have 2 U.S. dollars and 7 Laotian kips.
   - After removing 1 U.S. dollar, we now have 1 U.S. dollar and 7 Laotian kips.

   Be sure to write tests for error conditions.

54. The money bag object in the previous exercise can be represented as an object in which the property names are standard currency codes (see `http://www.iso.org/iso/support/currency_codes_list-1.htm`) such as USD (United States dollar), BHD (Bahraini dinar), ERN (Eritrean nakfa), TJS (Tajikistani somoni), and DKK (Danish krone), and whose values are the amounts of that particular currency. The bag can have function properties (methods) such as

   - `m.add(currency, amount)`—add a certain amount of a certain currency to the bag,

- `m.remove(currency, amount)`—remove a certain amount of a certain currency from the bag, and

- `m.amountOf(currency)`—return the amount of a given currency in the bag.

Write QUnit tests for a money bag.

55. Write a function to compute the nth prime number. Also write a QUnit test asserting that the first prime is 2, the second is 3, the tenth is 29, and the one millionth is 15485863.

56. Change the algorithm you used in the previous exercise to compute the nth prime number. Validate the algorithm with the same unit test from the previous exercise. Reflect on how having a working unit test in place affected your productivity. Did it make you more confident? Did it catch any bugs? Do you feel you arrived at a working algorithm more quickly?

CHAPTER 8

Distributed Computing

CHAPTER CONTENTS

Introduction

So far in this text, we have focused entirely on programs (applications) that run on a single computer. But many of the programs you use every day, especially those that run inside web browsers, actually do quite a bit of computation on a remote computer (the *server*) in addition to the computation done by the script in the browser. An application in which computation is split among separate, communicating, physical machines is called a *distributed application*.

Distributed programming requires the programmer to think about a number of issues that do not arise in simpler applications: making sure the various executing components are ready to exchange data before they communicate, ensuring that one component doesn't end up waiting too long for another to finish a task, and dealing with communication failures. This chapter looks briefly at the topic of distributed computing in general before discussing how to write distributed applications in JavaScript with a programming methodology called Ajax. By the end of this chapter, you will be able to write interesting scripts that employ Ajax to communicate with remote systems.

8.1   Distributed Computing Models

The general problem of dividing an application into separate physical machines can be modeled in several ways:

- In a *peer-to-peer* system, two (or more) computers each run essentially the same program. This program can both send data to other programs of its kind and receive data from other programs of its kind. Examples of peer-to-peer systems include file-sharing networks such as Gnutella, Internet phone applications such as Skype, instant messaging and chat applications, and the venerable Usenet.

- A *grid computing* system, or *computational grid*, employs large numbers of computers to tackle a single problem, typically one of great complexity or with an extremely large amount of data, but which can also be broken up into sufficiently autonomous subtasks. A computational grid can be viewed as a generalized peer-to-peer system, although the programs being run and interactions across specific machines may vary depending on how the computation is organized. Grid computing is most frequently used in scientific computing and simulations, although systems with large numbers of simultaneous participants, ranging from massively multiplayer online role-playing games (MMORPGs) and virtual world environments to popular-science applications such as SETI@home and Folding@home, have also been given the "grid" label.

- In a *client–server* system, a server runs code at the request of multiple clients, which rely on that server to get work done.

- A *thin client* system is a type of client–server system where the client "application" is very generic, like a web browser. The server generates not only the data for the client to use but also the instructions for how the client should render its entire user interface.

- A *thick client* is designed for a specific application. Many games, tax preparation software, fancy email clients, and music libraries are thick clients. Unlike a web browser, which can host any kind of application, these thick clients perform only the function for which they were designed. They communicate with a server to store data, but most of the work of rendering a fancy display is done in the client. These applications were quite common in the early days of personal computing because networks were slow and servers were not powerful enough to handle too many clients simultaneously. They are enjoying a resurgence today on "smart" embedded and mobile devices.

- A *rich Internet application*, or RIA, shares aspects of both thin and thick clients. Like a thin client, it runs in a web browser; like a thick client, it does much computation on its own. Examples include Google Docs, Google Maps, and the web version of Twitter.

Because the predominant environment for JavaScript is the web browser, the vast majority of JavaScript applications are thin client or rich Internet applications.

Review and Practice

1. What is the difference between a grid computing system and a client–server system?

2. What makes a rich Internet application different from a thin client application?

8.2   Data Interchange Formats

Because distributed applications are split among different physical machines, we have to think about some things differently. We don't exactly define a function, say `squareRoot`, on one machine and just call it from another machine. In fact, it is very common for the two machines to be running code in different languages. Clients tend to favor JavaScript and ActionScript these days (Visual Basic and Delphi in the old days), and many server applications run Java, PHP, Ruby, Python, or hundreds of other languages, including JavaScript itself.[1]

While there are ways to make distributed applications look as if clients are making function calls (these are called *remote procedure calls* [RPCs] or *remote method invocations* [RMIs]), at some level the two applications are interchanging streams of bytes.[2] What can the data that are being exchanged look like? Normally we like applications that exchange text; this makes the exchanged data easy for us (humans) to read and allows us to debug any communication or protocol issues a little more easily.

8.2.1   Plain Text

The simplest representation for exchanging information is plain text—sequences of encoded bytes that are decoded as codepoints in some character set (review Section 3.4.1 if you need a quick refresher). The resulting characters are then

---

[1]While many concepts in this text are applicable to JavaScript on both clients and servers, our emphasis remains on client-side JavaScript. If you want to get a firsthand taste of server-side JavaScript, you will want to look at Node.js (`http://nodejs.org`).

[2]At an even lower level, the two *machines* are exchanging streams of bytes that contain a lot of information to make the communication reliable. For details, check out the *OSI network model* [Zim80].

simply viewed as that: characters. No additional interpretation or structure is expected beyond "a sequence of characters."

For example, you might wish to publish a "fortune" server that responds to client requests with a pithy adage or a "message of the day." A client may send the following text to the server:

```
Fortune?
```

to which the server may reply:

```
It is easier to ask for forgiveness than permission.
```

The data exchanged are exactly the characters required to form the strings "Fortune?" and "It is easier to ask for forgiveness than permission." For a hypothetical "fortune" server like this one, plain text fits the bill exactly.

Now, suppose there is a "timekeeper" server on the network that reliably and consistently tracks the current date and time. If this server responds to date/time queries in plain text, you may receive this sequence of characters:[3]

```
Sunday, February 22, 2015 17:37:43-PST
```

You, a human reader, can immediately make sense of this piece of text (well, most of it, at least—knowledge of time zones and their abbreviations notwithstanding), and this is the main strength of exchanging data in this manner: it is easily readable by people.

Plain text falls short when you want machines to perform additional computation, processing, or interpretation on the data. In this simple date example, you can easily identify the month, date, time, day of the week, year, and other aspects of the returned text. Machines need to do a little more work. In particular, *parsers* need to be implemented in order to derive additional meaning from a piece of text. Parsing a consistently expressed date string is one thing, but what if the data may also look like this:

```
Sunday, the 22nd of February, 2015 AD
```

---

[3]This service is in fact a defined standard, called the `daytime` protocol.

or this:

```
Today is the twenty-second day of the second month, a Sunday in the
    year 2015.
```

Because plain text does not have any prescribed organization beyond being a sequence of characters, it becomes cumbersome when the data being exchanged have additional structure or organization. An online storefront, for example, may return information about items for sale. Such items have distinct values such as a name, manufacturer, price, and availability. One option for going beyond plain text is a *name and value* format, such as:

```
name=Acme Roadrunner Trap
manufacturer=Acme Corporation
price=$500.00
availability=in stock
```

But what if the storefront also needs to respond to product searches? More than one item for sale may be returned. In addition, what if the items have attributes that are themselves structured, such as a manufacturer address? For data exchange needs such as these, additional formats are available. On a certain level, all of these formats are "plain text," but the expected organization of information goes beyond just "a sequence of characters." Certain sequences of characters are expected in certain places or in a certain order, and these sequences help to identify more complex structures in the data.

8.2.2   XML

If the data you need to get back are complex, plain text gets harder to work with. Take, for example, the online storefront from the previous section. In response to a product search, the system may want to return:

- Products matching the search, with associated information such as price and availability

- A "what other people bought" list based on the user's keyword(s)

- A list of product categories related to the search

Consider how this list would look in plain text. How would you represent the product data? How would you indicate when the list of products stops and when you are now listing what other people bought? How about the product categories after that?

Just for the sake of argument, let's take a stab at it. Let's break up our results with "markers" for "products," "suggestions," and "categories." Then, because we may have multiple entries for each item, let's use a blank line to separate them:

```
*** products ***
name=Acme Roadrunner Trap
manufacturer=Acme Corporation
price=$500.00
availability=in stock

name=Acme Roadrunner Decoy
manufacturer=Acme Corporation
price=$750.00
availability=backorder

*** suggestions ***
name=Ultimate Fake Tunnel
manufacturer=Ultimate Fakers Corporation
price=$200.00
availability=in stock

*** categories ***
Cages

Traps

Signs
```

So far so good, and certainly, for this online storefront alone, you can build a distributed application based on a representation such as this. But what if you want to build multiple types of applications? What if you want them all to work together? And finally, what if you don't want to keep inventing new ways to represent potentially complex data? It would be beneficial to come up with not only a general scheme for representing structured, complex, or multivalued data, but also one that can be widely adopted and standardized. One such standard is XML, short for *eXtensible Markup Language*.

XML "Look-and-Feel"

Markup refers to how distinct sections of data are identified or *delimited*. Here is a possible XML representation of our search result example:

```
<searchResult>
  <products>
    <product name="Acme Roadrunner Trap"
      manufacturer="Acme Corporation"
      price="500.00"
      availability="in stock" />

    <product name="Acme Roadrunner Decoy"
      manufacturer="Acme Corporation"
      price="750.00"
      availability="backorder" />
  </products>

  <suggestions>
    <product name="Ultimate Fake Tunnel"
      manufacturer="Ultimate Fakers Corporation"
      price="200.00"
      availability="in stock" />
  </suggestions>

  <categories>
    <category>Cages</category>
    <category>Traps</category>
    <category>Signs</category>
  </categories>
</searchResult>
```

A complete, individual package of XML data, like the search result shown above, is called a *document*. The "document" term applies to anything that is represented in XML, whether or not it complies with our conventional notion of what a document is.

XML documents, then, consist of *elements*—distinct parts of the document, each identified by a name. Elements may contain as many additional elements as needed to capture the meaning of the information in the document. Elements may also have *attributes*—characteristics or properties of that element.

Elements and attributes—that's what an XML document *is*. Now, how does it *look*? That's where the "markup" comes in.

Tags delineate the elements of an XML document. They serve the same function as bullets or section numbers in conventional outlines or tables of contents. Whereas humans can generally figure out where a heading or bullet item starts and ends, computers need more help. Thus, tags also explicitly state when an XML element ends.

A tag consists of a name without spaces, "bookended" by angle brackets (< >). There are three types of tags: *start* tags, *end* tags, and *standalone* tags. Start tags look like this:

```
<tagName>
```

The start tag *marks* the beginning of a particular element; everything from that point until the matching end tag belongs to that element. End tags look like this:

```
</tagName>
```

The main difference between a start tag and an end tag is the inclusion of a slash symbol (/) right after the opening angle bracket. Start and end tags must *pair up*; that is, for every start tag, there must be a matching end tag later on. The tags are matched based on the name they contain.

The structure of the data is communicated by what tags are within which tags. The technical term for this is *nesting*. Thus, in the preceding search result example, the `searchResult` element—which, as the top-level element, or the element with no container, also represents the document—*contains* three other elements directly: `products`, `suggestions`, and `categories`. The `products` element, in turn, consists of two `product` elements.

You may have noticed that the `product` elements are not marked up in the same way as `searchResult`, `products`, `suggestions`, or `categories`: they don't appear to have an end tag. When a single tag is enough to convey all of the information for an element, a shortcut called a *standalone* tag can be used. Standalone tags look like this:

```
<standaloneTagName/>
```

Note how the slash symbol is now right before the closing angle bracket. A standalone tag is simply a shortcut; it means the same thing as:

```
<standaloneTagName>
</standaloneTagName>
```

The `product` tags aren't just standalone; they also show how attributes are represented:

```
<product name="Acme Roadrunner Trap"
  manufacturer="Acme Corporation"
  price="500.00"
  availability="in stock" />
```

An XML attribute is written as a `name="value"` expression within a start or standalone tag. Attribute names, like tag names, cannot have spaces. Attribute values, in turn, must always be enclosed in double quotes ("). An equals sign (=) sits between the attribute name and value. The preceding `product` element has attributes `name`, `manufacturer`, `price`, and `availability`, with corresponding values "Acme Roadrunner Trap," "Acme Corporation," "500.00," and "in stock."

Start and end tags do not always enclose just other elements—the list of related categories in our search result example shows that plain text can reside between tags as well:

```
<categories>
  <category>Cages</category>
  <category>Traps</category>
  <category>Signs</category>
</categories>
```

This element *content* can be as long as needed and serves to capture lengthy amounts of data, text or otherwise. This allows XML great flexibility, capable of representing both database-like content (attributes) and free-form information (nonelement content between tags).

There is much more to XML than what has been described here. For more, we defer to the official XML specification [W3C08a]. Suffice it to say that XML also provides for *schemas* (formal definitions of what belongs in a document and how it is structured) and *validation* (automated checking of an XML format's correctness). We will see more XML and XML-like code after this chapter, but for now we have more data exchange formats to examine.

Processing XML in JavaScript

Web browsers provide a host object called `DOMParser` for processing XML data. `DOMParser` objects have a `parseFromString` function that takes an XML representation and turns it into a `Document` object. This `Document` object behaves just like the DOM for a web page—because it is, in fact, the same type of object, only based on the XML string and not the web page's source code:

```
var tinyXML =
    '<tinydoc name="test">' +
        "<body>hello</body>" +
    "</tinydoc>";

var parser = new DOMParser();
var tinyDoc = parser.parseFromString(tinyXML, "text/xml");

alert(tinyDoc.getElementsByTagName("tinydoc")[0].getAttribute("name"));
alert(tinyDoc.getElementsByTagName("body")[0].childNodes[0].nodeValue);
```

Note how the result of `parseFromString` behaves just like the `document` host object, but of course pertains to the XML document represented in the `tinyXML` variable rather than the web page itself. Distributed web applications that use XML for data exchange typically use `DOMParser` to convert an XML message into its DOM representation, then use the available DOM functions to access its information.

8.2.3 JSON

XML is standardized, flexible, and general—but it is also quite *verbose*, meaning that it sometimes requires more characters to get an idea across than one might expect. In our running search result example, we enclosed our list of product matches between `<products>` and `</products>` tags, and each product itself has the name `product` within its standalone tag:

```
<products>
  <product name="Acme Roadrunner Trap"
    manufacturer="Acme Corporation"
    price="500.00"
    availability="in stock" />

  <product name="Acme Roadrunner Decoy"
    manufacturer="Acme Corporation"
    price="750.00"
    availability="backorder" />
</products>
```

The extra verbiage also clutters up the overall text, making it harder to separate the actual information ("Acme Roadrunner Trap," etc.) from supporting text such as the tag names. When this is finally parsed as a `Document` object, getting to the desired information takes a lot of function calls and array navigation.

These caveats can be quite a drag, especially for large data sets that have to be represented in XML, then parsed as large `Document`s. You might be wondering: why take all this trouble, when, as we've seen in Section 3.6, JavaScript has a perfectly simple way to represent composite data structures (objects and arrays), as well as a concise way to define them from literals:

```
var dress = {
    size: 4,
    color: "green",
    brand: "DKNY",
    price: 834.95
};
```

```
var location = {
    latitude: 31.131013,
    longitude: 29.976977
};
```

```javascript
var part = {
    "serial number": "367DRT2219873X-785-11P",
    description: "air intake manifold",
    "unit cost": 29.95
};
```

```javascript
var p = {
    name: { first: "Seán", last: "O'Brien" },
    country: "Ireland",
    birth: { year: 1981, month: 2, day: 17 },
    kidNames: { 1: "Ciara", 2: "Bearach", 3: "Máiréad", 4: "Aisling" }
};
```

This precise question did in fact occur to others, particularly to JavaScript pioneer and expert Douglas Crockford. He proposed a pretty neat idea: let's just use this same notation for data interchange! Thus, JavaScript Object Notation, or JSON, was born, and it stands today as a very strong alternative to XML, especially if you don't need a lot of XML's rigor and just want to get data across. Our search result can thus look like this when sent across machines:

```json
{
  "products": [
    {
      "name": "Acme Roadrunner Trap",
      "manufacturer": "Acme Corporation",
      "price": 500,
      "availability": "in stock"
    },

    {
      "name": "Acme Roadrunner Decoy",
      "manufacturer": "Acme Corporation",
      "price": 750,
      "availability": "backorder"
    }
  ],

  "suggestions": [
```

```
{
    "name": "Ultimate Fake Tunnel",
    "manufacturer": "Ultimate Fakers Corporation",
    "price": 200,
    "availability": "in stock"
  }
],

"categories": [ "Cages", "Traps", "Signs" ]
}
```

From seeing this, we hope you will agree that there is not much more to learn about JSON beyond what you have seen in previous chapters. Just like in regular JavaScript, you delimit objects with curly braces ({ }) while arrays are enclosed in square brackets ([ ]). There is one major difference: the use of double quotes to delimit object property names is required.

To parse a JSON string, use the `JSON.parse` function (you got a preliminary taste of this in Section 7.3.1). This function returns a JavaScript object, exactly as if you had initialized it in code. Before running the following program, see if you can correctly anticipate what each of the `alert` function calls will display:[4]

```
var searchResultString = '{ \
  "products": [ \
    { \
      "name": "Acme Roadrunner Trap", \
      "manufacturer": "Acme Corporation", \
      "price": 500, \
      "availability": "in stock" \
    }, \
    { \
      "name": "Acme Roadrunner Decoy", \
      "manufacturer": "Acme Corporation", \
      "price": 750, \
      "availability": "backorder" \
    } \
  ], \
```

---

[4]You may also be thinking that, since a JSON string is valid JavaScript, "parsing" it via `eval` might be a good idea. The answer is no, this is not a good idea. Review Section 7.3.1 for the gory (*evil*) details.

```
  "suggestions": [ \
    { \
      "name": "Ultimate Fake Tunnel", \
      "manufacturer": "Ultimate Fakers Corporation", \
      "price": 200, \
      "availability": "in stock" \
    } \
  ], \
  "categories": [ "Cages", "Traps", "Signs" ] \
}';

alert(searchResultString);
var searchResult = JSON.parse(searchResultString);
alert(searchResult.products[0].availability);
alert(searchResult.suggestions[0].price);
alert(searchResult.categories[1]);
```

It is important to note that, despite its name, JSON is as much a cross-platform, cross-language data interchange format as XML is. While it originated in JavaScript, you can parse and form JSON strings in a variety of programming languages and systems, with the JSON object simply being the web browser/JavaScript implementation of such a functionality.

8.2.4 YAML

We close this section with a final data interchange format: YAML. YAML seeks a best-of-both-worlds approach to data interchange, seeking to combine (and improve on) the readability of JSON with some of the more advanced features of XML, that JSON does not have, such as XML's ability to link data items within the same interchange representation.

A brief digression on naming: The acronym (or subacronym) "YA" is conventionally interpreted in computer science circles as "*Yet Another*"—an in-joke of sorts about the field's habit of reinventing tools in search of better, faster, and/or more powerful implementations of the same task. "YAML" was originally viewed as "Yet Another Markup Language," in keeping with the typical YA meme. In the end, its designers changed YAML's meaning to the self-referential "YAML

Ain't Markup Language," to emphasize what distinguishes it from XML and its relatives.[5]

Our online storefront search result example would look like this in YAML:

```
---
products:
  - name: Acme Roadrunner Trap
    manufacturer: Acme Corporation
    price: 500
    availability: in stock

  - name: Acme Roadrunner Decoy
    manufacturer: Acme Corporation
    price: 750
    availability: backorder

suggestions:
  - name: Ultimate Fake Tunnel
    manufacturer: Ultimate Fakers Corporation
    price: 200
    availability: in stock

categories:
  - Cages
  - Traps
  - Signs
...
```

You may immediately notice a certain "cleanness" in this representation. It is strikingly devoid of "computerese" like XML's tags and angle brackets or even JSON's curly braces and commas. YAML achieves this by taking a page from the playbooks of programming languages such as Python and Haskell: *make spacing matter*. Substructures are communicated by *indenting* a line farther than the line before it. It's a clever insight—the human eye gets it, and in the manner that it is defined (more leading space than the previous line), it is also machine-processable. The amount of actual space used doesn't matter; indentation is simply compared to what was done in the previous line.

---

[5]Self-referential acronyms are themselves another (*yet* another?) computer science in-joke, with GNU ("GNU's Not Unix") being perhaps the most well-known example.

Actual character "markers" are very limited. The three dashes (---) separate "documents" (thus allowing more than one "document" to appear in a single YAML stream), while three periods (...) indicate the end of the YAML representation. Colons (:) separate property names or "keys" from their values, while individual dashes (-) indicate list (array) members. In the event that these characters may cause confusion elsewhere (such as when a property value contains a colon), double quotes can be used to delimit text.

Like XML and JSON, YAML is not bound to a programming language or platform; if you think about it, no data interchange format should be so connected, really. As a bonus, JSON is considered to be a subset of YAML, such that any YAML parser can also parse JSON without any issues. At this writing, other languages and platforms, such as Python, C, Java, Perl, and Ruby, are actually more mature in the YAML implementation department than JavaScript is. Languages and platforms, however, are constantly changing, so, right after reading this, you should do a web search for "JavaScript YAML parser" or "JavaScript YAML implementation" for the up-to-the-minute state of the YAML-in-JavaScript art.

Review and Practice

1. What types of data would be good matches for interchange via plain text? via XML? via JSON? via YAML?

2. How does the JavaScript object that is returned by `DOMParser.parseFromString` differ from the object that is returned by `JSON.parse`?

3. What characteristic of YAML serves as the most important factor in improving its human readability? Why?

8.3 Synchronous vs. Asynchronous Communication

Now that we have established some background for how distributed applications communicate, let's look at how this communication is carried out. There are two basic models:

- *Synchronous* communication involves strict, sequential exchange, with one party sending a message, waiting for a response, then possibly sending a response to that response as the other party waits. The word itself loosely translates as "at the same time," and that is another way to think about it:

the parties involved remain present and attentive throughout the communication exchange.

Conversations, in person or on the phone, are synchronous activities, as are situations where you are waiting in line for service.

■ *Asynchronous* communication involves interactions that do not require waiting or the parties' constant attention. A sending party may move on to other things immediately after sending a message; the receiving party may see the message any time later, then respond at any time.

Message exchanges, whatever the medium (e.g., snail mail, voice mail, texting, email), are asynchronous: you form and leave a message, then are free to do other things (including sending more messages) immediately after. You can check for responses at your leisure. Activities that follow a "drop-off-and-pick-up" sequence, such as calling in a restaurant order, having clothes dry-cleaned, or leaving your car at the shop, are also asynchronous in nature.

Web applications are client–server applications in which the browser plays the role of the client, fetching data from a server. Frequently, the browser's request is for a new page: you click a button or link and wait for the new page to be downloaded and displayed. This is synchronous communication; you can't really do anything (within that browser window) until the new page is ready.

You have likely encountered asynchronous communication also. Perhaps you clicked on a button or link and in response saw a spinning circle or flower animate in a small portion of the screen while the rest of the page was completely functional. You were able to carry out tasks without waiting for the server's response.

Asynchronous communication is carried out in web applications under the direction of JavaScript. The computing paradigm of making server requests for data that will be used on the current page, and not holding up user interaction while these data load, is now known as Ajax.

Review and Practice

1. State whether the following activities are synchronous or asynchronous:

    (a) Telephone conversation

    (b) Instant messaging session

    (c) Filing for and then receiving your tax refund

    (d) Driving across an intersection

    (e) Playing a hand of poker

2. State whether the following communication characteristics pertain to synchronous, asynchronous, or both models of communication:

(a) Ability to disconnect from communication medium in between sending and/or receiving of messages

(b) Predictable and consistent order of messages sent and received

(c) Ability to coordinate activities in real time

(d) Ability to "broadcast" messages to more than one party

(e) Potential to be used for sending or receiving very large amounts of information

8.4   Ajax

The name *Ajax* originated as the acronym for *Asynchronous JavaScript and XML*. As you will see in a moment, the phrase behind the acronym didn't turn out to be completely accurate, but the acronym itself sounded so cool that the capitalization was dropped and it simply became a name for this computing paradigm.

To see Ajax in action, you generally need look no further than any website that claims to use "Web 2.0" technology. Scrolling maps or lists, live updates, and dynamic filters that do not change addresses or load entire new pages are very likely using Ajax to accomplish these effects. As long as a server call is made within the context of a single web page, and the browser lets the user continue to interact while the data load and the page updates itself, we say the application is "using Ajax." The asynchronous server call is an "Ajax call."

We will now look at how to write Ajax applications. Before we begin, we'd like to state one catch to this connectivity: for security purposes, an Ajax application may retrieve information only *from the same server* that hosted the original Ajax web page. We will discuss this in detail in Section 8.6. Due to this security model, any Ajax code you invoke using our JavaScript runner page at `http://javascript.cs.lmu.edu/runner` is limited to services that are also available from that site. Not to worry—we've loaded it up with a few that you can use.

8.4.1   Ajax in jQuery

Our approach to Ajax is to first show it to you in the most hassle-free and compact form available—which means using a library at first. Fortunately, we have chosen a library that you have already encountered: jQuery.

We will begin with a simple plain text example, using jQuery's `ajax` method. We have talked about a "fortune" service; now it's time to try it:[6]

```
$.ajax({
    url: "../php/fortune.php",
    success: function (response) {
        $("#footer").html(response);

        // Compare the above jQuery call to:
        // document.getElementById("footer").innerHTML = response;
    }
});
```

Because the fortune service returns a different "fortune" every time it is requested, you can click Run repeatedly to see new things. The example is written so that each successive call puts the new fortune in the same location: the `div` element at the end of the page whose `id` is "footer." Notice also that because we have jQuery anyway, we have opted to manipulate the DOM the jQuery way, instead of using `document.getElementById`.

Before we break down the code, let's try one more thing. Reload the JavaScript runner page, then run the following:

```
$("body").append("<img id='loading' src='../images/loadera16.gif' \
                  style='display: none' />");
```

If you like, you can see what this small program did by using your browser's document inspector (*not* a "view source" command, but something that displays the web page as it currently stands, such as the Firebug add-on for Firefox, or the inspector pane in WebKit-based browsers such as Safari or Chrome). A successful run should have added an `img` element, invisible for now, to the end of the web page.

---

[6] The JavaScript runner page automatically loads the jQuery library into the JavaScript context. If you want to try this on a page that you write, be sure to include a `script` element that does this for that page (feel free to grab it from the JavaScript runner source).

Next, *without* reloading the page, replace the script in the text area with the following one:

```
$("#footer").html("");
$("#loading").show();

$.ajax({
    url: "../php/fortune.php",
    success: function (response) {
        $("#loading").hide();
        $("#footer").html(response);
    }
});
```

Now click   Run   as much as you like. You should see a quick glimpse of a "spinner" animation as the program waits for the fortune service to respond. The service doesn't take much time, so don't blink.

We wanted to throw in this animation so that you can recognize the "Web 2.0" activity that is taking place. Most such sites do something like this to give the user feedback that some action is taking place.

These examples show, in distilled and simplified form, the main elements of Ajax:

- An asynchronous request being made of a URL

- Action taken upon the arrival of a response, typically something that places the response on the web page

- Optionally, user interface feedback showing that the request has been sent and is waiting for an answer

In its jQuery form, Ajax's first two elements are captured in the argument to the `ajax` function. As you might have noticed from the function call, `ajax` takes a single argument: a JavaScript object that provides the settings for this particular Ajax transaction.

In the example, we provide two settings: `url`, a string that holds the URL of the web service to be accessed, and `success`, a function that holds the code to be run once the web service's response becomes available. The `ajax` function then does the work of connecting to the URL, waiting for a response, gathering up the result—in this case a plain text fortune—then calling the **success** function. It is important to note that **ajax** *returns right away*—that's what being asynchronous is all about. Other code can run after the **ajax** call, without waiting for the server response.

Here's a final quick tweak to show the "asynchronous" part (this one no longer uses the "loader" image, so you don't need the **img** setup code anymore):

```
$("#footer").html("");

$.ajax({
    url: "../php/fortune.php",
    success: function (response) {
        $("#footer").html($("#footer").html() + response);
    }
});

$("#footer").html($("#footer").html() + "Your fortune is: ");
```

Note how in this version we concatenate the **innerHTML** property of the **footer** element. This gives you an indication of the order in which the code runs. As you can see in Figure 8.1, "Your fortune is:" appears before the actual fortune, meaning that the last line of the script ran before the **success** function did.

Going back to the version of our Ajax script that uses an animated "loader" image, the user interface feedback is done in two parts: first, we set up the **img** element whose visibility means that an Ajax request is in progress. This is typically an animated image—though notice that the animation has nothing to do with the actual network communication. It is there solely to make the user aware that something is going on. Before making the jQuery **ajax** call, we make this element visible. In our example, we also clear out the **footer** element to show that we are expecting a new fortune to take its place.

When the data finally arrive, the function we designated in the **success** property of the **ajax** settings object makes the **img** element invisible once more. The page will now be ready for a new Ajax cycle.

At this point, you may be wondering: we've seen the *A* for asynchronous and of course we're using the *J* for JavaScript ... but where's the *X* for XML? That's just it—*XML isn't necessary*. Ajax programming doesn't really care about the

Your fortune, via Ajax (the actual "fortune" that you see will vary, of course).

data interchange format that is used by the responding server. In the case of our fortune server example, our needs are well served by plain text. If the web service being used returns something other than plain text, you would simply parse or process that response using a corresponding technique from Section 8.2 or some custom code, then transfer or assign the extracted information accordingly.

With jQuery, this processing is even done for you with common data interchange formats like JSON. To see this in action, we have prepared yet another web service, this time returning JSON as a result: `http://javascript.cs.lmu .edu/php/calendar.php`. Start by accessing that URL directly with your browser. If the web browser chooses to save the response as a file, go ahead and do so, then open that file with a favorite text editor. You should see something like this:

```
[
  {
    "month": "Jul",
    "day": 6,
```

```
    "movable": false,
    "description": "(Helen) Beatrix Potter born, 1866"
  },
  {
    "month": "Jul",
    "day": 6,
    "movable": false,
    "description": "First 'talkie' (talking motion picture) premiere
                    in New York, 1928"
  },
  {
    "month": "Jul",
    "day": 6,
    "movable": false,
    "description": "Lawrence of Arabia captures Aqaba, 1917"
  },
  {
    "month": "Jul",
    "day": 6,
    "movable": false,
    "description": "The Jefferson Airplane is formed in San Francisco,
                    1965"
  },
  {
    "month": "Jul",
    "day": 7,
    "movable": false,
    "description": "P.T. Barnum dies, 1891"
  },
  {
    "month": "Jul",
    "day": 7,
    "movable": false,
    "description": "First radio broadcast of \"Dragnet\", 1949"
  },
  {
    "month": "Jul",
    "day": 7,
    "movable": false,
    "description": "Saba Saba Day in Tanzania"
  },
```

```
{
    "month": "Jul",
    "day": 7,
    "movable": false,
    "description": "Ringo Starr (Richard Starkey) born in Liverpool,
                    England, 1940"
  }
]
```

Perfectly good JSON. In this situation, jQuery's `ajax` function not only takes care of the network communication for you, but upon detecting the JSON response, it also automatically sends the data to `JSON.parse` and returns the final JavaScript object in the `success` function directly! Here's a script to try in `http://javascript.cs.lmu.edu/runner`:

```
$("#footer").html("");
$.ajax({
    url: "../php/calendar.php",

    success: function (response) {
        $("#footer")
            .append("<table id='calendar' border='1'></table>");
        for (var i = 0; i < response.length; i += 1) {
            $("#calendar").append("<tr></tr>");

            var addCell = function (cellValue) {
                $("#calendar tr:last-child")
                    .append("<td>" + cellValue + "</td>");
            };

            addCell(response[i].month);
            addCell(response[i].day);
            addCell(response[i].description);
            addCell(response[i].movable ? "year-to-year" : "fixed");
        }
    }
});
```

Note how the `success` function now treats the `response` parameter as a JavaScript object—specifically, an array of objects, each of which is some event that takes place close to today. These events have `month`, `day`, and `description` properties. The `movable` property indicates whether or not that event changes dates from year to year.

Leveraging the already-structured response object, this sample script displays the event data in a `table` element. Note how it is a matter of iterating through the array of calendar events, with each event corresponding to a table row and each event property corresponding to a table cell or column. Thanks to jQuery, the JSON parsing (and a lot more!) has been done for us. We merely need to navigate the object.

8.4.2   Ajax Without a Library

For completeness, we conclude this section with a look at Ajax programming *without* the help of jQuery's `ajax` function. What you will see here is "raw" Ajax—how it looks using only the host objects available in the web browser. These days, there is very little reason to go raw in practice. You do need to see it, though, in order to understand the paradigm more deeply (and to appreciate how much of a favor jQuery's authors have done for you!).

Behind the scenes, jQuery's `ajax` function uses the `XMLHttpRequest` host object. Notice again that, despite its name, this object does not require XML. Type this script into our HTML "playground" page at `http://javascript.cs.lmu.edu/playground`, or skip the typing by going right to `http://javascript.cs.lmu.edu/playground/ajax`:

```
// Set up some objects that everyone will want to see.
var xmlHttp,
    status = document.getElementById("status"),

/*
 * This function handles changes to a request's state.
 */
stateChanged = function () {
    // Conveniently for us, the request's state is a value from 0 to 4.
    var actions = [
        function () { status.innerHTML += "Not initialized."; },
        function () { status.innerHTML += "Setup"; },
        function () { status.innerHTML += "...Sent"; },
        function () { status.innerHTML += "...In Process"; },
```

```
        function () {
            status.innerHTML += "...Complete";
            // Deal with the data here.
        }
    ];

    // Call the function that corresponds to the new state of the
    // request.
    actions[xmlHttp.readyState]();
};

// This is the main script sequence.
status.innerHTML = "";
if (XMLHttpRequest) {
    xmlHttp = new XMLHttpRequest();
    xmlHttp.onreadystatechange = stateChanged;

    // We expect a URL in Input 1.
    xmlHttp.open("GET", document.getElementById("input1").value, true);
    xmlHttp.send(null);
} else {
    status.innerHTML = "Sorry, no Ajax!";
}
```

To see this script in action, type any URL that starts with `http://javascript.cs.lmu.edu` (because this is the site that serves the playground page; the address of this very page, `http://javascript.cs.lmu.edu/playground/ajax`, should be fine). What happens? You should see text that builds into the following. The text may build so quickly that its appearance looks instantaneous, but after reading this section, you will realize that it did come in a step at a time:

Setup...Sent...In Process...In Process...In Process...Complete

Let's break down the script to see what this sequence means.

The script starts by declaring variables for the two objects that we will need later: the `XMLHttpRequest` that we will be using and the `status` area on the web page. Assigning the `status` variable is just for brevity (no need for `document.getElementById("status")` over and over again), but we definitely need to hold on to the `XMLHttpRequest`. After the variables comes the function `stateChanged`, followed by the main sequence.

After blanking out the status area, the script starts with:

```
if (XMLHttpRequest) {
```

For current browser versions, this line is a simple, elegant check for Ajax readiness. We simply test for the presence of the `XMLHttpRequest` host object. If `XMLHttpRequest` is defined, then the `if` condition evaluates to true and we go on with our Ajax activity; otherwise, it evaluates to false and the web page should handle the absence of Ajax in some graceful manner. In our example, the web page warns the user that Ajax is not available via the green status region.

If you wish to support older browsers that are Ajax-ready but use different request mechanisms, this line explodes into a nearly page-long function. For brevity's sake and because, as time goes on, older browsers will go into disuse anyway, we leave this more inclusive but much longer version for you to find on your own. One day this check might not even be necessary, as it may become fair to assume that *all* current browsers will be Ajax-capable. It certainly isn't necessary with the jQuery `ajax` function, since cross-compatibility is yet another thing that `ajax` does for you.

Once we know that we can "do" Ajax, the script goes ahead and creates a new object based on the `XMLHttpRequest` prototype. The remainder of that `if` block assigns one property and calls two functions; we will explain the functions first:

open   This function defines the connection that the `XMLHttpRequest` object is to make. The first argument is the *method* to be used for the connection (common ones are `"GET"`, `"PUT"`, and `"POST"`, but there are more); the second argument is the *URL* to access; and the third argument states whether the connection is to be asynchronous (i.e., whether to wait for it to finish before moving on). The sample script uses the `"GET"` method, takes as the URL whatever you typed into the Input 1 field before running the script, and says `true`. Of *course* we want an asynchronous connection—that's the first "A" in Ajax, after all.

send   This function actually initiates the connection and may include some content (its lone argument) if applicable. In the case of the preceding sample script, we send the request with no additional information.

This line reveals how asynchronous communication is made possible, and it should look somewhat familiar:

```
xmlHttp.onreadystatechange = stateChanged;
```

Stumped on why it might look familiar? It's because *Ajax is event-driven.* The onreadystatechange property holds the JavaScript function that is to be invoked when something—an event!—happens to the XMLHttpRequest object. It is the Ajax event handler. We can do things asynchronously because we leave it to XMLHttpRequest to inform us when something notable has taken place. Until then, our code can be off doing other things.

At this point, we can finally look at the stateChanged function, which we now know to be the event handler for whenever the "ready state" of the XMLHttpRequest changes. And readyState is, in fact, one more property of XMLHttpRequest, as can be seen in the body of stateChanged. In this sample script, all stateChanged does is display the current value of readyState on the scratch page's status component. The readyState property can take on values from 0 to 4, with each value corresponding pretty much to the text shown in the script. We cumulatively build the innerHTML of the status area here to show how an XMLHttpRequest's state progresses through its connection.

As written in this example, we never see the "not initialized" state because no event triggers stateChanged if the XMLHttpRequest was not initialized yet. The state changes to "setup" once open is called (try the script without the send() line). Then, we may get more than one stateChanged invocation with readyState at "in process." When the content at the URL has been fully loaded, the state becomes "complete."

You may get multiple "in process" state change events, even though the state didn't change, because "in process" is the state during which an XMLHttpRequest is receiving data from the URL's server. Since the incoming data may be substantial, a good XMLHttpRequest implementation should "keep you posted" in case there are *some* data in the pipeline and your web page application might want to do something with them.

That about covers the entire sample script, as it was given; if you understand the script, you generally understand XMLHttpRequest. Once the request object does its work and it settles into readyState === 4 (i.e., "completed," "loaded," "finished"), XMLHttpRequest's involvement technically ends. But from an Ajax perspective, there is one more thing to do: process the raw response data by invoking `DOMParser` for XML or `JSON.parse` for JSON, or by running custom code. That part is not included in the sample script. Upon reaching `readyState === 4`, the web service response can be found in the `XMLHttpRequest` object's `responseText` property.

Review and Practice

1. The fortune example that appends "Your fortune is:" to the `footer` element immediately after the Ajax call was meant to demonstrate the "asynchronous" aspect of Ajax. Does "Your fortune is:" *necessarily* get concatenated before the actual fortune? Why or why not?

2. Look up the full reference for jQuery's `ajax` function. Based on what you see, is there a reason to use `XMLHttpRequest` instead of `ajax`?

8.5   Designing Distributed Applications

Data interchange formats (plain text, XML, JSON, etc.) and connection mechanisms or paradigms (Ajax) are fundamental parts of distributed applications, but in the end they remain *parts*. Additional concepts and issues come into play when putting these parts together as an effective whole, and that's what this section is about.

8.5.1   Uniform Resource Identifiers

The act of *identifying* something through an easy-to-express mechanism, such as a sequence of symbols or characters, is something that we do in almost every aspect of daily life, computer-related or not. We give ourselves names, we guard our social security numbers, we scan UPC codes, and we give most of our products titles or brand names. In a distributed application, with multiple services, clients, and other components needing to come together coherently, the task of identification is so important that it is formalized into a concept known as a *uniform resource identifier*, or URI.

Definitions and Specification

A URI is a sequence of characters that allows us to uniquely identify some resources that we might need. There are two types of URIs: URLs, or *uniform resource locators*, serve not only to identify a resource but also to indicate how to "reach" or "contact" that resource—thus, the term "locator." URNs, or *uniform resource names*, serve solely as identifiers. Thus, a person's full name and social security number are URNs. Once you know what these strings are ("William Shakespeare," "Arthur Conan Doyle," "888-88-8888," "123-45-6789"), you generally know who is being talked about, but the strings themselves don't include information that helps you reach the person. Phone numbers (especially cell phone numbers) and street addresses, on the other hand, include "locator" information. You can dial a phone number and contact the desired party, or you can send snail mail to or visit an address by going to the named city, finding the street, and going to the numbered place.

For computing resources, a general *scheme* for expressing URIs has been defined and standardized [BLFM05]. Such URIs have the following format:

```
<scheme name> : <hierarchical part> [ ? <query> ] [ # <fragment> ]
```

The *scheme name* describes the mechanism, system, or category of the URI. It tells you what to do with or how to interpret the rest of the identifier string. The *hierarchical part* holds the main identifying information; it is so named because we frequently identify objects by gradual narrowing of scope. For people's names, we have a surname to roughly identify one's family or clan, followed by additional names to zero in on the exact individual. Street addresses start with a country and/or state, narrowing down to a city, then street, then address, and potentially an apartment, unit, or suite number.

This sequence of "scopes" is called the *path* to the resource and is most frequently separated by the forward slash character (/). An optional *authority* part may also encode supporting information such as a username and/or password, in case individual access to a resource might vary (or even be disallowed). A typical authority part precedes the path and looks like `username:password`, with the @ character between authority and path.

The optional *query* in a URI represents additional information that is not necessarily part of the path, and finally the *fragment* represents an identifier for a specific part or section of the resource.

The English Wikipedia web article on URIs, for example, has the URI `http://en.wikipedia.org/wiki/Uniform_resource_identifier`. The scheme is `http`, short for the Hypertext Transfer Protocol, and thus this URI is a URL, as this same string can be used to download and view the article. The URL contains only a path in its hierarchical part, and no query nor fragment. As an encyclopedia article, this resource has identifiable sections or segments. To see its *References* section, one appends the fragment `References` to the URL: `http://en.wikipedia.org/wiki/Uniform_resource_identifier#References`.

Programming with URIs

Distributed applications frequently have to build URIs from user input. For instance, a web page may have a text field for a keyword search, whose value must then be included in the query part of a URI. A direct Google query, for example, looks like this:

```
http://www.google.com/search?q=<searchterms>
```

If you were to embed an Ajax Google query into a program using search terms that the user types into an input field with an ID of `searchField`, you might expect code that looks like this:[7]

```
var searchTerm = $("#searchField").attr("value");

$.ajax({
    url: "http://www.google.com/search?q=" + searchTerm,
    success: function (response) {
        // Do what you want with the HTML that comes back.
    }
});
```

This will not quite work, however, due to character sets and encoding. From the standard URI scheme described earlier, some characters have special meanings (`:`, `?`, `#`, `/`, and `@`, to specifically name the ones mentioned previously). The URI scheme itself is limited to a restricted set of characters, requiring that codepoints outside of this set be reexpressed (encoded) using a special notation [BLFM05].

---

[7]Unfortunately, this cannot be run on the online JavaScript runner because of the same origin security policy (Section 8.6.2). You can, however, enter this URI, with a search term, directly into a web browser to see what comes back.

Spaces, for example, need to be rewritten as %20. The percent sign (%) indicates an encoded character, and the value 20 is the codepoint for the space character in hexadecimal (32 decimal).

Another set of "tricky" characters involves those that appear in HTML and JavaScript code: < and >, for example. Input that looks like an HTML tag—especially `script` elements because those then include JavaScript within—if improperly handled might be included in future web pages as is, meaning that the web browser will interpret them as code, and not as data. Rewriting such symbols so that they are perceived by the user as such without being interpreted by the computer as code is another reason why direct concatenation of values should be avoided (more on this in Section 8.6.3).

At this point, you might be thinking, wouldn't it be nice if we had a built-in converter that takes care of these details for us? If you are, then you are thinking right. There is indeed a family of functions that takes care of these character set issues for us. What's important is that you are aware that they need to be called:

- `encodeURI` takes a string that is intended as a URI and rewrites special characters as their equivalent % encodings.

- `decodeURI` does the reverse: it takes an encoded URI and converts encoded characters back.

- `encodeURIComponent` takes a string that is intended as a *part* of a URI, such that special scheme characters like ?, /, and friends are treated as if they *aren't* special—they get encoded like "everyone else."

- `decodeURIComponent`—well, you can probably guess, right? This reverses whatever `encodeURIComponent` does, of course.

These functions are properties of the `window` global object, like `alert`, `prompt`, and friends, so you just call them directly. Here's something you can try, using `http://javascript.cs.lmu.edu/playground`. Type various strings, URI-looking or not, into the   Input 1   text field, click   Run , and see what happens:

```
var input = document.getElementById("input1").value;
var status = document.getElementById("status");

status.style.textAlign = "left";
status.innerHTML = "<b>encodeURI:</b> " + encodeURI(input) + "<br/>" +
```

```
"<b>encodeURIComponent:</b> " + encodeURIComponent(input) +
"<br/>" +
"<b>decodeURI:</b> " + decodeURI(input) + "<br/>" +
"<b>decodeURIComponent:</b> " + decodeURIComponent(input);
```

Here are some strings to try:

- A web address, like `http://javascript.cs.lmu.edu`

- A full address with a query that has spaces and special characters, like `http://www.google.com/search?q=encodeURI/decodeURI in JavaScript`

- A web address with a fragment/section identifier, like `http://en.wikipedia .org/wiki/Uniform_resource_identifier#References`

- A non-URL string with spaces and some special scheme characters, like `roadrunner traps and/or decoys?`

- A non-URL string that looks exactly like HTML code, like `<i>Hello</i>` or even `<script>alert("Hello!");</script>`

- A non-URL string with accented or other characters, like ¿Déjà vu? (you may need to check with your operating system to see how you can insert such characters into the input field)

- A string consisting of the special URI scheme characters: `:///?#`

- An already-encoded string (copy the output of either of the `encode` functions, such as `%3A%2F%2F%3F%23`)

The important thing to note here is what `encodeURIComponent` and `decodeURIComponent` do differently from `encodeURI` and `decodeURI`—the `component` versions treat the URI scheme characters differently. Thus, properly encoding our hypothetical Ajax Google example from earlier in this section can take either of these forms:

```
var searchTerm = $("#searchField").attr("value");

$.ajax({
    url: encodeURI("http://www.google.com/search?q=" + searchTerm),
    success: function (response) {
        // Do what you want with the HTML that comes back.
    }
});
```

or:

```
var searchTerm = $("#searchField").attr("value");

$.ajax({
    url: "http://www.google.com/search?q=" + encodeURIComponent(
        searchTerm),
    success: function (response) {
        // Do what you want with the HTML that comes back.
    }
});
```

The bottom line: encode before you connect, especially if the URI may contain special characters or is built from user input.

8.5.2 REST

The previous section focused on the nuts and bolts of what URIs are, how they are formatted, and what is involved when programming with them. In this section, we discuss a particular "big picture" perspective for how URIs are designed and used. This "big picture," or architecture, is called *Representational State Transfer*, or REST.

Defined and described by Roy Fielding in his doctoral dissertation [Fie00], REST specifies characteristics and constraints that facilitate simplicity, scalability, portability, and a host of other positive properties for a distributed system. When a distributed system satisfies these characteristics and constraints, it is described as *RESTful*. Many, in fact, consider the entire World Wide Web to be a RESTful system.

What REST Is Not

It may be more instructive to start by describing distributed activities that are *not* RESTful. So-called *remote procedure call*, or RPC, systems, where interactions can take the form of anything that resembles a function call—especially one that embeds a verb and a noun in the request's name—are not RESTful. Some examples of non-RESTful requests:

- A `changePassword(username, oldPassword, newPassword)` request

- Any request that explicitly includes `get`, `set`, `add`, `update`, `delete`, or other data-related action in its name

- Requests that "build" a sequence of actions, with each action depending directly upon actions made before it and materially affecting actions that come after, such as an online adder that starts with a `setNumber(number)` request followed by a number of `add(addend)` calls

Instead of viewing distributed interactions as *activities* to be performed, REST's "coin of the realm" is the *resource*. A distributed system is viewed as a set of resources. These resources do change and interact over the life of the system, but *not across network boundaries*. Instead, the sole distributed item is a *representation* of some resource. Once this representation has been transferred from one distributed component to another, the resource may be modified *within that component*—say, within a web page. If the change to the resource (i.e., a change to its *state*) is to be made permanent, a *new* representation of that resource—the changed version or new *state*—gets sent over the network to the distributed component that is responsible for the permanent storage of that resource. The new representation specifies how the resource is to be changed, but the permanent change itself takes place within the component that provides that service.

Thus, instead of a service vocabulary that includes requests such as `getUser(username)`, `setUsername(oldUsername, newUsername)`, or `changePassword(username, oldPassword, newPassword)`, the service knows only of the resource `users/username`: "the `user` resource with the given `username`." A *representation* of that user's current *state* is communicated (*transferred*) from server to client; if the client determines that the user's information needs to change, it sends a new representation (of the new state) back to the server instead of using explicit `setUsername` or `changePassword` directives. The server is then responsible for modifying the user resource's state based on the new representation that is transferred by the client.

What REST Is

To round out this core idea of resources whose state is transferred among distributed components using some representation, a RESTful architecture must also have the following properties:

- *Strict client–server relationship.* All RESTful communication clearly designates one party as the client and the other as the server—the exact opposite of a "peer-to-peer" system, where communications can pertain to anything and can move in any direction. With REST, the *client* requests the latest state of some resource within the system—say, a product catalog, a linked friend account, or a blog entry—and the *server* provides this state.

  Another implication of this strict relationship is *layering.* While a client may request something from a server, which itself is a client to another server, and so on, a client is *not* supposed to see "beyond" the immediate server from whom it is requesting a resource's information. In other words, your server may actually be "in the middle," but you are not supposed to see that. Your server is your server is your server, and if that server requires the services of other parties in the distributed system, that is none of your business. Such layering facilitates powerful performance and abstraction capabilities. In other words, it is *separation of concerns* (yet again!) for the distributed set.

- *Statelessness.* At first glance, this may seem rather strange. Doesn't the "S" in REST stand for the very word *state*? This is true, and so it requires a little more explanation. Recall that the "T" in REST stands for *transfer*—that's the key. A RESTful system performs *state transfers*: the server passes (*transfers*) the *state* of some resource *at that moment in time* to the client. Once that transfer is completed, it is considered completely closed; it does not leave *side effects* that must be taken into account by future requests or communications. *That* is what is meant by "statelessness." Every client request has the same meaning, regardless of what comes before or after it: "Please transfer a representation of this resource, as it is at this moment, to me." So the *overall system* retains state (it would be quite limited if it didn't!), but communications between clients and servers in that system do not.

■ *Uniform interface.* In the previous section, we noted that requests with explicit verbs are not RESTful. This exclusion is part of the *uniform interface* requirement for REST architectures: *all* requests include an *identifier* for the resource involved and a clear and separate indication of the *representation* to use when transferring that resource's state. Resources that are related to or associated with other resources express this by including the identifiers for *those* resources (links, effectively) within their transferred representations.

There are additional properties and details, but those are more technical and can be found in more in-depth readings (or Fielding's dissertation itself). With the properties described here, however, did you notice a very direct correspondence between REST and the World Wide Web? The Web unequivocally separates its clients (web browsers) from its servers (well, web servers). The Web is more or less stateless: each web browser access stands on its own, starting with a given address and ending with a web page. While it is true that a degree of statefulness may be implied by certain addresses, in the end, the general cycle of "ask for a web page, get back a web page" is self-contained and free of side effects. Finally, the uniform interface sounds like none other than the URL: a standardized, consistent scheme for identifying web resources, which are also used as links if one resource (web page) is associated with another. None of this is coincidence.

REST and the Web

The affinity between REST and the Web is more than just skin-deep. The concepts that you have seen in this chapter so far, from data interchange formats to Ajax to URIs, come together in a specific way to form RESTful *web services* and *web applications*. Recall that REST stipulates a strict separation between clients and servers. In the REST perspective, web applications are actually *clients*—we load them into our web browsers, and as we use them, they request and manipulate information that is managed by web services, which play the role of the *servers*. In order for a web service to be RESTful, it must have the following essentials:

■ URIs (Section 8.5.1) serve to uniquely identify resources and collections of resources. URIs representing collections typically have a path element that ends in some plural noun. For example, a bookstore service may identify its collection of books as `http://bookstore.com/books`. Requesting this resource produces a list of available books, with each book then identified with its own URI.

Such URIs for individual resources or elements add to the path element of the collection from which they came, in a way that unambiguously identifies them. Books, for example, are given a unique ISBN code. Thus, a usable URI for an individual book may be the URI for the collection of books followed by that book's ISBN code, such as `http://bookstore.com/books/978-0763780609`.

The remaining parts of a URI can also be viewed in terms of a resource: the query part can be used to specify subcollections (e.g., the subcollection of books with "JavaScript" in their titles may have the URI `http://bookstore.com/books?title=JavaScript`), while the fragment part can be used to "home in" on a specific part of a resource. For example, Chapter 5 of the book specified in the previous paragraph may have the URI `http://bookstore.com/books/978-0763780609#chapter5`.

What's not included in RESTful URIs? As stated before, URIs that embed verbs or imply state that carries over from previous network accesses need to be rethought and rewritten. For example, a URI such as `http://bookstore.com/bookSearch.do?title=JavaScript` may get changed into the resource collection query described earlier, while a stateful calculator web service that maintains an accumulated sum may have to be rethought more deeply, since a URI such as `http://bookstore.com/addToCurrentNumber?addend=5` misses both the central resource concept and the requirement for statelessness.

- RESTful web service URIs *may* return fully formed web pages (HTML) in principle, but in practice HTML is not a very effective representational mechanism for resources, mainly because it does not separate "pure state" from ancillary information such as presentation style or layout. The data interchange formats that we have discussed before work better: plain text, XML, JSON, YAML, and more.

The aforementioned RESTful URIs, therefore, typically return one or more of these representational formats. Conveniently, the protocol that is used for communicating with web servers (Hypertext Transfer Protocol, or HTTP, as seen in the scheme names of our example URIs) has a standardized mechanism for requesting and indicating the type of content requested. Thus, a specific representation can be requested without "polluting" the URI, *and* a web service can provide multiple representations so that clients may work with the one that works best for them.

■ *Changes in resource state*, which in many ways are really the only things that a RESTful distributed system does, are nicely captured in the four "verbs" provided by HTTP: GET, PUT, POST, and DELETE. Most of us only know GET— it's the verb that we use when we ask our web browsers to visit a website or download information. GET is a no-brainer match for clients that need the current state of a particular resource. The other verbs are used when a client has changed the state of a resource and would like to transfer this new state to a server: PUT for changes to a known resource, POST for the creation of a new resource, and DELETE for the removal of a resource. Just like the specification of a desired representation mechanism, these verbs are not part of the URI, again preserving the "purity" of URIs as resource identifiers.

On the client side of the equation, let's note first that web services can support more than just web applications as clients. Most notable are "mobile apps" that read and manipulate the same information as their web equivalents; such applications typically add device-specific features that web browsers cannot provide. Native desktop applications can also use web services, and even *other* web services can make use of them. The uniform interface and standardized representations provided by RESTful web services afford them a great deal of flexibility and transparency in terms of what kinds of clients can use them.

Web applications—that is, interactive web pages that we load into a web browser—are ultimately no different from all of these other applications. They present a user interface that can be manipulated; when certain user actions require new information (the latest resource *state*), requests are made to the appropriate web services, which then provide (*transfer*) a *representation* (in plain text, XML, JSON, YAML, or others) of this latest state. This is where Ajax comes in: it (1) takes care of server communication and (2) does so *asynchronously* so that the web page does not "freeze" while waiting for the server's response. Depending on the chosen representation, DOMParser, JSON, or other libraries take care of converting the transferred state into JavaScript objects, which in turn make them easy to manipulate and display.

What may cause confusion is how these web applications are *delivered*. Unlike other "apps," which are typically installed first and then run by a double-click, finger tap, or other action, the web applications themselves *are also downloaded* from the network, on demand. The mechanism for downloading these applications is also HTTP, the same protocol used to communicate with web services. However, the *content* that is delivered is not a data interchange format as we have discussed them, but a combination of HTML, images, JavaScript, and other information that is meant to *display* something for the user, and not solely to convey information. The similarity of delivery, therefore, is where the resemblance ends. Once a modern web application for a RESTful distributed system has started within a web browser, it is no longer functionally different from a native mobile or desktop application. Event-driven programming, coupled with Ajax for network communication and the DOM for displaying information, makes web applications indistinguishable from other types of applications in terms of how they interact with web services, and for particularly well-designed and well-implemented web applications, they may well be indistinguishable from users' perspectives as well.

8.5.3 Separation of Distributed Application Concerns

RESTful or not (though we hope you'll agree that REST certainly helps), the virtue of separation of concerns is just as applicable in distributed computing— and perhaps even more so—as in the other paradigms that you have seen so far. For a simple example with code that is short enough to digest easily, we have written a small Ajax-style application that you can access at `http://javascript.cs.lmu .edu/ajax-sample`. This application provides web access to *Linux manual pages*— online documentation for Linux operating system commands and interfaces. You can search this documentation with keywords, then read full manual pages when you have found the command you want. Figure 8.2 shows this application in action, after the search term `processing` has been typed.

The web application starts with an empty search field. Ajax enables "as-you-type" behavior: start by typing `process`, for example, then continue typing until you have `processing` as the keyword. The web page updates the search results as you go. As you can see from Figure 8.2, the search results list the Linux manual pages whose one-line descriptions match the search term. Clicking on the links that

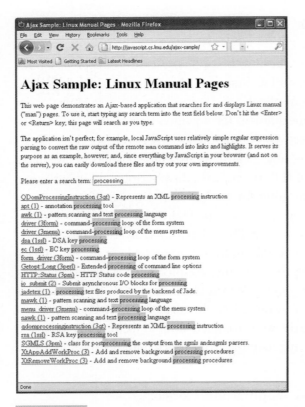

FIGURE 8.2

An Ajax-style Linux manual web application.

begin each result then leads you to the full manual page. For example, clicking on dsa (1ssl) leads you to documentation on processing DSA (digital signature algorithm) keys.

Web applications such as these are structured according to the following major components:[8]

■ First, one must determine the *model*—the information—that is supplied and used by the application. In our manual page lookup, we work with either a set of search results or the full text of a Linux manual page. If you follow the

---

[8]And, as your programming knowledge and experience broaden, you will notice a similar structuring for other types of applications as well.

`script` elements and their referenced JavaScript files, you will notice that, ultimately, the application requests the following URIs:[9]

- `http://javascript.cs.lmu.edu/php/man-keyword.php?keyword=` `<keyword>` for keyword searches, with `<keyword>` being replaced by the URI-encoded version of whatever the user has typed into the search field

- `http://javascript.cs.lmu.edu/php/man.php?entry=<entry>` `&section=<section>` to access the actual manual page's text; `<entry>` corresponds to the manual entry (command, library function, etc.) while `<section>` corresponds to the section identifier within the overall Linux manual

Ultimately, the text that these URIs return serves as the model for the application. You can access these URIs directly within your browser if you like; just fill in the query parameters with appropriate values. For example, a search for `processing` corresponds to the URI

```
http://javascript.cs.lmu.edu/php/man-keyword.php?keyword=
processing
```

which returns the following plain text (or something similar—server maintenance may change the available manual pages):

```
QDomProcessingInstruction (3qt) - Represents an XML processing
                                  instruction
apt (1)                 - annotation processing tool
awk (1)                 - pattern scanning and text processing
                          language
driver (3form)          - command-processing loop of the form system
driver (3menu)          - command-processing loop of the menu system
dsa (1ssl)              - DSA key processing
ec (1ssl)               - EC key processing
form_driver (3form)     - command-processing loop of the form system
Getopt::Long (3perl)    - Extended processing of command line
                          options
```

[9]Yes, this example is not RESTful. We want to show that, even without REST, any distributed application benefits from proper separation of concerns.

```
HTTP::Status (3pm)      - HTTP Status code processing
io_submit (2)           - Submit asynchronous I/O blocks for
                          processing
jadetex (1)             - processing tex files produced by the
                          backend of Jade.
mawk (1)                - pattern scanning and text processing
                          language
menu_driver (3menu)     - command-processing loop of the menu system
nawk (1)                - pattern scanning and text processing
                          language
qdomprocessinginstruction (3qt) - Represents an XML processing
                          instruction
rsa (1ssl)              - RSA key processing tool
SGMLS (3pm)             - class for postprocessing the output from
                          the sgmls andnsgmls parsers.
XtAppAddWorkProc (3) - Add and remove background processing
                          procedures
XtRemoveWorkProc (3) - Add and remove background processing
                          procedures
```

The entry for DSA key processing is called **dsa**, which can be found in section **1ssl** of the manual. Thus, this URI returns the full text of that manual page:

> http://javascript.cs.lmu.edu/php/man.php?entry=dsa&section=1ssl

The resulting text is too long to reproduce fully here, but if you use your browser, you can see it all. These are the data, or the **model**, that the web application uses.

■ You may have noticed that, despite the resemblance of the web application's search results (Figure 8.2) and manual page displays to the raw data returned by our web service, they remain distinct. With search results, for example, the entries and sections on the left have been presented as links, leading to the actual manual page text. In addition, the matched keywords are highlighted in the descriptions of the manual pages. This presentation is known as the *view* of the application.

The rule to follow is to never mix the model and the view. The main reason here is that any single piece of information can really be presented, formatted, or, well, *viewed* in many ways. Any information exchange that locks on some particular display is ultimately harder to work with and maintain. Thus, the web service URIs for this web application return only plain text. The web application code includes explicit conversion mechanisms that prepare this text for display on the web page. For search results, the `formatManKeywordResult` function performs this conversion programmatically. For the manual page text, which is best displayed using a fixed-width font, the response of the `man.php` service is assigned to the `innerHTML` property of a specific `pre` element because, by default, `pre` elements display their content using just such a font.

- The third major component of a well-separated web application is its *controller* code. Conceptually, controller activity is any response to user actions that determines how the application behaves—what it does, where it goes next, what information it retrieves. With web applications, this code is easy to identify: it is whatever gets invoked by event handlers, as seen in Chapter 6.

  Proper setting of event handlers within the web page (e.g., `onclick`, `onfocus`, `onkeyup`) allows the web browser to call the right JavaScript code when the user does something of interest or when a predetermined amount of time passes. Code triggered by these events can then either manipulate content completely locally (e.g., change the state of other controls, update their values, modify other displayed information) or initiate requests for new information from the network via Ajax. When this new information arrives, code is triggered again by an event handler—the `success` function in jQuery's `ajax` settings argument or the `onreadystatechange` function in the lower-level `XMLHttpRequest` object. This code updates the displayed content accordingly.

  "Control" does not necessarily have to be user-triggered, either. Web pages that exhibit "live update" behavior without explicit web browser reloads typically have ongoing activity, set up through the `setTimeout` or `setInterval` functions (first seen in Chapter 6 and explored further in Chapter 9), that gets triggered automatically at set time intervals. This also constitutes a form of control and ultimately has the same structure: at some point, a function gets called, and this function initiates an update of the web page's content.

Web applications that are structured in this manner are easy to maintain not only because their tasks are distinct and form natural boundaries for application components, but also because they can be distributed among software developers with different specialties. The model can be handled by web service and database experts; the view goes to web page design specialists and graphic artists. Finally, the controller can be the focus of JavaScript and DOM experts. While these groups do have to interact, their tasks are separate enough that, after some initial coordination, they can do their work relatively independently, coming together only to integrate their work and refine the overall application.

8.5.4   Server-Side Technologies*

In some respects, the material in this section is none of your business if you are a JavaScript programmer. If you have your URIs and you know what they provide, there is no need for you to know more of what these URIs' servers do. That is the beauty of strict client–server layering. Still, in certain contexts it may be beneficial to have *some* idea of what goes on "server-side," and that's the focus of this section.

Figure 8.3 illustrates the parts that frequently participate in server-side activities—that is, anything that happens from the time JavaScript code contacts a web service to the time it receives its response.

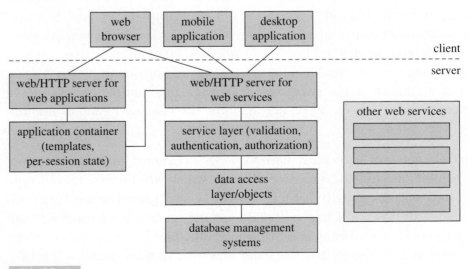

FIGURE 8.3

A sampling of server-side technologies.

The first point of contact for Web-based distributed applications is a web, specifically HTTP, server. Prominent examples of HTTP servers include the open source Apache and the commercial Internet Information Server (IIS) from Microsoft. This server receives web browser requests and figures out what to do with them. In the earliest days of the Web, these hosts were little more than file servers: URIs mapped directly to files, which were then delivered back. These days, a *lot* more can happen.

Most significantly, modern distributed applications may actually have web/ HTTP servers that perform *two* distinct functions. One category of web server is responsible for distributing the *web application*—that is, the sequence of web pages that users see and interact with through a web browser. A second category of web server then handles the *services* needed by that web application: information retrieval, heavy computation, and the like. When separated in this manner, the web application HTTP server may be as much a "client" of the service HTTP server as the browser itself (if connecting via Ajax) or, for that matter, any other type of application, such as a thick one running on a desktop or mobile computer. Systems with this division of labor among their HTTP servers are said to have a *service-oriented architecture* (SOA). The web application HTTP server takes care of assembling web pages and other resources for direct presentation to and interaction by the user, while the web service HTTP server takes care of the actual information management tasks required by an application.

In dynamic, distributed applications, and especially in those running within an SOA, web service HTTP servers function more as relays or routers than file servers: based on a web request's URI, the server determines another layer of software that should handle the request. This *service layer* runs small programs called *servlets* that use, as input, the information provided in the web request—not just the URI but also the HTTP verb (`GET`, `PUT`, `POST`, or `DELETE`) and other request parameters. The servlet then returns a response—HTML, image data, video, plain text, XML, JSON, YAML, whatever—that the web server relays back to the client (a web browser, a thick desktop or mobile application, or even another HTTP server). There is a lot of diversity here, the most venerable tools being shell and Perl scripts. Java software (yes, *that* Java, which has no real relationship with JavaScript outside of "branding") is also quite prevalent, as are PHP (formerly *Personal Home Page*, now *PHP: Hypertext Processor* in the fashion of self-referential acronyms like YAML and GNU), Python, Ruby, C# (Microsoft .NET), and, yes, even JavaScript frameworks.

Anything can happen at this layer: algorithms can run, documents can be generated on the fly, and other web services may even be contacted. In the end, the result must abide by whatever has been promised by the requested URI, for use by the web client as needed.

A very frequent subactivity at this layer is *data access*—the retrieval and manipulation of permanently stored (*persistent*) information. This *data access layer*, sometimes represented as *data access objects*, or DAOs, focuses on *CRUD*—the *c*reation, *r*etrieval, *u*pdating, and *d*eletion of data. At the "bottom" of most such data access layers are database management systems such as MySQL, PostgreSQL, Microsoft SQL Server, Oracle, or one of many available NoSQL servers. It should be noted that older client-server configurations considered these databases as the server; these days, as you can see, more layers of abstraction, or *tiers*, are involved.

At every boundary in this sequence—web browsers contacting web servers, to application or scripting layers, to other web services (possibly), to data access layers or objects, then database management systems and all the way back—additional *transparent* layers may exist. These layers are called transparent because they are not explicitly contacted for their services. Instead, they do their work "behind the scenes," taking care of optimization, security, or performance tasks such as caching, load balancing, or encryption and decryption. Their work is important and sometimes critical, keeping systems from getting overloaded, maintaining responsiveness, or protecting them from attackers. The transparency of their work is important, so that distributed application developers do not have to change their code based on the presence of or modifications to such utilities.

Review and Practice

1. What is the difference between a URL and a URN?

2. Would you agree that the *entire* World Wide Web is a RESTful system? Why or why not?

8.6   Security

Computer and information security is a crucial and complex area and has grown much more important with the advent of the World Wide Web and its accompanying distributed applications. In the broadest sense, security is the protection of resources (computers, networks, information, etc.) against access by unauthorized parties. Specific security terms derive from the resource that is being protected and the type of access that this protection seeks to prevent. For example, protecting information from being disclosed inappropriately is *confidentiality*; protecting information from being *modified* inappropriately is *integrity*. *Availability* involves the protection of a system from being rendered unusable, for reasons ranging from physical failures (power outages, hardware problems) to intentional denial-of-service attacks.

In this section, we review what is available, and what is not, regarding the security of distributed applications in general and the security of web browsers and JavaScript in particular. It is true that these issues exist for all computer systems, programming languages, and technology platforms; however, the sheer ubiquity of the World Wide Web magnifies their importance significantly.

8.6.1   The Web, the Bad, and the Sandbox

In principle, the primary concern with security and the Web is actually no different from software security in general: the prevention of malicious programs from running on your computer. When you run software on your computer, you are placing your trust in that software—that it won't read (much less share) information that it shouldn't, that it won't damage anything on your system, that it won't render your machine unusable, and so on.

The (humongous) trick with the Web is that it involves a piece of software—the web browser—that can contact any machine on the Internet with the greatest of ease and, thanks to JavaScript, can run programs delivered by those machines, potentially without your knowledge. This sheer ease of contact and software delivery explodes the size of the problem by many orders of magnitude. It also motivates the creation of the rules and controls you are about to see.

Of course, we can't *not* run programs on our web browsers. By doing so we would lose a vast amount of functionality that we currently enjoy. The idea, then, is to *limit* the activities that a program can perform—allow the ones that should generally be safe and disallow those that can lead to malicious behavior.

This limiting principle is called *sandboxing*. A *sandbox* is a well-defined "safe area" of functionality in which the sandboxed program is allowed to "play." For JavaScript programs that are downloaded from the Internet by a web browser, the following activities are prohibited:

- Reading or writing files on the user's computer, with the exception of *cookies*—short data segments—or *local storage* created by the same server that provided the JavaScript program.

- Accessing the browsing history of the user (JavaScript can move through it, but it cannot read where it is going).

- Under many circumstances, opening new browser windows (the often-activated "block pop-up windows" web browser setting)—and, even when it can open a window, such a window must be larger than 100 pixels on all sides, fit within the user's screen, and have a title bar.

- Closing windows that it did not open, under the already limited situations for which Javascript *is* allowed to open a window.

- Modifying the file chosen by the user with a web page file chooser element (i.e., an `input` element with a `type` attribute of `file`).

- Reading or writing files on the web server. All communications are limited to HTTP requests, which necessarily get processed by the web server before they result in any direct activity on the server's files.

- Interacting with resources, including network connections, whose servers and protocols are different from the server and protocol that delivered the JavaScript program. This is called the *same origin policy*, and because this policy is particularly relevant in the context of distributed applications, we will examine it further in the next section.

- Communicating directly with databases. This is just a corollary of the previous two limitations: if you can only use HTTP when connecting to a server *and* the only machine you can connect to is the server that provided your web page, then you certainly cannot talk to database servers directly.

- Hiding the source code (HTML, styles/visuals, JavaScript) or data (text, images) on a web page.

The JavaScript implementations within web browsers are supposed to enforce these sandbox limitations—which leads us to a final point about sandboxes. In the end, while we generally distrust JavaScript code from the web (since we otherwise wouldn't put it in a sandbox), we must trust our web browser. What can be done to maintain or affirm this trust? Ideally, we should not have to rely on a web browser developer's word alone. Security-oriented groups and individuals are of assistance here. They examine web browsers as they are released, using test programs, network monitors, and other tools to confirm that this software enforces the required protections. In this regard, an *open source* browser facilitates an even broader "plurality of trust." By providing not only finished, executable/double-clickable software but also its *source code*—that is, the human-readable code, typically in a programming language like C or C++, from which the web browser is built—a web browser developer can build a community that can see *exactly* what the web browser does, and when, and how. With more "eyes" on the code beyond its immediate developers', a web browser's overall security may be maintained more thoroughly and more quickly. Closed-source web browser developers must use other mechanisms, or more resources, to accomplish the same thing. This doesn't mean they can't also produce sufficiently secure web browsers; it just means they may need to take different approaches to get there.

Some web browsers implement a second type of sandbox that is useful to know about but is generally transparent to web page code. This sandbox protects web pages not from potentially unsafe network activity but from *each other*. Like any computer program, web page code may encounter fatal errors or crashes. Without a "process sandbox," pages with such issues may bring the entire web browser down with it, including pages that had no problems at all. When a process sandbox is implemented, well-behaved web pages are protected from misbehaving ones; crashes within the bad pages will terminate only those pages and not any other open, problem-free browser tabs or windows.

8.6.2   The Same Origin Policy

As mentioned in the previous section, the *same origin policy* of the JavaScript sandbox is particularly relevant to distributed applications. JavaScript programs can interact *only* with resources (documents, elements, services) with the same *origin* as the program itself, *origin* being defined as the combination of network protocol, port, and host. At first, this stipulation that a JavaScript program may only communicate with the web server and protocol that delivered it may seem to be severely limiting; this is the policy, for instance, that limits the Ajax code that you type into `http://javascript.cs.lmu.edu/runner` to contacting only URLs at `http://javascript.cs.lmu.edu`. The trade-off is necessary, however, in order to protect web users from potential malfeasance.

Imagine what could happen if this policy *weren't* around. Without this policy, any website could read the information you download from any other website. For example, if your web browser were displaying windows for your social network and your bank account, then scripts in either window would be able to read the data from the other. Your friends could find out exactly how much money you have or owe, and your bank could read your and your friends' status updates. Passwords could be gathered and stolen; fraudulent information could be displayed. These possibilities, and many more, motivate the same origin policy.

In terms of network connections and distributed applications, this policy forces a one-to-one relationship between a web application and its server. On the one hand, this simplifies certain interactions and is aligned with REST. On the other, this requires additional work to be done on the server, especially if the application involves the gathering of information from multiple sources.

Cross-Origin Resource Sharing

While the default behavior of web browsers is to restrict Ajax requests to the same origin policy, the *Cross-Origin Resource Sharing* (CORS) specification loosens this restriction if explicit permission is given by a web service [W3C09a]. The specification was motivated by the acknowledgment that, while the same origin policy is a necessary security measure for most web applications, legitimate capabilities like mashups (Section 8.6.4)—and services meant for such capabilities—are also significantly limited by it.

The CORS specification allows a web *service* to state whether other domains may use that service. `XMLHttpRequest` implementations that conform to this specification can then perform a "preflight check" for URLs that do not have the same origin. If the service for that URL grants permission, then the request can complete.

The central CORS site-check consists of the following:

1. The `XMLHttpRequest` includes an `Origin` header in its request, holding the domain of the web page whose code is making the request.

2. The web service includes, in its response, an `Access-Control-Allow-Origin` header, which lists the origins for which the service can be processed. This list can range from a specific list of domains all the way to absolutely everyone.

3. If `Origin` matches up with `Access-Control-Allow-Origin`, then the request goes through.

Additional headers in the specification facilitate finer-grained control, if desired. As usual, details can be found in the actual specification document.

To see this specification in action, run the following in `http://javascript` `.cs.lmu.edu/runner`:

```
$("#footer").html("");

$.ajax({
    url: "http://go.technocage.com/javascript/cors",
    success: function (response) {
        $("#footer").html(response);
    }
});
```

This Ajax request, despite going to a different origin from the runner page, *does* succeed. You should see a simple `Hello!` at the bottom of the page when you run this program. The web browser permitted this connection because this particular (trivial) web service responds with `Access-Control-Allow-Origin: *`, meaning that *any* web page from any domain may contact it.

In the end, as before, the effectiveness of the Cross-Origin Resource Sharing specification depends on the web browsers that implement it. If your web application relies on this ability, you will want to make sure the user's web browser supports CORS (which it should, unless it is absurdly out of date).

HTML Allows Cross-Site Requests

While the same origin policy may, at first glance, seem restrictive enough to keep all JavaScript network activity to the web page that served it, the reality turns out to be quite different. The first "contradiction" to the same origin policy is the observation that it applies primarily to JavaScript code, and not HTML. The second issue, hinted at here but examined more closely in the next section, involves how JavaScript code "gets into" a web page in the first place. Under certain circumstances it is possible for a web server to deliver JavaScript code that was written by someone else (with potential malicious intent).

But let's return to the fact that HTML—the DOM—is not actually covered by the same origin policy. As such, the following connections to different origins are possible:

- The downloading, *in HTML code*, of resources from other origins. That is, the same origin policy does not apply to web page elements that require content from other sites—images, plug-in data, nested web pages … and *JavaScript files*.

- The submission of an HTTP POST request, if that request is set up through a form element within the web page that is then submitted. The form element can specify URLs to which requests will be sent that do not meet the "same origin" criterion.

The first non–same origin "exception" (in quotes because, strictly speaking, it is not an exception to the rule but something that does not fall within what the rule covers, which is JavaScript code), when used with script elements, presents some interesting possibilities. Essentially, you can load and run JavaScript programs delivered by other sites as long as you use a script element to reference them (via the src attribute). Here's the interesting behavior: you can *create* this script element *on the fly* with JavaScript, just like any other DOM element. The script at the remote site can then be loaded and run. Because the creation of the script element and the script that it loads can happen at any time, and can depend on current program logic and state, this technique is known as *dynamic script loading*. Try the following code in http://javascript.cs.lmu.edu/runner:

```
var script = document.createElement("script");
script.type = "text/javascript";
script.src = "http://go.technocage.com/javascript/cross-site.js";
document.body.appendChild(script);
```

Note how it runs JavaScript code from an origin that is not the same as http://javascript.cs.lmu.edu. Yes, this code ran; what did it do? To find out, clear the text area and run the following code (without reloading the page):

```
alert(payload);
alert(payload.username);
alert(payload.password);
```

There is now a **payload** variable on the page, with properties **username** and **password**, whose values appear when the program is run. To see how this was done, load the earlier JavaScript code directly into your web browser:

```
http://go.technocage.com/javascript/cross-site.js
```

You should see the following:

```
var payload = JSON.parse('{ "username": "victim", "password":
                         "uh-oh!" }');
```

This code may seem harmless enough, but observe how the **payload** variable was defined: it is the output of a **JSON.parse** call. The included JSON might have been a *live* response—the result of a database query that the URI request triggers on the remote, not-the-same-origin site. "Not the same origin" is the key here. With standard Ajax, you *wouldn't* have been able to retrieve this JSON object due to the same origin policy. With the **<script>** tag and some complicity from the remote site (by "padding" additional JavaScript around the JSON data), we have gotten around that policy. This technique, called JSONP for *JSON with Padding*, effectively allows a JavaScript program to invoke a web service that is not of the same origin as its web page.

For maximum flexibility, JSONP is typically implemented with a *callback function* whose name is supplied by the client as part of the **script** URL. This way, different web applications can use the same service without being locked into particular function or variable names. Most JSONP-capable services have converged upon using the parameter name **callback** for this purpose. If this parameter is present in a web request, JSONP happens; otherwise, "bare" JSON comes back.

For example, Twitter provides a variety of services for querying its database of tweets, trends, and users. The following URL returns a JSON representation for trending topics in a given week (you can type it right into a web browser to see what it returns):

```
http://api.twitter.com/1/trends/weekly.json
```

However, due to the same origin policy, using Ajax to retrieve these data is prohibited. For example, typing the following into **http://javascript.cs.lmu .edu/runner** will not work:

```
$("#footer").html("");

$.ajax({
    url: "http://api.twitter.com/1/trends/weekly.json",
    success: function (response) {
        $("#footer").html(response);
    }
});
```

Fortunately, Twitter supports JSONP via the `callback` parameter. Type this code instead:

```
$("#footer").html("");

window.displayObject = function (data) {
    $("#footer").append($("<pre></pre>").text(JSON.stringify(data)));
};

var script = document.createElement("script");
script.type = "text/javascript";
script.src = "http://api.twitter.com/1/trends/weekly.json?callback=
             displayObject";
document.body.appendChild(script);
document.body.removeChild(script);
```

Note how *this* code works. It displays the returned JSON object, reconverted into a string, at the bottom of the page. This script even removes the temporary `script` element once it is done. Note also that the preceding code does not use jQuery's `ajax` function—it is doing "raw" JSONP. The good news is that jQuery *does* support JSONP transparently; you will see how in Section 8.7.2.

A similar non–same origin connection can be made by dynamically creating a `form` element. The `form` element's `action` property states the URL with which to connect, and its `method` specifies the type of HTTP request (verb) to make of that URL. The `form`'s `submit` function then makes the connection, including any parameters provided by `input` and other elements within the `form`. The element itself does not even have to be appended to the `document` object. Try the following code on the runner page:

```
var form = document.createElement("form");
form.action = "http://go.technocage.com/javascript/cross-site.js";
form.method = "get";
form.submit();
```

Note how you have made a connection to a different website. If that HTTP request had any side effects, like reading or writing data, then those side effects would indeed have taken place. The difference here from the `script` approach is that what you see next depends on the response of the contacted site; frequently it is whatever web page the `action` URL returns. Thanks to HTTP's *redirect* ability, however, that response can transparently take you to a *different* site—*including your own*. Try the following variant of the preceding program, which is identical except for the `action` URL:

```
var form = document.createElement("form");
form.action = "http://go.technocage.com/javascript/referback";
form.method = "get";
form.submit();
```

Running seems to do nothing; you go right back to `http://javascript.cs .lmu.edu/runner`. And yet something *did* happen: the server at the `action` URL did whatever the request asked it to do. It could have updated a database, performed a transaction, or even connected to other servers. And in the end, it *sent the web browser back to the original web page.*[10] Thanks to the redirect, most users would have missed this activity. Again, we have made a connection to a non–same origin site using JavaScript.

8.6.3   Cross-Site Scripting

For all the limitations imposed on JavaScript code, ranging from the same origin policy to the other "barriers" within the sandbox, techniques and vulnerabilities that compromise a web application's security still exist. In this section, we present what is arguably the most prevalent exploit on the Web—cross-site scripting, or XSS.

---

[10]Don't worry; the demo URL here does *nothing* other than send the web browser back. Really. *Trust us.*

Unlike other well-known exploits, like buffer overflows, man-in-the-middle attacks, and assorted types of forgeries or eavesdropping, XSS is truly and intrinsically Web-specific: it takes advantage of the specific confluence of mechanisms and behaviors that exist in the combination of technologies (HTML, JavaScript, web services, and more) behind current web applications. The seeds of XSS have, in fact, been distributed throughout the last two sections of this chapter. In the fashion of traditional detective stories, one can say that, at this point, you already have the information needed to implement an XSS exploit on a vulnerable web application.

Take a moment before reading on if you'd like to puzzle it out for a bit. What can you do, given what you know, to subvert all of the safeguards you have seen so far?

(Come back when ready.)

Whether you have figured it out or have given up trying, here goes. Most XSS attacks are founded on *code injection*—the insertion of JavaScript code into a web page, resulting in that code's running, under the same origin policy, as if it were a script delivered by the exploited web service. With such a program in place, the attacker can do anything that the web application can do—without any obvious sign that the malicious code does not belong to that application.

Injection by URL

One type of injection takes advantage of how a web application might "echo back" parameters such as search terms or other values that are included in its URLs. For example, suppose an online store can search by name and manufacturer, and such a search is expressed as a single URL as follows:

```
http://examplestore.com/search?name=<term1>&manufacturer=<term2>
```

Suppose, then, that the page that this website returns after such a search looks something like Figure 8.4, where, as a friendly reminder, the user's search terms are restated along with the list of possible results.

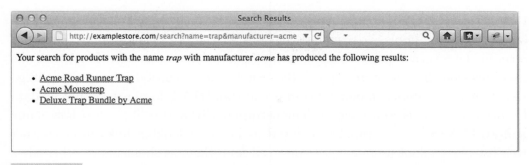

FIGURE 8.4

A search results page that "echoes back" parameters provided in the website's URL.

Here's the rub: if the developer of this website is not careful, an attacker can use the site's "echoed" parameters against it *by submitting parameters that can be interpreted as HTML*. To demonstrate this, we have created a website that has this vulnerability, at `http://javascript.cs.lmu.edu/php/vulnerable.php`. This site accepts `name` and `manufacturer` parameters, as with the preceding example. It doesn't do any real searches, of course, so don't be shocked if the search results never change. Go ahead and try it with the parameters shown in Figure 8.4: `http://javascript.cs.lmu.edu/php/vulnerable.php?name=trap&manufacturer=acme`.

Looks pretty much like what you would expect, yes? Now try `http://javascript.cs.lmu.edu/php/vulnerable.php?name=<u>trap</u>&manufacturer=<u>acme</u>`. See how the search terms are underlined now? That's because this particular website isn't very good about encoding user-provided values—a critical programming oversight that leads to XSS vulnerability. Note that while a real-world search engine may not return any search results for a URL such as this one, that wouldn't be the goal of an XSS attack. Instead, it has successfully *injected* HTML into the returned page! Now, consider what would happen if this injected HTML contained a `script` element: the returned (vulnerable) page would include the script and the browser would run it, as if it were generated by that very site. Same origin policy be damned—it has just been subverted!

Code-injecting URLs can get unwieldy to type, so we have put together a web page—hosted by another site, naturally—that lists these URLs. Go ahead and give them a try: `http://go.technocage.com/javascript/xss-urls.html`.[11] The referenced script example is particularly devious. It inserts a fake username/password form in the returned page—using a script *from a different website*. Further, if the user clicks on the button to "retry" the search, the submitted information can go to *yet another website*—again, allowed because an HTML form can submit its data to *any* server. This web page of demonstration URLs also illustrates how many real-world XSS attacks can be deployed as innocent-looking links from another website. Nonvigilant users may decide to click on them as shortcuts to other sites, not realizing they are injecting an undesirable script into the version of the web page that they see. Links such as these might also be included in an email, which is one of the main reasons why clicking on email links is to be avoided. Instead, navigate to the site of interest manually.

The exemption of HTML from the same origin policy, as described in the previous section, has been manipulated here into a mechanism for some serious malfeasance. Moral of the story: a vulnerable website, coupled with some clever URL manipulation by an XSS attacker, can lead to the execution of malicious code, with virtually no limitations.

Injection by Web Form

Injection by URL is just one of many ways in which an XSS attacker can add code where it was not intended. In fact, newer web browsers are more "vigilant" with such URLs, sometimes encoding them automatically and, in some cases, even detecting when a `script` fragment in the URL was also found in the returned page.

Another approach is code injection by web form: by observing the way a vulnerable site accepts form-based input and presents this input when the form is processed, an attacker can enter code into these fields such that the resulting page (or even future pages, in case the entered data are stored in a database and redisplayed during web searches or other operations on the website) runs malicious code. The principle is the same: get the targeted web application to accept infor-

---

[11] Web browsers are continuously improving their security capabilities, so don't be surprised if one or more of the script injection examples no longer works for you. For example, note how the examples switch the order of the `name` and `manufacturer` parameters so that the `script` element tags are out of order (and thus harder to detect). If your web browser does catch us, just look at the URL and the resulting web page, if the URL parameters did get through, to see how a script would have gotten injected into that page.

mation that gets regurgitated in subsequent web pages as executable JavaScript. In the prior section, the "point of entry" is a URL; in this one, it is a web form.

The "nonorigin" page at `http://go.technocage.com/javascript/xss-form.html` displays a form that posts data to our demonstration service at `http://javascript.cs.lmu.edu/php/vulnerable.php` (remember that forms are not bound by the same origin policy). Injection by web form is, by mechanism, no different from injection by URL: a connection is made to a vulnerable service, typically using the HTTP `POST` action, submitting parameters that result in a web page with malicious code. The example "prefills" at `http://go.technocage .com/javascript/xss-form.html` inject the same code, in fact, that the sample URLs at `http://go.technocage.com/javascript/xss-urls.html` do.

The choice between injection by URL, web form, or other means depends on a number of factors. First and foremost is the existence of a vulnerability at all. Some web applications may have it at the URL, while others my have it with HTTP `POST` requests. Another factor may be context of use: depending on the type of attack, the code may be meant to do its work upon immediate return of the web service (i.e., the injected code is meant to take effect immediately after the URL or web form is submitted), or, if the URL or web form saves information to a database, the code may be meant to appear in other web application pages. The bottom line is that, unless web applications specifically guard against code injection, XSS has the potential to completely undermine the objectives of the JavaScript sandbox and its same origin policy.

Defensive Programming Against XSS

The XSS problem is one that can be tackled on many levels. As you read this, new standards and technologies are being worked on for evolving distributed web applications toward better security and modularity, without detracting from the capabilities that most people expect of the Web today. Until these standards gain widespread support and adoption, however, application developers are left to include their own defenses.

The rules are fairly simple, actually. They are founded on the premise that the web browser is fundamentally insecure and that you should therefore examine everything that the browser sends to your web service, especially data provided by external sources such as users and other websites. Safeguards should be programmed into both the client and server sides:

- Server-side code must always *validate* requests received from web browsers. Expected input must be held to the most restrictive format that makes sense for the application.

- Both client- and server-side code must properly *encode* all exchanged information. You have seen the `encode` and `decode` functions that are available in JavaScript; server-side technologies have similar functions. Use them.

These safeguards should minimize the XSS risk for today's distributed applications, even as longer-term solutions are developed and adopted.

8.6.4   Mashups

While the restrictions and protections placed by web browsers on JavaScript network connections are generally necessary, they stand in direct conflict with some legitimate and powerful web application categories. In this section, we examine one such category: *mashups*. Mashups provide compelling new ways for combining and visualizing data from disparate sources, yet they rely on the very activities that the same origin policy and other web browser security features restrict.

A mashup web application is an application that retrieves two or more data sets, typically from distinct sources, and presents them in an integrated manner that encourages new insights and correlations—a web instance of the adage about a whole being greater than the sum of its parts. Mashups are also characterized by a high degree of interactivity and dynamic behavior: to navigate or adjust the mashup, users expect to be able to see display updates as they drag or adjust user interface controls "live"; the traditional "click-and-wait" web navigation cycle is not acceptable here. Examples of mashups include:

- A website that overlays restaurants over a map

- A website that displays a wide variety of events on a calendar

- A website that graphs numeric data such as stock prices alongside prominent news headlines from the same period

- A website that displays photographs taken at various tourist sites overlaid on a map

- A website that displays your social network and associates events, places, or groups with linked friends

- A website that customizes its advertisements according to its content and what it knows about you, such as your shopping history, your recent search terms, or how you reached that website

Figure 8.5 is a screenshot of a mashup, `http://www.flickrvision.com`, that uses the same data sources. Instead of displaying images based on map navigation,

FIGURE 8.5

`http://www.flickrvision.com`, another Flickr–Google Maps mashup.

`http://www.flickrvision.com` is time-based—as you watch the web application, images pop in and out of the map as they are uploaded. As we are rehashing aphorisms here, observe, from these two screenshots showing different presentations for the same data, how there is more than one way to skin (mash up?) a cat.

It should be noted that while many web applications (particularly search engines and web portals) may exhibit functionality that is similar to this, such applications may be collecting and hosting the data used on their own, and so they are architecturally no different from a typical client–server database application. The "spirit" of a mashup emphasizes the use of disparate services that are not necessarily designed to work together and are not even aware that they are being integrated with data from other services.

By its very nature, then, a mashup needs to bypass the same origin policy. The application web page itself can only be served by one site, while that same page must have access to more than one data source, and therefore more than one server. The same origin policy is here to stay, however, and so mashup implementations rely on one or more of the following workarounds—most of which, we hope you *aren't* surprised to learn, you have seen before:

- *Server-side integration.* This approach is the only one that hews strictly to the letter of same origin policy: use the server that provides the mashup web page as a relay for all of the services that the mashup combines. Thus, the web page need only contact a single server or origin. The set of "mashable" services is limited to the ones that the relay server "understands."

- *Cross-Origin Resource Sharing (CORS).* It's not hard to see why mashups and CORS are made for each other—the very principle behind CORS is the granting of explicit cross-origin permission by certain services. Services that are meant to be mashed up can simply allow any origin (or a specific list of known clients), and voilà, mashup applications can connect at will.

- *Dynamic script loading.* This is precisely the technique shown in Section 8.6.2. The browser-side mashup code can create `script` elements on the fly, with the scripts designed to return the mashable data. This relies on the accessed services' having such scripts available for use in this manner.

■ *JSONP.* Also seen in Section 8.6.2, JSONP is a specific use of dynamic script loading, with `script` references resolving to a JSON expression's being passed into some function in the browser-side mashup code. For greater customizability, the JSONP service may accept "prefix" or "postfix" parameters, indicating what JavaScript code should be "wrapped" around the JSON data representation. Having this customizability allows mashup applications to process the JSON in a manner that best fits their needs.

■ *XSS techniques.* If you think about it, JSONP is actually a form of "permitted" code injection, with XSS techniques constituting a broader set of alternative but similar methods. Thus, any other XSS technique—code injection by URL, code injection by HTTP `POST`, to name a couple—will also work, again as long as the participating service has available mechanisms for doing so. Somewhat ironically, mashups necessitate a sort of "invited" code injection—something that has led Douglas Crockford to characterize these applications as "self-inflicted XSS attacks" [Cro10].

Review and Practice

1. Choose three sandbox restrictions on JavaScript code other than the same origin policy, and explain why removing each restriction may pose a security risk.

2. Try to inject *two* distinct `script` elements into the demonstration vulnerable service at `http://javascript.cs.lmu.edu/php/vulnerable.php`: one in the `name` parameter and another in the `manufacturer` parameter. What happens, and why? You may need to open your web browser's error console or debug window to get a definitive answer.

8.7   Case Study: Events and Trending Topics

We conclude this chapter with a mashup case study: a web application that lines up the events reported by our homegrown calendar service at `http://javascript .cs.lmu.edu/php/calendar.php` with the publicly available, RESTful Twitter API (`https://dev.twitter.com/docs/api`). In particular, the application accesses Twitter's trending topics service, which provides the most popular topic searches on its website at a given time.

You can try out the mashup at `http://javascript.cs.lmu.edu/calendar-mashup`. Figure 8.6 displays a screenshot of the application in action.

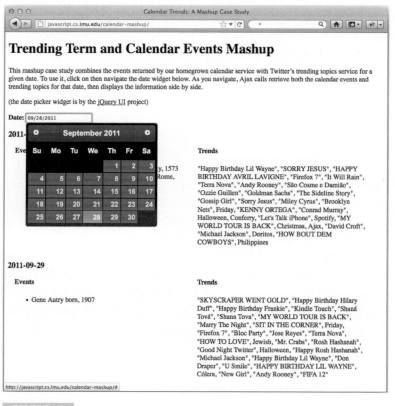

FIGURE 8.6

The Events and Trending Topics mashup case study.

The case study mashup works by having the user select a date. Date selection triggers an Ajax connection that requests information from each service. Calendar events and trending topics for the same day are then displayed side by side.

For a bird'seye view, the web application's source code—except for externally included libraries—is shown here:

```
<!DOCTYPE HTML>

<html>
  <head>
    <meta charset="UTF-8" />
    <title>Calendar Trends: A Mashup Case Study</title>

    <!-- Styles needed by the date widget. -->
    <link rel="stylesheet" type="text/css"
        href="http://ajax.googleapis.com/ajax/libs/jqueryui/1.8.9/
              themes/ui-darkness/jquery-ui.css"/>

    <!--
      Very simple styles just to put the events and trends side by
      side.
    -->
    <style type="text/css">
      .date { clear: both; }
      .category {
        width: 45%;
        margin: 0 1em;
        display: inline-block;
        vertical-align: top;
      }
      .category h4 { margin-top: 0; }
    </style>

    <script type="text/javascript"
      src="http://code.jquery.com/jquery-latest.min.js"></script>
    <script type="text/javascript"
      src="http://ajax.googleapis.com/ajax/libs/jqueryui/1.8.9/
            jquery-ui.min.js"></script>
    <script type="text/javascript" src="date.js"></script>
```

```
<script type="text/javascript">
  $(function () {
    // Make the Ajax animation invisible.
    $("#ajaxAnimation").hide();

    // Set up the date picker.
    $("#datepicker").datepicker({
      onSelect: function (dateText) {
        // Set up the model variable.
        var mashup = {};

        // Set up the function that displays the data in the model.
        var displayMashup = function () {
          var mashupHtml = "";
          $.each(mashup, function (dateKey, mashupItem) {
            mashupHtml += "<h3>" + dateKey + "</h3>";

            // Write out the events.
            mashupHtml += "<div class=\"date\">";
            mashupHtml += "<div class=\"category\">
            <h4>Events</h4>";
            mashupHtml += "<ul>";
            $.each(mashupItem.events, function (i, mashupEvent) {
              mashupHtml += "<li>" + mashupEvent + "</li>";
            });
            mashupHtml += "</ul></div>";

            // Write out the trends.
            mashupHtml += "<div class=\"category\">
            <h4>Trends</h4>";
            mashupHtml += "<p>";
            $.each(mashupItem.trends, function (i, mashupTrend) {
              if (i > 0) {
                mashupHtml += ", ";
              }
              mashupHtml += mashupTrend;
            });
            mashupHtml += "</p></div></div>";
          });
```

```
              $("#results").html(mashupHtml);
          };

          // Grab the date.
          var date = new Date(dateText);

          // Clear the content of the results element.
          $("#results").html("");

          // Show some Ajax feedback animation.
          $("#ajaxAnimation").show("fast");

          // Start with calling the calendar service. We then
          // contact Twitter after we've received and processed
          // the calendar results. Note how the two services have
          // differing formats for their date parameters.
          $.getJSON("http://javascript.cs.lmu.edu/php/calendar.php",
            { date: date.toString("yyyyMMdd") },
            function (result) {
              // Process the calendar results first: our model data
              // are JavaScript objects with date strings as
              // properties. Each property is then an object that
              // consists of events and, later, Twitter trends.
              mashup = {};
              $.each(result, function (i, event) {
                // Each element has only a month and a day. We
                // convert that into a date string with the chosen
                // year.
                var dateString = event.month + " " + event.day +
                  ", " + date.toString("yyyy");

                // Use the date as a property, then add events to its
                // value.
                var dateKey = new Date(dateString).toString("yyyy-\
MM-dd");

                if (mashup[dateKey]) {
                  mashup[dateKey].events.push(event.description);
                } else {
                  // Initialize the mashup single-date object.
                  mashup[dateKey] = {
                    events: [ event.description ],
```

```
                  trends: []
                };
            }
        });

        // Now we can grab the Twitter trends. Because this is
        // outside the page's domain, we need a technique that
        // works around the same origin policy. Here, we use
        // JSONP since it is easily supported by jQuery: just
        // append "callback=?" to the URL for the getJSON
        // function.
        $.getJSON(
          "http://api.twitter.com/1/trends/weekly.json?
           callback=?",
          {
            date: date.toString("yyyy-MM-dd"),
            exclude: "hashtags"
          },
          function (result) {
            // For every date in the result, we locate a pre-
            // existing date, then add the topic to that date.
            $.each(result.trends, function (dateKey,
              trendArray) {
              if (mashup[dateKey]) {
                $.each(trendArray, function (i, trend) {
                  mashup[dateKey].trends.push(trend.query);
                });
              }
            });

            // With the data gathering complete, we can finally
            // display the mashup.
            displayMashup();
            $("#ajaxAnimation").hide("fast");
          }
        );
      }
    });
  }
});
```

```
    </script>

  </head>

  <body>
    <h1>Trending Term and Calendar Events Mashup</h1>

    <p>This mashup case study combines the events returned by our
    homegrown calendar service with Twitter&rsquo;s trending topics
    service for a given date. To use it, click on then navigate the
    date widget below. As you navigate, Ajax calls retrieve both the
    calendar events and trending topics for that date, then displays
    the information side by side.</p>

    <p>(the date picker widget is by the <a
    href="http://jqueryui.com">jQuery UI</a> project)</p>

    <p><label for="datepicker"><b>Date:</b></label>
      <input type="text" id="datepicker" />
      <img id="ajaxAnimation" src="../images/loadera16.gif" /></p>

    <div id="results"></div>
  </body>
</html>
```

8.7.1   Date Selection User Interface

Date selection is accomplished with the help of the jQuery UI project (`http://jqueryui.com`), which provides a library of reusable, customizable "widgets" for web applications. As its name implies, jQuery UI is built on jQuery and uses many of its design principles and core functionality. The application also provides a simple animation graphic to indicate when an Ajax connection is in progress.

To use jQuery and jQuery UI, their JavaScript files are referenced in the page's `head`. The open source Datejs library (`http://www.datejs.com`) is also referenced, for flexible formatting of `Date` objects as strings:

```
<script type="text/javascript"
  src="http://code.jquery.com/jquery-latest.min.js"></script>
<script type="text/javascript"
  src="http://ajax.googleapis.com/ajax/libs/jqueryui/1.8.9/
     jquery-ui.min.js"></script>
<script type="text/javascript" src="date.js"></script>
```

Setting up the date widget and Ajax animation consists of HTML tags and corresponding JavaScript. The web page body contains the following tag for the text field that will invoke the date widget:

```
<p><label for="datepicker"><b>Date:</b></label>
   <input type="text" id="datepicker" />
   <img id="ajaxAnimation" src="../images/loadera16.gif" /></p>
```

Notice that there is actually nothing jQuery UI-specific about the HTML. All of the "magic" resides in the following JavaScript fragment from the last, long `script` element in the page's `head`. This code makes full use of the selectors, added functionality, and shorthand of the jQuery library (Section 7.5):

```
$(function () {
  // Make the Ajax animation invisible.
  $("#ajaxAnimation").hide();

  // Set up the date picker.
  $("#datepicker").datepicker({
    onSelect: function (dateText) {
      /* The rest of the program logic goes here. */
    }
  });
});
```

The `script` element starts with jQuery's `$(document).ready` substitute for the `onload` event, further abbreviated with the `$(function () { })` shorthand.

First off, the function hides the Ajax animation `img` element with the ID selector `#ajaxAnimation`. Compare that selector-plus-`hide` call to its non-jQuery equivalent:

```
document.getElementById("ajaxAnimation").style.display = "none";
```

The second jQuery call sets up the jQuery UI date widget. It selects the `#datepicker` text `input` element and calls the jQuery UI-installed `datepicker` function to set it up. In jQuery style, all of the settings and customized behavior for this date widget are enclosed in a JavaScript object that is passed as the single argument to `datepicker`.

For our case study mashup, the only option that needs to be set for the date widget is its date selection event handler, passed in the `onSelect` property of the `datepicker` argument. The entirety of the application's remaining logic is within this function.

8.7.2 Ajax Connection

The `onSelect` function starts with a couple of definitions that will be used later:

```
// Set up the model variable.
var mashup = {};

// Set up the function that displays the data in the model.
var displayMashup = function () {
  /* We'll see this later. */
};
```

Things really get started right after the `displayMashup` function definition, with these lines:

```
// Grab the date.
var date = new Date(dateText);

// Clear the content of the results element.
$("#results").html("");

// Show some Ajax feedback animation.
$("#ajaxAnimation").show("fast");
```

In plain English, what happens, line by line, is:

- A `Date` object is parsed from the `dateText` argument that is passed into the `onSelect` function by the date widget. This is the string representation of the date that the user chose from the calendar widget.

- The element reserved for the mashup data, given an ID of "results" and thus using the jQuery selector `#results`, is emptied of any content. Calling jQuery's `html` function with an empty string does this very concisely.

- We use jQuery's `show` function to display our Ajax animation image, thus giving the user visual feedback that we are waiting for network requests to complete. jQuery's `show` and `hide` functions actually do more than just set an element's `display` property; they also perform smooth transitional animation as the selected elements appear or disappear. In this case, we customize this animation by passing `fast` as an argument to `show`.

At this point, we make our network request. Instead of jQuery's general-purpose `ajax` function, we use its shorthand equivalent for JSON requests, `getJSON`. Because this function assumes that we are connecting to a service that uses JSON as a data representation, we do not need to supply as much information as we would for `ajax`. `getJSON` does still call `ajax`, but prefills a number of settings that are common to JSON services.

The `getJSON` call immediately follows our displaying of the Ajax animation image and looks like this:

```
$.getJSON("http://javascript.cs.lmu.edu/php/calendar.php",
  { date: date.toString("yyyyMMdd") },
  function (result) {
    /* Event processing and more Ajax --- coming up next. */
  }
);
```

`getJSON` accepts three arguments: the URL of the JSON service, any parameters for the request, and a handler function for processing the service's response. As with `ajax`, that `result` object is the already-parsed version of the JSON data representation that was transferred over the network.

From the preceding code, we can see that our mashup contacts the calendar service first. Previously, we accessed the service without any parameters, and, as we saw in Section 8.4.1, doing so produces the events for today and tomorrow. When a `date` parameter is included, with the date formatted as `yyyyMMdd` (e.g., July 28, 2011, would be `20110728`), the service returns the events for that date and the day after. `getJSON` takes these parameters in the form of a JavaScript object, seen in the second line of the preceding code—an object with a single property, called `date`, whose value is the `date` object that we parsed previously, formatted as required by the calendar service.

The final `getJSON` argument, which is the handler code that should run when the JSON request completes, consists of two primary steps:

1. It processes the array of events returned by the calendar service (the `result` argument).

2. It initiates an Ajax request to the Twitter trending topics service.

Since we are focusing on Ajax connections in this section, we will skip right to the second Ajax request for now:

```
$.getJSON("http://api.twitter.com/1/trends/weekly.json?callback=?",
  {
    date: date.toString("yyyy-MM-dd"),
    exclude: "hashtags"
  },
  function (result) {
    /* Trending topic processing and mashup display ---
       coming up in the last two sections. */
  }
);
```

This is another `getJSON` call, this time to the Twitter trending topic service at `http://api.twitter.com/1/trends/weekly.json?callback=?`. Note that this network connection is typically disallowed due to the same origin policy, so we need to use one of the workarounds seen in Section 8.6.2. In our case study, we go with JSONP, which is supported by the Twitter service. Appending `?callback=?` to the service URL tells the `getJSON` function that JSONP is to be used; `getJSON` does the rest (yet another reason for jQuery's indispensability in modern web application programming).

The Twitter trending topic service is given two parameters: `date` and `exclude`. The `date` parameter, expected in `yyyy-MM-dd` format, specifies the day for which trending topics are to be reported. The `exclude` parameter asks the service to return topic strings only, and not Twitter hashtags (single-word strings that begin with a `#` sign). The handler function given to this `getJSON` call processes the trending topic object that is returned and performs the final mashup display.

As we end this section and before we conclude with how the JSON results are processed, mashed up, and displayed, notice the sequential approach taken in this case study: one JSON request is performed first, and the second one is performed *strictly after* the first one—something that is guaranteed by making the second request within the result-handling function of the first one. This design choice was made because the processing of Twitter trending topics cannot take place until calendar events processing completes. The alternative would be to structure the `onSelect` event handler as follows:

```
$.getJSON("http://javascript.cs.lmu.edu/php/calendar.php",
  { date: date.toString("yyyyMMdd") },
  function (result) {
    /* Event processing. */
  }
);


$.getJSON("http://api.twitter.com/1/trends/weekly.json?callback=?",
  {
    date: date.toString("yyyy-MM-dd"),
    exclude: "hashtags"
  },
  function (result) {
    /* Trending topic processing. */
  }
);
```

When written in this manner, the execution order of the event and trending topic processing functions (the result handlers of the calendar and Twitter JSON requests, respectively) cannot be determined beforehand; such is the nature of asynchronous communication. We can either write code that will work regardless of execution order or enforce such an order and write the code with that assumption. The case study chooses the latter, trading potential performance gains (since both connections will share some concurrent time) for code simplicity (algorithms that do not assume specific sequences of events are generally more complex and harder to read, not to mention program).

8.7.3 Result Processing

The JSON objects returned by the services used by our mashup case study are organized in ways that are determined by the developers of those services. As seen in Section 8.4.1, the calendar service returns an array of event objects, each with `month`, `day`, `movable`, and `description` properties. The Twitter trending topics service, in turn, returns a single object with a `trends` property, which consists of one property for every date in the requested time span. Finally, each of those properties is an array of topic objects, with `name` and `query` properties.

To properly "mash up" these objects, they must be processed in a manner that correlates them according to the objective of the mashup application. In our case study, we want to line up the recorded events from the calendar service with the Twitter service's trending topics for the equivalent date(s). The goals of our result handler functions, therefore, are to

- do whatever processing or computation is necessary in order to reflect the correlation that we are trying to accomplish, and

- display this correlated information on the web page.

As stated in the previous section, we explicitly start with the data received from the calendar service. Here is the processing code for that result handler:

```
// Process the calendar results first: our model data are
// JavaScript objects with date strings as properties.  Each
// property is then an object that consists of events and,
// later, Twitter trends.
mashup = {};
$.each(result, function (i, event) {
  // Each element has only a month and a day.  We convert
  // that into a date string with the chosen year.
  var dateString = event.month + " " + event.day +
```

```
      ", " + date.toString("yyyy");

    // Use the date as a property, then add events to its
    // value.
    var dateKey = new Date(dateString).toString("yyyy-MM-dd");
    if (mashup[dateKey]) {
      mashup[dateKey].events.push(event.description);
    } else {
      // Initialize the mashup single-date object.
      mashup[dateKey] = {
        events: [ event.description ],
        trends: []
      };
    }
});
```

The strategy for implementing a mashup involves determining a *model* that best represents the information received from the various services. This model should clearly capture how the mashed-up data sets correlate with each other and should also make it easy to convey that information visually on the web page.

Since the whole point of this application is to correlate events and trending topics from the same date, we design our "mashed up" product as an object with one property for each date in the data set, named using the date formatted as yyyy-MM-dd. The value of each property shall be an object with two arrays: one for events and another for trends. For example, a model consisting of data for October 31, 2011, and November 1, 2011, would look like this:

```
{
  "2011-10-31": {
    "events": [ "Halloween", "Nevada Day" ],
    "trends": [ "ghosts", "Vegas", "party" ]
  },

  "2011-11-01": {
    "events": [ "All Saints Day", "Samhain" ],
    "trends": [ "In memoriam", "Happy new Celtic year" ]
  }
}
```

Our processing code, then, needs to "convert" the event data from the calendar service into the appropriate `events` arrays under their corresponding dates, then add the trending topic data from Twitter into the appropriate `trends` arrays for those same dates. With that plan in mind, let's go back to the processing code.

We start by initializing the variable that holds our model. In our case study, that variable is called `mashup`:

```
mashup = {};
```

You might recall that this variable was declared at the very beginning of the date widget's `onSelect` function to ensure that the code after that, particularly the `getJSON` result handler functions, is referring to the same object.

We know that the calendar service returns an array of events, each with a `month`, `day`, and `description`. Our mashup does not need the `movable` property, so we will largely ignore it. The approach we take is to iterate through this array, depositing the `description` for each event under the corresponding date-named property in the `mashup` variable:

```
$.each(result, function (i, event) {
  // Each element has only a month and a day.  We convert
  // that into a date string with the chosen year.
  var dateString = event.month + " " + event.day +
    ", " + date.toString("yyyy");

  // Use the date as a property, then add events to its
  // value.
  var dateKey = new Date(dateString).toString("yyyy-MM-dd");
  if (mashup[dateKey]) {
    mashup[dateKey].events.push(event.description);
  } else {
    // Initialize the mashup single-date object.
    mashup[dateKey] = {
      events: [ event.description ],
      trends: []
    };
  }
});
```

For iterating through the array, we use jQuery's **each** function. It is more concise and less error-prone than a **for** statement. The **each** function takes the object or array to be iterated over and a function that specifies what should be done for each property value or element in that object. That function takes two arguments: the index/property in the array or object and the value at that index/property.

In this function, and thus for each event returned by the calendar service, we construct a date string using that event's **month** and **day** properties, appending the year chosen by the user. This date string is converted into a **Date** object, then reformatted to the desired **yyyy-MM-dd** representation. This string is then used as a property name for the **mashup** variable: if that property already exists, then the event's **description** is **push**ed to the end of the **events** array; if not, then a new { **events, trends** } object is created and assigned to that date.

As seen in the previous section, the code then initiates an Ajax request to the Twitter trending topics service. In *that* request's result handler function, we have the following code:

```
// For every date in the result, we locate a preexisting
// date, then add the topic to that date.
$.each(result.trends, function (dateKey, trendArray) {
  if (mashup[dateKey]) {
    $.each(trendArray, function (i, trend) {
      mashup[dateKey].trends.push(trend.query);
    });
  }
});

// With the data gathering complete, we can finally
// display the mashup.
displayMashup();
$("#ajaxAnimation").hide("fast");
```

The processing code also uses the **each** function, this time iterating through the **trends** property of the service's JSON response. As an aside, note how the use of JSONP is completely transparent to our code; jQuery did everything from our initial connection request up to the calling of the result handler function.

For this **each** invocation, the values passed into the iteration function are the date-string properties in the **trends** object. Conveniently, these date strings are already in the same **yyyy-MM-dd** format that is used by the **mashup** model object (yes, that was part of the plan). Thus, the code simply accesses `mashup[dateKey]` and `pushes` the `trend` objects' `query` string to the `mashup[dateKey].trends` array. The initial `if` condition ignores trending topics from dates that were not part of the calendar service's response.

With the `mashup` object completed after the `each` function call, the application can now display the fruits of its labor on the web page. We come full circle to the `displayMashup` function that was defined early in our `onSelect` date widget handler, with which we conclude our case study walkthrough. Once `displayMashup` finishes its work, we can finally dismiss our Ajax animation image with a `hide` call.

Observe how the trending topics processing code has a strict sequential relationship with the calendar events processing code: it is the calendar events code that sets up the "skeleton" for the `mashup` model object, with the trending topics processing code just filling in the blanks. It is also the trending topics code, "knowing" that it is the last set of instructions, that calls `displayMashup` and finally closes the entire Ajax sequence by putting away its animated feedback image. Imagine how both routines would have looked if we could not make any assumptions about which one ran first.

8.7.4 Data (Mashup) Display

You might have noticed that, aside from the displaying of the Ajax animation image, none of the processing done so far—the Ajax requests, the `each` iterations, the `mashup` object manipulations—has been visible to the user. Our case study design intentionally separates all data manipulation activities from display activities. While this separation is not absolutely required—one can imagine processing code that directly manipulates the DOM as the calendar events and trending topics are manipulated—it is a commonly used "dividing line." This way, changing your mind about how the mashup data are presented does not interfere with how you correlate the original responses from the web services used.

Returning to the `displayMashup` function, we have:

```
var displayMashup = function () {
  var mashupHtml = "";
  $.each(mashup, function (dateKey, mashupItem) {
    mashupHtml += "<h3>" + dateKey + "</h3>";

    // Write out the events.
```

```
mashupHtml += "<div class=\"date\">";
mashupHtml += "<div class=\"category\"><h4>Events</h4>";
mashupHtml += "<ul>";
$.each(mashupItem.events, function (i, mashupEvent) {
  mashupHtml += "<li>" + mashupEvent + "</li>";
});
mashupHtml += "</ul></div>";

// Write out the trends.
mashupHtml += "<div class=\"category\"><h4>Trends</h4>";
mashupHtml += "<p>";
$.each(mashupItem.trends, function (i, mashupTrend) {
  if (i > 0) {
    mashupHtml += ", ";
  }
  mashupHtml += mashupTrend;
});
mashupHtml += "</p></div></div>";
  }

$("#results").html(mashupHtml);
};
```

The function centers on HTML tags that get accumulated in the `mashupHtml` variable as the code iterates over the `mashup` object. For each property of `mashup`, which we know to correspond to a date, the function

1. creates a heading (`h3`) element with the date,

2. creates an event list (`ul` element) where each event is a list item (`li` element), and

3. creates a comma-separated trend list presented as a paragraph (`p` element).

Once the HTML string is complete, it is sent to the element whose ID is `results` using jQuery's `html` function. This finally results in something that the user sees (Figure 8.6). As seen in the previous section, when this function returns, the entire cycle concludes with the rehiding of the animated Ajax image.

Review and Practice

1. How does the case study ensure that the Twitter trending topic Ajax connection of the mashup code takes place after the calendar event Ajax request?

2. What does the jQuery `each` function do?

3. How would the case study code change if the date headings in the mashup display were to change to a fully spelled-out `month day, year` format (e.g., `March 12, 2011`)?

Chapter Summary

- Distributed computing concerns applications that divide their work among separate physical machines.

- In order to get the work done, the machines involved in a distributed application must agree on how data will be interchanged among them. Common data interchange formats for web applications include plain text, XML, JSON, and YAML.

- There are two models for distributed application communication. Synchronous communication involves strict, sequential exchange where communicating parties must be present and wait for each other as information travels back and forth. Asynchronous communication allows communicating parties to leave messages for each other without having to wait for a response, allowing them to move on with other activities in the meantime.

- Ajax was once an acronym for *Asynchronous JavaScript and XML* but has since evolved into a term in its own right, denoting a style of web programming that uses JavaScript objects to perform asynchronous information interchange.

- Ajax has a "native" library based on the `XMLHttpRequest` host object but is generally much easier to program with libraries such as jQuery.

- Distributed web applications use Uniform Resource Identifiers, or URIs, to unambiguously identify services, hosts, and other resources on a network.

- Representational State Transfer, or REST, is a distributed application architecture approach that structures a distributed system as a strict sequence of client–server relationships and views all communication as the transfer of object state *at that moment in time* from one machine to the next. REST has been known to facilitate simplicity, scalability, and portability in a distributed system.

- REST concepts map very well to web technologies and standards such as URIs and HTTP.

- Separation of concerns remains a major virtue when designing and developing distributed applications.

- The World Wide Web, as a highly distributed system that makes it extremely easy to exchange information, requires a number of mechanisms to protect users from malicious code and unauthorized eavesdropping. A "sandbox" limits the activities that a JavaScript program may do.

- The *same origin policy* is an important JavaScript limitation that keeps its code from reading or manipulating information from sources other than the web server that delivered the current web page. It is not an *HTML* limitation, however, and JavaScript can be used to create HTML dynamically.

- Techniques for working around the same origin policy primarily involve the coordinated use of JavaScript-generated HTML elements such as `script` and `form`.

- Cross-site scripting, or XSS, is a security vulnerability that allows JavaScript code to be *injected* by an outsider into a web page. Once injected, this code gains the same rights and privileges as any other JavaScript code that was delivered by the web page.

- A mashup is a popular type of distributed application that combines diverse yet correlatable information from different web services and servers into an integrated, unified display.

Exercises

1. The original Napster application made the peer-to-peer distributed system a household word (relatively speaking). Do some research on how the original Napster worked and state why the system was described as such.

2. Machines that participate in a peer-to-peer distributed system are sometimes called *servents*, a "word mashup" of "server" and "client." Explain why this term makes sense for that system model.

3. Look up the meaning of the term *crowdsourcing* and compare its meaning to a grid computing system. How similar or different are these terms?

4. Do a little research into the following applications and state whether they use a thin client, a thick client, a rich Internet application, or more than one of the three:

   (a) Amazon
   (b) eBay
   (c) Facebook
   (d) Gmail
   (e) iTunes
   (f) LinkedIn
   (g) Second Life
   (h) Twitter
   (i) World of Warcraft
   (j) YouTube

5. Is the choice among a thin client, a thick client, and a rich Internet application mutually exclusive? State why or why not.

6. Could there be such a thing as a JavaScript *thick* client? State why or why not.

7. State whether or not the following types of data are suitably communicated using plain text representations:

(a) A news item

(b) A list of movies

(c) A short story

(d) The box score of a basketball game

(e) A user's network of friends

(f) The URL of a particular website

(g) The order status of a purchased item

(h) The order information for a purchased item

(i) The closing price for a stock

(j) A month's worth of closing prices for a stock

8. Do a little research on XML and JSON to find out one or more things that can be done with XML but not with JSON. Describe each XML-only capability and state how having this capability may (or may not) affect a distributed application.

9. Similarly to the previous exercise, find one or more things that can be done with JSON but not with XML. Describe each JSON-only capability and state how having this capability may (or may not) affect a distributed application.

10. Take the following data interchange representations and provide reasonable "translations" of each representation to the other two structured formats described in this chapter. Online parsers are available for each format (search for "online XML/JSON/YAML parser") so that you can check your work.

(a) XML to JSON and YAML

```
<character name="Ulf Pendragor"
    class="barbarian"
    strength="48" intelligence="42" />
```

(b) JSON to XML and YAML

```
{
    "ISBN": "978-0763780609",
    "title": "An Introduction to Programming with JavaScript",
    "author": [ "Ray Toal", "John Dionisio" ],
```

```
    "year": 2012
}
```

(c) XML to JSON and YAML

```
<weather date="2015-10-31" zip="90096">
  <condition description="cloudy" />
  <temperatures>
  </temperatures>
</weather>
```

(d) YAML to XML and JSON

```
---
movies:
  - title: Citizen Kane
    director: Orson Welles
    starring:
      - Orson Welles
      - Joseph Cotten
      - Dorothy Comingore

  - title: The Third Man
    director: Carol Reed
    starring:
      - Orson Welles
      - Joseph Cotten
      - Alida Valli

tv:
  - series: I Love Lucy
    episode: Lucy Meets Orson Welles
    director: James V. Kern
    starring:
      - Lucille Ball
      - Desi Arnaz
...
```

(e) JSON to XML and YAML

```
[
  "A nickel ain't worth a dime anymore.",
  "I never said most of the things I said.",
  "Even Napoleon had his Watergate.",
  "I always thought that record would stand until it was
   broken.",
  "Half the lies they tell about me aren't true."
]
```

(f) YAML to XML and JSON

```
---
- name: Excalibur
  type: sword
  wielder: Arthur

- name: Mjolnir
  type: hammer
  wielder: Thor

- name: Durendal
  type: sword
  wielder: Roland
...
```

(g) JSON to XML and YAML

```
{
  "year": 1896,
  "city": "Athens",
  "country": "Greece",
  "events": [
    "athletics", "cycling", "fencing",
    "gymnastics", "shooting", "swimming",
    "tennis", "weightlifting", "wrestling"
  ],
  "organizer": "Demetrius Vikelas"
}
```

(h) XML to JSON and YAML

```
<haikus>
  <haiku>
    <first>Kochira muke</first>
    <second>Ware mo sabishiki</second>
    <third>Aki no kure</third>
  </haiku>
  <haiku>
    <first>None is traveling</first>
    <second>Here along this way but I,</second>
    <third>This autumn evening.</third>
  </haiku>
</haikus>
```

(i) YAML to XML and JSON (this may require a little research)

```
---
- number: XXV
  couplet: |
    Then happy I, that love and am beloved,
    Where I may not remove nor be removed.

- number: LXXX
  couplet: |
    Then if he thrive and I be cast away,
    The worst was this, my love was my decay.
...
```

(j) XML to JSON and YAML (this may require a little research)

```
<template>
  <title>Informal Letter</title>
  <salutation><![CDATA[Dear <recipient/>]]></salutation>
  <complimentary-close>Sincerely</complimentary-close>
  <signature><![CDATA[<sender/>]]></signature>
</template>
```

11. Take the XML representations from Exercise 10, whether supplied by the text or constructed by you as an answer, and do the following:

(a) Write a JavaScript runner program that uses `DOMParser` to convert the XML representation into a `Document` object.

(b) Extend your program so that it uses `getElementsByTagName` to retrieve and display two element types (your choice) from the resulting `Document`.

(c) Extend your program so that, for each element retrieved by `getElementsByTagName`, your program also displays all of the element's `childNodes` array members, if any.

(d) You may have noticed that, in performing the previous three tasks, you ended up using the same code over and over again, with only the XML representation and the tag names changing. Refactor your program so it is fully contained within a function called `processXML`. The `processXML` function should accept three arguments: `xmlString`, `firstTagName`, and `secondTagName`. `xmlString` is the XML representation to process, `firstTagName` is the first tag name to find and display, and `secondTagName` is the second tag name to find and display. Have your runner script call `processXML` in this manner:

```
processXML(
    prompt("Please enter the XML representation to
            process:"),
    prompt("Please enter the first tag to find:"),
    prompt("Please enter the second tag to find:"));
```

This way, a single program can process all 10 XML representations from the previous exercise!

12. Take the JSON representations from Exercise 10, whether supplied by the text or constructed by you as an answer, and do the following:

(a) Write a JavaScript runner program that uses the `JSON` object to convert the JSON representation into a JavaScript object.

(b) Extend your program so that it retrieves and displays two subproperties or array members (your choice) from the resulting object.

(c) Extend your program so that, using the jQuery `each` function, your program also displays all properties/members, if any, for each subproperty or array member retrieved in the previous task.

(d) You may have noticed that, in performing the previous three tasks, you ended up using the same code over and over again, with only the JSON representation and the sequence of property keys changing. Refactor your program so it is fully contained within a function called `processJSON`. The `processJSON` function should accept three arguments: `jsonString`, `firstKeySequence`, and `secondKeySequence`. `jsonString` is the JSON representation to process, while `firstKeySequence` and `secondKeySequence` are strings of comma-separated values (such as `"city"`, `"movies,1,starring,0"`, or `"events,2"`) representing the sequence of properties to access in order to reach the desired value. Have your runner script call `processJSON` in this manner:

```
processJSON(
    prompt("Please enter the JSON representation to \
process:"),
    prompt("Please enter the first comma-separated sequence \
 of property keys/indices:"),
    prompt("Please enter the second comma-separated \
 sequence of property keys/indices:"));
```

This way, a single program can process all 10 JSON representations from the previous exercise! (*Hint:* The `split` function will turn your comma-separated string of property keys/indices into an array fairly easily.)

(e) Are there certain properties that the generalized program from the preceding task will *not* be able to retrieve? Explain your answer briefly.

13. Type the following program into the JavaScript runner page and run it multiple times, taking note of the output for each run:

```
$.ajax({
    url: "../php/fortune.php",
    success: function (response) {
        alert("First fortune call: " + response);
    }
});
```

```
$.ajax({
    url: "../php/fortune.php",
    success: function (response) {
        alert("Second fortune call: " + response);
    }
});
```

The first "a" in "Ajax" is supposed to stand for "asynchronous." How does the preceding program's output tell you that the network connections are indeed asynchronous?

14. In some cases, asynchronous communication is *not* desired. Fortunately, jQuery accommodates "synchronous Ajax" (is that an oxymoron?) through the `async` option. If `async: false` is supplied with an `ajax` call, then communication is done synchronously.

Modify the program in Exercise 13 so that the calls are done with `async: false`, then run it multiple times. What behavior did you expect, and did the new program behave as expected?

15. If your main concern for the program in Exercise 13 is to ensure that the first fortune always appears first, is it sufficient to add `async: false` to the first `ajax` call only? Why or why not?

16. There is another way to modify the program in Exercise 13 to ensure that the first fortune always appears first, *without* using the `async: false` option. Figure that way out and implement it.

17. When introducing Ajax functionality into a web page, proficiency with development tools, such as the Firebug add-on for Firefox or the Developer Tools suite in WebKit-based browsers such as Safari or Chrome, becomes as important as ever because a lot of activity is now invisible to end-user eyes.

    (a) Open your web browser of choice and learn how to reveal its development tools by looking it up on the Web. Web browsers and their user interfaces are ever-evolving, so you may as well get the hang of looking up specifics like this instead of relying on static book instructions.

    (b) Locate and open the *Console* panel of the developer tools.

(c) Use the JavaScript runner page to run this program:

```
$.ajax({
    url: "../php/fortune.php",
    success: function (response) {
        console.log(response);
    }
});

$.ajax({
    url: "../php/calendar.php",
    success: function (response) {
        console.log(response);
    }
});
```

The direct results of these connections should appear in the developer console. If not, track down what may have gone wrong and retry until you see the results.

(d) Locate the network connection viewer in your developer tools. At this writing, Firebug places them in the *XHR* tab of the *Net* panel. WebKit-based browsers display network connections in the   Network   section.

(e) Your two connections to `fortune.php` and `calendar.php` should be visible. Note the wealth of additional information that gets exchanged, beyond just the URL and the response content; in particular, *headers* provide supplementary information about the request and response. What are the values of the following headers?

- `User-Agent` (request header)
- `Accept` (request header)
- `X-Requested-With` (request header)
- `Referer` (request header)
- `Server` (response header)
- `Content-Length` (response header)
- `Content-Type` (response header)

18. As you have seen, much of the power behind web services lies in the ability to supply *parameters* with the request. Parameters are like function arguments: they provide additional information that customizes or affects the resulting output.

In Section 8.7, we showed that our homegrown `calendar.php` service accepts a single parameter, `date`, that specifies the day for which calendar events are being requested. The date is supposed to be in `yyyyMMdd` format—that is, a four-digit year, followed by a two-digit month and a two-digit day, without spaces or punctuation.

(a) You can supply parameters directly in the URL—no JavaScript required. Open the network connection viewer in your web browser tools suite and type the following URLs. Note the request and response that appear:

- `http://javascript.cs.lmu.edu/php/calendar.php?date=19800312`
- `http://javascript.cs.lmu.edu/php/calendar.php?date=20000728`
- `http://javascript.cs.lmu.edu/php/calendar.php?date=20111031`
- A `calendar.php` URL corresponding to your birthday
- A `calendar.php` URL corresponding to today

(b) To supply parameters in the jQuery `ajax` function, include a `data` property in your submitted options. Run the following program, making sure you keep your developer tools open so you can see all the action:

```
$.ajax({
    url: "../php/calendar.php",

    data: {
        date: "19800312"
    },

    success: function (response) {
        console.log(response);
    }
});
```

(c) Modify and run the program in part 18b for each date given in part 18a.

19. Write a program for the JavaScript runner page that connects to the `fortune.php` service every 10 seconds and displays the new fortune in the `footer` element within that page.

20. Modify the program in Exercise 19 so it works in the JavaScript DHTML playground page at `http://javascript.cs.lmu.edu/playground` instead of the JavaScript runner page.

21. Modify the program in Exercise 20 so the refresh frequency is customizable: have the program set up the `input1` text field element on that page so a user can type a number of seconds into that field. The program should then change its refresh frequency accordingly. Watch out for nonnumeric or invalid input (e.g., negative numbers)!

22. Modify the program in Exercise 20 so the "fortune" retrieval is now *on-demand*: have the program add a `button` element to the page such that a new "fortune" is retrieved and displayed only when the user clicks on that button. (*Hint:* Programmatic addition of a button was shown in Section 6.3.2. You might also prefer to do this using jQuery; this information is easy to find on the Web.)

23. Write a program for the JavaScript DHTML playground page that connects to the `calendar.php` service with a user-selected date. The date should be entered via the `input1` text field element; make sure your program validates the value of that field as a legitimate date expression and then processes that date so it is passed into `calendar.php` in the expected format. The received events should then be displayed on the page.

24. Modify the program in Exercise 23 so that, instead of a user-entered date, date navigation is accomplished using Previous Day and Next Day buttons. Add these buttons programmatically to the JavaScript DHTML playground page, and set them up so that, when clicked, the Previous Day button retrieves and displays events from `calendar.php` for the day before the current one, and the Next Day button does the same for the day after the current one. Be sure to update the current date so subsequent clicks move further backward and forward in time, respectively.

25. The full range of available `options` for the jQuery library's `ajax` function shows that it takes a general-purpose, "everything but the kitchen sink" approach to making network connections within a web page. However, simpler uses of Ajax occur often enough that *shorthand* functions are also available for certain combinations of option values and common end-result actions like displaying the retrieved information within a web page element. These shorthand functions are documented in `http://api.jquery.com/category/ajax/shorthand-methods`.

Using this documentation as reference, write the following in the JavaScript runner page:

(a) A program that uses the `get` shorthand function to retrieve a fortune from the `fortune.php` service and displays it in the element whose ID is "footer"

(b) A program that uses the `load` shorthand function to retrieve a fortune from the `fortune.php` service and displays it in the element whose ID is "footer"

(c) A program that uses the `load` shorthand function to retrieve events from the `calendar.php` service and displays them in the element whose ID is "footer"

(d) A program that uses the `get` shorthand function to retrieve events from the `calendar.php` service and displays them via the `alert` function

26. The responses of the `calendar.php` service are handled differently by the jQuery Ajax shorthand functions `load` and `get`. What is the difference?

27. Use the `getJSON` shorthand function to retrieve events from the `calendar.php` service and display these as an unordered list (i.e., a `ul` element containing one `li` element for each returned event) within the `footer` element.

28. Modify the program in Exercise 27 so it asks the user for a desired date and retrieves/displays the list of events on that date (according to the `calendar.php` service).

29. Write your own shorthand function—call it `myGet`—that uses the general-purpose `ajax` function and acts very similarly to `get`. (*Hint:* Read the `get` documentation.)

30. Write your own shorthand function—call it myGetJSON—that uses the general-purpose ajax function and acts very similarly to getJSON. (*Hint:* Read the getJSON documentation.)

31. Come up with a new, reasonably useful Ajax shorthand function, write up some reference documentation for it, then implement it. Write a demo program that shows your shorthand function at work, and include that demo's source code as an example in your function's documentation.

32. Write your own shorthand function—call it getTheHardWay—that does *not* use the jQuery library at all but still acts very similarly to get. (*Hint:* Use XMLHttpRequest.)

33. Write your own shorthand function—call it getJSONTheHardWay—that does *not* use the jQuery library at all but still acts very similarly to getJSON. (*Hint:* Use JSON.parse.)

34. Choose five of your closest friends or relatives and state at least one "URN" and one "URL" for each of them.

35. Consider "snail mail" addresses, not including zip codes, such as 123 Elm Street, Fun City, California, U.S.A. Some addresses are houses, while others have multiple residences with an additional unit or apartment number (e.g., 123 Elm Street #221B). Further, each home has different kinds of rooms or spaces, such as bedrooms, bathrooms, outdoor areas, etc. Areas may also be described through other characteristics such as colors or the kind of floors they have.

    Viewing snail mail addresses as a snailmail scheme per the URI definition in Section 8.5.1, consider the following:

    (a) Based on the preceding description, identify the aspects of a snail mail address that would comprise its hierarchical part, potential queries, and possible fragments.

    (b) Would snail mail URIs be URNs or URLs?

    (c) How would you write the address "900 Brown Ave., Edge City, New York, U.S.A." as a snailmail URI?

    (d) How would you write the address "255 Tuazon Blvd., Apt. 343, Santiago, Chile" as a snailmail URI?

(e) How would you write "the bedrooms in 414 Main Street, Ontario, Canada" as a `snailmail` URI? (*Hint:* Think of "bedrooms" as a query for `roomType=bedroom`.)

(f) Suppose five people live at a particular snail mail address: Reed, Steve, Diana, Jane, and Pam. How would you include this information in a `snailmail` URI? (*Hint:* One can think of residents as "users" of a location.)

(g) How would the use of a zip code affect the `snailmail` URI scheme, both conceptually and in the way a `snailmail` URI would look?

36. Consider a `book` URI scheme, where the hierarchical portion of the URI consists of an author's last name, then first name, then finally the book's title. The fragment portion, if present, refers to a chapter in the book. For example, the URI for *The Moonstone* by Wilkie Collins would be `book://Collins/Wilkie/TheMoonstone`, while the third chapter in that book, simply called "III," would be `book://Collins/Wilkie/TheMoonstone#III`.

    Are these `book` URIs considered URNs or URLs? Why or why not?

37. Manually encode the following strings as URIs and then as URI components. You may need to refer to character encoding tables to determine the correct encoded equivalents for certain characters. Check your work by comparing your answers to what `encodeURI` and `encodeURIComponent` produce.

    (a) `http://www.com`

    (b) `nearby movies`

    (c) `https://account.bank.com?userid=sam`

    (d) `is P=NP?`

    (e) `http:friend or foe?`

38. Manually decode the following strings as if they were encoded URIs and then as if they were encoded URI components. You may need to refer to character encoding tables to determine the correct encoded equivalents for certain characters. Check your work by comparing your answers to what `decodeURI` and `decodeURIComponent` produce.

    (a) `Unicode%20table`

(b) `https%3A%2F%2Fwww.myfriends.com`

(c) `http://supersearch.com`

(d) `2%2B2%3D5`

(e) `2B%7C~2b%3Athat's%20the%20%3F`

39. State whether the following URIs are RESTful. If not, state why not.

  (a) `http://api.chatter.net/post-comment?text=Hello`

  (b) `http://coolstore.mall.cc/stores/452`

  (c) `https://www.lo.tsomo.ney/accounts/checking/456A-2981`

  (d) `https://login.gamenetzone.ly/leaderboard/editscore.xml`

  (e) `http://methodrun.popstack.net/libraries?tag=JavaScript`

40. Suppose our sample `fortune.php` service had a top-level URI of `http://javascript.cs.lmu.edu/fortunes` while behaving in exactly the same manner (i.e., when you send a GET request to that URI, you get a random "fortune" back). Does that make `http://javascript.cs.lmu.edu/fortunes` RESTful? Why or why not?

41. The Linux manual services at `http://javascript.cs.lmu.edu/php/man-keyword.php` and `http://javascript.cs.lmu.edu/php/man.php`, described in Section 8.5.3, are certainly not RESTful. How might you change their URIs so that the service does follow REST? (*Hint:* Think of the Linux manual as a document consisting of sections and entries, and note that keyword searches are queries on this document.)

42. Many modern distributed applications separate their concerns into web services that provide only data, and web clients that access these services. REST, with its focus on resources and heavy use of HTTP, is a clear fit for separated web services. Would REST make sense for the URLs of a web *client*? Why or why not?

43. The same origin policy prevents code from one website from making connections to another website. The responsibility for enforcing this policy necessarily falls on the web browser application that is being used.

    With developer tools activated (especially the console and the network connection display), run the following program using the JavaScript runner page in at least three different web browsers:

```
$.ajax({
    url: "http://api.twitter.com/1/trends/weekly.json",
    success: function (response) {
        alert(response);
    }
});
```

Double-check that this service does indeed return data by accessing the URL `http://api.twitter.com/1/trends/weekly.json` *directly* from each web browser.

How does each browser handle the disallowed Ajax connection? Are errors reported? What data (if any) get returned?

44. The `bit.ly` URL shortening service converts any conventional web URL into a shortened version (that starts with `http://bit.ly`, of course). You can access many of the service's functions using Ajax, through its published API. This API provides full support for CORS, thus exempting it from the same origin policy and allowing JavaScript code from any website to use `bit.ly` for URL shortening and expansion, among other operations, via Ajax.

    Visit `bit.ly`'s API website at `http://code.google.com/p/bitly-api/wiki/ApiDocumentation` and look up the service's `shorten` call. Then write an Ajax program within the JavaScript runner page that retrieves the shortened version of any conventional web URL. Prove to yourself that CORS support was indeed provided by examining your Ajax call's response headers. (*Note:* Be sure to read the service's rules on URL encoding.)

    You will need a free `bit.ly` account to access `bit.ly`'s services. The account provides you with an *API key* that allows you to make `bit.ly` service calls; you will find this in the *Settings* page of your `bit.ly` account.

45. Modify the program you wrote in Exercise 44 so it instead *expands* a shortened URL. For input, you may use any `bit.ly` URL, including the ones you generated yourself using the original URL expansion program.

46. Write interactive versions of your `bit.ly` `shorten` and `expand` programs for use with the JavaScript DHTML playground page, such that the URL to expand or shorten is taken from the `input1` element.

47. Create an HTML file with the HTML equivalent of the `script` element created by the JavaScript code on page 412 (the one that runs `http://go.technocage.com/javascript/cross-site.js`) in its `head`. Within the page's `body` element, include an inline `script` element that displays the `username` and `password` properties of the `payload` variable. Open the HTML file in a browser to check if it behaves as expected.

48. The sample JSONP program on page 414 shows how jQuery provides an alternative to `document.createElement`: passing an HTML fragment into the `$` function creates the elements defined by that fragment. Try this in the JavaScript runner, for example:

```
$("#footer").append($("<div id='demo'><span>Hello!</span>
    </div>"));
```

Use this form of web page manipulation to run the `http://go.technocage.com/javascript/cross-site.js` script.

How can you tell whether the script did or did not run? Does your program otherwise behave exactly like this example, which appends a `div` element to `#footer`?

49. Use JSONP to access the Twitter Search service at `http://api.twitter.com/1/search.json` from a JavaScript runner program. You may pattern your code after the sample given on page 414.

The service takes a `q` parameter for the search term and of course the JSONP `callback` parameter. Full documentation is available at `https://dev.twitter.com/docs/api/1/get/search`.

50. Adapt the program you wrote in Exercise 49 for use with the JavaScript DHTML playground page, such that the search term to use is taken from the `input1` element.

51. The CORS-capable `bit.ly` URL shortening services mentioned in Exercise 44 also support JSONP via the `callback` parameter (read the API documentation for details). Use the `script`-element-creation technique to access the `bit.ly` `shorten` and `expand` services from the JavaScript runner page.

52. Use the built-in JSONP support provided by jQuery's `getJSON` function to access the `bit.ly` `shorten` and `expand` services from the JavaScript runner page.

53. Knowing now that `bit.ly` supports both CORS and JSONP, which approach do you prefer, and why?

54. Write your own JSONP convenience function, defined as follows:

```
var myGetJSONP = function (url, successFunction) {
    // Put your implementation here.
};
```

You may *not* use the jQuery `getJSON` function in your implementation (obviously).

Show that your function works by making JSONP calls with the Twitter and `bit.ly` services you have used in previous exercises.

55. Using the inline script injection technique, write URLs for the `http://javascript.cs.lmu.edu/php/vulnerable.php` service that do the following:

    (a) Send the web browser to some arbitrary website. (*Hint:* Look up the `location.href` property.)

    (b) Prompt the user for two strings and display the concatenated result (*Hint:* Don't forget about URI encoding.)

    (c) Insert *the very URL that you used* for `http://javascript.cs.lmu.edu/php/vulnerable.php` into the web page that is returned by that web service. (*Hint:* Play with `document.write`.)

56. Here's a little secret about the cross-site scripting site at `http://go.technocage.com/javascript`: aside from the "real" JavaScript programs `cross-site.js` and `xss-form-onload.js`, *every other URL ending in* `.js` will produce the form injection script used by `http://go.technocage.com/javascript/xss-urls.html` and `http://go.technocage.com/javascript/xss-form.html`. Try these URLs to see for yourself:

    ■ `http://go.technocage.com/javascript/whatever.js`

- `http://go.technocage.com/javascript/totallyrandomname.js`

- `http://go.technocage.com/javascript/WowItReallyIsTheSameCode.js`

Take advantage of this `http://go.technocage.com/javascript` "feature" to write at least three other `http://javascript.cs.lmu.edu/php/vulnerable.php` URLs that have the same form-injection effect as `http://go.technocage.com/javascript/xss-urls.html` and `http://go.technocage.com/javascript/xss-form.html`.

57. The Twitter API features a simple search service that can locate tweets based on a free-text term. You can read about it in `https://dev.twitter.com/docs/api/1/get/search`. The service's URL is `http://api.twitter.com/1/search.json` and the free-text parameter name is `q` (e.g., `http://api.twitter.com/1/search.json?q=JavaScript`).

Write a JavaScript runner program that mashes up the `http://javascript.cs.lmu.edu/php/fortune.php` service with the Twitter search service by passing text from a fortune into the `q` parameter of `http://api.twitter.com/1/search.json`, then displays its results on the web page. You will need to use the JSONP approach seen in Section 8.7.

"Fortunes" can get fairly long, so you may wish to process the fortune text first, by extracting its longest words and using those as the `q` parameter.

58. Section 8.7 showed a sample mashup program that displays calendar event information alongside Twitter trending topics for the same date. Write a different Twitter–`calendar.php` mashup, this time using *text* from the returned calendar events for a given date as the `q` parameter for the Twitter search service at `http://api.twitter.com/1/search.json`.

As with the previous exercise, processing of the calendar text may be necessary in order to yield a decent number of matching tweets. For calendar events, using the capitalized words in the returned calendar text may work well, as such words represent people, places, or other proper nouns.

59. As you may have inferred from Section 8.6.4, the photo site Flickr (`http://www.flickr.com`) provides a rich API for accessing its image streams. Like `bit.ly`, you will need an API key to use it. Information for getting

this key, as well as the API itself, can be found at `http://www.flickr.com/services/api`. Focus on the REST request format with a JSON response.

When returning JSON, the Flickr API uses JSONP: it expects that a function called `jsonFlickrApi` has been defined, which takes a single argument representing the JSON object that is returned by Flickr.

The `flickr.photos.search` operation performs what its name implies: it searches Flickr's photos and returns information on the photos that match the search parameters (see `http://www.flickr.com/services/api/flickr.photos.search.html` for details). Searching with the `text` parameter returns pictures whose title, description, or tags contain the provided value.

Using `flickr.photos.search` with the `text` parameter, write a mashup program that retrieves a fortune from `http://javascript.cs.lmu.edu/php/fortune.php`, then performs a Flickr photo search using the returned fortune. For best results, you may have to "distill" the fortune somewhat, say to its three longest or most repeated words. The program should display the photo data returned by `flickr.photos.search`. (Displaying the photos themselves takes more work; see the next exercise.)

Rerunning the program will, of course, retrieve a new "fortune," and thus return a new set of photo data.

60. Extend your Flickr–`fortune.php` mashup so that the photos themselves are displayed as dynamically created `img` elements that are appended to the JavaScript runner page. (You may need to look ahead to Section 9.2.1 if you have never before worked with images in web pages.) Read the documentation in `http://www.flickr.com/services/api/misc.urls.html` for information on how to build URLs from the photo data returned by `flickr.photos.search`.

CHAPTER 9

Graphics and Animation

CHAPTER CONTENTS

Introduction

Many JavaScript applications involve performing computations and showing results by manipulating the DOM of a web page. Effective event handling, as seen in Chapter 6, based on both user activity and the passage of time, facilitates interactivity, with JavaScript as the connecting technology. We have seen, so far, that our options for displaying information to the user have been generally text or images that are stored (or generated) on a server. This range of elements is adequate for conventional documents and forms but falls short for applications such as games, simulations, visualization, and animation.

This chapter aims to introduce you to the visual, graphics, and animation technologies that are available in modern, standards-compliant web browsers. These options range from additional visual and graphical properties within the HTML DOM to full-fledged graphics technologies that allow you to draw and fill lines, curves, polygons, or other shapes, perform sophisticated image processing and compositing operations, and even render hardware-accelerated three-dimensional (3D) objects. All this, manipulated entirely within your browser, with no additional software.

9.1   Fundamentals

Certain concepts and techniques are common to all graphics and animation subsystems. This section introduces the core set that underlies the specific technologies in this chapter.

9.1.1   Coordinate Spaces

All computer graphics operations are generally performed within the context of a *coordinate space*—that is, a two-dimensional (2D) or 3D region within which colors, lines, shapes, or other entities are placed. A specific location within that space can be represented with sequences of numbers called *coordinates*, with one number for each dimension of the space. Thus, 2D coordinates are represented by an *ordered pair* (x, y), while 3D coordinates are represented by an *ordered triple* (x, y, z). By convention, the x in 2D or 3D coordinates represents a horizontal location ("left to right"), while y is vertical ("up to down"). In 3D, z is typically referred to as *depth*, representing the "front-to-back" dimension. The special coordinates $(0, 0)$ and $(0, 0, 0)$ are designated as the *origin* of the space.

The direction along which a coordinate grows also varies based on the graphics system. A typical convention is to have x-coordinates increase to the right. In 2D graphics systems, y-coordinates usually increase in the downward direction. In some 3D graphics systems, the y-coordinate increases *upward*, with the z-coordinate increasing as it moves *toward* the viewer. These are all conventions, however, and there is no hard-and-fast rule on directionality and coordinate values; it is thus another thing to note when learning about a new graphics technology.

Coordinate spaces give us an unambiguous mechanism for designating positions and sizes—an understandably crucial part of being able to tell a computer where to draw something. Figure 9.1 illustrates typical 2D and 3D coordinate spaces.

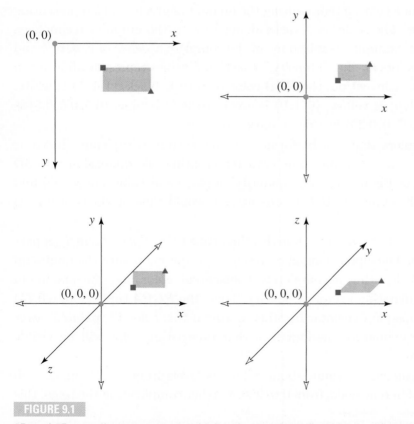

FIGURE 9.1

2D and 3D coordinate spaces, each showing a rectangle with opposite corners $(2, 1)$ (indicated by the small square) and $(4, 2)$ (indicated by the small triangle) in 2D, or $(2, 1, 0)$ and $(4, 2, 0)$ in 3D.

In the physical world, we tend to attach *units* to coordinates and distances. A location on the earth is typically given in degrees (latitude and longitude); lengths or distances may be measured in inches, meters, miles, or even light-years, with "square" or "cubic" versions of these units representing areas and volumes, respectively. Computer graphics systems vary in their use of units. Keep an eye on them in later sections.

9.1.2   Colors

If coordinate spaces define *where* or *how big* a visual entity may be, colors form the basis of *what* that entity looks like. Without going into a deeper discussion of the physics of light and color, suffice it to say that in most computer graphics systems, a color is represented by the ordered triple (r, g, b), with r representing the amount of red in a color, g representing the amount of green, and b representing the amount of blue. The scale used varies depending on the graphics technology. One convention, for example, uses 0 to mean the complete absence of r, g, or b and 1 for any of these colors at "full intensity." Fractional values represent all levels in between. Under this convention, the RGB color $(0, 0, 0)$ is black, $(1, 1, 1)$ is white, $(1, 0, 0)$ is red, $(1, 1, 0)$ is yellow, $(0, 1, 0)$ is green, $(0, 0, 1)$ is blue, $(0.5, 0.5, 0.5)$ is a medium gray, $(0.25, 0, 0.25)$ is a deep, dark violet, etc.

The range of colors that can be formed by this system is typically shown as a *color cube*, with red, green, and blue each representing one dimension in a 3D coordinate space (see Figure 9.2). To "quantify" a particular color, one would find that color within the cube; its RGB representation would then be the coordinates of that color.

Some graphics systems accept a fourth value, called the *alpha channel*, as part of a color definition. The alpha channel represents transparency, with the minimum value (typically 0) denoting a completely transparent color and the maximum value (typically 1) denoting complete opacity. Thus, the *RGBA* tuple $(1, 0, 1, 0.75)$ represents a 75% opaque magenta. In other words, if this color is "painted" over another color, approximately one-fourth of that preexisting color will be visible beneath the magenta.[1]

While it is convenient to think about colors as levels from 0 to 1, many web technologies use a different scale, from 0 to 255. Further complicating the issue, this

---

[1]The specific computation that takes place can actually vary quite a bit, but that's for a computer graphics book to handle, not an introduction to programming.

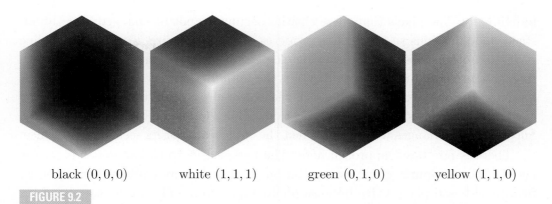

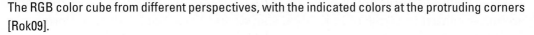

black $(0, 0, 0)$ white $(1, 1, 1)$ green $(0, 1, 0)$ yellow $(1, 1, 0)$

FIGURE 9.2

The RGB color cube from different perspectives, with the indicated colors at the protruding corners [Rok09].

range is sometimes represented in hexadecimal, from 00 to FF (refer to Section 3.3.4 for a refresher). When expressed in this manner, an RGB color starts with a pound/number sign (#) then lists the two-hexadecimal-digit red, green, and blue values in that order. The example RGB colors in Figure 9.2, when written this way, would be #000000 for black, #FFFFFF for white, #00FF00 for green, and #FFFF00 for yellow. The expression #000033 would be a dark blue, #808080 a medium gray, #FFE6E6 a light pink, and so on.

9.1.3   Pixels vs. Objects/Vectors

There are two main approaches for describing a computer graphics image or "scene": it can be represented as a discrete grid of colored squares or *pixels* (e.g., images from a digital camera or scanner) or as a set of geometric or other objects, each with different properties and characteristics (e.g., pictures created by drawing programs like Adobe Illustrator, Dia, OmniGraffle, or Microsoft Visio).

With the pixel-based or *image-space* perspective of a scene, all operations end up changing the color(s) of one or more pixels. With such a perspective, a *drawCircle* function would calculate a set of pixels that best approximates a circle and would color that set accordingly. The notion of a circle dissipates after that. Once the circle is colored, only the pixels remain.

With the *object-space* perspective (also known as *vector-based graphics*), a computer graphics scene is viewed as a collection of entities that can be manipulated individually. The pixels that these entities occupy cannot be changed directly; instead, modifications to an object's properties, such as its size, location, color, line style, and others, result in objectwide changes in its appearance. In this perspective, a *drawCircle* function would retain the notion of a circle after it is called. A mechanism would exist through which the drawn circle could be retrieved as a circle, and properties such as radius, location, color, etc., could be changed directly. Such property changes would then affect the circle's and/or its scene's appearance.

There is no "best" approach here. The perspective to choose depends on the needs of the computer graphics application. A digital photo editor is better served by a pixel-based perspective because photographs store only pixels, not shapes or objects, while a diagramming program is better served by objects because diagrams are manipulated in terms of individual shapes and lines. Some advanced programs combine both perspectives, but at any given moment, the user does retain one approach or the other.

The general trade-off between pixels and objects/vectors is that the pixel-oriented approach gives you absolutely fine control over how a scene looks—literally down to the dots that make up the picture—while the object-based approach typically uses fewer machine resources (there tend to be millions of pixels in a picture as opposed to a few hundred objects) and provides for *resolution independence*. Object-based graphics can be scaled up or down and, because the objects are redrawn every time, they can always be drawn for maximum detail or smoothness. Figure 9.3 illustrates this trade-off. In the figure, the same circle, with a radius of 25 pixels, is drawn with a pixel-based technology, then with an object-based technology. The picture is then magnified a few times over.

The web page shown is in fact drawn using two technologies that we will cover in this chapter: the pixel-based `canvas` element and the object-based Scalable Vector Graphics, or SVG, standard. In case you are wondering, the full code to the page is shown here:

```html
<!DOCTYPE html>
<html>
  <!-- This page requires a fully HTML5-compliant web browser.
       Make sure to zoom in as much as possible to see the
       pixel-vs.-object difference. -->
  <head>
    <meta charset="UTF-8"/>
    <title>Pixel vs. Object</title>
```

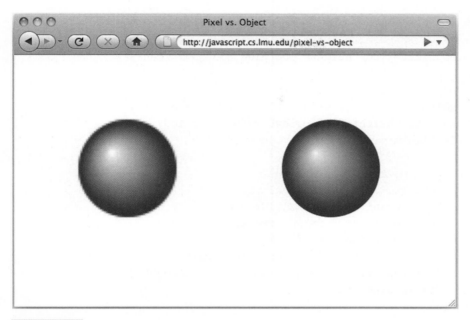

FIGURE 9.3

Comparison of a shaded circle with pixel-based (left) vs. object-based (right) approaches.

```
    <script>
      window.onload = function () {
        var canvas = document.getElementById("canvas");
        var renderingContext = canvas.getContext("2d");

        // Image-space circle.
        var radialGradient = renderingContext.createRadialGradient
            (42, 42, 1, 50, 50, 25);
        radialGradient.addColorStop(0, "white");
        radialGradient.addColorStop(1, "#880000");

        renderingContext.fillStyle = radialGradient;
        renderingContext.beginPath();
        renderingContext.arc(50, 50, 25, 0, Math.PI * 2, true);
        renderingContext.fill();
      };
    </script>
  </head>
```

```
<body>
  <!-- Pixel-space circle will go here. -->
  <canvas width="100" height="100" id="canvas"></canvas>

  <!-- Object-space circle. -->
  <svg xmlns="http://www.w3.org/2000/svg" version="1.1"
    width="100" height="100" viewBox="0 0 100 100"
    style="width: 100px; height: 100px;">

    <defs>
      <!-- First, define the gradient. -->
        <radialGradient id="radialGradient"
          cx="50" cy="50" r="25" fx="42" fy="42"
          gradientUnits="userSpaceOnUse">
            <stop offset="0%" stop-color="white" />
            <stop offset="100%" stop-color="#880000" />
        </radialGradient>
    </defs>

    <!-- Then, us it. -->
    <circle cx="50" cy="50" r="25" fill="url(#radialGradient)" />
  </svg>
</body>
</html>
```

In the end, the final representation is based on the display technology used for viewing computer graphics. Today, these technologies are almost all pixel-based, and so even object- or vector-based graphics get converted into pixels (a process called *rasterization* or *scan conversion*) as they reach the computer display.

9.1.4 Animation

At its core, animation involves showing a sequence of images quickly enough that the viewer perceives the illusion of motion, with "quickly enough" being around 30 or more images, or *frames*, per second. Differences between successive images should be fairly small, allowing the brain to "fill in the blanks" from one frame to the next.

When the images are pixel-based, the approach to animation is typically to redraw frames in their entirety, since any pixel can change at any time. Under certain circumstances, only the parts of the frame that change can be redrawn, if those parts are known.

For object- or vector-based animation, object properties such as position, size, color, and others are changed in small amounts at each "frame" or interval. The object-based graphics system then takes care of redisplaying the objects.

Review and Practice

1. Based on how colors are "quantified" as described in Section 9.1.2, state how the following color changes would be performed on some (r, g, b) value:

   - Make the color brighter
   - Make the color darker
   - Make the color a gray level

2. What is the difference between pixel- and object-based graphics? What factors or features would make you choose one over the other?

9.2   HTML and CSS

Chapter 6 introduced how web pages are really trees or outlines of *elements* that can be created using either HTML or JavaScript. These elements make up what is called the *Document Object Model*, or DOM.

In that chapter, the DOM was viewed as a mechanism for creating user interfaces. In this chapter, we add a new dimension to the DOM: we view it as a *visual medium*. Using the terminology of the previous section, the DOM can be used as an object-based computer graphics system, with the spectrum of possible web elements serving as the objects to display, and *Cascading Style Sheets*, or CSS, serving as the mechanism for determining how these objects look.

9.2.1   HTML Elements for Graphics

Chapter 6, and in particular Section 6.2, showed you how to build web pages consisting of elements such as paragraphs (p), push buttons (`input` with `type="button"` or `button`), text fields (`input` with `type="text"`), lists (`select`), and others. These elements are not typically what one would associate with computer graphics, however. In this section, we look at other elements that are better suited for general-purpose visuals.

The `img` Element

The `img` element includes ready-made image files such as screenshots, digital photos, or any other (web-compatible) visual content in a web page. This element's most important attribute is `src`, which specifies the image file to include, as either an absolute web address or a path relative to the location of the web page. In HTML, `img` is specified as follows:

```
<img src="http://javascript.cs.lmu.edu/images/bookcover.jpg" />
```

This causes the image file located at `http://javascript.cs.lmu.edu/images/bookcover.jpg` to appear wherever the tag is located in the web page.

As with all web page elements, you can also create an element in JavaScript and append it to the web page. The following code is meant to be run in our JavaScript runner page at `http://javascript.cs.lmu.edu/runner`; it creates an `img` element that is identical to the previous HTML example and adds it to the web element whose `id` is "footer" (yes, this is a try-it-yourself example):

```
var footer = document.getElementById("footer");
var image = document.createElement("img");
image.src = "http://javascript.cs.lmu.edu/images/bookcover.jpg";
footer.appendChild(image);
```

The `div` Element

The `div` element serves as a sort of counterpoint to `img`; instead of an element that displays prepared content, `div` is more of a blank slate. It can be viewed as a "graphics-from-scratch" building block.

Specifying a `div` element in HTML is trivial:

```
<div></div>
```

Or, for use in `http://javascript.cs.lmu.edu/runner` (adjust accordingly when using this code fragment on a different web page):

```
var footer = document.getElementById("footer");
var div = document.createElement("div");
footer.appendChild(div);
```

In this minimal form, however, the result is as trivial as the mechanism: you get nothing more than a box with zero height. Instead, the usefulness of `div` comes from using it as a generic container for other elements and the customization of its visual properties. The `div` element truly is the blank slate of the DOM.

The next few sections illustrate just how this blank slate can be turned into a wide variety of object-based graphics displays on a web page.

9.2.2 CSS

CSS, or *Cascading Style Sheets*, is the visual or *presentation* technology of the Web. You have already used some CSS: it is effectively the DOM property named `style`. By touching `style`, whether in JavaScript or HTML (as the `style` attribute within most tags), you are touching CSS.

The *C* in CSS stands for *cascading*, which tries to express how the `style` property or attribute may be applied at many levels, ranging from a single, unique element (*this* particular `div`; *that* exact `img`) to all elements of a particular type (all `p` elements; all `h1` elements) to all elements with the same `class`, which is a new way to group or categorize elements that we have not seen before. Specific `style` values may also be applicable only to elements at a certain point in the web page, such as only `a` elements that are inside `p` elements.

To illustrate some ways by which `style` can be assigned, we will use an easily discernible, easy-to-understand visual property: `border-style`. The `border-style` property represents how an element's boundaries are rendered. Known border styles include `dotted`, `dashed`, `solid`, `double`, `groove`, `ridge`, `inset`, `outset`, and `none` (for no border at all).

Individual Elements

Individual elements can be given specific visual properties in the following ways:

- The `style` attribute for elements created using HTML tags

- The `style` property for elements created or accessed through the DOM

- A *CSS rule* that selects a single element by its `id` attribute/property

These ways are illustrated in the following examples; all of them pertain to the JavaScript runner page at `http://javascript.cs.lmu.edu/runner`, and they all have the identical result of setting the border of the `introduction` element to `solid`.

In its original form, this element is specified in HTML as follows:

```
<p id="introduction">
    <!-- Text and other tags go here. -->
</p>
```

Modifying the tag as shown here gives this element a `solid` border:

```
<p id="introduction" style="border-style: solid">
    <!-- Text and other tags go here. -->
</p>
```

Alternatively, you can run the following code to set `border-style` through JavaScript. Note how the hyphenated property name is replaced by its "camel case" version; that is, hyphens are removed and the letter that follows is capitalized (can you explain why this change is necessary?):

```
document.getElementById("introduction").style.borderStyle = "solid";
```

This code fragment uses `getElementById` to retrieve the `introduction` element, then assigns the string `"solid"` to the `borderStyle` subproperty of that element's `style` property.

Style assignment by CSS rule involves modifying the HTML again. For this approach, the pound sign (#) is shorthand for "the element whose `id` is ... ," and the curly braces ({ }) enclose the CSS properties to be applied:

```
<head>
    <!-- Other head elements go here. -->
    <style type="text/css">
        #introduction {
            border-style: solid
        }
    </style>
</head>
```

For both the HTML attribute and CSS rule approaches, multiple `style` properties can be set by separating them with semicolons (`;`):

```
<p id="introduction" style="border-style: solid; color: red">
    <!-- Text and other tags go here. -->
</p>
```

Or:

```
<head>
    <!-- Other head elements go here. -->
    <style type="text/css">
        #introduction {
            border-style: solid;
            color: red
        }
    </style>
</head>
```

Test yourself: see if you can figure out how to set multiple style properties in JavaScript. No worries if you can't; you will learn how soon enough.

Elements of the Same Type

To assign the same visual properties to all elements of the same type, say all `p` elements, you may use either JavaScript or a CSS rule. Because this `style` assignment affects multiple elements uniformly, the "in-tag" approach does not apply.

The `document` object's `getElementsByTagName` function returns an array of every element with the same type/tag. You can then use a `for` statement to assign the `style` subproperties for every element in that array (you can try this yourself at `http://javascript.cs.lmu.edu/runner`):

```
var pElements = document.getElementsByTagName("p");
for (var i = 0; i < pElements.length; i += 1) {
    pElements[i].style.borderStyle = "solid";
}
```

Assignment by CSS rule uses the same `style` element as in the previous section, only this time the *selector* preceding the { } block should be the name of the tag:

```
<head>
    <!-- Other head elements go here. -->
    <style type="text/css">
        p {
            border-style: solid
        }
    </style>
</head>
```

Note a key difference between the JavaScript and CSS rule approaches: the JavaScript approach changes the style for the existing elements *at the time the code is executed*. If subsequent JavaScript code creates a new `p` element and appends it to the document, that element *will not* have the assigned `style` subproperties.[2]

Other CSS Selectors

Beyond individual property setting and setting by element type, the remaining mechanisms for modifying CSS visual properties mainly involve the selector that begins CSS rules. Because our focus here is computer graphics and not web page authoring, we only summarize some of them here:

- A selector that begins with a period (.), such as `.helpbox` or `.menuitem`, applies to web elements that have been assigned a `class` attribute:

```
<p class="helpbox">A CSS rule that begins with .helpbox
    will affect this p element.</p>
```

- Multiple selectors separated by commas (,) allow you to apply the same set of visual properties to distinct groups of elements:

```
p, .helpbox, #mainInstruction {
    background-color: rgb(250, 250, 192);
    border-style: outset
}
```

---

[2]There *is* a JavaScript technique for creating or modifying CSS rules, but we have chosen to leave that as something for you to look up.

Just to throw in some new things, note the fairly self-explanatory `background-color` property, and how it is set using an `rgb` expression (one of many RGB representations that CSS accepts; this version takes color component values as integers from 0 to 255).[3]

- Multiple selectors separated by *greater-than* signs instead of commas constitute *containment* instead of a list: a selector of `p > a`, for example, affects only `a` elements that are inside `p` elements. To specify properties for `div` elements are contained within another `div` that is in turn contained in a top-level `div`, you would use the selector `div > div > div`.

CSS is, on one level, simple in principle, yet surprisingly deep, powerful, and complex on another. We have attempted to cover the basic mechanisms here; if you are interested in more (about selectors and properties alike), we suggest the official CSS home page for definitive, no-holds-barred coverage [W3C10a]. A quick web search will also reveal a large number of learning, tutorial, and reference sites.

jQuery's $

With this wide array of approaches for assigning visual properties, we hope that some of the motivation and accomplishment behind jQuery (Section 7.5) becomes clear: thanks to jQuery's $ function, setting the properties of just the right collection of elements becomes much simpler to do. This is what effective library design achieves—it can take an existing mechanism for getting things done and, with the right functions and objects, make programming such activities easier, faster, and more powerful.

9.2.3 Visual Properties

At this point, we turn to CSS properties that specifically facilitate visual effects beyond document layout or user interface appearance. In addition, we will emphasize CSS property manipulation from JavaScript as opposed to the HTML and CSS rule approaches seen previously. All examples are designed for the JavaScript runner page at `http://javascript.cs.lmu.edu/runner`.

---

[3]In yet another pesky detail that we don't have space to fully address, not all colors can be represented by all web browsers. For the purposes of this chapter, however, we won't worry about this issue.

Size and Spacing

The `width` and `height` properties, as you might expect, can set the size of a web element's content to something other than its default. Units must be provided along with the dimensions; we will stick to pixels (`px`) here and leave you to learn about other units on your own. Borders also have a size property: `border-width`. As with `width` and `height`, units are required.

Related to size is the *spacing* around a web element. Two types of space are available: *margin* and *padding*. Margin refers to the space around an element that is *outside* the border, while padding refers to the space between an element's border and its content. Since web elements have four sides (top, left, bottom, and right), there are four properties for each type of spacing: `margin-top`, `margin-left`, `margin-bottom`, and `margin-right` for margin, and (obviously enough) `padding-top`, `padding-left`, `padding-bottom`, and `padding-right` for padding. "Shortcut properties" `margin` and `padding` are also assignable, to one, two, or four number-plus-unit expressions separated by spaces: one-value expressions set all four sides, two-value expressions set vertical and horizontal spacing, and four-value expressions can set all four sides to different values in a single assignment.

The following `http://javascript.cs.lmu.edu/runner` example provides some code that manipulates these size and spacing properties for the `div` element whose `id` is "footer." Note how the overall area that is occupied by an element is ultimately the combined space determined by `width`, `height`, `border-width`, `padding`, and `margin`. Type in this code and play around (recall, again, the "camel case" rule for how hyphenated CSS property names are modified when accessed via JavaScript):

```
var footer = document.getElementById("footer");
footer.innerHTML = "Fun with sizes and spaces";
footer.style.width = "100px";
footer.style.height = "100px";
footer.style.borderStyle = "outset";
footer.style.borderWidth = "2px";
footer.style.marginLeft = "300px";
footer.style.marginTop = "100px";
footer.style.paddingRight = "50px";
footer.style.paddingBottom = "200px";
```

Color, Images, Opacity, and Visibility

Color and images form another broad category of CSS properties. Color properties can be set using expressions ranging from preset keywords (red, blue, black, white, etc.) to, as you have seen, an rgb triplet. Web elements have three independently settable colors: foreground, background, and border. We will let JavaScript runner code do the talking now:

```
var footer = document.getElementById("footer");
footer.innerHTML = "Fun with color";
footer.style.color = "yellow";
footer.style.backgroundColor = "rgb(0, 0, 200)";
footer.style.borderStyle = "inset";
footer.style.borderColor = "rgb(150,150, 150)";
```

In addition to solid colors, an element's background can be set to a preloaded *image file* if available. Image files are specified in CSS using a url expression: the keyword url followed by the image's, well, URL enclosed in parentheses. Here's some more code, using an image that we know exists somewhere on http://javascript.cs.lmu.edu:

```
var footer = document.getElementById("footer");
footer.innerHTML = "Fun with color";
footer.style.height = "128px";
footer.style.color = "yellow";
footer.style.backgroundImage =
    "url(http://javascript.cs.lmu.edu/images/bookcover.jpg)";
```

Notice how background images repeat by default, and what can be seen depends on the size of the element. The background-repeat property controls how (or whether) a background image repeats within its web element's area. Separate images can also be assigned to borders via the border-image property, using a similar mechanism. We will leave that for you to look up and discover.

A final, related pair of properties pertains to opacity and visibility. You can set the opacity of a web element via the opacity property. This is equivalent to the aforementioned *alpha channel* with colors. In CSS, this property can take values from 0 to 1, with 1 indicating complete opacity and 0 indicating complete transparency (i.e., the element is effectively invisible but still takes up space).

The following example plays with the title/header of the JavaScript runner page as well as the overall visible portion of the page (i.e., its `body` element). Note how opacity is not a matter of "lightness" or "darkness"—it does interact with overlapping elements, such as the underlying color of the web page. Play with the code, trying out different color and opacity values to see how they affect each other:

```
var header = document.getElementById("header");
document.body.style.backgroundColor = "rgb(0, 80, 0)";
header.style.color = "cyan";
header.style.opacity = "0.5";
```

An `opacity` of 0 makes an element completely transparent, but it remains *present* on the web page; that is, it still takes up space. Compare this to the `display` property, which determines whether an element is even there (i.e., *displayed* or not). A value of `none` takes the element away from the page's *display*. Other values make it visible, the most common one being `block`:

```
var header = document.getElementById("header");
header.style.display = "none";
```

Note the difference between an `opacity` of 0 and a `display` of `none`.

More Advanced Visual Effects

Borders, solid colors, and images make up the primary graphics properties of most web elements. With CSS Level 3 (CSS3) or greater, additional properties become available that greatly expand the range of possible visuals in "pure" HTML and CSS (i.e., visuals that a compatible web browser can generate by itself, without requiring a predrawn image file).

CSS3 is sufficiently new that your web browser may not support the exact property names given here. If the code examples do not initially work, try appending a *prefix* to the property name: `Moz` for the Mozilla family of web browsers (Firefox, Flock, etc and `Webkit` for the WebKit family (Safari, Chrome, etc.). At the HTML attribute and CSS rule level, you will need hyphens before and after each prefix (e.g., `-moz-` or `-webkit-`).

Drop shadows are an easy way to immediately add some dimensionality to a web page. CSS3 drop shadows consist of four values: the shadow's color, its *horizontal offset*, its *vertical offset*, and its *blur radius*. The offsets are the distances by which the shadow is, well, *offset* from the web element. The blur radius is effectively the "softness" of the shadow: the larger, the softer.

The following example gives the `footer` element of the JavaScript runner page a relatively soft, grayish drop shadow that falls to the right and below it (note the expected units for the offsets and blur radius):

```
var footer = document.getElementById("footer");
footer.innerHTML = "Getting fancy";
footer.style.boxShadow = "rgb(128, 128, 128) 3px 5px 10px";
```

Again, if this code does not work as is, remember to assign the value to `MozBoxShadow` for Firefox, Flock, and other Mozilla browsers and to `WebkitBox Shadow` for Safari, Chrome, and other WebKit browsers.

The CSS3 `border-radius` property facilitates rounded corners—the effect of which may be greater than you might expect in terms of eliminating the "boxy" default appearance of many web elements. In its simplest form, `border-radius` takes a single length value. This results in a web element's corners being drawn as quarters of a circle whose radius is the given length:

```
var footer = document.getElementById("footer");
footer.innerHTML = "Styling outside the box...";
footer.style.borderStyle = "outset";
footer.style.borderWidth = "2px";
footer.style.borderRadius = "10px";
```

There's quite a bit of flexibility here. More complex forms of `border-radius` allow for distinct horizontal and vertical radii (thus making the corners appear as *quarter ellipses* instead of quarters of a circle) as well as different radii *for each corner*. Plus, `border-radius` and `box-shadow` play well together. See what happens when you combine the previous two examples to create a rounded, drop-shadowed `div` element.

We wrap up our quick tour of CSS3 with *gradient backgrounds*—perhaps the trickiest of the properties we are reviewing but well worth the learning curve. CSS3 approaches gradient backgrounds as *browser-generated images*; that is, they can be used for any property that also takes a `url` expression for an online image file. Thus, gradients can be used with `background-image`, `border-image`, and other properties that typically take an image URL.

As with `border-radius`, the CSS3 expression for a gradient can range from simple-but-standardized to complicated-but-customized. We will stay with simple here, leaving the full gamut of options to reading outside of this text:

```
var footer = document.getElementById("footer");
footer.innerHTML = "Look, ma, no images!";
footer.style.backgroundImage =
    "linear-gradient(white, rgb(200, 0, 0), rgb(128, 0, 0))";
document.body.style.backgroundImage =
    "linear-gradient(left, lightgray, white)";
```

In this simplest form, a gradient is a comma-separated list of colors. The web element then transitions as smoothly as possible across these colors in a particular direction (top to bottom) by default. Different directions can be specified by including a starting point as the first parameter, as seen in the gradient that is assigned to the document's `body` element. In this example, the "starting color" begins at the left side of the element and travels to the right.

Older web browsers actually take differing expressions for gradients, among other values and properties that are available only in the latest standards. The Mozilla/Firefox family of web browsers expects the usual `-moz-` prefix, such as `"-moz-linear-gradient(white, rgb(200, 0, 0), rgb(128, 0, 0))"`, while the WebKit family of web browsers uses the `-webkit-` prefix and expects the type of gradient (`linear`, `radial`) as a parameter.

Dealing with these backward-compatible property variations is straightforward though verbose: *set them all*. Web browsers know to ignore a setting or value that they do not recognize. Thus, a functional workaround until all web browsers converge upon the latest standards is to set every known property variant (CSS3, `-moz-`, `-webkit-`, and others potentially) and, in the case of gradients, assign multiple gradient variations. Here is a code example:

```
var footer = document.getElementById("footer");
footer.innerHTML = "Look, ma, no images!";

// Mozilla version: WebKit ignores this.
document.body.style.backgroundImage =
    "-moz-linear-gradient(left, lightgray, white)";
footer.style.backgroundImage =
    "-moz-radial-gradient(25% 50%, circle," +
```

```
    "white 0%, rgb(200, 0, 0) 50%, rgb(128, 0, 0) 100%)";

// WebKit version: Mozilla ignores this.
document.body.style.backgroundImage =
    "-webkit-gradient(linear, 0% 0%, 100% 0%," +
    "color-stop(0, lightgray), color-stop(1, white))";
footer.style.backgroundImage =
    "-webkit-gradient(radial, 25% 50%, 0, 50% 100%, 750," +
    "color-stop(0, white), color-stop(0.5, rgb(200, 0, 0))," +
    "color-stop(1, rgb(128, 0, 0)))";

// CSS3 version: the latest browsers take this.
document.body.style.backgroundImage =
    "linear-gradient(left, lightgray, white)";
footer.style.backgroundImage =
    "radial-gradient(25% 50%, circle," +
    "white 0%, rgb(200, 0, 0) 50%, rgb(128, 0, 0) 100%)";
```

It's an intimidating number of settings (and we haven't even covered all of them!), but the effort leads to a great deal of flexibility in coloring and/or displaying web elements—all without running a paint program or image editor.

9.2.4 Absolute Position

When web pages are designed as documents and user interfaces, they tend to follow default sizing, flow, and positioning rules. This is a good thing for those purposes, as consistency and device/window independence are paramount for such applications. In computer graphics, however, we want greater flexibility and sometimes even complete freedom from those constraints and conventions.

To make DOM elements support pixel-level positioning, do the following:

1. Determine the element that serves as the *container* for the overall graphics display.

2. Set the **position** style property of the container element as **relative**. This can be done directly within the HTML as follows:

```
<div style="position: relative">
    <!-- Other elements go here. -->
</div>
```

Alternatively, `position` can be set with CSS rules. The web page at `http://javascript.cs.lmu.edu/basicanimation` uses this approach, with the CSS rules placed in a different file instead of written "inline" within a `style` element. This is analogous to using the `script` tag with a `src` attribute.

3. Elements within the container element must, in turn, have *their* `position` style property set to `absolute`.

4. Initial position and size may also be set. The four style properties `left`, `top`, `width`, and `height` facilitate this—they mean exactly what their names say. The positions should be followed by an appropriate unit of measure, typically pixels (`px`). The properties `left: 0px` and `top: 0px` correspond to the upper-left corner of the container element. Direct HTML setting of these properties looks like this:

```
<div style="position: absolute; left: 10px; top: 20px;
                              width: 100px; height: 50px">
    <!-- Elements within the animated element. -->
</div>
```

The preceding HTML defines a 100- × 50-pixel object whose top-left corner is 10 pixels from the left edge of its containing element and 20 pixels from the top edge. As with any web element, these properties can be set using CSS rules instead of within the HTML tags.

Alternatively, you can also set `right` and `bottom` properties. These reveal a subtle difference in the way positioning properties behave in CSS: they represent *distances from their respective boundaries*. Thus, `right: 0px` actually aligns an element's right side *with the right side of its container*. Similarly, `bottom: 5px` places an element's bottom at 5 pixels above the bottom of the containing element.

JavaScript code can, of course, assign these style properties directly, and such assignments immediately result in the corresponding change on the web page:

```
// Assume that the box variable already refers
// to some absolutely positioned element within
// a relatively positioned one.
box.style.left = "15px";
box.style.top = "25px";
```

If the `box` variable refers to the same element previously defined by the HTML tags, then this JavaScript fragment immediately moves that element 5 pixels down and to the right.

9.2.5 Case Study: Bar Chart

We conclude our discussion of HTML and CSS computer graphics with a couple of case studies, starting with a simple bar chart program. The program consists of a single function, `createBarChart`, that takes an array of data items, each of which is an object with `color` and `value` properties, and creates a DOM element that holds a bar chart of the given array. You can find the finished program at `http://javascript.cs.lmu.edu/barchart`. Figure 9.4 displays how it looks in Firefox for Mac OS X, along with its HTML code.

Data items can be specified easily through JavaScript's object notation:

```
document.body.appendChild(createBarChart(
    [ { color: "red", value: 50 },
      { color: "blue", value: 100 },
      { color: "green", value: 75 } ]));
```

The program was designed in this manner to make it easy to display different and possibly multiple bar charts without having to touch the main code, which is encapsulated completely within the `createBarChart` function. The function itself creates a self-contained web element that displays the bar chart. It starts simply enough, creating a `div` element with its `position` CSS property set to `relative`:

```
var chart = document.createElement("div");
chart.style.position = "relative";
```

The function then sets the height of the containing element. This height is determined by the column with the largest value. For a little vertical clearance, 10 pixels are added to the final height:

```
var height = 0;
for (var i = 0; i < data.length; i += 1) {
    height = Math.max(height, data[i].value);
}
chart.style.height = (height + 10) + "px";
```

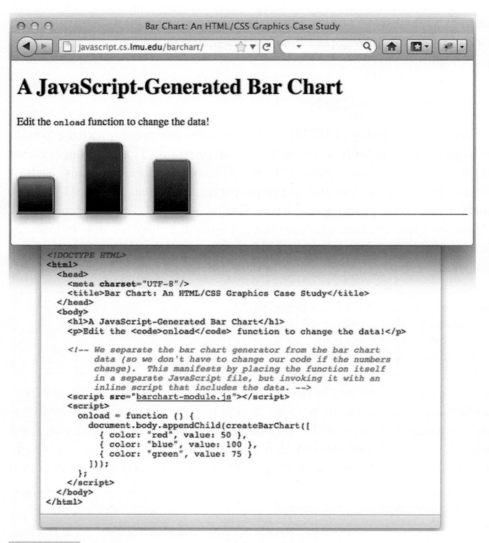

The bar chart case study.

After a little visual styling on the containing element, the columns in the bar chart are set up. This entails iterating through the array of data items and creating a column for each data item. That column has a standardized width, while its height is determined by the **value** property of the data item and its color is determined by the `color` property. Finally, the column is positioned at the bottom of the containing `div`:[4]

```
var dataItem = data[i];
var bar = document.createElement("div");
bar.style.position = "absolute";
bar.style.left = barPosition + "px";
bar.style.width = barWidth + "px";
bar.style.backgroundColor = dataItem.color;
bar.style.height = dataItem.value + "px";
bar.style.borderStyle = "ridge";
bar.style.borderColor = dataItem.color;

bar.style.boxShadow = "rgba(128, 128, 128, 0.75) 0px 7px 12px";
bar.style.borderTopLeftRadius = "8px";
bar.style.borderTopRightRadius = "8px";
bar.style.backgroundImage =
    "linear-gradient(" + dataItem.color + ", black)";

bar.style.bottom = "0px";
chart.appendChild(bar);
```

This case study is not meant to be a completely customizable bar chart program, but we hope that it effectively illustrates many of the HTML and CSS graphics mechanisms that we have shown in this section.

9.2.6 Case Study: Towers of Hanoi Display

This case study represents a possible start for a browser-based Towers of Hanoi puzzle (discussed in Section 10.2.2). In addition to providing yet another example of object-based computer graphics in HTML and CSS, this case study shows how separation between visual properties or presentation and the actual data or model for the puzzle can be accomplished. This separation facilitates "reformatting" of the graphics display without having to touch any JavaScript.

The web page can be found at `http://javascript.cs.lmu.edu/hanoi`. Figure 9.5 shows the page as rendered by Firefox for Ubuntu.

---

[4]The actual implementation also accommodates CSS3 variations for certain browsers, but we redact that here in favor of the standard CSS3 properties and expressions.

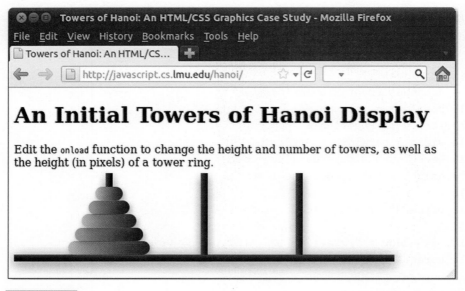

FIGURE 9.5
The Towers of Hanoi case study.

As with many of the case studies in this book, we have tried to keep the HTML minimal (Figure 9.6). Three things are notable though:

- Note the **link** tag that refers to a *hanoi.css* file.

- As before, **onload** is an *event handler*, and so the **hanoi** function call *returns another function*. That function is called only when the web page has finished loading.

- The parameters passed to the **hanoi** function correspond to the number of tower rings, the number of towers, and the physical height, in pixels, of the rings.

The separate CSS file facilitates modifications to the colors, borders, shadows, and other visual properties of the Towers of Hanoi display without touching the JavaScript code—separation of concerns, yet again. The one visual attribute that is visible to the **hanoi** function is the height of each ring. This is done because tower and ring positioning are dependent on this value, and JavaScript necessarily handles that, especially if this program were to be made interactive (e.g., movable rings, implementation of Towers of Hanoi rules, determination of winning/victory state).

FIGURE 9.6

HTML source for the Towers of Hanoi case study.

Compare the following sample rule from *hanoi.css*, for example, against what can be seen in Figure 9.5. It defines the visual properties that are shared by all rings and supports properties for web browsers that do not yet support standardized CSS3 property names:

```css
.ring, .oddring {
    border-radius: 10px;
    -moz-border-radius: 10px;
    -webkit-border-radius: 10px;
    box-shadow: rgba(128, 128, 128, 0.5) 2px 4px 7px;
    -moz-box-shadow: rgba(128, 128, 128, 0.5) 2px 4px 7px;
    -webkit-box-shadow: rgba(128, 128, 128, 0.5) 2px 4px 7px;
}
```

Beyond that, the program itself is conceptually simple: it represents the overall puzzle as an array of "towers," where each tower (member of the **towers** array) is in turn an array of "rings." The rings are actually **div** elements, given a class of **ring** or **oddring**. The CSS rules use this class to "format" these **div** elements consistently:

```javascript
var towers = [];
for (var i = 0; i < towerCount; i += 1) {
    towers.push([]);
}

var ringWidth = (height + 1) * ringHeight;
for (i = 0; i < height; i += 1) {
    // Each ring is a div element, and we identify it with an ID.
    var ring = document.createElement("div");
    ring.id = height - i - 1;
    ring.style.width = ringWidth + "px";
    ring.style.height = ringHeight + "px";

    // For variety, we'll display odd and even rings differently.
    // The class attribute in HTML tags is accessed via the property
    // name className in JavaScript.
    ring.className = (i % 2 == 0) ? "ring" : "oddring";
    towers[0].push(ring);

    // The next ring is smaller.
    ringWidth -= ringHeight;
}
```

Once this array of arrays has been built, the overall containing **div** element is created. Tower elements are created and added to the container, followed by the rings. Finally, in anticipation of some work toward implementing a functional version of this puzzle, the code that positions each ring is placed in a function:

```javascript
var positionRings = function () {
    towerLeft = positionIncrement;
    for (i = 0; i < towerCount; i += 1) {
        var bottom = towerWidth;
        for (j = 0; j < towers[i].length; j += 1) {
            ring = towers[i][j];
            ring.style.left = // We use parseInt to chop off the units.
                (towerLeft - (parseInt(ring.style.width) / 2)) + "px";
```

```
            ring.style.bottom = bottom + "px";
            bottom += ringHeight;
        }
        towerLeft += positionIncrement;
    }
};
```

Note how the function works by iterating through each tower in the `towers` array. For each such tower, the rings are then positioned. Its separation as a function allows for easy updating of the display in case the rings are moved among towers.

Review and Practice

1. What is the difference, if any, between an `img` element and an image that is assigned to the `background-image` CSS attribute? Can you tell which is which in a web browser window without looking at the source tags?

2. How are the `left`, `top`, `bottom`, `right`, `width`, and `height` properties related in absolute positioning? Do they interact with each other at all (i.e., Are there cases where changing one of these properties automatically affects another?)?

3. Look up and describe the CSS attributes that are available for web page text (font styles, sizes, alignment, etc.). Try these out on your own.

9.3 Animation in HTML and CSS

The simplest way to do animation with HTML and CSS is to manipulate the DOM at intervals. By repeatedly modifying certain visual properties of DOM elements with a time-based `setInterval` event handler, animation can be performed within a web page. Small changes, made gradually and frequently enough, are interpreted by the brain as continuous motion or change.

The general approach to web page animation can be summarized as follows:

1. Set up the DOM element to be animated. This primarily entails setting its properties such that it can be moved or otherwise modified in a fine-grained, gradual manner.

2. Define a function that serves as the "entry point" into the animation.

3. Within the function, call `setInterval` with a function that modifies the DOM element in terms of what should happen in a single animation "frame." Smooth movement is typically perceived at or near 30 frames per second; this translates to a `setInterval` parameter of 30–40 milliseconds.

4. If desired, set up an event handler or other condition that stops the animation. Stopping the animation involves holding on to the identifier returned by `setInterval`.

`http://javascript.cs.lmu.edu/basicanimation` illustrates this general approach as well as the specific concepts described in the remainder of this section.

9.3.1   Constant Velocity

The simplest form of motion animation involves *constant velocity*; that is, at each preset interval throughout the animation sequence, an object moves by a fixed amount. Diagonal movement can be achieved by modifying both the `left` and `top` style properties at each animation "frame."

In the `http://javascript.cs.lmu.edu/basicanimation` example for constant velocity, the animated box `cv-box` moves left to right and back, at a speed that can be entered by the user in the `cv-velocity` text field. For ease of modification, the interval to use is assigned to a `millisecondsPerFrame` variable (set to 30 in the example):

```javascript
var startConstantVelocityAnimation = function () {
    // Grab the desired velocity.
    var velocity =
        parseFloat(document.getElementById("cv-velocity").value);

    // Grab the object to animate, and initialize if necessary.
    var box = document.getElementById("cv-box");
    box.style.left = box.style.left || "0px";

    // Start animating.
    var intervalID = setInterval(function () {
        var newLeft = parseInt(box.style.left) + velocity;
        if ((newLeft < 0) || (newLeft > maxLeft)) {
            velocity = -velocity;
        } else {
```

```
            box.style.left = newLeft + "px";
        }
    }, millisecondsPerFrame);

    // Toggle the start button to stop animation.
    setupButton(document.getElementById("cv-button"), "Stop Animation",
        function () {
            clearInterval(intervalID);

            // Toggle the start button to stop animation.
            setupButton(document.getElementById("cv-button"),
                "Start Animation", startConstantVelocityAnimation);
        }
    );
};
```

Note how the box's `left` property is initialized to `0px` if it has not already been set. The function that is repeatedly called by `setInterval` increments this property by the desired velocity (assumed to be in pixels per interval), reversing the direction whenever the box hits the left or right boundary. The `px` suffix is appended to the new `left` property to indicate the desired unit of measure.

The return value of `setInterval` is saved in the `intervalID` variable so that the user can stop the animation, triggered in this example by a `click` event handler that calls `clearInterval` with `intervalID`.

9.3.2 Fading In and Out

Animation is not just about position; *any* value that can be changed little by little over time is a candidate for animation. In the most general case, multiple values can in fact change in an animation.

As an example of an alternative animation property, we choose the `opacity` style property to implement fade-ins and fade-outs. As seen in Section 9.2.3, when `opacity` is 0, its associated element is completely transparent (invisible). When it is 1, the element is completely opaque. Every value in between represents how much you can "see through" that element. Fade animations correspond to the opacity of an object: when it starts out completely transparent or opaque, and as it appears or disappears, its value is increased or decreased a little at a time.

The fade-in/fade-out example in `http://javascript.cs.lmu.edu/ basicanimation` manipulates `opacity` in virtually the same way as a box's position: it starts the opacity at an appropriate value, then adds to/subtracts from that opacity over time until it reaches the target value.

Because the page starts with the fade example box being visible, the first effect that can be tried is the fade-out. In the following `setInterval` invocation, the key variable is `fadeRate`, or the degree by which the element gets more transparent with each frame. Note how it fulfills the same role as velocity when doing motion animation:

```javascript
var intervalID = setInterval(function () {
    // Calculate the new values.
    var newOpacity = parseFloat(box.style.opacity) - fadeRate;
    if (newOpacity <= 0) {
        // Upon reaching maximum transparency, stop the animation and
        // toggle the function of the fade button.
        newOpacity = 0;
        clearInterval(intervalID);
        setupButton(document.getElementById("fade-button"),
            "Fade In", startFadeInAnimation);
    }

    box.style.opacity = newOpacity;
}, millisecondsPerFrame);
```

Most of the function actually has to do with *ending* the animation, not the animation itself! Opacity is decreased by `fadeRate` at each frame—that's it. The web browser takes care of the rest. Since this is a fade-out, we end the animation when `newOpacity` reaches or goes below 0. As with motion animation, we end the animation by calling `clearInterval(intervalID)`, then toggle the fade button to do a fade-in when it is next clicked.

Fading in is hardly any different: we start the opacity at 0 and increase it instead, stopping when the opacity reaches 1. The code is so similar that we will leave it for you to infer or just examine online.

9.3.3   Animating Other Properties

The suite of available CSS properties, some of which were introduced in Section 9.2.3, offers a wide selection of animation possibilities. These can be modified over time via `setInterval`, individually or in combination, to produce a variety of animation effects:

- Because colors (e.g., `color`, `background-color`, `border-color`) can be expressed in terms of red, green, and blue values, appropriate gradual modification of these values can produce color transition effects for different aspects of a web element.

- The `width` and `height` properties allow for size animation. Just remember that, like `left`, `top`, `right`, and `bottom`, these properties need a unit of measure, such as `px`, in order to work properly.

- Properties such as `border-width`, `margin`, and `padding` can animate web element spacing and layout.

- Text-related properties, which are not covered in this chapter, can animate blocks of text, ranging from their font size to their style and color.

In principle, any property that has a visual effect that can be changed in small increments over time is a candidate for animation. Once you have gotten the general pattern for animation using `setInterval` and `clearInterval`, with help from how functions are objects in JavaScript, setting these up is straightforward and satisfying.

9.3.4   Ramped (or Eased) Animation

Many systems implement animation through *tweening*: the user specifies the start and end states of an animated object (called the object's *key frames*) and the desired duration of the animation, and the software computes the frames in between. The center of this computation is the *tweening function*, which, when given a start state, an end state (or, equivalently, the amount of change in state), the target duration, and the current time in the animation, returns the intermediate or "tweened" state that the object should have. The actual tweening algorithm is then a matter of iterating from time 0 to the total duration, periodically calling the tweening function at the current time and setting the animated object's state to whatever the tweening function returns.

By encapsulating an animated object's behavior within a tweening function, more sophisticated changes such as acceleration, oscillation, or anything else can be implemented without changing the overall structure of the animation code. The `http://javascript.cs.lmu.edu/basicanimation` eased animation example implements "ease in," "ease out," and "ease in and out"—acceleration, deceleration, and symmetrical acceleration followed by deceleration. The tweening functions for these effects are shown here [Pen06]:

```
var quadEaseIn = function (currentTime, start, distance, duration) {
    var percentComplete = currentTime / duration;
    return distance * percentComplete * percentComplete + start;
};

var quadEaseOut = function (currentTime, start, distance, duration) {
    var percentComplete = currentTime / duration;
    return -distance * percentComplete * (percentComplete - 2) + start;
};

var quadEaseInAndOut = function (currentTime, start, distance,
        duration) {
    var percentComplete = currentTime / (duration / 2);
    return (percentComplete < 1) ?
        (distance / 2) * percentComplete * percentComplete + start :
        (-distance / 2) * ((percentComplete - 1) *
            (percentComplete - 3) - 1) + start;
};
```

The approach of these functions is to start by determining how far along in the animation we are, which is done by dividing the current time by the total duration. This results in a value from 0 to 1, effectively the percent complete. When easing in, we multiply the distance by the square of this value, offset by the start position. When easing out, we multiply by the *negative* of the distance since we are decelerating. Easing in and out divides the overall distance in half, returning the "ease in" value in the first part of the animation and returning the "ease out" value in the second part. The functions are quadratic—i.e., they are based on the square of the amount of time that has passed—because simple acceleration in elementary physics affects an object's location in that manner.

Note that constant velocity animation is simply a linear tweening function: the object's state for a given frame is directly proportional to the number of elapsed frames. And ultimately, we are not locked in at all, to elementary physics or otherwise, when it comes to what we do in the tweening function. As long as the function puts the object in the desired start state at `currentTime === 0` and puts the object in the desired end state (or close enough) at `currentTime === duration`, the function can do anything it wants, really. The main condition is that the "trajectory" of the values returned by the tweening function has a recognizable smoothness. In other words, it must produce sufficiently small changes over time, which is the essence of animation.

As you might have supposed by now, tweening functions can apply to *any* animatable property, not just movement. Fades, changes in color, changes in size—the animation possibilities explode when the code is structured around a "pluggable" tweening function. The results are elegant in design and powerful in functionality because JavaScript treats functions as objects and the DOM supports a wide variety of "tweenable" properties.

If you would like to explore these tweening possibilities further, Robert Penner has developed a library of tweening/easing functions [Pen06] (the examples shown here are based on his work), and the Tweener open source project has implemented these functions in JavaScript and other languages [Twe10].

9.3.5 Declarative CSS Animation

The latest CSS standard supports specific *declarative* versions of the animation techniques shown in this section [CSS09a, CSS09b]. By "declarative," we mean that a web page can simply state—"declare"—that certain animations should take place under certain circumstances. Standards-compliant web browsers can take those declarations and act upon them without needing further code from the web page. In a sense, declarative CSS animations focus on *what* should happen without having to specify *how* it happens.

Because this type of animation does not involve JavaScript at all, we will cover it no further than through a brief example. The simplest form of declarative CSS animation is the *transition*—tweening that occurs when an element changes from one style to another. Such transitions involve the *property* to be animated, the *duration* of the animation, and the *timing function* (equivalent to the tweening or easing functions from the previous section). The following code demonstrates this:

```html
<!doctype html>
<html>
  <head>
    <meta charset="UTF-8"/>
    <title>Declarative CSS Animation Demonstration</title>
    <style>
      span {
        font-size: 48px;
        transition: text-shadow 2s ease;
        -moz-transition: text-shadow 2s ease;
        -webkit-transition: text-shadow 2s ease;
      }

      span:hover {
        text-shadow: 0px 0px 18px red;
      }
    </style>
  </head>
  <body>
    <span>Follow</span> <span>the</span>
    <span>unearthly</span> <span>glow!</span>
  </body>
</html>
```

Declarative functionality is generally simpler and less error-prone than actual programmed functionality, but this does not mean the programming goes away. It simply means the software has been able to structure its programmed components well enough that "declaring" *what* to do is easily mapped to the code or functions that show *how* it is done. Thus, learning how to program these effects (i.e., the subsections before this one) remains relevant even as declarative approaches become more sophisticated—because ultimately, *someone* has to get around to programming all of those declared behaviors!

Review and Practice

1. What role does `setInterval` play in web animation?

2. The `setInterval` function returns an identifier that can be used to refer to the particular repetition that the function call initiated. Name a situation in which knowing this identifier can prove useful.

3. Is it possible to write a tweening function as described in Section 9.3.4 such that the tweened object appears to move back and forth over time? Why or why not? Test your answer by downloading and modifying the code in `http://javascript.cs.lmu.edu/basicanimation`.

4. Does declarative CSS animation obviate the need to know how to program animation effects directly? Why or why not?

9.4   The canvas Element

For web browsers that support it, the `canvas` element provides web pages with a dynamically paintable area. JavaScript applications have full, pixel-level control of `canvas` elements and work with them through functions that provide very similar functionality to image editing software. One can think of `canvas` as a mechanism for "scripted painting." An extensive online tutorial for the `canvas` element can be found in [Moz09], while [WW10] provides the latest version of its specification.

9.4.1   Instantiating a `canvas`

As with all web page elements, `canvas` can be created either through tags in HTML or through explicit creation and inclusion in the document by JavaScript code. The `canvas` element has two distinct attributes—`width` and `height`—both expressed in pixels. When left unspecified, a `canvas` defaults to a `width` of 300 pixels and a `height` of 150 pixels.

An HTML `<canvas>` tag looks like this:

```
<canvas width="200" height="200">
A canvas element should appear here, in browsers
that support it.
</canvas>
```

This `width` and `height` represent the *drawable region* of the `canvas`, not its visible size. Thus, `<canvas width="200" height="200">` represents an area that is evenly divided into 200 columns across and 200 rows down, *regardless of how big that canvas appears on the web page.* If CSS or other mechanisms change a `canvas` element's presentation or layout size to something other than its designated `width` and `height`, then its contents are scaled up or down to that size.

Note the role of the text between the start and end tags: browsers that do not support the `canvas` element will not recognize the `canvas` tags and will display any text in between. You can use this behavior to give the user some kind of warning or notice that the web page needs `canvas` element support in the web browser. Web browsers that do support `canvas` will not display this text because there would be a `canvas` right in its place!

In pure JavaScript, creating and configuring a `canvas` element is very similar to most other elements:

```
var canvas = document.createElement("canvas");
canvas.innerHTML = "A canvas element should appear here," +
    " in browsers that support it.";
canvas.width = 200;
canvas.height = 200;
document.body.appendChild(canvas);
// ...or wherever else you'd like the canvas to go.
```

9.4.2   The Rendering Context

The bridge between your JavaScript code and what users see in a `canvas` element is the *drawing, graphics,* or *rendering context.* This concept is in fact common to many computer graphics programming environments.

If `canvas` is a programmer's version of an image-editing or paint application, then a rendering context is the programmer's analog for the *state* of that application: the current tool, the selected color, the current font, etc. Typical interaction with a graphics context involves setting relevant values such as color, drawing style, and font. An actual drawing operation can then be requested, and that operation is performed using those values. These operations then result in user-visible changes to what is in the `canvas`.

In a design choice that should no longer be surprising, the rendering context is represented as a JavaScript object. It is acquired through the `getContext` function of the `canvas` element. `getContext` requires one parameter: the type of context that is being requested. This section focuses on the 2D rendering context (indicated by passing `"2d"` to `getContext`); see Section 9.6 for its 3D counterpart:

```
// Assume that the canvas variable holds a valid canvas, whether
// created manually, accessed via document.getElementById, or obtained
// by any other method.
var renderingContext = canvas.getContext("2d");
```

Once the code has a rendering context, drawing can begin in earnest. This small program paints a red 50×25 rectangle with an upper-left corner located at $(5, 5)$ of whatever `canvas` element provided the rendering context referenced by the `renderingContext` variable:[5]

```
renderingContext.fillStyle = "rgb(255, 0, 0)";
renderingContext.fillRect(5, 5, 50, 25);
```

This program illustrates the general pattern for `canvas` use: set up the rendering context and call a drawing function. The setup here involves a single property, `fillStyle`, which determines how drawn items are, well, *filled* when drawn. In the example, this is a solid swath of full-intensity red.

The drawing function used here is `fillRect`; it draws a solid rectangle, according to the current value of the `fillStyle` property. For arguments, `fillRect` expects the x- and y-coordinates of the rectangle's upper-left corner followed by its width and height.

`fillStyle` can also take colors that have alpha transparency; use `rgba` for those. Add the following two lines to draw a half-opaque green rectangle on top of the red rectangle:

```
renderingContext.fillStyle = "rgba(0, 255, 0, 0.5)";
renderingContext.fillRect(30, 20, 40, 50);
```

The `canvas` rendering context has a wide variety of properties, some more of which you will see in later sections. You may find that multiple properties need to be set at any given time, but you will want to revert to whatever values they had

---

[5]You may choose to run this code on a canvas you created manually (i.e., the last code sample from the previous section), or you may prefer to execute it from an HTML file with a `<canvas>` tag. To emphasize the interchangeability of these approaches, we leave that choice to you.

soon after. The **save** and **restore** functions are good for those: call **save** when you want to "mark" the rendering context's properties at a certain point, change the rendering context as needed, then call **restore** when done. This is particularly useful if you have separated your drawing routines into functions:

```
var drawingFunction = function (renderingContext) {
    renderingContext.save();
    /* Do anything you want; change anything you want. */
    renderingContext.restore();
    /* It's as if nothing has changed! */
};
```

9.4.3   Drawing Rectangles

In addition to **fillRect**, the **strokeRect** and **clearRect** functions are variations on the theme of painting rectangles. **strokeRect** paints only an "outlined" or "bordered" rectangle, while **clearRect** performs the equivalent of "erasing" a rectangle.

The following program presumes an existing **canvas** variable that holds a **canvas** element and shows these three functions in action. For reference, Figure 9.7 illustrates what you should see.

```
var renderingContext = canvas.getContext("2d");
renderingContext.fillStyle = "rgb(255, 0, 0)";
renderingContext.fillRect(10, 10, 100, 50);
renderingContext.fillStyle = "rgba(0, 255, 0, 0.5)";
renderingContext.fillRect(50, 20, 100, 50);
renderingContext.clearRect(20, 15, 75, 40);
renderingContext.strokeRect(25, 25, 75, 40);
```

Properties other than **fillStyle** influence the appearance of a painted rectangle, such as **strokeStyle**, **globalAlpha**, **lineWidth**, **lineCap**, **lineJoin**, and **miterLimit**. Feel free to look up and experiment with these to see how they change the appearance of a drawn rectangle.

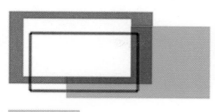

Fun with canvas rectangles.

9.4.4   Drawing Lines and Polygons

If `canvas` only did rectangles, then it would not functionally surpass HTML/CSS. Virtually everything you can do with a `canvas` rectangle can be done with `div` elements. With *paths*, however, `canvas` begins to truly shine.

A *path* is essentially a sequence of points. Points may or may not be connected by lines—it depends on how they are specified. As with the rectangle drawing functions, all of this action centers around a rendering context. A new path is started by calling `beginPath`. Functions such as `moveTo`, `lineTo`, `arc`, and others then specify points on that path. An optional `closePath` call ensures that the last point specified connects a line to the first point specified. Calls to `stroke` and `fill` either draw the lines in the current path or paint in the region delineated by the lines in that path, respectively. The general pattern for path drawing code thus looks like this:

```
var renderingContext = canvas.getContext("2d");
renderingContext.beginPath();
/* Specify your points. */
/* Optional. */ renderingContext.closePath();
/* One or both: */
renderingContext.stroke();
renderingContext.fill();
```

A variety of functions aids in specifying points. The simplest one, conceptually, is `moveTo`. The `moveTo` function takes 2D coordinates (`x`, `y`) and adds those to the path, without doing any drawing. Calling `moveTo` is like lifting a pencil off the paper and placing it at the location you specify.

The `lineTo` function, in turn, moves the "pencil" *without* lifting it, thus drawing a line connecting the current and new locations. A `stroke` call then draws those

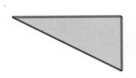

FIGURE 9.8

A rudimentary path example.

lines, while a `fill` call paints in the region enclosed by those lines. The following code, for example, paints a cyan right triangle with a black outline (Figure 9.8):

```
var renderingContext = canvas.getContext("2d");
renderingContext.fillStyle = "rgb(0, 255, 255)";
renderingContext.strokeStyle = "black";
renderingContext.beginPath();
renderingContext.moveTo(10, 10);
renderingContext.lineTo(110, 10);
renderingContext.lineTo(110, 60);
renderingContext.closePath();
renderingContext.fill();
renderingContext.stroke();
```

Typing, running, and experimenting with this code (using whatever mechanism you prefer for creating the `canvas` element) gives you a good feel for how paths work. Specifically, try the following changes, and see if you can predict the outcome:

- Remove the `closePath` function call.

- Interchange the `fill` and stroke calls.

- Change the `fillStyle` and `strokeStyle` rendering context properties.

- Add more `moveTo` and `lineTo` calls after calling `fill` or `stroke`, then call `fill` or `stroke` again.

- Insert a new `beginPath` function call (with a new initial `moveTo` call, if necessary) *before* the `moveTo` and `lineTo` calls in the previous task.

Mix and match these changes as you like. Consider your experimentation time complete when you can accurately predict what you will see for each permutation you make.

9.4.5 Drawing Arcs and Circles

Arcs and curves are part of `canvas`'s path functionality. For circles and arcs, use the `arc` function. The `arc` call of `arc(x, y, radius, startAngle, endAngle, anticlockwise)` has, as its parameters:

- the center of the arc, `(x, y)`,

- the `radius` of the arc,

- the start and end angles of the arc (`startAngle`, `endAngle`), given in radians, and

- whether these angles are connected clockwise (`anticlockwise === false`) or counterclockwise (`anticlockwise === true`).

Calling `arc` is equivalent to calling `lineTo(x, y)` and then drawing the arc, so call `moveTo(x, y)` first if you want the arc or circle to stand alone. If the use of radians gives you high school trigonometry flashbacks, the `Math` object defines a `PI` property, so you can convert from degrees to radians with a minimum of fuss using the expression `(Math.PI / 180) * degrees`. Note that a full circle or disc can be drawn by having a `startAngle` of 0 and an `endAngle` of `Math.PI * 2`.

As with `lineTo`, `arc` by itself does not draw anything. Finish things off with `stroke` to draw the curve defined by the arc, or with `fill` to draw a solid "pie slice."

The following example, adapted from [Moz09], provides a nice selection of what `arc` can do (you should get something that looks like Figure 9.9). Make sure you

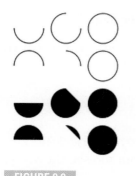

FIGURE 9.9

Variations on a canvas arc theme [Moz09].

run this on a **canvas** element with a width of at least 150 and a height of at least 200 (can you see why?):

```
var renderingContext = canvas.getContext("2d");
for (var i = 0; i < 4; i += 1) {
    for (var j = 0; j < 3; j += 1) {
        renderingContext.beginPath();
        var x = 25 + (j * 50),
            y = 25 + (i * 50),
            radius = 20,
            startAngle = 0,
            endAngle = Math.PI + ((Math.PI * j) / 2),
            anticlockwise = ((i % 2) === 0) ? false : true;

        renderingContext.arc(x, y, radius,
            startAngle, endAngle, anticlockwise);

        if (i > 1) {
            renderingContext.fill();
        } else {
            renderingContext.stroke();
        }
    }
}
```

Once you have this working, as given, try the following modifications:

- Change the value of **radius**.

- Change the constants in the expressions for **x** and **y**.

- Remove the **beginPath** call at the beginning of the inner loop.

- Replace the **if** statement at the end of the inner loop with just a call to **fill** or **stroke**, also without **beginPath**.

- Interchange the value of the **anticlockwise** variable.

- Add a **closePath** function call right before calling **stroke**.

As before, consider your understanding complete if you can foresee the visual results of each code change you make.

9.4.6 Drawing Bézier and Quadratic Curves

The final path-specific functions involve Bézier curves, of the quadratic `quadraticCurveTo` and cubic `bezierCurveTo` varieties. The mathematics of these curves is beyond the scope of this text, and admittedly, they are easier to work with in interactive draw programs, which allow you to manipulate them in real time.

Suffice it to say that both curves start at the current point in the path (e.g., a point set by `moveTo`) and end at a new point. In addition, `quadraticCurveTo` takes the coordinates of one *control point* (`cp1x`, `cp1y`) while `bezierCurveTo` takes two control points (`cp1x`, `cp1y`, `cp2x`, `cp2y`). In both cases, the control point coordinates come first, with the destination endpoint given as the last two parameters.

The following example draws a rectangle, with quadratic Bézier curves drawn over it. The vertices of the rectangle serve as control points for quadratic curves, with their adjacent corners serving as endpoints. Run this code on a `canvas` with a width of at least 200 and a height of at least 100:

```
var renderingContext = canvas.getContext("2d");
renderingContext.strokeStyle = "rgba(0, 0, 0, 0.25)";
renderingContext.lineWidth = 0.5;
renderingContext.strokeRect(20, 20, 160, 60);

renderingContext.strokeStyle = "rgb(128, 0, 0)";
renderingContext.lineWidth = 1.0;

renderingContext.beginPath();
renderingContext.moveTo(20, 20);
renderingContext.quadraticCurveTo(180, 20, 180, 80);
renderingContext.moveTo(180, 20);
renderingContext.quadraticCurveTo(180, 80, 20, 80);
renderingContext.moveTo(180, 80);
renderingContext.quadraticCurveTo(20, 80, 20, 20);
renderingContext.moveTo(20, 80);
renderingContext.quadraticCurveTo(20, 20, 180, 20);
renderingContext.stroke();
```

The next code fragment illustrates an alternative path. Adjacent vertices of the rectangle in this example serve as control points for cubic Bézier curves, with

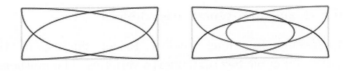

FIGURE 9.10

Quadratic and Bézier curves.

their opposite corners serving as endpoints. Because the resulting curves are harder to tell apart, they are done as separate paths so that different colors can be used to draw them. This code also needs a **canvas** with a width of at least 200 and a height of at least 100. Figure 9.10 illustrates how these quadratic and Bézier curve code examples should look.

```
renderingContext.strokeStyle = "rgb(128, 0, 0)";
renderingContext.beginPath();
renderingContext.moveTo(20, 20);
renderingContext.bezierCurveTo(180, 20, 180, 80, 20, 80);
renderingContext.stroke();

renderingContext.strokeStyle = "rgb(0, 128, 0)";
renderingContext.beginPath();
renderingContext.moveTo(180, 20);
renderingContext.bezierCurveTo(20, 20, 20, 80, 180, 80);
renderingContext.stroke();

renderingContext.strokeStyle = "rgb(0, 0, 128)";
renderingContext.beginPath();
renderingContext.moveTo(180, 80);
renderingContext.bezierCurveTo(180, 20, 20, 20, 20, 80);
renderingContext.stroke();

renderingContext.strokeStyle = "rgb(128, 0, 128)";
renderingContext.beginPath();
renderingContext.moveTo(180, 20);
renderingContext.bezierCurveTo(180, 80, 20, 80, 20, 20);
renderingContext.stroke();
```

The **canvas** element's path-based functions provide a powerful library of routines for drawing almost any geometric entity. While the functions are object-based ("arc," "line," "quadratic curve," etc.), **canvas** is ultimately pixel-oriented; therefore, once these paths are drawn, it is not possible to go back and modify them the way one can set a new position for a `div` element. Once drawn or filled, the shapes become pixels and can only be manipulated as pixels from that point on.

If the ability to draw lines, arcs, circles, and curves does not seem to make up for the loss of object-based modification, the other broad `canvas` functionality should: the ability to manipulate images.

9.4.7 Working with Images

The `canvas` element can draw preexisting image files in a variety of ways. If you find that the CSS variations for displaying an `img` element start falling short of your vision, displaying the image in a `canvas` element may be the way to go.

What `canvas` does *not* do is load the image data itself. Why replicate that work, after all, when the `img` element and other JavaScript objects can do it already? So that's where we start.

Specifying an Image Source

Mechanisms for bringing an image into a `canvas` element include, but are not limited to:

- An `img` element on the web page. This can be accessed by `id` or through any other means of "walking" through the DOM.

- Another `canvas` element on the web page. Same here; you can use any approach to get to that element.

- An `Image` object created on the fly. But be sure to wait until it is fully loaded before using it. See the upcoming *Implementation Notes* section for more details on this.

Placing the content of one `canvas` onto another is particularly powerful. You can use that method for magnified or thumbnail views, for example. Tiles, overlays, and other visual effects constitute other possibilities.

If an `img` element is to be used solely as a "source image" for a `canvas` element, you can load it without its being visible on the web page by setting its `style.display` property (Section 9.2.3):

```
<!--
   For canvas use only.  Note the "display: none" property and the
   assigned id attribute.
-->
<img id="coverimg" src="/images/bookcover.jpg" style="display: none" />
```

Drawing an Image

With any of the aforementioned image sources in hand, drawing them on a `canvas` element is a matter of calling one of these rendering context functions:

- drawImage(image, dx, dy) draws the image such that its upper-left corner is located at (dx, dy) on the canvas.

- drawImage(image, dx, dy, dw, dh) *scales* the image to width dw and height dh.

- drawImage(image, sx, sy, sw, sh, dx, dy, dw, dh) draws a *slice* or *subimage* of the original image with its upper-left corner at the location (dx, dy), width dw, and height dh. The slice to be drawn has its left corner at (sx, sy) on the original image, with width sw and height sh, again on the original image.

Figure 9.11, which is part of the official `canvas` specification [WW10], summarizes these image-drawing options.

A sample page at `http://javascript.cs.lmu.edu/canvas-image` illustrates canvas image drawing along with other canvas functions that were seen previously. For fun, we have thrown in some rendering context properties that you have not seen yet but whose purpose should be fairly apparent. Figure 9.12 illustrates what you should see.

The page, which illustrates a hypothetical game in which images of eyes are matched, uses two invisible `img` elements as image sources:

```
<img id="girl-image" src="girl.jpg" alt="girl" style="display: none" />
<img id="boy-image" src="boy.jpg" alt="boy" style="display: none" />
```

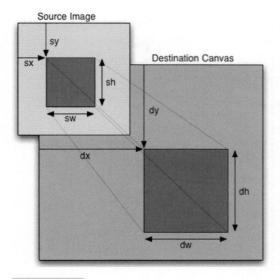

FIGURE 9.11

`drawImage` variations [WW10].

FIGURE 9.12

Canvas image drawing and other functions/properties.

Once the page has loaded, the original images are drawn and scaled on the canvas, with the eyes in each image drawn individually, thanks to the slicing variant of the **drawImage** function. The code for drawing the images, along with variable initialization and rendering context property settings, is shown here:

```
var canvas = document.getElementById("canvas");
var girlImage = document.getElementById("girl-image");
var boyImage = document.getElementById("boy-image");

var renderingContext = canvas.getContext("2d");
renderingContext.shadowOffsetX = 0;
renderingContext.shadowOffsetY = 4;
renderingContext.shadowBlur = 16;

renderingContext.shadowColor = "rgba(120, 120, 255, 0.5)";
renderingContext.drawImage(boyImage, 262, 12, 240, 320);
renderingContext.drawImage(boyImage, 177, 510, 100, 60,
    273, 400, 100, 60);
renderingContext.drawImage(boyImage, 380, 488, 100, 60,
    142, 400, 100, 60);

renderingContext.shadowColor = "rgba(255, 120, 120, 0.5)";
renderingContext.drawImage(girlImage, 12, 12, 240, 320);
renderingContext.drawImage(girlImage, 250, 365, 100, 60,
    400, 400, 100, 60);
renderingContext.drawImage(girlImage, 445, 315, 100, 60,
    12, 400, 100, 60);
```

To emphasize that only a **canvas** element can facilitate this visual with just the two **img** elements, translucent green triangles indicate which eye is which. The property setup and the code for the first triangle are shown here:

```
renderingContext.shadowColor = "rgba(120, 120, 120, 0.5)";
renderingContext.shadowOffsetX = 4;
renderingContext.fillStyle = "rgba(80, 200, 80, 0.5)";
renderingContext.beginPath();
renderingContext.moveTo(12, 400);
renderingContext.lineTo(112, 400);
renderingContext.lineTo(166, 117);
renderingContext.fill();
```

Implementation Notes

Image data can sometimes be large enough to require consideration of something we have ignored so far: download time. Note that images cannot be drawn until the image data have actually *arrived* at the web browser. For `img` elements in a web page, waiting for a `load` event before doing the heavy graphics lifting does the trick. For dynamically created `Image` objects, such as:

```
var image = new Image();
image.src = "/images/bookcover.jpg";
```

be sure to wait until the image file has fully downloaded before you use it on a canvas. Fortunately, this is easy—`Image` objects can report the `load` event, indicating when their image data have been completely read:

```
var image = new Image();
image.onload = function () {
    var renderingContext = canvas.getContext("2d");
    renderingContext.drawImage(image, 0, 0);
};
image.src = "/images/bookcover.jpg";
```

Note how the event handler is assigned *before* the `src` property. This ensures that the function does get called when image loading is complete.

A self-contained example, written for the JavaScript runner page at `http://javascript.cs.lmu.edu/runner`, is shown here:

```
var canvas = document.createElement("canvas");
canvas.width = 512;
canvas.height = 512;
document.body.appendChild(canvas);

var image = new Image();
image.onload = function () {
    var renderingContext = canvas.getContext("2d");
    renderingContext.drawImage(image, 0, 0);
};
image.src = "/images/bookcover.jpg";
```

9.4.8   Transformations

Suppose you needed to draw a particular visual multiple times on a **canvas** element. Congratulations if your first thought was to place that code inside a function—your programming instincts are showing! Here, for example, is a function that draws a basketball. It takes a rendering context as an argument, so it can be used on any **canvas** on the web page. Note also how we are throwing in a few more rendering context possibilities that you have not seen before; by now you should be able to generally infer what's happening, and if not, you should be able to look them up to get the details:

```
var drawBasketball = function (renderingContext) {
    renderingContext.save();
    var gradient = renderingContext.createRadialGradient
        (-15, -15, 5, 15, 15, 75);
    gradient.addColorStop(0, "rgb(255, 130, 0)");
    gradient.addColorStop(0.75, "rgb(128, 65, 0)");
    gradient.addColorStop(1, "rgb(62, 32, 0)");
    renderingContext.fillStyle = gradient;

    renderingContext.beginPath();
    renderingContext.arc(0, 0, 50, 0, 2 * Math.PI, true);
    renderingContext.fill();

    renderingContext.strokeStyle = "black";
    renderingContext.lineWidth = 1;
    renderingContext.beginPath();
    renderingContext.moveTo(0, -49);
    renderingContext.bezierCurveTo(30, -35, 30, 35, 0, 49);
    renderingContext.moveTo(-49, 0);
    renderingContext.bezierCurveTo(-35, -30, 35, -30, 47, -15);
    renderingContext.moveTo(-35, 35);
    renderingContext.bezierCurveTo(0, -30, 50, -20, 45, 20);
    renderingContext.moveTo(-28, -40);
    renderingContext.bezierCurveTo(10, -35, 25, -35, 29, -40);
    renderingContext.stroke();
    renderingContext.restore();
};
```

Note how most of the function's code is "bracketed" between **save** and **restore** function calls. This is a good graphics programming habit, as it ensures that the state of the system prior to calling your function is preserved after your function returns. It is the computer graphics equivalent of "leave things the way you found them."

You might also have noticed that the basketball is centered at (0, 0); it was easier to figure out the coordinates of the various points in this ball with (0, 0) as a reference. However, calling this function as is would produce the image shown in Figure 9.13.

One might be tempted to add x and y parameters to the function, representing the desired center of the basketball, then adjust all of the values according to x and y. But there are other reasonable variations to this function: we may want basketballs of different sizes, or we may want to rotate the ball. Adding more and more parameters to this function to represent size and rotation, plus the needed adjustments to the drawing routines to accommodate such arguments, would turn this function's code into a morass of variables, arithmetic, and incomprehensibility.

There must be an easier way—and there is: *transformations*. A transformation is a manipulation of the *coordinate space* within which points are being drawn. The points are positioned *relative to* the transformed space, meaning that, depending on the current transformation, the *same code* can produce different visual results.

FIGURE 9.13

A naïve call to the drawBasketball function.

There are three basic transformations, each implemented by a different rendering context function:

- **translate(x, y)** moves the origin (0, 0) of the **canvas** element's coordinate space by (x, y). All points are then positioned as offsets from the new "origin."

- **rotate(angle)** turns the *axes* of the coordinate space—i.e., the left/right direction (*x*-axis) and the up/down direction (*y*-axis)–by the given **angle**. The vertical and horizontal can thus become diagonal, and all points specified after a rotation are drawn relative to this new vertical/horizontal orientation.

- **scale(x, y)** resizes the dimensions of the coordinate space by the given scale factors **x** and **y**. Thus, a unit of 1 grows or shrinks by this scale factor.

The beauty of transformations is that they accumulate. For example, calling **translate(5, 10)** followed by **translate(3, -2)** results in (0, 0) being ultimately located at (8, 8). The exact mathematics that defines how transformations behave is standard issue for a computer graphics course; look there for those computational details. For the purposes of this discussion, the intuitive/visual perspective will suffice.

Now, back to our basketball example. With transformations in our tool belt, we can write code that looks like the following to produce what you see in Figure 9.14 (the code assumes a canvas that is at least 550 units wide and 350 units high):

```
var renderingContext = canvas.getContext("2d");
var xStep = 25, yStep = -100;

// Start the ball at the bottom left of the canvas.
renderingContext.translate(50, 300);
for (var i = 0; i < 19; i += 1) {
    drawBasketball(renderingContext);
    // Move the ball by the current step values.
    renderingContext.translate(xStep, yStep);
    yStep += 25;

    // Check to see if the ball needs to bounce.
    if (yStep > 100) {
        yStep = -100;
    }
}
```

FIGURE 9.14

Transformations on a basketball, part 1.

We may feel like being clever by trying to rotate the ball a little each time we display it. We might also feel like scaling the ball along the vertical direction to convey the impression that it compresses slightly after a bounce. We may then initially modify our code as shown (asterisks indicate the specific additions/changes):

```
  var renderingContext = canvas.getContext("2d");
  var xStep = 25, yStep = -100;

  // Start the ball at the bottom left of the canvas,
* // and compressed vertically due to a bounce.
  renderingContext.translate(50, 300);
* renderingContext.scale(1, 0.5);
  for (var i = 0; i < 19; i += 1) {
      drawBasketball(renderingContext);
*     // Rotate and scale the ball.
*     renderingContext.rotate(10 * Math.PI / 180); // 10 degrees.
*     renderingContext.scale(1, 1.1);
      // Move the ball by the current step values.
      renderingContext.translate(xStep, yStep);
      yStep += 25;

      // Check to see if the ball needs to bounce.
      if (yStep > 100) {
```

```
            yStep = -100;
        }
    }
```

Disappointingly, however, this code produces Figure 9.15.

What went wrong? The problem is that this code neglects how transformations "add up." Remember that transformations are *cumulative*. Just as each `translate` call moves the origin *relative to* where it already was, based on prior `translate`s, so do `rotate`s and `scale`s. Thus, each subsequent rotation *rotated not only the ball itself but also its position relative to the prior origin*. Ditto with the scaling.

The fix for this can be found in functions that you have already seen: `save` and `restore`. First off, the current transformation is part of the rendering context's state, and is thus preserved by `save` and `restore` alongside the other properties that you have seen. Second, `save` and `restore` are themselves cumulative: they form a *stack* of rendering context states, such that multiple calls to `save` each produce a distinct "marker" for how the rendering context was at that time. Matching calls to `restore` retrieves each state in the reverse order. It's like having multiple undos and redos on a typical computer application.

By always "resetting" the current transformation to a previous state, we can perform our `rotate`s and `scale`s, which are relative to just the ball, outside of the `translate`s. However, this must change the values that we send to our transformations. Instead of increments, we must set them to "absolute" values—that is,

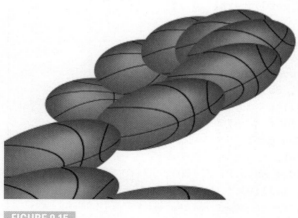

Transformations on a basketball, part 2.

FIGURE 9.16

Transformations on a basketball, part 3.

values that are not relative to each other but are based solely on each iteration of the `for` loop.

Figure 9.16 illustrates what we want, as produced by the following code. This finished version of the program can be found as a complete web page at `http://javascript.cs.lmu.edu/canvas-transforms`.

```javascript
var renderingContext = canvas.getContext("2d");
var xStep = 25, yStep = -100;

// We now have variables to represent the absolute position,
// rotation, and scaling of the ball.
var x = 50, y = 300, angle = 0;
var compression = 0.5;

// Start the ball at the bottom left of the canvas.
for (var i = 0; i < 19; i += 1) {
    // Always return to the same state after each iteration.
    renderingContext.save();

    // Move the ball to the current position.
```

```
        renderingContext.translate(x, y);

        // Scale and rotate the ball.
        renderingContext.scale(1, compression);
        renderingContext.rotate(angle);

        // *Now* draw.
        drawBasketball(renderingContext);

        // Calculate the new position, rotation, and scale.
        x += xStep; y += yStep; yStep += 25;
        angle += 10 * Math.PI / 180; // 10 degrees.
        compression += (compression <= 0.9) ? 0.1 : 0;

        // Quick check to see if the ball has hit the "floor."
        // This results in a "bounce."
        if (y + yStep > 300) {
            compression = 0.5;
            y = 300; yStep = -100;
        }

        renderingContext.restore();
}
```

At this point, if you haven't done so already, you will want to try transformations for yourself. You can download the self-contained code from `http://javascript.cs.lmu.edu/canvas-transforms` and play with the transformation code in there: make it move differently, make it rotate faster or in a different direction, resize the ball differently, etc. Or, you can write something completely new from scratch. It is fair to say that, more than anything you have seen about the `canvas` element so far, it is the use of transformations that benefits the most from practice and experience.

When, one day, you have learned about the underlying mathematics that powers transformations, you will want to look up the `transform` and `setTransform` functions. These functions allow the specification of transformations in their most general form, allowing you to manipulate what is drawn beyond what `translate`, `rotate`, and `scale` provide.

9.4.9   Animation

The broad strokes of canvas animation—or any JavaScript animation, for that matter—do not actually differ much from what is described in Section 9.3. You still need to plan out the incremental modifications that are needed for each "frame," and you need to make these modifications rapidly and repeatedly, typically using `setInterval`. What's different with a `canvas` element corresponds to what's different between pixel-based and object-based graphics: instead of modifying the properties of discrete objects, the code needs to *redraw the entire canvas* at each "frame."

As mentioned before, `canvas` element drawing functions such as `fillRect`, `arc`, `drawImage`, and others do not actually create distinct rectangles, curves, or other visible shapes. They merely "paint" the individual pixels that correspond to these objects. Once called, you are left with the `canvas` element again—no more, no less. Animating a `canvas` element thus involves

- planning the data structure(s) for your animated scene, such that it can be drawn in its entirety within a single function,

- writing a "new frame" function that modifies your data structure(s) to reflect advancement to the next state in the animated sequence and then repaints the affected `canvas` element, and

- calling `setInterval` so that it repeatedly calls the "new frame" function at a sufficient frequency (at least 30 frames per second).

Note how the techniques for updating your scene—constant velocity, ramped/eased change, etc.—remain the same. It is only the display mechanism that changes slightly, again due to the `canvas` element's "all or nothing" nature.

The code at `http://javascript.cs.lmu.edu/canvas-animated` applies these principles—and it's based on the transformation example from the previous section! The key difference is that, instead of a `for` loop that draws each basketball instance on top of the prior basketballs, we have a `nextFrame` function that clears the `canvas` element first, then draws the basketball and updates its position, rotation, and scale. A `setInterval` call sets up the repeated invocation of `nextFrame` at a sufficient frequency:

```
/* Note how, aside from the conversion of the for loop into a
   nextFrame function, the code has not otherwise changed much
   from the transformation example.  The only other differences
   are adjustments to the values: they make smaller changes to
   accommodate the frequency with which the canvas is redrawn. */

var renderingContext = canvas.getContext("2d");
var xStep = 2.5, yStep = -10.0;

// Variables to represent the absolute position, rotation, and
// scaling of the ball.
var x = 5, y = 300, angle = 0;
var compression = 0.5;

var nextFrame = function () {
    // Always return to the same state after each iteration.
    renderingContext.save();

    // Clear the canvas.
    renderingContext.clearRect(0, 0, canvas.width, canvas.height);

    // Move the ball to the current position.
    renderingContext.translate(x, y);

    // Scale and rotate the ball.
    renderingContext.scale(1, compression);
    renderingContext.rotate(angle);

    // *Now* draw.
    drawBasketball(renderingContext);

    // Calculate the new position, rotation, and scale.
    x += xStep; y += yStep; yStep += 0.25;
    angle += Math.PI / 180; // 1 degree.
    compression += (compression <= 0.95) ? 0.05 : 0;

    // Quick check to see if the ball has hit the "floor."
    // This results in a "bounce."
    if (y + yStep > 300) {
        compression = 0.5;
```

```
        y = 300; yStep = -10.0;
    }

    // One more check to see if the ball has gone "off-canvas."
    // This moves the ball back to the left side.
    if (x > canvas.width) {
        x = 50;
    }

    renderingContext.restore();
};

// One hundred frames per second!
setInterval(nextFrame, 10);
```

9.4.10 canvas by Example

For a full-fledged `canvas` example, we have implemented yet another variant of our tic-tac-toe case study; this version can be found at `http://javascript .cs.lmu.edu/tictactoe/canvas`. This version is organized similarly to the version in Section 7.4 in that it is designed to have minimal dependence on the HTML page that references its script.

The main highlight of this version is its use of a `canvas` element instead of a `table` as the display mechanism for the tic-tac-toe board. This change has the following consequences:

- With one distinct web element for each tic-tac-toe cell in prior versions, no additional computation was necessary to find the cell that corresponded to a click: the browser did this for you! With the single `canvas` element containing the entire tic-tac-toe grid, however, the location of the mouse click determines the affected cell.

  As if this weren't enough of a twist, many browsers today do not actually have a standard, consistent mechanism for delivering mouse click coordinates. There are also some gotchas involving whether or not a web page is currently scrolled, which affects the reported click location.

  To address this compatibility issue, we have adapted code from [Pil10] that takes browser variations and scrolling into account:

```
var getCursorPosition = function (event) {
    var x, y;
    if (event.pageX || event.pageY) {
        x = event.pageX;
        y = event.pageY;
    } else {
        x = event.clientX + document.body.scrollLeft +
            document.documentElement.scrollLeft;
        y = event.clientY + document.body.scrollTop +
            document.documentElement.scrollTop;
    }

    x -= board.offsetLeft;
    y -= board.offsetTop;

    return { 'x': x, 'y': y };
};
```

The `click` handler for the canvas calls this function to get a reliable `(x, y)` location for the mouse click:

```
var set = function (event) {
    // Start with our cross-browser coordinate finder.
    var location = getCursorPosition(event);

    // Continues...
```

We will leave the details on `getCursorPosition` to [Pil10]. It is also possible that, by the time you read this, web browsers will have converged on a consistent standard for reporting mouse click coordinates.

■ The members of the `squares` array must thus include their coordinates within the `canvas`, since they are no longer web page elements, as seen in the assigned `onload` function. We choose to store their upper-left corners and assume they are all the same size:

```
var indicator = 1;
var y = 0;
```

```
for (var i = 0; i < 3; i+=1) {
    var x = 0;
    for (var j = 0; j < 3; j+=1) {
        squares.push({ x: x, y: y, indicator: indicator });
        indicator += indicator;
        x += board.width / 3;
    }
    y += board.height / 3;
}
```

- Finally, we now need a `getSquare` function that locates the square that contains a detected mouse click:

```
var getSquare = function (x, y) {
    var cellWidth = board.width / 3;
    var cellHeight = board.height / 3;
    for (var i = 0; i < squares.length; i+=1) {
        if ((x > squares[i].x) && (x < squares[i].x + cellWidth)
                && (y > squares[i].y) && (y < squares[i].y +
                cellHeight)) {
            return squares[i];
        }
    }

    return null;
};
```

One might view these changes as disadvantages of the `canvas` approach: the management of cell locations was given to us "for free" when we worked within the DOM. Now that we have "taken over" the entire game board with a single `canvas`, we have to implement these functions ourselves.

In addition, the `nodeValue` property, which used to hold the symbol within a square and thus the string to be displayed, gives way to a `paint` function that paints a particular cell state: empty, X, or O. This gives us maximum flexibility in what to display inside a cell. These `paint` functions are taken from a `squarePainters` array that is mapped according to the strings that were originally used in `nodeValue` and are still used by `turn` and `score`. Each `paint` function takes x and y parameters, representing the upper-left corner of the square to be drawn. As an example, here is the function that paints the X symbol:

```javascript
function (x, y) {
    // X's are dark blue diagonals with drop shadows.
    boardContext.save();
    boardContext.lineWidth = 5;
    boardContext.strokeStyle = "rgb(0, 0, 120)";
    boardContext.shadowOffsetX = 0;
    boardContext.shadowOffsetY = 1;
    boardContext.shadowBlur = 3;
    boardContext.shadowColor = "rgba(0, 0, 0, 0.75)";

    // We draw within a region whose margin is the grid thickness.
    var cellWidth = board.width / 3 - (gridThickness << 1),
        cellHeight = board.height / 3 - (gridThickness << 1),
        side = Math.min(cellWidth, cellHeight),
        xCorner = side >> 2,
        xSize = side * 3 >> 2;

    // The translate call helps to simplify the path coordinates.
    boardContext.translate(x, y);
    boardContext.beginPath();
    boardContext.moveTo(xCorner, xCorner);
    boardContext.lineTo(xCorner + xSize, xCorner + xSize);
    boardContext.moveTo(xCorner, xCorner + xSize);
    boardContext.lineTo(xCorner + xSize, xCorner);
    boardContext.stroke();

    boardContext.restore();
}
```

The result of all of this code can be seen in Figure 9.17, which shows a canvas-based tic-tac-toe game in progress.

What cannot be seen in the figure is an additional touch: animation. You will have to visit http://javascript.cs.lmu.edu/tictactoe/canvas to see this for yourself. Whenever the player makes a move, the new X or O does not just appear—it does so with some kind of animation.

The overall animation strategy is the same: when the animation needs to "play," a particular function, in this case animate, is called. In this example,

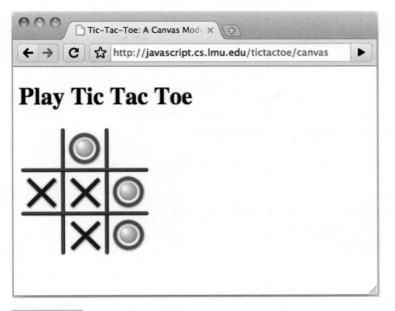

FIGURE 9.17

A canvas-based tic-tac-toe case study.

we trigger the animation when the player makes a move, which in turn is when the click event is handled by the set function:

```
var set = function (event) {
    // Start with our cross-browser coordinate finder.
    var location = getCursorPosition(event);
    var square = getSquare(location.x, location.y);
    if (square) {
        if (square.paint !== squarePainters['\xA0']) {
            return;
        }

        // Animate the incoming mark.
        animate(square);
    }
};
```

Note how a *lot* of the old set code is gone. We will get to that in a moment. The animate function should be somewhat recognizable: most of it consists of a `setInterval` call to a "next frame" function. The animation lasts for a particular number of frames (i.e., interval function calls), then ends when that number of frames is reached:

```
var nextFrame = setInterval(function () {
    // The "empty square" painter serves as our eraser.
    squarePainters['\xA0'](square.x, square.y);

    // The current mark is drawn using some intermediate rendering
    // context state.
    boardContext.save();
    tweeners[turn](frameCount / frameTotal, square.x, square.y);
    squarePainters[turn](square.x, square.y);
    boardContext.restore();

    // Are we done?
    frameCount += 1;
    if (frameCount > frameTotal) {
        clearInterval(nextFrame);
        finishTurn(square);
    }
}, 1000 / 30);
```

What may appear unusual is the reference to the `tweeners` variable. Recall, from Section 9.3.4, that a common animation approach involves the definition of a "tweening" function whose role is to determine, based on an absolute time slice and other parameters, the state of the animation at a particular frame. In this case, the time slice is represented by the percent completion of the animation (`frameCount / frameTotal`). The `tweeners` variable is an object with functions for the X and O marks:

```
var tweeners = {
    'X': function (animationFraction, x, y) {
        /* Tweening code for X goes here. */
    },

    'O': function (animationFraction, x, y) {
        /* Tweening code for O goes here. */
    },
};
```

The appropriate `tweeners` function for the current turn is called in order to set up the rendering context, after which the aforementioned `squarePainters` function is called. Since much of the animation setup consists of changes to the rendering context, this code is bracketed by a `save/restore` pair.

Finally, the concluding portion of the former `set` function, which updates the score, checks for a winning condition, and/or moves on to the next turn, has been separated into a `finishTurn` function. This function is called when the designated number of animation frames has passed.

These `paint` and `animate` functions, alongside the additional code for dealing with coordinates, represent the primary trade-off with using `canvas` for an application such as this: is the visual flexibility that is afforded by `canvas` worth the additional code that HTML, CSS, and the DOM and its events otherwise provide automatically or more easily? In the end, the answer to this question can only be determined on a case-by-case basis. For this particular case study, you be the judge: do you prefer this version of tic-tac-toe over the ones you have seen earlier in the text? The strength of this preference, in relation to the increased code complexity, then determines whether all that additional work was worth it!

Review and Practice

1. What is the difference between the `width` and `height` attributes of the `canvas` tag/element, and its `width` and `height` properties in CSS?

2. What happens to the displayed content within a `canvas` element when the web browser's magnification or zoom level is increased?

3. In the canvas-based tic-tac-toe case study, parts of the `set` function were separated into a `finishTurn` function, which is called after the animation has concluded. Why is this necessary? That is, why couldn't the code in `finishTurn` simply follow the `animate` call in `set`?

9.5 SVG

SVG, short for *Scalable Vector Graphics*, is yet another graphics technology standard for web pages [W3C09b]. SVG bridges a gap between HTML/CSS and the `canvas` element: like HTML/CSS, it is object-based and therefore does not get "blocky" or "jaggy" when magnified, but like `canvas`, SVG can handle a wider variety of shapes and visual elements than HTML/CSS.

Like HTML, SVG is expressed as a sequence of *tags* with corresponding *attributes*. An SVG drawing thus resembles an HTML document at the source code level, though the specific tags and attributes differ. Like HTML and `canvas`, an SVG drawing can also be "built" using pure JavaScript code. Finally, SVG animation resembles HTML animation more than `canvas` animation: because it is object-based, animation in SVG consists of making small, frequent changes to individual SVG elements, as opposed to the draw/redraw approach required by the pixel-based `canvas`. Plus, SVG can perform *declarative* animation—certain elements can state the type of animation that is to take place, and the animation "just happens," with no additional programming.

9.5.1   Seeing SVG in a Web Browser

The following listing shows the code/tags that produce the SVG drawing shown in Figure 9.18:

```
<svg version="1.1" xmlns="http://www.w3.org/2000/svg">

    <circle cx="100" cy="50" r="40"
        stroke="black" stroke-width="2" fill="blue"/>

    <rect x="20" y="75" width="250" height="100"
        rx="40" ry="20" fill="red" opacity="0.25"/>

    <line x1="100" y1="50" x2="270" y2="175"
        stroke="rgb(255, 255, 80)" stroke-width="10px"
        stroke-linecap="round"/>

</svg>
```

This drawing can be made to appear in an SVG-capable web browser using any of the following mechanisms:

■ The SVG code can be saved as a separate file (with a file name suffix of `.svg`) then opened directly by the browser. When the `.svg` file is opened directly, no other content is shown because, well, there isn't anything else! This approach suffices for experimentation or testing, or when all of the desired content can be captured in the SVG drawing.

FIGURE 9.18

A simple (abstract) SVG drawing.

- The SVG file can also be referenced within an HTML file using an `iframe` element. For example, to include an SVG file named *diagram.svg* within a web page, you may use the following tag:

```
<iframe src="diagram.svg" width="500" height="500"></iframe>
```

The `width` and `height` attributes are optional, but you will probably use them most of the time in order to control the space occupied by the SVG drawing.

- The SVG code can be included directly (i.e., inlined) among the HTML tags; inline SVG is, in fact, part of the latest HTML standard specification [W3C08b]. Note that SVG elements are not considered to be a part of HTML, per se. Instead, they are viewed as *embedded content*, with their own distinct *namespace*:

```
<!-- HTML DOCTYPE, html, and head above this line. -->
<body>
    <!-- Some HTML can go here. -->
    <svg xmlns="http://www.w3.org/2000/svg" version="1.1"
      viewBox="0 0 100 100" width="400" height="400">
        <linearGradient id="backgroundGradient"
          x1="0%" y1="5" x2="0%" y2="20" gradientUnits=
```

```
            "userSpaceOnUse">
            <stop offset="0%" stop-color="rgb(255, 200, 200)" />
            <stop offset="40%" stop-color="red" />
            <stop offset="100%" stop-color="rgb(60, 0, 0)" />
        </linearGradient>
        <rect x="5" y="5" width="20" height="20"
          fill="url(#backgroundGradient)" />
    </svg>
    <!-- More HTML can go here. -->
</body>
<!-- Other closing tags below this line. -->
```

In case you are wondering, the SVG part of that code fragment looks like Figure 9.19.

- You can also build an SVG drawing "out of thin air" using JavaScript. This approach is structurally similar to what you have seen before, except with a variant of **createElement** called **createElementNS**. "NS" stands for "namespace" here. As mentioned before, SVG is not strictly a part of HTML and so its elements must explicitly conform to the SVG language:

```
var svgns = "http://www.w3.org/2000/svg";

var svg = document.createElementNS(svgns, "svg");
svg.setAttribute("width", 256);
svg.setAttribute("height", 256);
svg.setAttribute("viewBox", "0 0 50 50");

var shape = document.createElementNS(svgns, "circle");
shape.setAttribute("cx", 25);
```

FIGURE 9.19

An SVG rectangle with a gradient.

```
shape.setAttribute("cy", 25);
shape.setAttribute("r",  10);
shape.setAttribute("fill", "green");
svg.appendChild(shape);

document.body.appendChild(svg);
```

There is no accompanying figure for the preceding code because you can run it, as is, in `http://javascript.cs.lmu.edu/runner` and see the result for yourself. Note also the fairly straightforward correspondence between SVG tags and `createElementNS`, and SVG attributes and `setAttribute`. This means that, given any SVG drawing, conversion from SVG tags to dynamically created JavaScript and back should not be too complicated.

As you might have inferred, the specific mechanism of choice ultimately depends on how your web page is structured and how its assets are created or managed. Thus, the remainder of this section will focus on the SVG tags and attributes themselves, without cluttering in any information that pertains only to how the SVG drawing is linked to or written inline. Of course, when behavior needs to be dynamic, the programmatic approach will be the way to go.

9.5.2 SVG Case Study: A Bézier Curve Editor

A walkthrough of SVG's elements, attributes, and capabilities, as we have done with HTML/CSS and the `canvas` element, can get quite tedious because they are conceptually similar to and share some overlap with these technologies, differing only in terms of syntax and specific details. Instead, we take a different approach: we present a self-contained, fairly extensive case study that shows many of SVG's features and highlight points of interest within that case study. The official SVG specification [W3C09b], among other resources and tutorials that are easy to find on the Web, should fill in the gaps and provide specifics.

Our case study is a rudimentary Bézier curve editor, and it has been implemented as a single `.svg` file. You can access this document at `http://javascript .cs.lmu.edu/curve-editor.svg` (note the suffix). Successfully loading it should produce something that looks like Figure 9.20.

The editor is meant to work similarly to those found in drawing programs such as Adobe Illustrator: dragging the bluish squares modifies the endpoints or vertices

FIGURE 9.20

An SVG Bézier curve editor.

of the curve, while dragging the greenish circles modifies the control points of the curve. The curve itself is animated so that it appears to "glow" red; we put that there to demonstrate SVG's declarative animation feature. Dotted gray lines relate the control points to their associated vertices.

Viewing the source code to `http://javascript.cs.lmu.edu/curve-editor` `.svg` reveals tags and attributes that should look familiar yet different. This is how it starts:

```
<svg version="1.1" xmlns="http://www.w3.org/2000/svg"
  xmlns:xlink="http://www.w3.org/1999/xlink" onload="editorSetup();">
    <!-- Generalized functionality for editing curves. -->
    <script xlink:href="curve-editor.js" />
```

The overall tag (and thus element) is `svg`. Like `html`, this serves as the top-level container for the drawing's content. Note the `onload` attribute, which specifies code that will run when document loading is complete (see what we mean by "familiar yet different"?). We will look at the `editorSetup` function later.

The first element within the SVG document is `script`. In another case of déjà vu, this element works very similarly to its namesake in HTML. Note here that a `script` element that refers to a separate file uses an `xlink:href` attribute instead of `src`. We will look at what is inside *curve-editor.js* later on, but suffice it to say that this tag results in similar behavior to its HTML equivalent: it reads the script and executes its code. Top-level variables remain available for later.

The tags that follow show how gradients are expressed as first-class elements. Identifiers (the `id` attribute) facilitate references to them later in the drawing.

Note any similarities to the CSS gradients from Section 9.2.3—this is by design:

```
<linearGradient id="vertexGradient" gradientUnits="objectBoundingBox"
  x1="0" y1="0" x2="1" y2="1">
    <stop offset="0%" stop-color="rgb(0, 0, 200)" />
    <stop offset="10%" stop-color="blue" />
    <stop offset="100%" stop-color="black" />
</linearGradient>

<radialGradient id="controlGradient" gradientUnits="objectBoundingBox"
  cx="0.5" cy="0.5" r="0.5" fx="0.3" fy="0.3">
    <stop offset="0%" stop-color="white" />
    <stop offset="50%" stop-color="green" />
    <stop offset="100%" stop-color="black" />
</radialGradient>
```

9.5.3   Objects in the Drawing

Most of the remaining tags in the case study pertain to the objects within the drawing. Comments have been elided for brevity here because the focus is on the elements themselves and not necessarily their specific roles in the program:

```
<line id="startConnector" stroke="gray" stroke-dasharray="5,3" />
<line id="endConnector" stroke="gray" stroke-dasharray="5,3" />

<path id="path" fill="none" stroke="black" stroke-width="2">
    <animateColor attributeName="stroke" dur="5s"
      repeatCount="indefinite"
      values="black;rgb(220, 0, 0);black" />
    <animate attributeName="stroke-width" dur="5s"
      repeatCount="indefinite"
      values="2;4;2" />
</path>

<rect id="startVertex" x="40" y="27" width="10" height="10"
  fill="url(#vertexGradient)" />
<rect id="endVertex" x="195" y="195" width="10" height="10"
  fill="url(#vertexGradient)" />
```

```
<circle id="startControl" cx="25" cy="122" r="5"
  fill="url(#controlGradient)" />
<circle id="endControl" cx="150" cy="200" r="5"
  fill="url(#controlGradient)" />
```

The elements in the preceding listing represent objects to be rendered within the SVG drawing. These elements are drawn using a "painter's model"; that is, they are drawn one at a time and in the order that they appear. Later elements may partially or totally obscure earlier ones. Thus, the `line` elements will end up at the "bottom" of the drawing, with the `circle` elements up top.

Four types of elements are shown here: `line`, `path`, `rect`, and `circle`. Per the SVG specification, each element comes with attributes that are specific to it (e.g., `x`, `y`, `width`, and `height` for `rect`, or `cx`, `cy`, and `r` for `circle`). Some attributes are available across the board as well, such as `id` and presentation values such as `fill` and `stroke`. Note how the `fill` attributes of the `rect` and `circle` elements refer, by `id`, to the gradients we saw earlier.

The `path` element also contains `animateColor` and `animate` elements. These illustrate the *declarative animation* feature of SVG. Instead of requiring explicit code for periodically changing the attributes of an element, SVG accepts descriptions of *how* these attributes change over time. The browser then does the rest. The tags in this example make the `path` element (a similar construct, conceptually, to the paths from Section 9.4.4) cycle its stroke color from black to reddish and back (`animateColor`), and also oscillate its stroke width between 2 and 4 (`animate`).

9.5.4   Reading and Writing Attributes

This being a programming text after all, our case study does not just produce a static diagram but also allows you to change it. As mentioned, the Bézier curve shown can be modified by dragging the square or circle "handles," with the squares controlling vertices and the circles linked to control points. This functionality is delivered through the code contained in *curve-editor.js* and within the `script` element at the end of the `.svg` file.

The code in *curve-editor.js* is separated because it is designed for use with any Bézier curve path element within a document. The functions within this file are parameterized so that they are not connected to any particular `path`, `rect`, `circle`, or `line` elements. The only assumptions made by this code are that `rect` elements are used as vertex "handles," `circle` elements are used for control point "handles," and `line` elements exist for visually connecting each vertex to its corresponding control point.

The "meat" of this code is the `updateCurve` function, which changes a given `path` element according to the positions of two `rect` and `circle` element pairs. The function also expects two `line` elements, updating their endpoints so they connect the corresponding `rect` and `circle` elements:

```javascript
var updateCurve = function (startVertexElement, endVertexElement,
  startControlElement, endControlElement,
  startConnectorElement, endConnectorElement, path) {
    // Grab the data needed for the path.
    var startVertex = getCenter(startVertexElement),
        endVertex = getCenter(endVertexElement),
        startControl = getControlCenter(startControlElement),
        endControl = getControlCenter(endControlElement);

    // Build the path data string.
    var pathData = "M" + startVertex.x + "," + startVertex.y + " ";
    pathData += "C" + startControl.x + "," + startControl.y + " ";
    pathData += endControl.x + "," + endControl.y + " ";
    pathData += endVertex.x + "," + endVertex.y;

    // Assign the new data string to the path.
    path.setAttribute("d", pathData);

    // Update the indicator lines.
    updateConnector(startConnectorElement, startVertex, startControl);
    updateConnector(endConnectorElement, endVertex, endControl);
};
```

The function starts by retrieving the data needed to update the curve: two vertices and two control points. The vertex coordinates are derived from the centers of the vertex elements, while the control point coordinates come from the centers of the control point elements. The vertex elements are `rect`s, and according to the SVG specification, rectangles are described through their upper-left corner (x, y), their `width`, and their `height`. Thus, deriving their centers requires a little arithmetic:

```
var getCenter = function (vertex) {
    return {
        x: +vertex.getAttribute("x") + (vertex.getAttribute("width")
            / 2),
        y: +vertex.getAttribute("y") + (vertex.getAttribute("height")
            / 2)
    };
};
```

Note how the centers are returned as objects with coordinates stored in x and y properties. A similar approach was taken in the `getCursorPosition` function of the `canvas` implementation of tic-tac-toe (Section 9.4.10).

The `circle` element, on the other hand, is defined by its center (cx, cy) and radius r. Thus, deriving its center in order to get control point coordinates is simpler. A similar (x, y) object is returned:

```
var getControlCenter = function (control) {
    return {
        x: control.getAttribute("cx"),
        y: control.getAttribute("cy")
    };
};
```

With the desired coordinates read into the `startVertex`, `endVertex`, `startControl`, and `endControl` variables, these values can now be written out to the affected elements—specifically, the `path` that displays the actual curve and the connector `line`s between the vertices and control points.

You have seen paths before: conceptually, these *are* the same paths seen in Section 9.4.4 and beyond. With the `canvas` element, a path is initiated by calling the `beginPath` function. Functions such as `moveTo`, `lineTo`, `arc`, `quadraticCurveTo`, and `bezierCurveTo` then build up the points within the path, concluding with a `fill` or `stroke` call.

The SVG equivalent of a path is structurally the same: a `path` element declares the existence of the path, and that element includes a sequence of "buildup" commands that ultimately define it. The path then gets drawn using whatever presentation or style attributes (or defaults) are assigned to it.

Letter	Command
M	move to
L	line to
H	horizontal line to
V	vertical line to
C	curve to
S	smooth curve to
Q	quadratic Bézier curve to
T	smooth quadratic Bézier curve to
A	elliptical arc
Z	close path

Table 9.1

Available `path` Element Commands

Unlike the sequence of function calls in a `canvas` path, however, the key information for the SVG `path` element is expressed as a single, potentially large string assigned to a particular attribute, simply named `d` (loosely "data"). The `d` attribute consists of *path commands*. The specific command is designated by a single letter followed by whatever parameters are required by that path command. Table 9.1 lists what is available.

Many path command parameters consist of 2D coordinates, and these coordinates can be either absolute (i.e., an exact location within the SVG drawing) or relative (i.e., a displacement or offset from the previously mentioned point). Uppercase command letters indicate absolute coordinates and lowercase command letters indicate relative ones.

In the case of our Bézier curve editor, we need only the `M` *move to* command followed by a single `C` *curve to* command. In all cases, coordinates are absolute, so both letters are capitalized. The `M` command takes the coordinates of the first vertex, and the `C` command lists the two control points followed by the second vertex. The string is built through simple concatenation:

```
// Build the path data string.
var pathData = "M" + startVertex.x + "," + startVertex.y + " ";
pathData += "C" + startControl.x + "," + startControl.y + " ";
```

```
pathData += endControl.x + "," + endControl.y + " ";
pathData += endVertex.x + "," + endVertex.y;

// Assign the new data string to the path.
path.setAttribute("d", pathData);
```

The `setAttribute` call assigns the final string to the `path` element's `d` attribute, which automatically updates the display.

The remainder of `updateCurve` positions the two `line` elements that connect the start and end vertices to their corresponding control points. The `updateConnector` function assigns the (x, y) coordinates to the appropriate endpoints of each `line` element, simply named $(x1, y1)$ and $(x2, y2)$:

```
var updateConnector = function (connectorElement, vertex, controlPoint)
    {
    connectorElement.setAttribute("x1", vertex.x);
    connectorElement.setAttribute("y1", vertex.y);
    connectorElement.setAttribute("x2", controlPoint.x);
    connectorElement.setAttribute("y2", controlPoint.y);
};
```

In general, reading and writing SVG elements is a matter of calling `getAttribute` and `setAttribute`, respectively. While this mechanism looks somewhat different from the direct reading and assigning of properties in HTML, the behavior is otherwise the same: the web browser keeps all of these attributes updated, such that reading them always provides the current value, and setting them triggers the corresponding changes to the displayed drawing.

A missing detail: How does one get a "hold" of the elements to be read or written? The answer is quite similar to how it can be done with HTML and is part of the discussion in the next section.

9.5.5 Interactivity (aka Event Handling Redux)

The final aspect of our case study involves the code required to connect the user's actions to changes in the SVG elements, thus resulting in updates to the displayed Bézier curve. As with prior HTML examples, we set things up through a `load` event handler:

```
var editorSetup = function () {
    /* Function and variable definitions. */
    ...

    return function () {
        document.getElementById("startVertex").onmousedown =
            getStartDragHandler(updateVertex);
        document.getElementById("endVertex").onmousedown =
            getStartDragHandler(updateVertex);
        document.getElementById("startVertex").onmouseup =
            endDragHandler;
        document.getElementById("endVertex").onmouseup =
            endDragHandler;
        document.getElementById("startControl").onmousedown =
            getStartDragHandler(updateControl);
        document.getElementById("endControl").onmousedown =
            getStartDragHandler(updateControl);
        document.getElementById("startControl").onmouseup =
            endDragHandler;
        document.getElementById("endControl").onmouseup =
            endDragHandler;
        updateSampleCurve();
    };
}();
```

Skipping to the end at first, we see that the `load` event handler finishes up with a call to `updateSampleCurve`. This function is a simple "sync," ensuring that the current curve does correspond to the current locations of the vertex and control point "handles." It is a call to `updateCurve`, with the specific elements that are declared in this SVG drawing:

```
var updateSampleCurve = function () {
    updateCurve(document.getElementById("startVertex"),
        document.getElementById("endVertex"),
        document.getElementById("startControl"),
        document.getElementById("endControl"),
        document.getElementById("startConnector"),
        document.getElementById("endConnector"),
        document.getElementById("path"));
};
```

The rest of the `load` event handler is a sequence of event handler assignments, specifically for the `mousedown` and `mouseup` events of certain elements. We see here that accessing elements within the SVG drawing is equivalent to accessing the elements of a web page: the variable `document` is available for the SVG drawing as a whole, and that drawing has a `getElementById` function that returns the element with the given ID. SVG does in fact conform to the Document Object Model, so manipulating an SVG drawing programmatically is very similar to doing so in HTML.

The event handlers are coordinated around supporting mouse drags: holding down a mouse button over a vertex or control point "handle," moving the mouse, then letting go of the button when the new position has been finalized by the user. Thus, it makes sense that the expressions that assign handlers to `mousedown` events have the words "start drag" in them, while the `mouseup` handlers refer to a single `endDragHandler` function.

The general sequence of a drag operation in this Bézier curve editor is as follows:

1. When the mouse button is held down, we save the element over which this took place—this is the element that will be dragged.

2. While the element is being moved (we will see how this is tracked in a moment), take note of the new position and update the curve accordingly.

3. When the mouse button is lifted, the drag operation ends by "letting go" of the dragged element and stopping the mouse movement–update cycle.

We thus require a variable over the course of the mouse drag to store the current "drag element":

```
var dragElement = null;
```

Let's look at how drags are started. In this curve editor, two types of elements can be dragged: `rect` elements for the curve vertices and `circle` elements for its control points. The only difference between these two drag operations is the set of attributes needed to update the state of the curve. For `rect` elements, we need to access the upper-left corner (x, y) and size (`width` and `height`), while for `circle` elements, we only need the center (cx, cy). We thus place these activities under separate `updateVertex` and `updateControl` functions, respectively. Each function takes an **event** parameter. This is the mouse motion event that we capture while the drag is taking place. Both functions read the position of the mouse and set the new location of the dragged element accordingly:

```
var updateVertex = function (event) {
    dragElement.setAttribute("x", event.clientX - dragElement.
        getAttribute("width") / 2);
    dragElement.setAttribute("y", event.clientY - dragElement.
        getAttribute("height") / 2);
};

var updateControl = function (event) {
    dragElement.setAttribute("cx", event.clientX);
    dragElement.setAttribute("cy", event.clientY);
};
```

The **getStartDragHandler** function sets up these functions when the mouse button is pressed:

```
var getStartDragHandler = function (moveFunction) {
    return function (event) {
        dragElement = event.target;
        document.onmousemove = function (event) {
            moveFunction(event);
            updateSampleCurve();
        };
    };
};
```

In essence, when the mouse button is pressed, the pressed element, **event.target**, is assigned to the **dragElement** variable. The **mousemove** event is then tracked using either **updateVertex** or **updateControl** (or whatever is passed in the **moveFunction** parameter). Then, after the mouse moves and the dragged element is updated, the curve is redisplayed via **updateSampleCurve**.

Letting go of the mouse button requires the same actions, regardless of the element being dragged. Thus, **endDragHandler** is not a function that in turn returns the handler function but is the event handler itself:

```
var endDragHandler = function (event) {
    document.onmousemove = null;
    dragElement = null;
};
```

In other words, we stop tracking mouse movement over the SVG drawing and clear out our reference to the outgoing `dragElement`.

9.5.6   Other SVG Features

As mentioned earlier in this section, we have opted to highlight specific aspects of SVG through a case study rather than walk through a laundry list of features and capabilities. Thus, while the case study can provide a feel for SVG, it certainly cannot cover everything SVG can do. The following are some features that may pique your interest in further reading:

- SVG supports element grouping, similar to the *Group* function found in many drawing programs. Grouping allows multiple elements to be treated, and thus manipulated, as one.

- Like `canvas`, SVG also supports transforms. Transformations can be assigned as a per-element attribute, and they can also be animated declaratively.

- SVG supports image processing *filters*, allowing the objects within the drawing to be manipulated at the pixel level. Filter elements for blurs, color manipulation, and general convolution are available, and many of these effects can be animated declaratively.

- CSS can be used with SVG just as it is used with HTML: it can establish common sets of attribute values, or styles, for certain types or groups of elements. Like groups, CSS makes it easier to control the appearance of multiple elements without explicitly setting attributes for them individually.

As mentioned, the official SVG specification provides full details and many examples [W3C09b]. Other SVG tutorials, articles, and resources are also fairly easy to find on the Web.

1. Look up the `width`, `height`, and `viewBox` attributes of the top-level `svg` element. How are they related?

2. Is it possible to put a `div` element in an SVG drawing, or to put a `circle` element in an HTML document? Why or why not?

3. Read up on the SVG g element. In what ways is it similar to a `canvas` element's 2D rendering context? In what ways is it different?

9.6   3D Graphics with WebGL

In theory, 3D graphics algorithms sit squarely on top of 2D graphics technologies: they take 3D information and compute how this can be presented on a 2D display in a manner that our eyes and brains interpret as a 3D view. But while it is completely possible to implement these 3D algorithms in software alone, using a 2D pixel-level graphics technology such as the `canvas` element, the sheer computational scale and complexity of these algorithms make this approach impractical for general use. Still, it is worth mentioning that software-only 3D libraries in JavaScript have been implemented, if only as proofs of concept. One such project, OpenJSGL, implements some of the 3D fixed-function OpenGL pipeline in pure JavaScript, painting on a standard 2D `canvas` element [Bur08]. The functionality is accurate, but, because all calculations are done in JavaScript, performance is an issue for anything beyond the most rudimentary 3D programs.

The key to 3D graphics with JavaScript, then, is to connect JavaScript functions as directly as possible to the underlying graphics hardware. The technology that does this is WebGL. As its name implies, it connects web browsers to the OpenGL 3D graphics standard [Khr09]. This standard has widespread, well-established hardware support and is available on almost all modern platforms and devices, ranging from mobile and embedded devices all the way up to the most specialized graphics workstations and gaming consoles [Khr10].

This section presents and walks through a WebGL case study that you can run on any WebGL-capable browser. However, since 3D programming concepts and techniques are themselves way beyond the scope of this text, we focus primarily on how the program connects to HTML and JavaScript instead of the specific 3D code. Consider it a teaser; if you find yourself hooked, your next step would be to study computer graphics in general. The concepts are the same, regardless of the programming language. WebGL makes these technologies available to a web browser (and thus JavaScript) without the need for additional software or plug-ins.

9.6.1   WebGL Is the 3D `canvas`

As hinted at in Section 9.4.2, WebGL is implemented as the *3D* graphics rendering context for the `canvas` element. Thus, the first step in using WebGL is to create a `canvas` element within a web page. This step is identical to its 2D counterpart.

Once the `canvas` element is ready or retrieved (say, by `getElementById`), calling `getContext` with `"webgl"` as the parameter instead of `"2d"` returns the 3D WebGL rendering context:

```
var gl = canvas.getContext("webgl");
```

This rendering context is completely different from the 2D version, with totally different concepts and functions. In fact, programmers familiar with OpenGL will recognize the 3D rendering context better than programmers familiar with 2D `canvas` programming. Note the chosen name for the variable that holds the rendering context: `gl` is a nod to the OpenGL roots of WebGL.

What does remain similar to `canvas` in WebGL is event handling: mouse and other events are reported to the `canvas` element in exactly the same way as in 2D. Thus, assigning functions to `mousemove`, `mousedown`, and friends remains the same.

With this context in mind, let's look at a case study.

9.6.2   Case Study: The Sierpinski Gasket

We have chosen to render the 3D version of a fractal called the *Sierpinski gasket* for our WebGL case study. The rendering can be rotated in 3D and features a simple lighting model. The case study can be accessed at `http://javascript.cs.lmu.edu/webgl-sierpinski`; WebGL-enabled browsers should display something similar to Figure 9.21. If you are using an older web browser that does not support WebGL, you will immediately see a somewhat unceremonious `alert` dialog informing you of that fact.

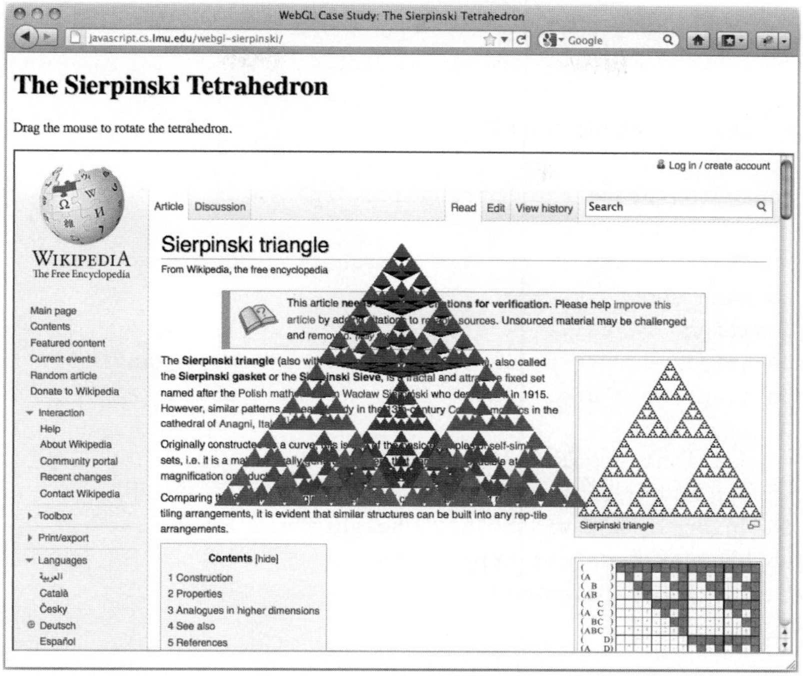

FIGURE 9.21

FIGURE 9.21

The 3D Sierpinski gasket, implemented using WebGL and rendered over the Wikipedia article about the Sierpinski triangle.

The HTML for this page is fairly straightforward, and we include it here in its entirety:

```
<!DOCTYPE HTML>
<html>
  <head>
    <meta charset="UTF-8"/>
    <title>WebGL Case Study: The Sierpinski Tetrahedron</title>
    <script src="matrix4x4.js"></script>
    <script src="sierpinski.js"></script>
    <script>
      window.onload = function () {
        // All of the action is in the startSierpinski function.
        startSierpinski(document.getElementById("sierpinski"));
      };
```

```
    </script>
  </head>
  <body>
    <h1>The Sierpinski Tetrahedron</h1>

    <p>Drag the mouse to rotate the tetrahedron.</p>

    <!-- Some HTML/CSS trickery to put the tetrahedron on top of the
         Wikipedia page about it. -->
    <div style="position: relative; width: 100%">
      <iframe src="http://en.wikipedia.org/wiki/Sierpinski_triangle"
        style="position: absolute; width: 100%; height: 600px;">
      </iframe>
      <div style="position: absolute; width: 100%; top: 5em;
                  text-align:center;">
        <canvas id="sierpinski" width="512" height="512">
          Your web browser does not support the
          <code>canvas</code> element! Sorry.
        </canvas>
      </div>
    </div>
  </body>
</html>
```

Note how, at this level, the page and code are identical to their 2D counterparts.
A `canvas` tag with an `id` of `sierpinski` defines the element, and this element is
retrieved from the DOM through `getElementById`. All other activities take place
in the `startSierpinski` function.

The `startSierpinski` function can be found in *sierpinski.js*. The other file
referenced by the web page, *matrix4x4.js*, is a Mozilla-authored script that defines
a number of useful 3D graphics utility functions. Because our focus here is on
JavaScript programming and not computer graphics theory, we will look primarily
at *sierpinski.js*.

The `startSierpinski` function has been written to accommodate a start-to-
end read-through as much as possible. It should be noted that "real-world" 3D
graphics code may not be as monolithic as `startSierpinski`, making use of a
wide variety of reusable utility scripts and supporting files.

The function begins with—surprise—a `getContext` call. A `null` 3D rendering
context triggers the error dialog regarding the web browser's (lack of) WebGL
support:

```
var startSierpinski = function (canvas) {

    // Grab the WebGL rendering context.
    var gl = canvas.getContext("webgl");
    if (!gl) {
        alert("No WebGL context found...sorry.");

        // No WebGL, no use going on...
        return;
    }
    ...
```

With the `gl` context in hand, the function then starts setting up the "scene." Here we see the first block of code that will be more recognizable to OpenGL programmers than to 2D `canvas` programmers:

```
gl.enable(gl.DEPTH_TEST);
gl.clearColor(0.0, 0.0, 0.0, 0.0);
gl.viewport(0, 0, canvas.width, canvas.height);
```

Note the arguments to the `clearColor` function call: in WebGL, this function sets the background color that will be used for any part of the 3D scene that is not occupied by an object. The color is expressed in RGBA format, with each component ranging from 0.0 to 1.0. As you might recall, the *A* in this format represents the *alpha channel* or transparency level. Setting the alpha channel of `clearColor` to 0.0 produces the "object-on-top" effect in the case study. The `canvas` element is still rectangular but is now invisible except where 3D objects are present.

Because we are not going into 3D in depth here, we will leave further specifics of these functions to a computer graphics or OpenGL programming text. We just wanted to throw some of this in so you can get a feel for how the API looks.

9.6.3 Defining the 3D Data

The next section of the program takes care of defining the gasket itself. The entry point to this functionality is the `divideTetrahedron` function:

```
var vertices = [];
var normals = [];
divideTetrahedron(vertices, normals,
    [ 0.0, 3.0 * Math.sqrt(6), 0.0 ],
    [ -2.0 * Math.sqrt(3), -Math.sqrt(6), -6.0],
    [ -2.0 * Math.sqrt(3), -Math.sqrt(6), 6.0 ],
    [ 4.0 * Math.sqrt(3), -Math.sqrt(6), 0.0 ],
    5);
```

Conceptually, the 3D Sierpinski gasket starts out as a tetrahedron (the four arrays that are passed as arguments in the preceding listing). This tetrahedron is then split into four tetrahedrons, consisting of the original four vertices and the six midpoints between these vertices. The new tetrahedrons are then split in the same way, and so on without a limit. We cannot do this ad infinitum, of course, so our code uses a depth value that states how many times the base tetrahedron should be split. In the preceding listing, this depth is 5.

Once divideTetrahedron is done, we will have the triangles that make up the gasket in the vertices variable and the *normal vectors* of these triangles in the normals variable. Because we are skipping the graphics theory, we will have to leave the normal vectors at that.

The 3D data must then be passed to the graphics card. This transfer activity is supported by a family of related functions that are made available by the 3D graphics context:

```
var vertexBuffer = gl.createBuffer();
gl.bindBuffer(gl.ARRAY_BUFFER, vertexBuffer);
gl.bufferData(gl.ARRAY_BUFFER, new Float32Array(vertices),
    gl.STATIC_DRAW);

var normalBuffer = gl.createBuffer();
gl.bindBuffer(gl.ARRAY_BUFFER, normalBuffer);
gl.bufferData(gl.ARRAY_BUFFER, new Float32Array(normals),
    gl.STATIC_DRAW);
```

Without going into computer graphics specifics, this listing allocates space in the graphics card for the 3D data (createBuffer) and then sends the JavaScript-built arrays to those buffers using bufferData. Float32Array is a support object that comes with WebGL and is used for passing native JavaScript data into the graphics hardware.

9.6.4   Shader Code

In OpenGL, the actual 3D graphics operations that are to be performed are specified in *shaders*—custom code that determines how a 3D object is displayed in its associated `canvas` element. Shaders are written in a specialized language called GLSL, short for *GL Shading Language*. The next major section of `startSierpinski` has to do with setting up these shaders, starting with their source code:

```
var vertexShaderSource =
    "#ifdef GL_ES\n" +
    "precision highp float;\n" +
    "#endif\n" +

    "attribute vec3 vertexPosition;" +
    "attribute vec3 normalVector;" +

    "uniform mat4 modelViewMatrix;" +
    "uniform mat4 projectionMatrix;" +
    "uniform mat4 normalMatrix;" +
    "uniform vec3 lightDirection;" +

    "varying float dotProduct;" +

    "void main(void) {" +
    "    gl_Position = projectionMatrix * modelViewMatrix *
        vec4(vertexPosition, 1.0);" +
    "    vec4 transformedNormal = normalMatrix * vec4(
        normalVector, 1.0);" +
    "    dotProduct = max(dot(transformedNormal.xyz,
        lightDirection), 0.0);" +
    "}";

var fragmentShaderSource =
    "#ifdef GL_ES\n" +
    "precision highp float;\n" +
    "#endif\n" +
```

```
"varying float dotProduct;" +

"void main(void) {" +
"    vec4 color = vec4(1.0, 0.0, 0.0, 1.0);" +
"    float attenuation = 1.0 - gl_FragCoord.z;" +
"    gl_FragColor = vec4(color.xyz * dotProduct * attenuation,
    color.a);" +
"}";
```

Note how the shaders themselves are just long strings—after all, they are also just computer programs, albeit somewhat specialized ones. In practice, the shader code is more strictly separated for easier maintenance.

The shader source strings are then processed by WebGL, and life goes on if no errors are encountered during that time. In another case of "connecting worlds," successful shader setup concludes with the definition of a number of variables that serve as "bridges" to the variables in the shader code:

```
gl.uniform3f(gl.getUniformLocation(shaderProgram, "lightDirection"),
    0, 1, 1);

var vertexPosition = gl.getAttribLocation(shaderProgram,
    "vertexPosition");
gl.enableVertexAttribArray(vertexPosition);
var normalVector = gl.getAttribLocation(shaderProgram, "normalVector");
gl.enableVertexAttribArray(normalVector);

var modelViewMatrixLocation = gl.getUniformLocation(shaderProgram,
    "modelViewMatrix"),
    projectionMatrixLocation = gl.getUniformLocation(shaderProgram,
    "projectionMatrix"),
    normalMatrixLocation = gl.getUniformLocation(shaderProgram,
    "normalMatrix");
```

The first line of this listing not only accesses a shader variable (`lightDirection`) via `getUniformLocation`, but also assigns the vector $\langle 0, 1, 1 \rangle$ to it using `uniform3f`. The remaining lines mostly store the "locations" of these variables in JavaScript.

9.6.5   Drawing the Scene

With the Sierpinski data calculated and loaded, the gasket can now be displayed on the `canvas` element. That's what the next section of code in *sierpinski.js* handles:

```javascript
var modelViewMatrix = new Matrix4x4(),
    projectionMatrix = new Matrix4x4();
    viewerLocation = { x: 0.0, y: 0, z: 20.0 },
    rotationAroundX = 0.0, rotationAroundY = -90.0;

var drawScene = function () {
    // Clear the display.
    gl.clear(gl.COLOR_BUFFER_BIT | gl.DEPTH_BUFFER_BIT);

    // Set up the viewing volume.
    projectionMatrix.loadIdentity();
    projectionMatrix.perspective(45, canvas.width / canvas.height,
      11.0, 100.0);

    // Set up the model-view matrix.
    modelViewMatrix.loadIdentity();
    modelViewMatrix.translate(-viewerLocation.x, -viewerLocation.y,
      -viewerLocation.z);
    modelViewMatrix.rotate(rotationAroundX, 1.0, 0.0, 0.0);
    modelViewMatrix.rotate(rotationAroundY, 0.0, 1.0, 0.0);

    // Set up the normal matrix.
    var normalMatrix = modelViewMatrix.copy();
    normalMatrix.invert();
    normalMatrix.transpose();
    gl.uniformMatrix4fv(normalMatrixLocation, gl.FALSE,
      new Float32Array(normalMatrix.elements));

    // Display the gasket.
    gl.bindBuffer(gl.ARRAY_BUFFER, vertexBuffer);
    gl.vertexAttribPointer(vertexPosition, 3, gl.FLOAT, false, 0, 0);
    gl.bindBuffer(gl.ARRAY_BUFFER, normalBuffer);
    gl.vertexAttribPointer(normalVector, 3, gl.FLOAT, false, 0, 0);
    gl.uniformMatrix4fv(modelViewMatrixLocation, gl.FALSE,
        new Float32Array(modelViewMatrix.elements));
```

```
    gl.uniformMatrix4fv(projectionMatrixLocation, gl.FALSE,
        new Float32Array(projectionMatrix.elements));
    gl.drawArrays(gl.TRIANGLES, 0, vertices.length / 3);

    // All done.
    gl.flush();
};
```

The main take-home of this section is the `drawScene` function, which does the actual displaying of the Sierpinski gasket. The variables outside of `drawScene` (`modelViewMatrix`, `projectionMatrix`, `viewerLocation`, `rotationAroundX`, and `rotationAroundY`) represent *shared state*, which is also accessed by event handler code.

9.6.6   Interactivity and Events

The last part of our case study's code deals with events. The program has a single interaction scenario: the user can drag the mouse within the 3D scene in order to see the Sierpinski gasket from all angles. All of the event handler code in the `startSierpinski` function supports this single scenario:

```
var xDragStart, yDragStart,
    xRotationStart, yRotationStart;
var cameraRotate = function (event) {
    rotationAroundX = xRotationStart + yDragStart - event.clientY;
    rotationAroundY = yRotationStart + xDragStart - event.clientX;
    drawScene();
};

canvas.onmousedown = function (event) {
    xDragStart = event.clientX;
    yDragStart = event.clientY;
    xRotationStart = rotationAroundX;
    yRotationStart = rotationAroundY;
    canvas.onmousemove = cameraRotate;
};

canvas.onmouseup = function (event) {
    canvas.onmousemove = null;
};
```

This segment adds event handlers for `mousedown` and `mouseup` events within the `canvas` element. The outline of a drag is as follows: when the mouse button is held down, its position is noted and a `mousemove` handler is then assigned to the `canvas`. The `mousemove` event handler is the `cameraRotate` function, and this function updates the current rotation according to the movement of the mouse. Upon updating the values, `cameraRotate` calls `drawScene` in order to refresh the display. Figure 9.22 illustrates the Sierpinski gasket after a typical rotation drag.

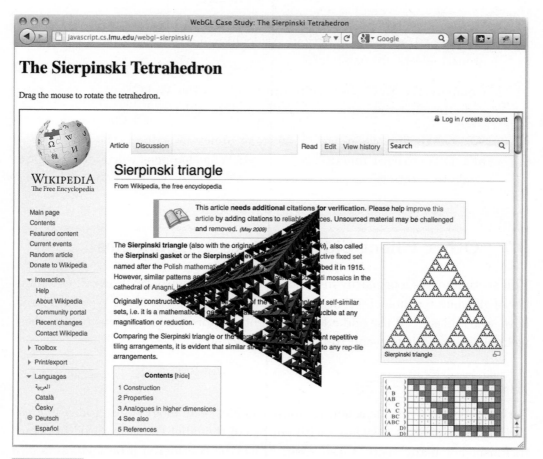

FIGURE 9.22

The 3D Sierpinski gasket, rotated.

With the event handlers set up and ready to go, the function ends with an initial rendering of the 3D scene. Note how, up to this point, *none of the preceding code has yet had a visible effect*:

```
drawScene();
```

With this function call, the Sierpinski gasket appears before the user for the first time and the `startSierpinski` function ends. Subsequent activities are now entered through the event handlers, and these handlers in turn call `drawScene` whenever the rotation angle changes.

Review and Practice

1. Download the case study files and experiment with the color that is passed into the `clearColor` function. Aside from invisibility, what other background effects are possible?

2. Compare the SVG case study drag code to the WebGL case study drag code. In what ways are they similar and/or different?

3. What happens when the `drawScene` function call at the end of the `startSierpinski` function is removed? What happens when an attempt is made to rotate the scene?

9.7   Other Client-Side Graphics Technologies

This section serves a primarily historical or contextual purpose: it describes a number of graphics technologies that, while not considered to be official Web standards, have seen widespread use and adoption. In other words, a lot of websites use these technologies, and it is useful to place them in context.

9.7.1   Flash

Perhaps the most prevalent nonstandard graphics technology in use today is *Flash* [Ado10]. Many might take issue with our use of the label "nonstandard" in regard to Flash. For many years, Flash could in fact be considered a de facto standard for web graphics and animation.

Architecturally, Flash is a web browser *plug-in*; it is a separate piece of software that registers itself with the web browser. HTML tags such as `<embed>` or `<object>` would then identify resources that are meant for display by Flash. Once downloaded by the browser, the data in these resources get sent to the Flash plug-in.

Categorically, Flash started as an object/vector-based animation package. Using separate Flash authoring software, content creators would define objects, shapes, and other components in a 2D, time-based "stage." Moving or changing these objects in different frames would define the desired animation, using *tweening* techniques that are very similar to those discussed in Section 9.3.4. At the conclusion of the authoring process, the original "Flash movie" or `.fla` file would be exported as a compressed, optimized `.swf` file. These are the files that web browsers would download and relay to the Flash plug-in.

As time and adoption progressed, Flash expanded to include other functionalities such as video playback and database access. The visual authoring tools were augmented with their own programming language, ActionScript, which, like JavaScript, is based on the ECMAScript standard. In many respects, the Flash plug-in has become a full-fledged, general-purpose program execution environment, contained within, yet distinctly separate from, the web browser's native HTML/ DOM, CSS, and JavaScript technologies.

9.7.2 Java

Not strictly a graphics technology, Java was an early candidate for general-purpose web browser programming, and its early popularity is in fact the reason that JavaScript is so named, despite its having very little resemblance or relationship to Java itself. The complete Java *platform* consists of its eponymous programming language, whose code is then compiled into a special *byte code* format that runs on a *virtual machine*—a software layer that abstracts out the actual computer hardware on which Java programs execute into a standardized, unified set of features and specifications [LY99]. This platform includes but is not restricted to pixel- and object-based graphics technologies, many of which, at the time, surpassed what web pages could do. For this reason, early attempts at generalized, web-based computer graphics applications turned to Java as the implementation base.

Earlier versions of HTML included an `applet` element, which provided information for loading Java code into a web browser. This code is written in the Java programming language, then compiled into the aforementioned byte code format. Web browsers would then pass this code into their own built-in Java virtual machines for execution.

While this mechanism sounds similar to the plug-in approach, it is important to note that Java was originally viewed as "in-the-box" web browser functionality, and not as a separately installed software package, similarly to how the JavaScript interpreter and host objects are included today. As Java waned in popularity, it stopped being an expected (non-plug-in) web browser feature and itself "moved out" as a plug-in, running as a "peer" to Flash and other plug-in technologies.

Java is primarily used today as a general-purpose but nonbrowser programming platform. It is used particularly frequently with server-side applications, taking on the computational and data access workload whose output eventually finds its way into web pages and applications.

9.7.3   VML

VML, which stands for *Vector Markup Language*, is functionally equivalent to SVG. It is mentioned here because, as of this writing, Microsoft's Internet Explorer web browser does not support SVG natively, but it does support VML.[6]

This SVG/VML schism may normally make web authors who wish to create cross-browser, object-based graphics throw up their arms in exasperation, if it weren't for a library called Raphaël [Bar10]. Raphaël "wraps" object-based graphics in JavaScript functions that transparently invoke SVG calls in standards-compliant web browsers and VML calls in Internet Explorer. Like jQuery, Raphaël stands as another example of effective library design that delivers genuine time (and headache) savings for web development.

Review and Practice

1. What is the difference between a plug-in and "built-in" web browser technology?

2. Would you consider JavaScript's name to be a misnomer? Why or why not?

---

[6]It is possible that, by the time you read this, Internet Explorer will have native support for SVG. Nevertheless, this section's discussion of Raphaël should remain of interest.

Chapter Summary

- The latest HTML and CSS web standards provide a wealth of visual options that used to require custom, prerendered image files: drop shadows, rounded borders, gradient fills, and much more.

- Time-based events, particularly as triggered by `setInterval`, plus well-planned, gradual changes to the data or properties that have visual effects, form the basis of computer animation in any technology.

- The `canvas` element is the standard web browser technology for creating graphics that require pixel-level control, and is ideal for manipulating or creating images of arbitrary content within the browser.

- SVG facilitates the creation of object-based graphics well suited for diagrams, schematics, or applications that require maximum smoothness or sharpness regardless of magnification or zoom level.

- WebGL adds 3D graphics to the `canvas` element, effectively connecting JavaScript programs to acceleration hardware that is necessary for adequate 3D performance.

- The common thread across these latest technologies is that they are "built in" to modern, standards-compliant browsers and are interoperable through JavaScript. Earlier technologies required additional software or plug-ins whose integration and interaction with web pages may have varied widely.

Exercises

1. Find an online color picker tool (`http://www.colorpicker.com/`, for example) and practice your color conversion skills. "Estimate" the RGB representations for the following colors, then use the color picker to see the actual RGB values:

   (a) Brown

   (b) Orange

(c) Purple

(d) Fuchsia

(e) Maroon

(f) Dark green

(g) Navy blue

(h) Gold

(i) Lavender

(j) Light gray

Most online color picker tools use the hexadecimal #rrggbb format, so be ready to express colors using that notation.

2. Use the same color tool from the previous exercise to convert from RGB to a color: visualize the colors specified by the following hexadecimal RGB representations, then enter them into the color picker to see how close you were to the actual color:

(a) #993300

(b) #FF9900

(c) #6600CC

(d) #CC33FF

(e) #990033

(f) #003300

(g) #000099

(h) #FFCC00

(i) #CCCCFF

(j) #F5F5F5

Don't worry if your "color sense" isn't too great—that's why color picker tools exist, after all!

3. State whether the following types of visuals are best represented as pixels or as objects/vectors:

(a) Bar graphs

(b) Faces

(c) Floor plans

(d) Street maps

(e) Terrain maps

(f) Clouds

(g) Circuit diagrams

(h) Planetary and satellite orbits

(i) Granite surfaces

(j) Mathematical functions

4. Write the CSS selector that specifies the following web page elements:

(a) The web page element whose `id` attribute is `header`

(b) The web page element whose `id` attribute is `sidebar`

(c) All `h1` elements in a page

(d) All `img` elements in a page

(e) All elements whose `class` attribute is `selected`

(f) All `p` elements within a `div` element

(g) All `span` or `label` elements

(h) All `input` elements

(i) `div` elements and elements whose `class` attribute is `block`

(j) Elements whose `class` attribute is `details` that are inside the element whose `id` attribute is `results`

5. The screenshot in Figure 9.23 displays three `div` elements with exactly the same `margin`, `padding`, and `border` CSS properties. Mark it up to show which areas make up the `div`s' border, content, margin, and padding.

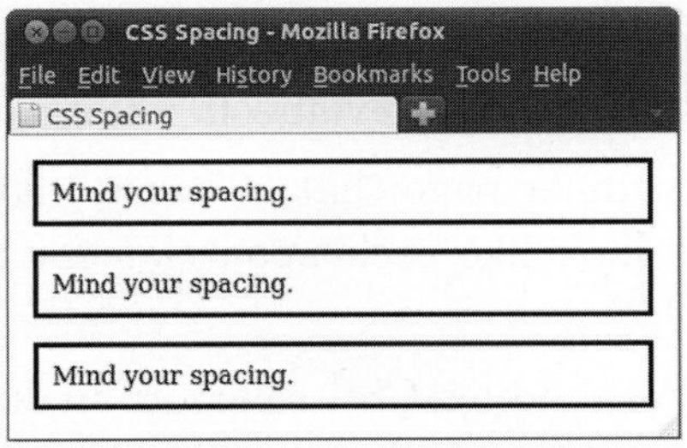

FIGURE 9.23

Three `div` elements, for Exercise 5.

6. The screenshot in Figure 9.24 displays nine **span** elements with different background, shadow, and border radius CSS properties. For each element:

   (a) Replicate the element's appearance as closely as possible using CSS style rules in an HTML file that you write yourself.

   (b) Write a program in the JavaScript runner page that makes the **footer div** element on that page look like the element.

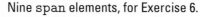

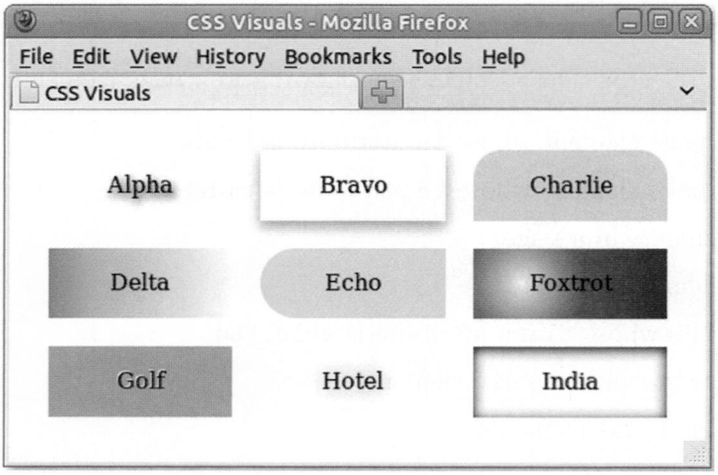

FIGURE 9.24

Nine **span** elements, for Exercise 6.

7. The screenshot in Figure 9.25 displays 15 **span** elements, each with some combination of 7 specific CSS properties and values.

   (a) Based on the figure, infer the seven CSS properties that are mixed and matched by each **span** element.

   (b) Replicate each **span** element's appearance as closely as possible using CSS style rules in an HTML file that you write yourself.

   (c) Write programs in the JavaScript runner page that, in turn, make the **footer div** element on that page look like each **span** element in the figure.

   (d) What HTML attribute (with corresponding CSS selector) makes the mixing and matching of visuals shown in this figure fairly easy to do?

FIGURE 9.25

Fifteen span elements, for Exercise 7.

8. Use some combination of spacing, border, and absolute positioning/sizing CSS properties to write HTML pages that display reasonable, if simplified, facsimiles of the following objects:

   (a) A telephone keypad

   (b) A piano keyboard (12 keys minimum)

   (c) A set of dominoes

   (d) The six individual faces of a die

   (e) A QWERTY keyboard

   (f) Your favorite console game controller (Don't worry about exactly matching button shapes; rectangles and rounded rectangles are okay for those.)

9. The Dutch painter Piet Mondrian is known for his distinct, geometric compositions, some of which are shown in Figure 9.26. Use some combination of background, spacing, border, and absolute positioning/sizing CSS properties to write HTML pages that resemble Mondrian's paintings.

FIGURE 9.26

A sample of works by Piet Mondrian.

10. The tic-tac-toe case study shown in Section 6.7 is essentially a simple HTML/CSS graphics display. Use the visual properties described in this section (and even others that are available but not explicitly mentioned here) to improve the aesthetic appearance of that program (e.g., colors, borders, drop shadows).

11. Make the following modifications to the bar chart case study in Section 9.2.5:

    ■ Add labeled axes with tick marks

    ■ Include a numeric display for each column (i.e., display the value of that column numerically as well as visually)

    ■ Separate common visual properties as CSS rules

12. Read up on the DOM and CSS manipulation capabilities of jQuery and re-implement the bar chart and Towers of Hanoi case studies (Sections 9.2.5 and 9.2.6, respectively) so they use jQuery's functions instead of the "raw" DOM. For example, the code fragment on page 485, plus some of its succeeding code from the case study, would now look like this:

```
var chart = $("<div></div>").css({
        position: "relative",
        borderBottomStyle: "solid",
        borderBottomWidth: "1px"
    });
```

After porting the two case studies, answer this question: given the choice, which approach/API do you prefer, and why?

13. Look up the rules of the Towers of Hanoi puzzle (Section 10.2.2 or on the Web) and enhance the Towers of Hanoi case study into a functioning version. You may either implement a drag-and-drop gesture for moving rings around or have the user click on a ring to move and then click on the destination tower (while enforcing the rules of the puzzle of course!). Finally, implement a win condition tester that pops up an alert and resets the puzzle once all the rings have moved to a new tower.

14. Implement a simple "box drawing program" web page using a combination of HTML, CSS, and JavaScript. When the user opens the page, he or she should be able to draw, move, and resize boxes within some designated drawing area. (*Tip:* Set the drawable area's `user-select` CSS property to `none` so that mouse drags are not interpreted as page selection actions. You may also look up and use the `cursor` CSS property to provide some feedback on what operation will be initiated if the user begins a mouse drag at the current location.)

15. If you have access to a touch event-capable web browser, implement a similar box drawing web page as in the previous exercise, but have it respond to touch events rather than to mouse events.

    To test your work, you may need to have a web server for hosting your touch-capable box drawing program, as some devices that have touch-capable web browsers cannot open web pages as local files.

16. If you have access to a multitouch event-capable web browser, enhance the touch-capable box drawing web page from the previous exercise so that multiple touches can operate on multiple boxes. That is, enable more than one box at a time to be drawn, moved, or resized, based on the placement and location of the user's fingers.

17. Download the `http://javascript.cs.lmu.edu/basicanimation` files and experiment with different values for the `millisecondsPerFrame` variable. For what values of `millisecondsPerFrame` do the animations start looking "jerky" or "stuttery"? Is there a point of diminishing returns where decreasing `millisecondsPerFrame` no longer makes a perceivable difference?

18. Download the `http://javascript.cs.lmu.edu/basicanimation` files and modify the constant velocity animation example so that the object moves diagonally instead of just horizontally.

19. Modify the constant velocity animation example so that the animated object appears to bounce within its containing element, similarly to 2D Pong games from the 1970s and 1980s.

20. Implement a tweening function that moves an object based on the *cube* of the elapsed time instead of the square. How would you characterize the resulting movement?

21. Many animation effects have such utility that the jQuery library "cans" them in easy-to-use functions such as `slideUp`, `slideDown`, `fadeIn`, and `fadeOut`. Implement your own workalike functions (without using jQuery, of course), with each of them taking the element to animate as a parameter:

```
var mySlideDown = function (element) {
        /* Your implementation here. */
    },

    mySlideUp = function (element) {
        /* Your implementation here. */
    },

    myFadeIn = function (element) {
        /* Your implementation here. */
    },

    myFadeOut = function (element) {
        /* Your implementation here. */
    };
```

(*Hint:* Yes, you may use the `http://javascript.cs.lmu.edu/basicanimation` files as a starting point.)

22. One of the optional parameters that the jQuery animation functions can accept is an easing function, precisely like the ones described in Section 9.3.4. However, the jQuery functions accept function *names* instead of the functions

themselves, thus limiting the possible choices to a fixed set like `"swing"` or `"linear"`.

Extend the workalikes you wrote in Exercise 21 so they accept *actual* easing functions. Use the function definition described in Section 9.3.4:

```
var myWorkalike = function (element, easingFunction) {
        // Your implementation here, where easingFunction
        // is called as follows:
        var position = easingFunction(currentTime, start,
                        distance, duration);
    };
```

Demonstrate the flexibility of your animation functions by calling them with inline easing function objects.

23. Because JavaScript animations happen concurrently by virtue of the `setInterval` function, program execution proceeds immediately, even while an animation is still going on. Sometimes this is not desirable; you may, for example, want something to happen only after some element has completely faded in or out.

To address this issue, the jQuery animation functions accept *callbacks*—functions that are called strictly *after* a particular animation has concluded. Extend your workalikes from Exercise 21 by having them accept optional callback functions as parameters:

```
// If you did the previous exercise, you may retain the
// easingFunction parameter here.
var myWorkalike = function (element, callbackFunction) {
        // Your implementation here, where callbackFunction
        // is called as follows once the animation concludes:
        callbackFunction();
    };
```

24. Add the following animation effects to the tic-tac-toe case study shown in Section 6.7:

   ■ "Fade-ins" for X's and O's as the player clicks on the grid

- "Fade-outs" for X's and O's as a new game is set up

- Any sort of "ending animation" (color changes, movement, etc.) upon the conclusion of a game

If you did any of the preceding animation-workalike exercises, you may use what you wrote there to make this exercise easier.

25. Write short JavaScript `canvas` programs that draw the following on a `canvas` element of your choosing. Exact dimensions, positions, and color values are up to you, as long as what you draw corresponds reasonably to the plain English descriptions:

   (a) A blue square at the center of the `canvas`

   (b) A black border surrounding the perimeter of the `canvas`

   (c) A 50% translucent red rectangle overlapping a 50% translucent green rectangle

   (d) An orange "X" whose lines span the upper-left to lower-right corners and lower-left to upper-right corners of the `canvas`, respectively

   (e) A solid brown hexagon

26. Write short JavaScript `canvas` programs that draw the following on a `canvas` element of your choosing. Exact dimensions, positions, and color values are up to you, as long as what you draw corresponds reasonably to the plain English descriptions:

   (a) A grid of lavender squares, one `canvas` pixel apart, filling the entire `canvas` (there is more than one approach to drawing this)

   (b) A "graph paper"-style grid consisting of light green lines that fills the entire canvas (again, there is more than one approach)

   (c) A honeycomb pattern at least three hexagons across and three hexagons down

   (d) A polka-dot pattern with pink dots on a brown background

   (e) A simplistic number "8" consisting of overlapping purple circles

27. Write short JavaScript `canvas` programs that draw the following objects on a `canvas` element of your choosing. Exact dimensions, positions, and color

values are up to you, as long as what you draw corresponds reasonably to the plain English descriptions:

(a) A "fake 3D" green wireframe cube at the bottom right of the `canvas`

(b) A "fake 3D" solid cube, with its three visible faces colored in varying shades of gray, at the top center of the `canvas`

(c) Reasonable facsimiles of a baseball, a golf ball, and a tennis ball, painted with gradients for a 3D effect

(d) A yellow smiley face with a radial gradient to give it a faux spherical effect

(e) A ringed planet, painted with gradients for a 3D effect

28. Write short JavaScript `canvas` programs that draw the following "scenes" on a `canvas` element of your choosing. Exact dimensions, positions, and color values are up to you, as long as what you draw corresponds reasonably to the plain English descriptions:

(a) A simple sunset scene, with a reddish sun setting into a green horizon under a gray-blue sky

(b) A similar sunset scene as part (a), but with the sun setting into a dark blue "ocean" horizon and with a partial reflection showing on the ocean surface

(c) A red "sphere" (i.e., a circle with a radial gradient) and the fake 3D solid cube from Exercise 27b, with recognizably shaped gray "shadows" underneath

(d) Two stick-figure people, one wearing a black hat and another with long hair

(e) A simple skyline scene, where black buildings with yellow-lit windows are set against a dark blue sky (*Tip:* Try using a loop that draws buildings with random sizes and window counts from left to right.)

29. Implement a simple pixel-based paint program web page using the `canvas` element. Allow the user to choose colors and brush sizes. Color and brush size selection may be implemented outside of the `canvas`, using buttons, drop-down menus, or other appropriate web page elements with corresponding event handlers.

30. If you have access to a touch event-capable web browser, implement a painting web page as in the previous exercise, but have it respond to touch events rather than mouse events.

31. If you have access to a multitouch event-capable web browser, enhance the touch-capable painting web page from the previous exercise so that multiple touches generate multiple simultaneous brush strokes, based on the placement and location of the user's fingers.

32. Gather up some photos of yourself, your family, or your friends, and arrange them into a photo collage on a `canvas` element. How does this approach to arranging and scaling images compare to using absolutely positioned `img` elements using HTML and CSS only?

33. Many 2D games rely on *sprites* for their displays. A sprite is a reusable image that is moved and drawn within a 2D game scene as needed. The images within the sprites themselves can be swapped out to simulate motion within the sprite, such as a character's legs while walking or a vehicle's turning wheels. The technique very closely resembles traditional cel animation.

    Find a library of emoticon images on the Web and use those images to implement an animated emoticon face on a `canvas` element. Emoticon image sets are ideal for this kind of work (without having to draw your own sprites) because they are similarly sized and come in large varieties. Remember that you can use *slices* or *subimages*, which will come in handy if an emoticon image set is provided as one large image file.

    Make sure you respect any copyrights or licenses for the images you find (i.e., don't post your assignment for public consumption unless you are allowed to do so).

34. Package and adapt the five JavaScript object-drawing programs that you implemented in Exercise 27 into reusable functions that behave well when used with transforms. Demonstrate your functions' reusability by repeatedly calling them from a program that makes interesting changes to the active `canvas` transformation, similarly to what was shown in Section 9.4.8.

35. The so-called *instance transformation* is a very prominent one in computer graphics. It enables the arbitrary positioning, orienting, and resizing of any

shape, all without distorting it. It is, in fact, a "combo" transformation consisting of a scaling, a rotation, and a translation, in that order.[7]

Implement an `instanceTransformation` function that can take any `canvas` graphics routine, represented as a function, and apply the instance transformation before drawing it, using a given scale factor, rotation angle, and (x, y) location:

```
var instanceTransformation = function (graphicsDrawingFunction,
        scale, rotation, xTranslation, yTranslation) {
    // Scale, then rotate, then translate...
    // ...then draw (i.e., call graphicsDrawingFunction).
    //
    // And remember to leave things as you found them!
};
```

Show that your implementation works correctly by drawing a "scene" using a series of `instanceTransformation` calls:

```
instanceTransformation(square, 2, Math.PI / 4, 10, 10);
instanceTransformation(circle, 1, 0, 50, 25);
instanceTransformation(square, 4, 0, 20, 40);
```

36. Rewrite the skyline scene you implemented in Exercise 28e so the entire skyline is drawn using repeated calls to a *single* `drawBuilding` function, with transformations doing the repositioning and resizing.

37. Take one of the sunset scenes you implemented in Exercise 28 and rewrite it so it presents an *animated* sunset: show the sun starting higher in the sky, and move it until it sinks below the horizon. For full effect, you may want to gradually change the color of the ground and the sky as the sun sets.

---

[7]Mathematically, the transformations are written right to left, yielding $M = TRS$, where M is the instance transformation, T is translation, R is rotation, and S is scaling. A computer graphics course will explain everything if you are interested.

38. Implement a `canvas`-based "eyes" program that draws two cartoon eyes with pupils that follow the mouse cursor within the `canvas` element. The pupils should move independently, resulting in cross-eyes when the cursor is between the two eyes.

    If this description isn't sufficiently clear, look up the *xeyes* program on the Internet.

39. Implement a `canvas`-based analog clock program. The clock should have a second hand and correspond to the computer's system time. Be creative with the clock's design and appearance—it's a graphics exercise after all!

40. Implement a `canvas`-based program that displays raindrops falling from top to bottom. Make sure they accelerate as they fall, the way real raindrops do (i.e., their velocity increases at a constant rate).

41. Make the raindrops program you wrote in Exercise 40 interactive: moving the mouse horizontally within the `canvas` element should change the size of the raindrops, while moving the mouse vertically should change the speed with which they fall.

42. Implement a `canvas`-based "hangman" program. While the cumulative "hangman" picture should most certainly be done within the `canvas` element, you might prefer to implement the interactive section, consisting of letter selection and the word-in-progress, with non-`canvas` HTML and CSS. This implementation choice is up to you.

    This chapter is about computer graphics after all, so feel free to exercise some creativity with your hangman scene. You don't have to limit yourself to stick figures and line drawings.

43. Write SVG-based versions of the visuals requested in Exercise 25 in two forms:

    (a) Declarative SVG tags and markup

    (b) Programmatic construction with JavaScript

    As before, exact dimensions, positions, and color values are up to you, as long as what you draw corresponds reasonably to the plain English descriptions.

44. Write SVG-based versions of the visuals requested in Exercise 26 using programmatic construction with JavaScript. As before, exact dimensions, positions, and color values are up to you, as long as what you draw corresponds reasonably to the plain English descriptions.

    Which of these visuals, if any, can also be directly declared using SVG tags and markup? Characterize the differences between the programmed and marked-up versions.

45. Write SVG-based versions of the objects requested in Exercise 27 in two forms:

    (a) Declarative SVG tags and markup
    (b) Programmatic construction with JavaScript

    As before, exact dimensions, positions, and color values are up to you, as long as what you draw corresponds reasonably to the plain English descriptions.

46. Write SVG-based versions of the visuals requested in Exercise 28 in two forms (note the sole exception):

    (a) Declarative SVG tags and markup (except for the skyline, 28e)
    (b) Programmatic construction with JavaScript

    As before, exact dimensions, positions, and color values are up to you, as long as what you draw corresponds reasonably to the plain English descriptions.

    How do the SVG markup versions of these visuals differ from their programmatically constructed JavaScript counterparts?

47. Implement an SVG-based analog clock program, functionally similar to the `canvas`-based clock from Exercise 39.

48. Implement an SVG-based raindrop program, functionally similar to the `canvas`-based version from Exercise 40.

49. Implement an SVG-based *interactive* raindrop program, functionally similar to the `canvas`-based version from Exercise 41.

50. Implement an SVG-based "hangman" program, functionally similar to the `canvas`-based version from Exercise 42. For the SVG version, it may be easier to also implement letter selection and word-in-progress within SVG, so take a second look at that if you opted for HTML elements in Exercise 42.

51. Modify the SVG case study's `.svg` file (Section 9.5.2) so it displays two editable curves. Are changes to the *curve-editor.js* script necessary? What would it take to modify the case study so it displays any particular number of Bézier curves?

52. The C *curve to* command of the `path` element can take more than two control points and vertices to produce a single curve with any number of twists and turns. Modify the SVG case study in Section 9.5.2 so it displays and edits a three-vertex, three-control point curve. What would it take to modify the case study so it displays and edits a curve with any particular number of vertices and control points?

53. Overall, what types of graphics applications are better served by a 2D `canvas` element? What graphics applications are best done with SVG?

54. Would you say that having WebGL "ride off" the `canvas` element is a good idea? Compare this design decision, for example, to one where a hypothetical, completely different `canvas3d` element is used for 3D graphics on a web page.

The remaining exercises all involve making modifications to the WebGL case study from Sections 9.6.2 to 9.6.6, available online at `http://javascript.cs.lmu.edu/webgl-sierpinski`. Download and copy its HTML and JavaScript source code to your computer prior to taking on the following tasks.

55. Modify the WebGL case study code so that, instead of the vanilla `alert` that pops up if a WebGL context could not be retrieved, a friendlier, less-disruptive element appears right within the page.

While this task does not particularly require WebGL, it does give you some practice with displaying useful feedback when unexpected situations take place. Make sure the element is prominent enough to be noticed but not too intrusive or intimidating. An explanation of the problem would be good; you can use the "three-point rule" for good error messages: state the error, state its most likely possible cause(s), and state possible courses of action for rectifying the error (e.g., "Please use a web browser that supports WebGL 3D graphics.").

Test your modified WebGL case study on a web browser that you know does *not* support WebGL, or, in the absence of such a browser, just program an artificial condition that makes the error message element appear.

56. Modify the WebGL case study code so the program displays a solid tetrahedron instead of the Sierpinski gasket. You may need to review Sections 9.6.2 to 9.6.6 to recall how the `divideTetrahedron` function works.

57. The WebGL `drawArrays` function is the function that finally triggers the actual display of the 3D object onto the `canvas` element. Its first argument, given in the WebGL case study code as `gl.TRIANGLES`, tells `drawArrays` to render every three vertices as a solid triangle.

    (a) Replace `gl.TRIANGLES` with `gl.LINES`. What appears on the web page instead?

    (b) Do some Internet research on the other values that `drawArrays` will accept for its drawing mode outside of `gl.TRIANGLES` and `gl.LINES`. Play with those values and rerun the Sierpinski gasket every time to see how it is drawn for each value.

58. This line in the `fragmentShaderSource` variable determines the color of the Sierpinski gasket:

```
vec4 color = vec4(1.0, 0.0, 0.0, 1.0);
```

    The color is given as an RGBA value with individual color components ranging from 0.0 to 1.0 (review Section 9.1.2 if needed). Modify the code so the drawn 3D object appears green.

59. Modify the WebGL case study code as shown here so the program directly assigns the `vertices` and `normals` variables and produces a 10×10 square that can be rotated in 3D:

```
var vertices = [
  -5, 5, 5, -5, 5, -5, -5, -5, -5, -5, -5, -5, -5, -5, 5, -5,
    5, 5
];

var normals = [
  -1, 0, 0, -1, 0, 0, -1, 0, 0, -1, 0, 0, -1, 0, 0, -1, 0, 0
];
```

The arrays are somewhat verbose because the WebGL case study expects the data to be given in terms of triangles. Thus, the "square" is really given as two triangles, one with vertices $(-5, 5, 5)$, $(-5, 5, -5)$, and $(-5, -5, -5)$, and another with vertices $(-5, -5, -5)$, $(-5, -5, 5)$, and $(-5, 5, 5)$. The triangle vertices are given in counterclockwise order with respect to the "fronts" of the triangles, which face the same direction as the negative x-axis, or the vector $\langle -1, 0, 0 \rangle$. For reasons we cannot explain now, this vector must be repeated once for every vertex of every triangle, and the `normals` array therefore repeats $\langle -1, 0, 0 \rangle$ six times.

(a) Verify that your modified copy of the WebGL case study code now draws the preceding square. You may delete the `divideTetrahedron` function entirely if you wish.

(b) Extrapolate these arrays so the program draws a $10 \times 10 \times 10$ *cube* that is centered on the origin. (*Tip:* Work things out on a piece of graph paper first.)

60. Assign `mouseover` and `mouseout` event handlers to the WebGL case study such that the WebGL `canvas` background becomes an opaque dark blue when the mouse hovers over it, then reverts to transparent when the mouse leaves. (*Hint:* Recall/review what was said about the WebGL context's `clearColor` property.)

CHAPTER 10

Advanced Topics

CHAPTER CONTENTS

Introduction

For this last chapter we present a collection of interesting and important topics in programming that we've not yet come across. Each topic is discussed in the context of JavaScript, but most are of a very general nature and applicable to programming in many other languages. We have chosen five topics: regular expressions, recursion, caching, MapReduce, and the dynamic creation of event handlers.

We have titled the chapter "Advanced Topics" not because these topics are difficult (at least, no more so than closures or asynchronous computation, which you've seen earlier) or usable only by skilled programmers, but because they add a great deal of power to your programming repertoire and should eventually be learned. By the end of this chapter, you will have a working knowledge of these five topics and be able to employ them in scripts of your own.

10.1   Regular Expressions

We can often recognize good programmers by the code they *don't* write in addition to the code they *do* write. In Section 4.3.4, we saw how you could avoid writing `if` and `switch` statements by using objects for value lookup. In Chapter 6, we saw how JavaScript's event mechanism freed you from having to write code to listen for and dispatch events. In these situations, you specified *what* you wanted or what you wanted to happen instead of *how* you got data or how you caused actions to occur. JavaScript, like most modern programming languages, has a feature that allows you to omit control code in another common situation: finding patterns within text.

10.1.1   Introducing Regular Expressions

A *regular expression*, or *regex*, is a pattern describing a set of strings. JavaScript regexes are delimited with slashes (`/.../`). We will begin with examples:

- `/dog|rat|cat/` matches any string containing "dog" or "rat" or "cat" because the "|" character means *or*.

- `/colou?r/` matches any string containing "color" or "colour" because the question mark means *optional*.

- `/go*gle/` matches any string containing "ggle," "gogle," "google," "goooogle," "gooooogle," and so on because the asterisk means *zero or more*. The plus sign is related; it means *one or more*: `/go+gle/` will not match "ggle," though it will match "gogle," "google," and so on.

- `/b[aeiou]b/` matches any string containing "bab," "beb," "bib," "bob," or "bub" because the square brackets mean *one of*.

- `/^Once/` matches any string *beginning with* "Once" (indicated by the caret).

- `/ss$/` matches any string *ending with* "ss" (indicated by the dollar sign).

- `/^dog$/` matches any string that begins and ends with "dog"; in other words, it matches *only* the string "dog."

- `/^[A-PR-Y0-9]{10}$/` matches only a string of 10 characters, each of which is an uppercase letter A through P or R through Y, or a decimal digit.

- `/^z{3,5}$/` matches "zzz," "zzzz," and "zzzzz" only.

- `/[^md5]+/` matches any string of one or more characters, each of which is not an "m," not a "d," and not a "5." The construct `[^...]` means a character other than those listed.

- `/\d+\D:\u262f/` matches any string containing one or more digits followed by a nondigit, a colon, and a yin yang symbol (U+262F). Specifically, `\d` (digit) is short for `[0-9]` and `\D` (nondigit) for `[^\d]`.

- `/i..d/` matches any four-character sequence starting with an "i" and ending with a "d." The dot (`.`) means any character except the line break (U+000A, or `\n`).

The `test` method on regexes will tell you whether or not a regex matches a string, returning `true` or `false`, while the `search` method on strings will return the position in the string of the first match (or `-1` if there's no match).

```
/\s+a\s+/.test("one   a day")      ⇒ true
/^[0-9]+/.test("U2 - War")         ⇒ false
"JavaScript".search(/[N-Z]/)       ⇒ 4
"Brendan".search(/[Ee]ich/)        ⇒ -1
```

Construct	Stands For
\u*hhhh*	The character with codepoint *hhhh*
\x*hh*	The character with codepoint *hh*
\t	The tab character; same as \u0009
\n	The linefeed character; same as \u000A
\v	The vertical tab character; same as \u000B
\f	The form feed character; same as \u000C
\r	The carriage return character; same as \u000D
\s	The same as [\t\n\v\f\r\u00A0\u2028\u2029]
\S	The same as [^\s]
\d	The same as [0-9]
\D	The same as [^\d]
\w	The same as [A-Za-z0-9_]
\W	The same as [^\w]

Table 10.1

A Selection of Regex Pattern Constructs

A \s (seen in the first regex example) matches any one of several *space characters*. Like \d and \D, it is one of several special constructs in the regex pattern language. Several of these are listed in Table 10.1.

Regexes can be used in the `split` and `replace` operations on strings:

```
"ladedada".split(/ad/)              ⇒  ["l","ed","a"]
"Lots   of    spaces".split(/\s+/)  ⇒  ["Lots","of","spaces"]
"Hello".replace(/[aeiou]/, "u")     ⇒  "Hullo"
"Aloha".replace(/^/, ">> ")         ⇒  ">> Aloha"
```

The second operation here splits a string across any sequence of one or more spaces; the third produces a string just like a given string with the first lowercase Latin vowel replaced with a u;[1] and the fourth produces a string like a given string, with ">> " at the beginning.

---

[1]Yes, you will see how to do a "replace all" operation later in this section.

1. List the strings matched by the regex /M(rs?|(is)?s)/.

2. Explain why s.replace(/$/, "!") produces the same result as s + "!".

10.1.2   Capture

The regex **test** and string **search** methods only tell you whether a match appears and where the match is, respectively, but will not tell you which portion of your text matched. For this, use the string **match** method or the regex **exec** method. These methods *capture* the portion of the string that matches your regex, as well as any pieces of it that you enclose in parentheses.

Here's an example. A United States postal code consists of five digits, followed by a dash and then four digits. The following script shows how we can capture each of the two parts of the zip code:

```
var usZipCode = /(\d{5})-(\d{4})/;
var address = "6233 Hollywood Blvd, Los Angeles, CA 90028-5310 USA";
var result = address.match(usZipCode);
alert(result.length + " matches");   // Alerts 3 matches
alert(result[0]);                     // Alerts 90028-5310
alert(result[1]);                     // Alerts 90028
alert(result[2]);                     // Alerts 5310
```

The **match** method returns an array whose first element (at index 0) contains the entire portion of the text that matched. The remaining items (at positions 1, 2, and so on) contain those parts of the matched text corresponding to the parenthesized portions of the regex. The capture at index k corresponds to the kth left parenthesis in the string. The following regex has six left parentheses, so the match result is an array indexed from 0 to 6:

```
var regex = /a(((bc)d(e))(f(gh)))i/;
var text = "abcdefghijk";
alert(text.match(regex).join(",")); // abcdefghi,bcdefgh,bcde,bc,e,fgh,
                                     // gh
```

For regex r and string s, the invocation r.exec(s) is virtually equivalent to s.match(r). Both return **null** if there is no match.

Capturing requires the regex engine to do a fair amount of work; this negatively impacts performance in those situations where parentheses are needed for grouping but not capture. For example, it is possible to write a United States postal code without the dash and final four digits. A regex that can match both forms is

```
\d{5}(-\d{4})?
```

Here the parentheses are required because *both* the dash and the four-digit suffix are in the scope of the optional part. But parentheses will cause the matcher to capture and remember this part if it exists—a relatively expensive operation. If you do not need to know this matched portion, you should use the *noncapturing* group expression, (?: ...), like so:

```
\d{5}(?:-\d{4})?
```

Review and Practice

1. Give a regex for 10-digit numbers that allows you to capture the first three digits.

2. For the regex /(\d{5})(?:-(\d{4}))?/, give the result match array after matching against (a) 90069 and (b) 90045-2659.

10.1.3   Quantifiers

The symbols ?, *, and + are known as *quantifiers* because they match a certain number of times:

- a? matches zero or one a,

- a* matches zero or more a's, and

- a+ matches one or more a's.

These quantifiers match *greedily*; that is, they match as many characters as possible. To match as few characters as possible—that is, to match *reluctantly*—use ??, *?, and +?:

$$"aaaaaah".match(/a+/) \Rightarrow "aaaaaa"$$
$$"aaaaaah".match(/a+?/) \Rightarrow "a"$$
$$"aaaaaah".match(/a*/) \Rightarrow "aaaaaa"$$
$$"aaaaaah".match(/a*?/) \Rightarrow ""$$
$$"aaaaaah".match(/a?/) \Rightarrow "a"$$
$$"aaaaaah".match(/a??/) \Rightarrow ""$$

Review and Practice

1. Evaluate the expressions

   (a) `"zooooom".match(/o+m/)` and

   (b) `"zooooom".match(/o+?m/)`.

   Explain any differences in the results.

2. Evaluate the expressions

   (a) `"<a><b></b></a>".match(/<.*>/)` and

   (b) `"<a><b></b></a>".match(/<.*?>/)`.

   Explain any differences in the results.

10.1.4 Backreferences

You can use the forms \1 through \9 to refer to the captured groups later in the regex itself. This requires an example:

```
var regex = /(\S+)\s+\1/;
var text ="I think that that was okay";
alert(text.match(regex)[0]);    // Alerts that that.
```

The \1 refers to whatever was matched by the \S+. So our regex defines a pattern composed of one or more nonspace characters, followed by one or more space characters, followed by exactly the same sequence of nonspace characters found earlier. That is, it finds repeated words.

Review and Practice

1. What does the regex /(.)(.)\2\1/ describe? Give examples of strings that it matches.

2. Describe the meaning of the regex /<[A-Za-z]+>[^<]*<\/\1>/.

10.1.5   Regex Modifiers

You can attach *modifiers* to a regex to change its behavior. JavaScript has three such modifiers:

1. i (meaning `ignoreCase`)

2. g (meaning `global`)

3. m (meaning `multiline`)

The following example repeatedly prompts the user to enter either "truth" or "dare," using the i modifier to match any combination of uppercase or lowercase letters (e.g., "trUTh," "DarE"):

```
while (!prompt("Truth or dare?").match(/^(truth|dare)$/i)) {
    alert('Just "truth" or "dare" please.');
}
alert("Thanks --- interesting choice!");
```

The g modifier makes a regex apply globally—that is, everywhere it matches. Here's an example that shows the effect of this modifier on the **replace** operation.

Without **g**, only the first match is replaced; with **g**, all matches are:

```
"Rascally rabbit".replace(/[LlRr]/, "w")    ⇒    "wascally rabbit"
"Rascally rabbit".replace(/[LlRr]/g, "w")   ⇒    "wascawwy wabbit"

"Aloha Nui".replace(/[aeiou]/g, "*")        ⇒    "Al*h* N**"
"Lots   of     spaces".replace(/\s+/g, " ") ⇒    "Lots of spaces"
"(800) 555-1212".replace(/\D/g, "")         ⇒    "8005551212"
```

Modifiers can also be combined:

```
"Rascally rabbit".replace(/[LR]/gi, "w")  ⇒  "wascawwy wabbit"
```

The **m** modifier changes the behavior of the ^ and $ markers. Normally these match the beginning and ending of an entire string, respectively. But with **m**, these *also* match just after and just before line breaks. We will leave you with an example:

```
"pig\npup\nrap\npot".replace(/^p/g, "b")   ⇒   "big\npup\nrap\npot"
"pig\npup\nrap\npot".replace(/^p/gm, "b")  ⇒   "big\nbup\nrap\nbot"
```

Review and Practice

1. Write a regex that means exactly the same as `/truth|dare/i` without using the **i** modifier.

2. Write an expression (containing a regex) that replaces all w's with v's and all v's with w's.

10.1.6   The RegExp Constructor

The notation `/.../` is shorthand for **new RegExp("...")**.[2] The explicit **RegExp** constructor is required when the pattern depends on data not known until the script is running. Here we are turning some user input into a pattern to use later:

---

[2]We should say "very nearly shorthand for," because within the double quotes that define a string, you would have to escape certain characters that you can write plainly inside the slashes with the `/.../` notation.

```
var name = prompt("What's your name?");
var pattern = new RegExp("^" + name + "$");
```

Review and Practice

1. Why, in the example in this section, would defining the pattern as /^name$/ be wrong?

2. Does the expression RegExp.prototype.isPrototypeOf(/abc/) evaluate to true or false? Why?

10.1.7   More on Regular Expressions

This completes our brief tour of regex support in JavaScript. We have not covered everything there is to know by any means—you will eventually want to familiarize yourself with a complete reference, such as https://developer.mozilla.org/en/JavaScript/Guide/Regular_Expressions or the ECMAScript reference itself—but we hope we have managed to give you an idea of what regexes can do. The exercises at the end of the chapter will give you some opportunities to use additional regex concepts, such as lookahead.

Taking the time to learn regular expressions will pay dividends; you might find yourself turning 100 lines of text processing code into less than 10. Like all programming constructs, though, regexes can be both used and abused. There are ways of writing regular expressions for which matching is terribly slow. Regex performance is beyond the scope of this text, but good references on this topic do exist.

10.2   Recursion

We now turn to a programming technique you may sometimes find very hard to live without—recursion.

FIGURE 10.1

A recursive figure.

10.2.1 What Is Recursion?

Generally speaking, *recursion* occurs when something refers to, or is composed of, "smaller" copies of itself, such as the triangle in Figure 10.1. This triangle is made up of three copies of itself, each scaled by a factor of 0.5 in both the x and y directions.[3]

In addition to recursive figures, you will often see

- *recursive definitions*, in which a term is used in its own definition;

- *recursive datatypes*, in which the instances of a datatype have fields of the type itself; and

- *recursive functions*, in which the body of a function contains a call (or calls) to itself.

---

[3]The recursive definition of this shape means it is something more than a (one-dimensional) curve but something less than a (two-dimensional) surface; in fact, this particular figure has dimension $\ln 3 / \ln 2 \approx 1.5849625$.

A recursive definition is not the same as a circular definition. The latter is useless because it defines a term exactly as itself, such as

A *quux* is a quux.

A proper recursive definition, on the other hand, has at least one part (called a *basis*) that does not rely on self-reference, in addition to a part that builds on previously defined objects. The basis provides a starting point for building up the (often infinite) set of items that satisfy the definition. Here are some examples:

A *natural number* is either 0 or the successor of a natural number.

A *palindrome* is either a string of length 0, a string of length 1, or a string of the form *cpc* where *c* is a character and *p* is a palindrome.

A *descendant* of a person *p* is either a child of *p* or a descendant of a child of *p*.

In computer science, and programming, recursive datatypes and recursive functions are quite common. We would like to start with a realistic example, but it pays to start simple. We will start with the classics.

Review and Practice

1. In each of the preceding recursive definitions, identify the basis.

2. Give a recursive definition for an arithmetic expression involving integers, addition, multiplication, subtraction, and division. Allow parentheses, too.

10.2.2   Classic Examples of Recursion

Factorial

One of the iconic examples of recursion in the world of computer science is the *factorial* function. The factorial of a positive integer is computed like so:

$$factorial(n) = 1 \times 2 \times 3 \times \cdots \times (n-1) \times n$$

while the factorial of any nonpositive integer is just 1. Now notice:

$$factorial(n) = \underbrace{1 \times 2 \times 3 \times \cdots \times (n-1)}_{factorial(n-1)} \times n$$

so

$$factorial(n) = \begin{cases} 1, & \text{if } x \leq 1, \\ factorial(n-1) \times n, & \text{otherwise.} \end{cases}$$

In JavaScript we can write this as:

```
/*
 * Returns the factorial of n.  Precondition: n is a nonnegative
 * integer.
 */
var factorial = function (n) {
    return n <= 1 ? 1 : factorial(n-1) * n;
};
```

This is a proper, noncircular recursive function. It has a basis—a way to return a value without a recursive call—and it makes recursive calls with arguments that show progress toward the basis.

The recursive definition of this function is shorter than the alternative approach that uses a **for** loop, a loop variable, and a variable to hold the ultimate answer; however, it is much less efficient. Look at the amount of work it has to do:

$$
\begin{aligned}
factorial(4) &= factorial(3) \times 4 \\
&= factorial(2) \times 3 \times 4 \\
&= factorial(1) \times 2 \times 3 \times 4 \\
&= 1 \times 2 \times 3 \times 4 \\
&= 2 \times 3 \times 4 \\
&= 6 \times 4 \\
&= 24
\end{aligned}
$$

Function calls are not cheap. For this function, stick with the simpler iterative version.

Review and Practice

1. Write a nonrecursive version of the factorial function.

2. Suppose your friend, while writing the recursive factorial function, wrote the body like this:

   ```
   return n <= 1 ? 1 : factorial(n) * n;
   ```

   What happens when you call `factorial(4)`? Why? What property of proper recursive functions is violated here?

Greatest Common Divisor

Modern cryptography relies heavily on several mathematical functions. One of these, the *greatest common divisor* (GCD) of two integers a and b, is the largest positive integer that evenly divides both a and b (see Figure 10.2). How do we write this function?

The direct approach is to first ensure b is smaller than a (by swapping their values if necessary), then checking

1. Does b evenly divide a and b?

2. Does $b - 1$ evenly divide a and b?

3. Does $b - 2$ evenly divide a and b?

and so on, down to 1. As soon as you get a yes answer, you're done. But this approach only works for relatively small numbers, because it takes only "one step at a time." If you run this algorithm on the values five quadrillion and five quadrillion

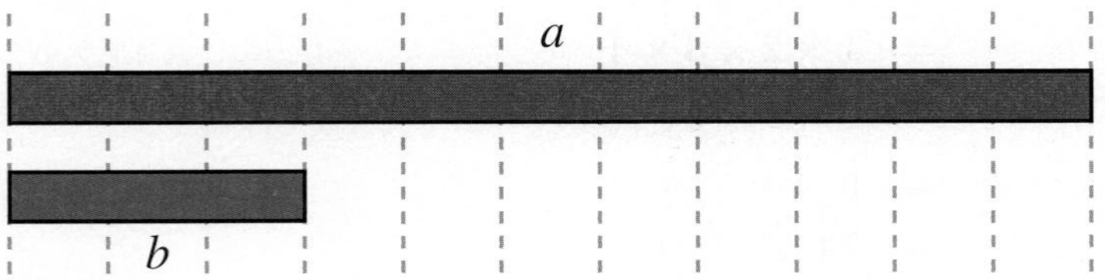

FIGURE 10.2

The GCD of a and b evenly divides both a and b.

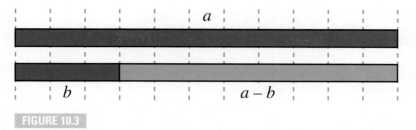

FIGURE 10.3

The GCD of a and b is the same as the GCD of b and $a - b$.

and one, you will never see it finish (at least not on an ordinary computer). How about a more clever algorithm?

Figure 10.3 shows us that a better algorithm does exist. In order for a value to evenly divide both a and b, it must also evenly divide $a - b$. In fact, the problem of computing $gcd(a, b)$, where $a > b$, can be reduced to computing $gcd(a - b, b)$. (The figure should suggest the truth of this fact to you, but if you are skeptical, consult a mathematics text for a proof.) Notice that if $b > a$ this same idea applies: you reduce $gcd(a, b)$ to $gcd(a, b - a)$. What if $a = b$? That's easy—the gcd is a (or b). And look at that! This is the basis of our recursion. Here is the JavaScript implementation:

```
/*
 * Returns the greatest common denominator of a and b. Precondition:
 * a and b are both nonnegative integers.
 */
var gcd = function (a, b) {
    if (a === b) {
        return a;
    } else if (a < b) {
        return gcd(a, b-a);
    } else {
        return gcd(a-b, b);
    }
};
```

If you prefer conditional expressions, you can do a *one-liner*:

```
/*
 * Returns the greatest common denominator of a and b. Precondition:
 * a and b are both nonnegative integers.
 */
var gcd = function (a, b) {
    return a === b ? a : a < b ? gcd(a, b-a) : gcd(b, a-b);
};
```

Let's see this improved algorithm in action:

$$
\begin{aligned}
gcd(140, 21) &= gcd(119, 21) \\
&= gcd(98, 21) \\
&= gcd(77, 21) \\
&= gcd(56, 21) \\
&= gcd(35, 21) \\
&= gcd(14, 21) \\
&= gcd(14, 7) \\
&= gcd(7, 7) \\
&= 7
\end{aligned}
$$

That's a little better. We are going down in steps of 7, rather than 1, but do you notice how we kept subtracting 21 over and over? Can we improve on this? Yes, and Figure 10.4 shows how. For a value to divide both a and b, with $a > b$, it has to also evenly divide the remainder of $a \div b$, namely $a \bmod b$ (because it evenly divides *all* the b's). So, $gcd(a, b) = gcd(b, a \bmod b)$ when $a > b$.

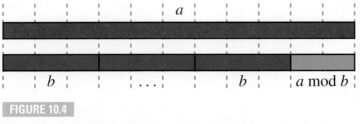

FIGURE 10.4

The GCD of a and b is the same as the GCD of b and $a \bmod b$.

Let's work out how this will go:

$$
\begin{aligned}
gcd(140, 21) &= gcd(21, 7) \\
&= gcd(7, 0) \\
&= 7
\end{aligned}
$$

Wow! We got down to an answer much quicker. And we uncovered what the basis of the recursion should be. When we take the remainder of $a \div b$, a value of 0 means that b evenly divides a. So if b gets to 0, our answer is a:

```
/*
 * Returns the greatest common denominator of a and b. Precondition:
 * a and b are both nonnegative integers.
 */
var gcd = function (a, b) {
    return b === 0 ? a : gcd(b, a % b);
};
```

Wait—what if $a < b$? The function still works! Here's a concrete example that should convince you:

$$
\begin{aligned}
gcd(21, 140) &= gcd(140, 21 \bmod 140) \\
&= gcd(140, 21)
\end{aligned}
$$

When $a < b$, the first recursive step swaps the arguments. That's a rather nice surprise.

In the end-of-chapter exercises, you will have several opportunities to explore the performance of this modulo-based algorithm relative to the two previous algorithms.

As an aside, you might like to know that this algorithm has been around for quite a while. It is called the Euclidean algorithm after Euclid of Alexandria ($E\upsilon\kappa\lambda\epsilon\acute{\iota}\delta\eta\varsigma$), who described it in his famous work *Elements*, written around 300 BCE, although it is quite likely others before Euclid used it as well.

Review and Practice

1. Give the derivation of $gcd(25, 2)$ under each of the three algorithms (trying all divisors, subtraction-based, and modulo-based) in this section.

2. Perform the derivation of $gcd(1, 30)$ under each of the three algorithms in this section.

Towers of Hanoi

Among the top 10 quintessential computer science memes, right up there with the powers of two and the Fibonacci numbers, is the Towers of Hanoi. In Figure 10.5 a player is moving six discs from the left stack to the right stack, using the middle stack for storage. The rules of the game prohibit small discs from ever going on top of large discs.

We can write a script to play the game quite easily—if we employ recursion. Think about how you would move 6 discs from the left stack to the right stack. First you would move the top 5 discs from the left stack to the center stack, then move the bottom disc all the way to the right, then move the 5 discs from the center to the right. See Figure 10.6. How do you move 5? By first moving 4 discs. And to move 4, you must first move 3. You need to remember to not recurse when you are down to zero.

In general, moving n discs from stack A to stack B requires first moving $n - 1$ to the temporary stack (let's call it C), then the bottom disc from A to B, and

FIGURE 10.5
Playing the Towers of Hanoi game.

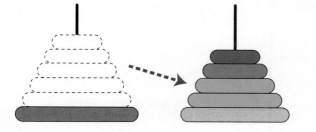
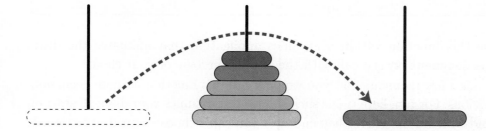
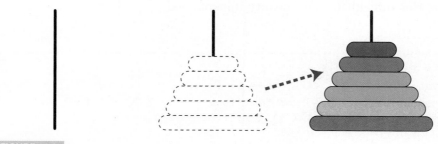

FIGURE 10.6

Steps in the Towers of Hanoi game.

finally the stack of $n - 1$ from C to B. The function is a direct translation of this rule—though of course we have to include a basis to make sure the function can finish:

```
/*
 * Displays HTML instructions for moving n disks from tower a
 * to tower b using tower c as the temporary holding place.
 * Precondition: n is an integer, and a, b, and c are distinct
 * strings.
 */
var hanoi = function (n, a, b, c) {
    if (n !== 0) {
        hanoi(n - 1, a, c, b);
        document.write("Move from " + a + " to " + b + "<br />");
        hanoi(n - 1, c, b, a);
    }
};
```

To use this function within a graphics application that animates the discs, replace the `document.write` call with the animation logic of your choice.

Think for a few moments how you would write this function without recursion. It's not obvious. For fun, here is one such solution. It assumes your discs all start on tower 0 and will end up where they end up—you can't choose your destination. It employs the little-used shift, binary conjunction, and binary disjunction operators. We will leave this difficult-to-read beauty unexplained.

```
var hanoi = function (n) {
    for (var t = 1; t < 1 << n; t += 1) {
        document.write("Move from " + ((t & t - 1) % 3) + " to " +
            (((t | t - 1) + 1) % 3) + "<br />");
    }
};
```

Binary Search

If you have ever used a paper phone book, you know that it is pretty easy to find a phone number given a name, but to find the name for a given phone number is not worth your time. Because the phone book is sorted by name, you can search for a certain name n by first opening the book to the middle; if the name you see there is n, you are done. If it is alphabetically greater than n, you search (recursively!) the first half; otherwise you search the latter half. This is called *binary search* because at each "step" you reduce the search problem to that of searching one of two halves of the original list.

Let's see this idea in action searching a JavaScript array. Figure 10.7 shows the steps taken in finding the value 42 in an array. Each step searches the range $[m, n)$ (that is, m inclusive to n exclusive) by looking first at the midpoint $\lfloor (m + n)/2 \rfloor$. Here's the code (note the precondition):

```
/*
 * Returns an index position of the value x in the array a,
 * or -1 if x is not in a. Precondition: array a is sorted.
 */
var binarySearch = function (a, x) {

    /*
     * Returns an index position of the value x in the array a
     * between the index first (inclusive) and last (exclusive).
     */
    var search = function (first, last) {
        // Basis: if your range is empty, you haven't found it
        if (first >= last) {
            return -1;
```

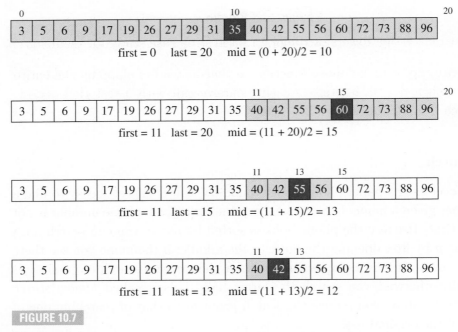

FIGURE 10.7

Binary search.

```
    }

    // Find the midpoint and recurse if necessary
    var mid = Math.floor((first + last) / 2);
    if (a[mid] === x) {
        return mid;
    } else if (a[mid] < x) {
        return search(mid + 1, last);
    } else {
        return search(first, mid);
    }
};

// Searches for x in the whole of a.
return search(0, a.length);
}
```

This function turned out to be a little bit long, and there's no way you should use code like this without a unit test. Tests need to cover the cases where the values are present and not present for all kinds of different reasons. Here's the QUnit test script we used:

```
$(document).ready(function () {

    module("Binary Search");

    // Test empty array
    test("Empty array", function () {
        ok(binarySearch([], 100) === -1);
    });

    // Test one-element array
    test("One-element array", function () {
        ok(binarySearch([5], 5) === 0);
        ok(binarySearch([5], 8) === -1);
    });

    // Tests that all values, in every position, can be found, and that
    // we get -1 for values below, in between, and above all positions.
    test("Larger array", function () {
        var a = [0, 10, 20, 30, 40, 50, 60, 70, 80, 90, 100];
        for (var i = 0; i < a.length; i += 1) {
            ok(binarySearch(a, a[i]) === i, "Found " + a[i]);
        }
        for (var x = -5; x <= 105; x += 10) {
            ok(binarySearch(a, x) === -1, x + " should be missing");
        }
    });
});
```

Review and Practice

1. Give a trace for the array in Figure 10.7 that shows how the value 63 is not found during a binary search.

2. What is the maximum number of recursive calls taken when performing a binary search on an array of size 1000?

10.2.3   Recursion and Family Trees

We will now look at examples for which recursion leads to solutions that are far simpler than their iterative counterparts and arguably as efficient. We will create family trees, defining people with objects. Each person will have a name, a mother, and a father. In real life, people would also have birthdays, identification numbers, and other properties, but these will just get in the way of showing off recursion. Let's introduce our new type with a constructor:

```
var Person = function (name, mother, father) {
    this.name = name;
    this.mother = mother;
    this.father = father;
}
```

Figure 10.8 shows an example family. Note the convention of using `null` to indicate the unknown. Now, let's write a function to determine whether or not one person is an ancestor of another. We would start like so:

```
var Person.prototye.isAncestorOf = function (p) {
    // ... Code goes here ...
}
```

What's next? Many beginning programmers might jump right in to writing a loop. They might first check p's mother, then p's mother's mother, then p's mother's mother's mother, and so on, but then realize they have to check fathers as well. They would quickly find out this isn't a matter of writing one mother loop and one father loop; there are many, many "paths" to consider. How can we possibly navigate around a tree like this?

This is where a recursive definition of ancestry comes to the rescue:

q is an **ancestor** of p if and only if q is p's mother or p's father or an ancestor of p's mother or an ancestor of p's father.

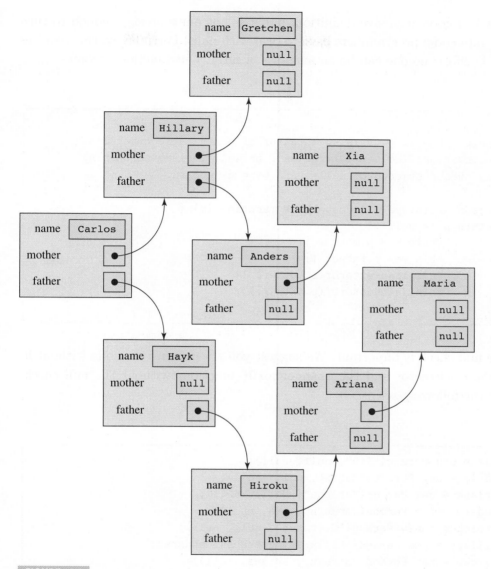

FIGURE 10.8

A family tree of objects.

This is a good recursive definition, but it is not quite precise enough to turn directly into code: programmers have to deal with nulls! Fortunately, this requires very little effort: no one can be an ancestor of **null**. Our function becomes:

```
/*
 * Returns true if this is an ancestor of p and false otherwise.
 * Precondition: The family tree must be well formed, containing
 * only person objects or nulls, and with no cycles.
 */
var Person.prototype.isAncestorOf = function (p) {
    return p != null &&
            (this === p.mother ||
            this === p.father ||
            this.isAncestorOf(p.mother) ||
            this.isAncestorOf(p.father));
}
```

The null check is important. We suggest you try running the code without it. Enter the constructor and the **isAncestorOf** function (without the null check) and try the following script:

```
var xia = new Person("Xia", null, null);
var maria = new Person("Maria", null, null);
var ariana = new Person("Ariana", Maria, null);
var anders = new Person("Anders", xia, null);
var gretchen = new Person("Gretchen", null, null);
var hillary = new Person("Hillary", gretchen, anders);
var hiroku = new Person("Hiroku", ariana, null);
var hayk = new Person("Hayk", null, hiroku);
var carlos = new Person("Carlos", hillary, hayk);
alert(ariana.isAncestorOf(hillary));
```

Add the null check back in and you should see the script alert **false**.

Review and Practice

1. Why would you expect the ancestor function to be difficult to write without recursion?

2. What happens when you implement the ancestor function without the null check and call it with two people for whom you expect the function to return false?

3. One way to violate the precondition of the ancestor function is to create a "cycle," say, by making someone his or her own grandparent. What would you expect the function to do in this case?

10.2.4   When Not to Use Recursion

Sometimes writing recursive functions results in much cleaner and much shorter code than equivalent nonrecursive functions. (Try writing ancestor and descendant functions on family trees without it!) But sometimes, recursive formulations are wasteful. We have already seen that the recursive version of factorial required more computational work than its iterative counterpart. However, there's a case when this extra work is extreme. Recall the Fibonacci sequence we saw earlier in the text. The first two values are 0 and 1, and each remaining value is the sum of the previous two:

$$0, 1, 1, 2, 3, 5, 8, 13, 21, 34, 55, 89, 144, 233, \ldots$$

A recursive function to find the kth Fibonacci value (we will index from 0) is:

$$fib(k) = \begin{cases} k, & \text{if } x = 0 \text{ or } x = 1, \\ fib(k-2) + fib(k-1), & \text{otherwise.} \end{cases}$$

Translated directly to JavaScript we have:

```
/*
 * EVIL function to compute the kth Fibonacci number.  Precondition: k
 * is a nonnegative integer less than 75. (Beyond the 75th Fibonacci
 * number, the values are outside the range of contiguous integers
```

```
 * JavaScript can represent exactly.
 */
var fib = function (k) {
    return (k <= 1) ? k : fib(k - 1) + fib(k - 2);
}
```

Why is this evil? Let's trace the actions of the JavaScript engine as it evaluates `fib(5)`:

```
fib(5) = fib(4) + fib(3)
       = fib(3) + fib(2) + fib(3)
       = fib(2) + fib(1) + fib(2) + fib(3)
       = fib(1) + fib(0) + fib(1) + fib(2) + fib(3)
       = 1 + fib(0) + fib(1) + fib(2) + fib(3)
       = 1 + 0 + fib(1) + fib(2) + fib(3)
       = 1 + 1 + fib(2) + fib(3)
       = 2 + fib(1) + fib(0) + fib(3)
       = 2 + 1 + fib(0) + fib(3)
       = 3 + 0 + fib(3)
       = 3 + fib(2) + fib(1)
       = 3 + fib(1) + fib(0) + fib(1)
       = 3 + 1 + fib(0) + fib(1)
       = 4 + 0 + fib(1)
       = 4 + 1
       = 5
```

Computing the value of `fib(5)` requires 15 function calls! But it gets worse: computing `fib(10)` takes 177 calls, `fib(20)` takes 21,891 calls, `fib(30)` takes two and a half million calls, and `fib(50)` requires over 40 billion. If you enter the preceding script into a shell and try to compute `fib(70)`, your browser will either crash or show an alert box saying "a script is taking too long."

The problem, which you can see from this derivation, is that many of these calls are redundant. In calling `fib(5)`, we also call `fib(4)` once, `fib(3)` twice, `fib(2)` three times, `fib(1)` five times, and `fib(0)` three times. In the next section, we will see a way to call the function for each argument only once. Alternatively, you can just use plain old iteration (though it won't be a one-liner anymore!):

```
/*
 * Returns the kth Fibonacci number.  Precondition: k is a
 * nonnegative integer less than 75.
 */
var fib = function (k) {
    if (k <= 1) {
        return k;
    }
    var a = 0;
    var b = 1;
    for (var i = 2; i <= k; i += 1) {
        var old_a = a;
        a = b;
        b = old_a + b;
    }
    return b;
}
```

Review and Practice

1. The computation of `fib(50)` with the evil function requires 40,730,022,147 calls. If a certain JavaScript engine could execute 1 million calls per second, how long would it take for this computation to complete?

2. Implement and run the evil Fibonacci function with an argument of 70. Try it on various browsers. What happens?

10.3   Caching

A good rule of thumb in designing efficient programs is if you have just performed a nontrivial computation, and the same computation is likely to be requested later, then save your result (in a variable, most likely). The next time the computation is requested, just return the saved result. We call the storage for this already-computed data a *cache*.

What kinds of things can we cache? Function results make good examples.[4]

---

[4]Sometimes you will see the term "memoization" used when a function is set up to use a cache for its previously computed results.

Where can we cache function results? Since, functions are objects, why not make the cache a property of the function object? Here's a prime number function with a cache:

```
/*
 * Determines whether n is prime.  Only considers integer values in the
 * range 2 through 10 billion, and throws an exception if the argument
 * isn't.
 */
var isPrime = function (n) {
    if (n < 2 || n > 1e10 || n % 1 !== 0) {
        throw new Error("I don't feel like testing that value");
    }

    // If we've computed this before, return cached value.
    if (isPrime.cache[n] !== undefined) {
        return isPrime.cache[n];
    }

    // Otherwise, compute it.  Start by assuming true...
    var answer = true;
    for (var test = 2; test <= Math.sqrt(n); test += 1) {
        if (n % test === 0) {
            // Found a divisor.  It's composite.  Stop looking.
            answer = false;
            break;
        }
    }

    // Save the answer in the cache and return it.
    isPrime.cache[n] = answer;
    return answer;
}
isPrime.cache = {}
```

Unit tests for this function can include tests that the cache was (and was not) filled:

```javascript
$(document).ready(function () {

    module("Primes");

    test("Known primes", function () {
        ok(isPrime(2), "2 is prime");
        ok(isPrime(3), "3 is prime");
        ok(isPrime(5), "5 is prime");
        ok(isPrime(7), "7 is prime");
        ok(isPrime(11), "11 is prime");
        ok(isPrime(3571), "3571 is prime");
        ok(isPrime(433494437), "433494437 is prime");
    });

    test("Known composites", function () {
        ok(!isPrime(2345346438), "A big even number is composite");
        ok(!isPrime(3553), "3553 is composite");
        ok(!isPrime(9901 * 9901), "9901^2 is composite");
    });

    test("Checking the cache", function () {
        ok(isPrime.cache[2345346438] === false, "2345346438 got
            cached");
        ok(isPrime.cache[3553] === false, "3553 got cached");
        ok(isPrime.cache[11] === true, "11 got cached");
        ok(isPrime.cache[13] === undefined, "13 wasn't cached");
    });
});
```

Caching sounds like just the thing to help us with those evil recursive functions that perform repeated computation—like the Fibonacci function from the last section:

```javascript
/*
 * Returns the kth Fibonacci number, using recursion and a cache.
 * Precondition: k is a nonnegative integer less than 75.
 */
```

```
var fib = function (k) {
    // Use cached result if we've computed fib(k) before.
    if (fib.cache[k] !== undefined) {
        return fib.cache[k];
    }

    var answer = k;
    if (k > 1) {
        answer = fib(k - 1) + fib(k - 2);
    }

    // Cache the answer and return it.
    fib.cache[k] = answer;
    return answer;
}
fib.cache = {}
```

You should try out this function. It can compute `fib(70)` immediately, while the uncached version would never finish in a reasonable amount of time. But this power comes with a risk: caches can fill up. Making millions of (differing) calls to a memoized function will start using up more and more memory. We encourage you to think about ways to deal with this problem.

Caching is extremely important in large-scale distributed systems, especially those using databases. Querying a database and fetching data are fairly expensive, so caches are routinely set up to hold the results of frequent queries. In these situations, though, not only must you worry about caches filling up, but you must also worry about the data changing in the database while the cache is still active; therefore an expiration time is placed on some caches. Details are outside the scope of this text, but this is certainly an important area of software design you are likely to encounter some day.

Review and Practice

1. What happens if we don't include the assignment to `isPrime.cache` in the first example from this section?

2. Implement and test the improved Fibonacci function in this section.

10.4 MapReduce

One extremely interesting area of study in computing is the processing and analysis of massive data stores—stores containing many trillions or quadrillions of bytes of data. Data at this scale can never be stored in a single database or processed on a single computer; processing must be distributed among a *cluster* of hundreds or thousands of computing nodes.

One of the companies dealing with "Big Data," Google, introduced a software framework called *MapReduce* [DG04] for distributed computation. The name MapReduce comes from two well-known functions, `map` and `reduce`. We cannot cover all the details of massively distributed computation in this short chapter, but we will look in detail at these two functions, as well as their friend `filter`, because of the way they inspired this popular framework.

10.4.1   Using `map`, `filter`, and `reduce`

We will start with short, quick definitions:

- **Map** applies a certain operation to each element of an array. For example,

$$map(square, [3, 4, 10, -5, 8]) \Rightarrow [9, 16, 100, 25, 64]$$

- **Filter** keeps only those array elements that meet a certain condition. For example,

$$filter(odd, [3, 6, 9, -11, 4]) \Rightarrow [3, 9, -11]$$

- **Reduce** computes a single result by applying a binary operator cumulatively to the array elements. For example,

$$reduce(plus, [3, -8, 1, 20]) \Rightarrow 3 + (-8) + 1 + 20 = 16$$

In ECMAScript 5, `map`, `filter`, and `reduce` are all properties of `Array.prototype`. We will illustrate them with three examples (you will generate a few more in the end-of-chapter exercises).

Example 1. Compute the sum of the squares of all odd elements in an array:

```
var square = function (x) {return x * x;};
var odd = function (x) {return x % 2 === 1;};
var plus = function (x, y) {return x + y;};

[3, 5, 2, 0, 9, 8, 6, 1].filter(odd).map(square).reduce(plus);
```

Example 2. Given a list of words, return a string containing the capitalizations of all three-letter words, chained together with hyphens:

```
var capitalize = function (s) {return s.toUpperCase();};
var isThreeLetterWord = function (s) {return s.length === 3;};
var addHyphen = function (s, t) {return s + "-" + t;};

["the","really","old","cat","is","home"].
    filter(isThreeLetterWord).
    map(capitalize).
    reduce(addHyphen);
```

Example 3. Given a list of words, return the word that appears most often (without taking case into account), along with the number of times it appears:

```
var count = {};
var alwaysTrue = function (s) {return true;}
var record = function (s) {
    s = s.toLowerCase();
    if (count[s]) count[s] += 1; else count[s] = 1;
    return [s, count[s]];
};
var moreFrequent = function (p, q) {return p[1] > q[1] ? p : q};

["the","rAT", "A","car","bat","rat","the","rat","Rat","a"].
    filter(alwaysTrue).
    map(record).
    reduce(moreFrequent);
```

These examples share some structure in common. Let's capture the commonality:

```
/*
 * Given an array a, filters with function f, then maps it with m,
 * then reduces it with r.
 */
var mapreduce = function (a, f, m, r) {
    return a.filter(f).map(m).reduce(r);
}
```

Notice that `filter` and `map` return arrays, but `reduce` returns a value made by combining array elements. When operating on empty arrays, `filter` and `map` can return empty arrays, but what does `reduce` do? Answer: It throws a `TypeError`, unless you supply a second argument—the so-called "default value"—to return for an empty array. Technically, this additional argument is more than just the empty-array return value: it is used as the first argument for the first reduction call. Formally:

$$[a_1, a_2, \ldots, a_n].reduce(f, x) = f(f(f(x, a_1), a_2), \ldots)$$

Or, using a concrete example:

$$[7, 6, 10].reduce(plus, \mathbf{3}) = \mathbf{3} + 7 + 6 + 10$$

When the array is empty, there are no array elements to reduce with the default value, so the call just returns the default value.

Review and Practice

1. In your own words, explain what the map, filter, and reduce operations do.

2. Write a function, using `map`, that accepts an array of two-element arrays and returns a new array whose elements are like those of the original array, only reversed. For example, given `[[4,3], [9,1], [2,6]]`, your function should produce `[[3,4], [1,9], [6,2]]`.

3. Write a function, using `reduce`, that takes an array of strings and returns the string made by piecing together the first character of each string element.

10.4.2 Implementation

We hope you see that *using* map, reduce, and filter is easy, but suppose you needed to implement these functions yourself. Perhaps your JavaScript installation does not have these functions. Or perhaps you were building your own JavaScript engine from scratch. You can add these three functions to Array.prototype yourself. Here is a first attempt at adding map:

```
/*
 * A first attempt at Array.prototype.map
 */
if (!Array.prototype.map) {
    Array.prototype.map = function (f) {
        var result = [];
        for (var i = 0; i < this.length; i += 1) {
            result.push(f(this[i]));
        }
        return result;
    };
}
```

This code assigns a mapping function to the map property provided the property does not already exist. The implementation is inefficient, though. Every time push is called, new space has to be allocated to grow the result array. We can do better by preallocating the space, using the Array constructor directly:

```
/*
 * A second attempt at Array.prototype.map
 */
if (!Array.prototype.map) {
    Array.prototype.map = function (f) {
        var result = new Array(this.length);
        for (var i = 0; i < this.length; i += 1) {
            result[i] = f(this[i]);
        }
        return result;
    };
}
```

It turns out that this is still far from the real, professional implementation! We need to handle the cases where (1) we are passed an object with a corrupted `length` property, (2) the parameter `f` is not a function, and (3) someone has deleted one of the array properties. We can speed up a little by precomputing the length of the array so we don't have to use it multiple times. Now we're at:

```
/*
 * A third attempt at Array.prototype.map
 */
if (!Array.prototype.map) {
    Array.prototype.map = function (f) {
        var len = this.length >>> 0;
        if (typeof fun != "function") {
            throw new TypeError();
        }
        var result = new Array(len);
        for (var i = 0; i < len; i += 1) {
            result[i] = f(this[i]);
        }
        return result;
    };
}
```

The real `Array.prototype.map` is more general than the version we are developing here; details can be found in the ECMAScript 5 Specification, and full implementations of `map`, `filter`, and `reduce` are provided in Mozilla's Developer Center JavaScript pages.

Review and Practice

1. Determine the meaning of the expression `this.length >>> 0` in the code for `map`. (A web search should turn up the answer.)

2. What would happen in the `map` implementation from this section if the `typeof` check were not included and a nonfunction were passed in?

10.4.3 MapReduce in Large-Scale Data Processing

Why are functions like these important? For one thing, they operate on entire arrays—saving you from having to code your own loops to process the array elements individually. Secondly, as we mentioned at the beginning of the chapter, the MapReduce style of programming is often used for the processing of massive data sets: creating large search indexes, carrying out searches, sorting, analyzing documents, computing analytics, and so on. One of the reasons for this is that the `map` and `filter` operations are inherently *parallel operations*; that is, given a set of 20 million items to process, the data set can be distributed to, say, 2000 machines, each of which processes its own slice of 10,000 items. The entire job runs (nearly) 2000 times faster than the original job—meaning a job that would take 33 hours can be done in 1 minute. With more machines, your speedup can be more dramatic.

Review and Practice

1. Do some research to determine what kinds of MapReduce jobs are run at Google.

2. The open source project *Hadoop* (`http://hadoop.apache.org`) contains its own MapReduce framework (though different from Google's). Do some research to find out what interesting jobs are run with Hadoop.

10.5   Dynamically Creating Event Handlers

We will close this chapter with a case study illustrating a common programming mistake. We hope you will follow along and perhaps be able to recognize the bug before we point it out.

The scenario is this: we place a number of user interface elements, indexed from $0 \ldots n-1$, on a page so that when one is triggered, some information unique to the triggered element is displayed. For example, we might have a map with numbered points of interest as in Figure 10.9, for which hovering over an icon brings up a corresponding pop-up.

To show the fundamentals behind this scenario, without cluttering the presentation with the details of graphics and mashups covered in previous chapters, we will create a simple page whose "markers" are numbered buttons, each representing a different state of Australia. Clicking a button will alert the full name of the state, as in Figure 10.10.

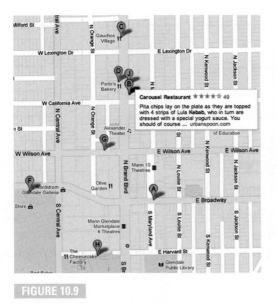

FIGURE 10.9

A map with points of interest.

FIGURE 10.10

An application with buttons triggering similar events.

Our HTML page will reference two scripts: one to define the data and one to define the interaction:

```
<!doctype html>
<html>
  <head><title>Australian States</title></head>
  <body>
    <script src="australian_states.js"></script>
    <script src="australian_states_ui.js"></script>
  </body>
</html>
```

In a real-life application, our data might be stored on a server and fetched on demand with an Ajax call. To keep the application manageable, we will embed the data in the *australian_states.js* script like so:

```
var states = [
    "New South Wales",
    "Queensland",
    "South Australia",
    "Tasmania",
    "Victoria",
    "Western Australia"
];
```

Now for the user interface. For our first attempt, we will attach separate event handlers to each button. Each handler will be a function that, we hope, will alert the name of the correct state:

```
/*
 * A failed attempt to create buttons labeled 0...5 that each alert
 * the name of an Australian state when clicked.
 */
onload = function () {
    for (var i = 0; i < states.length; i += 1) {
        var button = document.createElement("button");
        button.appendChild(document.createTextNode(i));
        button.onclick = function () {alert(states[i]);};
        document.body.appendChild(button);
    }
}
```

Before reading on, examine the script and try to figure out what will happen. Then execute the script and hit every button, and see if you are correct.

*   *   *

Why did every button click alert **undefined**? Let's trace through the script to find out. The second line says we need to do something for every element in the **states** array. The first time through the loop, we create a button labeled "0" and attach a click handler whose action is to alert the value of **states[i]**. But pay attention here: we do not evaluate **states[i]** yet! We go through the loop of creating buttons and assigning click handlers for the remaining entries in the **states** array. By the time the document is loaded, the web page is rendered, and a person is ready to click the button, the value of i is 6. And **states[6]** is indeed **undefined**.

If we really want each button to have its own personal event handler that knows what to alert, we can create each handler as a closure, passing in the value to use for the new closed-over variable:

```
/*
 * A script to provide buttons labeled 0...5, each alerting the name
 * of an Australian state when clicked. Each event handler is a
 * closure.
 */
onload = function () {
    for (var i = 0; i < states.length; i += 1) {
        var button = document.createElement("button");
        button.appendChild(document.createTextNode(i));
        button.onclick = function (i) {
            return function () {alert(states[i]);};
        }(i);
        document.body.appendChild(button);
    }
};
```

While this closure-based solution is interesting, you may have noticed a simpler solution. Instead of assigning a separate function object to each button (functions are relatively expensive to create), you can create a single function; however, this function has to get the array index at *click* time, not at *function creation* time. How can you do this? Remember that buttons are objects, and objects can have arbitrary properties. Simply create a property for each button to hold the array index. When the handler is called, the **this** expression will refer to the button, and the desired index is one property lookup away:

```
/*
 * A script to provide buttons labeled 0...5, each alerting the name
 * of an Australian state when clicked.
 */
onload = function () {
    var showInfo = function () {
        alert(states[this.stateIndex]);
    }
    for (var i = 0; i < states.length; i += 1) {
        var button = document.createElement("button");
        button.appendChild(document.createTextNode(i));
        button.stateIndex = i;
        button.onclick = showInfo;
        document.body.appendChild(button);
    }
};
```

Review and Practice

1. Draw a picture showing all the objects in the closure-based script in this section.

2. Rewrite the closure-based script in this section so that instead of passing i to the event handler generator, you pass in the string to alert.

Chapter Summary

- Regular expressions describe patterns of text. Several powerful operations on regular expressions can be used to significantly reduce the amount of code you would ordinarily have to write for text processing.

- Recursion is the phenomenon of objects being comprised of copies of themselves. We may encounter recursive definitions, recursive datatypes, and recursive functions.

- Proper recursive functions must include a basis (a way to return without making a recursive call), and each recursive call must make progress toward that base case.

- Recursion should not be used to replace a trivial loop, nor should it be used when it causes certain calls to be made repeatedly.

- Caching is the technique of saving a result the first time it is computed and looking up this saved result when the same computation is subsequently requested.

- The use of the higher-order array functions `map`, `filter`, and `reduce` can simplify the writing of many common operations. These functions have inspired modern systems for processing Big Data.

- There are times when event handlers must be created to use data that are not known until run time. Closures are a common and elegant solution for these situations.

Exercises

1. Write a function that takes in a string s and returns whether s contains at least one of the following substrings: `"dog"`, `"cat"`, or `"rat"`.

2. Give a regular expression that matches a Latin letter (uppercase or lowercase) followed by four decimal digits.

3. Give regular expressions for the following (in each case "digit" refers to a basic decimal digit 0 through 9):

    (a) A string of 16 digits beginning with 51, 52, 53, 54, or 55

    (b) A string of either 13 or 16 decimal digits beginning with a 4

    (c) A string of 15 digits beginning with 300–305, 36, or 38

    (d) A string of 16 digits beginning with 6011 or 65

4. Write a function that removes all basic Latin vowels from a string (the basic Latin letters are those with codepoints in the range U+0000 through U+007F). For example,

$$\texttt{removeLatinVowels("Argentina")} \;\Rightarrow\; \texttt{rgntn}$$

5. Which of the following two functions do you think is better? Why?

```
var isAllDigits = function (s) {
    return /^\d*$/.test(s);
}
```

```
var isAllDigits = function (s) {
    return ! /\D/.test(s);
}
```

6. What does the regex /(.)\1(.)\2(.)\3/i match? Can you think of any English words that are matched by this regex?

7. Write a function that takes in an array of strings and outputs another array of strings that is just like the input, except that (1) any strings that are empty or consist entirely of spaces are dropped, and (2) any strings that begin with a # are dropped. Use the replace method and regular expressions.

8. Here is another prime number function. Note the precondition:

```
/*
 * Returns whether or not n is prime.  Precondition: n is a
 * positive integer greater than 1.
 */
var isPrime = function (n) {
    return ! /^1?$|^(11+?)\1+$/.test(new Array(n+1).join("1"));
};
```

Test this function in a runner page or shell to convince yourself that it works. (Use numbers less than 100,000.) Try to explain how it works. What happens when your input value is in the millions or billions? The regex used in the function is due to a programmer named Abigail. Find, on some web page, other instances of Abigail's work. EXTRA CREDIT: Most of it is in a language called Perl; try your hand at porting some of it to JavaScript.

9. One regex form we did not discuss in this chapter was the (?=) form, known as *positive lookahead*. In particular, the form X(?=Y) (for substrings X and Y) matches an occurrence of X only if followed by an occurrence of Y. Explain then (in general terms), what this script is doing:

```
var pattern = /Hillary(?=\s+Clinton)/g;
var text = "Once Hillary Clinton was talking about Sir\n" +
    "Edmund Hillary to Hillary Makasa and then Hillary\n" +
    "Clinton had to run off on important business.";
alert(text.replace(pattern, "Secretary"));
```

Are there other ways to do the same thing?

10. Another regex form not discussed in this chapter is the *negative lookahead*—
    X(?!Y) matches occurrences of X not followed by Y. Use this form to write
    a function that, when given a string, returns the number of q's not followed
    by a u.

11. Do some research about the evils of JavaScript's eval function. Make a list
    of attacks that can be performed on a web page that does not sanitize the
    input to eval.

12. Can you ever have a problem sending a JSON string to eval? For example,
    go to http://search.twitter.com/search.json?q=uruguay and look at
    the result. Could that string be safely passed to eval and the result of the
    evaluation assigned to a variable? Why or why not? If you argue that eval
    should not be used here, what would you use in its place?

13. Give a recursive definition for an odd integer. (*Hint*: Use 1 as the basis.)

14. Give a recursive definition of the shape in Figure 10.1.

15. The following four definitions do not have the form of a proper recursive
    definition, yet they are not necessarily circular. Determine, for each, what
    set of numbers they define:

    - $x =_{def} \cos(x)$

    - $x =_{def} x$

    - $x =_{def} x + 1$

    - $x =_{def} 6 - x^2$

16. Here is an alternative recursive version of the factorial function:

```
/*
 * Returns the factorial of n. Precondition: n is a nonnegative
 * integer.
 */
var factorial = function (n) {
    var f = function (i, a) {
        return i === n ? a : f(i + 1, a * (i + 1));
    };
    return f(0, 1);
}
```

Trace out the computation of `factorial(6)`. We have started it for you:

```
factorial(6) = f(0, 1)
             = f(1, 1)
             = . . .
```

How does this compare to the derivation using the classic recursive formulation?

17. Give an iterative implementation of Euclid's GCD algorithm. You may state that the two arguments must be nonnegative as a precondition.

18. How many recursive calls are required to compute the GCD of 611,953 and 611,951 using (a) the naïve algorithm, (b) the algorithm using subtraction, and (c) the algorithm using modulo?

19. How many recursive calls are required to compute the GCD of 611,953 and 2 using (a) the naïve algorithm, (b) the algorithm using subtraction, and (c) the algorithm using modulo?

20. How many recursive calls are required to compute the GCD of 611,953 and 305,477 using (a) the naïve algorithm, (b) the algorithm using subtraction, and (c) the algorithm using modulo?

21. How many moves are required to legally move 3 discs in the Towers of Hanoi puzzle? How many to move 5 discs? 10? n?

22. Write a binary search function without recursion.

23. Suppose you had a sorted array of 1000 elements on which you are about to perform a binary search. If you are lucky, the element you are searching for will appear in the array exactly in the middle; in this case you have found an item in "one probe." What is the maximum amount of probes required to find an element in your array (or to determine your desired item is not present)? Suppose you had a billion elements in your array. What is the maximum number of probes required now?

24. Another perennial favorite recursive algorithm is finding the minimum number of coins required to produce a certain amount of money. The euro currency, for example, has coins with denominations of 1, 2, 5, 10, 20, 50, 100, 200, and 500 euro cents; therefore, the minimum number of coins to produce €9.84 is eight (one €5, two €2, one 50c, one 20c, one 10c, and two 2c).

   (a) Write a function that takes in an amount of euro cents and returns the minimum number of euro coins that make up that amount.

   (b) Suppose your coin denominations are 1, 9, 15, and 19 cents. What is the minimum number of coins required to make 18 cents? To make 45 cents?

   (c) Modify your algorithm in part (a) to handle the 1, 9, 15, and 19 set of denominations.

   (d) Write a function that takes in an array of coin denominations and an amount of money, and returns the minimum number of coins required to make the given amount.

25. An alternative approach to building family trees is to store children, not parents, in each person object:

```
var Person = function (name) {
    this.name = name;
    this.children = [];
}
Person.prototype.addChild = function (child) {
    this.children.push(child);
}
```

Write (in `Person.prototype`) methods for:

- The number of known ancestors of a person
- The number of known descendants of a person
- Whether a person is a sibling of another
- Whether a person is a descendant of another

You may use as a precondition that the tree of people is well formed.

26. Write a recursive function to determine how many (known) ancestors a person in a family tree has.

27. Try to write an ancestor or descendant function on family trees without recursion. Why is this so much harder to do than it is to write a nonrecursive version of binary search?

28. How many function calls are executed when trying to compute the 100th Fibonacci number using the evil Fibonacci function from this chapter?

29. Apply the caching technique used for the Fibonacci function in this chapter to a factorial function.

30. Apply the caching technique used for the Fibonacci function in this chapter to a GCD function.

31. How do you use the `mapreduce` function from this chapter to perform an operation with a mapper and reducer but no filter? What if there is no mapper? No reducer?

32. Use the `mapreduce` function from this chapter to implement each of the following operations on an array a:

    (a) Return the concatenation of the reversal of all strings in a that have a length of at least 2.

    (b) Return the number of elements of a. (*Hint*: The mapper just produces 1, the filter does nothing at all, and the reducer is plain old `+`.)

    (c) Return the largest even number in a.

    (d) Return the reversal of a.

33. Read an article or two describing uses of MapReduce today. Look for articles that cover not only uses at Google but also open source versions of the framework, such as Hadoop.

34. Extend the little Australian states example in this chapter as follows:

    (a) Create an HTML page in which the background image is a map of Australia.

    (b) Position on the map small boxes labeled with a number (0...5), centered in each state.

    (c) When the mouse hovers over a box, show an information box for the state that contains the state name, its capital, its area, and its population. Feel free to use jQuery or any other library that helps you create fancy user interface effects.

35. Suppose your little brother or sister offered the following approach to the Australian states example in this chapter. What would you tell him or her?

```
onload = function () {
    for (var i = 0; i < states.length; i += 1) {
        var button = document.createElement("button");
        button.appendChild(document.createTextNode(i));
        button.stateIndex = i;
        button.onclick = function () {
            alert(states[this.stateIndex]);
        };
        document.body.appendChild(button);
    }
};
```

36. JSLint doesn't like the closure-based event-handling example we presented in this chapter. It seems to think functions within loops are sloppy. Find out why it thinks so (a web search will point you to the answer), and rewrite the script according to JSLint's recommendations.

37. Donald Knuth wrote: "Computer programming is an art, because it applies accumulated knowledge to the world, because it requires skill and ingenuity, and especially because it produces objects of beauty. A programmer who subconsciously views himself as an artist will enjoy what he does and will do it better." How can this quote be reconciled with the notion that good software is crafted (or engineered) and must conform to certain standards?

APPENDIX A

JavaScript Language Reference

Introduction

This appendix provides selected JavaScript reference information. It lists the complete set of reserved words, datatypes, operators, and statements. It gives a very light synopsis of the native objects and a handful of the host objects used in web programming. The purpose of this appendix is to provide brief and accessible tables and lists. No attempt is made to *explain* the material, though in some cases we provide short examples to illustrate how a feature might be used.

Versions of JavaScript

JavaScript 1.0 was created by Brendan Eich in 1996. New features were added over time as the language progressed through versions 1.1, 1.2, and beyond. Technically, "JavaScript" is a trademark referring to a dialect of the officially standardized ECMAScript [ECM99, ECM09] language.[1] The scripting language found in the popular Internet Explorer browser is officially named JScript, though everyone calls it JavaScript, too.

Roughly speaking, all major browsers today support the third edition of ECMAScript (ECMAScript 3). JavaScript and JScript are essentially ECMAScript 3 plus a large set of host objects to support web programming. Many browsers support the newer fifth edition of ECMAScript (see `http://kangax` `.github.com/es5-compat-table/` for details on ECMAScript 5 support).

---

[1]ECMAScript is the foundation of other languages, too, including ActionScript, which powers Adobe Flash.

ECMAScript is an evolving language, so expect future versions of JavaScript to contain many new features.

In the reference sections that follow, we first present reserved words, operators, statements, and native objects defined in the ECMAScript standards. We will use the superscript E5 to mark features that appear in ECMAScript 5 but not in ECMAScript 3. We will then present reference material for selected host objects common to most JavaScript web installations.

Reserved Words

JavaScript designates the following words as *reserved*. Reserved words may not be used as the name of a variable, and if used as a property name in ECMAScript 3, they must be quoted in an object literal and may not be used with the dot-notation.

abstract	boolean	break	byte	case	catch	char
class	const	continue	debugger	default	delete	do
double	else	enum	export	extends	false	final
finally	float	for	function	goto	if	implements
import	in	instanceof	int	interface	long	native
new	null	package	private	protected	public	return
short	static	super	switch	synchronized	this	throw
throws	transient	true	try	typeof	var	void
volatile	while	with				

Datatypes

There are six datatypes in JavaScript: Boolean, number, string, undefined, null, and object. Example values of each type appear in Table A.1. Three kinds of objects, namely arrays, functions, and regular expressions, have a special syntax.

Operators

Table A.2 lists all of the JavaScript operators, arranged from highest to lowest precedence.

Type	Example Values
undefined	`undefined`
null	`null`
Boolean	`false` `true`

number	`8`
	 `7.3342`
	 `6.02e23`
	 `0xffd32a`
	 `Infinity`
	 `NaN`

string	`"hello"`
	 `"She said 'nyet'"`
	 `'x = "4"'`
	 `"one\ntwo\nthree"`
	 `"Olé"`
	 `"Ol\xe9"`
	 `"\u043d\u0435\u0442"`
	 `"Buy some Chanel \u2116 5"`

object	`{ }`
	 `{name:"Spike", age:6, breed:"terrier"}`
	 `[ ]`
	 `[1, true, [1,2], {x:5, y:6}, "Hi"]`
	 `function (x,y) {return 2 * x + y;}`
	 `/^hello,? world$/i`

Table A.1

JavaScript Datatypes

Operators	Assoc.	Description
.	L	member
[]		member
()	N/A	call
new		create instance
++ --	N/A	postfix increment, postfix decrement
!	R	logical not
~		bitwise complement
- +		unary negation, unary plus
++ --		prefix increment, prefix decrement
typeof		type name
void		evaluate and return undefined
delete		delete
* / %	L	multiply, divide, modulo
+ -	L	add, subtract
<<	L	left shift
>>		arithmetic right shift
>>>		logical right shift
< <=	L	less than, less than or equal
> >=		greater than, greater than or equal
in		has property
instanceof		has type
== !=	L	sloppy equals, not ==
=== !==		equals and same type, not ===
&	L	bitwise and
^	L	bitwise xor
|	L	bitwise or
&&	L	AND-ALSO (short-circuit logical "and")
||	L	OR-ELSE (short-circuit logical "or")
?:	R	conditional
= += -=	R	assignment
*= /= %=		
<<= >>= >>>=		
&= ^= |=		
,	L	comma

Table A.2

JavaScript Operators

Statements

The following is a list of the JavaScript statements, together with sample usage patterns. The usage patterns are informal only; consult [ECM09] for the official syntax.

- **The empty statement** has no effect.

    ;

- **The expression statement** evaluates an expression and ignores the result. The expression may not start with the word `function`.

    expression;

- **The variable declaration statement** declares one or more variables and gives them initial values. If an initializer is not present, the corresponding variable gets the value `undefined`.

    `var` *name*;
    `var` *name*, *name*;
    `var` *name* = *expression*;
    `var` *name* = *expression*, *name*, *name* = *expression*;

- **The if statement** executes code conditionally.

    `if` (*expression*) *statement*
    `if` (*expression*) *statement* `else` *statement*

- **The iteration statement** executes code repeatedly.

    `while` (*expression*) *statement*
    `do` (*statement*) `while` *expression*;
    `for` (*expression*; *expression*; *expression*) *statement*
    `for` (*variable* `in` *object*) *statement*

- **The continue statement** jumps immediately to the beginning of the next iteration of the loop with the given label name or, if no label name is present, the currently executing loop.

```
continue;
continue labelname;
```

■ **The break statement** immediately exits the loop with the given label name or, if no label name is present, the currently executing loop.

```
break;
break labelname;
```

■ **The return statement** immediately exits the current function, returning the given expression or, if no expression is provided, the value `undefined`.

```
return;
return expression;
```

■ **The with statement** should not be used.

```
with (expression) statement
```

■ **The labeled statement** gives a name to a statement. Generally, loops are labeled so they can be referred to in `break` and `continue` statements.

```
labelname : statement
```

■ **The switch statement** jumps to the first label that is `===` to a given expression.

```
switch (expression) case-clauses
```

Each *case-clause* has one of the two following forms:

```
case expression : statement
default : statement
```

Only one `default` clause may appear.

■ **The throw statement** throws a value, disrupting the current control flow.

```
throw expression;
```

- **The try statement** executes a block, but if anything is thrown inside the block and a catch clause is present, the catch will be executed with the thrown object bound to the name. If a `finally` block is present, it will be executed whether or not anything was caught.

  try *block* `catch` (*name*) *block*
  try *block* `finally` *block*
  try *block* `catch` (*name*) *block* `finally` *block*

- **The block statement** executes its statements sequentially.

  { *sequence-of-statements* }

Function Declarations

Scripts are sequences of statements and function declarations. A function declaration declares a variable with a given name and assigns a function value. It may appear only at the top level of a script or function body. Function declarations are not managed consistently among different browsers. We recommend avoiding them.

  `function` *name* (*parameters*) *block*

Native Objects

This section lists the native objects of JavaScript together with the names of their properties. In some cases we give a general description of some of the properties in order to convey how the properties might be used. These property descriptions are not intended to be complete; consult the ECMAScript Language Specifications for the missing details.

The Global Object

The ECMAScript language specifies that the global object is to contain the following properties:

Object	Properties
The global object	NaN Infinity undefined eval parseInt parseFloat isNaN isFinite encodeURI encodeURIComponent decodeURI decodeURIComponent Object Array Function Math JSON^{E5} Number Boolean String Date Error EvalError RangeError ReferenceError TypeError SyntaxError URIError

A particular implementation of ECMAScript, such as JavaScript, is allowed to add additional properties to the global object. When JavaScript is used in a web environment, the global object is a window object. Window objects are described later in this appendix.

Array

The **Array** object is the constructor for all arrays.

Object	Properties
Array	length prototype isArray^{E5}
Array *instances*	length
Array.prototype	constructor toString toLocaleString concat join pop push reverse shift slice sort splice unshift indexOf^{E5} lastIndexOf^{E5} every^{E5} some^{E5} forEach^{E5} map^{E5} filter^{E5} reduce^{E5} reduceRight^{E5}

A summary of some of the more common array operations follows. As noted earlier, we have omitted some technical details and advanced capabilities in the interest of brevity.

For an arbitrary expression e, array a, string s, function f, and numbers i, j, and n:

- `Array.isArray`(e) produces `true` if e is an array, or `false` otherwise.

- a.`toString`$()$ produces the same result as a.`join(",")`.

- a.`concat`$(a_1, a_2, \ldots, a_n)$ produces a new array containing the elements of a followed by the elements of a_1 followed by the elements of a_2 and so on.

- a.`join`(s) produces a string comprising all of the elements of a separated by s. If s is `undefined`, then `","` is used as the separator.

- a.`pop`$()$ removes and produces the last element from a.

- a.`push`$(e_1, e_2, \ldots, e_n)$ adds each of the e_i's to the end of a, and produces the new length of a.

- a.`reverse`$()$ reverses a itself, and produces a.

- a.`shift`$()$ removes and produces the first element of a.

- a.`slice`(i, j) produces a new array containing the elements of a from index i inclusive to j exclusive. i and j can be negative, in which case they refer to positions relative to the end of the array (with -1 being the last position, -2 the second to the last, and so on).

- a.`sort`(f) sorts array a according to the comparison function f. If f is `undefined`, then the elements of a are treated as strings.

- a.`splice`$(i, n, e_1, \ldots, e_n)$ replaces the n elements of a starting at index i with $e_1, \ldots, e_n$.

- a.`unshift`$(e_1, \ldots, e_n)$ adds the e_i's to the front of a, producing the new length of a.

- a.`indexOf`(e) produces the first index in a at which e appears (testing for membership with `===`), or -1 if e does not appear in a. a.`indexOf`(e, i) finds the first index of e starting the search at index i within a.

- a.lastIndexOf(e) works similarly to indexOf but produces the first position of e found by searching backward from the end of the array. a.lastIndexOf(e, i) searches backward starting at position i.

- a.every(f) produces true if $f(x)$ is truthy for all elements x of a, or false otherwise. The elements of a are tested in order, and the testing will stop as soon as a test is falsy.

- a.some(f) produces true if $f(x)$ is truthy for at least one element x of a, or false otherwise. The elements of a are tested in order, and the testing will stop as soon as a test is truthy.

- a.forEach(f) calls $f(x)$ for each element x of a, in order.

- a.map(f) produces $[f(a_0), f(a_1), f(a_2), f(a_3), \ldots]$.

- a.filter(f) produces a new array containing all elements x of a for which $f(x)$ is truthy.

- a.reduce(f, x) produces $f(x, f(a_0, f(a_1, f(a_2, f(a_3, \ldots))))) $. If the second parameter is not supplied, the call produces $f(a_0, f(a_1, f(a_2, f(a_3, \ldots))))$, but will throw a TypeError if a is empty.

Boolean

Objects created with the Boolean constructor wrap primitive Boolean values. Use of Boolean objects is never a good idea. Do not use this constructor.

Object	Properties
Boolean	length prototype
Boolean *instances*	*none*
Boolean.prototype	constructor toString valueOf

Date

The Date constructor creates objects that represent instances in time. These instances are describable by a proleptic Gregorian calendar only, and with no adjustment for leap seconds.

Object	Properties
Date	length prototype parse UTC now ^{E5}
Date *instances*	*none*
Date.prototype	constructor toString toDateString toTimeString toLocaleString toLocaleDateString toLocaleTimeString valueOf getTime getFullYear getUTCFullYear getMonth getUTCMonth getDate getUTCDate getDay getUTCDay getHours getUTCHours getMinutes getUTCMinutes getSeconds getUTCSeconds getMilliseconds getUTCMilliseconds getTimezoneOffset setTime setFullYear setUTCFullYear setMonth setUTCMonth setDate setUTCDate setDay setUTCDay setHours setUTCHours setMinutes setUTCMinutes setSeconds setUTCSeconds setMilliseconds setUTCMilliseconds setTimezoneOffset toGMTString toISOString ^{E5} toJSON ^{E5}

Error Objects

Objects constructed with Error, EvalError, RangeError, ReferenceError, SyntaxError, TypeError, or URIError are designed to be thrown.

Object	Properties
Error	length prototype
Error.prototype	constructor name message toString
EvalError	length prototype
EvalError.prototype	constructor name message toString
RangeError	length prototype
RangeError.prototype	constructor name message toString
ReferenceError	length prototype

Object	Properties
ReferenceError.prototype	constructor name message toString
SyntaxError	length prototype
SyntaxError.prototype	constructor name message toString
TypeError	length prototype
TypeError.prototype	constructor name message toString
URIError	length prototype
URIError.prototype	constructor name message toString

Function

The `Function` object is the constructor for all functions.

Object	Properties
Function	length prototype
Function *instances*	length prototype
Function.prototype	constructor toString apply call bind^{E5}

For function f, array a, object x, and expressions a_i:

- f.`toString()` produces a textual description of f.

- f.`apply`(x, a), where a is an array, calls $f(a_0, a_1, a_2, \ldots)$ in a context in which the expression `this` evaluates to x.

- f.`call`$(x, a_0, a_1, a_2, \ldots)$ calls $f(a_0, a_1, a_2, \ldots)$ in a context in which the expression `this` evaluates to x.

- f.`bind`$(x, a_0, a_1, a_2, \ldots)$ produces a new function that acts like $f(a_0, a_1, a_2, \ldots)$ with the expression `this` inside the call evaluating to x.

JSON

The `JSON` object contains two functions for turning JavaScript objects to and from their textual representations.

Object	Properties
JSON^{E5}	parse^{E5} stringify^{E5}

- `JSON.stringify(o)` produces the (textual) representation of object o.

- `JSON.parse(s)` produces the object described by string s.

Math

The `Math` object contains a number of mathematical constants and functions.

Object	Properties
Math	E PI SQRT1_2 SQRT2 LN2 LN10 LOG2E LOG10E abs sin cos tan acos asin atan atan2 exp log ceil floor min max pow random round sqrt

A basic description of each of these properties follows. Note that when `NaN` is used as an operand, the result will be `NaN`. In addition, both `Infinity` and `NaN` are possible results even for finite arguments; for example, `Math.acos(2)` $\Rightarrow$ `NaN`.

Value	Meaning
`Math.E`	The value e, $\approx 2.718281828459045$
`Math.PI`	The value π, $\approx 3.141592653589793$
`Math.SQRT1_2`	The value $\sqrt{\frac{1}{2}}$, $\approx 0.7071067811865476$
`Math.SQRT2`	The value $\sqrt{2}$, $\approx 1.4142135623730951$
`Math.LN2`	The value $\ln 2$, $\approx 0.6931471805599453$
`Math.LN10`	The value $\ln 10$, $\approx 2.302585092994046$
`Math.LOG2E`	The value $\log_2 e$, $\approx 1.4426950408889634$
`Math.LOG10E`	The value $\log_{10} e$, $\approx 0.4342944819032518$
`Math.abs(x)`	The absolute value of x, $|x|$
`Math.sin(x)`	The sine of x radians
`Math.cos(x)`	The cosine of x radians
`Math.tan(x)`	The tangent of x radians
`Math.acos(x)`	The angle in $0 \ldots \pi$ (radians) whose cosine is x
`Math.asin(x)`	The angle in $-\frac{\pi}{2} \ldots \frac{\pi}{2}$ (radians) whose sine is x
`Math.atan(x)`	The angle in $-\frac{\pi}{2} \ldots \frac{\pi}{2}$ (radians) whose tangent is x. Note `Math.atan(+∞)` $\Rightarrow \frac{\pi}{2}$ and `Math.atan(-∞)` $\Rightarrow -\frac{\pi}{2}$.

Value	Meaning
`Math.atan2(`y, x`)`	The angle from the positive x axis to the vector $\langle x, y \rangle$, expressed in radians as a value in $-\pi \ldots \pi$
`Math.exp(`x`)`	e^x
`Math.log(`x`)`	$\ln x$
`Math.ceil(`x`)`	The smallest integer greater than or equal to x
`Math.floor(`x`)`	The largest integer less than or equal to x
`Math.min(`$x, y, \ldots$`)`	The minimum of the zero or more operands given. $-\infty$ if no operands are given. `NaN` if any of the operands is `NaN`.
`Math.max(`$x, y, \ldots$`)`	The maximum of the zero or more operands given. $+\infty$ if no operands are given. `NaN` if any of the operands is `NaN`.
`Math.pow(`x, y`)`	x^y
`Math.random()`	A random number greater than or equal to 0 but less than 1
`Math.round(`x`)`	The closest integer to x. If x is equidistant to two different integers, then the smallest of those two.
`Math.sqrt(`x`)`	$\sqrt{x}$

Number

Objects created with the `Number` constructor wrap primitive number values. You never need to create number objects explicitly; simply evaluating an expression of the form $n.p$ where n is a (primitive) number and p is a property will implicitly create an object to hold n.

Object	Properties
Number	`length prototype MAX_VALUE MIN_VALUE NaN NEGATIVE_INFINITY POSITIVE_INFINITY`
Number *instances*	*none*
Number.prototype	`constructor toString toLocaleString valueOf toFixed toExponential toPrecision`

For numbers n, k, and r:

- **Number.MAX_VALUE** is the largest finite JavaScript number, $(2 - 2^{-52}) \times 2^{1023} \approx 1.7977 \times 10^{308}$.

- **Number.MIN_VALUE** is the smallest representable number greater than zero, $2^{-1074} \approx 5 \times 10^{-324}$.

- **Number.NEGATIVE_INFINITY** is $-\infty$.

- **Number.POSITIVE_INFINITY** is ∞.

- **Number.NaN** is NaN.

- n.**toString**(r) produces the string for n with radix r. If r is missing, it defaults to 10. If $r < 2$ or $r > 36$, it throws a **RangeError**.

- n.**toLocaleString**() produces the string for n using formatting conventions of the current locale.

- n.**valueOf**() produces n.

- n.**toFixed**(k) produces the string for n with k digits after the decimal point.

- n.**toExponential**(k) produces the string for n with one digit before the decimal point and k digits after.

- n.**toPrecision**(k) produces the string for n, in either decimal or exponential form, using k digits of precision.

Object

The **Object** constructor is invoked for all objects created with an object literal.

Object	Properties
Object	length prototype getPrototypeOf ^{E5} getOwnPropertyDescriptor ^{E5} getOwnPropertyNames ^{E5} create ^{E5} defineProperty ^{E5} defineProperties ^{E5} seal ^{E5} freeze ^{E5} preventExtensions ^{E5} isSealed ^{E5} isFrozen ^{E5} isExtensible ^{E5} keys ^{E5}
Object *instances*	*none*
Object.prototype	constructor toString toLocaleString valueOf hasOwnProperty isPrototypeOf propertyIsEnumerable

For objects x and y, and string p:

- `Object.getPrototypeOf`(x) produces the prototype of x.

- `Object.getOwnPropertyDescriptor`(x, p) produces the property descriptor of own property p within x, or `undefined` if p is not an own property of x.

- `Object.getOwnPropertyNames`(x) produces an array of the names of all own properties of x.

- `Object.keys`(x) produces an array of the names of all *enumerable* own properties of x.

- `Object.preventExtensions`(x) makes x nonextensible. `Object.isExtensible`(x) produces `true` if x is extensible and `false` otherwise. A nonextensible object cannot have new properties added.

- `Object.seal`(x) seals x, and `Object.isSealed`(x) produces whether x is sealed. A sealed object is nonextensible and each of its properties is nonconfigurable.

- `Object.freeze`(x) freezes x, and `Object.isFrozen`(x) produces whether x is frozen. A frozen object is sealed and cannot have any property value changed; it is truly immutable.

- `Object.create`(*proto*) produces a newly created empty object with prototype *proto*. `Object.create`(*proto*, *specs*) produces a newly created object with prototype *proto* and properties set as if by calling `Object.defineProperties`$(x, specs)$.

- `Object.defineProperty(`x, p, d`)` adds property p to object x with descriptor d, or if p is already an own property of x, changes its descriptor to d (if x isn't sealed or frozen).

- `Object.defineProperties(`x`,`$\{p_1 : d_1, \ldots, p_n : d_n\}$`)` essentially invokes `Object.defineProperty(`x, p_i, d_i`)` for each i.

- x`.toString()` produces a string representation of x, producing things like `"[object Object]"` and `"[object Math]"`; this method is intended to be overridden.

- x`.valueOf()` produces a primitive (generally a string or number) representation of x; this method is intended to be overriden.

- x`.hasOwnProperty(`p`)` produces `true` if p is an own property of x, and `false` otherwise.

- x`.isPrototypeOf(`y`)` produces `true` if y is the prototype of x, and `false` otherwise.

- x`.propertyIsEnumerable(`p`)` produces `true` if p is an own property of x and enumerable, and `false` otherwise.

RegExp

The `RegExp` object is the constructor for all regular expression objects.

Object	Properties
RegExp	length prototype
RegExp *instances*	source global ignoreCase multiline lastIndex
RegExp.prototype	constructor toString exec test

For regex r and string s:

- r`.exec(`s`)` looks for matches of r in s, producing a match array on success or `null` if no match. The match array contains, at index 0, the entire match, with properties 1, 2, and so on (if present) containing each of the captures.

The array also contains the properties `index` (the index in s where the match starts) and `input` (whose value is that of s). It may also update properties in r, such as `lastIndex`.

- r.`test`(s) produces `true` if s contains a match for r, or `false` otherwise.

- r.`toString`() produces some sort of representation of the regex.

- r.`source` produces the text of the pattern.

- r.`global` produces `true` if the regex is to be tested against all possible matches in a string, or `false` if at most one.

- r.`ignoreCase` produces `true` if case should be ignored while matching, or `false` if it should not.

- r.`multiline` produces `true` if a multiple-line string should be treated as multiple strings (that is, `^` and `$` are allowed to match the beginning and ending of lines), or `false` otherwise.

- r.`lastIndex` produces the next index at which to start looking for matches (only set if `global` is `true`).

String

Objects created with the `String` constructor "wrap" primitive string values. You never need to create string objects explicitly; simply evaluating an expression of the form $s.p$ where s is a (primitive) string and p is a property will implicitly create an object to hold s.

Object	Properties
String	length prototype fromCharCode
String *instances*	length
String.prototype	constructor toString valueOf charAt charCodeAt concat indexOf lastIndexOf localeCompare match replace search slice split substring toLowerCase toLocaleLowerCase toUpperCase toLocaleUpperCase trim[E5]

The following are some of the more common string operations. As usual, some technical details have been omitted for brevity's sake; you can find missing information in an ECMAScript reference.

For strings s and t, regex r, and numbers c, n, and k:

- `String.fromCharCode(`c`)` produces a string whose sole character has codepoint c.

- s`.toString()` produces s.

- s`.valueOf()` produces s.

- s`.charAt(`k`)` produces a string whose sole character is the character at position k (starting from 0) within s, or `""` if k is out of range.

- s`.charCodeAt(`k`)` produces the codepoint of the character at position k (starting from 0) within s, or `NaN` if k is out of range.

- s`.concat(`$s_1, s_2, \ldots, s_n$`)` produces the string formed by concatenating each of the s_i's together, in order. If $n = 0$, it produces `""`.

- s`.indexOf(`t`)` produces the smallest index at which t appears as a substring of s, or -1 if t is not a substring of s. s`.indexOf(`t, k`)` produces the first index at which t appears in s at or after position k (or -1 if not present).

- s`.lastIndexOf(`t`)` produces the largest index at which t appears as a substring of s, or -1 if t is not a substring of s. s`.lastIndexOf(`t, k`)` produces the largest index at which t appears in s before or at position k (or -1 if not present).

- s`.localeCompare(`t`)` produces a negative value if s appears before t in the sort order for the current locale, 0 if s and t are the same, and a positive number if s appears after t.

- s`.match(`r`)` produces the match or array of matches, or null if there is no match, of the regex r in s, depending on the form of r. If r includes the global flag, a simple array of matches is produced; otherwise the call produces the same result as r`.exec(`s`)`.

- s`.replace(`r, t`)` produces a new string like s but with some or all of the matches of r replaced with t.

- s.search(r) produces the index of the first match of r within s, or -1 if no match.

- s.slice(i, j) produces a new string consisting of the slice of s from index i inclusive to j exclusive. If j is undefined, then it is treated as l, the length of s. Negative values of i and j are treated as $l + i$ and $l + j$, respectively.

- s.split($sep, limit$) produces an array of substrings of s, split in s by sep. If present and positive, $limit$ caps the size of the produced array.

- s.substring(i, j) produces a new string consisting of the slice of s from index i inclusive to j exclusive. If j is undefined, then it is treated as l, the length of s. If $i > j$ at function entry, then these values are effectively swapped.

- s.toLowerCase() and s.toUpperCase() produce the string like s but with all characters lowercased or uppercased, respectively, using Unicode case rules.

- s.trim() produces the string like s but with all leading and trailing whitespace removed.

Web Host Objects

JavaScript host objects generally do have prototypes and constructors, so this reference lists properties for each "type" of host object.

Browser Objects

Browser windows generally have the following properties (there may be more, but these are the more common ones):

Type	Properties
Window	screen location history navigator window self parent top document length frames name status defaultStatus closed innerWidth innerHeight outerWidth outerHeight pageXOffset pageYOffset screenX screenY screenLeft screenTop opener alert blur clearInterval clearTimeout close confirm createPopup focus moveBy moveTo open print prompt resizeBy resizeTo scrollBy scrollTo setInterval setTimeout

When JavaScript is used to control a web browser, its global variable itself is a representation of the browser window. This object will contain all the properties of a regular window object, all of the ECMAScript-required global properties (`Math`, `parseInt`, etc.), and a special property `window`, which refers to itself.

The common types for the browser itself, its current location and history, and the display screen on which it resides are as follows:

Type	Properties
Screen	width height availWidth availHeight colorDepth pixelDepth
Location	href protocol host hostname pathname port search hash assign reload replace
History	length go back forward
Navigator	appName appCodeName appVersion platform userAgent cookieEnabled javaEnabled taintEnabled

DOM Nodes

JavaScript web implementations expose host objects for the DOM, which is made up of nodes. Nodes have the following properties:

Type	Properties
Node	nodeName nodeValue nodeType parentNode childNodes firstChild lastChild previousSibling nextSibling attributes ownerDocument namespaceURI prefix localName insertBefore replaceChild removeChild appendChild hasChildNodes cloneNode normalize isSupported hasAttributes

The "subtypes" of Node include all of the preceding properties and may include several of their own:

Type	Properties
Document	doctype implementation documentElement title referrer domain URL body images applets links forms anchors cookie createElement createDocumentFragment createTextNode createComment createCDATASection createProcessingInstruction createAttribute createEntityReference getElementsByTagName importNode createElementNS createAttributeNS getElementsByTagNameNS getElementById open close write writeln getElementsByName
Element	tagName getAttribute setAttribute removeAttribute getAttributeNode setAttributeNode removeAttributeNode getElementsByTagName getAttributeNS setAttributeNS removeAttributeNS getAttributeNodeNS setAttributeNodeNS getElementsByTagNameNS hasAttribute hasAttributeNS
Attr	name specified value ownerElement
Text	data length substringData appendData insertData deleteData replaceData splitText
Comment	data length substringData appendData insertData deleteData replaceData
CDATASection	data length substringData appendData insertData deleteData replaceData splitText

Type	Properties
Processing-Instruction	target data
DocumentType	name entities notations publicId systemId internalSubset
Document-Fragment	none
Notation	publicId systemId
Entity	publicId systemId notationName
Entity-Reference	none

HTML Objects

Each of the elements in an HTML document has the properties of `Node` and `Element`, plus the following:

Type	Properties
HTMLElement	className clientHeight clientWidth dir id innerHTML lang offsetLeft offsetParent offsetTop onblur onclick ondblclick onfocus onkeydown onkeypress onkeyup onmousedown onmousemove onmouseout onmouseover onmouseup onresize scrollHeight scrollLeft scrollTop scrollWidth style title

Specific HTML elements add their own properties to those inherited from `Node`, `Element`, and `HTMLElement`, many of which we list here along with their properties. We omit elements and properties that are not used in modern HTML because their functionality is best handled with CSS. We also omit elements that do not have any properties other than those inherited from `HTMLElement`.

Element	Properties
<a>	accessKey charset coords href hreflang name rel rev shape tabIndex target type blur focus

Element	Properties
`<area>`	`accessKey alt coords href noHref shape tabIndex target`
`<base>`	`href target`
`<blockquote>`	`cite`
`<button>`	`accessKey disabled form name tabIndex type value`
`<del>`	`cite dateTime`
`<fieldset>`	`form`
`<form>`	`elements length name acceptCharset action enctype method target submit reset`
`<frame>`	`frameBorder longDesc marginHeight marginWidth name noResize scrolling src contentDocument`
`<frameset>`	`cols rows`
`<head>`	`profile`
`<iframe>`	`frameBorder height longdesc marginHeight marginWidth name scrolling src width contentDocument`
`<img>`	`alt height isMap longDesc name src useMap width`
`<input>`	`defaultValue defaultChecked form accept accessKey alt checked disabled macLength name readOnly size src tabIndex type useMap value blur focus select click`
`<ins>`	`cite dateTime`
`<label>`	`form index htmlFor`
`<legend>`	`form accessKey`
`<link>`	`disabled charset href hreflang media rel rev target type`
`<map>`	`areas name`
`<meta>`	`content httpEquiv name scheme`
`<object>`	`code archive codeBase codeType data declare height name standby tabIndex type useMap width contentDocument`

Element	Properties
`<optgroup>`	disabled label
`<option>`	defaultSelected disabled form index label selected text value
`<param>`	name type value valueType
`<q>`	cite
`<script>`	text htmlFor event charset defer src type
`<select>`	type selectedIndex value length form options disabled multiple name size tabIndex add blur focus
`<style>`	disabled media type
`<table>`	caption tHead tFoot rows tBodies border cellPadding cellSpacing frame rules summary width createTHead deleteTHead createTFoot deleteTFoot createCaption deleteCaption insertRow deleteRow
`<tbody>`	align ch chOff vAlign rows insertRow
`<tfoot>`	align ch chOff vAlign rows insertRow
`<thead>`	align ch chOff vAlign rows insertRow
`<td>`	cellIndex abbr align axis ch chOff colSpan headers rowSpan scope vAlign
`<textarea>`	defaultValue form accessKey cols disabled name readOnly rows tabIndex type value blur focus select
`<th>`	cellIndex abbr align axis ch chOff colSpan headers rowSpan scope vAlign
`<title>`	text
`<tr>`	rowIndex sectionRowIndex cells align ch chOff vAlign insertCell

Events

Events that occur in the browser are objects of "type" Event, which have the following properties. Properties marked with an asterisk are not supported by the Internet Explorer browser. Properties marked with a superscript M appear in mobile browsers.

Type	Properties
Event	altKey bubbles* button cancelable* clientX clientY ctrlKey currentTarget* metaKey relatedTarget screenX screenY shiftKey target* timeStamp* touches^{M,*} type

Styles

Finally, each style object features a very large number of properties. Some notes about them:

- Some properties are "shorthand" properties, combining multiple "atomic" properties into a single property expression. If a property name can also be found as a prefix for other property names, such as `background` for `background-attachment`, `background-color`, `background-image`, and others, then that property name is likely for a shorthand property.

- Many properties also break down by direction: `top`, `left`, `bottom`, and `right`. For these properties, their shorthand equivalents can set all of them to the same value, each of them individually, or each dimension individually (horizontal, vertical).

- Properties that have hyphens in CSS are rewritten in camel case when accessed by JavaScript (e.g., `border-color` in CSS is `borderColor` in JavaScript).

- Some properties are only available in certain versions or levels of CSS. Since most current web browsers are up to the latest standards, we have chosen not to distinguish properties among these versions. It is still useful to note this, however, in case an older web browser appears to have problems. Such browsers may have no support for a newer property at all, or they may have prefixes for that property, such as `-moz-` or `-webkit-`.

- The following list is not completely comprehensive; as always, the final authority is the latest official specification from the W3C.

Type	Properties
Style	background background-attachment background-clip background-color background-image background-origin background-position background-repeat background-size border border-bottom border-bottom-color border-bottom-left-radius border-bottom-right-radius border-bottom-style border-bottom-width border-collapse border-color border-image border-image-outset border-image-repeat border-image-slice border-image-source border-image-width border-left border-left-color border-left-style border-left-width border-radius border-right border-right-color border-right-style border-right-width border-spacing border-style border-top border-top-color border-top-left-radius border-top-right-radius border-top-style border-top-width border-width bottom box-decoration-break box-shadow caption-side clear clip color content cursor direction display empty-cells float font font-family font-size font-size-adjust font-stretch font-style font-variant font-weight hanging-punctuation height left letter-spacing line-height list-style list-style-image list-style-position list-style-type margin margin-bottom margin-left margin-right margin-top marquee-direction marquee-play-count marquee-speed marquee-style max-height max-width min-height min-width opacity outline outline-color outline-style outline-width overflow overflow-style padding padding-bottom padding-left padding-right padding-top position quotes right table-layout text-align text-align-last text-decoration text-emphasis text-indent text-justify text-outline text-shadow text-transform text-wrap top unicode-bidi vertical-align visibility white-space white-space-collapse width word-break word-spacing word-wrap z-index

Canvas

The two-dimensional rendering context of a **canvas** element has the following properties and functions.

Type	Properties
Function properties	arc arcTo beginPath bezierCurveTo clearRect clip closePath createImageData createLinearGradient createPattern createRadialGradient drawFocusRing drawImage fill fillRect fillText getImageData isPointInPath lineTo measureText moveTo putImageData quadraticCurveTo rect restore rotate save scale setTransform stroke strokeRect strokeText transform translate
Nonfunction properties	canvas fillStyle font globalAlpha globalCompositeOperation lineCap lineJoin lineWidth miterLimit shadowBlur shadowColor shadowOffsetX shadowOffsetY strokeStyle textAlign textBaseline

APPENDIX B

Numeric Encoding

Introduction

This appendix explains various ways in which numbers can be represented and encoded in computer systems in general, and JavaScript in particular. It covers binary, decimal, and hexadecimal numerals, the representation of noninteger values, and the details behind JavaScript's belief that $0.1 + 0.2 \neq 0.3$.

Place Value

A *number* is an abstraction of a quantity; a *numeral* is a representation of a number. For example, the number seventy-six can be denoted by the Roman numeral LXXVI, the Hindu-Arabic decimal numeral 76, the Hindu-Arabic hexadecimal numeral 4C, or the Hindu-Arabic binary numeral 1001100.

Hindu-Arabic systems represent numerals as a sequence of *digits* with an optional *radix point*. The number of digits in such a system is referred to as the *base*; for example, the base of a system with digit set $\{0, 1, 2, 3, 4, 5, 6, 7, 8, 9\}$ is 10. Each digit in the numeral resides at an *index position*, which increases by one as we move left, with index position 0 just to the left of the radix point. For example:

3	2	1	0		−1	−2	−3
8	7	0	4	.	1	7	9

The *place value* of index position p is simply the base raised to the power p. The numeric value of a numeral is found by multiplying each digit by the place value of its index position. For the preceding numeral we have:

$$8 \times 10^3 + 7 \times 10^2 + 0 \times 10^1 + 4 \times 10^0 + 1 \times 10^{-1} + 7 \times 10^{-2} + 9 \times 10^{-3}$$
$$= 8704.179$$

Binary and Hexadecimal Numerals

The binary (base-2) and hexadecimal (base-16) numeral systems are very common in computing. The digits in the binary system are 0 and 1; they are called binary digits, or *bits* for short. Here are some binary numerals:

$$
\begin{aligned}
1101.1 &= 1 \times 2^3 + 1 \times 2^2 + 0 \times 2^1 + 1 \times 2^0 + 1 \times 2^{-1} = 13.5 \\
1.101 &= 1 \times 2^0 + 1 \times 2^{-1} + 1 \times 2^{-3} = 1.625 \\
100001.001 &= 2^5 + 2^0 + 2^{-3} = 33.125 \\
10000000 &= 2^7 = 128
\end{aligned}
$$

Hexadecimal digits are {0, 1, 2, 3, 4, 5, 6, 7, 8, 9, A, B, C, D, E, F}; examples include:

$$
\begin{aligned}
\texttt{A4C.8} &= 10 \times 16^2 + 4 \times 16^1 + 12 \times 16^0 + 8 \times 16^{-1} = 2636.5 \\
\texttt{2.48} &= 2 \times 16^0 + 4 \times 16^{-1} + 8 \times 16^{-2} = 2.28125 \\
\texttt{CAFE53} &= 12 \times 16^5 + 10 \times 16^4 + 15 \times 16^3 + 14 \times 16^2 + 5 \times 16^1 + 3 \times 16^0 \\
&= 13303379
\end{aligned}
$$

In JavaScript, you may use hexadecimal numerals *for integers only*; to do this, prefix the numeral with `0x`—for example, `0x2c9`, `0xa`, `0x7fff`.

Your JavaScript interpreter may treat integers beginning with a zero as base-8, or *octal*. For this reason, we recommend you never write an integer with a leading zero, unless you are writing the number zero itself!

Numbers in JavaScript

Binary systems are so common in computing because it is easy to produce hardware components (often electronic) that can exist in one of two states. For example, a high voltage could represent a 1 and a low voltage could represent a 0. All data, whether numeric or textual (or anything else), are ultimately stored or transmitted as sequences of bits. JavaScript stores numbers as sequences of 64 bits, partitioned into three sections as follows:

s 1 bit	e 11 bits	f 52 bits

Here s stands for sign, e for exponent, and f for fraction. Since e is an 11-bit field, you can think of it as a value in $0 \ldots 2047$, and f (with 52 bits) as a value in $0 \ldots 2^{52} - 1$ (about 4.5 quadrillion). The value of the number stored is determined by the following algorithm:

1. If $e = 0$, then the number stored is $(-1)^s \times f \times 2^{-1074}$.

2. If $1 \leq e \leq 2046$, then it is $(-1)^s \times (1 + f \times 2^{-52}) \times 2^{e-1023}$.

3. If $e = 2047$ and $f = 0$, then it is $(-1)^s \times \infty$.

4. If $e = 2047$ and $f \neq 0$, then it is `NaN`.

Saying $(-1)^s$ is just a fancy way to say that $s = 0$ means the number is positive, and $s = 1$ means the number is negative. Let's look at an example. The number "negative forty-nine plus three hundred and seventy-five thousandths" (decimal -49.375) is encoded as follows:

1. 49 in decimal is `110001` in binary.

2. 0.375 is three-eights, which is `0.011` in binary.

3. 49.375 is therefore $110001.011_2 \times 2^0$.

4. This can also be written $1.10001011_2 \times 2^5$. The fractional part, `10001011`, will fill the left portion of the f field, and we must choose an e so that $e - 1023 = 5$. So $e = 1028$.

5. The number is negative, so $s = 1$.

Writing it out, we have

1 10000000100 1000101100000000000000000000000000000000000000000000

This process looks fairly complicated, and while you *could* compute the representation of given numbers by hand, the average programmer never has to. Working with algorithms such as these and building hardware to encode and perform arithmetic on these representations are generally tasks for computer engineers. Still, JavaScript programmers need to have a sense of the ramifications of this encoding scheme, namely the limits to numeric size and accuracy.

Because bit strings can get quite long, people prefer to write them using hexadecimal. There is a trivial mapping from binary to hex: every group of 4 bits maps to one hex digit ($0000 \rightarrow 0$, $0001 \rightarrow 1$, $0010 \rightarrow 2$, ... $1111 \rightarrow F$). Thus every 64-bit sequence can be written as a sequence of 16 hex digits. Our encoding of -49.375 would be written as C048B00000000000.

Size and Accuracy Limits

The fact that numbers are crammed into fixed-size components means

- we will have a smallest representable number,

- we will have a largest representable number, and

- there will be gaps in the set of representable numbers.

We can determine the largest and smallest representable finite numbers in JavaScript. The largest finite number is found by maxing out the f field and using 2046 for the e field (because 2047 is treated specially). The bits would be

0 01111111111 1111111111111111111111111111111111111111111111111111

or, if you prefer hex, 7FFFFFFF. See if you can use the preceding rules to determine the decimal representation.

The smallest number greater than zero is

0 00000000000 0000000000000000000000000000000000000000000000000001

which is hex 00000001. The rules we have discussed will tell you that this number is 2^{-1074}.

In addition to numeric size limits due to fixed-size storage locations, there are accuracy limits as well: not every number can be exactly represented. You might already be familiar with this phenomenon. Suppose you are only allowed to do arithmetic with five places after the decimal point. To represent the number $\frac{2}{3}$ in decimal with a fixed number of available digits, you would "round up" and write 0.66667.

Roundoff Error

Computing with approximations leads to *roundoff error*. Try adding $\frac{2}{3}$ to $\frac{2}{3}$ in our hypothetical situation of being limited to five places after the decimal point:

$$
\begin{array}{r}
0.66667 \\
+\quad 0.66667 \\
\hline
1.33334
\end{array}
$$

Oops—we wanted 1.33333. A similar thing happens in JavaScript. JavaScript is really good at representing numbers that are powers of 2, but not so good at powers of 10. In particular, tenths show up as repeating fractions in binary. Consider:

$$
\begin{array}{rcl}
0.1 & \rightsquigarrow & \text{3FB999999999999A} \\
0.2 & \rightsquigarrow & \text{3FC999999999999A} \\
0.3 & \rightsquigarrow & \text{3FD3333333333333}
\end{array}
$$

To store 0.1 and 0.2 we had to round up the last digit from a 9 to an A. This means 0.1 + 0.2 = 3FD3333333333334, which in decimal is 0.30000000000000004. These errors are unavoidable when working with numbers in fixed-size binary representations. When your applications demand numbers of larger size and absolute precision, you need to develop your own (or use someone else's) software. For instance, you can represent incredibly large numbers as plain old JavaScript arrays with each element an integer in $0 \ldots 9$. Addition and multiplication involve manipulating the "digits" just as you learned how to do in grade school. Your code may run hundreds of times slower than the native JavaScript arithmetic, but size and accuracy will be limited only by the amount of memory available to your JavaScript environment.

APPENDIX C

Unicode

Introduction

This appendix provides an overview of the Unicode character set, the native character set of the JavaScript language. As Unicode contains over 100,000 characters and continues to grow, we won't list every character; rather, we will cover the basics of codepoints, blocks, categories, encoding, and decoding. The goal is to provide just enough material for you to use many of the features of the character set effectively.

Basic Concepts

A *character* is a named symbol, such as LATIN SMALL LETTER C WITH CEDILLA, GURMUKHI SIGN ADAK BINDI, or SOUTH WEST BLACK ARROW. Do not confuse a character with a *glyph*, which is just a picture of a character. For example, the glyph Σ can be used for GREEK CAPITAL LETTER SIGMA as well as SUMMATION SIGN.

A *character set* is a collection of characters, called its *repertoire*, each of which is assigned a unique integer called its *codepoint*. Popular sets today include *ASCII* (a set with 128 characters); *ISO8859-1*, also known as Latin-1 (256 characters); *Windows-1252* (also 256 characters); and *Unicode* (over 100,000 characters and growing).

Each character set assigns codepoints to characters in its own fashion; therefore, a single character can have different codepoints in different character sets. For example, the character LEFT DOUBLE QUOTATION MARK is assigned codepoint 201C (hexadecimal) in Unicode, but 93 (hexadecimal) in Windows-1252.

Example Unicode Characters

The following is an arbitrary selection of Unicode characters. You can find the complete repertoire and character mapping at `http://unicode.org/`. We have followed the Unicode convention of writing characters as four- or six-character hexadecimal numerals, prefixed by U+:

U+0025	PERCENT SIGN
U+002B	PLUS SIGN
U+0054	LATIN CAPITAL LETTER T
U+005D	RIGHT SQUARE BRACKET
U+00B0	DEGREE SIGN
U+00C9	LATIN CAPITAL LETTER E WITH ACUTE
U+02AD	LATIN LETTER BIDENTAL PERCUSSIVE
U+039B	GREEK CAPITAL LETTER LAMDA
U+0446	CYRILLIC SMALL LETTER TSE
U+0543	ARMENIAN CAPITAL LETTER CHEH
U+05E6	HEBREW LETTER TSADI
U+0635	ARABIC LETTER SAD
U+0784	THAANA LETTER BAA
U+094A	DEVANAGARI VOWEL SIGN SHORT O
U+09D7	BENGALI AU LENGTH MARK
U+0BEF	TAMIL DIGIT NINE
U+0D93	SINHALA LETTER AIYANNA
U+0F0A	TIBETAN MARK BKA- SHOG YIG MGO
U+11C7	HANGUL JONGSEONG NIEUN-SIOS
U+1293	ETHIOPIC SYLLABLE NAA
U+13CB	CHEROKEE LETTER QUV
U+2023	TRIANGULAR BULLET
U+20A4	LIRA SIGN
U+2105	CARE OF
U+213A	ROTATED CAPITAL Q

U+21B7	CLOCKWISE TOP SEMICIRCLE ARROW
U+2226	NOT PARALLEL TO
U+2234	THEREFORE
U+265E	BLACK CHESS KNIGHT
U+01D122	MUSICAL SYMBOL F CLEF
U+01D34A	TETRAGRAM FOR EXHAUSTION

When programming, you will often need to look up the codepoint for the character or characters you want to use. You can use a standard web search for this, search a specific website such as `http://www.fileformat.info/info/unicode/`, or use an application like *gucharmap*. Some programmers like *code charts*, examples of which follow:

20-2f		!	"	#	$	%	&	'	(	)	*	+	,	-	.	/
30-3f	0	1	2	3	4	5	6	7	8	9	:	;	<	=	>	?
40-4f	@	A	B	C	D	E	F	G	H	I	J	K	L	M	N	O
50-5f	P	Q	R	S	T	U	V	W	X	Y	Z	[	\	]	^	_
60-6f	`	a	b	c	d	e	f	g	h	i	j	k	l	m	n	o
70-7f	p	q	r	s	t	u	v	w	x	y	z	{	|	}	~	

a0-af		¡	¢	£	¤	¥	¦	§	¨	©	ª	«	¬		®	¯
b0-bf	°	±	²	³	´	µ	¶	·	¸	¹	º	»	¼	½	¾	¿
c0-cf	À	Á	Â	Ã	Ä	Å	Æ	Ç	È	É	Ê	Ë	Ì	Í	Î	Ï
d0-df	Ð	Ñ	Ò	Ó	Ô	Õ	Ö	×	Ø	Ù	Ú	Û	Ü	Ý	Þ	ß
e0-ef	à	á	â	ã	ä	å	æ	ç	è	é	ê	ë	ì	í	î	ï
f0-ff	ð	ñ	ò	ó	ô	õ	ö	÷	ø	ù	ú	û	ü	ý	þ	ÿ

400-40f	È	Ë	Ђ	Ѓ	Є	Ѕ	І	Ї	Ј	Љ	Њ	Ћ	Ќ	Ѝ	Ў	Џ
410-41f	А	Б	В	Г	Д	Е	Ж	З	И	Й	К	Л	М	Н	О	П
420-42f	Р	С	Т	У	Ф	Х	Ц	Ч	Ш	Щ	Ъ	Ы	Ь	Э	Ю	Я
430-43f	а	б	в	г	д	е	ж	з	и	й	к	л	м	н	о	п
440-44f	р	с	т	у	ф	х	ц	ч	ш	щ	ъ	ы	ь	э	ю	я
450-45f	è	ë	ђ	ѓ	є	ѕ	і	ї	ј	љ	њ	ћ	ќ	ѝ	ў	џ
460-46f	Ѡ	ѡ	Ѣ	ѣ	Ѥ	ѥ	Ѧ	ѧ	Ѩ	ѩ	Ѫ	ѫ	Ѭ	ѭ	Ѯ	ѯ
470-47f	Ѱ	ѱ	Ѳ	ѳ	Ѵ	ѵ	Ѷ	ѷ	Ѹ	ѹ	Ѻ	ѻ	Ѽ	ѽ	Ѿ	ѿ

2600-260f	☀	☁	☂	☃	☄	★	☆	☇	☈	☉	☊	☋	☌	☍	☎	☏
2610-261f	☐	☑	☒	☓	☔	☕	☖	☗	☘	☙	☚	☛	☜	☝	☞	☟
2620-262f	☠	☡	☢	☣	☤	☥	☦	☧	☨	☩	☪	☫	☬	☭	☮	☯
2630-263f	☰	☱	☲	☳	☴	☵	☶	☷	☸	☹	☺	☻	☼	☽	☾	☿
2640-264f	♀	♁	♂	♃	♄	♅	♆	♇	♈	♉	♊	♋	♌	♍	♎	♏
2650-265f	♐	♑	♒	♓	♔	♕	♖	♗	♘	♙	♚	♛	♜	♝	♞	♟
2660-266f	♠	♡	♢	♣	♤	♥	♦	♧	♨	♩	♪	♫	♬	♭	♮	♯
2670-267f	♰	♱	♲	♳	♴	♵	♶	♷	♸	♹	♺	♻	♼	♽	♾	♿
2680-268f	⚀	⚁	⚂	⚃	⚄	⚅	⚆	⚇	⚈	⚉	⚊	⚋	⚌	⚍	⚎	⚏

c760-c76f	읠	읡	읢	읣	읤	읥	읦	읧	음	읩	읪	읫	읬	읭	읮	읯
c770-c77f	의	읱	읲	읳	이	익	읶	읷	인	읹	읺	일	읽	읾	읿	
c780-c78f	잀	잁	잂	잃	임	입	잆	잇	있	잉	잊	잋	의	잍	잎	잏
c790-c79f	자	작	잒	잓	잔	잕	잖	잗	잘	잙	잚	잛	잜	잝	잞	잟
c7a0-c7af	잠	잡	잢	잣	잤	장	잦	잧	잨	잩	잪	잫	재	잭	잮	잯
c7b0-c7bf	잰	잱	잲	잳	잴	잵	잶	잷	잸	잹	잺	잻	잼	잽	잾	잿

| 1d300-1d30f | ⚊ | ⚏ | ⚍ | ⚌ | ☰ | ☱ | ☲ | ☳ | ☴ | ☵ | ☶ | ☷ | | | |

(chart of trigram/hexagram glyphs, rows 1d300–1d356)

Code charts do have one serious limitation: they show only glyphs, not character names. In fact, many Unicode characters have *no* visible glyphs and show up blank in the chart! Four of these glyph-less characters appear in the preceding charts: U+0020 SPACE, U+007F DELETE, U+00A0 NO-BREAK SPACE, and U+00AD SOFT HYPHEN. You can find the complete set of beautifully formatted code charts for the entirety of Unicode, augmented with a list of character names, at `http://unicode.org/charts/`.

Unicode Blocks

The designers of Unicode partitioned the space of available codepoints into blocks to group similar characters together. A small sampling of blocks follows; for the complete set (there are approximately 200 blocks in all), see `http://unicode.org/Public/UNIDATA/Blocks.txt`.

0000..007F	Basic Latin
0080..00FF	Latin-1 Supplement
0250..02AF	IPA Extensions
0400..04FF	Cyrillic
0900..097F	Devanagari
0E80..0EFF	Lao
16A0..16FF	Runic
1700..171F	Tagalog
1B80..1BBF	Sundanese
20A0..20CF	Currency Symbols

2200..22FF	Mathematical Operators
2600..26FF	Miscellaneous Symbols
2800..28FF	Braille Patterns
30A0..30FF	Katakana
4E00..9FFF	CJK Unified Ideographs
ABC0..ABFF	Meetei Mayek
12000..123FF	Cuneiform
1D100..1D1FF	Musical Symbols
1F000..1F02F	Mahjong Tiles
100000..10FFFF	Supplementary Private Use Area-B

New blocks and new characters are added to the repertoire with each new version of Unicode. Unicode is designed to use only codepoints in the range 0...10FFFF, with 66 codepoints guaranteed to never be assigned to any character, ever. (The permanently unassigned codepoints are FDD0–FDEF, FFFE, FFFF, 1FFFE, 1FFFF, 2FFFE, 2FFFF, 3FFFE, 3FFFF, 4FFFE, 4FFFF, 5FFFE, 5FFFF, 6FFFE, 6FFFF, 7FFFE, 7FFFF, 8FFFE, 8FFFF, 9FFFE, 9FFFF, AFFFE, AFFFF, BFFFE, BFFFF, CFFFE, CFFFF, DFFFE, DFFFF, EFFFE, EFFFF, FFFFE, FFFFF, 10FFFE, and 10FFFF.) This means there is room for 1,114,046 characters, though as of Unicode Version 5.2, only approximately 100,000 characters have been allocated.

Unicode Categories

Every character is a member of a particular character category. Each category has a two-character code. The Unicode categories are as follows:

Code	Name	Examples
Lu	Letter—uppercase	1041B DESERET CAPITAL LETTER ETH
Ll	Letter—lowercase	161 LATIN SMALL LETTER S WITH CARON
Lt	Letter—titlecase	1F2 LATIN CAPITAL LETTER D WITH SMALL LETTER Z
Lm	Letter—modifier	2B2 MODIFIER LETTER SMALL J
Lo	Letter—other	62F ARABIC LETTER DAL

Code	Name	Examples
Nd	Number—decimal digit	9EE BENGALI DIGIT EIGHT
Nl	Number—letter	2168 ROMAN NUMERAL NINE
No	Number—other	F30 TIBETAN DIGIT HALF SEVEN
Pc	Punctuation—connector	203F UNDERTIE
Pd	Punctuation—dash	2013 EN DASH
Ps	Punctuation—open	28 LEFT PARENTHESIS
Pe	Punctuation—close	29D9 RIGHT WIGGLY FENCE
Pi	Punctuation—initial quote	2018 LEFT SINGLE QUOTATION MARK
Pf	Punctuation—final quote	2E03 RIGHT SUBSTITUTION BRACKET
Po	Punctuation—other	55A ARMENIAN APOSTROPHE
Sm	Symbol—math	D7 MULTIPLICATION SIGN
Sc	Symbol—currency	0AF1 GUJARATI RUPEE SIGN
Sk	Symbol—modifier	1FFD GREEK OXIA
So	Symbol—other	2105 CARE OF
Me	Mark—enclosing	20DD COMBINING ENCLOSED CIRCLE
Mc	Mark—spacing combining	110B8 KAITHI VOWEL SIGN AU
Mn	Mark—nonspacing	1D17C MUSICAL SYMBOL COMBINING STACCATO
Zs	Separator—space	20 SPACE A0 NO-BREAK SPACE 2003 EM SPACE
Zl	Separator—line	2028 LINE SEPARATOR
Zp	Separator—paragraph	2029 PARAGRAPH SEPARATOR
Cc	Other—control	08 BACKSPACE 0A LINE FEED
Cf	Other—format	200F RIGHT TO LEFT MARK 2062 INVISIBLE TIMES
Cs	Other—surrogate	*all characters in* U+D800...U+DFFF
Co	Other—private use	*all characters in private use blocks*
Cn	Other—not assigned	*(no characters in this category)*

Some programming languages (JavaScript is not one of them) have a mechanism for matching characters from a given category in their regular expressions. A recommended reference for looking up characters by category is `http://www.fileformat.info/info/unicode/category/`.

Character Encoding

When data are stored in memory, stored in a file, or transmitted over a network, all the hardware ever sees is raw bits. We require some kind of context to determine whether those bits represent text, numbers, objects, code, or something else. Representing high-level information in bits is called *encoding*; interpreting the bits as high-level data is called *decoding*. In Appendix B we saw how numbers were encoded in JavaScript; here we will look at the encoding of character data. There are three basic strategies for encoding Unicode text: UTF-32, UTF-16, and UTF-8. We will illustrate them by looking at how they encode the following example string:

m ↑ ℵ ◇

This string is made up of four characters, which are, in order:

U+006D LATIN SMALL LETTER M
U+010939 LYDIAN LETTER C
U+05D0 HEBREW LETTER ALEF
U+2662 WHITE DIAMOND SUIT

In UTF-32, we use 32 bits (4 bytes) to describe each character, simply placing each character's codepoint (in order) into 32 bits. Our example string is encoded as follows:[1]

00 00 00 6D 00 01 09 39 00 00 05 D0 00 00 26 62

UTF-32 is easy to understand, and because it is a *fixed-length* encoding (meaning every character is encoded in the same number of bytes), it is easy to find the

---

[1]For simplicity, we are omitting any discussion of endianness; the interested reader can get full details at `http://unicode.org/faq/utf_bom.html`.

memory address of the kth character in a string. (Do you see how?) However, UTF-32 uses up a lot of memory. An alternate encoding, UTF-16, uses only 16 bits for characters in the range U+0000...U+FFFF and 32 bits for the rest. Because the vast majority of textual interchange uses low-codepoint characters, a UTF-16 encoding almost always takes up half the space as the equivalent UTF-32 encoding.

Here is the UTF-16 encoding algorithm. To encode the character with codepoint c

1. if $0 < c < \text{FFFF}$, then the encoding is the 16-bit representation of c;

2. otherwise, because the maximum codepoint of Unicode is 10FFFF, we know $10000 < c < 10\text{FFFF}$. Let $x = c - 10000$ (hex). This is guaranteed to be a 20-bit number. (You might want to verify this.) Distribute the 20 bits of x into a 32-bit word as follows:

   110110*bbbbbbbbbb* 110111*bbbbbbbbbb*

Applying this algorithm to our example string, we get

00 6D D8 02 DD 39 05 D0 26 62

You might find it odd that the character U+010939 is encoded as D8 02 DD 39; after all, wouldn't that decode into *two characters*, namely U+D802 and U+DD39? In a way it does, but the Unicode mapping classifies all characters in the range U+D800 to U+DFFF as *surrogate characters*. A surrogate isn't "really" a character—it just stands for other characters. UTF-16 manages to use character pairs from this range to stand for characters in the (much larger) range U+010000 to U+10FFFF.

Because UTF-16 uses 2 bytes for some characters and 4 for others, it is a *variable-length* encoding scheme. Another variable-length encoding scheme is UTF-8. In this scheme:

- U+0000...U+007F are encoded in 1 byte.

- U+0080...U+07FF are encoded in 2 bytes.

- U+0800...U+FFFF are encoded in 3 bytes.

- U+010000...U+10FFFF are encoded in 4 bytes.

Encoding works as follows. Codepoints up to 7F require 7 bits; in UTF-8 these 7 bits are packed into a single byte like so:

0*bbbbbbb*

Values up to 7FF require 11 bits, which are allocated in 2 bytes like so:

110*bbbbb* 10*bbbbbb*

Values up to FFFF take up 16 bits, spread out like this:

1110*bbbb* 10*bbbbbb* 10*bbbbbb*

Finally, values up to the Unicode maximum of 10FFFF need 21 bits:

11110*bbb* 10*bbbbbb* 10*bbbbbb* 10*bbbbbb*

While UTF-8 may look complex, remember that the encoding and decoding are done in software libraries so you don't have to deal with this in your own scripting. However, practicing encoding and decoding by hand can be a good thing—a great way to really learn and comprehend a real and very successful encoding scheme! You can begin by trying to encode our example string. If you did it properly, you should have produced:

6D F0 90 A4 B9 D7 90 E2 99 A2

In practice, UTF-8 is an excellent encoding scheme for English text because all English letters occupy codepoints 00 through 7F and thus require only 1 byte of encoding. Characters from many other modern languages occupy codepoints 80 through 7FF, taking up 2 bytes in UTF-8. CJK (Chinese Japanese Korean) characters, however, mainly occupy codepoints 3000 through A4CF, requiring 3 bytes in UTF-8.

Character Decoding

Text that gets encoded for storage or transmission needs to be decoded later. In web applications, for example, the client (web browser) will request a page containing text from a server. The server encodes its text into a byte stream and transmits this to the client, along with information stating how the client should interpret those bytes. In Figure C.1, a web browser's request for a page has been fulfilled by a server, along with metadata saying the bytes are encoded using UTF-8. The browser receives this information and *decodes* the UTF-8 byte stream, displaying the page as intended.

If the programmer writing the server application forgets to inform the client of the encoding that was used, the client must guess the encoding. While this isn't always difficult, this extra burden on the client isn't nice, so server programmers should take care to inform clients of their chosen encoding schemes.

Many web browsers even allow human users to choose a decoding method, which can produce amusing results. In Figure C.2, a Firefox user has gone to the View → Character Encoding menu item and selected ISO-8859-1. Oops!

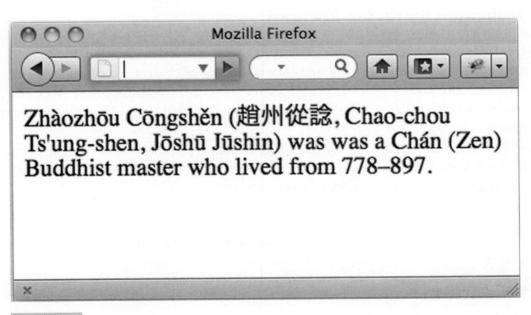

FIGURE C.1

A web page viewed with the proper decoding.

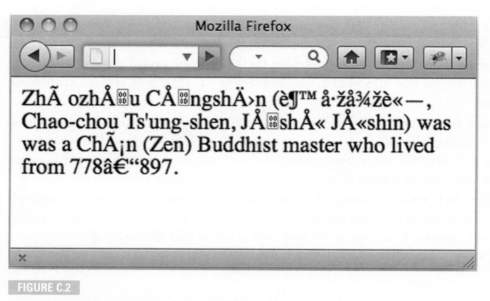

FIGURE C.2

A web page viewed with the incorrect decoding.

Unicode Character Escapes

One effective way to avoid encoding–decoding mismatches is to work entirely with characters in the range 00...7F and take advantage of character escapes.[2] We will show how this is done in XML, HTML, and JavaScript. Other document types and programming languages have some form of escaping, but we will not cover them here.

In XML and HTML, simply place the decimal representation of the codepoint of the desired character between &# and ; or the hexadecimal representation between &#x and ;. For example, to render the text

$$E \propto m$$

in XML or HTML, we notice that the codepoint of the PROPORTIONAL TO symbol is 221D (hex) or 8733 (decimal). We can therefore write either

```
E&#x221d;m
```

---

[2]Most of the character sets in use today, including ASCII, ISO8859-1 through ISO8859-15, Windows-1252, and Unicode, all have the same character mappings in this range.

or

```
E&#8733;m
```

In JavaScript, we use \u followed by *exactly four hexadecimal digits*, which means our example text is written

```
E\u221dm
```

Only four digits? How can we handle characters with codepoints above FFFF? Consider the character U+01D13E MUSICAL SYMBOL EIGHTH REST. In HTML or XML, we simply write 𝄾. However, \u1d13e in JavaScript renders as two characters: LATIN SMALL LETTER SIDEWAYS O WITH STROKE followed by LATIN SMALL LETTER E. Do you see why?

In fact, strings in JavaScript are not really sequences of characters, but rather *sequences of 16-bit fragments of UTF-16 encoding*! Therefore, to represent the Lydian word 𐤀𐤐𐤌, you would write

```
var s = "\ud802\udd20\ud802\udd2d\ud802\udd2c";
```

Although only a three-*character* string, the UTF-16 encoding is made up of six 16-bit components, which is all JavaScript really cares about. Therefore:

$$\text{s.length} \quad \Rightarrow \quad 6 \qquad (\text{not } 3)$$
$$\text{s.charAt(2)} \quad \Rightarrow \quad \text{"\ud802"} \quad (\text{not "o"})$$

So when JavaScript counts characters, it counts surrogates as individual characters. It really shouldn't do this, but the language isn't perfect, and unless you are using characters in the range U+010000 ... U+10FFFF, you won't notice the difference anyway. Nonetheless, it is a distinction you need to be aware of.

Glossary

Ajax A style of web programming where requests are made to a server and responses, possibly but not necessarily in XML, are processed at some later time without leaving the current web page. (The term was created as a catchy shorthand for <u>A</u>synchronous <u>J</u>avaScript <u>a</u>nd <u>X</u>ML.)

Algorithm A description of an always-terminating computational process composed of a finite number of steps.

Animation The process of creating and displaying a sequence of still images that change by small amounts but at frequent intervals, thus evoking the perception of movement.

Argument An expression passed to a function in a call.

Array An indexed collection of values. In JavaScript, arrays are indexed with integers beginning at 0. A true JavaScript array has a `length` property that, if assigned a value by a script, will expand or shrink the collection.

Asynchronous A form of communication in which a client issues a request and does not wait for the server to complete the request.

Binary Having exactly two fundamental parts. The binary numeral system, for example, has exactly two digits, 0 and 1.

Boolean One of the two values `true` or `false`. Can also refer to the type containing the values `true` or `false`.

Broken Not working according to specification.

Bug A mistake in the writing of a program that causes the program to perform incorrectly.

Callback A function designed to be executed "at some later time" during an asynchronous request.

Canvas The web page element to use for creating and displaying pixel-based computer graphics. WebGL also uses `canvas` as the target element for hardware-accelerated 3D graphics output.

Character A named symbol, such as PLUS SIGN, MUSICAL SYMBOL F CLEF, CHEROKEE LETTER QUV, or WHITE CHESS KNIGHT. Do not confuse a character with a *glyph*, which is a picture of a character. For example, the two distinct letters LATIN CAPITAL LETTER P and CYRILLIC CAPITAL LETTER ER can both be represented with the glyph P; similarly the distinct characters GREEK CAPITAL LETTER SIGMA and N-ARY SUMMATION can both be represented with the glyph Σ.

Character set A collection of characters, each of which is tagged with a unique integer called its *codepoint*. For example, in the Unicode character set, the character CYRILLIC SMALL LETTER YU has codepoint 2116 (or 44E in hex). Popular character sets in use today are Unicode, ASCII, and ISO-8859-1.

Closure An expression containing variables together with context providing values to those variables. In JavaScript, closures are nested functions containing references to variables in (textually) enclosing functions.

Collection An item of data that is made up of constituent data items.

Constructor A function that creates a new object. In JavaScript, the term is generally used for functions designed to be used with the `new` operator.

Crash The premature and unexpected termination of a program.

CSS The visual, formatting, and presentation technology standard for web pages. Acronym for <u>C</u>ascading <u>S</u>tyle <u>S</u>heets.

DOM The representation of the structure and content of a document, usually a web page, as an object. SVG (Scalable Vector Graphics) drawings also conform to the DOM. Acronym for <u>D</u>ocument <u>O</u>bject <u>M</u>odel.

DRY Code that is free from multiple nontrivial fragments of code saying essentially the same thing. Acronym for <u>D</u>on't <u>R</u>epeat <u>Y</u>ourself.

Effects Visual or auditory happenings that enhance a user's experience, such as the hiding or revealing of text or images through fading or sliding. Sometimes abbreviated as "fx."

Encoding A system for representing information in an alternative form, typically to conform to particular constraints, rules, or criteria. Examples include UTF-8 for character data and IEEE 754 for floating-point numbers.

Event An action, such as a page load, button press, keystroke, or touch, to which a script may wish to respond. The passage of time and the arrival of data over the network, though not strictly "actions," are also occurrences that are handled similarly to events.

Event-driven A programming paradigm where code is distributed across multiple events and must be read not sequentially (beginning to end) but in terms of what events may "fire" during the life of the program.

Evil Code that contains one or more serious, often blatant, violations of proper coding practices.

Exception An object that is thrown to indicate that an unusual, abnormal, or unexpected situation has occurred. Throwing an exception disrupts the normal control flow of a script.

Expression A fragment of code that is evaluated.

Function Code that can be called, generally with arguments.

Garbage Memory that was previously allocated to store information in a script but that cannot be used again because variables that once referenced the space no longer do so.

Hack A quickly written, and possibly ugly, solution to a coding problem that "just works," *or* a particularly ingenious solution to a coding problem using a nonobvious technique that both works perfectly and impresses other programmers.

Hairy Code that is complicated to the point of being impossible to understand.

Hex Short for *hexadecimal.* A system of denoting numerals using a base of 16. Traditionally the digits are 0, 1, 2, 3, 4, 5, 6, 7, 8, 9, A, B, C, D, E, and F. The prefix "hexa-" is Greek; the Latin prefix is not commonly used.

HTML A markup language for structured documents. Acronym for Hypertext Markup Language, although HTML documents contain more than just text.

HTTP A generic, stateless, application-level protocol for data transmission, most notable for its support of hypermedia. It is the primary protocol for the World Wide Web. Acronym for Hypertext Transfer Protocol.

Hypermedia A collection of media elements linked together in such a way that they can be navigated to and from each other by some agent.

Immutable The characteristic of an object that may not have any of its properties added or deleted or reconfigured in any way, nor have any of its properties' values changed.

Integer One of the set of "countable numbers" $\{\ldots-3,-2,-1,0,1,2,3,\ldots\}$. JavaScript can accurately represent all integers in the range -9007199254740992 $\ldots 9007199254740992$; outside of this range, some, but certainly not all, integers can be represented.

JSON A notation for the description of structured data, consisting of objects (collections of key–value pairs), arrays (simple lists), numbers, strings, Booleans, and the value `null`. It is more compact than XML. Acronym for JavaScript Object Notation.

Loop A chunk of code that is performed repeatedly, generally (but not necessarily) until some condition is true.

Magic The execution of complex but highly useful behavior that appears to happen of its own accord or be triggered by simple code that is seemingly unrelated.

Numeral A representation of a number. JavaScript allows both decimal (e.g., `76`) and hexadecimal (e.g., `0x4C`) numerals, though hexadecimal representations can only be used for integers.

Object In JavaScript, a value made up of named properties.

Object-oriented Code characterized by a focus on data, rather than algorithms or processes. Optionally carries the connotation of supporting classification hierarchy and information hiding.

Parameter A variable in a function that is initialized to the value of its corresponding argument when a function is called.

Prototype An object holding properties intended to be shared by a number of similar objects. In JavaScript, each object created by applying the operator `new` to a function will, by default, have the same prototype.

Regular expression A pattern of text intended to be matched during search or replace operations. In programming languages, a regular expression is not an arbitrary pattern but one built from a restricted set of basic pattern forms. Also known as a *regex* or *regexp*; the plural form *regexen* is sometimes heard.

Reserved word A word or identifier that cannot be used as the name of a variable.

Same origin policy A security policy in which scripts are not allowed to communicate with hosts other than the host from which they were downloaded.

Sandbox An environment in which untrusted code is run to avoid affecting the integrity of the overall system.

Scope The range of program text in which a particular name refers to a particular variable.

Script A sequence of statements intended to be executed as a single unit. Also called a *program*.

Server A program that continuously runs, responding to requests from other programs as they come in. The term can also be applied to machines that run server programs.

Statement A unit of execution within a script. The JavaScript statements are the empty statement, variable declaration, expression evaluation, block, `if`, `for`, `while`, `continue`, `break`, `return`, `with`, `switch`, `throw`, and `try`.

String A text value. Strings can be viewed as a sequence of symbols or characters. Thus, they have length, and individual characters in the string can be accessed by a numeric index starting from zero.

SVG A standard markup language for creating object- or vector-based computer graphics. Acronym for <u>S</u>calable <u>V</u>ector <u>G</u>raphics.

Synchronous A form of communication in which the parties involved actively coordinate and wait for each other as they exchange information

Tag A central expression in markup languages. Tags delimit—indicate the start and end of—specific sections or *elements* within a markup document. A *start tag* is recognizable as a name and attributes enclosed in angle brackets (`< >`) while an *end tag* includes a forward slash after the first angle bracket (`</ >`) and contains only the tag name.

Tweening The automated computation of intermediate states between a designated beginning and end. Used extensively in computer animation to avoid repositioning or modifications at a frame-by-frame level.

Type A particular set of values. All values in JavaScript belong to one of six types: `undefined`, `null`, Boolean, number, string, or object.

Unicode An internationally standardized character set, containing hundreds of thousands of characters. It is the native character set of JavaScript.

Unit test Code that runs other code under several scenarios, comparing the actual behavior with expected behavior. A unit test framework will run an entire suite of unit tests, reporting the number of times the actual and expected behaviors did not agree (i.e., the number of test failures).

User agent Software that does work on behalf of a (generally human) user. Often simply a technical term for a web browser.

Variable A named container for a value. A variable can be updated by assigning it a new value.

WebGL A bridge technology for connecting JavaScript code and the HTML `canvas` element to hardware-accelerated 3D graphics. Its name is derived from OpenGL, a popular 3D graphics technology standard.

XML A language for the description of structured data. Acronym for <u>E</u>xtensible <u>M</u>arkup <u>L</u>anguage.

YAML A language for the description of structured data, emphasizing human readability. Acronym for <u>YAML</u> <u>A</u>in't <u>M</u>arkup <u>L</u>anguage.

Bibliography

[Ado10]   Adobe Systems Inc. Flash home page.
           `http://www.adobe.com/products/flash/`, 2010. Accessed on June
           30, 2010.

[App11]   Apple, Inc. Safari web content guide. `http://developer.apple.com/`
           `library/safari/#documentation/AppleApplications/Reference/`
           `SafariWebContent/Introduction/Introduction.html`, 2011.
           Accessed on January 2, 2011.

[Bar10]   Dmitry Baranovskiy. Raphaël—JavaScript library.
           `http://raphaeljs.com`, 2010. Accessed on June 21, 2010.

[Bec02]   Kent Beck. *Test-Driven Development: By Example*. Addison-Wesley
           Professional, 2002.

[BLFM05]   Tim Berners-Lee, Roy Fielding, and Larry Masinter. Uniform
           resource identifier (URI): Generic syntax.
           `http://tools.ietf.org/html/rfc3986`, January 2005. Accessed on
           July 7, 2010.

[Bra07]   Brad Bird, screenwriter *Ratatouille*. Pixar Animation Studios, 2007.

[Bur08]   Andrés Buriticá. OpenJSGL.
           `http://sourceforge.net/projects/openjsgl/`, 2008. Accessed on
           June 28, 2010.

[Che10]   Ben Cherry. JavaScript: Better and faster.
           `http://www.bcherry.net/talks/`, 2010. Accessed on August 11,
           2010.

[Cri70]   Francis H. C. Crick. "Central dogma in molecular biology." *Nature*, 227:561–563, 1970.

[Cro01]   Douglas Crockford. Javascript: The world's most misunderstood programming language. `http://javascript.crockford.com/javascript.html`, 2001. Accessed on May 24, 2008.

[Cro08a]   Douglas Crockford. *JavaScript: The Good Parts*. O'Reilly Media, Inc., 2008.

[Cro08b]   Douglas Crockford. JavaScript: The world's most misunderstood programming language has become the world's most popular programming language. `http://javascript.crockford.com/popular.html`, 2008. Accessed on May 24, 2008.

[Cro10]   Douglas Crockford. "Really, JavaScript?" In *JSConf US 2010*, Washington, D.C., April 2010.

[CSS09a]   CSS Working Group. CSS animations module level 3. `http://www.w3.org/TR/css3-animations`, 2009. Accessed on March 26, 2011.

[CSS09b]   CSS Working Group. CSS transitions module level 3. `http://www.w3.org/TR/css3-transitions`, 2009. Accessed on March 26, 2011.

[Den07]   Peter J. Denning. "Computing is a natural science." *Communications of the ACM*, 50(7):13–18, 2007.

[DG04]   Jeffrey Dean and Sanjay Ghemawat. "Mapreduce: Simplified data processing on large clusters." In *OSDI '04: Sixth Symposium on Operating System Design and Implementation*, San Francisco, 2004.

[ECM09]   ECMA. *Standard ECMA-262, ECMAScript Language Specification, 5th Edition*. Ecma International, December 2009. `http://www.ecma-international.org/publications/files/ECMA-ST/ECMA-262.htm`.

[ECM99] ECMA. *Standard ECMA-262, ECMAScript Language Specification, 3rd Edition*. Ecma International, December 1999. `http://www.ecma-international.org/publications/files/ECMA-ST-ARCH/ECMA-262,%203rd%20edition,%20December%201999.pdf`.

[Fie00] Roy Fielding. "Architectural Styles and the Design of Network-Based Software Architectures." PhD dissertation, University of California, Irvine, 2000.

[Fow03] Martin Fowler. *UML Distilled: A Brief Guide to the Standard Object Modeling Language*. Addison Wesley, Reading, Massachusetts, 3rd edition, September 2003.

[Fuc09] Thomas Fuchs. Extreme JavaScript performance. `http://www.slideshare.net/madrobby/extreme-javascript-performance`, 2009. Accessed on August 9, 2010.

[Goo11] Google, Inc. Android Developers home page. `http://developer.android.com`, 2011. Accessed on January 2, 2011.

[ISO04] ISO. *ISO 8601:2004—Data elements and interchange formats—Information interchange—Representation of dates and times*. International Standards Organization, 2004.

[Khr09] Khronos Group. WebGL—OpenGL ES 2.0 for the web. `http://www.khronos.org/webgl`, 2009. Accessed on June 28, 2010.

[Khr10] Khronos Group. OpenGL 4.0. `http://www.khronos.org/opengl`, 2010. Accessed on June 28, 2010.

[Knu74] Donald E. Knuth. "Structured programming with go to statements." *Computing Surveys*, 6(4):261–301, December 1974.

[Lon10] Jarod Long. A JavaScript prototypal inheritance pattern that doesn't suck. `http://www.iokat.com/posts/2/`, 2010. Accessed on January 1, 2011.

[LY99] Tim Lindholm and Frank Yellin. *The Java Virtual Machine Specification*. Prentice Hall, 2nd edition, 1999.

[Mac09]   Bruce J. MacLennan. Computation and nanotechnology: Toward the fabrication of complex hierarchical structures. `http://www.cs.utk.edu/~mclennan/papers/CAN-TR.pdf`, 2009. Accessed on February 7, 2009.

[Moz09]   Mozilla Developer Center. Canvas tutorial. `https://developer.mozilla.org/en/canvas_tutorial`, 2009. Accessed on June 7, 2010.

[MS03]   Robin Milner and Susan Stepney. Nanotechnology—computer science opportunities and challenges. `http://www-users.cs.york.ac.uk/~susan/bib/ss/nonstd/rsrae03.htm`, 2003. Accessed on February 7, 2009.

[New99]   Joseph M. Newcomer. Optimization: Your worst enemy. `http://www.flounder.com/optimization.htm`, 1999. Accessed on August 16, 2011.

[Nor01]   Peter Norvig. Teach yourself programming in ten years. `http://norvig.com/21-days.html`, 2001. Accessed on August 16, 2011.

[Ope02]   Open Source Initiative. The open source definition. `http://www.opensource.org/docs/osd`, 2002. Accessed on May 24, 2010.

[Pen06]   Robert Penner. Robert Penner's easing equations. `http://www.robertpenner.com/easing`, 2006. Accessed on March 21, 2010.

[Pil10]   Mark Pilgrim. *Dive into HTML 5*. `http://diveintohtml5.org`, 2010. Accessed on June 17, 2010. Available on paper as *HTML5: Up and Running*. O'Reilly Media, 2010.

[PL07]   Alfred S. Posamentier and Ingmar Lehmann. *The Fabulous Fibonacci Numbers*. Prometheus Books, Amherst, NY, 2007.

[Rok09]   RokerHRO (Wikimedia contributor). textposcolorcube.pov. `http://roker.dingens.org/wikipedia/colorcube`, 2009. Accessed on May 26, 2010.

[Spo06]   Joel Spolsky. Can your programming language do this?
          `http://www.joelonsoftware.com/items/2006/08/01.html`, 2006.
          Accessed on May 31, 2008.

[Twe10]   Tweener Developers. Tweener. `http://code.google.com/p/tweener`,
          2010. Accessed on March 22, 2010.

[W3C02]   W3C. XHTML 1.0 The Extensible Hypertext Markup Language
          (Second Edition). `http://www.w3.org/TR/xhtml1/`, 2002. Accessed
          on August 16, 2011.

[W3C08a] W3C. Extensible Markup Language (XML) 1.0 (Fifth Edition).
          `http://www.w3.org/TR/REC-xml`, 2008. Accessed on August 16, 2011.

[W3C08b] W3C SVG Working Group. Inline SVG in HTML5 and XHTML.
          `http://dev.w3.org/SVG/proposals/svg-html/svg-html-proposal`
          `.html`, 2008. Accessed on August 16, 2011.

[W3C09a] W3C. Cross-origin resource sharing. `http://www.w3.org/TR/cors`,
          2009. Accessed on July 17, 2010.

[W3C09b] W3C. Scalable Vector Graphics (SVG) 1.1 specification.
          `http://www.w3.org/TR/SVG`, 2009. Accessed on June 21, 2010.

[W3C10a] W3C. Cascading style sheets. `http://www.w3.org/Style/CSS`, 2010.
          Accessed on May 29, 2010.

[W3C10b] W3C. HTML5: A vocabulary and associated APIs for HTML and
          XHTML. `http://www.w3.org/TR/html5/`, 2010. Accessed on August
          16, 2011.

[W3C10c] W3C Geolocation Working Group. DeviceOrientation event
          specification.
          `http://dev.w3.org/geo/api/spec-source-orientation.html`,
          2010. Accessed on January 2, 2011.

[W3C11a] W3C Geolocation Working Group. W3C Geolocation Working Group
          home page. `http://www.w3.org/2008/geolocation`, 2011. Accessed
          on January 2, 2011.

[W3C11b] W3C Web Events Working Group. W3C Web Events Working Group home page. http://www.w3.org/2010/webevents, 2011. Accessed on January 2, 2011.

[W3C99] W3C. HTML 4.01 specification. http://www.w3.org/TR/html4/, 1999. Accessed on August 16, 2011.

[WW10] W3C and Web Hypertext Application Technology Working Group (WHATWG). The canvas element. http://dev.w3.org/html5/spec/the-canvas-element.html#the-canvas-element, 2010. Accessed on June 7, 2010.

[Zak09a] Nicholas Zakas. Speed up your JavaScript. http://www.youtube.com/watch?v=mHtdZgou0qU, 2009. Accessed on August 9, 2010.

[Zak09b] Nicholas Zakas. Writing efficient JavaScript. http://www.slideshare.net/nzakas/writing-efficient-javascript, 2009. Accessed on August 9, 2010.

[Zim80] Hubert Zimmermann. "OSI reference model—The ISO model of architecture for open systems interconnection." *IEEE Transactions on Communication*, 28(4):425–432, April 1980.

Index

Credits

Chapter 1

1.1 Adapted from Francis H. C. Crick. Central dogma in molecular biology. Nature, 227:561–563, 1970.; **1.2** Used with permission from Microsoft; 1.3 U.S. Army Photo.

Chapter 2

2.1 Firefox logo® is a registered trademark of the Mozilla Foundation; **2.3** Firefox logo® and Mozilla logo™ are registered trademarks of the Mozilla Foundation; **2.4** Mozilla logo™ is a registered trademark of the Mozilla Foundation/Courtesy of Jesse Ruderman; **2.8** Firefox logo® is a registered trademark of the Mozilla Foundation; **2.13** Courtesy of Douglas Crawford.

Chapter 4

4.7 Firefox logo® and Mozilla logo™ are registered trademarks of the Mozilla Foundation; **4.8** Firefox logo® is a registered trademark of the Mozilla Foundation/Courtesy of Jesse Ruderman; **4.9** Firefox logo® is a registered trademark of the Mozilla Foundation/Courtesy of Jesse Ruderman.

Chapter 6

6.1 Firefox logo® is a registered trademark of the Mozilla Foundation; **6.3** Mozilla logo™ is a registered trademark of the Mozilla Foundation; **6.10** Mozilla logo™ is a registered trademark of the Mozilla Foundation.

Chapter 7

7.13 Firefox logo® is a registered trademark of the Mozilla Foundation/Courtesy of Jesse Ruderman; **7.17** Courtesy of Jörn Zaefferer, Query Testing Team; **7.18** Courtesy of Jörn Zaefferer, Query Testing Team.

Chapter 8

8.4 Mozilla logo™ is a registered trademark of the Mozilla Foundation; **8.5** Mozilla logo™ is a registered trademark of the Mozilla Foundation/© Flickrvisio; **8.6** Firefox logo® and Mozilla logo™ are registered trademarks of the Mozilla Foundation.

Chapter 9

9.4 Firefox logo® and Mozilla logo™ are registered trademarks of the Mozilla Foundation; **9.21** "Sierpinski Triangle." *Wikipedia.org*, accessed November 8, 2011 at http://en.wikipedia.org/wiki/Sierpinski_triangle; **9.22** "Sierpinski Triangle." *Wikipedia.org*, accessed November 8, 2011 at http://en.wikipedia.org/wiki/Sierpinski_triangle; **9.24** Firefox logo® is a registered trademark of the Mozilla Foundation; **9.25** Firefox logo® is a registered trademark of the Mozilla Foundation; **9.26A** © Fedorov Oleksiy/ShutterStock, Inc.; **9.26B** © Reinhold Leitne/ShutterStock, Inc.; **9.26C** © Cienpies Design/ShutterStock, Inc.

Chapter 10

10.9 © 2011 Google; **10.10** Firefox logo® and Mozilla logo™ are registered trademarks of the Mozilla Foundation.

Appendix C

C.1 Firefox logo® and Mozilla logo™ are registered trademarks of the Mozilla Foundation; **C.2** Firefox logo® and Mozilla logo™ are registered trademarks of the Mozilla Foundation.